THE

LITERARY LIFE AND CORRESPONDENCE

OF

THE COUNTESS OF BLESSINGTON.

BY

R. R. MADDEN, M.R.I.A.

AUTHOR OF

"TRAVELS IN THE EAST," "INFIRMITIES OF GENIUS," "THE MUSSULMAN," "SHRINES AND SEPULCHRES," "THE LIFE OF SAVONAROLA," ETC.

"L'homme marche vers le tombeau, trainant apres lui, la chaine de ses esperance, trompèes."

IN THREE VOLUMES.

VOL. III.

LONDON:
T. C. NEWBY, PUBLISHER, 30, WELBECK STREET,
CAVENDISH SQUARE.
1855.

Library of Congress Cataloging in Publication Data

Madden, Richard Robert, 1798-1886.
The literary life and correspondence of the Countess of Blessington.

1. Blessington, Marguerite (Power) Farmer Gardiner, Countess of, 1789-1849. I. Title.
DA536.B66M3 1973 828'.7'09 [B] 78-148279
ISBN 0-404-07720-X

Reprinted from the edition of 1855, London
First AMS edition published in 1973
Manufactured in the United States of America

International Standard Book Number:
Complete Set: 0-404-07720-X
Volume III: 0-404-07723-4

AMS PRESS INC.
NEW YORK, N. Y. 10003

THE

LITERARY LIFE AND CORRESPONDENCE

OF

THE COUNTESS OF BLESSINGTON.

IN THREE VOLUMES.

VOL. III

AMS PRESS
NEW YORK

From a Photograph by Count D'Orsay.

STANNARD & DIXON 7, POLAND S^T

THE TOMB OF MARGUERITE COUNTESS OF BLESSINGTON

CONTENTS OF VOL. III.

CHAPTER I.

PAGE

Notice and Letters of the Marquess Wellesley . . . 1

CHAPTER II.

Notice and Letters of the late and present Dukes of Wellington . 13

CHAPTER III.

Notices and Letters of Sir Edward Bulwer Lytton and Sir Henry Bulwer, G.C.B. 27

CHAPTER IV.

Notices and Letters of Isaac D'Israeli, Esq.—The Right Honourable Benjamin D'Israeli, M.P.—Charles Dickens, Esq. . 75

CHAPTER V.

Notices and Letters of Lord Abinger to Lady Blessington—Letters of Lord Durham—Lord John Russell—Lord Brougham—Lord Lyndhurst—The Marquis of Lansdowne—Lord Glenelg—Sir J—— H——, respecting a communication of Lady Blessington to Lord Anglesey—Letters signed G.—The Marquis of Normanby—The Earl of Westmoreland—Viscount Lord Strangford —Letter signed D. to Lady Blessington—Letter from Lady

PAGE

Blessington to Sir Robert Peel—Sir Robert Peel's Statement —Letters signed F. B. to Lady Blessington—Letters signed H. —Letters signed C.—Reference to Lady Blessington's Correspondents 108

CHAPTER VI.

Notices and Letters of Dr. Samuel Parr, LL.D.—Sir Thomas Lawrence, R.A.—Thomas Moore, Esq.—Thomas Campbell—B. W. Procter, Esq. (Barry Cornwall) 146

CHAPTER VII.

Notices and Letters of Joseph Jekyll, Esq., F.R.S., L.F.S.A.—Jack Fuller—The Hon. W. R. Spencer—Henry Luttrell, Esq. —George Colman, Esq.—Theodore Hook — James Smith—Horace Smith 172

CHAPTER VIII.

Notices and Letters of Captain Marryatt, R.N., C.B., &c.—A. Fonblanque, Esq.—John Galt—Nicholas Parker Willis, Esq.—Frederick Mansell Reynolds, Esq. 215

CHAPTER IX.

Notice and Letters of Dr. William Beattie, M.D.—Letters from Lady Blessington to R. R. Madden—Letters from R. R. Madden to Lady Blessington 255

CHAPTER X.

Notices and Letters of B. Simmonds, Esq. and John Kenyon . 289

CHAPTER XI.

Miscellaneous Letters 303

CHAPTER XII.

Epistolary Curiosities, &c. 329

CHAPTER XIII.

Correspondence with the Mathews 343

APPENDIX.

No. I.

PAGE
Letters to and from Lord Blessington 376

No. II.

Letters of Sir William Gell to Dr. Frederic Forster Quin . 386

No. III.

Latin Lines to Lady Blessington, by W. S. Landor . . 399

No. IV.

Notice of Thomas Stewart, Esq., subsequently the Abbé Stewart, nephew of Sir W. Drummond 400

No. V.

Statuary, Vases, and Bronzes, the property of General Count D'Orsay, the father of Count Alfred, confiscated in 1793, and appropriated by the state; claimed by the Count in July, 1844 401

No. VI.

Notice of Count D'Orsay's Gore House Picture . . . 405

No. VII.

Lord Byron's Yacht, "The Bolivar," (subsequently Lord Blessington's property). Account of, by Mr. Armstrong, Author of "The Young Commander," "The Two Midshipmen," &c. . 405

No. VIII.

Notices of Lords Holland, Grey, Lansdowne, Erskine, and Mr. Perry, in the hand-writing of Count D'Orsay:—probably the production of Lady Blessington 408

No. IX.

Notices of Madame du Deffand and Madame Geoffrin . . 410

No. X.

PAGE

Notice of Edward Rushton, of Liverpool—Lines on his death, by a correspondent of Lady Blessington . . . 414

No. XI.

Observations of a distinguished English writer on the labours of Monsieur Eugene Sue 419

No. XII.

Separate Notices of some of the Eminent or Remarkable Persons who were Correspondents, Friends, or Acquaintances of Lady Blessington 420

No. XIII.

Account of a Scene witnessed by Thomas Moore and the Editor . 506

No. XIV.

Further observations on the death of L. E. L. . . . 511

No. XV.

Assassination of the Abbé Stewart in Italy—Reference to a recent Murder in London 534

A MEMOIR

OF THE

LITERARY LIFE AND CORRESPONDENCE

OF THE

COUNTESS OF BLESSINGTON.

CHAPTER I.

THE MARQUESS WELLESLEY.

RICHARD COLLEY WESLEY, first Marquess Wellesley (eldest son of Yarrell, second Baron Wesley, and subsequently to the birth of said Richard, Earl of Mornington), was born in Dublin, the 20th of June, 1760, and died in London, in 1842, in his eighty-third year.* To his mother's excellent understanding and great mental accomplishments is chiefly to

* In "Pue's Occurrences," a weekly paper, published in Dublin, No. 50, from June 17th to June 21st, 1760, I find the following notice among the births—(June 20th, 1760)—"In Grafton Street, the Lady of the Right Honourable the Lord Mornington was safely delivered of a son and heir, to the great joy of that family." This is the first time, as far as I know, that the above notice has been referred to in relation to the place of birth of the Marquess. A great deal of confusion of dates, names, and of ideas that have led Colonel Gurwood, Mr. Peter Cunningham, and other writers, into error, have arisen, as I imagine, from there being a traditional account of a son of Lord Mornington born in Grafton Street, in the house lately occupied by the Royal Irish Academy, and, from some cause or other, that son being erroneously supposed to be Arthur Wesley, the third son of Lord Mornington.

be attributed the careful cultivation of the Marquess Wellesley's elegant tastes for literature and classical learning. His first display of oratorical talent was in an eloquent academical address, pronounced at Eton, in 1778, and, two years later, he gained the University prize for the best composition in Latin verse. At a subsequent period of his career, the Provost of Eton College, Dr. Goodall, before a committee of the House of Commons on academic education, spoke of the Marquess Wellesley as "infinitely superior to Porson in Greek composition." The Marquess, he said, as a genuine Greek scholar, exhibits the exquisite style and manner of Xenophon. He sat in the Irish House of Peers from the date of his succession to the title of his father, the Earl of Mornington, in 1781, for a few years. In 1784, he was sworn in a Member of the Privy Council; in 1786, he was appointed one of the Lords of the Treasury. He sat in the English House of Commons, for several boroughs, from the year 1784, and distinguished himself particularly at the time of the Regency question by his advocacy of the English view of it, and at the period of the French Revolution, by his denunciations of its excesses. He married, in 1794, his first wife, the daughter of M. Pierre Roland, by whom he had previously several illegitimate children. A separation took place soon after the marriage, and the Marchioness died in 1816, leaving no legitimate issue. In 1795, he was appointed a member of the Board of Control: and subsequently Chief Governor of India.

In 1797 he was created Baron Wellesley, in the peerage of

The notice I discovered in "Pue's Occurrences" disposes of that error; but there remains another to get rid of. The house of Lord Mornington, in Grafton Street, was not the one which became the property of the Royal Irish Academy. The Academy's premises were built on the site of that house, in fact, the house in which the Marquess of Wellesley was born, has long ceased to exist. A writer of great research and accuracy, in his second article on "the Streets of Dublin," treats largely of this locality.

Great Britain, and in 1799, Marquess Wellesley, in the peerage of Ireland, on account of his great services in the office of Governor-General of India. In 1805, after a career of unparalleled successes, signal civil and military triumphs, and services of the highest importance, thwarted and distrusted, and interfered with in his great and comprehensive schemes and governmental measures by the Court of Directors, he resigned his office and returned to England, when he had attained the forty-fifth year of his age.

In the latter part of 1809, he was appointed Ambassador to Spain. He landed at Cadiz the day the battle of Talavera was fought, but remained only a short time in Spain, and on his return home was appointed Secretary of State for Foreign Affairs. His known opinions in favour of Catholic Emancipation did not leave him long in office, and for fifteen years he continued in opposition to government.

In December 1821 the Marquess of Wellesley was appointed Lord Lieutenant of Ireland. From 1807 up to that period, Ireland was governed for the interests, and in the interests solely, of Orangeism, nominally by the Duke of Richmond, but virtually by the Attorney-General, Saurin, and an English Chancellor, Lord Manners, who was wholly under the control of the former.

The Marquess of Wellesley in 1822 struck a blow at the Orange ascendancy regime, from which it never recovered. From 1807, up to that period, Ireland had been governed by William Saurin, of Huguenot descent, a black-letter lawyer of eminence, of much astuteness in his profession, but of a narrow mind, illiberal and unenlightened, a partizan of Orangeism without disguise or any affectation of impartiality in his high office—an open adherent of that system, deriving all his power from its fanaticism, and exercising all his influence for its objects, under the cloak of zeal for the interests of religion. All the administrative power of the state was placed by him and the Chancellor, the governors of the chief governor, in the hands of Orangemen. The Duke of Richmond, who had been appointed Viceroy in 1807, and held his office till 1813, had delegated his authority to the Chancellor, Lord Manners, and by Lord Manners, the chief power and control of the government, civil and military, and religious, had been transferred to Saurin.

Such was the power in Ireland which the Marquess of Wellesley found more difficulty in dealing with, than that of Tippoo Saib in India. And yet at the period of his arrival in that country as Governor-General, the sovereignty of India had to be disputed with three native powers, and Sultans of vast resources. But the struggle of one power alone, of Orangeism in Ireland, with Saurin for its legal sultan, cost the illustrious statesman more trouble than all the strife of his government in India, and his wars with the princes of the Mahrattas and Nizam. He broke the stubborn neck of Orange influence and insolence, however, though at an infinite cost of trouble, vexation, and disquiet. And this attainment perhaps, after all, is the greatest achievement of the illustrious Marquess.

Lady Blessington had reason to know that such was the opinion of the Marquess: among her papers she has left a very remarkable piece of evidence of the fact, of unquestionable authenticity, in the following statement of the Marquess to her in March 1840.

" *Bushe is one of the first men produced by our country.* " *When I went to Ireland in* 1821, *I found him depressed* " *by an old Orangeman, named Saurin, then Attorney-Ge-* " *neral by* title, *but who had been really Lord Lieutenant* " *for* fifteen *years. I removed Saurin, and appointed Bushe* " *Lord Chief Justice.*

" *Saurin set up a newspaper to defame me,* ' *The Evening* " *Mail,' which (notwithstanding the support of Lord*

"*Manners and the Orangemen) has not* yet *ruined or* "*slain me.*"

Of one of the principal opponents of the Marquess, in his Irish Government, a few words may not be misplaced here.

Thomas Manners Sutton, first Lord Manners, a younger son of Lord George Manners Sutton, third son of the third Duke of Rutland, who was born in 1756, and died in 1842, in his 87th year, was Lord Chancellor of Ireland, from the death of Mr. Fox till the retirement of Lord Liverpool. For twenty years, he enjoyed greater patronage and emoluments than ever fell to the lot of any legal functionary in Ireland. His patron, Spencer Perceval, who was Attorney-General in 1802, when Colonel Despard was prosecuted successfully for high treason, discovered in the peculiar talents of the then Solicitor-General, Lord Manners, the qualities which fitted him, in his opinion, for the high office of Lord Chancellor in Ireland.

The whole Orange party and ascendancy throughout the country received the new Lord Chancellor with acclamation. The great Indian General, Sir Arthur Wellesley, the late Duke of Wellington, who at the same time was appointed Chief Secretary, was not less favourably received by the same party: poor deluded innocents! no prophetic vision of theirs peering into futurity, and the part that Chief Secretary was to play in 1829.

Manners was an ornamental Chancellor—of a grim countenance, somewhat ghastly, painfully suggestive of the aspect that a resuscitated mummy might be expected to assume in the act of reviving, and was remarkable for courtesy on the bench. He bowed oftener to the bar, bent his gaunt form lower, spoke in milder accents, stood more perpendicularly at the close of a long sitting, and smiled with greater labour, than any keeper of the seals in Ireland had ever done before. He imparted great dignity, and gave a gentlemanly character to the exercise of his vast patronage, for all the purposes of party and intrigue, and the jobbery interests, which were protected and promoted by his subordinate in legal office. But his decisions in Chancery were found entitled to little respect in Westminster Hall; and of his administration of justice, it can be said with truth—it gave very general satisfaction to the Orangemen of Ireland. William Saurin, who was made Attorney-General in 1809, and who retained his office for sixteen of the years that Lord Manners was Chancellor, the uncompromising adversary of Catholic claims, and most virulent of all the opponents of them, was at once taken to the private councils of the Chancellor, Lord Manners, on his arrival, and became his "guide, philosopher, and friend." Daily the business of the government of Ireland was done by the two legal functionaries of kindred spirits,—"Arcades Ambos," as they regularly walked down every morning from Stephen's Green to the Four Courts, and returned to their homes, after a visit to the Castle every evening, with arms linked, and solemn steps and bended brows, settling affairs of state, and arranging the things that were to be done by the facile, convivial, and pleasure-loving Chief Governor and Viceroy, the Duke of Richmond, who thus allowed himself "to be led by the nose as tenderly as asses are."

The well-known partiality of this dignified Judge for the Attorney-General, had the effect to be expected from it, on the Solicitors of the Court of Chancery, Mr. Saurin having "the ear of the Court," and a supposed influence over the Lord Chancellor out of Court. Mr. Saurin, who was known to be a man of some intellectual power, and the Lord Chancellor Manners one of very little strength of mind, and capable of being influenced by one of a very different calibre of understanding, briefs poured in, on the favoured Attorney-General, and men of the highest standing in their profession were cast into the shade, in the court, of the exceedingly courteous Lord Chancellor Manners.

In January, 1822, the Marquess Wellesley being Viceroy, the Attorney-Generalship of William Saurin came to an end. But his power, as the confidential adviser of the Lord Chancellor, and the acknowledged head and legal guide of the Orange ascendancy faction, continued to be exercised and pitted against the government of the Marquess Wellesley for a period of six years, namely, from 1822 to 1828, when the Liverpool ministry broke up, and Lord Manners was succeeded by Sir Anthony Hart.

The conqueror of Tippoo Saib and the Nizam, having resolutely encountered the hostile power of Irish Orangeism, that had been previously deemed indomitable in Ireland, and having succeeded largely in his warfare with that system, though not to the full extent of his desires, after an administration of justice and wisdom of six years' duration, was recalled in 1828, when his brother, the Duke of Wellington, took the office of First Lord of the Treasury.

The Marquess married a second time, in 1825, the eldest daughter of Richard Caton, Esq., of Maryland, in America, and widow of Robert Patterson, Esq., a Roman Catholic lady, by which marriage there was no issue.

During the whole of the Duke of Wellington's administration, the Marquess remained in retirement.

In 1833, Lord Grey being Prime Minister, the Marquess, in his 74th year, once more took on him the office of Lord Lieutenant of Ireland, and retained office for the period of one year. He returned to England when Peel came into office, in December, 1834.

In 1835, he accepted the office of Lord Chamberlain, for the sake, it is said, of its emoluments; and with that humiliating step, his public life may be said to have closed.

An elegant volume of his Latin Poems, entitled "Primitiæ et Reliquiæ," many of them written after he became an octogenarian, were privately printed a short time before his death;

and perhaps, but for the care of one whom he loved like a father, and watched over with all the affectionate interest of a true and faithful friend—Mr. Alfred Montgomery—these remarkable poems never would have seen the light of day.

"Some of these had been recently written, and they exhibit in an astonishing degree his unimpaired vigour of intellect, and his unaltered elegance of taste. One poem in this volume justly attracted universal admiration."*

This eminent man passed much of his time, in the latter portion of his life, in the vicinity of Eton.

The Marquess lived and died in straitened circumstances, leaving a great name, which will yet be honoured as that of one of the most illustrious men of his time; perhaps, as that of the first British statesman of his age.

By the will of the Marquess Wellesley, Alfred Montgomery, Esq., his private secretary, was left £1000, "in regard of his affectionate, dutiful, and zealous services." And the residue of his property was left to the Marchioness Wellesley, whose death took place in the latter part of 1853.

By a codicil to the will, the Marquess bequeathed to his secretary, Mr. Montgomery, all his manuscripts, enjoining the public use of a portion of them in the following terms:—

"*And I desire him to publish such of my papers as shall tend to illustrate my two administrations in Ireland, and to protect my honour against the slander of Melbourne and his pillar of state—O'Connell.*"

To Lord Brougham he bequeathed his Homer, in four volumes, and earnestly desired him to assist in publishing his MSS., saying, "I leave my memory in his charge, confiding in his honour and justice."†

The property was sworn under £6000.

* Memoirs of Eminent Etonians; with Notices of the Early History of Eton College. By Edward S. Creasy, M.A. Bentley.

† Gentleman's Magazine, December, 1844, p. 654.

LETTERS FROM THE MARQUESS WELLESLEY TO LADY BLESSINGTON.

"Kingston House, June 9th, 1839.

"MY DEAR LADY BLESSINGTON,

"Your little volume of wisdom, genius, and just sentiment, has delighted me; I have read it with great admiration, and (although in my seventy-ninth year) with instruction, and I hope with self-correction.

"It is very amiable to think of me so often in the midst of all your higher occupations, but your thoughts are chiefly directed towards the happiness of others, and I am proud of the share which your kindness allots to me.

"If your definition of a *Bore* be correct, you never can have encountered one of those Pests of Society. For '*when were you thinking only of yourself?*'

"Ever your most grateful
"And devoted servant,
"WELLESLEY."

"Kingston House, November 9th, 1839.

"MY DEAR LADY BLESSINGTON,

"Your beautiful and magnificent present contains such a crowd of wonders, that it will require almost a season before I can finish my wonderments at the whole collection.

"The poetry (which I have read, none of your Ladyship's) is very beautiful and interesting; the plates, printing, binding, all chefs-d'œuvre of their kind.

"I have not been able yet to appreciate the prose. A thousand thanks for your kindness in thinking of me. As to the play, I do not admire it, and I do not wish to criticise it.

"I have not been well lately, otherwise I should much sooner have acknowledged your Ladyship's goodness and munificence.

"I am truly grateful for your protection of my dear young friend, Alfred Montgomery, who is truly grateful for it, and I sincerely believe truly worthy of it.

"I am too happy always to render any service to your Ladyship; and I regret the approaching expiration of the privilege of franking, principally as it will deprive me of the pleasure of obeying your commands.

"Ever, my dear Lady Blessingtor,
"Your faithful, obliged,
"And devoted servant,
"WELLESLEY."

"Kingston House, January 1st, 1840.

"MY DEAR LADY BLESSINGTON,

"I have suffered such continual pain, that I have been unable to offer my heartfelt acknowledgments for all your kindness and favour. Writing on this day, it would be impossible to omit the most ardent wishes for many happy returns of this season to you; if half the happiness you dispense to others is returned to yourself, you will be among the happiest of the human race. This is no great demand upon the gratitude of the world, to compromise your just claims, by the payment of one half.

"Your commendation of my humble tribute to the adored 'Shrine of my Education,' has raised me in my own estimation. The sentiments flow from the very source of my heart's blood, and therefore must be congenial with the feelings of one whose works abound with similar emotions. I am sure you understand the Latin; you could not write as you do, if you had not approached those pure springs of all beauty, sublimity, virtue, and truth.

"I feel most gratefully the honour you confer on me, when you desire to publish my verses in your beautiful annual collection; but I am averse to any publication; and I therefore hope that you will not attribute my declining this distinction to any want of a sense of its high value.

"Your protégé, Alfred, is still in Staffordshire, hunting and shooting with Lords Anglesey, Hatherston, &c. I expect him this week.

"Believe me ever,
"My dear Lady Blessington,
"With true attachment and gratitude,
"Your devoted servant,
"WELLESLEY."

"Kingston House, March 27th, 1840.

"MY DEAR LADY BLESSINGTON,

"Being anxious to obey your Ladyship's kind command, I send you some verses, which I have lately addressed to my dear and highly-respected friend, Lord Chief Justice Bushe (though nominally to his grand-daughter, Miss Fox). You will not understand them, unless you first read the Packet (No. 1) containing a letter from the Chief Justice, with some verses from Miss Fox.

"If your Ladyship thinks my verses worth notice, they are at your disposal.

"They have been sent to Ireland, of course, but with a notice, that they are not published. It is, however, to be expected that the Chief Justice will be desirous of communicating them to his friends.

"If your Ladyship should think them worthy of your notice, I think I could obtain permission from the Chief Justice to publish his letter, and his grand-daughter's verses, and my original letter to his Lordship at the same time....

"WELLESLEY."

"Kingston House, 10th May, 1840.

"MY DEAR LADY BLESSINGTON,

"You must think me very insensible, or worse, to have left your beautiful poetry unpraised for so long a time; nothing less than absolute inability to write could excuse me; but the sad truth is, that I have been in such a state of suffering from pain for some time past, (although my complaints are said not to be dangerous), as to be quite disqualified for human society.

"I am restrained from giving utterance to all estimation of your verses by their excessive kindness to me; although I know your sincerity so well, that I am sure you think all you say; and I have too much respect for your judgment to be disposed to dispute its justice, when pronounced in my favour.

"Military laurels, by common consent of mankind, occupy the pinnacle of the Temple of Living Fame; and no statesman should envy a living hero, particularly if the great Captain should happen to be his own brother. But the page of history is wide enough to contain us all; and posterity will assign his proper place to each.

"I think Mrs. and Miss Fox a great deal too squeamish. The verses are really creditable to the young lady's genius; and the publication of them is my act, and not hers; therefore, there is no question affecting her modesty.

"Mrs. Malaprop (the original from whom Sheridan drew his character) resided at Bath; and there, somebody having mentioned a young lady, twelve years old, who was perfect in all accomplishments, she observed:—'For my part, I don't like those *praycooshus* young ladies.' This day the Chief Justice told me in the council chamber, Dublin Castle.

"Your Ladyship may be assured that I will omit no effort to obtain the Chief Justice's consent, and if I should fail (which I do not expect), you may rely on my endeavours to make ample amends, and fully to discharge so clear a debt of honour.

"Ever, my dear Lady Blessington,

"Your truly devoted servant,

"WELLESLEY."

"Kingston House, 3rd August, 1841.

"MY DEAR LADY BLESSINGTON,

"I return the verses, with a high sense of the value of your approbation; they were an Etonian exercise in the fifth form, which was *sent up for good.* I translated them the other day (or rather sleepless night), at the desire of Lady Maryborough.

"I am very much better, but I shall never think myself recovered, until I have been able to pay my duty to you.

"Ever, dear Lady Blessington,

"Your grateful and devoted servant,

"WELLESLEY."

CHAPTER II.

THE DUKE OF WELLINGTON.

ARTHUR WESLEY, third son of the Earl of Mornington, was born May the 1st, 1769,—but not at Dangan Castle, co. Meath, Ireland, as Burke erroneously states.*

* In the Public Register, or Freeman's Journal, of Saturday, May the 6th, 1769, there is the following brief announcement: "*Birth :—In Merrion Street, the Right Hon. the Countess of Mornington, of a son.*"

This newspaper was half-weekly, and only one publication could occur between Saturday, the 29th of April, and Saturday, May the 6th.

In Enshaw's Gentleman's Magazine, a monthly periodical published in Dublin, in the number for May, 1769, the following entry, in the list of births, is to be found. "*April 29, the Countess of Mornington, of a son.*"

In the Dublin Mercury, of Thursday, May the 4th, 1769, the same announcement is made, in the same words.

The parish books of St. Peter's Church, Dublin, contain the registry of the baptism, in the following words, at the foot of a page headed "Christenings, 1769."—"*April 30, Arthur, son of the Right Hon. Earl and Countess of Mornington ;*" and signed, *Isaac Mann, Archdeacon.* The east side of Upper Merrion Street was then, as it now is, included in the parish of St. Peter.

The house, No. 24, about the centre of the east side of Upper Merrion Street, now occupied by the Ecclesiastical Commissioners, was formerly the town residence of the father of the late Lord Cloncurry, who in his Memoirs makes mention of an entertainment given by his father to the Lord Lieutenant, "*at Mornington House, a residence in Merrion Street, which he had purchased from Lord the late Marquess Wellesley.*"

Mr. Burke, in his Peerage, erroneously records his Grace's birth at

Young Wesley was sent to Eton, afterwards to the Military College of Angers.

Whatever proficiency he may have made in military studies, in classical and literary attainments no pretensions to progress have ever been set up for him. The natural bent of his genius was in the direction of the former pursuits.

He entered the army at the age of eighteen, and the Irish House of Commons before he was twenty-two. In 1790, being then a Captain in the army, he was returned for the borough of Trim.

The 10th of January, 1793, the Hon. Mr. Wesley made his maiden speech, seconding a motion for an address to His Majesty, returning most cordial thanks for the royal message, recommending, amongst other matters for consideration, the situation of His Majesty's Catholic subjects to the serious attention of the Irish Parliament.

Mr. Wesley said :—"At a time when opinions were spreading throughout Europe, inimical to Government, it behoved us, in a particular manner, to lay before our gracious Sovereign our determination to support and maintain the constitution; he took notice that, under the present reign, this country had risen to a state of unexampled prosperity. He said that the augmentation of the forces, as mentioned in the speech, had, from the circumstances of the times, become necessary. He reprobated, in very severe terms, the conduct of the French towards their King, and their invasion of the territories of sovereign princes, and their irruption into the

Dangan Castle, county Meath, on the 1st of May, 1769; and in Dublin it was a generally received opinion that his Grace was born in a house that formerly stood on the site of the late Royal Irish Academy House, in Grafton Street.

The fact of the birth of the late Duke of Wellington, at No. 24, Upper Merrion Street, has been clearly established, in a pamphlet on the subject, by John Murray, Esq., A.M., LL.D., published in 1852.

Austrian Netherlands. He applauded the conduct of the administration of this country, for issuing the proclamation of the 8th of November, and he condemned the attempt of a set of men, styling themselves National Guards, and appearing in military array; a set of men unknown in the country, except by their attempts to overthrow the Government; the conduct of the administration, on that occasion, entitled them to the confidence of the people. In regard to what had been recommended in the speech from the throne, respecting our Catholic fellow-subjects, he could not repress expressing his approbation on that head; he had no doubt of the loyalty of the Catholics of this country, and he trusted that when the question would be brought forward, respecting that description of men, that we would lay aside all animosities, and act with moderation and dignity, and not with the fury and violence of partizans."*

Between the first effort in the Irish Parliament, in favour of the Catholic claims in 1793, and the final successful one in the British House of Commons in 1829, a great military career was accomplished, and a vast renown achieved.†

* Irish Parliamentary Debates, p. 5 1793.

† In 1787, he had received his first commission of Ensign. In the list of promotions, 1792, we read—" Honble. Arthur Wesley, from 58th Regiment of Foot, to be Captain, vice Crofton, in the 13th Regiment of Dragoons." After various promotions, he wa sappointed Lieutenant Colonel of the 33rd Foot in 1793. He served on the Continent, at the head of a brigade, in the Low Countries, and at Malines in 1794, and in 1797 joined his regiment in India.

After triumphant campaigns in the Mysore, the Nizam's territories, those of the Mahratta chiefs in the Deccan, Major-General Sir Arthur Wellesley resigned his command, and returned to England in March, 1805.

He married Lady Catherine Pakenham, third daughter of the Earl of Longford, in 1806; accepted the office of Chief Secretary for Ireland, with special privileges, in April, 1809, the Duke of Richmond being then Lord Lieutenant. Was second in command under Lord

From 1817, the Duke's services, being no longer needed in the field, were called into activity in conferences and congresses with the statesmen and sovereigns of foreign powers. In 1818, he and Lord Castlereagh attended the congress of Aix-la-Chapelle. As plenipotentiary from the British Government, the Duke assisted at the congress of Verona in 1822. He was appointed Master-General of the Ordnance in 1819. He succeeded the Duke of York, as Commander in Chief, in 1826.

Cathcart, in the expedition to Copenhagen, still retaining the office of Secretary of Ireland, in the summer of 1807. Landed in Corunna, with the rank of Lieut.-General, and the title of Sir Arthur Wellesley, 20th July, 1808. After the Treaty of Cintra, at the end of this campaign, returned to England in disgust, in the latter part of 1808. Resumed the duties of Chief Secretary for Ireland, and his seat in Parliament, January, 1809. After Sir John Moore's defeat, was appointed to the chief command of the army for the defence of Portugal, resigned his Irish office, and arrived in the Tagus in April, 1809, in which year he was created Baron Douro of Wellesley, and Viscount Wellington.

Having driven the French out of Portugal, gained victory after victory, and well-deserved honours and rewards, he entered Madrid with something like regal triumph in July, 1812, in which year he was created Earl of Wellington, and a few months later, Marquess of Douro, Duke of Wellington. The decisive battle of Vittoria was fought the 20th of June, 1813. A brief and brilliant campaign ended in the expulsion of the French army, 120,000 men, from Spain, in October, 1813. The British army, under the Duke of Wellington, bivouacked triumphantly on the soil of France, in November, 1813.

At the dissolution of Napoleon's empire, the Duke was dispatched to Paris, and appeared at the Tuilleries as British ambassador, in the early part of 1814. Six months later, he represented his country in the great congress of the Continental Allied Sovereigns.

On Napoleon's escape from Elba, in 1815, the command of the English army destined for the invasion of France was given to him.

The crowning victory of the great Duke was gained at Waterloo, in June, 1815. Foreign honours and distinctions innumerable,—a Principality— a Field-Marshal's baton — liberal grants and unparalleled popularity and pre-eminence at home—marked the general sense of his great services.

Being accused of having sought the office of Premier, when held by Mr. Canning, he declared, in his place in the House of Lords, in 1827, he was "sensible of being unqualified for such a situation," and that he "should have been mad to think of it."

Eight months later, he was Prime Minister of England. At the opening of the session, the policy of the Duke's Government, in favour of Catholic Emancipation, was announced from the throne, 5th February, 1829. The Relief Bill passed both houses, and received the royal assent, within two months of that period. The declaration against Parliamentary Reform was made at the commencement of the session, November, 1829. The downfall of the old Toryism for ever, and of the Wellington party for ten years, dated from 1830.

The 7th of June, 1832, the royal assent was given to the Reform Bill, and on the 18th of the same month the Duke of Wellington was assaulted by the populace in Fenchurch Street, and nearly dismounted; and for the first time in his life, turned his back on assailants.

On the fall of the Whigs, he resumed his place in the Cabinet, but without special office of any kind, in 1841.

On the accession of the Whigs to power, the command of the army again reverted to him on the death of General Lord Hill. He gave no factious opposition to any government, except to that of Mr. Canning. He said that "he knew the Queen's government must be carried on," so he assisted the Whigs when he thought they deserved support; and whenever the Court was in any difficulty, the Duke was invariably sent for, and was relied on to the last for sure counsel in all dilemmas.

September the 14th, 1852, the greatest General of his age terminated his career of glory, aged eighty-three years.

Wellington's best fame rests on the confidence in his plain

dealing, and direct, straight-forward views of public duty, and of obligation to truth and fairness, with which he had the ability to inspire men of all grades, and in all circumstances, throughout the whole of his career in private and in public, and alike in a military and a civil capacity.

Sir Robert Peel pronounced a noble eulogy on his illustrious friend, in which, with the instinct of a great and wise man, setting forth truth as the most glorious of all virtues, he said—the Duke "was the truest man he had ever known." This was a great eulogy; the Duke's memory may dispense with any other.

LETTERS FROM THE LATE DUKE OF WELLINGTON TO LADY BLESSINGTON.

"London, March 3rd.

"My dear Lady Blessington,

"Notwithstanding the circumstances which I mentioned to your Ladyship yesterday, and that I, in fact, have no personal knowledge of your brother, which always renders it difficult to recommend to another the person, in respect to whom one labours under this disadvantage; I have at your desire, written the enclosed letter to Sir Hudson Lowe, which I hope will answer the purpose of drawing his attention to him.

"Ever your Ladyship's
"Most faithful servant,
"Wellington."

"London, February 6th, 1830.

"I am going out of town myself to-morrow morning, but I have desired my servant to attend you with this note; and the only drawing that I have of Lady D——, which has not been engraved.

"Ever yours, most faithfully,
"Wellington."

"London, Dec. 15, 1837.

"I enclose a letter for Sir John Hervey. I am afraid that it will not be of much use to Captain P——, as I am not much acquainted with Sir John Hervey.

"Believe me ever
"Yours, most sincerely,
"WELLINGTON."

"London, May 24th, 1838.

"I am delighted to learn that my recommendation of Captain P—— to Sir John Hervey has been of use to him.

"I received with gratitude your beautiful present, and perused it with delight.

"I have been very remiss in having omitted to thank you for sending it to me. I beg you to forgive me, and to thank you now for the gratification which the perusal of this work gave me.

"Believe me ever yours,
"Most sincerely,
"WELLINGTON."

"London, June 12th, 1838.

"Nothing will give me greater satisfaction than to receive any body that you recommend to me.

"Foreigners are not exactly aware of our habits, they think that we sit up to receive visits and compliments as they do. Unfortunately, I don't find the day long enough to be able to receive all who are really under the necessity of seeing me. However, I will receive Mons. Rio, or any body else you will send to me.

"I return Monsieur de Chateaubriand's account of [ ]*

"Believe me to be
"Yours, most sincerely,
"WELLINGTON."

"London, June 14th, 1838.

"It has given me the greatest pain to have been under the necessity of sending away Mons. de Rio without receiving him.

"I know how unpleasant it is to a gentleman to [ ]†

* Word illegible all but two first letters, He.—R. R. M.

† Three words illegible.—R. R. M.

and as I had so many people with me and waiting, I thought it best to request him to call on any other day.

"I cannot but feel, however, that there is no time so uselessly employed by a visitor, and him upon whom the visit is inflicted, as in these visitations of ceremony.

"Believe me to be
"Yours, most sincerely,
"WELLINGTON."

"January 16th, 1839.

"I am much flattered by your Ladyship's recollection, evinced by your recommendation of a gentleman to be appointed Provost of Worcester College, Oxford.

"Since I heard of the vacancy in that office, which it becomes my duty to fill, in my capacity of Chancellor of the University, I had been considering the qualifications of the several candidates, not less than seventy in number; and consulting with archbishops, bishops, and the heads of the University, in respect to the choice to be made.

"I acknowledge that it never occurred to me to refer to the ladies, and I return my thanks to the one who has assisted me with her counsel.

"I am apprehensive, however, that I cannot hold out expectations to Mr. Landor that he will be appointed.

"The Provost of Worcester College has the government of that institution. The qualifications required to enable him to perform the duties of the office are various, and quite different from those which have attracted your attention towards Mr. Landor. In the choice which I shall make, I must satisfy not only the College and its visitors, but the University, the Church, and the public at large.

"I hope, therefore, that you will excuse me if I decline to attend to your wishes upon this occasion.

"Believe me ever your
"Most faithful servant,
"WELLINGTON."

"London, March 2d, 1839.

"You are one of that kind part of the creation which don't feel the difference between conferring a favour and asking a favour.

"You are right; he from whom the favour is asked, ought to be as much delighted with the occasion afforded of gratifying the fair solicitor, as he would be by the favour conferred.

"I am very much amused by your recollection of my note upon your recommendation of Mr. Landor.

"I return my best thanks for your present. I will peruse it with much interest.

"Believe me ever

"Yours, most faithfully,

"WELLINGTON."

"London, April 5th, 1844.

"After I had written to you yesterday, or rather sent my note, I learned last night, that my daughter-in-law is going out of town, and I enclose a note directing my housekeeper to shew my house to Monsieur P——— on to-morrow, Tuesday.

"Since writing the above, I have received your note of the 4th. I will certainly go and see the statue of Napoleon, at the first leisure moment I may have. This day, if possible.

"Ever yours, most faithfully,

"WELLINGTON."

"London, August 3rd, 1844.

"I have this evening received your note of yesterday.

"My daughter-in-law is now inhabiting the apartments in this house, in which the pictures are placed.

"And I should certainly prefer that she should not be disturbed by persons coming to look at them; she will probably go out of town in a short time, and I will then send you an order directing my housekeeper to shew the house to Monsieur Pleyel.

"If, however, she should be going away, I will send you an order forthwith for the admission of ———.

"Believe me ever

"Yours, most faithfully,

"WELLINGTON."

"London, November 22, 1844.

"I am very grateful for the beautiful work which you have been so kind as to send me.

"I should be delighted to see the new work of art just finished by Count D'Orsay: would you be so kind as to tell me where I could see it?

"Believe me ever
"Yours, most faithfully,
"WELLINGTON."

"London, February 21st, 1845.

"I was very sorry that I had not the pleasure of finding your Ladyship at home, when Count D'Orsay was so kind as to shew me his beautiful sketches some days ago.

"I have delayed to thank you for your kind note, in hopes that I might be able to call upon you at a particular hour.

"But I am sorry to say I cannot yet do so; but I hope that it may be in my power to do so by to-morrow morning.

"Believe me ever
"Yours, most faithfully,
"WELLINGTON."

"London, June 19th, 1845.

"I am very much obliged to you! Count D'Orsay will really spoil me, and make me vain in my old age! by sending me down to posterity by the exercise of every description of talent with which he is endowed!

"I will certainly call upon you at the very first moment I can.

"Ever yours sincerely,
"WELLINGTON."

"London, July 22, 1845, at night.

"I have just now received your note of this day, upon the melancholy death of Lord C———. I had learned with much concern of his pecuniary embarrassments occasioned by the fire in 1834. It appears to me that you are mistaken, in supposing that when he was created a Peer, provision was made for him by the grant of a pension from the Civil List. As well as I recollect, the ——— of ———, his father had been enabled to grant to him the reversion of an office in the ——— of ———, the emoluments of which were then considered in making the usual provision for him when he should no longer be the ——— of ———.

" But my recollection of the transaction is very imperfect; and, after all, I judge from your statement, that when he retired from the ———, the usual provision was made for him from the Consolidated Fund, under the authority of the provisions of an act of parliament. I am certain that the grant could not have been given from the Civil List, because I know that the total that the minister can grant, in any one year, from that fund, is £12,000 a year. You have done quite right in applying to Sir Robert Peel. No grant can be made from the Consolidated Fund, excepting under authority of the provisions of an act of parliament, which act must originate in the House of Commons. But the House will not take into consideration the investigation of a grant of money, which is not, in the first instance, recommended by the Crown. I am not aware of any precedent of a grant from the Consolidated Fund to the widow of a deceased grantee, and whatever the merits and services of Lord ———, I think it very probable that Sir Robert Peel might think it unreasonable to expect to prevail on the House to make such a grant to Lord ———'s widow and child, in addition to the provision made from the same fund to his son, who succeeds to the title, and not consistent with a due performance of his duty to the Queen to make the attempt.

" In respect to your desire that I shall suggest to Sir Robert Peel to make this arrangement, I am convinced that Sir Robert Peel requires no suggestion from me to induce him to adopt every measure in his power, and consistent with his duty, to mark the respect for the memory and affection for the person of the late Lord C———. I have told you what I think of the nature of the case, and of the difficulties in which Sir Robert Peel may find himself placed; if he should think it necessary, and that my opinion could be of any use to him, I am certain that he will speak to me, knowing as he does, the regard I have always felt for my departed friend!

"But feeling, as I do, that in my position in the House of Lords, I can do nothing which can relieve him from the pressure of the difficulties which will exist in the House of Commons, it appears to me that I ought not to interfere, unless and till Sir Robert should require my opinion and assistance. Solicitation is out of the question. It is not desired by you, and would not be listened to by Sir Robert Peel; and as I know I can do nothing to assist him and overcome the difficulties of the case, I am convinced I do that which is best for the case as well as most becoming, by delaying to make a suggestion till I shall be required. Believe me ever

"Yours, most sincerely,

"WELLINGTON."

"London, January 19, 1847, at night.

"I received your note of this day when I returned home, at too late an hour to communicate on this day with Mr. Tuffett; but I will do so on Monday. You are quite right. Count D'Orsay's work is of a higher description of art than is described by the word portrait! But I described it by that word, because the likeness is so remarkably good, and so well executed as a painting, and that this is the truest of all artistic ability, truest of all in this country. I am really not a judge of the effect of my name in the newspapers, but I am sensible of the effect produced by any manifestations of interest in an officer I might wish dealt with favourably. Believe me,

"My dear Lady Blessington,

"WELLINGTON."

"London, June 19th, 1847.

"I shall be delighted to see a good engraving of Count D'Orsay's picture of the Queen on horseback.

"But I should prefer not to take any steps to attain that object till it is seen what the Queen and the Prince themselves do as to the object of your wishes.

"Unless it should be decidedly disadvantageous to the Count to wait a little longer, I would recommend him to do so.

"Let me know what he determines.

"Ever yours, most faithfully,

"WELLINGTON."

"London, August 7th, 1849.

"I have received your Ladyship's note, and am much concerned to learn that the gentleman in question is unwell.

"I don't know at what time my daughter-in-law will return.

"But if you will write me a note when the gentleman will be sufficiently well to look at pictures in gentlemen's houses, I will send you an order by my servant to shew them, if my daughter-in-law should not be at the moment inhabiting the apartments.

"Ever yours, most faithfully,

"WELLINGTON."

LETTER FROM LORD FITZROY SOMERSET TO LADY BLESSINGTON.

"Horse Guards, June 11, 1848.

"DEAR LADY BLESSINGTON,

"The Duke of Wellington will be happy to consider your nephew H. F——, a candidate for a commission by purchase, and to introduce him into the service when his other very numerous engagements may permit.

"Believe me, very faithfully

"Yours, FITZROY SOMERSET."

THE DUKE OF WELLINGTON.

(LATE MARQUIS OF DOURO.)

The eldest son of the late Duke of Wellington, by a daughter of the second Lord Longford, who died in 1831, was one of the most intimate friends of the Countess of Blessington. He was born in 1807; completed his education at Trinity College, Cambridge; was returned to parliament, and represented Aldborough in 1829-30-31, and again entered parliament for Norwich in 1837, which place he represented till 1852. He married, in 1839, Lady Elizabeth Hay, daughter of the Marquis of Tweedale; was aide-de-camp to his father from 1842 to 1852, and in the latter year, succeeded to the title. He was appointed Master of the Horse to the Queen,

January, 1853, Lieutenant-Commandant of the Victoria (Middlesex) Rifles, August, 1853.

Lady Blessington, whose insight into character was not the least remarkable of her qualities, said of the Marquis of Douro, that "he had a fund of common sense, of rich humour, and of good nature, sufficient for half-a-dozen elder sons of the nobility."

It is difficult to touch on the character of a man whose position in society, however exalted, is that of a private individual, bearing an historic name, and having no personal distinction apart from it. Free from ostentation, simple in his tastes and manners, reserved in society, but fond of it, and easily drawn towards those who shine in it, naturally generous and warm-hearted, keenly perceptive of the ridiculous, of a very original turn of mind, shrewd and sensible, a close observer of character, with a profound admiration and respect for the memory of his illustrious father, the qualities of this young nobleman were calculated to render him a favourite in such circles as those of Gore House, and with those who presided over them.

FROM THE MARQUIS OF DOURO.

"Tuesday.

"My dear Lady Blessington,

"I have shewn your verses to the most brilliant German Professor in the world, and he can make nothing of them. I therefore restore them to you, resisting the temptation to *compose* a translation, which certainly never could be detected.

"Yours sincerely,

"Douro."

CHAPTER III.

SIR EDWARD BULWER LYTTON.

EDWARD LYTTON BULWER, born in 1805, the third son of William Earle Bulwer, Esq., of Heydon Hall and Wood Dalling, Norfolk, (Brigadier-General), by his marriage in 1798, with Elizabeth Barbara, daughter and sole heiress of Richard Warburton Lytton, Esq., of Knebworth Park, Herts,* succeeded to the Knebworth estates, by the will of his mother, who died the 19th December, 1844, and taking the surname of Lytton, by sign manual, became the representative of his mother's family, and the head of the two other ancient houses, of Lytton of Knebworth, and of Robinson, or Norreys.

In 1838, on account of his literary merit, he was created a Baronet. He married, 29th August, 1827, Rosina, only surviving daughter of Francis Wheeler, Esq., of Lizzard Connel, county Limerick, and had issue, Edward Robert, born 8th November, 1832, and a daughter, named Emily Elizabeth, deceased. Bulwer's precocious poetical talents, like those of Byron, manifested themselves before he was

* This venerable lady, Mrs. Elizabeth Barbara Bulwer Lytton, died at her house, in Upper Seymour Street, at the age of seventy, 19th December, 1844. There is no trait in the character of Sir Edward Bulwer Lytton more remarkable or creditable than that of strong filial attachment, with all its feelings of high respect and tender affection, which, at every period of his career, he appears to have entertained for his mother.

seven years of age. He was placed at private schools in the neighbourhood of Knebworth, at an early age; was for some time under the care of private tutors, preparatory to his being sent to college, and completed his education at Cambridge. He wrote a poem on "Sculpture," while he was at college, which obtained the prize for poetry. One of his earliest productions was a collection of small poems —"Weeds and Wild Flowers," which was printed in 1826, when he was twenty-one years of age, but was not published. This production was followed by "O'Neil, the Rebel," in 1827. His next work was "Falkland;" but the name and fame of Bulwer only became known after the publication of "Pelham," in 1828.* A writer in Bentley's Miscellany, apparently conversant with Bulwer's labours, and acquainted with his habits and modes of application to study, observes, "Bulwer worked his way to eminence—worked it—through failure, through ridicule. His facility is only the result of practice and study. He wrote at first very slowly, and with great difficulty: but he resolved to master the stubborn in-

* The "Disowned" was published in 1829, and "Paul Clifford" in 1830. At various intervals from the latter date, appeared, "Eugene Aram," "The Siamese Twins, a serio-comic Poem;" "Conversations of an Ambitious Student," "England and the English," "The Pilgrim of the Rhine," "The Last Days of Pompeii," an historico-descriptive novel; "The Crisis," a political brochure; "Rienzi, or the Tribune;" "The Duchess de la Valiere," a drama; "The Lady of Lyons," a drama; "Richelieu," a drama; "Money," a drama; "Ernest Maltravers," "Alice, or the Mysteries;" "Athens," "Leila, or the Siege of Grenada;" "Calderon, the Courtier;" "Night and Morning," "Day and Night," "Last of the Barons," "Zanoni," "Eva, the Ill-omened Marriage, and other Tales and Poems;" "Harold," "Lucretia;" "The New Timon," and "King Arthur," [two politico-satirical poems, without the author's name;] "Letters to John Bull," in favour of Protection; and a drama, written for private representation, "Not so Bad as we Seem;" were followed by two of his latest and best novels, "The Caxtons," and "My Novel."

strument of thought, and mastered it. He has practised writing as an art, and has re-written some of his essays, unpublished, nine or ten times over. Another habit will shew the advantage of continuous application. He only writes about three hours a day, from ten in the morning till one—seldom later. The evenings, when alone, are devoted to reading, scarcely ever to writing. Yet what an amount of good hard labour has resulted from these three hours. He writes very rapidly, averaging twenty pages a day of novel print."

I very much question the fact, that Sir Edward restricts his literary labour to three hours a day. I am very sure that if double the amount of time were given to the performance of the same amount of labour as he must go through—mind and body would suffer less from its accomplishment. The composition of a work, and the transcription of MS. to the extent of twenty printed pages, in three hours, is too much for a continuance of many days; the time allowed for the labour is too short for its performance, without an excessive wear and tear of mental and physical energies.

A writer in Fraser's Magazine, reviewing Sir B. Brodie's "Psychological Inquiries," makes the following observations on mental labour:—

"Cuvier was usually engaged for seven hours daily in his scientific researches, these not having been of a nature to require continuous thought; and Sir Walter Scott devoted about six hours daily to literary composition, and then his mind was in a state to enjoy lighter pursuits afterwards. When, however, after his misfortunes, he allowed himself no relaxation, there can be little doubt, as Eubulus observes, that his over-exertion contributed, as much as the moral suffering he endured, to the production of the disease of the brain which ultimately caused his death.

"One day, when he was thus exerting himself beyond his

powers, Sir Walter said to Captain Basil Hall, who also suffered and died from disease in the brain—

" 'How many hours can you work?'

" 'Six,' answered the Captain.

" 'But can't you put on the spurs?'

" 'If I do, the horse won't go.'

" 'So much the better for you,' said Scott, with a sigh. 'When I put on the spurs, the horse *will* go well enough; but it is killing the horse."

The fact is, it is as impossible to lay down rules for the management of the mind, and the regulation of its labour, as we do for the management of the body, and the uses and application of its powers. The same amount of labour of the mind that one man could endure during six hours of the day, for a considerable time, without detriment to his health, bodily or physical, would prove fatal to another in half that period.

Sir Bulwer Lytton first entered parliament for St. Ives, and next represented Lincoln.

From 1841 to 1852, he remained out of parliament, and in the latter year, was returned for his native county, Hertford.

Few English writers whose compositions consist chiefly of works of imagination, have attained such an eminence in literature as he has done. From "Pelham" to "My Novel," we have a series of works, extending to about fifty volumes, any one of which productions might suffice to make a reputation for an ordinary novelist.

But it is to the aggregate of the works of Sir E. B Lytton, we must look for the evidences of those remarkable intellectual qualities which are destined to make the productions of a man of his stamp live in after-ages.

The author's consciousness of possessing such qualities is not only sufficiently evident in those novels; it is rather prominently obtrusive in some of them. But the author cannot be more fully persuaded of the fact than his readers, that his writings are destined to influence his times, and that living proofs of his intellectual powers will long survive the latter.

One of the most characteristic features of Bulwer's writings is, the singular combination of worldly experience—a perfect knowledge of life, and especially of life in the upper circles of society, a thorough acquaintance with its selfishness and specious fallacies —*ses miseres et ses bassesses*, with the vast amount of genuine poetry that prevails in his prose writings. With the exception of Scott's novels, "Ivanhoe," and "The Bride of Lammermoor," especially, no works of fiction in the English language abound with so many passages of true poetry as the novels of Bulwer. The greatest misfortune that the Republic of Letters has suffered perhaps, for the past twenty years, is the calamity of Bulwer belonging to the aristocracy and to politics, being a Baronet, a Member of Parliament, and a man of a plentiful estate. Intellectual gifts like his, of the highest order, were never given for some sections only of society, that are highly favoured and peculiarly privileged, but for mankind at large, and for greater and higher purposes than providing entertainment for the leisure hours of the upper classes. They were given for the promotion of higher interests than those material ones of the Manchester school of philosophy, and the aims and ends of a Godless spirit of utilitarianism, pretending to care for poverty, and to be actuated and directed by Christian motives. They were given to advance the true interests of the masses of the people of his own land especially; to enable him to contribute to their enlightenment, to spiritualize and purify their minds, and to elevate their condition—physical as well as moral.

If I am not greatly mistaken, this opinion peeps through many pages of every work of fiction that has been published by Sir E. B. Lytton during the past twelve or fifteen years. Like all men of great intellectual endowments, the consciousness of the existence of those powers, and the sense of the great obligations they impose on their possessor, are continually struggling for expression, and unconsciously find it frequently in his writings.

We are reminded in them, perpetually, that the author has the power, and knows that he possesses it, of doing greater and better things in literature than any that he has attempted or achieved.

The popularity of this prolific author has endured for upwards of twenty years. For one reader of his works prepared to cavil with their merits, twenty will be found to admire them. No man who ever occupied the position that Sir E. B. Lytton has done in literary life, considering the fame he has acquired, coming frequently before the public, and always with claims to notice, that rather force themselves on attention than solicit an indulgent reception, and insinuate themselves into the good graces of the public, has escaped more lightly the penalty of notoriety—that tax of envy and censure which pre-eminent ability pays for the privilege of distinction: and this observation is made with a knowledge of all the little wars of criticism that little men in periodical literature have waged on him.

As a literati *sui generis*, his aims and turn of mind, style and mode of philosophizing in fiction, must be well studied, before the peculiarities of his genius can be properly comprehended. It is only by those, whose knowledge of him in private enables them to appreciate his benevolent disposition, his readiness to acknowledge the merits of his literary cotemporaries and competitors, to serve the unfortunate, and to encourage struggling merit, that any apparent anomalies in his literary character can be reconciled.

By Lady Blessington, his talents and his worth were held in the highest estimation.

LETTERS FROM SIR EDWARD BULWER LYTTON TO LADY BLESSINGTON.

"Paris, 31 August, 1833.

"MY DEAR LADY BLESSINGTON,

"You were kind enough to wish that I should sometimes write to you, and I take an early opportunity of doing so, because I read in the papers of your loss, and I sympathize most sincerely in it.* I trust the robber did not take any of those beautiful little treasures which used to ornament your rooms, and for which, I know, you must have formed an absolute attachment;—an attachment which, unlike others in general, cannot be easily replaced; for, somehow or other, we seem to value the relics of people at a higher rate than themselves; and one would regret more, perhaps, to lose a portrait of Madame de Sevigné, than many of her contemporaries may have felt when they lost Madame de Sevigné herself.

"Paris is much better than it was last year; it is beginning to recover from its glorious revolution. It is all very fine to say liberty is useful to trade, but whenever liberty stretches herself, she always kicks poor trade out of doors. Louis Philippe amuses himself by making fine speeches, in answer to fine addresses; the people look on, and laugh. For France, however it may seem to change, is never employed but in two things, either laughing or crying. As for the theatres, they are carrying indecency to the utmost. Queen Caroline and Bergami delight us at one theatre, and something worse at another.

"Do you know, I find Paris a melancholy place; if one has seen it in one's earliest youth, it reminds one of the vast interval of mind that has elapsed. Say what we will, there is nothing

* Robbers had entered the house in Seamore Place at night, and from Lady Blessington's drawing-room carried away trinkets, consisting of seals, snuff-boxes, smelling bottles, &c., to the value of upwards of £1000. Lady Blessington afterwards received a letter from one of the thieves at the hulks, giving an account of the robbery, and stating that when the jewels were broken up and sold piecemeal, the party divided £700 among them.—R. R. M.

like youth; all we gain in our manhood is dullness itself compared to the zest of novelty, and the worst of it is, the process of acquiring wisdom is but another word for the process of growing old. Adieu, dear Lady Blessington,

"Ever truly yours,

"E. L. B."

"Bath, January 19, 1833.

"A thousand thanks for your kind letter, which was a new corroboration of the maxim, that they who have every right to be pleased with themselves, have a natural fascination in pleasing others.

"One's vanity is a quarrelsome companion, and always falling out with one; you reconcile it to oneself with the same art which others employ in widening the breach, and sharpening the contest. I may not say that I disbelieve the countless obliging things you say of me, but I may say at least that I know how little I deserve them, and in proportion to my demerits I estimate your kindness, and am affected by your praise. But I will not dwell more on that part of your letter, however tempting, lest you should think I am recurring to the old trick of authors, and seeking in modesty an excuse for egotism.

"I can fully sympathize with poor Count D'Orsay in the horror that must have seized upon him, when he saw himself an ex-minister, on the wrong side of fifty (I suppose), and an author 'who could not be offered any thing fit for a gentleman to receive!' He has been singularly unlucky of late. It seems as if there were a magical conspiracy against him. He is not only killed, but transformed; he is not only to be a dead man, but a Pythagorean; they want to make him believe, not only that the soul is out of his own body, but that it is transmigrated into the body of Baron D'Haussez. I don't wonder at his anxiety on the matter, and have already written to assure him that the mistake was only orthographical. * * * * knew the difference between D'Orsay and D'Haussez, but he did not know how to spell the difference between them.†

† The Baron D'Haussez, ex-minister of Marine of Charles X., was a frequent visitor at Seamore Place in 1832 and 1833.—R. R. M.

"And now, dear Lady Blessington, adieu. Many repeated thanks, warm and sincere, for all your kindness to me.

"E. L. B."

"Hotel Vittoria, Naples, November 26th.

"Behold me then at Naples, beautiful, enchanting, delicious Naples, the only city in all Italy, (except old Verona, whose gable ends and motley architecture, and hanging balconies, still speak of Shakespeare and of Romeo) which is quite to my heart. I freeze in the desolate dullness of Rome, with its prosing antiquaries and insolent slaves. In Venice I fancy myself on board a ship, viz. 'in a prison, with the chance of being drowned.' In Florence I recognize a bad Cheltenham. In Naples, I for the first time find my dreams of Italy. Your magic extends even here, and the place to which you have given me letters of introduction, seems to catch a charm from your beauty, and an endearment from your kindness. What a climate, and what a sea; the humour and gaiety of the people delight me. I should be in paradise if it were not for the mosquitos. But these, in truth, are terrible tormentors; they even seem to accustom themselves to me, and behave with the polite indifference of satiety; they devour me piecemeal; they are worse than a bad conscience, and never let me sleep at nights. I am told, for my comfort, that when the cold weather comes they will vanish, and leave me alternating between the desire to enjoy the day, and the hope to rest at night.

"I presented your letter to Sir William Gell, who kindly asked me to breakfast, where I found him surrounded with his dogs, amidst which he wheels himself about (for he is entirely unable to stand) in his large chair, and seems to enjoy life, enough to make a man in the possession of the use of his limbs hang himself with envy. I never knew so popular or so petted a man as Sir William Gell; every one seems to love him—yet there is something artificial and cold about him *au fond*, pardon me for saying so.

"Old Matthias is here, employing his eighty-first year in putting T———'s poems into Italian verse. These old men have time to amuse themselves, we young ones are so busy that we seem as if we had not a moment to live.

"While I thank you for your introduction to Sir William Gell, I ought not to forget that to Landor, who was particularly kind to me, and whom I liked exceedingly. One is at home instantly with men of real genius; their oddities, their humours, don't put one out half so much as the formal regularity of your half-clever prigs. But Landor, thanks to your introduction, had no humours, no oddities, for me. He invited me to his villa, which is charmingly situated, and smoothed himself down so much, that I thought him one of the best-bred men I ever met, as well as one of the most really able: (pity, nevertheless, so far as his talent is concerned, that he pets paradoxes so much: he keeps them as other people keep dogs, coaxes them, plays with them, and now and then sets them to bite a disagreeable intruder.)

"He gave me two letters, to his friend T——— M———, and to a Miss M———, and I confess I felt a melancholy in leaving him. How much he might do! What a true, bold, honest genius he has! It makes me sad to see men like him indolent and happy. I fancy their career is blighted, yet it is perhaps just the reverse. We, the noisy, the active, the ambitious, it is we who fulfil not our end,

"'and wear
Our strength away in wrestling with the air.'

"Mr. Craven too, has been most kind. How well he plays! I was not aware that he was an author, by-the-by, till I saw his book bound in calf's skin. It seemed, on looking into it, pleasant and well written.

"Pray tell me how your Annual succeeds? I hear no news, I read no papers. Dumb to me the new oracles of my old Magazine. Politics reach me not. I miss the roar of London. I feel how much, while I have joked at the English, I love England. What a country! what force! what energy! what civilisation! How it shames the talkative slaves here. But it is time to end.

"E. L. B."

"January 24, 1835.

"It is certainly a blessed thing that one is not absolutely at the mercy of other people. The reports concerning me appear to 'progress' in a regular climax. First, I had not a shilling, and an execution was in my house; then I was bought by the Tories, and now I am dead! They have taken away fortune, honesty, and lastly, life itself. Such are the pleasures of reputation!

"Just before you sent, Lady C—— B—— was also pleased to despatch a message to know at what hour I had departed this world? Three other successive deputations arrived, and this morning, on opening a Lincoln paper, I found that there too it had been reported 'that their excellent representative was no more.' I consider that I have paid the debt of nature—that I am virtually dead—that I am born again with a new lease—and that the years I have hitherto lived are to be struck off the score of the fresh life I have this morning awakened to.

"I believe, my dearest friend, that you were shocked with the report, and would, in your kind heart, have grieved for its truth. So would four or five others; and the rest would have been pleased at the excitement; it would have been something to talk about before the meeting of Parliament.

"The author of the 'Seaport Sketches' was very foolish, begging his pardon. Literature has many mansions; and I am sure 'Pompeii' is not one of the best of them. As well might I burn my books, after reading Don Quixote.

"I am delighted to see M—— in 'the Keepsake.' What is it? I guess, an Essay on Friendship, or Roman History, or Hume's Philosophy. After all this promise, all the assurances that M. was to be a great author by-and-bye, out he comes, at the age of fifty, in a sketch for 'the Keepsake!'

"I am now going to plunge into Histories of China, light my pipe, read a page, and muse an hour, and be very dull and melancholy for the rest of the evening. Still it is some consolation to think one is not—dead!

"E. L. B."

"December, 1834.

"I am rejoiced that Lord D—— admires Fonblanque as he deserves. Honour, wisdom, and genius!—what a combination to reconcile one to mankind, and *such* honour, *such* wisdom, and *such* genius as Fonblanque; the three highest attributes, in the highest degree!

"You say you think I am less pleased by praise of myself than you are; I know not that—but this I do know, that kindness does more than please—it conquers, it subdues me; and in you I see enough to falsify a thousand theories, and for ever to deprive me of the only true philosophy, viz. indifference to all things.

"E. L. B."

"January 19th, 1835.

"....If I should be well enough the day after to-morrow, I should then be enchanted if you would let me accompany you in your drive for an hour, and revive me by your agreeable news of politics, literature, and the world. Ten thousand thanks for D'Orsay's offer. But Phæton is not quite strong enough to manage Apollo's horses—'souls made of fire, and children of the sun'—as William * * * * 's nose long testified.

"I have just landed from the three-volume voyage of 'Peter Simple.' The characters are exaggerated out of all truth, and the incidents, such as changing children, shutting up the true heir in a madhouse, &c. are at once stale and impossible. But, despite this, he (Marryatt) has a frank, dashing genius, and splashes about the water in grand style. He writes like a *man*, and that is more than most of the other novelists do, who have neither the vigour of one sex, nor the refinement of the other. * * *, to wit, now and then swaggers, but it is always in petticoats!

"E. L. B."

"January 23, 1835.

"Verily, my dearest friend, you regale me like Prince Prettyman, in the Fairy Isle. I owe you all manner of thanks for a most delicate consideration, in the matter of twelve larks, which flew hither on the wings of friendship yesterday; and scarcely had I recovered from their apparition, when lo, the rushing pinions of a brace of woodcocks.

"Sappho, and other learned persons, tell us that Venus drove sparrows; at present, she appears to have re-modelled her equipage upon a much more becoming and attractive feather.

I own that I have always thought the Dove himself a fool to a Woodcock, whom, for his intrinsic merits, I would willingly crown king of the tribe. As for your Eagle, he is a Carlist of the old regime, a mere Bourbon, good for nothing, and pompous; but the woodcock, *parlez moi de ça.* He has the best qualities, both of head and heart; and as for beauty, what opera-dancer ever had such a leg? I have given their two majesties into Rembault's honourable charge, and hope they will be crowned to-morrow, as a matter of *course.*

"Many thanks for the volume of Monsieur de B——. You are right. I never saw a cooler plagiarism in my life. I shall certainly retaliate upon M. De B—— the moment I can find any thing in him worth stealing! Yet the wretch has talent, and his French seems to me purer and better (but I am a very poor judge) than that of most of his contemporaries. But then he has no elevation, and therefore no true genius, and has all the corruptions of vice without her brilliancy. Good Heaven! has the mighty mischief of Voltaire transmigrated into such authorlings. *They* imitate his mockery, his satire! They had much better cobble shoes!

"I don't (pardon me) believe a word you say about the 'Two Friends.' If it have no passion, it may be an admirable novel nevertheless. Miss Edgeworth has no passion;—and who in her line excels her?

"As to your own doubts, they foretell your success. I have always found, one is never so successful as when one is least sanguine. I fell in the deepest despondency about 'Pompeii' and 'Eugene Aram;' and was certain, nay, most presumptuous about 'Devereux,' which is the least generally popular of my writings. Your feelings of distrust are presentiments to be read backward; they are the happiest omen. But I will tell you all about it—Brougham-like—when I have read the book. As to what I say in the preface to 'Pelham,' the rules that I lay down may not suit all. But it may be worth while just to scan over two or three commonplace books of general criticism, such as Blair's 'Belles Lettres,' Campbell's 'Rhetoric,' and Schlegel's 'Essay on the Drama,' and his brother's on 'Literature.'

"They are, it is true, very mediocre, and say nothing of novels to signify; but they will suggest to a thoughtful mind a thousand little maxims of frequent use. Recollect, all that is said of poetry and the drama may be applied to novels; but after all, I doubt not you will succeed equally without this trouble. Reflection in one's chamber, and action in the world, are the best critics. With them, we can dispense with other teachers; without them, all teachers are in vain. 'Fool!' (says Sidney in the Arcadia), 'Fool! look in thy heart and write!'

"E. L. B."

"1835.

"I had fancied the air (of Acton) would revive me, but I am miserably ill to-day, and have sent for the 'leech,' as the poets call a doctor, why, I don't know, except because when he once fastens on us, we can't shake him off till he has got enough of our substance! I suspect that epidemic mystery, the Influenza, to be mine enemy on this occasion; and to add to my misfortunes, while I am dying to go to bed, I am obliged to go to the House. After all, life is a troublesome business, and I often long to shut up shop and retire from the profession."

(No date.)

"I am slowly preparing my unwieldy masses of History for the press. Fiction begins to lose all charm for me—I mean, to write it. The reading is still delightful, especially when one meets with friends.

"I spend all the day by the water-side, with the sun full in my face. I feel as if I were drinking life from it like a fountain. Nature meant me for a salamander, and that is the reason I have always been discontented as a man—I shall be a salamander in the next world."

"Paris, January 5, 1836.

"I have been out little at present, though such of the world as I have encountered seem inclined to pet the lion if he will let them. But a gregarious lion, after all, would be but a sheep in disguise. Authors are made to be ascetics, and it is in vain to struggle, as I once did, against the common fate—

made to go through the world sowing dreams to reap disappointments, to sacrifice grave interests to generous whims, to aspire to be better, and wiser, and tenderer, than others; though they may seem worse, and more visionary, and harsher, and so at last to shut up their souls in patient scorn, and find that even appreciation and justice come too late. In politics here, all seem to think France tolerably calm, and the ministry tolerably safe. I went to see the Chamber opened the other day, and was amused at the *Frenchness* of all I saw. The King's shrugs and grins, and then the 'vives emotions,' which replied to his well-turned periods. I have been supine and idle here, save in the composition of a long poetical epistle to you; I like it tolerably, and will send it by the next bag.* I have some thoughts of launching on the public a volume of Poems. What do they say of things in England? Here, there is a general feeling that the Whigs cannot stand. For my part, I think a republic certain, if perpetual changes in government are to keep men always unsettled, and play the deuce with trade and quiet.

"E. L. B."

"September 17, 1836.

"Here I am, rusticating calmly amongst the apples of Devonshire. I made an agreeable and prolonged tour through Hampshire by the New Forest; and skirting the Dorsetshire coast, arrived safely at my present abode, some few miles from the sea. My avocations are as simple as my history. I *literatize* away the morning, ride at three, go to bathe at five, dine at six, and get through the evening as I best may, sometimes by correcting a proof. Apropos of novels, have you read L. Ritchie's 'Magician?' It is full of wild interest and vigorous power. It reminded me a little of Victor Hugo. I am very anxious to hear how your 'Thoughts' proceed, and whether you have finally resolved to omit them from the tales for Saunders and Ottley.

"I see *le cher* D'Orsay amongst the spectators at the Giant

* The Poetical Epistle will be found at the end of this correspondence.—R. R. M.

Balloon—so I perceive he has renounced his grouse-shooting project.

" As for poor Mrs. Graham, I never knew, till her accident, how famous a thing it was to go up in balloons. Regular bulletins of her health in all the papers, and daily inquiries in Poland Street; yet, if she had hurt herself tumbling down stairs, nobody would have cared two straws. Nay, if even the great Talfourd were lying ill with a concussion in the brain, I doubt whether he would excite half the commiseration bestowed on this foolish woman falling topsy turvey out of the clouds.* Why going in a balloon should make people more celebrated than going in a ship, I cannot imagine. But why the world should not care a pinch of snuff about half-a-score people being drowned every week, and yet make all this bother about an accident out of a bladder, is still more puzzling. It can't be that the danger is greater in balloons than ships, for more people are drowned in a week, than are killed from a balloon in a century. As D———— would say, 'these mysteries are not for mortals.' Only think of the newspapers giving * * * * a sinecure, and then taking it away again. That was the refinement of cruelty; if I were he, I would never forgive the Government; it is no crime not to give an hungry man a piece of bread, but it is a monstrons shame to thrust it in his mouth, and then bob it out again.

" What villanous weather—wind and rain—rain and wind—I suspect that rain and wind are to an English heaven what beefstakes and mutton chops are to an English inn. They profess to have every thing else, but you are sure to have the steak to-day and the chop to-morrow. I have only had one glimpse of the sun since I have been here, and it was then so large, that I took it for a half sovereign, which I had lost the day before.

" There is such a cottage eight miles hence (not to be sold though); I longed for you and D'Orsay to see it. It belongs to a Mr. Fish. Out of nine acres he has made a little paradise;

* At an interval of seventeen years from the accident above referred to, I witnessed another fall topsey-turvey out of the clouds, and a descent on a stack of chimnies, of the same adventurous lady, in Dublin, 1853, with similar results.— R. R. M.

but he has especially availed himself of an immense verandah, so contrived as to seem a succession of bowers, through which are seen different prospects—a fountain, a lawn, an aviary, or the sea.

"Tell D'Orsay he (Mr. Fish) must have a vast deal of life to spare, for he beats you and the Count hollow in his animals. What think you of half-a-dozen kangaroos, or fifty parrots, or two buffaloes! or two Cape sheep, or a South American camel! or a pelican, or two emews! besides a whole wilderness of antelopes and gazelles, in a park about as long as your library? They give me a temporary consumption only to look at them pumping away all the oxygen into their exhausted lungs. I am sure I left a great part of my vitality at Fish Cottage.

"Pray write and tell me all your news, I shall soon wing my way homewards, when you will see as much of me as has escaped Mr. Fish's pelicans and South American camel. I long to have a breeze from the Isle of Beauty, and when I receive your letter shall fancy it summer. Long after youth leaves one for good, it comes back for a flying visit, in every recollection of friendship, in every association of grace.

"E. L. B."

[No date, but must have been written in 1837.]

"I was sure that your woman's heart would feel much for poor Lord R——'s sudden and striking death. These funeral knells make the only music in life that is faithful to the last, more and more frequent as we journey on, till the dull heart ceases to hear them, and the most sensitive accustoms itself to the chime. I spent my son's holidays at Brighton; and now he has left me, I have wandered on to this most solitary spot, where the air is milder, though I am not sure yet that it agrees with me.

"I am most concerned to hear you have been so serious a loser by Mr. Heath's death. But I wish, at least, that the annuals themselves may be continued by some one. They satisfy an elegant want of so large a part of the community, that I do not think they can be suffered to drop, and I sincerely and earnestly hope you may get satisfactory terms from some publisher of capital and enterprise. "E. L. B."

"Margate, September 24, 1837.

"People walk about here in white shoes, and enjoy themselves as much as if they were not Englishmen. I lodge over a library, and hear a harp nightly, by which the fashionable world is summoned to raffle for card-racks and work-boxes. It commences at nine, and twangs on till eleven; at twelve I am in the arms of Morpheus.

"An innocent life enough, very odd that one should enjoy it *mais tous les goûts sont respectables!* Though Margate itself be not exactly the region for you to illumine, I cannot help thinking that some grand solitary villa on this cheerful coast would brace and invigorate you. The air is so fine, the sands so smooth, and there is so much variety in the little island.

"I have been reading 'Trevelyan;' it is pretty and natural How is *le beau Roi* Alfred? I can fancy him on the Margate pier, with the gaze of the admiring crowd fixed upon him. But he would be nothing without white shoes.

"I am now going to stroll along the sands, and teaze shrimps, which abound in little streamlets, and are singularly playful, considering that they are born to be boiled.

"E. L. B."

"Margate, October 3rd, 1837.

"I have been whiling away the time here, with nothing much better than the mere enjoyment of a smooth sea and fair sky, which a little remind me of my beloved Naples! Margate and Naples—what association! After all, a very little could suffice to make us happy, were it not for our own desires to be happier still. If we could but reduce ourselves to mechanism, we could be contented. Certainly I think as we grow older, we grow more cheerful, externals please us more, and were it not for those dead passions which we call memories, and which have ghosts no exorcism can lay, we might walk on soberly to the future, and dispense with excitement by the way. If we cannot stop time, it is something to shoe him with felt, and prevent his steps from creaking.

"E. L. B."

"Paris.

"This place seems in no way changed, except that the people I knew, have grown three years younger; the ordinary course of progression in France,

"'Where lips at seventy still shed honey;'

and even as much, if not more, honey than in the previous years. The politics of the place are simply these. The king, by setting each party against the other, has so contrived to discredit all, as to have been able to get a ministry entirely his own, and without a single person of note or capacity in it. Ancient jealousies were for awhile strong enough to prevent the great men who were out from uniting against the little men who were in. But present ambition is stronger than all past passions, and at last a league is formed of all the ci-devant ministers against the existing ones.

"I must tell you a *bon mot* which Madame de L——— told me. 'Je n'ai pas besoin de tant de *rossignols* dans ma chambre,' said the king, speaking of the orators he despises. 'Mais votre Majesté,' said Monsieur ——, 's'ils ne chantent pas, ils sifflent.'

"E. L. B."

"Cork. [No date.]

"Certainly they ought to give Lord Durham a dinner in London, and wherever I may be, I will come to attend it. But it is impossible any one could think of asking me to preside at it; there are a thousand more worthy. Mulgrave, if he had not been in office, would have been the man; as it is, I think Sir Henry Parnell would be the best. They ought not to select any city or metropolitan member, for then it appears too exclusively local and commercial; and Lord Durham should carefully avoid committing himself about the corn laws, or against the agricultural interest. But this to ourselves. As it is, he ought certainly to have the dinner; and it matters not one rush whom they have for president, so long as his name is known; for if they set up a man of straw, the room would be equally crowded, and with people equally respectable. Durham has written his horoscope in people's hearts—they only want the occasion to tell him of his destiny.

"P.S. I have been enchanted with the upper Lake of Killarney, and a place called Glengariff; and I think that I never saw a country which nature more meant to be great. It is thoroughly classical, and will have its day yet. But man must change first.

"E. L. B."

"January, 1841.

"I shrink from returning to London, with its fever and strife. I am tired of the stone of *Sisyphus*, the eternal rolling up, and the eternal rolling down. I continue to bask delighted in the light of Schiller. A new great poet is like a discovery of a lost paradise. It reconciles us to the gliding away of youth, when we think that, after all, the best pleasures are those which youth and age can enjoy alike—the intellectual.

"Kind love to D'Orsay, and best regards to all your circle.

"E. B. L."

[No date.]

"It is a sin against nature, your being ill—like a frost in summer. *I* am used to it. Oh! I saw L. E. L. to-day. She avows her love to her betrothed frankly, and is going to Africa, where *he* is governor of a fortress. Is not that grand? It is on the Gold Coast, and his duty is to protect black people from being made slaves. The whole thing is a romance for Lamartine. Half Paul and Virginia, half Inkle and Yarico. Poor Miss Landon! I do like and shall miss her. But she will be happier than in writing, which seems to me like shooting arrows and never hitting the right mark, but now and then putting out one's own little boy's eye. Love to dear D'Orsay.

"E. B. L."

[The Water Cure.]

"Malvern, June, 1844.

"As yet I can say nothing certain of the experiment in my own case; but my faith is confirmed by all I see around me, and believe this to be the safest and best establishment. Certainly it would be unwise to try it near London, within reach of its annoyance or excitement, for the stimulus to the nerve and brain is so astonishing, that any extra demand upon either must be extremely prejudicial.

"Fortunately the frame accustoms itself to the practice; an extraordinary and child-like calm comes over us, and the indisposition to mental labour is most strong and most salutary.

"The villas about here, for those who, like you, could not reside in the house (where there is little accommodation), are beautiful, and the landscape almost equals the view from the Simplon.

"Dr. Wilson considers the restoration (effected by this mode of cure) sure, speedy, and permanent. Three blessings this system gives very soon—sleep, appetite, and a capacity for vigorous exercise.

"E. B. L."

"Grand Parade, Brighton, November 22nd, 1844.

"Literature, with me, seems dead and buried. I read very little, and write nought. I find stupidity very healthy.

* * * * * * * * * * *
* * * * * * * * * * *
* * * * * * * * * * *

"To unite as we do, miracles with logic, is a mistake. As I grow older, and I hope wiser, I feel how little reason helps us through the enigmas of this world. God gave us imagination and faith, as the two sole instincts of the future. He who reasons where he should imagine and believe—prefers a rush-light to the stars.

"E. B. L."

"Malvern, Saturday, 13th April, 1845.

"I have been here for the last seven weeks, courting the watery gods; and though this system always reduced me for the time, I hope to get the re-action I did before. I leave on Wednesday evening, probably travelling all night, and shall be in town for a few days. My water-doctor is coming with me, principally to see the opera on Thursday and Saturday. He is extremely desirous to obtain a presentation to you, and is really a very gentlemanlike, intelligent person, and worth hearing on his own system.

"E. B. L."

"Rome, February 12th, 1846.

"According to the promise you were kind enough to invite from me, I write to you from my wandering camp, amidst the hosts who yearly invade *la belle Italie.* I performed rather a hurried journey to Genoa, and suffered more than I had anticipated from the fatigue. So there I rested and sought to recruit; the weather was cold and stormy—only at Nice had I caught a glimpse of genial sunshine. With much misgiving, I committed myself to the abhorred powers of steam at Genoa, and ultimately re-found about two thirds of my dilapidated self at Naples. There, indeed, the air was soft, and the sky blue; and the luxurious sea slept calmly as ever round those enchanting shores, and in the arms of the wondrous bay. But the old charms of novelty are gone. The climate, though enjoyable, I found most trying, changing every two hours, and utterly unsafe for the early walks of a water-patient, or the moonlight rambles of a romantic traveller. The society ruined by the English and a bad set. The utter absence of intellectual occupation gave me the spleen, so I fled from the balls, and the treacherous smiles of the climate, and travelled by slow stages to Rome, with some longings to stay at Mola, which were counteracted by the desire to read the newspapers, and learn Peel's programme for destroying his friends the farmers. The only interesting person, by the way, I met with at Naples, was the Count of Syracuse, the King's brother; for he is born with the curse of ability, (though few discover, and fewer still acknowledge it), and has been unfortunate enough to cultivate his mind, in a country and in a rank where mind has no career. Thus he is in reality afflicted with the ennui which fools never know, and clever men only dispel by active exertions. And it was melancholy to see one with the accomplishments of a scholar, and the views of a statesman, fluttering away his life amongst idle pursuits, and seeking to amuse himself by billiards and *lansquenet.* He has more charming manners than I ever met in a royal person, except Charles the Tenth, with a dignity that only evinces itself by sweetness. He reminded me of Schiller's Prince, in the 'Ghost Seer.'

"And so I am at Rome! As Naples now a second time disappointed me, so Rome (which saddened me before) revisited, grows on me daily. I only wish it were not the Carnival, which does not harmonize with the true charm of the place, its atmosphere of art and repose. I pass my time quietly enough, with long walks in the morning, and the siesta in the afternoon. In the evening I smoke my cigar in the Forum, or on the *Pincian* Hill, guessing where Nero lies buried—Nero, who, in spite of his crimes, (probably exaggerated), has left so gigantic a memory in Rome, a memory that meets you everywhere, almost the only Emperor the people recall. He must have had force and genius, as well as brilliancy and magnificence, for the survival. And he died so young.

"I was more shocked than I can express by poor G——'s startling fate. It haunted and preyed on me for many days and nights.

"I am now steering homeward; this stupendous treachery of ——'s recalls my political fervour. I long again to be in public life. I thought the old illusions were dispelled; and the career of a politician is neither elevating nor happy.

"E. B. L."

"Lyons, April 10th, 1846.

"I expect to arrive in England the last week in April. I am much struck with Lyons; there are few cities in Italy to compare with it, in effect of size, opulence, and progress.

"But Italy has improved since I was there last. Life is more active in the streets, civilization re-flowing to its old channels. Of all Italy, however, the improvement is most visible in Sardinia. There the foundations of a great State are being surely and firmly laid. The King, himself, approaches to a great man, and though priest-ridden, is certainly an admirable Governor and Monarch. I venture to predict, that Sardinia will become the leading nation of Italy, and eventually rise to a first-rate power in Europe. It is the only State in Italy with new blood in its veins. It has youth,—not old age, attempting to struggle back into vigour in Medea's caldron.

"I have been indolently employing myself, partly on a version of a Greek play, partly on a novel, anxious to keep my mind distracted from the political field, which is closed to me. For, without violent opinions on the subject, I have great misgivings as to the effect of Peel's measures on the real happiness and safety of England, and regard the question as one in which political economy—mere mercantile loss and gain, has least to do. High social considerations are bound up in it; no one yet has said what I want said on the matter. Nevertheless, I was much delighted with Disraeli's very able, and indeed remarkable, speech. I am so pleased to see his progress in the House, *which I alone predicted the night of his first failure.* I suppose Lord George Bentinck is leading the agriculturists; I cannot well judge from Galignani with what success.

"This letter has remained unfinished till to-day, the 13th, when I conclude it at Joigny. More and more struck with the improvement of France, as I pass through the country slowly. It is a great nation indeed; and to my mind, the most disagreeable part of the population, and the part least improved, is at Paris.

"E. B. L."

"Knebworth, December 24, 1846.

"I am extremely grateful, my dearest friend, for your kind letter, so evidently meant to encourage me, amidst the storm which howls around my little boat.* And, indeed, it is quite a patch of blue sky, serene and cheering through the very angry atmosphere which greets me elsewhere. I view it as an omen, and sure I am, at least, that the blue sky will endure, long after the last blast has howled itself away.

"Perhaps, in some respects, it is fortunate that I have had so little favour shewn to me, or rather so much hostility, in my career. If I had once been greeted with the general kindness and indulgent smiles that have, for instance, rewarded —— I should have been fearful of a contrast in the future, and, satisfied at so much sunshine, gathered in my harvests, and broken up my plough. But all this vituperation goads me on. Who can keep quiet when the tarantula bites him?

"I write this from a prison, for we are snowed up all round;

* The allusion here is to the poem of the "New Timon."

and to my mind, the country is dull enough in the winter, without this addition to its sombre repose. But I shall stay as long as I can, for this is the time when the poor want us most.

"E. B. L."

"(No date.)

"I cannot disguise from you that I have strong objections in writing for an annual, of which a principal is, that in writing for one, I am immediately entangled by others, who, less kind than you, conceive a refusal unto them, when not given to all, is a special and deadly offence.

"Another objection is, that unless you edit a work of that nature, you have all sorts of grievous remonstrances from your publishers, or friends, assuring you that you cheapen your name, and Lord knows what! And, therefore, knowing that you greatly exaggerate the value of my assistance, I could have wished to be a reader of your 'Book of Beauty,' rather than a contributor. But the moment you seriously ask me to aid you, and gravely convince yourself that I can be of service, all objection vanishes. I owe to you a constant, a generous, a forbearing kindness, which nothing can repay; but which it delights me to prove that I can at least remember. And consequently you will enroll me at once amongst your ministering genii of the lamp.

"You gave me my choice of verse or prose—I should prefer the first; but consider well whether it would be of *equal service* to you. That is my sole object, and whichever the most conduces to it, will be to me the most agreeable means. You can therefore consider, and let me know, and lastly, pray give me all the time you can spare.

"To prove to you that I am a mercenary ally, let me name my reward. Will you give me one of the engravings of yourself in the 'Book of Beauty.' It does not do you justice, it is true, but I should like to number it among those mementoes which we keep by us as symbols at once of reality and the ideal. Alas! all inspiration dies except that of beauty.

"E. B. L."

"Craven Cottage, Fulham. [No date.]

"It was most kind in you to think of my misfortune,* and to offer to my ark so charming a resting-place. I heard with sincere gratitude of your visit this morning. The Thames has been pleased to retire to his own bed to-day, and has therefore left me less in fear from an invasion of mine. Though fond of philosophy, I cannot say that I am much pleased with these last 'Diversions of *Pearly*.' However, I have escaped better than I could have anticipated, and as I am informed the Thames never did such a thing before, in the memory of this generation, I have the comfort of believing that an inundation is like the measles and smallpox—a visitation once happily over, to be classed among those memories of the past, which are only revived in the persons of our posterity. At present I am making an embankment, that I think will baffle the river gods in any ulterior malicious designs upon their unfortunate neighbour.

"Like the escaping mariner of old, I hope soon to render my homage to a shrine, where abide the tutelary powers whom we call the 'Graces,' in prosperity, and by the fairer name of the 'Charities,' in distress.

"E. B. L."

"January 25th, 1849.

"I am very much obliged to you, my dearest friend, for your kind and gracious reception of 'King Arthur.' It contains so much of my more spiritual self—that it is more than the mere author's vanity, it is the human being's self-love that is gratified by your praise. It is to a hard, practical, prosaic world that the fairy king returns after his long sojourn, on the oblivious lake, and if he may yet find some pale reflexion of his former reign, it will take long years before the incredulous will own that he is no impostor.

"E. B. L."

* An inundation of the Thames.

"ONE OF THE CROWD."

AN EPISTLE FROM PARIS, TO THE COUNTESS OF BLESSINGTON, JANUARY 1, 1836.

Referred to in a letter dated 5th January, 1836.

Behind me sorrow, and before me strife,
What sudden smoothness lulls the waves of life?
Hemm'd by the gloom that shadows either side,
One track the moon-beams from the dark divide.
Never for him whose youth in haunted dells
Heard, tho' far off, Corycian oracles,
Whom the still Nine made dreamer at his birth,
Can the soft magic all forsake the earth.
Tho' on the willow hang his silent lute,
Tho' song's wild passion lies subdued and mute,
Still for the charm revealing heaven he sighs,
And feels the poet which his life belies.

Here, where the wheels of wild contenders roll,
And one vast dust-cloud hides from each the goal,
Where gusts of passion mock all guiding laws,
And sport alike with forest-kings and straws,
Apart and lone amid the millions round,
I hear the uproar and survey the ground,
And for one hour, spectator of the time,
Affect the sage, and would be wise in rhyme.
What change, since first my boyhood's careless glance
Rov'd her gay haunts, has dimm'd the smile of France?
Where are the bland address, the happy ease,
The minor morals of the wish to please?
These, the fair magic of the mien, no more
Deck the fierce natures which they masked of yore
Enter yon shop, whose wares arrest your eye,
The smileless trader bullies you to buy:
At Cafès scarce the blunt, bluff garçons stir;
All now are equal, you're no longer—Sir!

While, if thro' streams of mud miscall'd a street
You wend your way, what swaggering shapes you meet.
Grim, lowering, wild, along the gay Boulevard,
Sweep hordes of dandies bearded like the pard ;
And, as each step the herds unyielding bar,
Puff in your loathing face the rank cigar!
If haply creeping by the cleaner wall,
Some tiptoed damsel meet the whiskered Gaul,
He stalks the *trottoir* with a Sultan's air,
Peers thro' the veil and revels in the stare:
The wall on this side, and on that the mud,
Behold the weaker vessel in the flood!*

The change displeases! let it not amaze,
Behold the fruit of the "*Three Glorious Days.*"
Well, freedom won,—let freedom pardoned be
For rugged manhood,—Sons of Hampden—*Free*!
The people triumphed,—what do they possess?
A venal Chamber and a shackled Press!
On the scar'd ear of earth for this alone
Crash'd the great ruins of the Bourbon throne.
All France herself one standing army made,
All freedom fettered, to the fears of trade!†

All! nay, deny not some substantial gain;
Such patriot blood has not been spilt in vain.
Flags of *three* hues instead of *one* are reared—
Jean gains no vote, but once he wore no beard.

Sick of these tricks of state, which seem to dim
The stars of empire for a madman's whim—

* The rudeness in manner which characterized the Parisians at the date referred to in the text, was too ungenial to the natural character of the population to last long; it was consistent only with the mock freedom which for a time deluded the French people, under the reign of Louis Philippe.

† It is the grossest injustice to call Louis Philippe a tyrant. He is the representative of the Fears of the Bourgeoisie! By their favour he rose, by their interests he governs, and by their indifference he may yet fall.

These fools that take a riot for reform,
And furl the sail which bore them thro' the storm—
Turn we from men to books?—no more, alas!
Wit's easy diamond cuts the truthful glass;
The pointed maxim—the Horatian style,
That won the heart to wisdom with a smile,
Are out of date—the Muses clad in black,
See language stretch'd in torture on the rack.
Sense flies from sadness, when so very sad,
And what burlesque like gravity run mad?
An author took his fiction to the trade,
Mournful the theme, from love and murder made.
"Sir," quoth the bookwife, "this is somewhat cold;
Man loves a maid and slays her; sad but old!
We want invention! make the man an ape,
Some mighty spirit in a monkey shape.
Picture what scenes! the subject could not fail,
A soul divine made desperate by—a tail!"

Invent some monster—some unheard-of crime,
And *this* is "*nature*"— "*this the true sublime!*"
The same in books as action, still they make
The mightiest clamour for the smallest stake.
Each frigid thought in streams of fury flows,
And tritest dialogue raves with "ahs and ohs."

Yet these the race—these sucklings of romance,
That sneer at all, that gave her fame to France,
That hoot, the screech owls, from their perch obscene,
Thy sun Corneille, thy starry pomp, Racine!
* * * * prates of Rousseau with a patron's air,
But pigmy * * * * scoffs at great Voltaire!

Eno' of these—in quiet let them lie,
Peace to their ashes, while we speak they die!
I grant to * * * * all that art can do,
For schools that style the "extravagant" "*the true.*"
And duped to bogs by their divining rod,

Dig for the natural, where they find the *odd.**
I grant Alphonso can at moments touch,
Tho' not to tears, he whines himself too much.
His pathos pranks it with a parson's air,
A drop of Byron, to a quart of Blair!
I grant that René's high soul'd author knows,
To paint the lily and perfume the rose.
A gorgeous troop of glittering words to raise,
And stalk to fame in all the pomp of phrase.
But at the best, in him we can but hail
A *he* Corinna, or a *she* De Stael!
Yet these, whate'er their light, are on the wane,
Too wild for Europe, but for France too plain.
Romance and horror, now are out of fashion,
Balzac has made *philosophy* the passion!
And all the town,—sweet innocent! endures
Are two-sex'd seraphs, "*dans immenses malheurs.*"
Relieved, we hasten from these frenzies fine,†
This whirl of words—these nightmares of the Nine,
To own that France with pride may point to all
Beranger's verse, and half the prose of Paul.‡
What then! I hear some sombre critic say—
The grave offends you, you prefer the gay.
No! give the cypress or the rose its hue,
I like them both, but I must have the *true.*
Your gay is natural, and your grave is forced,
What stuff like sentiment from sense divorced?

Back from the things without, my soul recedes—
How daily more on self the reason feeds?

* See Victor Hugo's Preface to Cromwell, in which we are assured that the true spirit of poetry lies in the grotesque.

† See the "Seraphitas," of M. de Balzac.

‡ Paul Courier. The author, in allowing these lines upon the French writers to remain, thinks it right to say, that in the spirit of a juster and maturer criticism, he should, were he writing on the same subject now, qualify, though not wholly withdraw, the blame, and accord due praise to the unquestionable genius, which, if it does not redeem all faults, defies and survives all depreciation. (1854.)

As years creep o'er us, less and less we note
The toy and rattle from our reach remote:
Less we observe, and more remember! Man
The one same, endless marvel that we scan:
But to the stranger heart incurious grown,
We centre all our study on our own.
Ah! first when youth ran high, and, sparkling up
Life's very foam could overflow the cup,
When the heart's ocean, bright with April skies,
Glass'd every glance from woman's starry eyes,
When foe or friend alike was blithely made,
And all the thought could prompt, the act obey'd;
When earth was new, and life unpall'd could give
Each hour a something to the next to live;
When ev'n in trifles, thought could truth discern,
And pleasure taught philosophy to learn;—
Then, first these scenes I rov'd delighted o'er,
Chang'd are the scenes, the visitant much more!
Man and his motives grown a well-read book,
The jaded task fatigues the languid look,
Foes cannot rouse, new friends can but presume,
Life's wrinkled cheek hath lost its heavenly bloom;
And half in sorrow, half in scorn, I see
That change on earth, which is but change in me!
Dull trash this world!—I lay it on the shelf,
Come my own heart—none reads too oft *himself!*

Can all the stars this outward earth illume?
E'en day itself leaves half our orb in gloom,
But one lone lamp lights up the spirit's vault,
The egotist hath wisdom in his fault.
When grief or thought the burthened soul oppress,
It is a sweet religion——*to confess!*
To the charm'd ear of Poesy—the Priest,
We pour our sighs, and quit the shrine released.
For who can bare to mortal eye the soul?
This is the true confessional,—*the scroll!*
Here in our art we find a strange relief,
And in revealing half forget our grief.

Blame not communion with ourselves, it grows
Not from the wish to *nurse* but *vent* our woes,
And he who makes a mirror of his mind
Does but condense the likeness of mankind.
Still young in years, my heart hath run through most
That youth desires to feel, and age to boast;
Enough of fortune, and of gentle birth,
To share the sabbaths, as the toils of earth;
Enough of health and hardihood to call
Each man my mate, and feel at home with all;
Life's various shades it has been mine to view,
Till the wide pallet proffers nought of new.
Art and ambition, eulogy and blame,
Excite no longer:—I have gained a name:
The name once made, our toils can scarce exalt
One merit granted,—or atone one fault.
And, oh! how still the censure and the praise,
(For *both* make fame) our own tormentors raise;
First we enjoy, and afterwards endure,
Ache at the glare and sigh to be obscure.

What then, is life so dark a web, whose white
The fates unravel as we near the night?
Springs like the banyan, every high desire
To bend once more, and mingle with the mire?
Is it in vain, as up the steep we wind,
That each firm step some folly leaves behind?
Is it in vain we pierce the secret maze,
"And scorn delight, and love laborious days?"
No, for the while the prospect fades below,
Near and more near the heavens before us glow,
Like Chaldee's seers,* our starry lore takes birth
Where most the drear monotony of earth;
Around, all tame,—above we raise the scope,
And learn the vast astrology of Hope.
'Tis worth a youth of suffering, care, and strife,
To win some spot beyond the storms of life;

* It was the vast flatness of the Chaldean soil that conduced to, and favoured their astronomical science.

A cell unseen—where Thought—a hermit grown,
Sits musing o'er the perils it hath known;
And—(faintly heard without the tempest's roar)
Trims the soul's lamp, and cons some sacrd lore.
And if no more on passion's stream we waft
The laughing Chrishna on his lotos raft,*
Heav'd by each wave, and woo'd by every wind,
Life leaves not all its softer gods behind;
Our buried youth, rays never quenched illume:
And love's lone watchlight burns in fancy's tomb.
Better we prize, as lighter gains depart,
That mine of wealth—the treasure of a heart.
And feel we know not, till around us sweeps,
Day after day, the darkness of the deeps,
Till the false raven that from death we bore,
Left us in peril, and returned no more;
How blest the olive of the welcome Dove,
And what new worlds are promised us by love!

Thus at the worst, experience is not gloom,
And golden fruits replace the purple bloom:
And oft, methinks, that as we grow more wise,
We fit our souls for ends beyond the skies;
For Heaven—the vulgar scarcely paint aright,
As some inactive torpor of delight,
Where thought's high travail we for aye dismiss,
Lull'd in the Sybarite's indolence of bliss.

Nobler, be sure, our nature and our doom!
Each gain we make we bear beyond the tomb.
Just as our spirits may exalt us here,
Trained to high purpose in a holier sphere;
Proceeding on from link to link, until
We serve the *word*, but comprehend the *will*.
No longer blinded to the part we play,
Benighted wanderers yearning for the day,

* The Indian God of Love is represented as floating on the lotos leaf down the Ganges; and offerings on lotos leaves are yearly sent to drift down the river.

Each step before us blackness,—life and death—
Joy—grief—the glaciers hanging on a breath ;
Slaves to the Present's wheel revolving, bound,
Now whirl'd aloft—now dash'd upon the ground;
Self to itself a riddle ;———all unknown
Whither we tend or wherefore we should groan ;
But by the struggles of our mind below
To *guess* at knowledge, trained at last—*to know.*
The end august ordained to our survey,
Where once we groaned, we glory, to obey,
And—lost all leaven of the earth we trod,
Endue the Seraph as we near the God!

Can the same joys reward, or doom await
Mind's various ranks in Heaven's mysterious state ?
What dungeon star could fetter, cheek by jowl,
Some Lord's dull spark, and Shakespeare's sunlike soul?
Say, cans't thou guess what mighty tasks await
The Bard's freed spirit at the Eternal Gate ?
Reserved (how know'st thou) when from clay redeemed,
To rule the worlds of which it here but dreamed.
From power to power, from light to light ascend—
Take death from genius—where can genius end ?

Accept the doctrine—and no more surprise,
In fate or soul, man's stern disparities.
No more we sigh to ask why genius wears
Proud hearts away " in crosses and in cares."
Why the same fates that Sidney's murderer raise,
Bring Milton " darkness and the evil days."
Why Dante from La Scala's board is fed,
And Otway chokes with the unwonted bread :
No more we wonder, when across the night
Some meteor spirit casts a moment's light;
And seems—as darkness closes round the sky—
Born but to blaze, to startle, and to die.
Look but to *earth*, and bootless we might call
Iskander's rise, or bright Rienzi's fall;

When Brutus found the virtue he adored,
At length a name—and perish'd on his sword,
In vain for Rome did her great Roman bleed,
The wasted drops brought forth no dragon seed.
How oft, through life, we meet with souls whose fire
But lit the shrine of one divine desire.
In vain they panted, struggled, toil'd, and wrought,
The monomaniacs of some god-like thought.
How many martyrs to mankind, whose name
Died with their dust—uncanonized by fame!
But if a stern philosopher be Fate,
That schools us harshly at life's outer gate,
Before (the dark noviciate o'er) we win
The master-science of the shrine within,
If Heaven be not the rest to our career,
But its new field—then life at once is clear.
Then solv'd the riddle.—We in vain for earth
May toil and strive—*Heaven* claims us from our birth;
And every toil but nerves the soul to climb
Alp upon Alp beyond the walls of Time!
For if ev'n matter, if the meanest clod,
Knows nought of waste in the vast schemes of God:
How much more wanted to the wondrous whole,
Each spark of thought—each monad of the soul!
By one great nature's toil all space may gain,
And worlds attest—"*man ne'er aspires in vain!*"
Never, O earth, for merely human ends
Heaven to thine orb, some rarer spirit sends.
On Plato's soul did day celestial break,
That boys thro' Phædo might arrive at Greek?
Was godlike Pericles* but born to rule
The smooth Orbilius of a brawling school,
To curb or fawn upon the riot throng,
To build a shrine, or patronize a song?
No!—here we read the first leaf of the scroll,
To guess the end we must peruse the whole;
No—though the curtain fall, your judgment stay,
'Twas but the prologue! Now begins the play!

And ere you ask what some score lives may mean,
Death, raise the curtain! Heaven, present the scene!

* * *
* * *
* * *

In youth " we babbled of green fields"—the pure
Air—where the muse might court " *la belle nature*,"
And ask'd, in Harold's hollow prayer, to dwell
With our lone fancies, by the flood and fell!
But, now, old Berkeley's true disciples grown,
Our sense and soul make all the world we own.
What boots it that yon moonlight casts its glow
O'er grave fiacres freezing in a row,
Or the long wall beside whose jealous gate,
Th' unenvied sentry holds his silent state?
What matters where the outward scene may be?
Earth has no Eden which we may not see!
Waves Thought his wand—and lo before my eyes
Heaves the soft lake, or bend the purple skies,
Or summer shines upon that quiet shade
Where Love sad altars to Remembrance made,
Where its wild course the heart to ruin ran,
And youth grew rich by usury on the man!
Let Syntax Pilgrims rove from clime to clime,
And hunt o'er earth the beauteous and sublime.
Fools! not on Jura's giant heights they grow,
Nor found, like weeds, where Leman winds below!
Where the Faun laughs thro' vines, they are not hid,
Nor mummied up in Memphian pyramid.
Dig where you will, how fruitless is your toil!
Are thoughts and dreams the minerals of the soil?
Within our souls the real landscape lies,
There, rise our Alps—*there*, smile our southern skies;
There, winds the true Ilyssus, by whose stream
We cull the hyacinth, and invite the dream;
Revive the legend and the truth of old,
" Live o'er each scene, and be what we behold."

The New Year's Eve!—Night wanes; more near and near
Creeps o'er the breathless world the coming year!
Lo! what full incense of the hope and prayer,
Ascends from earth to earth's appointed heir!
With tearless eyes we see the dark hours fling
In Time's vast vault the old discrownëd King,
Hail to the Son!—Alas!, with prayers as vain
Men asked all blessings from the Father's reign.

Still the soul's faith Hope's rising sun invites,
We fawn on fate—the future's parasites!
For me, at least, the courtier creed is o'er,
And wise experience whispers "wish no more!"
Life hath no compass;—thro' the dark we sail,
Float passive on, and leave to God the gale;
Come calm or storm, at least no power beside
Can yield the haven, or appease the tide!

E. L. B.

In a letter addressed to Lady Blessington by E. L. Bulwer, from Paris, dated 1st of January, 1836, the foregoing poetical epistle was enclosed, which, though of an earlier date than several other letters of his, has been placed at the end of this correspondence, with the view of drawing more particular attention to it.

SIR HENRY BULWER, G.C.B.

Henry Bulwer, the elder brother of Sir Edward Bulwer Lytton, and second son of W. E. Bulwer, Esq., was born in 1803 or 1804.

Studious and reserved in early years, he entered on the active business of life, prepared by his habits to surmount obstacles, and to bring to grave subjects of inquiry, sedateness of mind, solid information to all collateral branches of such subjects, and a perfect knowledge of their bearings on the researches we are engaged in.

He entered parliament in 1830, as representative of Wilton. In 1831 and 1832 he represented Coventry, and from 1834 till 1837, Marylebone. Politics, however, did not engross all his attention.

The great works of this gentleman are, "The Monarchy of the Middle Classes," which appeared in 1834, and "France, Social, Literary, and Political," published in 4 vols. in 1836. In accurate statistical information, philosophical views, perspicuity in dealing with very extensive official returns and reports, and making a minute analysis of the civil and military administrations of France, no publication of modern times that treats of that country bears any comparison with the work of Henry Bulwer. With all the evident marks of genius in his productions, there are indications also of nervous irritability in his writings, and of many of the peculiarities of valetudinarianism, bordering on eccentricity, manifested in inequalities of style, occasional vagueness, and a frequent falling-off in the vigour and originality of the writer. A small work of his, giving an account of his travels in Greece, "An Autumn in Greece," was published previously to the works above mentioned.

He has contributed much to reviews, magazines, and annuals, and one of his earliest anonymous productions, a "Life of Lord Byron," prefixed to the Paris edition of the poet's works in English, exhibited a great deal of tact and literary talent.

He served in the Second Life Guards, was attached to the mission at Berlin in August, 1827; to the embassy at Vienna in 1829, at the Hague in 1830, at Paris in 1832; was appointed Secretary of Legation at Brussels, in 1835; was Chargé d'Affairs there in 1835 and 1836; Secretary of Embassy at Constantinople in 1837; at St. Petersburgh in 1838; at Paris, June, 1839; was for some time Minister Plenipotentiary in 1839, 1840, and 1841; was appointed Envoy Extraordinary and Minister Plenipotentiary at Madrid, June,

1843, which post he continued to hold till the rupture of diplomatic relations between England and Spain in 1848; was made a Privy Councillor in 1845, and a K.C.B. in 1848. Sir Henry Bulwer was appointed Minister Plenipotentiary at Washington in 1849; made a G.C.B. in 1851; and was transferred to Florence in the same capacity in January, 1852, and was accredited to the courts of Modena and Parma.*

In his various embassies, Sir Henry Bulwer has performed his high duties with firmness, decision, manliness of character, and signal ability, without making any unnecessary display of those qualities; but, on the contrary, making natural amenity, quietude of manner, and amiability of disposition, apparently his most remarkable characteristics. In 1848, when the soldier-statesman, Narvaez, was in power, during the intrigues of some of the foreign embassies in Spain, and commotions occasioned by them, Sir H. Bulwer had frequent remonstrances to address to the Spanish ministers from his government; and his firmness and efficiency in the discharge of his duties, gave such offence to the arbitrary sword-law despot, then at the head of affairs in Spain, that he ordered the British minister to quit Madrid, on pretence of interference in plots and conspiracies against the government. For two years, the office of British minister at Madrid was left vacant. This violent proceeding of Narvaez was atoned for subsequently by an *amende honorable*, the terms of which were said to have been dictated by Lord Palmerston.

Sir Henry Lytton Bulwer possesses prepossessing, unpretending manners, and the air of inspiring confidence and retaining it. He is gentle in his bearing, of a languid appearance, and retiring deportment, yet of a strong will, and firm determination, and indomitable courage on great occasions: but irresolute, and uncertain in the ordinary affairs of every-day life. In conversation he is highly amusing and well in-

* The Foreign Office List for 1854, p. 33.

formed, and, notwithstanding an apparent thoughtlessness, something of an assumed indolence of mind, (in the face of society, and in the company of very intimate friends), and a remarkable playfulness of manner and disposition—few men are more observant and reflective, and deeper thinkers.

Habitual delicacy of health has been in his case productive of absence of mind on many occasions, and little *contretemps* which have given rise to misconceptions on the part of strangers and persons slightly acquainted with him; and thus offence has been sometimes taken at things either said or done by the diplomatist distraught in society, where no offence whatever was intended.

Sir Henry married, a few years ago, a daughter of Lord Cowley.

Few persons who were in the habit of meeting Mr. Henry Bulwer in London fashionable society in 1833 and 1834, as I have had that honour, on several occasions, in Seamore Place, who remember the young reserved man of a meditative turn, slight, pale, studious-looking, of a sickly cast of countenance, of a plaintive, valetudinarian sort of aspect, would be prepared for the varied and well-deserved successes of the elder brother of Sir Edward Bulwer Lytton in diplomacy, politics, and literature, which have attended his later career.

LETTERS FROM LADY BLESSINGTON TO HENRY LYTTON BULWER, ESQ.

"Seymour Place, London, Nov. 6, 1834.

"My dear Mr. Bulwer,

"It has given me great pleasure to hear from you, and it gives me scarcely less, to be able to tell you of the perfect success of your book. I read it with all the acuteness of the *critic*, increased by the nervous anxiety of the friend; and feeling satisfied of its merit, I was only desirous of drawing general attention to it, as far as lay in my power, by recommending it to all my acquaintances, and commenting on it, in my salon, every evening. Many people are too idle or indolent to take the trouble of judging for themselves; a book must be pointed out to them, as worthy of being read; and the rest, the merits of a good book will insure. Yours has been a regular *hit*, as the booksellers call it; a better proof of which I cannot give you, than that on Saturday last, a copy of the first edition was not to be procured for love or money. It is not only praised, but *bought*, and has placed you very high on the literary ladder. Go on and prosper; your success furnishes an incitement, that the first work of few authors ever gave, and it would be unpardonable not to persevere in a path that offers such brilliant encouragement. I ought not to omit mentioning, that in Mr. Fonblanque you have had as judicious a critic as an anxious friend. His good taste, and friendly zeal on this occasion, have secured him my friendship; admiration for his brilliant talents, and respect for his unflinching honesty, he had long since now. Lay this man to your heart, for be assured he is worthy of it. He is one of those extraordinary men, too good for the age in which they are born, too clever not to be feared, instead of loved, and too sensitive and affectionate not to be grieved that it is so.

"I never fear genius and worth, it is only the egotistical irritability of mediocrity that I fear and shun. It grieves me when I see men like Fonblanque misunderstood, or undervalued, and it is only at such moments that I am ambitious: for I should like to have *power*, wholly and *solely*, for doing justice to merit, and drawing into the sunshine of fortune those who ought to be placed at the top of her wheel, with a drag to prevent that wheel revolving. 'Pompeii' has covered its author with glory; every one talks of, every one praises it. What a noble creature your brother is; such sublime genius, joined to such deep, such true feeling. He is too superior to be understood in this age of pigmies, where each little animal thinks only of self and its little clique, and are jealous of the giants who stood between them and the sun, intercepting from them all its rays. 'Without these giants,' say they, 'what brightness would be ours, but they keep all the sun to themselves.' Poor Miss Landor! for poor I must call the person who has either bad taste enough, or bad feeling enough, to abuse your book; how severely punished she must be by its success.

"Strange to say, I have just been interrupted by E——— E———, who came to spend the evening with me, and who has only now left me. I told him what you stated, and he has requested me to inform you that he never has said an unkind word, or what he thinks could be tortured into unkindness, of you to any human being. He says that of this he can speak so positively, that he defies any one to assert the contrary, and that if you will name your informant, he will refute him. For the expressions of his constituents at Coventry, he says, he cannot be responsible, and has no control over political differences, always producing hostile expressions, if not feelings.

"M. Blessington."

"January 18, 1836.

"I have great pleasure in telling you, your book gains ground every day. The influential papers take extracts from it daily, and every one reads it.

"I heard from E—— E—— last week; he says the Whigs were never so firmly seated as at present. The new Peerages have given great dissatisfaction, particularly that of Lady ——. I saw Mr. E. J. Stanley last evening, and he appeared in very good spirits, which looks well for his party. He is a good person, and well disposed towards you.

"I heard from your brother on Friday, from Paris; he sent me an epistle in verse, which is a *chef-d'-œuvre*, worthy of the first of our poets.

"M. Blessington."

"Gore House, September 17, 1840.

"I am never surprised at evil reports, however unfounded, still less so at any acts of friendship and manliness on your part. One is more than consoled for the mortification inflicted by calumnies, by having a friend so prompt to remove the injurious impressions they were likely to make. Alfred is at Doncaster, but he charges me to authorize you, to contradict, in the most positive terms, the reports about his having participated in, or even known of the intentions of the Prince Louis. Indeed, had he suspected them, he would have used every effort in his power to dissuade him from putting them into execution. Alfred, as well as I, entertain the sincerest regard for the Prince, with whom for fourteen years we have been on terms of intimacy; but of his plans we knew no more than you did. Alfred by no means wishes to conceal his attachment to the Prince, and still less that any exculpation of himself should in any way reflect on him; but who so well as you, whose tact and delicacy are equal to your good nature, can fulfil the service to Alfred that we require?

"Lady C——— writes to me, that *I* too am mixed up in the reports. But I defy the malice of my greatest enemy to prove that I even dreamt of the Prince's intentions, or plans.

"Do you remember a friend of the Guiccioli's, a certain Marquis de Frassigny, or some such name, an elderly man, who lived in the Rue Neuve des Capucines? At the request of the Guiccioli, I sent two or three letters from her to him, under cover to Lady C———, because he happened to live within two doors of Lady C———, to save the sous for the petite poste. You know how foreigners attend to these little savings; and lo! and behold, no sooner does Lady C——— hear of the reports at Paris, than she conjures up an idea that this same Marquis de Frassigny (for it is some such name) is no other than the Marquis de C—— Channell, with whom the Prince Louis has been mixed up, but whose name I never heard of until I saw it in the papers. Tell me if you remember this same Frassigny? Have you heard from the Guiccioli lately, for I have not? Is it true that Dr. Lardner is gone to America? I have not heard from Edward since he went abroad, have you?

"I have been in Cambridgeshire for some weeks, and have only just returned. Alfred will write to you the moment he returns, but, *en attendant*, you are authorized and requested to contradict the rumours.

"M. BLESSINGTON."

"Gore House, April 13, 1843.

"Of all the kind letters received on the late bereavement, that has left so great a blank in my life, none have so much touched me as yours; for I know how to appreciate the friendship which prompts you to snatch from time so actively and usefully employed as yours always is, a few minutes for absent and sorrowing friends. This last blow, though not unexpected, has, nevertheless, fallen heavily on me, and the more so, that the insidious malady, which destroyed my poor dear niece, developed so many endearing qualities in her sweet and gentle nature, that her loss is the more sincerely left. Two months before this last sad event, we lost her little girl, that sweet and interesting child, whose beauty and intelligence (though, poor thing! she was deaf and dumb) you used to admire. This has indeed been a melancholy year to me.

"Alfred's position, as you may well imagine, would of itself fill me with chagrin, and the protracted illness of two beings so dear to me, closed by their deaths, has added the last blow to my troubles. May you, my dear Henry, be long spared from similar trials, and be left health and long life to enjoy your well-merited reputation, in which no one more cordially rejoices than

"Your sincere, affectionate friend,

"M. Blessington."

LETTERS OF SIR HENRY LYTTON BULWER TO LADY BLESSINGTON.

"December, 1841.

"My dear Lady Blessington,

"I think D'Orsay wrong in these things you refer to: to have asked for London especially, and not to have informed me how near the affair was to its maturity when St. Aulaire went to the D. of B———'s, because I might then have prepared opinion for it here; whereas I first heard the affair mentioned in a room, where I had to contend against every person present, when I stated what I think—that the appointment would have been a very good one. But it does not now signify talking about the matter, and saying that I should have wished our friend to have given the matter rather an air of doing a favour than of asking one. It is right to say, that he has acted most honourably, delicately, and in a way which ought to have served him, though, perhaps, it is not likely to do so. The French Ambassador did not, I think, wish for the nomination. M. Guizot, I imagine, is, at this moment, afraid of any thing that might excite discussion and opposition, and it is idle to disguise from you that D'Orsay, both in England and here, has many enemies. The best service I can do him is by continuing to speak of him as I have done amongst influential persons, viz., as a man whom the Government would do well to employ; and my opinion is, that if he continues to wish for and to seek employment, that he will obtain it in the end. But I don't think he will obtain the situation he wished for in London, and I think it may be some little time before he gets such a one as he ought to have, and that would suit him. The Secretaryship in Spain would be an excellent thing, and I would aid the Marshal in any thing he might do or say respecting it. I shall be rather surprised, however, if the present man is recalled. Well, do not let D'Orsay lose courage. Nobody succeeds in these things just at the moment he desires: ———, with his position here (speaking of a French nobleman), has been ten years getting made ambassador, and at last is so by a fortunate chance. Remember also how long it was, though I was in Parliament, and had some little interest, before I was myself fairly launched in the *diplomatic career*. Alfred has all the qualities for success in any thing, but he must give the same trouble and pains to the pursuit he now engages in, that he has given to other pursuits previously. At all events, though I speak frankly and merely what I think to him, I am here and always a sincere and affectionate friend, and most desirous to prove myself so. With respect to ———, for recommending whom you seem to reproach me, my opinion remains unchanged; and I still think him the best person, if not the only one, you could have employed. I know he spoke frequently to Guizot. I believe he also spoke to the King; and upon the whole, I believe that what he said to ——— was partly correct.

"HENRY BULWER."

In reference to this subject, Sir Henry Bulwer observes, in a recent communication to the Editor—"It was altogether a great pity D'Orsay was not employed, for he was not only fit to be so, but to make a most useful and efficient agent, had he been appointed. H. B."

"Hotel Douvres,
"Rue de la Paix, October 2.

"I have been staying very recently at Versailles, roving about those beautiful gardens and woods, which I delight in, and have but just now come to Paris, where, however, I hear there are many English; but as Landor is going to England, you will probably see him, and hear more than I can tell you.

"In literature there is nothing new here, but a new novel, 'Jacques,' from Mde. Dudevant (G. Sand). She is really a curious woman. Mrs. ————, a poet, who was said to be on intimate terms with her last year, is now, as it is reported, succeeded by a doctor, the consequence being a new doctrine, supported by a new work, demonstrating that the affections of the heart are to be separated from the pleasures of the senses. The poet represents the heart, the doctor the senses.

"HENRY BULWER."

No date.

"I shall seem an ungrateful man; but I have a head, alas! as well as a heart, and the former aches at writing what the latter wishes written. A thousand kind things in return for those you say to me. Praise from you is worth having, because it is sincere, and because I have a sincere affection for the person who bestows it. I got here well, and am often thinking of my sojourn under your hospitable roof, with the most agreeable recollections; and often wishing that my nest had been built a little nearer to your groves.

"Think sometimes of an absent friend, whom you may ever believe

"Yours most affectionately,
"HENRY BULWER."

"Hampton.

"I just received your note. It is not, as you may suppose, from carelessness and forgetfulness, that you have not had my contribution. I have begun twenty tales about that abominable sixteenth century, and none of them have pleased me but one, which I thought would not please you. It was full of horrors, magic, murder, and the East. It is now burnt, and I am writing as hard as I can, something which you will have to burn, if you like, on Monday evening. But I am a bad contributor, for I can't write at all times, nor on all subjects, though you can command me in all things.

"Henry Bulwer."

"May 6, 1849.

"I was very glad to get your letter. I never had a doubt (I judged by myself) that your friends would remain always your friends, and I was sure that many who were not Alfred's, when he was away, would become so when he was present. It would be great ingratitude if Prince Louis forgot former kindnesses and services, and I must say, that I do not think him capable of this.

"I think you will take a house in Paris or near it, and I hope some day there to find you, and to renew some of the many happy hours I have spent in your society. I shall attend the sale, and advise all my friends to do so. From what I hear, things will probably sell well. I am sure that Samson will execute any commission for you when he goes to Paris, and I gave Douro your message, who returns it. The ——, of whom you speak, made their appearance at the court ball; the lady dressed rather singularly. Her hair à-la-Chinoise, and stuck with diamonds. All the women quizzed her prodigiously, until they found out she was the last Parisian fashion. In fact, she looked remarkably well, and people were quite right in saying nothing could be so becoming, directly they ceased thinking that nothing could be so ridiculous.

* * * * * * *

"My own plans are still very uncertain, but I think of going to ——— by Paris. What little I hear about the New Chamber and the President's prospects is good, and I liked a letter by Lucien Buonaparte the other day much. It is a pity, however, a great pity, this quarrel with Napoleon; and I can't quite approve of publishing a private letter in the newspaper, and dismissing a man from his post on account of his leaving it, before hearing the reasons he had to give for doing so.

"HENRY BULWER."

CHAPTER IV.

ISAAC D'ISRAELI, ESQ.*

THE author of "The Curiosities of Literature," Isaac D'Israeli, of honoured memory, the literary historian, was born at Enfield, near London, in May, 1766, and was the only son of Benjamin D'Israeli, a Venetian merchant, of the Jewish persuasion, long established in England.

English Literature is therefore indebted to Italy, Judaism, and Venetian commerce, for two of its most distinguished sons; and English politics and statesmanship to the same old sources, for a public man, who has achieved for himself an eminent position, and the leadership of a great party.

Isaac D'Israeli was sent, at an early age, to Holland: he passed some years of boyhood in Amsterdam and Leyden; acquired there a great knowledge of languages, and *some* knowledge, but not a very extensive acquaintance, with the classics.

On his return to England, he applied himself a great deal to books, and made his first known appearance in print in the "Gentleman's Magazine," for December, 1786. That article of four pages, entitled "Remarks on the Biographical Accounts of the late Samuel Johnson, LL.D.," bore the signature J.D.I.

* The particulars of the career of the elder D'Israeli, given in this sketch, are gathered chiefly from a highly interesting Memoir, published in the "Gentleman's Magazine," for July, 1848, which has been ascribed to his distinguished son; and also from numerous references to him in Lady Blessington's papers.

But long previously, and subsequently to the date of that Essay, his leading passion was a love of poetry, and an ambition to write poetry. He began to discover that he was not destined to succeed in that line, so early as 1788; but he went on, in spite of fate, wooing the Muses, whom he had made divers vows to abandon; and in 1803, published a volume of "Narrative Poems," in 4to.

In 1799, appeared "Love and Humility, a Roman Romance;" also "The Lovers, or the Origin of the Fine Arts;" and in a second edition of these productions, in 1801, he introduced "The Daughter, or a Modern Romance."

Another novel, the date of which is unknown, called "Despotism, or the Fall of the Jesuits," was published by him. It would be interesting to know how that subject had been treated by him.

But several years earlier, his predilection for literary criticism had manifested itself in his studies and pursuits. So early as 1791, he published the first volume of "Curiosities of Literature," consisting of anecdotes, characters, sketches, and observations, literary, critical, and historical. In 1793, the second volume appeared, with "A Dissertation on Anecdotes." A third volume, some years later, completed the work. In 1823, a second series, however, was published; and up to 1841, went through twelve editions.

In 1795, appeared his "Essay on the Manners and Genius of the Literary Character:" in 1796, "Miscellanies, or Literary Recreations:" in 1812 and 1813, his "Calamities of Authors," in two volumes: in 1814, in three volumes, "Quarrels of Authors, or some Memoirs of our Literary History, including Specimens of Controversy, to the reign of Elizabeth:" in 1816, "An Inquiry into the Literary and Political Character of James the First."

These are the great works on which rests the fame of Isaac

D'Israeli; but one of his works, entitled, "Commentaries on the Life and Reign of Charles the First," in two volumes 8vo., 1828, obtained more popularity, for a time, than any of the works above-mentioned. For this work, in 1830 increased to four volumes, very eulogistic of Charles the First, the author got from Oxford the honorary degree of D.C.L., the public orator of the university, in conferring it, using the words—"Optimi Regis, optimo defensori."

In 1839, while meditating a more comprehensive and elaborate work on the "History of English Literature," he was totally deprived of sight. This terrible calamity was compensated for, to some small extent, by the constant attendance on him of his daughter. With her aid as an amanuensis, he produced "The Amenities of Literature." Mr. D'Israeli was a fellow of the Society of Antiquaries, and a member of some other learned societies.

He had a literary controversy, in 1837, with Mr. Bolton Corney, (the author of a production entitled "Curiosities of Literature Illustrated," a literati who works in the mine of old bookish knowledge), which controversy troubled a good deal the tranquillity of Mr. D'Israeli, and shook a little the implicit confidence which the public reposed in all his statements respecting what is called "Secret History," the originality of curious matter, alleged to have been discovered in ancient documents, and the authenticity and dates of manuscripts and books referred to by him. Mr. Corney's object was to pull down the fame of the elder D'Israeli: that object he has not been able to effect, but he assuredly has shewn a tendency in Mr. D'Israeli to that sort of vanity which prompted Bruce to represent a travelling companion as dead, who was living at the time of his representation of his death, in order to enhance the value of the discovery of the source of the Nile, in his anxiety to appropriate the sole merit of that discovery, to be able to say with Coriolanus—"Alone I did it." D'Israeli, unquestionably, claimed as discoveries of his own, that never were in print, matters which subsequently were found to exist in published books.

He had made some previous attempts, anonymously, at romance writing. In 1797, he published "Vaurien, a Satirical Novel:" subsequently, "Flim Flams, or the Life of my Uncle," an extravaganza after the manner of Rabelais; and "Megnoon and Leila," the earliest English romance purporting to represent Oriental life, with strict attention to costume.

Mr. D'Israeli, in 1847, lost his wife. This lady, whom he married in February, 1802, was a sister of George Bassevi, Esq., of Brighton, a magistrate for Sussex, and aunt of the late eminent architect, George Bassevi, Esq., who was killed in Ely Cathedral, in 1845. At the time of the death of the elder D'Israeli, in his 82nd year, the 19th of July, 1848, he was still engaged in literary pursuits: the love of ancient books—old ragged veterans—was with him truly the "ruling passion, strong in death;" and when Mr. Corney and his labours shall be utterly forgotten, the services of Isaac D'Israeli to English literature will be remembered and well regarded. He died at the residence of his son, Benjamin, at Bradenham House, tenderly watched over in his last illness by that affectionate son, and deeply lamented by him long after his decease.

He left three sons:—the eldest of whom is now member for Buckinghamshire; the second son is a clerk in the Registry Office in Chancery; and the youngest an agriculturist in Buckinghamshire. An only daughter died, while travelling in the East with her eldest brother.

One of the best likenesses of Isaac D'Israeli is that by Count D'Orsay, engraved in the "Illustrated London News," of January 29th, 1848. A whole-length, by Alfred Crowquill, appeared in "Fraser's Magazine," some years prior to 1848; and a portrait of him in very early life, by Drummond, was published in "The Mirror," for January, 1797.

LETTERS FROM I. D'ISRAELI, ESQ., THE AUTHOR OF "THE CURIOSITIES OF LITERATURE," TO LADY BLESSINGTON.

"November 10th, 1838.

"MY DEAR LADY BLESSINGTON,

"I am the most unworthy receiver of your ever beautiful Book, and the kindness of remembering me is—

Plus belle que la Beautè.

"I hope you read some time ago a note from me, to announce to you a Friesic version of some very tender philosophy on Life and Death, composed by you in the 'Book of Beauty,' of 1834.

"The object was to show the analogy between our Saxon, or Friesic, and our English—freed of all foreign words. I do not know whether you will rejoice to understand, that of seventy and seven words, carefully counted, of which your stanzas consist, you have not more than eight foreigners; so that you wrote pure Saxon, which they say is the rarest and most difficult affair possible—most of our writers being great corruptors of the morality of words, or, as they say, of language. I put "the eight foreigners" down, like the Polish gentlemen's paws, whose patriotism, I see, is in a quarrel—

"Pain," "hours," "joy," "scold," "vanish," "sceptred," "empire," "brief."

"You see, my dear Lady, what a charming thing it is to be simple and natural, for then you are sure to write Saxon. Shakespeare wrote Saxon, for he knew how to write; Addison did not know anything of Saxon, and the consequence is, that Addison never wrote English. I hope Saxon will not go out of fashion; but whether it does or not, you must continue to write such stanzas as these on Life and Death.

"I. D'ISRAELI."

"1, St. James' Place, 5th February.

"I write to you from the sofa, where I have been laid prostrate by my old enemy, and fairly captured, almost ever since I had the pleasure of being with you.

"Could I have bound these *arthritic* heels of mine with the small light pinions of the only god who wore wings to his, I should ere now have made a descent on Gore House; but I have nothing now left, I fear, but to dwell on "Imaginary Conversations.'"

"I. D'ISRAELI."

THE RIGHT HON. BENJAMIN D'ISRAELI, M.P.

The eldest son of the distinguished literati, who was the subject of the preceding notice, Benjamin D'Israeli, was born in 1805. The literary tastes and talents of the father had been transmitted to the eldest son, and given early promise, in this instance, of intellectual powers of the highest order, which were not disappointed.

He travelled in Germany at an early age, and subsequently, in 1826, Italy and the Levant. In 1829 and 1830, he visited Constantinople, Syria, and Egypt, accompanied as far as Syria by his sister.

In 1831, on his return to England, he found the country involved in the Reform agitation. He became a candidate for the borough of Chipping Wycombe, on principles neither Whig nor Tory, but in general rather theoretically Radical, and on two points of the charter, quite practically so; on the hustings, a far-advanced Reformer, an advocate of short parliaments, and vote by ballot. He was defeated at this election, and also at a subsequent one.

The author of "Vivian Grey," "The Young Duke," "Henrietta Temple," "Venetia," "Contarini Fleming," "Coningsby," "Sybil," "Tancred," "The Wondrous Lady of Alroy," &c. &c. &c., the former votary of the Muses, the late Chancellor of the Exchequer, was one of the most intimate literary friends of Lady Blessington. Many years ago (upwards of twenty), I frequently met Mr. D'Israeli at Lady Blessington's abode, in Seamore Place. It required no ghost from the grave, or rapping spirit from the invisible world, to predicate, even then, the success of the young D'Israeli in public life. Though in general society he was habitually silent and reserved, he was closely observant. It required generally a subject of more than common interest to produce the fitting degree of enthusiasm to animate him and to stimulate him into the exercise of his marvellous powers of conversation. When duly excited, however, his command of language was truly wonderful, his power of sarcasm unsurpassed; the readiness of his wit, the quickness of his perception, the grasp of mind that enabled him to seize on all the parts of any subject under discussion, those only would venture to call in question who had never been in his company at the period I refer to.

The natural turn of his mind was then of an imaginative, romantic kind; but his political pursuits were beginning to exert a controlling influence over this tendency, and it then only occasionally broke through the staid deportment of the sombre politician, and the solemn aspect of grave and thoughtful conservatism. The struggles of an early literary career, the strife of a political one, in more advanced years, the wear and tear of a mind whose ruling passion was ambition, have now given a premature character of care and weariness of spirit to the outward, as well as the inner man of Mr. D'Israeli. I have met few men, in any country, with more unmistakable marks of genius than he possesses. If strong convictions, sound principles, steadfast opinions, and settled purposes in political action, were always found associated with exalted intellectual qualities like those of Mr. D'Israeli, there is no man in this country who would be more formidable to his opponents, or serviceable to the state.

A man who sets out in a parliamentary career without birth, fortune, political influence, or commercial interests at his back, determined not to be tabooed, not to be intimidated, discouraged, or run down by any party, or by all factions, in the House of Commons, and who triumphs solely by his intellectual power over all impediments, to his unfailing and *undiscourageable* efforts, must have the true elements of greatness in his composition. If such a man lends the powers that are in him to any party for objects that are not generous, grand, and good, he is not faithful to himself, or likely to be enabled to be eminently useful to his country.

One of the earliest works of fiction of Mr. D'Israeli was "Contarini Fleming," which appeared in 1833, a psychological romance. In 1834 appeared, "A Vindication of the British Constitution;" a thing that never has been defined or vanquished, but is perpetually vindicated. In 1835, on the establishment of a Conservative ministry, Mr. D'Israeli was a candidate for the borough of Taunton—declared himself in favour of Conservative principles, and was considered a supporter of Peel. At this election he made an attack on Mr. O'Connell, which was not prudent, nor one likely to pass with impunity. Mr. O'Connell replied, and the result was a challenge to the son of Mr. O'Connell: the offending party having long previously made a declaration, after a rencontre fatal to his antagonist, that he would fight no more. That challenge was declined by O'Connell's son. The correspondence ended with the intimation to O'Connell—"We shall meet at Philippi:" the thrashing floor of the House of Commons being evidently intended by Mr. D'Israeli, by the allusion to the Thracian field of Philippi, a place, no doubt, thus fitly designated, and designed to be the arena of many future tustles of the young Octavius of New England with the elder Dan, the Brutus of old Ireland, the scene of many contemplated Philippics, Peelics, and *O'Connell-licks*, all *in petto.*

In 1837, Mr. D'Israeli, the grandson of the worthy Venetian of the Hebrew nation, being highly popular with the ultra-Protestant Tory party, generally, and the champions of genuine uncorrupted Christianity of Maidstone, as maintained by the

Earl of Winchelsea of Battersea-fields celebrity, in particular, was returned to parliament, greatly indebted to Mr. O'Connell's abuse and uncomplimentary genealogical allusions for their favour. Octavius of young England arrived at Philippi, burning, as he was expected to be, with chivalrous ardour in defence of Protestant ascendancy and the corn-laws, and took his place on the Conservative side of the great field of politics, vulgarly called the House of Commons. Brutus, of old Ireland, *semper paratus* for assault or for defence, was on the opposite side, *fornenst* Octavius. And, lo! Greek met Greek for many nights, and no great "tug of war" ensued, and not a grease mark on the floor indicated a spot where any portion of the substance of the Maidstone combatant had been consumed, or so much as the tip of the tail of the Kilkenny animal, denoted that any deadly contest had taken place, and the dreadful practice had existed that would prevail, no doubt, more extensively among honourable gentlemen in Philippi, namely, of swallowing up one another in the heat of a debate, if they had not adopted the more discreet plan of swallowing their own words, and dealing with their political principles as tourists do with poached eggs on a fast day, when they are travelling, like Mr. Whiteside and Lord Roden, "for their sins," in Romish countries.

But there was a far more remarkable prophecy of Mr. D'Israeli, than the one about the meeting at Philippi, on his seizing the first opportunity, after his return, that presented itself of addressing the house. The attempt was a failure; but whether the fault of the audience or the orator, is of little moment. Mr. D'Israeli, with the inspiration of a true man of genius, believed in his own powers, and felt they must ultimately prevail. He turned to the hooters, the groaners, the hissers, the collective wisdom that crows like cocks and neighs like horses, the white-chokered, white-vested young gentlemen of the Lower House, who have dined and *wined*, and towards midnight are to be found kicking their heels on the benches in the body of the House, or recumbent in the side galleries, the noisy members, the much-excited, half-dreaming portion of the collective wisdom—and he said to the conscript fathers, calmly, and with emphasis : "*The time will come when you shall hear me.*" The man who uttered words like these at the onset of his career in the House of Commons, and set to work right in earnest to verify his prediction, is assuredly no common man. They were words of grave offence to the hereditary governing class, the old English family legislators, who have acquired prescriptive right to rule this land. The literary parvenu was disliked and despised by them. He could not refer to half-a-dozen grandfathers of great fortunes and large estates in support of his pretensions; to big-wigged progenitors who had been successful lawyers, famous courtiers, or descendants of celebrated courtezans, in ancient times: he could only go back to a father who had ennobled himself by the exercise of his genius, and had left a commodity of a great literary name to a son highly gifted, to keep in honour and respect.

But the worst of it, in the opinion of the old aristocratic parties who divide the advantages and privilege of governing the country between them, the son of a mere author, who dared to address the words to them—"*The time will come when you shall hear me*"—accomplished his prediction, he compelled them to hear him with profound attention. He forced his way into the councils of the nation, and of his sovereign, and compelled the Conservative party to adopt him for their chief.

But they hate him not the less for that compulsion, and their antagonists, who fear him quite as much as the others hate him, find fault with him for his inconsistency. He is a political apostate, a renegade, a man of no fixed principles, of no immutability of opinion, and fidelity to party interests.

But, in common fairness, let us ask, Which of the great leaders of the rival parties in the state, are perfectly consistent in their political opinions on the Corn Laws, on the Appropriation of Surplus Ecclesiastical Revenues, on Vote by Ballot? are faithful even to the great questions of Civil and Religious Liberty, of Reform, and of Free Trade, and consistent with themselves at different periods, in relation to the same subject? If public men be in earnest when they express detestation of change of political opinion in public men, let it be clearly understood they are sincere; and being so, that they denounce inconsistency alike in Whig or Tory, in great lords of the soil, and scions of a great stock, which may have given law-makers to the realm for many ages, as well as in a man of no other riches but his talents; of no other hereditary honours but those he has derived from his father's literary reputation; who owes more to nature and his father, the son of a mere author, than he does to Nell Gwynne, and all his grandmothers *antipassati* for several centuries gone by.

The brilliant wit of Sheridan, the sparkling repartee of Canning, the rich humour of O'Connell, racy of the soil that gave him birth, it is in vain to look for in the oratory of D'Israeli. But in sarcastic power, ability to make sharp, sudden-telling attacks on opponents, D'Israeli has no superior, and few equals. The peculiar talent, something " more than kith and less than kin" to wit, which distinguishes D'Israeli in debate in parliament, in his harangues on the hustings, and in his communications in the press, is that which he exhibits on many public occasions: of grave irony—irony indulged in with such solemnity of manner, with such apparent seriousness of intention, as well as such a seeming sense of profound importance attached to the object or opinions he desires to be thought in earnest in espousing, that the uninitiated in state mysteries allow their judgment to be led away by the specious reasoning of the plausible and able politician.*

If his literary impugners and political adversaries be sincere in their scorn, when they sneer at a Chancellor of the Exchequer, and the leader of a great political party in the House of Commons, because he has written works of fiction, poems for annuals, critiques for reviews in early life, continues to be addicted to literary pursuits, and being a man of brilliant imagination, cannot in their estimation be a profound politician,—let them condemn the exercise of all talent in

* One of the most admirable specimens of this grave irony is to be found in a letter of Mr. D'Israeli, recently published, expressive of a deep interest in the views of the members of an association at Blackburn, who are anxious to have the Emancipation Act of 1829 repealed, or neutralized by new restrictive legislation. In his letter, Mr. D'Israeli expresses a hope that the required steps will be taken by Lord John Russell:—

" In that case (he says), I should extend to him the same support which I did at the time of the Papal aggression, when he attempted to grapple with a great evil; though he was defeated in his purpose by the intrigues of the Jesuit party, whose policy was on that occasion upheld in Parliament with eminent ability and unhappy success by Lord Aberdeen, Sir James Graham, and Mr. Gladstone.

" I still retain the hope that Lord John Russell will seize the opportunity, which he unfortunately lost in 1851, and deal with the relations in all their bearings of our Roman Catholic fellow-subjects to our Protestant constitution. But, however this may be, there can be no doubt, that sooner or later, the work must be done, with gravity, I trust, and with as little heat as possible in so great a controversy, but with earnestness and without equivocation: for the continuance of the present state of affairs must lead inevitably to civil discord, and, perhaps, to national disaster."

Irony more gravely humorous than is to be found in this letter of Mr. D'Israeli to poor Mr. Christopher Robinson, of Blackburn, is not to be met with. It would be easier to conceive than to describe the inward glee that must have been felt at the successful composition of this admirably ironical epistle, that was intended to outdo the famous Durham letter, and to make a little party capital, during the recess.

literary pursuits, that is not connected with politics, on the part of men devoted to public affairs.

On that ground, Blackstone should be condemned for his sentimental verses, Sir William Jones for his translations of Persian poetry, Addison for his essays, Canning for his epigrams, Lord Brougham for all he has written that is not of law and politics, Lord John Russell for his biography of Moore, and his drama of Don Carlos.

Is it the novel only, that gentlemen object to? are all works of fiction unprofitable productions? Is the mere writing of a novel an evidence of puerility of mind? If the object of the author of such a work be the delineation of life and manners, a portraiture of some particular phase of society, and a representation of some grand life-like scene of heroic action or historical event, the prose-writer's aim and end will not differ materially from the epic poet's.

But suppose a young man starting into life, instead of devoting his time and talents to literary pursuits of any kind, to verse-making, book-reviewing, drama-composing, or novel-writing, gave himself up to horse-racing, gambling, to profligacy, and after a career of debauchery for some years, stopped short at the verge of ruin, entered on politics, and took his place in the House of Commons;—would he be entitled to more consideration than a man whose antecedents have been altogether different?

Are better things to be expected of him, than of the young author of works of fiction? Are higher hopes to be built on his experience of life, than on that of a young man who has sown his wild oats in another field—on one even of the lightest soil of literature?

The works of Mr. D'Israeli are of unequal merit; but they bear the stamp of an original mind, of power far superior to the exhibition he cares to make of it, in any of the works of fiction written by him. His "Vivian Grey" was written at the age of twenty-one. His "Contarini Fleming" is, perhaps, the best of his productions. His "Harriet Temple" contains some incidents of his own career, and depicts also, slightly dealing with it, the character of Count D'Orsay with much truth.

Mr. D'Israeli was introduced into Parliament for Maidstone, by the late Windham Lewis, Esq., M.P. for Green Meadow, county Glamorgan, who formerly represented that borough: and was left executor by that gentleman. Mr. D'Israeli married the widow of Mr. Lewis. She was the only daughter of John Evans, Esq., of Braceford Park, Devonshire; and with her Mr. D'Israeli acquired an independent fortune.*

LETTERS FROM THE RIGHT HON. BENJAMIN D'ISRAELI TO LADY BLESSINGTON.

"October 4, 1834.

"DEAR LADY BLESSINGTON,

"I see by the papers that you have quitted the shores of the 'far resounding sea,' and resumed your place in the most charming of modern houses. I therefore venture to recall my existence to your memory, and request the favour of hearing some intelligence of yourself, which must always interest me.

"Have you been well, happy, and prosperous? And has that pen, plucked assuredly from the pinion of a bird of Paradise, been idle or creative? My lot has been, as usual, here; though enlivened by the presence of ——, who has contrived to pay us two visits, and ——, who also gave us a fortnight of his delightful society.

* The second son of Mr. Isaac D'Israeli, is a clerk in the Register Office, in Chancery; the youngest, an agriculturist in Buckinghamshire. His only daughter, the devoted attendant and amanuensis of her aged and blind father, in the latter years of his life, died when travelling in the East with her brother, Mr. Benjamin D'Israeli. An admirable sketch of Mr. Isaac D'Israeli, by Count D'Orsay, was published in 1848, in "Bentley s Miscellany."

" I am tolerably well, and hope to give a good account of myself and doings when we meet, which I trust will be soon.

" How goes that ' great lubber,' the Public ? and how fares that mighty boar, the World? Who of my friends has distinguished or extinguished himself or herself? In short, as the hart for the waterside, I pant for a little news, but chiefly of your fair and agreeable self.

" D'Israeli."

" September 11.

" I send you a literary arabesque, which is indeed nonsense. If worthy of admission, it might close the volume, as fairies and fireworks dance and glitter in the last scene of a fantastic entertainment. I wish my contribution were worthier, but I get duller every day.

" This villa of Hadrian is doubly cheering, with an Italian sky.

" D'Israeli."

No date.

" Ever since your most agreeable dinner party (after pleasure comes pain), I have been a prisoner with the influenza: a most amazing infirmity in these troublesome times, when one likes to move about, and gather all the chit-chat which is always wrong. I wish you would write me a little confidential note, and tell me what the opposition mean to do, and what is to happen.

" D'Israeli."

" August 15.

" I am delighted with ' Agathon ;' it left me musing, which is a test of a great work. I invariably close such in a reverie. Wieland indeed always delights me. I sympathize with him much. There is a wild oriental fancy blended with his western philosophy, which is a charming union. I like a moral to peep out of the mildest invention, to assure us, that while we have been amused, we have all the while been growing a little wiser.

" The translation of the ' Agathon' is very clumsy.

" D'Israeli."

"I think the 'Manuscrit Vert' sad stuff. The author's constant efforts to be religious are very unfortunate. I fear that faith is not his practice. His hero seizes every inopportune occurrence to assure us that he believes in God. His evident conviction is the general one, that even this article of faith is by no means common in France. His hero and heroine are moulded in the German school, and are personifications of abstract ideas. The hero, because he believes in God, represents spiritualism; the heroine, because she instantly knows every man she meets, is materialism, forsooth! The lady is not a Philina, and altogether the author is a fool.

"*I have not made up my mind about Pickersgill and the Three Brothers. When I see more, more I will say. At present, I am inclined to believe that the work is a translation from the German.** Altogether, in a season of sorrow, your kind parcel has much amused me. Shall I send the books back to Hookham?

"D'ISRAELI."

* The subject of the authorship of this very remarkable, but very little known novel, was first brought to the attention of Lady Blessington by me. On reading this novel, by no means fashionable or advantageously known in the novel-reading world, I was greatly struck with the originality and genius of the author of this production. Finding the novel had been published by Stockdale, a London bookseller, father of the Harriet Wilson Memoirs publisher, of unenviable notoriety, who, at the period I refer to, was living in a small street between the Haymarket and Regent Street, I called on the latter about twenty years ago, and requested him to inform me who the author was of the novel in question, from which it was very obvious Byron had borrowed the story, and many of the ideas of his poem, "The Deformed Transformed." Stockdale told me, the author was a very young man, of considerable talent, and some eccentricity; his name was Pickersgill; his father was a merchant of London. He, Stockdale, never saw him but once, when he brought the MS. to his father for publication. The MS. lay in his father's hands for some years before it was published. There was a loss by the publication. The father of the author called on Stockdale, and wished to have the work suppressed. What became of the author, my informant, the son of the publisher, never learned.—R. R. M.

No date.

"I have not forgotten for a moment either you or Mrs. Fairlie; but from the evening I saw you last, I have lived in such a state of unpoetic turmoil, that I could not bring my mind to the charming task. I have seized the first unbroken time this morning to write the enclosed; and if Mrs. F. think them worthy of her acceptance, she can put to them any heading she likes.

"I should be mortified if the 'Book of Beauty' appeared without my contribution, however trifling. I have something on the stocks for you, but it is too elaborate to finish well in the present tone of my mind; but if you like a Syrian sketch of four or five pages, you shall have it in two or three days.

"I am in town only a day or two, and terribly hurried; but I hope to get to K. G. before the election.

"D'ISRAELI."

"Tuesday.

"I have intended to return the books, and send you these few lines every day, and am surprised that I could have so long omitted doing any thing so agreeable as writing to you.

"We are all delighted with the portraits: my sister is collecting those of all my father's friends: her collection will include almost every person of literary celebrity, from the end of the Johnsonian era: so your fair face arrived just in time. I am particularly delighted with P——'s portrait, which I have never seen before.

"I have read the article on Coleridge, in the 'Quarterly;' but do not agree with you in holding it to be written by ———. It is too good; his style has certainly the merit of being peculiar. I know none so meagre, harsh, and clumsy, or more felicitous in the jumble of common-place metaphors. I think the present reviewal must be by N——— C———, a cleverish sort of fellow, though a prig.

"You give me the same advice as my father ever has done, about dotting down the evanescent feelings of youth; but, like other excellent advice, I fear it will prove unprofitable. I have a horror of journalizing, and indeed of writing of all description.

"Do you really think that Jekyll is ninety? He has a son, I believe, of my standing.

"As you are learned in Byron, do you happen to know who was the mother of Allegra?

"D'Israeli."

No date.

"Until the Whigs are turned out, it seems that I never shall be able to pay you a visit; and therefore I shall wish for that result with double ardour. Irish Corporation and Constabulary Bills, and other dull nonsense, have really engrossed my time for the last three weeks; yet I have stolen one single moment of sunshine for the muse, and I send you some lines, which I hope you may deem worthy of insertion in your volume.

"D'Israeli."

"Tuesday morning.

"Alas! alas! you have made me feel my fetters even earlier than I expected. No dinners I fear, on Tuesday, for me in future, certainly not on this, as I must be at my post in a very few hours.

"Last night was very animating and interesting, and John Russell flung over the Radicals with remorseless vigour.

"D'Israeli."

"My father I find better than I expected, and much cheered by my presence. I delivered him all your kind messages. He is now very busy on his 'History of English Literature,' in which he is far advanced. I am mistaken if you will not delight in these volumes. They are full of new views of the History of our Language, and indeed of our Country, for the History of a State is necessarily mixed up with the History of its literature.

"For myself, I am doing nothing. The western breeze favours an alpine existence, and I am seated with a pipe under a spreading sycamore, solemn as a pacha.

"I wish you would induce Hookham to entrust me with Agathon, and that mad Byronian novel.

"What do you think of the modern French novelists? And is it worth my while to read them? And if so, what do you recommend me? What of Balzac? Is he better than Sue and George Sand Dudevant? And are these inferior to Hugo?

"D'ISRAELI.'

"March 21, 1837.

"Although it is little more than a fortnight since I quitted your truly friendly society and hospitable roof, both of which I shall always remember with deep and lively gratitude, it seems, to me at least, a far more awful interval of time. I have waited for a serene hour to tell you of my doings; but serene hours are rare, and therefore I will not be deluded into waiting any longer.

"In spite of every obstacle, I have not forgotten the fair Venetia, who has grown under my paternal care, and as much in grace, I hope, as in stature, or rather dimensions. She is truly like her prototype—

"'——*The child of love,*
Tho' born in bitterness, and nurtured in convulsion;'

but I hope she will prove a source of consolation to her parent, and also to her godmother, for I consider you to stand in that relation to her. I do not think that you will find any golden hint of our musing strolls has been thrown away upon me; and I should not be surprised if, in six weeks, she may ring the bell at your hall door, and request admittance, where I know she will find at least one sympathizing friend.

"I watch for the appearance of your volumes, I suppose now trembling on the threshold of publicity.

"In a box of books from Mitchell, that arrived lately down here, in the 'Life of Mackintosh,' I was amused and gladdened by the sight of some pencil notes, in a familiar handwriting. It was like meeting a friend unexpectedly.

"I have, of course, no news from this extreme solitude. My father advances valiantly with his great enterprise; but works of that calibre are hewn out of the granite with slow and elabora e strokes. Mine are but plaster of Paris casts, or rather statues of snow, that melt as soon as they are fabricated.

"D'Orsay has written me kind letters, which always inspirit me.

"D'ISRAELI."

"December 31, 1848.

"I took the liberty of telling Moxon to send you a copy of the new edition of the 'Curiosities of Literature,' which I have just published, with a little notice of my father. You were always so kind to him, and he entertained such a sincere regard for you, that I thought you would not dislike to have the copy on your shelves.

"I found, among his papers, some verses which you sent on his eightieth birthday, which I mean to publish some day, with his correspondence, but the labour now is too great for my jaded life.

"I must offer you our congratulations on Guiche's marriage, which is, we hope, all you wish; and also on the success of the future Imperator.

"D'ISRAELI."

"April 25, 1849.

"We returned to town on the 16th, and a few days after, I called at Gore House, but you were gone. It was a pang; for though absorbing duties of my life have prevented me of late from passing as much time under that roof as it was once my happiness and good fortune through your kindness to do; you are well assured, that my heart never changed for an instant to its inmates, and that I invariably entertained for them the same interest and affection.

"Had I been aware of your intentions, I would have come up to town earlier, and specially to have said 'adieu!' mournful as that is.

"I thought I should never pay another visit to Paris, but I have now an object in doing so. All the world here will miss you very much, and the charm with which you invested existence; but for your own happiness, I am persuaded you have acted wisely. Every now and then, in this life, we require a great change; it wonderfully revives the sense of existence. I envy you; pray, if possible, let me sometimes hear from you.

"D'ISRAELI."

CHARLES DICKENS, ESQ.

Charles Dickens! The public might dispense with any other notice of this gentleman, or of his ancestry, than the announcement of his name, and the statement of the fact that he is the author of "Sketches by Boz," "Pickwick," "Nicholas Nickleby," "American Notes," "Oliver Twist," "Master Humphrey's Clock," "Barnaby Rudge," "Dombey and Son," "The Chimes," "Christmas Carols," "Cricket on the Hearth," "Battle of Life," "Martin Chuzzlewit," "David Copperfield," "Bleak House," "Hard Times," &c. Little need be added to this great eulogy.

Charles Dickens was born in 1812, at Landport, Portsmouth.

His father's official duties obliged him to reside alternately at the principal naval stations of England;* and no doubt the varied bustling scenes of life witnessed by Charles Dickens in his early years, had an influence on his mind, that gave to him a taste for observation of manners and mental peculiarities of different classes of people engaged in the active pursuits of

* Mr. John Dickens (the father of Charles and W. L. Dickens) died in Keppel Street, Russell Square, March 31st, 1851, aged 65. Up to the period of his death, he enjoyed a pension from the Government. In early life, he held an office in the Navy Pay Department, at Chatham Dockyard. At an advanced age, rather, he became connected with the London Press, and for many years was known as one of its own efficient and respected members. He retired from it for a time, and settled at Alphington, near Exeter; but returned to London, to assist in the establishment of the Daily News.

Mr. W. L. Dickens is resident engineer of the Malton and Drayton Railway.

life, and quickened a naturally lively perception of the ridiculous, for which he was distinguished even in boyhood.

It is curious to observe how similar opportunities of becoming acquainted practically with life, and the busy actors on its varied scenes, in very early life, appear to influence the minds of thinking and imaginative men in after-years. Goldsmith's pedestrian excursions on the Continent, Bulwer's youthful rambles on foot in England, and equestrian expeditions in France, and Maclise's extensive walks in boyhood, over his native county, and the mountains and valleys of Wicklow a little later, were fraught with similar results.

Charles Dickens was intended by his father to be an attorney. Nature and Mr. John Dickens happily differed on that point. London law may have sustained little injury in losing Dickens for "a limb." English literature would have met with an irreparable loss, had she been deprived of him whom she delights to own a favourite son.

Dickens, having decided against the law, began his career in "the gallery," as a reporter on "The True Sun;" and from the start made himself distinguished and distinguishable among "the corps," for his ability, promptness, and punctuality.

He was next employed on "The Morning Chronicle," but not only as a reporter, but a writer in the evening edition of that paper. The piquant "Sketches of English Life and Character," which afterwards appeared in a distinct form, as "Sketches by Boz," were published in that journal.

Success was at once achieved. The next production was still more successful; "The Pickwick Papers," the earliest, and the best but one, of all the works of Charles Dickens.

"Nicholas Nickleby" followed, and introduced the incomparable "Squeers" to the public. "Oliver Twist" came next; and that prominent characteristic of the author—sympathy with the poor, and a powerful will to war with wrong and injustice—found an ample field for their exercise, in the pages of this work.

"Master Humphrey's Clock," with the admirably drawn "Old Curiosity Shop," and the most charming of all the female progeny of Dickens' imagination, "Little Nell," succeeded "Nickleby."

"American Notes, for General Circulation," the result of a transatlantic trip, made their appearance on the author's return to England in 1842.

"Martin Chuzzlewit" made its débût in numbers, in 1843.

And in 1844, Dickens went to Italy, for recreation and restoration of energies of mind and body over-worked: and in January, 1846, began to publish in the newly-established paper, "The Daily News," edited by him, the results of his Italian tour—"Pictures of Italy."

There are some sketches worthy of Dickens in those "Pictures," of ridiculous touring personages of the Bull family, and their roamings amidst the ruins of the Eternal City—their misadventures in classic lands—the constant *losings*, in particular, of a worthy English gentleman, with an umbrella eternally under his arm, in ancient tombs and temples; and incessant searches for him on the part of an anxious wife, always perspiring with solicitude and fatigue in her pursuits after her missing husband.

Since 1846, the success of "Dombey and Son," "David Copperfield," "Bleak House," and "Hard Times," bear ample testimony to the undiminished popularity and inexhausted powers of Charles Dickens; and perhaps the success of his weekly paper, "Household Words," is no less indicative of both than any of those distinct works.

The following notice of Dickens is by a lady intimately acquainted with him, who claims kindred with the late Countess of Blessington, and who stands near to her also in relationship of mind and form:—"His immense power of observation, from the humblest to the most important details, his genuine originality of thought and expression, are amongst the most striking of his attributes. Warm-hearted, impulsive, and generous, of buoyant spirits, the keenest intelligence, and quickest perception of every thing worthy of notice, of the ridiculous as well as of the beautiful; his independence of spirit, his natural elasticity and constitutional energy of mind, vivacity of manner in conversation, and perfect freedom from all affectation, enhance the value of his other excellent qualities."

"In him a variety of gifts and graces are combined, such as are rarely found united in the same individual. In all his domestic relations, as son, husband, father, and brother, his conduct is unexceptionable. His character seems to have some self-sustaining principle in it, in all positions he is placed in. His countenance is, I think, the most varying and expressive I ever saw."

LETTERS FROM CHARLES DICKENS, ESQ. TO LADY BLESSINGTON.

"Devonshire Terrace, June 2nd, 1841.

"Dear Lady Blessington,

"The year goes round so fast, that when anything occurs to remind me of its whirling, I lose my breath, and am bewildered. So your hand-writing last night had as startling an effect upon me, as though you had sealed your note with one of your own eyes.

"I remember my promise, as in cheerful duty bound, and with Heaven's grace will redeem it. At this moment, I have not the faintest idea how; but I am going into Scotland on the 19th to see Jeffrey, and while I am away, (I shall return, please God, in about three weeks), will look out for some accident, incident, or subject for small description, to send you when I come home. You will take the will for the deed, I know; and remembering that I have a 'Clock,' which always wants winding up, will not quarrel with me for being brief.

"Have you seen Townshend's magnetic boy? You heard of

him, no doubt, from Count D'Orsay. If you get him to Gore House, don't, I entreat you, have more than eight people—four is a better number—to see him. He fails in a crowd, and is *marvellous* before a few.

"I am told that down in Devonshire there are young ladies innumerable, who read crabbed manuscripts with the palms of their hands, and newspapers with their ankles, and so forth; and who are, so to speak, literary all over. I begin to understand what a blue-stocking means; and have not the smallest doubt that Lady —— (for instance) could write quite as entertaining a book with the sole of her foot as ever she did with her head.

"I am a believer in earnest, and I am sure you would be if you saw this boy, under moderately favourable circumstances, as I hope you will, before he leaves England.

"Believe me, dear Lady Blessington,

"Faithfully yours,

"CHARLES DICKENS."

"Devonshire Terrace, 10th March, 1844.

"I have made up my mind to 'see the world;' and mean to decamp, bag and baggage, next midsummer, for a twelvemonth. I purpose establishing my family in some convenient place, from whence I can make personal ravages on the neighbouring country, and, somehow or other, have got it into my head that Nice would be a favourable spot for head-quarters.

"You are so well acquainted with these matters, that I am anxious to have the benefit of your kind advice. I do not doubt that you can tell me whether this same Nice be a healthy place the year through, whether it be reasonably cheap, pleasant to look at and to live in, and the like. If you will tell me, when you have ten minutes to spare for such a client, I shall be delighted to come to you, and guide myself by your opinion. I will not ask you to forgive me for troubling you, because I am sure beforehand that you will do so.

"I beg to be kindly remembered to Count D'Orsay and to your nieces. I was going to say 'the Misses Power,' but it looks so like the blue board at a Ladies' School, that I stopped short. CHARLES DICKENS."

"Covent Garden, Sunday, Noon. (P.M. 1844.)

"Business for other people (and by no means of a pleasant kind) has held me prisoner during two whole days, and will so detain me to-day, in the very agony of my departure for Italy again, that I shall not even be able to reach Gore House once more: on which I had set my heart..I cannot bear the thought of going away, without some sort of reference to the happy day you gave me on Monday, and the pleasure and delight I had in your earnest greeting. I shall never forget it, believe me. It would be worth going to China—it would be worth going to America, to come home again for the pleasure of such a meeting with you and Count D'Orsay—to whom my love—and something as near it to Miss Power and her sister as it is lawful to send.

"It will be an unspeakable satisfaction to me (though I am not maliciously disposed), to know under your own hand at Genoa, that my little book made you cry. I hope to prove a better correspondent on my return to those shores. But better or worse, or any how, I am ever, my dear Lady Blessington, in no common degree, and not with an every-day regard, yours,

"CHARLES DICKENS."

"Milan, Wednesday, November 20th, 1844.

"Appearances are against me. Don't believe them. I have written you, in intention, fifty letters, and I can claim no credit for any one of them (though they were the best letters you ever read), for they all originated in my desire to live in your memory and regard.

"Since I heard from Count D'Orsay, I have been beset in I don't know how many ways. First of all, I went to Marseilles, and came back to Genoa. Then I moved to the Peschiere. Then some people, who had been present at the scientific Congress here, made a sudden inroad on that establishment, and over-ran it. Then they went away, and I shut myself up for one month, close and tight, over my little Christmas book, 'The Chimes.' All my affections and passions got twined and knotted up in it, and I became as haggard as a murderer, long before I wrote 'The End.' When I had done that, like '*The* man of Thessaly,' who having scratched his eyes out in a quickset hedge, plunged into a bramble-bush to scratch them in again, I fled to Venice, to recover the composure I had disturbed. From thence I went to Verona and to Mantua. And now I am here—just come up from underground, and earthy all over, from seeing that extraordinary tomb in which the Dead Saint lies in an alabaster case, with sparkling jewels all about him to mock his dusty eyes, not to mention the twenty franc pieces which devout votaries were ringing down upon a sort of skylight in the cathedral pavement above, as if it were the counter of his Heavenly shop.

"You know Verona? You know everything in Italy *I* know. I am not learned in geography, and it was a great blow to me to find that Romeo was only banished five-and-twenty miles. It was a greater blow to me to see the old house of the Capulets, with some genealogical memorials, still carved in stone, over the gateway of the court-yard. It is a most miserable little inn, at this time ankle-deep in dirt; and noisy Vetturini and muddy market carts were disputing possession of the yard with a brood of geese, all splashed and bespattered as if they had their yesterday's white trousers on. There was nothing to connect it with the beautiful story, but a very unsentimental middle-aged lady (the Padrona, I suppose), in the doorway, who resembled old Capulet in the one particular, of being very great indeed in the family way.*

* The author of the erudite work, "Descrizione de Verona, e delle Sue Provincia," (8vo. 1820, vol. ii. p. 102,) throws some doubt on the tradition that makes the old structure commonly referred to as the mansion of the ancient Capelli or Capelleti family; and refers to an old house in a street between the Piazza Delle Erbe è San Sebastiano, as more probably the Casa Capelleti. "Un pileo o Capello in Marmo della forma onde è lo stemma dei Capello Patrizi Veneti, quasi come a serraglio dell arco sta sul interna porta di detto luogo. Se lo stepo fosse stato lo Stemma dei nostri Cappelleti o Capelli, potrebbesi su questo fatto formar qualche attra coughiettura." Note on preceding passage, p. 115, vol ii. For an interesting account of the tragical denouement, in 1303, of the loves of "Romeo de' Monticoli è Giulietta de Capelletti," the reader is referred to vol. i. p. 256, of the same work; and for an account of the tomb of the lovers in the "Orfanotrofiá delle Franceschine," in Verona, to p. 140, same vol.—R. R. M.

"The Roman amphitheatre there, delighted me beyond expression. I never saw any thing so full of solemn, ancient interest. There are the four-and-forty rows of seats, as fresh and perfect as if their occupants had vacated them but yesterday—the entrances, passages, dens, rooms, corridors; the numbers over some of the arches. An equestrian troop had been there some days before, and had scooped out a little ring at one end of the arena, and had their performances in that spot. I should like to have seen it, of all things, for its very dreariness. Fancy a handful of people sprinkled over one corner of the great place; (the whole population of Verona wouldn't fill it now); and a spangled cavalier bowing to the echoes, and the grass-grown walls! I climbed to the topmost seat, and looked away at the beautiful view for some minutes; when I turned round, and looked down into the theatre again, it had exactly the appearance of an immense straw hat, to which the helmet in the Castle of Otranto was a baby: the rows of seats representing the different plaits of straw, and the arena the inside of the crown.

"I had great expectations of Venice, but they fell immeasurably short of the wonderful reality. The short time I passed there, went by me in a dream. I hardly think it possible to exaggerate its beauties, its sources of interest, its uncommon novelty and freshness. A thousand and one realizations of the thousand and one nights, could scarcely captivate and enchant me more than Venice...

"Your old house at Albaro—Il Paradiso—is spoken of as yours to this day. What a gallant place it is! I don't know the present inmate, but I hear that he bought and furnished it not long since, with great splendour, in the French style, and that he wishes to sell it. I wish I were rich, and could buy it. There is a third-rate wine shop below Byron's house; and the place looks dull, and miserable, and ruinous enough.

"Old ——— is a trifle uglier than when I first arrived. He has periodical parties, at which there are a great many flower-pots and a few ices—no other refreshments. He goes about, constantly charged with extemporaneous poetry; and is always ready, like tavern-dinners, on the shortest notice and the most reasonable terms. He keeps a gigantic harp in his bed-room, together with pen, ink, and paper, for fixing his ideas as they flow,—a kind of profane King David, but truly good-natured and very harmless.

"Pray say to Count D'Orsay everything that is cordial and loving from me. The travelling purse he gave me has been of immense service. It has been constantly opened. All Italy seems to yearn to put its hand in it. I think of hanging it, when I come back to England, on a nail as a trophy, and of gashing the brim like the blade of an old sword, and saying to my son and heir, as they do upon the stage: 'You see this notch, boy? Five hundred francs were laid low on that day, for post horses. Where this gap is, a waiter charged your father treble the correct amount—and got it. This end, worn into teeth like the rasped edge of an old file, is sacred to the Custom Houses, boy, the passports, and the shabby soldiers at town-gates, who put an open hand and a dirty coat-cuff into the coach windows of all Forestieri. Take it, boy. Thy father has nothing else to give!'

"My desk is cooling itself in a mail coach, somewhere down at the back of the cathedral, and the pens and ink in this house are so detestable, that I have no hope of your ever getting to this portion of my letter. But I have the less misery in this state of mind, from knowing that it has nothing in it to repay you for the trouble of perusal.

"CHARLES DICKENS."

"Genoa, May 9, 1845.

"Once more in my old quarters; and with rather a tired sole to my foot, from having found such an immense number of different resting places for it since I went away. I write you my last Italian letter for this bout, designing to leave here, please God, on the ninth of next month, and to be in London again, by the end of June. I am looking forward with great delight to the pleasure of seeing you once more; and mean to come to Gore House with such a swoop as shall astonish the Poodle, if, after being accustomed to his own size and sense, he retain the power of being astonished at any thing in the wide world.

"You know where I have been, and every mile of ground I

have travelled over, and every object I have seen. It is next to impossible, surely, to exaggerate the interest of Rome: though, I think, it *is* very possible to find the main source of interest in the wrong things. Naples disappointed me greatly. The weather was bad during a great part of my stay there. But if I had not had mud I should have had dust, and though I had had sun, I must still have had the Lazzaroni. And they are so ragged, so dirty, so abject, so full of degradation, so sunken and steeped in the hopelessness of better things, that they would make Heaven uncomfortable, if they could ever get there. I didn't expect to see a handsome city, but I expected something better than that long dull line of squalid houses, which stretches from the Chiaja to the quarter of the Porta Capuana; and while I was quite prepared for a miserable populace, I had some dim belief that there were bright rags among them, and dancing legs, and shining sun-browned faces. Whereas the honest truth is, that connected with Naples itself, I have not one solitary recollection. The country round it charmed me, I need not say. Who can forget Herculaneum and Pompeii?

"As to Vesuvius, it burns away in my thoughts, beside the roaring waters of Niagara; and not a splash of the water extinguishes a spark of the fire; but there they go on, tumbling and flaming night and day; each in its fullest glory.

"I have seen so many wonders, and each of them has such a voice of its own, that I sit all day long listening to the roar they make, as if it were in a sea shell; and have fallen into an idleness so complete, that I can't rouse myself sufficiently to go to Pisa on the twenty-fifth, when the triennial illumination of the Cathedral and Leaning Tower, and Bridges, and what not, takes place. But I have already been there; and it cannot beat St. Peter's, I suppose. So I don't think I shall pluck myself up by the roots, and go aboard a steamer for Leghorn.

"Let me thank you heartily for the 'Keepsake' and the 'Book of Beauty.' They reached me a week or two ago. I have been very much struck by two papers in them. One, Landor's 'Conversations,' among the most charming, profound, and delicate productions I have ever read. The other, your lines on Byron's room at Venice. I am as sure that you wrote them from your heart, as I am that they found their way immediately to mine.

"It delights me to receive such accounts of Maclise's fresco. If he will only give his magnificent genius fair play, there is not enough cant and dullness even in the criticism of art from which Sterne prayed kind Heaven to defend him, as the worst of all the cants continually canted in this canting world—to keep the giant down, an hour.

"Our poor friend, the naval governor, has lost his wife, I am sorry to hear, since you and I spoke of his pleasant face. And L. B., what a terrible history that was! F—— did himself enduring honour by his manly and zealous devotion to the interests of that orphan family, in the midst of all his pains and trouble. It was very good of him.

"Do not let your nieces forget me, if you can help it; and give my love to Count D'Orsay, with many thanks to him for his charming letter. I was greatly amused by his account of ————. There was a 'cold shade of aristocracy' about it, and a dampness of cold water, which entertained me beyond measure.

"CHARLES DICKENS."

"Devonshire Terrace, March 2, 1846.

"Many thanks for the letters! I will take the greatest care of them, though I blush to find how little they deserve it.

"It vexes me very much that I am going out on Friday, and cannot help it. I have no strength of mind, I am afraid. I am always making engagements, in which there is no prospect of satisfaction.

"Vague thoughts of a new book are rife within me just now; and I go wandering about at night into the strangest places, according to my usual propensity at such a time, seeking rest, and finding none. As an addition to my composure, I ran over a little dog in the Regent's Park yesterday (killing him on the spot), and gave his little mistress, a girl of thirteen or fourteen, such exquisite distress as I never saw the like of.

"I must have some talk with you about those American singers. They must never go back to their own country without your having heard them sing Hood's 'Bridge of Sighs.' My God, how sorrowful and pitiful it is!

"Best regards to Count D'Orsay and the young ladies.

"CHARLES DICKENS."

"Devonshire Terrace, May 19, 1846.

"If I had not a good reason for delaying to acknowledge the receipt of the book you so kindly sent me, I should be a most unworthy dog. But I have been every day expecting to be able to send you the enclosed little volume, and could get no copies until last night, in consequence of their running very fine against the subscription and demand. May you like it!

"I have been greatly entertained by the femme de chambre, who paints love with a woman's eye (I think that the highest praise), and sometimes like a female Gil Blas. The spirit of our two fair friends M. and S. shines through their representative. I would have identified the former any where.

"Count D'Orsay's copy of the pictures, with my cordial remembrance and regards. CHARLES DICKENS."

"48, Rue de Courcelles, Paris,
"January 24, 1847.

"I feel very wicked in beginning this note, and deeply remorseful for not having begun and ended it long ago. But *you* know how difficult it is to write letters in the midst of a writing life; and as you know too (I hope) how earnestly and affectionately I always think of you, wherever I am, I take heart on a little consideration, and feel comparatively good again.

"F—— has been cramming into the space of a fortnight, every description of impossible and inconsistent occupation in the way of sight-seeing. He has been now at Versailles, now in the Prisons, now at the Opera, now at the Hospitals, now at the Conservatoire, and now at the Morgue, with a dreadful insatiability. I begin to doubt whether I had any thing to do with a book called 'Dombey,' or ever sat over number five (not finished a fortnight yet) day after day, until I half began, like the monk in poor Wilkie's story, to think it the only reality in life, and to mistake all the realities for short-lived shadows.

"Among the multitude of sights, we saw our pleasant little

bud of a friend, Rose Cheri, play Clarissa Harlowe, the other night. I believe she did it in London just now, and perhaps you may have seen it. A most charming, intelligent, modest, affecting piece of acting it is: with a Death superior to any thing I ever saw on the stage, except Macready's ' Lear.' The theatres are admirable just now. We saw ' Gentil Bernard,' at the Variétés last night, acted in a manner that was absolutely perfect. It was a little picture of Watteau, animated and talking from beginning to end. At the Cirque, there is a new show-piece, called the ' French Revolution,' in which there is a representation of the National Convention, and a series of battles (fought by some five hundred people, who look like five thousand), that are wonderful in their extraordinary vigour and truth. Gun-cotton gives its name to the general annual jocose review at the Palais Royal, which is dull enough, saving for the introduction of Alexander Dumas, sitting in his study, beside a pile of quarto volumes about five feet high, which he says is the first tableau of the first act of the first piece to be played on the first night of his new theatre. The revival of Molière's ' Don Juan,' at the Français, has drawn money. It is excellently played, and it is curious to observe how different *their* Don Juan and Valet are, from our English ideas of the master and man. They are playing ' Lucretia Borgia' again, at the Porte St. Martin; but it is poorly performed, and hangs fire drearily, though a very remarkable and striking play. We were at V. H.'s house last Sunday week, a most extraordinary place, looking like an old curiosity shop, or the property-room of some gloomy, vast old theatre. I was much struck by H——— himself, who looks like a genius as he is, every inch of him, and is very interesting and satisfactory from head to foot. His wife is a handsome woman, with flashing black eyes. There is also a charming ditto daughter of fifteen or sixteen, with ditto eyes. Sitting among old armour and old tapestry, and old coffers, and grim old chairs and tables, and old canopies of state from old palaces, and old golden lions going to play at skittles with ponderous old golden balls, they made a most romantic show, and looked like a chapter out of one of his own books.

" CHARLES DICKENS."

CHAPTER V.

LORD ABINGER.

THE Right Honourable Sir James Scarlett, Baron Abinger, a Privy Councillor, Lord Chief Baron of the Exchequer, &c. &c. was born in Jamaica, where his family had been long resident, and held considerable property. A younger brother of his, Sir Robert Scarlett, had been for many years Chief Justice of the island.

James was sent to England, at an early age, for education. He graduated in Cambridge in 1790, and in 1794 was called to the bar. He rose rapidly in his profession as an advocate, and obtained a silk gown in 1816. He offered himself for the borough of Lewes in 1812, but lost the election; and again in 1816 contested the borough, and was defeated. In 1818, he entered parliament for Lord Fitzwilliam's borough of Peterborough. His success in parliament, however, was far from answering the expectations of his friends. In 1822, he stood for the borough of Cambridge, and was defeated; but was immediately after re-chosen for Peterborough.

In 1822, in Mr. Canning's administration, he was made Attorney-General, and was knighted the same year. From this period, Sir James manifested very strongly and conspicuously Conservative principles. In 1828, he ceased to be Attorney-General, and was succeeded by Sir Charles Wetherell. In May, 1829, Sir Charles made a violent speech in opposition to Catholic Emancipation, and was dismissed by the Duke of Wellington. Sir James Scarlett was appointed by the Duke to succeed Sir Charles Wetherell, who again offered himself to the borough of Peterborough, and was re-elected.

The new Attorney-General was soon called on to file criminal informations against "The Morning Journal," "The Atlas," and other papers, for libels on the Duke of Wellington and Lord Chancellor Lyndhurst. In 1830, on the Whigs coming into office, Sir James Scarlett's office of Attorney-General was conferred on Mr. Denman. In 1831, Sir James offered himself to the electors of Cockermouth, and was returned by them.

The following year, he stood for Norwich, on the Tory interest, and was returned also.

A tender appeal in behalf of Sir James Scarlett to the ladies of Norwich, in the contest of 1832, and in favour also of a brother candidate, is one of the most amusing specimens of grave rigmarole electioneering eloquence on record:—

"*To the Ladies of Norwich.*—'None but the brave deserve the fair.'—If ever the sweets of social virtue, the wrath of honest zeal, the earnings of industry, and the prosperity of trade, had any influence in the female breast, you have now a happy opportunity of exercising it to the advantage of *your* country—*your* cause. If ever the feelings of a parent, wife, sister, friend, or lover, had a sympathy with the *public virtue*, now is *your* time to indulge the *fonder passion.* If ever you felt for the ruin and disgrace of England, and for the *miseries and deprivations* occasioned by the obnoxious Reform Bill, you are called on, by the most tender and affectionate tie in nature, to exert *your* persuasive influence on the mind of a father, brother, husband, or lover: tell them not to seek filial duty, congenial regard, matrimonial comfort, nor *tender com-*

pliance, till they have saved *your* country from *perdition!* —*posterity* from *slavery!* History furnishes us with instances of *female patriotism!* equal to any in the page of *war* and and politics. O! may the generous and beatific charms of female persuasion prevail with the *citizens of Norwich*, to espouse the cause of real liberty—of

"STORMONT AND SCARLETT."*

The ex-Attorney-General's and Lord Stormont's electioneering eloquence on this occasion, and the enthusiastic warmth of its expression, is gravely commented on in the periodical in which this epistolary gem has been preserved:—

"'If ever the sweets of social virtue,' say these gallant champions of the close borough system, 'the wrath of honest zeal, the earnings of industry, and the prosperity of trade, had any influence in the female breast, you have now a happy opportunity of exercising it to the advantage of your country—your cause.' The idea of exercising female breasts to the advantage of the country is, at all events, original, and the hint in the following paragraph, that 'now is the time to indulge the fonder passion,' is of exceedingly questionable morality."

In December, 1834, when Peel came into power, Sir James was made Chief Baron, with a peerage, by the title of Baron Abinger, and his son succeeded to the seat for Norwich.

In the House of Peers, Lord Abinger spoke but seldom, and then chiefly on legal questions. He was irregular in his attendance in the house, and evinced there by his votes his repugnance to liberalism, and his strong sympathy with conservative views and old Tory political principles. As an advocate, it is universally admitted, Sir James Scarlett was unrivalled. He had those qualifications for legal eminence, which

* New Monthly Magazine, August, 1832.

have such an extraordinary effect in attracting attention to the merits of "young men behind the bar." He had an intelligent air, and a prepossessing personal appearance. He had one of those compact, business-looking faces, that look well with a wig. Sir James, moreover, had an appearance of confidence in himself, which begets a feeling of confidence in others. He had a twinkling expression of sagacity in his look, and a humorous aspect, which told amazingly with juries. He had, above all, a discriminative knowledge of human character, and a keen perception of character, which enabled him to deal with juries and jurors individually and collectively, that gave him singular advantage over other advocates in addressing himself to the feelings, interests, biases, and prepossessions of people in a jury box. The consummate art of his advocacy was exhibited in sinking the professional character of the advocate, elevating the merits of his case, adapting his suggestions and inferences to the prevailing opinions or prejudices of the jury, and appearing before them in an easy, nonchalant manner, speaking colloquially of matters that he happened to have become conversant with, enlarging on points useful to his case without any apparent sophistry, or slurring over others that were hurtful to it in a way the least calculated to draw observation to the astuteness practised in tiding over the difficulties he had to deal with. He abstained from all attempts at oratorical display.

On the bench, "he was not an ornamental judge, but he made a useful one." In more than one sense of the word, he did not make a *shewy* judge. During the latter years of his life, and from his elevation to the bench, Lord Abinger had grown very robust and florid. A severe attack of illness had latterly caused him to wear a black patch over one of his eyes, and his infirmity obliged him to walk with a stick, and to move his lower extremities apparently with great difficulty. He was seized with paralysis within two hours after presiding as one of the Judges of the Norfolk Circuit, on the 2nd of April, 1844, and in four days more he died of this attack.

Lord Abinger married, in 1793, the third daughter of Peter Campbell, Esq., of Kilmoray, in Argyleshire, by whom he had issue, three sons and two daughters. He married secondly, in 1843, the widow of the Rev. Henry John Ridley, of Ockley.

His Lordship's eldest son, the Honourable Robert Campbell Scarlett, now Lord Abinger, was born in 1794; his second son, Colonel the Honourable James Yorke Scarlett, served in the 5th Dragoon Guards; his youngest son was Secretary of Legation to the British Embassy in Florence in 1844. One of his daughters, who married Lord Campbell, in 1821 (whilst Sir John Campbell), was created a Peeress in 1836. His third daughter is the widow of Lieutenant-Colonel Sir E. Currey, K C.B. The will of Lord Abinger, strange to say, which was in his Lordship's own hand-writing, though extremely short, was yet informally executed. No executor was appointed by him. The property was sworn under £18,000.

The eminence of Lord Abinger in the legal profession, and his judicial position, are better known than his literary tastes, the kindness of his disposition, and the urbanity of his manners.

"I remember," (says Lady Blessington, in her "Diary in France,") "how much struck I was with Sir James Scarlett's countenance, when he was first presented to me. It has in it such a happy mixture of sparkling intelligence and good nature, that I was immediately pleased with him, even before I had an opportunity of knowing the rare and excellent qualities for which he is distinguished, and the treasures of knowledge with which his mind is stored. I have seldom met any man so well versed in literature as Sir James Scarlett, or with a more refined taste for it; and when one reflects on the arduous duties of his profession—duties which he has ever fulfilled with such credit and advantage to others—it seems little short of miraculous, how he could have found time to have made himself so intimately acquainted, not only with the classics, but with all the elegant literature of England and France."

LETTER FROM J. SCARLETT, ESQ. TO LADY BLESSINGTON.

"Saturday, February 2nd, 1822.

"MY DEAR MADAM,

"Accept my best thanks for having rendered the amusements of an amateur more interesting than I have yet found them. To say of your little production that it is lively and well written, is the lowest degree of praise to which it is entitled. It proves to me that you were destined for higher things.

"I wish I could accept your proposal for Monday, the 10th; but the Speaker has pre-occupied me for that day.

"Ever yours truly,

"J. SCARLETT."

LETTERS FROM LORD ABINGER TO LADY BLESSINGTON.

"New Street, Tuesday.

"MY DEAR LADY BLESSINGTON,

"I lost no time in complying with your desire; the answer expressed a general disposition favourable to your wish, but represented that an insurmountable obstacle had been thrown in the way of any reparation by D'Orsay's letter. If that can be re-called, I think something might be done. May it not be said or written by the Count, that the note was addressed in a moment of excitement, from reading the article; and that, upon reflection, he desired to withdraw it, that no traces might remain of any design to irritate by strong expressions; and to leave it to his own feelings, an unbiassed judgment, whether it would not be proper to qualify the conclusion, by a more temperate expression of an opinion than was probably formed on a partial view of the work?

"If the letter could be thus withdrawn, the course would be left open to you, to take an obvious way of setting matters right. I have not read the article; but from what I heard of it, it appears to me the critic has unjustly imputed to the author the whole faults of one of the characters, which is the most condemned.

"The views of society and of morals, when taken by Miss M——, and examined according to her standard, are not necessarily the views of the author.

"It may with more candour be supposed, that she expresses her own sentiments in the language of the characters that are held up as better examples.

"This is ground enough for an honourable *amende*. I am so much engaged, that I really have not time to call on you.

"Adieu, ever yours,

"ABINGER."

"New Street, Sunday.

"I can refuse you nothing. A very severe and lasting cold and cough almost unfit me for company; but if I do not get worse, I will surely join you on Friday, hoping that you will excuse my propensity to *bark*, as it does not arise from hydrophobia; on the contrary, I drink nothing but water.

"I have made acquaintance with 'the Two Friends,' and relish them much. In truth, I have devoted two successive midnight hours to them, and left them only when they were about to go to their chambers after marriage. I like the book; the characters are well drawn, the incidents well imagined, the interest well kept up, the sentiments of a high moral cast, and the composition occasionally rises into great elegance, and is always marked by correct feeling, well expressed. After so much of commendation, you will, I know, receive as well one critical remark.

"Had I been at your elbow when you wrote, I would not have allowed you to make use of two or three words, which I dislike; one is *agreeability*, which, if English, is not agreeable, and therefore does not suit you. But it is not English: agreeableness is the right word. Another is the word *mentally*, which, though a good word, has been so much abused by indifferent writers, that I have taken a dislike to it, and would banish it from the novels of my friends. I do not recollect any other.

"I am very glad to hear what you say of Burdett. I expected it of him, and hope that many will follow his example, though it is not the lot of many to possess his high and honourable feeling.

"The 'Law Magazine' has been sent to me, with the proper title-page cut open. Surely I ought to be satisfied with it, but it is too flattering. I cannot imagine, however, where the writer picked up the notion that, when I was Attorney-General, I entertained any project of increasing the expense of admissions—(to the bar, I presume). Such a thought never entered my head, nor did I ever hear it discussed by anybody. I certainly did propose a regulation, which was afterwards adopted, and of which I have heard no complaint. That regulation was, to submit candidates for admission to the Law Societies to a previous examination, with a view to ascertain their fitness by education to become members of a learned profession. It must be this to which the writer alludes.

"ABINGER."

"Lancaster, 16th August, 1835.

"A thousand thanks for your kind letter, which reached me yesterday. It is always a satisfaction to think that there is somebody two or three hundred miles away, that cares about you. I seem, at this distance from home, and surrounded by ceremonies and frivolities, as if I were in a foreign land, where nobody took any interest about me, which makes a letter from you, at all times agreeable, doubly charming.

"I am much flattered with the opinion you have given of my little contribution to Mackintosh's Life. I think, however, that I owe some part of your commendation to your partiality for me, and therefore I am the more pleased by it. I must say, however, that it does not look so well in print as I hoped it would, and that I see much to correct in it. I believe, however, that I have given a true character of Mackintosh's mind, which was candour itself. You will find, in the main, that Sydney Smith agrees with me, though he falls into the satirical vein to enliven his praise. Why mention so unimportant a trifle as the manner of shaking hands with his friends? It is true enough, that he presented a flat, unbending hand, as most Scotchmen do; but it is equally true, that in a moment he put you at ease by his conversation, which had nothing either cold or reserved about it. Though he possessed a great power in conversation, and brought more originality into it than any other man I ever knew, yet it was his great object to draw other men out, and learn what they had to say about what they best knew. The conduct of the Whigs towards him was ungrateful. I have not said half what I thought of it. After all, I think the most entertaining part of the Memoirs his own Letters and Journals. Some of the former will give you a notion of the depth and compass of his mind.

"I find everything tranquil in the North, and no exertion whatever in favour of the Corporation Bill. The partizans for it are few, and led by the old hacknied Whig and Radical spouters, who have ceased to possess the countenance and support of any respectable person. Nothing will be a more fatal error in the Peers than to take counsel of Fear. They ought to consider the Radical and some of the Whig leaders in the House of Commons as bent upon their destruction, and that every step taken by the instigation of such persons, is a step towards ruin. If the power of the House of Commons is to be wielded by Hume and O'Connell, the day of battle must come; and it is better that it should come while the Peers are erect, than when they are prostrate.

"As soon as I can dispose of my business, I shall bend my way towards town, where I shall hope for the happiness of seeing you.

"ABINGER."

"Abinger Hall, October 21, 1836.

"I would not thank you for your last kind present, till I had learned the value of it, by reading the book. My words are not a mere compliment then, as I must acknowledge that I read it with pleasure, not only from the interest of the stories, but from the style, which is perspicuous, sprightly, and agreeable, exactly suited to such a work.

"But allow me to remark, that the greater part of the loves are those of a young gentleman, though he was an elderly gentleman when he told his stories. I believe he is a true sketch of many vain old bachelors. To make the loves of an elderly gentleman agreeable in narration, would be as difficult, I fear, as to make them tolerable in reality. There are, however, four letters of Rousseau, called *Lettres d'un Sexagenaire,* in which he has undertaken, by the force of his style and sentiment, to make the passion of a writer at that age interesting. I wish you would look at them, and tell me if he has been successful.

"I have been but two half-days in town since the 13th of August, but shall return by the first of next month to my Italian House. Soon after, you will see, or, at least, hear of me, at Gore House. I have been wandering in Germany and Switzerland with my youngest son, and would call my tour pleasant, had it not been accompanied by too much rain and cold.

"Returning through Paris, the first person I encountered on emerging from the hotel was Lady Canterbury. She made us pass the evening with her, and dine there the next day.

"My Lord seems very happy, and has a beautiful house. His eldest son was with him; they do not talk of returning; she read me a portion of a letter from you respecting the affair at Gaston Hall.

"I remained but three days at Paris, and, on my landing at Dover, found L——— preparing for Paris; where, if you believe some of the French papers, he, together with P———, has been conspiring with the King of the French, to turn out the Whigs. I wish with all my heart, they may succeed before it is too late.

"Au revoir, adieu,

"ABINGER."

"Lincoln, March 6, 1837.

"I am not a greater believer in their resignation, because the Whigs profess an intention to resign. Their first object is to keep their places, at any sacrifice of principle; their second is to place the country in such a state as to give the greatest embarrassment to their successors and to the King. I believe some among them call this patriotism.

"ABINGER."

"New Street, March 8, 1838.

"As you place yourself in my hands touching your communication with Barnes, I shall play the part of a loyal, as well as faithful ambassador, in using the best discretion to advance your object. I shall not therefore send your letter, not because I do not concur in the remarks it contains, but because it has a tendency to rip up the old quarrel, by putting him under the necessity either of recanting his criticism, or of vindicating it. Now, I think the peace is a good peace, and promises to be lasting, unless disturbed by a recurrence to former differences. It is better, therefore, to allow me to make your acknowledgments in general terms of civility. He knows already my sentiments on the fallacy of the former critique. He must also know yours, and the recurrence to it looks as if you made it of more importance than it becomes you to do. I will come and see you as soon as I can.

"ABINGER."

"Maidstone, July 26, 1840.

"I delayed replying to your letter, in the hope that I might have something to say, which would be agreeable to you. I find, on casting up my accounts of patronage in the revising barristers' department, that I cannot find a vacancy for Mr. H———.

"I wish I could have complied with your other request, but I assure you, I have not been able to read or write without effort, in consequence of the state of my eyes; and all the poetry of former times, which you suppose finds place in my portfolio, has long been committed to the flames.

"I make a vow, however, to pay my respects to Gore House, the first moment that I can possibly spare after my return to town.

"ABINGER."

LETTERS FROM LORD DURHAM TO LADY BLESSINGTON.

"Cowes, June 14, 1835.

"DEAR LADY BLESSINGTON,

"I thank you much for your very agreeable letter, which I received this morning, and for your kind inquiries after my health, which is wonderfully improved, if not quite restored, by this fine air, and *dolce far niente* life. I anticipate with horror the time when I shall be obliged to leave it, and mix once more in the *troublous* realities of *public life.*

"Pray remember me most kindly to Lord Lyndhurst when you see him: a constant source of regret with me is, that our political path has hitherto been on separate lines, for I think him decidedly the most powerful and most efficient man in our House; and as a lawyer, there is not his equal on the Bench or at the Bar.

"I am sorry to hear you give so unfavourable account of the reputation of the ministry. They mean well, and if they are not stronger in intellect and efficiency, it is probably not because they do not wish to strengthen themselves, but because they would not be permitted.

"Your estimate of the three books, Miss Kemble's, De Lamartine's, and Bulwer's, is a most just one. The latter is full of first-rate genius.

"Ellice leaves me to-day; he will tell you what a charming life this is.

"Yours very truly,

"D."

"Peterhoff, September 3, 1836.

"I thank you most sincerely for your kind remembrance of me, and for the announcement of the successful termination of my appeal.

"I don't pretend to deny that I am much pleased at the result; but if the decision had been unfavourable to me, I should have still been satisfied, because I should have been certain that the equity of the case was against me in truth, if Lord Lyndhurst had so decided it. We differ in politics, it is true, but there can be but one opinion as to his unrivalled abilities as a lawyer; indeed, I should have been perfectly content long ago to have left the matter to his sole arbitration. If he had decided against me in Chancery, I never should have appealed to the Lords.

"Pray remember me to Lord Lyndhurst when next you see him, and tell him that my admiration of his talents is only equalled by my regret that their exercise——but I must not get into politics, so will leave my sentence unfinished.

"I have been very unwell lately, and confined to my bed, by a return of a rheumatic fever, which I had in the winter. This detestable climate is not to be endured but by persons possessing constitutions of platina or granite.

"What a state of confusion seems to exist in England; when will people be tired of all these petty party broils? To one looking on at a distance, it all appears very mean and indignified. The paramount interests of a great country like ours, ought not to be made the sport of party passions and selfish quibbles.

"Adieu! when you have a spare moment at Kensington, give me the benefit of it.

"D."

"Louth Castle, August 21, 1837.

"I enclose you an extract from a letter which I received this day, in answer to my complaint.

"I told you in London that I had had even more trouble about this affair, than all those of my embassy.

"However, I think, it is now concluded according to your desire.

"'The delay that has occurred in notifying the permission to dedicate is not owing to any neglect of the Librarian, but has arisen from the uncertainty whether any, except historical works, would be permitted. In order, however, to obviate this difficulty, Mrs. Fairlie's work has been looked upon as Historical Biography, and probably before you receive this, you will have heard that the permission is granted.'

"D."

"Cleveland Row, Saturday night.

"I have to thank you most sincerely for giving me an opportunity of making Mr. Bulwer's acquaintance. I have long admired his genius, and highly-estimated his pre-eminent abilities. They have never been sufficiently brought into play by those who have the power to make them as useful to the country as they are honourable to himself.

"With these feelings, I cannot but be delighted to think that I shall meet him on Tuesday.

"D."

"Cleveland Row, February 28, 1837.

"I return you Mr. ——'s papers. I can only repeat to you in writing, what I have already told you in conversation, that I have no direct means of serving him. You will perceive, that I value my own independence too much to solicit any place, even for my nearest relative or dearest friend.

"Durham."

On the back of this note there were some very remarkable lines, written by Lady Blessington, beginning with the words—

"At midnight's silent hour, when bound in sleep," &c.

with many erasures, and the traces apparently of many tears.

The lines will be found in the Chapter headed "Notice of the Career of Lady Blessington," vol. i.

"Lambton Castle.

"I had written to D'Orsay, to say how sorry I was that a party at home prevented my accepting your kind offer.

"I should have liked the quiet dinner above all things, and shall, whenever you propose it to me again, being most anxious to become acquainted with Mr. B.

"D."

"Lambton Castle, August 23, 1837.

"I enclose you the Royal permission. It would be right that Mrs. Fairlie shall address a letter of thanks herself to Mr. Glover.

"D."

"Harrington House, August 17, 1837.

"My Lord,

"I am informed by Col. Cavendish, that the information of the Queen's permission for Mrs. Fairlie to dedicate her forthcoming work, entitled 'Portraits of the Children of the English Nobility,' to her Majesty, should be communicated to your Lordship; and I have therefore the honour to state, that Mrs. Fairlie's request has been very graciously acquiesced in, and that she has permission to dedicate the work to Her Majesty.

"I have the honour to be, my Lord,

"Your most obedient servant,

"E. H. Glover, H. M. Libr."

From Lord Durham.

"January 24, 1838.

"I really have no appointment within my gift, and it pains me extremely to receive hundreds of applications to which I can only return the same answer. I should be ashamed of myself if I planted a colony of British officials in Canada; all Canadian places ought to be given to Canadians; and this will be the case, with rare exceptions, the nomination of which will rest with the Government.

"My own private staff, if I may so express myself, is settled; and if it was not, the absence of pecuniary emoluments would render these employments more onerous than valuable.

"There is an expression in Mr. J. F——'s note, that which refers to 'my intention of providing for him.' I am not aware of having expressed any such intention, of having given any such promise.

"The only recollection I have of the matter is, that you forwarded me some documents relating to Mr. F.'s application to Lord Palmerston, and that I declined mentioning his name, unless the subject was under discussion, when I would certainly do what I could to serve him. This I was anxious to do on his brother's account, whom I admire and esteem beyond most men; but as to any promise of provision, I am certain I would not be so thoughtless as to make it. I never violate a promise; but never make one hastily.

"I am, as you may imagine, overwhelmed with business; but still must devote a greater portion of my time than I could otherwise spare to relieve myself from the possibility of an imputation of having failed in performing that which I promised.

"I send Mrs. Fairlie the picture as she requests; will you give her my compliments, and also my best regards to my little friend?

"D."

"January 27, 1838.

"I return you the note, which completely confirms my recollection of what was my answer to you. I repeat again, that I have no places to bestow which it would become me to offer, or Mr. F. to accept. My own private secretaries are those who were with me before. The nomination of the one or two higher posts is in the Government, with my approval, of course; but as they belong to the legal and parliamentary class, they could not affect Mr. ———.

"My power of direction of control of administration is as you say unlimited, awfully unlimited; but I have no power of creating places, no power of making any appointment where no vacancies exist, or of fixing on Canadian revenues English officials.

"What therefore can I do? I dare not make a place expressly for Mr. F. I presume he does not wish to cross the Atlantic without the certainty of profitable employment. Pity me; for, in addition to the load of business which presses on me, I have all the misery of refusing requests from many whom I should be too happy to serve.

"D."

"Cleveland Row, Friday night.

"I return you the two notes, with many thanks for your kind communication of them.

"I fear you greatly overrate my means of justifying the good opinion entertained of me. But I will do my best.

"I am very anxious to cultivate the acquaintance of your two friends, and have to-night sent to ask them to meet the D. of Sussex here at dinner. His R. H. is no favourite of yours,

I know; but I have always found him a steady and kind-hearted friend.

"Ellice and I start for Paris on Friday next. Can I take any thing for you?

"I have not been able to call on you before to-day, being detained at home, by business and visitors, all the morning, and in the evening, I am generally too unwell to go out.

"D."

LETTER FROM LORD JOHN RUSSELL TO LADY BLESSINGTON.

"Woburn Abbey, February 5, 1838.

"DEAR LADY BLESSINGTON,

"Although I am *in opposition*, I have got my head so muddled with politics, that I cannot turn my mind with any effect to higher and more agreeable pursuits. In short, I am quite unfit to contribute to 'The Book of Beauty,' and am almost reduced to the state of 'the beast.'

"This it is—to get harnessed in the state car.

"I remain, yours faithfully,

"J. RUSSELL."

LORD BROUGHAM.

Henry, Baron Brougham and Vaux, of Brougham Hall, county Westmoreland—formerly Lord High Chancellor of England—will be known to posterity as Henry Brougham—the early champion of the Anti-slavery cause, Queen Caroline's counsel—the indomitable opponent of Castlereagh's policy—the faithful friend and bold defender of civil and religious liberty, while in the House of Commons.

With these titles to respect and honour, he may dispense with the labours of heraldry, in favour of the antiquity of his race, and Mr. Burke's successful effort to trace up his family, and their possessions in Westmoreland, to the Saxon Burghams before the Conquest.

His father, Henry Brougham, Esq. (who died in 1810), by his marriage with a sister of Robertson, the historian, Mary Syme (who died in 1839), had five sons, of whom Henry, born September 19, 1778, was the eldest.

He married, in 1819, the eldest daughter of Sir John Eden, niece of Lord Auckland, and widow of John Spalding, Esq., by whom he had two daughters—Eleanor Sarah, who died in 1820, and Eleanor Louisa, who died in 1839.

After a long career of professional labours, and of public services, this distinguished man was appointed Lord Chancellor, and created a peer of the realm, on the accession of the Grey administration in 1830, and retired with his party in 1834.

The great tendency to make war on people who seek to be pre-eminent in different pursuits, has been eloquently noticed by Cicero, and bitterly experienced by Lord Brougham.

Men smile complacently at the little jealousies of women, who are supposed to take offence at the union of beauty, esprit, literary talents, poetic genius, or intellectual gifts of any very superior order, in the same individual of their own sex. But men—able men too in politics, and in high legal and literary position, feel not unfrequently their merits rebuked in the presence of great successes of men of their own profession or especial avocation, who have acquired pre-eminence in other pursuits.

Lord Brougham, in one of his Historical Sketches, says—"The true test of a great man—that, at least, which must secure his place amongst the highest order of great men—is his having been in advance of his age."

By this standard, if his Lordship be judged, no doubt he will be found to be a man of more than ordinary greatness—a man of gigantic intellect, the like of which it will be in vain to look for among the great men of this country of the present century. He was in advance of his age on the Slavery question, on that of Catholic Emancipation, of Law Reform, Charitable Bequests' Reform, of National Instruction, of London Collegiate Education.

But there is another true test of a great man in a prominent public position; the power of enduring hatred and hostility in high places—of resisting envy, defamation, and ridicule, year after year, throughout a long and arduous career, systematically arrayed against him in the press; and of confronting powerful opponents in parliament, boldly and successfully, and almost singly, in many signal conflicts.

Lord Brougham is said to be hot and hasty, vehement, impetuous, and offensively earnest in discussion. The great Lord Chatham has been taxed with similar defects; and like him, Lord Brougham merges all minor imperfections in the countervailing merits of his vast powers of impulsive oratory and persuasive argument. His command of language, extent of information on every subject, in every science, embracing the whole circle of knowledge; his felicity in extracting arguments and illustrations from that vast store of varied information; his never-failing memory, marvellous ability of grappling with all the difficulties of a question, of seeing at a glance all its bearings, of sustaining a state of perpetual mental activity, of encountering opposition, utterly fearless of all opponents, of bearing down on his enemies, of sending forth torrents of words of overwhelming eloquence on any occasion, however sudden the emergency;—these peculiar talents and powers have seldom been equalled, never have been surpassed in parliament.

No man living in England has rendered so much service to the Anti-Slavery cause as Lord Brougham. On those services his character and fame might safely take their stand. In that sacred cause of justice and humanity, his efforts for the abolition of slavery and the slave trade, for nearly forty years, have been unremitting and unequalled in the display of intellectual powers that have been devoted to those great objects.

Lord Brougham is now seventy-six years of age. His gigantic intellect has lost none of its vigour: all his energies are as full of life and activity as they were thirty years ago.

One striking characteristic of Lord Brougham, that is noticeable now, as it was remarkable at the onset of his career, is his uniform, undeviating, unaffected, and undisguised detestation of meanness, cruelty, and baseness, wherever it is to be found, whether in the highest or the humblest station in society; and a generous and warm attachment to men of worth and genius, of high principle, and of a lofty enthusiasm in any cause in which the interests of truth are concerned, quite irrespective of the position of the parties who have won his esteem and his regard.

It was said of Wyndham, as a proof of his elevated intellectual character, that his personal friends were men of great powers of mind and high principles. "His soul lived, it may be said, in the highest region of intellect, and it could not have sustained itself there if it had not possessed a natural affinity for the noble and magnanimous."

LETTERS FROM LORD BROUGHAM TO LADY BLESSINGTON.

"Chateau, Tuesday, April 22, 1840.

"Dear Lady B.

"I fear you will think me very remiss in not sooner answering your kind letter, but I really had nothing to tell worth making you pay postage. You will justly enough say, that this should prevent me now, but I had rather you paid than think me ungrateful.

"News from hence you can expect none. Your account of Sir A. Paget's being better was highly agreeable to me, and it has been confirmed since, by accounts of his entire recovery. I am also very happy to find that Durham is getting well.

"The English have all broken up their encampment at Nice, and are hurrying homewards. Leader, who has been here some time, is gone to-day, and, I suppose, will be at home almost as soon as this reaches you. Pray give my kindest regards to Alfred, ———, and tell the latter I have seen the Colonel (Shaw) since last I wrote, and he complains of never hearing from him.

"We have had some share, though a small one, of the winter, which seems every where to have been so bad. It begun here on Lady-Day, but is now quite gone.

"In answer to your commands, I fear I must say no; indeed I am not in a condition to do any thing that is not absolutely necessary, and even doing that ——— was as much as I was up to, and possibly more.* I think of returning by slow journies through a district of France, which I have never seen, and some part of which is seldom visited. I shall set out in less than a week.

"Believe me sincerely yours,
"H. Brougham."

"November, 1843.

"The climate here is too delicious. I have Leader, Falconi, Meyrick, &c., and I expect Douro. The heat from eleven to two is too great, but we have delicious evenings and mornings. My spirits are getting round, for the first time these four dismal years.

"H. Brougham."

"Chateau Eleanor, November 28, 1843.

"I wish you would tell your clever, and, I believe, honest friend of the Paper, that I have given up both my prosecutions before he said a word. I did, because on reflection, I believed I should only oppress him to whom I really wished no harm, but should obstruct full and free discussion of public men's conduct and character. I also add, that whether his candid statement just sent me had appeared or no, I should have done this; but now he has shewn some repentance, I being his confessor, must prescribe a small penance, and it is this. Let him do something

* Lord B. had met with a severe family affliction not long previously.—R. R. M.

(no man can do so better), in furtherance of what is most near my heart, Law Reform, and especially of the Criminal Code.

" I have reason to believe (*entre nous*), that if the Liberal press give it a lift, the Government will do it; and this is enormously valuable.

" Let him do this, and he may abuse me weekly, and I never shall complain. " H. BROUGHAM."

LETTERS FROM LORD LYNDHURST.

" March 17, 1835.

" DEAR LADY BLESSINGTON,

" I would have called for the parcel yesterday for Lady Canterbury, but I was the whole of the day at the House of Lords. I make a rule of never attending public meetings and dinners. I have no objection to be a steward, and pay my contribution, if attendance will be dispensed with. Excuse me for this. I am most anxious always to do any thing you desire.

" Yours faithfully,

" LYNDHURST."

[No date.]

" I would dine with you with the greatest pleasure on Sunday, were it possible. But I am at Richmond, and have unluckily formed a party for that day, which I cannot desert. You judge me in one respect quite correctly. I am not a bigot either as to persons or things. I give men credit for sincerity when I can, and my spirit of toleration is most liberal and extensive. " LYNDHURST."

FROM THE MARQUIS OF LANSDOWNE.

" Berkeley Square, Saturday.

" DEAR LADY BLESSINGTON,

" I will certainly vote for Mr. Landon. Your recommendation, and the interesting circumstances you mention respecting his sister, with whose merits I am acquainted, at least, by reputation, are quite sufficient to interest me strongly in his favour.

" Believe me, very faithfully yours,

" LANSDOWNE.

FROM LORD GLENELG.

"Colonial Office, November 24, 1837.

"Dear Lady Blessington,

"I am very much obliged by your kind note, and beg you to believe, that it was not on account of Mr. Ellice alone that I took an interest in your friend. You would not do me justice if you thought so.

"It will give you pleasure to read the following passage from Sir J. Harvey's letter to me:—

"G. House.

"'It is very satisfactory to me to be enabled to add, that, independent of any personal introductory recommendations, the high qualities possessed by Mr. ——— are such as to render him eligible for any office in this colony, which it may be in my power to confer on him. I have accordingly had great pleasure in assuring Mr. ——— of the desire which I feel to serve him, whenever circumstances may enable me to do so.'

"I remain, dear Lady Blessington,
"Yours very truly,
"Glenelg."

"April 27, 1838.

"I am happy to say, Sir J. Harvey has appointed your friend to an office in the department of Crown Lands.

"You have probably heard of this. "Glenelg."

FROM SIR J——— H———, RESPECTING A COMMUNICATION OF LADY BLESSINGTON TO LORD ANGLESEY.

"Govt. House, Fredericton, New Brunswick,
"November 24, 1837.

"My dear Lord,

"Few circumstances connected with my advancement to this command have occasioned me such sincere satisfaction as your note of the 9th of September, with an enclosure from Lady Blessington. The Lady does tell her story with much natural and becoming feeling (as respects her friend), and therefore with eloquence. I had previously received a similar communication from Lady Canterbury; but I fear I must be ungallant enough to confess to your Lordship, that all the *billet* eloquence in the world—and few in it possess that talent in a higher degree than the fair ladies whose respective appeals are now before me—could have had half the weight with me that the slightest expression of a wish from you, my noble friend and kind patron would have.

"It shall go hard, but I will endeavour to find some situation for Captain P. ere long. He seems fit for any thing; his manners and conversation (and I will add, his appearance) most prepossessing; add to which, the interest which your Lordship has expressed in his welfare. You heard of the appeals of the two fair ladies, and an earnest recommendation to my notice from my friend Sir Henry Hardinge."

LETTERS SIGNED G.

"Downing Street, March 22, 1832.

"I had already received from Mrs. S—— a statement of the distressed situation of your friend and his family. I regret it most deeply, and the more, as I cannot, at present, hold out the means of relief.

"I have already more than once recommended him strongly to the Lord Lieutenant; but in Ireland, as here, the reductions which government has been, and is compelled to make, leave nothing in our power.

"I will speak to Mr. Ellice about the reference which you say is to be made to the Treasury, and if any assistance can with propriety be given in this manner, I shall be ready to concur in affording it. But it must depend upon the recommendation of the Board, after they have considered the case.

"G."

"DEAREST LADY BLESSINGTON,

"I have also been mortified to the greatest degree at having missed the only opportunities I could have had of seeing you, and it is still more vexatious, that I cannot call on you this morning. I have every minute engaged till the House of Lords, for which I am afraid I shall be so ill prepared, that if I am forced to speak, I shall certainly destroy any desire you may have had to hear me again. God bless you!

"Ever yours,
"G."

"Downing Street, February 15, 1833.

"I am sorry to say that the place of one of the Commissioners under the Bill for the Reform of the Church of Ireland, if it should pass, is not one for which it would be possible for me to recommend your friend.

"G."

FROM THE MARQUIS OF NORMANBY.

"Paris, March 27, 1848.

"My dear Lady Blessington,

"I forwarded without delay your packet to your correspondent, who has taken within these last few days to write so boldly, that if there is to be any 'terror,' he seems to desire to offer himself as the first victim. However, all is now very quiet for the moment here, though no one can see many weeks, or even days, into the future.

"It was very kind of you so to express yourself towards me, and to cite such an authority to be 'laudatus a laudato' (I make no excuse for quoting Latin to you), is always welcome.

"I see D'Orsay is helping to take care of our poor English exports.

"Yours very truly,
"Normanby."

FROM THE EARL OF WESTMORLAND.

"Berlin, January 21, —40.

"My dear Lady Blessington,

"I have written to recommend that the wishes in favour of your protegée should be attended to, and if Mrs. Percival will call at, or send to the Royal Academy, in Tenterden Street, she will learn what has been the decision of the Committee.

"I shall be most happy if I have succeeded in forwarding a wish of yours. I shall be very anxious to see the statue of Alfred, of which you speak; he is an extraordinary creature, with his talents of all sorts; coming out as a sculptor of high repute, and perfection is a singular proof of what I have said above. Pray remember me to him, and believe me very sincerely yours, "WESTMORLAND."

VISCOUNT LORD STRANGFORD.

His Lordship was born in 1780, and succeeded to the title in 1801. Having resided much in Portugal, and made himself familiar with the language, history, and literature of that country, he was selected, at an early age, as a fit person to represent the British nation at Lisbon in 1806, and next at Rio Janeiro. He was appointed Envoy Extraordinary and Minister Plenipotentiary at the Court of Sweden, in 1820; Ambassador to the Sublime Porte in 1820, and to Russia in 1825.

In 1803, he published "Poems from the Portuguese of Camoens, with Remarks on his Life and Writings," 8vo.; a work better appreciated by those acquainted with the Portuguese language and literature, than by those who are not. His Lordship, as an author, diplomatist, a man of fine taste and polished manners, is well and advantageously known to the public. He owes less for that advantage, to his intimate acquaintance and friendship with the late King of Hanover, up to the period of his death, than to his talents as a man of letters, and his abilities in his diplomatic career.

FROM VISCOUNT LORD STRANGFORD.

"Harley Street, Saturday Evening.

"Pray pity me—for I do deserve it—not for being very ill, which I really am, but for being obliged to give up all hope of waiting on you to-morrow.

"I caught a violent cold in being in the House of Lords on Tuesday, which ended in a fever, and since that direful Tuesday, I have been confined, not merely to my room, but to my bed, where I am 'at this present writing.' That odious House of Lords! as it is now constituted, it is only beneficial to Peers' eldest sons. Apropos thereof, I was very happy, and a little proud this morning, by learning that my George (who had the honour of making his bow one night last spring in your opera-box) has just been the successful candidate for the 'address,' as it is termed (in English ——), which is to be spoken before the King, at his annual visit to Eton on 'election.' This is rather a creditable exploit of my *primogenito's*, though I don't think he shews much worldly wisdom in starting in *these times*, on the 'loyal tack.'

"Ever, my dear Lady,
"STRANGFORD."

LETTER SIGNED D. TO LADY BLESSINGTON.

"F. Office, February 7, 1827.

"MY DEAR LADY BLESSINGTON,

"When I look at the date of your letter from Pisa, I feel quite ashamed. But the press of business during a stormy and troublesome period, must be my excuse for seeming incivility to many of those friends to whose wishes I am really most desirous to attend. Your recommendation has the greatest weight with me, both on account of the pleasure it would give me to oblige you, and because I am quite sure that you would not propose to me any person that was not perfectly fit for the situation in which you asked to see him placed. If, therefore, during the time that I continue in office, any opportunity shall occur that would enable me consistently, with engagements already taken, to provide for Mr. P. in the way you point out, I shall be most happy to avail myself of it, though I must also own to you, that the vacancies in the consulate line are so rare, and the claims already existing for them upon the office so numerous and powerful, that I cannot indulge a hope of being soon able to accomplish, as it would be scarcely less agreeable to me than it would be to yourself. Since I had the pleasure of hearing from you, I have received a very kind letter from Lord Blessington. Perhaps you will allow me to take the occasion of conveying to him, through you, my acknowledgment of it. Our friend Hare has been in England about six weeks. I find that during the last two years, he has received from you a great deal of attention and hospitality, with which I am the more gratified, because it is through me that he made an acquaintance that he found so advantageous to him. Lord B. mentions Count D'Orsay is still belonging to your party, and as preserving a friendly recollection of me. Pray be good enough to offer to him my compliments and regards.

" Believe me,
" My dear Lady Blessington,
" Yours most sincerely and faithfully,
" D."

FROM LADY BLESSINGTON TO SIR ROBERT PEEL.*

" Gore House, July, 1845.

" DEAR SIR ROBERT PEEL,

" In the heavy affliction that has just occurred to Lady C———, in the death of her husband, one of the most amiable and kind-hearted men that ever existed; the thought of the ill-provided state in which she is left, has, even during the first hours of a grief, as sincere as it is deep, induced me to address you, who were the friend of her departed husband. You are aware that poor dear Lord C———'s circumstances were in a most embarrassed state, so much so, that the anxiety and increasing uneasiness occasioned by them, and the knowledge that, at his death, his wife and child would be left so ill off, preyed so heavily on his mind, as to have produced the fatal event that occurred on Sunday last. I saw him a prey to anxiety and disappointment that weighed him to the earth, and, though deeply grieved, am not surprised at the sad catastrophe.

" You are aware that the pension he had reverts to his eldest son, but with a saving of one thousand a year to the country;

* From a copy among the papers of Lady B.—R.R.M.

but of this saving to the country might not you, as an act of kindness to an old friend, and of generosity to the widow and child of an old and faithful public servant, recommend some provision to be made for Lady C—— and her daughter.

"The health of poor Lady C—— is such, as to have little hope that her life will be long spared; therefore a pension to revert to Lord C——'s daughter, at her death, would not be unreasonable. The severe disappointment poor Lord C—— experienced in not being allowed compensation for the heavy losses he sustained by the fire at Palace Yard, led to the embarrassments of his affairs, and ever since embittered his life.

"To you I address myself in favour of the widow and daughter of your old friend, while yet he lies unburied, and while tears for his death almost blind me. But I think I best shew my regret for the departed by making an attempt to serve those so dear to him, and who are left so unprovided for. In a few days the Sessions will close, and before it does, I appeal to those good feelings which I am sure fill your breast, to take some step to obtain a provision for the widow and daughter of the late Lord C——.

"Believe me,
"Dear Sir Robert Peel,
"Yours faithfully,
"M. Blessington."

It was wholly impossible to carry Lady Blessington's wish into effect. The fund which benefitted by the death of Lord C—— was the Parliamentary Fund. The fund from which pensions are given, is that of the £1200 given by Parliament to the Queen for that purpose. As to providing for any child not his, it was wholly out of the question. But even *if* he had a child to be provided for, as well as a widow, nothing but a Bill could give that provision; and £3000 a year being secured to the son, who succeeded to the title, would be an answer to any application.

Lady Blessington wrote to a friend, on the 24th of July, that Sir Robert had stated to her—"How deeply he regretted that he could not feel justified in making any proposal to Parliament for a provision for the widow and daughter of his lamented friend Lord C——.

"He felt very confident that the attempt would not be a successful one.

"The provision made for a person holding the office which had been held by him on his retirement, was more liberal than that made for any other public servant. In the case of a minister of the Crown, entitled, from the inadequacy of his private means to claim a retiring allowance, the amount was limited to £2000 per annum; no provision whatever was made for the widow. The pensions granted to Mrs. Perceval and to Lady Canning, the widows of Prime Ministers dying while in the exercise of the highest functions, were special and exceptional cases.

"The provision made for Lord C——— was an annual pension of £4000 for his own life, and £3000 for his son, until his son should succeed to a lucrative sinecure office.

"He was not aware of any instance, in which a pension has been granted to a widow of a person holding such an office; and he was confident that the House of Commons, considering the liberality of the provision made for Lord C—— on his retirement, and contrasting it with the provision made for other public servants, would not consent to the establishment of the precedent, which such an arrangement as that which she proposed would constitute.

"He was compelled, therefore, very reluctantly, so far as private and personal feelings were concerned, to decline acceding to her suggestion."

From another letter of Lady Blessington, dated the 6th of August, 1845, it appears that her exertions for her deceased friend's family were not to be discouraged even by the very explicit statement just referred to; she renewed her application to Sir Robert, modifying it, however; but it was attended with no better success than the former. Sir Robert had stated to her:—

"He could not think it would be for the real advantage of the family of the late Lord, even if the means existed, that a provision should be made for his daughter from the Civil List.

"The whole sum available for the grant of pensions for the present year was £700.

"From such a fund was the vain attempt to be made, that had to meet the various claims upon the bounty of the Crown, founded upon personal service to the Crown; public service not otherwise provided for, and eminent literary and scientific merit.

"No pension granted (for the one to Madlle. D'Este stood upon special grounds) would probably exceed £200, and he did not think that a pension of such an amount would be an appropriate recognition of the services she would have considered."

Poor Lady Blessington writes, that she had made one more effort for a very limited provision for a daughter of Lord C—— by a former husband; but it failed, like the former. Sir Robert had plainly given her to understand:—

"The means did not exist at the present, at least, of making even the limited provision for the daughter, which alone could be made under any circumstances.

"Assurances had been already given, the fulfilment of which would entirely absorb the sum available for the current year."

LETTERS SIGNED F. B. TO LADY BLESSINGTON.

"February 24, 1829.

"Dear Lady Blessington,

"I send you a line, though I have nothing to say, nor time to say anything in, even if I had wherewithal, as Burns says in his letter to a friend, 'though it may serve for neither, and but just a kind memento.'

"Now pray remember me kindly, yea, most kindly, to Madame Crawford, to your amiable ladies, Milord, and to all the family of D'Orsay, *l'aimable baronne,* and pray make use of me on my return, if I can do anything, bring anything I can. Should D'Orsay want a horse, Lord Blessington a house, or any one anything; pray spare me not.

"I cannot omit expressing my wonder and gratification, at the astonishing change of the great Duke and Mr. Peel, converted into the Pacificator of Ireland! Let no man hereafter talk of the conversion of St. Paul as a miracle, nor woman either, not even Madame Krudner.

"Ever yours sincerely,
"F. B."

"April 1, 1832.

"You are very kind, and I should be very happy could I profit by it, but you have no idea of my state: not quite so bad as Theseus, who was fixed for ever, and immoveably, to his seat, but able to move only, crab-like, with the aid of crutches. What is very provoking, too, I am as well in health as anybody, and could I creep to your presence, in a becoming posture, no one would be more capable, or disposed to enjoy it.

"F. B."

[No date.]

"You make me renew past griefs; I really had forgot the most important use of knees. As you say, there seems to be a marvellous sympathy between the hinges of the knee and valves of the heart; the one indeed seems the safety-valve of the other, rather than a hinge at all. Certain it is, they move in wonderful accordance. You ask whether your observation is a satire on our sex? Philosophers say everything receives its nature from that of the recipient: if so, he who so takes it may, but those who, like me, witness it, don't feel it. I cannot answer the question.

"F. B."

"May 5th, 1832.

"Solomon says, that 'though you pound a fool in a mortar, yet will not his foolishness depart from him.'

"I am making a sad confession; but my spirits getting the better of my prudence the other day—only the other day, mind—I, having one or two people to dine with me, brought back my gout, which I had flattered myself I had got rid of; so that, with a short interval of promise, I am now nearly as when last I wrote to you, with the addition of recent experience, which makes, they say, fools wise; but I am past that age when men are said to be either fools or physicians; and as I am feelingly convinced that I am not the last, I fear my share of the alternative condemns me to Solomon's mortar, and certainly deprives me a second time of the pleasure you again so obligingly offer.

"F. B."

"19 July, 1832.

"I trust nothing will, and nothing *but death shall*, prevent me from having the pleasure of coming to you on Friday.

"F. B."

"August 14th, 1832.

"I am again confined to my own room, and this day, marked with chalk, must be marked with carbon. This is very sad, but such are the fickle terms on which we hold this tenement of clay. My repeated attacks seem to amount almost to a notice to quit. I don't mean to take it, however, but it certainly lowers its value. Well, the bill is carried. I should like so much to have talked it over with you, but it seems good otherwise to the gods.

"F. B."

"October 16, 1832.

"I am delighted you entertain so favourable an opinion of that most *deceptious* of all the human anatomy—the heart—and

I will confess that upon that subject, I would rely on a woman's opinion in preference to a physician.

"I am grieved at the state of Paris, poor Madame Crawford, and, indeed, the whole state of France. I hear all parties—ministers and anti-ministerialists—are in the greatest spirits, and equally confident of success. Lord A——— writes he is sanguine, and that is not natural to him. Lord E——— and a large party yesterday were full of exultation, so that we inhabit a sort of fools' paradise.

"I know the people will have the Reform, or more, and am only anxious for health to enjoy the difficulties that may arrive. I feel so well that it is quite ridiculous; and if I could but have got seated at your table on Saturday, I should not have been the guest least enjoying it.

"The Prince * is not only gossiping, but impertinent, affected, false, and not acquainted with the manners of good or bad society in England. It has all the appearance of a fictitious performance. A young lady just says that she should like to look at the two last volumes, so I will send for them in the morning. I am glad to hear of the recovery of Sir Walter Scott;—and as soon as I can move, except backwards, I shall move up to Seamore Place.

"F. B."

"June 25, 1833.

"A certain place, says Daniel, not the true prophet, but the false, is paved with good intentions. I fear in that regulated floor specimens of me will be found, and not rare. I will, however, encouraged by your unvarying indulgence, mend as fast as I can, assuring you the fault you so obligingly complain of, is neither voluntary nor unregretted, and moreover, carries with it its own punishment. The first opportunity I can lay hold of, shall terminate both the one and the other.

"F. B."

"Wednesday Evening, August 8, 1834.

"The brave General Rebinski is to dine with me on Friday,

* I presume, Prince Puckler Muskau.—R. R. M.

and, I believe, Prince Czartoriski. Perhaps D'Orsay would meet them. I will call in the evening to know. I don't know where you saw any report of what I said last night, but 'The Times' makes me talk sad nonsense, and say the reverse, in some instances, of what I did say.

"To make anything like the thing itself, it would be necessary to write a new speech, as far as the 'Times' is concerned; and this is a tiresome task; but I would do what I never did before, if it had a chance of serving the gallant, unhappy Poles.

"F. B."

"June 22, 1839.

"Many thanks for your obliging administration.

"What next! The King's death seems the deuce's own turn up. Lord Durham, it seems, is the violet in the lap of the new court. *Eh bien nous verrons.* Conjecture is useless and impossible indeed.

"F. B."

LETTER SIGNED H.

"August 8.

"Your very kind and flattering note gave me great pleasure. Believe me, that I long have wished to put an end to any estrangement that existed; and the happy and merry hours I passed at the Villa Gallo are too agreeably engraven on my memory, for me ever to feel anything but gratitude and affection for its inmates. I have often heard and known how kindly you and Alfred have spoken of me, and have often wished for an opportunity of breaking through the semblance of an enmity which I believe never really existed much on either side.

"Many, many thanks for your kind permission to come to Gore House, which I hope some morning or evening soon to avail myself of.

"The enclosed letter, I am very much obliged to you indeed for letting me see. I know no one whose happiness and prosperity I am more seriously glad to hear of, or who deserves better to be happy and prosperous; kind-hearted, generous, sincere and disinterested, full of the best qualities of her delightful country, without any of the faults that grow in that soil.

"Pray, when you next write, remember to convey to her my sincere congratulations upon her marriage and new position. I hope, the next time I go to Paris, to have an occasion of expressing them *vivâ voce.*

"Ever very faithfully yours,
"H———."

LETTERS SIGNED C.

"August 23rd, 1831.

"I am this moment, dear Lady Blessington, returned from J——. S———'s marriage; his wife is a piquante brunette, and decidedly pretty; he asked me to go as one of his witnesses; he had no Englishman to support him. I really thought I should have died while two little boys kept a white cloth over the head of J——, and he stood there the symbol of innocence.

"C."

"Rome, March 4, 1843.

"Many, very many thanks for your kind letter. You cannot conceive what real pleasure I received when your letter arrived; it was so very kind of you to write to me. We are now just returned after the Carnival, which has been very gay, and for which we have had decent weather, it only having poured two of the days, which we thought very fortunate, in this rainy climate. We had an excellent balcony opposite the Via Condotti, and from which we and our friends pelted away some thousand pounds of bonbons, &c.

"I think it most amusing to observe the effect it has on different people; some are so remarkably angry, some so dignified, and others enjoying it. I wish you could have seen Lord Winchelsea dressing at the Corso to call on some one, covered with white dust, and looking as if he were preparing a violent anti-Catholic speech for the House of Lords.

"A party of us, E., P., L., and F., went one day in a car; we were dressed as the priestesses in Norma, and we were attended by our servants as ancient Roman warriors; and I can assure you we made a great sensation. I went in the evening to Madame L ———'s in a woman's domino, with rather short petticoats, the latter garment being trimmed with lace, and being adorned with rose-coloured ribbons: of course I took occasion to shew it. I was beautifully *chaussée* with satin shoes, and completely mystified every one.

"I am so charmed to hear that Alfred bears up against his confinement with his usual fortitude. As to any success he may have in painting and sculpture, it does not in the least surprise me, as with his talents success crowns all his undertakings.

"C."

A vast number of letters exist—certainly several hundreds of letters—addressed to Lady Blessington, while she was residing in St. James's Square, in the Villa Belvedere in Naples, the Palazzo Negroni in Rome, the Hotel Ney in Paris, Seamore Place and Gore House, London; answers to invitations, to inquiries of a private nature, and applications of Lady Blessington in behalf of friends and protegées, which, however important, as shewing the extent and nature of her correspondence, or the influence exercised by Lady Blessington over the most eminent persons of her time, in statesmanship or in literature—have been withheld from publication, from a desire to insert no letters in these volumes, except on account of some intrinsic value and interest in such correspondence. These omitted letters include communications from Mr. Canning, Lords Hutchinson, Grey, Rosslyn, Beresford, Lyndhurst, Brougham, Durham, Jersey, Aberdeen, Morpeth, Glenelg, Westmoreland, Abinger, Normanby, Auckland, Chesterfield, Douro, Castlereagh, Strangford, Holland, Clanricarde, the Marquess Wellesley, the Duke of Wellington, Sir T. Lawrence, Sir Alured Clerk, Sir F. Burdett, Sir Edwin Landseer, Sir E. B. Lytton, Sir H. Bulwer, Sir W. Sommerville. Moore, Campbell, Rogers, Byron, Barry Cornwall, Lady Tankerville, Miss Landor, Mrs. Romer, Mrs. Sigourney, Mrs.

Mathews, Miss Louisa Sheridan, Madame Guiccioli, Madlle. Rachelle, Vicomte D'Arlincourt, the Duc D'Ossuna, le Prince Swartzenburg, le Prince Soutza, le Prince Belvidere, W. S. Landor, the Right Hon. B. D'Israeli, Dickens, Fonblanque, Forster, Serjeant Talfourd, the Hon. Spencer Cooper, Wilkie, Maclise, Wyatt, Uwins, Eugene Sue, Alfred de Vigny, Casimir de Lavigne, Col. D'Aguilar, Dr. Parr, Dr. Lardner, Dr. Quin, Dr. Beattie, James and Horace Smith, Macready, C. Greville, C. J. Matthews, Jekyll, Jack Fuller, Leitch Ritchie, Baillie Cochrane, Bernal Osborne, B. Simmonds, G. Mansel Reynolds, Theodore Hook, J. H. Jesse, Henry Chester, J. G. Wilkinson, Washington Irving, Kenyon, Luttrell, Hon. R. Spencer, Thackeray, Albert Smith, Jerdan, Haynes Bailey, &c. &c. &c.

CHAPTER VI.

DOCTOR SAMUEL PARR, LL.D.

This celebrated Greek scholar and eminent critic was born at Harrow-on-the-Hill, in 1746. He was educated at Harrow, and Emmanuel College, Cambridge. In 1769, he entered into orders. He established a school at Stanmore, and superintended schools in Colchester and Norwich, before he obtained the rectory at Asterby, in 1780; and a prebend's stall in the cathedral of St. Paul, in 1781. The perpetual curacy of Hatton, near Norwich, was conferred on him in 1785. In 1791, the riots at Birmingham, which proved destructive to the property of Dr. Priestly, extended to Hatton, and the property of Dr. Parr, on account of his friendship with Dr. Priestly, and his own liberal principles, was endangered. The following year, Dr. Parr exchanged his perpetual curacy at Hatton for a rectory in Northamptonshire. Early in 1793, he began to contribute to " The British Critic," and later wrote much in " The Classical Journal." In 1802, Sir Francis Burdett presented him to the rectory of Graffham, in Huntingdonshire. The Doctor's strong Whiggish principles, when Mr. Fox came into power, it is said, weighed down the merits of his erudition and theological acquirements in the estimation of the King, and prevented a bishopric being given him. He died in March, 1825, in his eightieth year, like the celebrated linguist and scholar Mezzofanti, leaving behind few records of his vast erudition. All the remains of Dr. Parr are comprised in a collection of Sermons, "A Tract on Education, and the plans pursued by Charity Schools," 4to., 1786. A Preface to Bellendenus de Statu, and "A Letter from Irenopolis to the Inhabitants of Eleutheropalis, or a Serious Address to the Inhabitants of Birmingham," in 1792. "Character of the late Charles James Fox, by Philopatris Varvicensis," 2 vols. 8vo. 1809; and some ephemeral pamphlets, occasioned by his critical disputes and controversies with Dr. Charles Combe and others.

> Of Bentley's feuds—of Porson's—Parr's
> Most Savage Greek and Latin wars,

few remains are left; and mankind would be nothing the worse if their battles had never been waged at all. Dr. Parr was renowned for his smoking, even more than Dr. Isaac Barrow. He would empty twenty pipes of an evening, in his own house; and when he was on his good behaviour in fashionable circles, it is said, he pined after the weed. About two years before his death, he was introduced by Mr. Pettigrew to Lady Blessington, and was so charmed by her appearance, manners, and conversation, that he would willingly, at any time, have relinquished his pipe ever after, for the pleasure of her society. After the first interview, he spoke to Mr. Pettigrew of her as "the gorgeous Lady Blessington."

FROM DR. PARR TO LADY BLESSINGTON.

"Hatton, January 26, 1822.

"May it please your Ladyship to accept the tribute of my best thanks for the present of a gorgeous cake, which does equal honour to your courtesy and your taste. It reached me last night. It seized the admiration of my wife, and two Oxford friends. They gazed upon its magnitude. They eulogized the colouring and the gilding of the figures with raptures. They listened gladly to the tales which I told, about the beautiful, ingenious, and noble donor. I perceive that your Ladyship's gift was sent by the Crown Prince coach, which I had pointed out, and upon which I depend chiefly. My wife and my cook, and her auxiliary, are waiting, with some anxiety, for a magnificent turbot, with which Lord Blessington intends to decorate the banquet.

"You may be assured that grateful and honourable mention of your names will be made in our toasts. I shall write to Lord Blessington when I know the fate of the fish.

"As it did not come by the Crown Prince, possibly it may be conveyed by the mail, which passes my door about nine, or by the Liverpool, which passes about the middle of the day.

"My village peal of eight bells is ringing merrily, and I wish that you and Lord Blessington were here, the witnesses of their music.

"I probably shall visit the capital in the spring, and with the permission of your Ladyship and Lord Blessington, I shall pay my personal compliments to you, in St. James's Square.

"I have the honour to be, with the greatest respect,

"My Lady, your Ladyship's faithful well-wisher,

"And much obliged humble servant,

"S. Parr."

"January 27, 1822.

"Ingenious and honoured Lady Blessington,

"Accept my praise as a critic, and my best thanks as a well-wisher, for the honour which you have done me, in sending me a most elegant poetical congratulation on the return of the anniversary of my birth-day. Lady Blessington, I have ventured to impress three kisses upon the precious communication, and I will order it to be preserved among my papers, as a memorial of your Ladyship's taste and courtesy. The cake, from its magnitude and its richness, would have adorned the table of a cardinal. Be assured, Lady Blessington, that not only was your name pronounced in the second toast, with that of the Duke of Sussex, and some other contributors to the dainties, but that I took an opportunity to speak about the gracefulness of your person and the lustre of your talents. I hope in the spring, that we shall meet together, and talk upon many interesting subjects, which must present themselves to our minds.

" Soon after the conclusion of my first letter, another coach brought me Lord Blessington's magnificent turbot, and a very eminent scholar bestowed a classical eulogium on the—

" 'Spatium admirabili rhombi.'

" Lord Blessington will tell you that the expression occurs in the fourth satire of Juvenal, and if you have a translation, pray amuse yourself with an account of Domitian's feast, and his guests and his wicked nature, when a huge fish had been presented to him, and he had summoned his trembling companions to the banquet. I am sure that Lord Blessington will like to refresh his memory, and after certain military outrages at Manchester, Hyde Park Corner, and Kensington, I shall applaud his Lordship for committing to memory the whole sixteenth satire of Juvenal. The composition is less adorned than many of the other satires. But his Lordship may take my word for it, that it came from the pen of Juvenal, and there will be found in it abundance of matter applicable to the odious and alarming occurrences which disgrace the government of the English Sardanapalus. Pray tell my Lord, that with allusion to the notorious voluptuary, a friend of his Lordship has put together a most proper and most poignant epitaph for George the Fourth. Give my best compliments to your lively sister, and permit me to have the honour to subscribe myself,

" Dear Madam, your faithful well-wisher,

" And respectful, obedient servant,

" S. PARR."

LETTER FROM MISS EMILY CALCRAFT TO LADY BLESSINGTON, IN RELATION TO DR. PARR.

" DEAR LADY BLESSINGTON,

" I have the pleasure to send you Mr. Horseman's excellent parody of a libel on Dr. Parr, together with his letter, and the Doctor's prompt and courteous reply. I beg you will excuse the paper having been much read; you are welcome, if you please, to copy it.

"I have transcribed for your Ladyship the brilliant oratorical passage which Lord Erskine was accustomed to ascribe to Viscount Strafford, and I have written a few lines to Dr. Parr's executors, which, should you determine upon addressing them, you may employ as the envelope of your communication.

"To these papers I venture to add two letters, containing most interesting traits of Dr. Parr's character. I trust to your good-nature to credit my showing them on this account, rather than because the notice taken in them of my pamphlet is so partial.

"I am, with great truth,
"Your Ladyship's obliged and sincere,
"EMILY CALCRAFT."

LETTER TO DR. PARR FROM THE REV. MR. HORSEMAN.

"Heydon Royston, August 20, 1821.

"REV. SIR,

"In a shameful and shameless newspaper, misnamed 'John Bull,' there appeared, last Monday, a miserable attack upon a character held in the highest estimation by the wisest and best of mankind. From a Tory acquaintance of mine this infamous paper reached me last Saturday, and to-day I happened to go to Royston, where I desired the agent at that place for the 'Cambridge Independent Press' newspaper, to forward to the proprietor for insertion in his next paper, what, upon the spur of the occasion, I hit off as I drove, in the shape of an answer.

"I take the liberty of sending you both these trifles for your amusement. It would give me far greater pleasure, had I the ability and opportunity to express, in a better way and more worthy of the very accomplished and distinguished personage so grossly and wretchedly libelled, my sincere admiration of his acute genius, his deep learning, his sound piety, and his unaffected virtue.

"I paid a delightful visit last November to your most excellent friend Mr. Coke, and hope again to accept the kindly proffered hospitality of Holkham, when it would very considerably add to my gratification, were I to have the good fortune to be honoured with an introduction to Dr. Parr, whom I have seen only at Oxford and Cambridge, with whose learned and liberal publications I am familiar, and of whose personal character I know enough to be anxious to know more. Should you think proper to notice the receipt of this communication, I shall be much flattered by a letter directed to the Rev. John Horseman, Heydon Royston.

"I have the honour to be, Rev. Sir,
"With the profoundest esteem,
"Your most obedient and very humble servant,
"JOHN HORSEMAN."

"The 'John Bull,' August 23, 1821.

"RECIPE FOR COMPOUNDING A POLITICAL RADICAL, D.D. A.S.S., &c., &c.

"To half of Busby's skill in mood and tense,
Add Bentley's *pedantry* without his sense;
From Warburton take all the spleen you find,
But leave his genius and his wit behind:
Squeeze Churchill's rancour from the verse it flows in,
And knead it stiff with Johnston's turgid prosing;
Add all the piety of Saint Voltaire,
Mix the gross compounds—Fiat—Dr. Parr."

Q. IN THE CORNER.

ANSWER.

"To more than Busby's skill in mood and tense,
Add Bentley's learning and his sterling sense;
From Warburton take all the wit you find,
But leave his grossness and his whims behind;
Mix Churchill's vigour as in verse it flows,
And knead it well with Johnston's manly prose;
Sprinkle the whole with pepper from Voltaire,
Strain off the scum, and—Fiat—Dr. Parr."

LETTER FROM DR. PARR TO THE REV. MR. HORSEMAN.

"Rev. Sir,

"I had left Hatton when your friendly and interesting letter arrived there. It has been forwarded to me in a large mass of papers, and I take an early opportunity of presenting to you the tribute of my respectful and thankful acknowledgments. Your retort on my slander is masterly, and to me it is the more pleasing, because I believe it to be the result of your own sincere conviction. I have never seen any one number of the 'John Bull,' but I hear that in profligate and malignant calumny it exceeds the vilest publications that ever disgraced the English press.

"While Ministers, Judges, Academics, Bishops, Priests, and Deacons are inveighing against the licentiousness of the Press, they would do well to recollect that 'John Bull' is more virulent in its spirit, and more mischievous in its consequences, than the worst effusions of scribbling Radicals. Upon my literary and intellectual powers I readily submit to the judgment of others, but I can safely and becomingly listen to the approving sentence of my conscience upon my principles, which are founded upon long and severe research, and upon my actions for the space of fifty-five years, during which time I have never truckled to power, nor preferred my personal interests to the sacred rights and social happiness of mankind. I ought to thank the writers of the 'John Bull' for stiring up an advocate so skilful and so distinguished as Mr. Horseman. If you should ever come into Warwickshire, my hope is, that you would permit me to receive you in my parsonage.

"S. Parr."

Extract from a Sermon of Dr. Parr on Repentance—transmitted to Lady Blessington by Miss Calcraft.

"The infinite importance of what he has to do, the goading conviction that it must be done, the utter inability of doing it, the dreadful combination in his mind of both the necessity and incapacity, the despair of crowding the concerns of an age into a moment, the impossibility of beginning a repentance which should have been completed, of setting about a peace which should have been concluded, of suing for a pardon which should have been obtained. All these complicated concerns, without strength, without time, without hope; with a clouded memory, a disjointed reason, a wounded spirit, undefined terrors, remembered sins, anticipated punishment, an angry God, an accusing conscience, altogether intolerably augment the sufferings of a body which stands little in need of the insupportable burden of a distracted mind to aggravate its torments."

SIR THOMAS LAWRENCE, R.A.

The first portrait painter of his age, Sir T. Lawrence, who had executed portraits of the greatest princes, and the principal personages of his day, mixed in the most distinguished circles, and had been received with honour in many European courts, was intimately acquainted with Lord Blessington in early life, and the late Lady Blessington from the period of her marriage to that of her departure from England, in 1822.

Two of his best portraits were those of Lord and Lady Blessington. He always considered the last as his *chef-d'œuvre.* When asked by Lord Blessington to copy it, he declined to do so, saying, "That picture could neither be copied or engraved." His assertion was afterwards fully verified. Of the three engravings that were made of that portrait by the first engravers of the day, Cousins, Reynolds, and another artist, not one was successful. In the wreck of the affairs of Lady Blessington, when every thing belonging to her was sold by auction, in 1849, at Gore House, I saw these two pictures sold. That of Lord Blessington was purchased by Mr. Fuller for £68, that of Lady Blessington, by the Marquess of Hertford for £336.

The portraits of Sir Thomas Lawrence, it is hardly needful to observe, are remarkable for the representation of mind and character, in the delineation of face and form, for the speaking looks, animated with spirit and intelligence in the expression of those he painted, for their giving his subjects a *distingué* air, and for his peculiar excellence in painting eyes, and rendering characteristic resemblances.

At the beginning of his career, his object was to imitate Reynolds, and some of his earlier pictures, in some degree, resembled those of Sir Joshua. Brilliancy of effect, ease and simplicity, the power of imparting nobility to physical perfections, and of making the mind discernible in the features he represented; these were the peculiar characteristics of his style. His manners and conversation were those of a gentleman accustomed to courts. In all matters his taste was exquisite; and in his office of President of the Royal Academy, he abstained from attempting reforms, however much needed, in his unwillingness to encounter formidable opponents.

Sir Thomas was born at Bristol, in 1769. He commenced the profession of a portrait painter, in Oxford, in 1787; removed to London, and rose rapidly to distinction from the year 1800. In 1814, he was charged by the Prince Regent to take portraits of the allied sovereigns who visited England; in 1815, he was knighted; in 1818, he was sent to Aix-la-Chapelle, to paint the principal members of Congress; in 1819, he visited Italy, and in the following year was elected President of the Academy. He died in January, 1830, in his sixty-second year.

A brother artist, and a friend of Lawrence, one thoroughly imbued with a spirit of criticism, thus speaks of the merits and works of Sir Thomas:

"Twenty years ago, his pictures (as Fuseli used to say) were like the scrapings of a tin-shop, full of little sparkling bits of light, which destroyed all repose. But after his visit to Italy, the improvement which took place was an honour to his talents. His latter pictures are by far his best. His great excellence was neither colour, drawing, composition, light and shade, or perspective—for he was hardly ever above mediocrity in any of these; but expression, both in figure and feature. Perhaps no man that ever lived contrived to catch the fleeting beauties of a face to the exact point, though a little affected, better than Lawrence. The head of Miss Croker is the finest example in the world. He did not keep his sitters unanimated and lifeless, but by interesting their feelings, he brought out the expression which was excited by the pleasure they felt.

"As a man, Sir Thomas Lawrence was amiable, kind, generous, and forgiving. His manner was elegant, but not high-bred. He had too much the air of always submitting. He had smiled so often and so long, that at last his smile had the appearance of being set in enamel. He indulged the hope of painting history in his day; but, as Romney did, and Chantry will, he died before he began; and he is another proof, if proof were wanting, that creative genius is not a passive quality, that can be laid aside or taken up as it suits the convenience of the possessor.

"As an artist, he will not rank high in the opinion of posterity. He was not ignorant of the figure, but he drew with great incorrectness, because he drew to suit the fashion of the season. If necks were to be long, breasts full, waists small, and toes pointed, Sir Thomas was too well bred to hesitate. His necks are therefore often hideously long, his waists small, his chests puffed, and his ancles tapered. He had no eye for colour. His tint was opaque, not livid, his cheeks were rouged, his lips like the lips of a lay-figure. There was nothing of the red and white which nature's own sweet and cunning hand laid on. His bloom was the bloom of the perfumer. Of composition he knew scarcely any thing; and perhaps, in the whole circle of art, there never was a more lamentable proof of these deficiencies than in his last portrait of the king."

FROM THOMAS LAWRENCE, ESQ. TO LORD MOUNTJOY.

"Greek Street, Sunday morning (1812).

"MY DEAR LORD,

"All other considerations apart (and those no slight ones), I confess to the strong temptation you hold out to me in the very venison itself! I beg its pardon for having written venison, like any other word, 'I own the soft impeachment.' Yet it does so unluckily happen, that I am engaged Monday, and Tuesday, and Wednesday, and Thursday, so that all hope of indulging my ruling passion is over with me this week. In return for your Lordship's kindness, I send you lines which I think not bad, certainly not the worse for being on my own side or view of the subject. With my respects to Lady Mountjoy,

"I remain, my dear Lord,

"Most faithfully and with true respect, yours,

"T. LAWRENCE."

ON WALTZING.

"What! the girl I adore by *another* embraced!
What! the balm of her breath shall another man taste!
What! prest in the whirl by another bold knee!
What! panting recline on another than me!
Sir, She's yours—you have brushed from the grape its soft blue,
From the rose-bud you've shaken its tremulous dew—
What you've *touch'd, you may take*—Pretty waltzer, adieu!"

"Greek Street, July 29, 1812.

"Without the preface of an apology, which your kind nature will either think needless, or make for me, I will at once state (but only from a necessity), that having, as your Lordship proposed, renewed your draft for £200, by keeping it back for an additional two months—I am applied to by the parties holding it respecting its non-payment.

"If it is convenient to your Lordship to give directions that it be now paid, why, I can only say, that I shall be a little assisted by it. If, however, it is not, will you in the course of to-morrow, favour me with another, at such time as your agents may enable the bankers to pay it? I will then get back the first and return it to you. I beg to say that the draft was not presented at the expiration of the first two months.

"I hope Lady Mountjoy continues quite well, and did not suffer from the lateness of the close of your bounteous entertainment of Sunday last. Believe me with the truest respect and attachment,

"My dear Lord,
"Most devotedly yours,
"T. LAWRENCE."

"Russell Square, 11 April, 1829.

"I will get a copy made from your portrait, at as reasonable a price as I can. I think your Lordship had better wait till, as you say, the quarter's revenue may be more flourishing. I have little doubt of the picture being well disposed of, but the present moment is the most inauspicious for application to the government.

"As a practice of the Museum, I see how strict is the attention to economy, even in apparently trivial details.

"Hayter's picture is more liked by me than by many amateurs; I see a great deal of merit in it; but its want of effect and breadth—indispensable qualities in our English school, (and properly so), makes the general eye indifferent to the careful finishing and excellence of its details.

"Ever, with the highest esteem and regard,
"T. LAWRENCE."

FROM SIR THOMAS LAWRENCE TO LADY BLESSINGTON.

"Russell Square, Monday evening.

"DEAR LADY BLESSINGTON,

"Do me the favour to sit to me at one o'clock to-day instead of twelve, and pray come with your pearl necklace.

"If you can spare the time, I shall want your Ladyship to remain till exactly four.

"I remain, dear Lady Blessington,

"Your very obedient and faithful servant,

"Thos. Lawrence."

"Russell Square, Saturday morning.

"Your charitable office is no sinecure; can you oblige me with one ticket for the Opera to-night?

"I avoid, if I can, to pay either in my own person or in that of a friend for this amusement; but my magnificent £1 is ready for any better purpose that your Ladyship may point out.

"Thos. Lawrence."

THOMAS MOORE, ESQ.

Moore's intimacy with Lord Blessington commenced so early as 1806. His Lordship's taste for private theatricals, and Moore's talent for epilogue writing and lyrical composition, led to their first acquaintance. Moore refers in his diaries to his early theatrical acquaintance with Lord Mountjoy.

In the Dublin "Evening Herald" of August 26, 1806, we find the following account of the theatricals at Lord Mountjoy's residence on the Mountjoy Forest estate, in the county of Tyrone, near Omagh. "Lord Mountjoy has seceded from the Kilkenny theatricals, and has opened a splendid theatre at Omagh. Fullam is acting manager, Mrs. Moore, Mrs. Chalmers, and Mrs. Fullam, are among the actresses."

Moore, in the introduction to Longmans' 8vo. edition of his poems (1840), mentions his schoolmaster, Samuel Whyte, being in request among the fashionables of Dublin and its neighbourhood, as a manager of the private theatricals, and a great encourager of a taste for acting among his pupils.

"In this line," says Moore, "I was long his favourite show scholar;" and among the play-bills embodied in his volume, to illustrate the occasions of his own prologues and epilogues, there is one of a play got up in the year 1790, at Lady Borrowes' private theatricals in Dublin, where, among the items of the evening's entertainment, is " an Epilogue, *A Squeeze at St. Paul's*, Master Moore."

Some curious particulars of Moore's early life were given to me in Wexford, about two years ago, by an old lady, a Miss Mary Doyle, a relative of the poet, then in her seventy-eighth year, and now in eternity. Miss Doyle stated her mother's name was Kate Corrin; she was a first cousin of Tom Moore's mother, who was a Miss Anastasia Codd; her father, Thomas Codd, was in the provision trade, and kept a slaughter-house in the Corn-Market. (The house still exists, and is now a public-house, called the Ark.)*

Immediately after the marriage of Mr. Moore with Miss Codd, they went to reside in Dublin. Mr. Moore was not a Wexford man. A few years later, Miss Doyle went up from Wexford to live with the Moores, and she lived many years with the family, about ten or twelve " off and on," upon several occasions. She remembers Tom's bed, when he was a mere boy, being covered with scraps of poetry, pinned on the curtains " all over them." Tom spent very little of his early days in Wexford, but when about the age of twelve years, went down on a visit to Mrs. Scallion, a relation.

Tom's earliest passion was for his cousin, Miss Mary Doyle. He was in the habit of writing verses in praise of her (she was about seventeen years of age at the time) ; *and some of the verses he wrote on her, and addressed to her, were published in some Magazines.*

This was the substance of Miss Doyle's statement ; and on

* At the death of Thomas Codd, the business was carried on by John Richards ; after Richards' death, by his daughter, Mrs. Hanlon, and she was succeeded by the present proprietor, who keeps a small public-house.

the next occasion of my visiting Wexford, and calling at her place of residence, with the view of making some further inquiries, I found she had died the day before, namely, on the 29th of November, 1852.

The lady in whose house she died, Mrs. Mary Frances Richards, a niece of the old lady, informed me that Miss Doyle was a person of strict veracity, and of the highest character. Whatever she said about being the object of the boyish fancies of Tom Moore, and the subject of many of his amatory poems, there could be no doubt of the fact. And even in her extreme old age, it gratified her to be reminded of it; and of the influence of her attractions—"for she was a great beauty in her youthful days."

But the strange part of the matter is, that Moore in his diary, though very circumstantial in his details respecting his boyhood, and the persons who frequented his father's house, and his early *penchants* too, and especially for a Miss Hannah Byrne, who was a good deal at his father's house, and to whom he addressed amatory poems—he says his first—never mentions his fair cousin, Miss Mary Doyle, at all, her residing many years at his father's house, nor alludes to the fact of his addressing verses to her on various occasions. Could he have confounded the name of Hannah Byrne, an early acquaintance of his family, with hers, in a remarkable reference to his first love?

In his diary, (vol. i. p. 22, of the Memoirs of Lord John Russell), he speaks of a Miss Hannah Byrne, who was a good deal at the house of his parents in his early days, to whom he addressed his first amatory effusions, and addressed her as Zelia, signing himself Romeo; the first of these which he published, appeared in 1793, in the Dublin "Anthologia Hibernica" Magazine.

On referring to the October number of that periodical, I find the following lines, which were the first poetic effusion of

Moore that appeared in print. They were written at his father's residence in Aungier Street, Dublin. They not only possess considerable beauty, but are singularly prophetic of the chord which he has struck with such delightful effect in after-years:—

TO ZELIA.

" 'Tis true my muse to love inclines,
And wreaths of Cypria's myrtle twines;
Quits all inspiring lofty views,
And chaunts what nature's gifts infuse;
Timid to try the mountain's height,
Beneath she strays, retir'd from sight;
Careless, culling amorous flowers,
Or quaffing mirth in Bacchus' bowers.
When first she raised her simplest lays,
In Cupid's never-ceasing praise,
The god a faithful promise gave—
That never should she feel love's stings,
Never to burning passion be a slave,
But feel the purer joy thy friendship brings."

When Lord Blessington removed to London, and was established in St. James's Square, in the latter part of 1820, or beginning of 1821, Moore renewed his acquaintance with his Lordship, and made that of Lady Blessington. He was a frequent and a favourite visitor there. In Lady Blessington's, journals, while residing in Paris, we find many references to the pleasure she received in renewed intimacy with Moore; and at a later period, Mr. Willis has made the world pretty familiar with the peculiar charm of Moore's society and conversation in Seamore Place.

There is a dash of genius, and much graphic truth in the following slight sketch of Moore by a man of kindred genius —B. R. Haydon.

"Met Moore at dinner, and spent a very pleasant three

hours. He told his stories with a hit-or-miss air, as if accustomed to people of rapid apprehension. It being asked at Paris who they would have as a godfather for Rothschild's child, 'Talleyrand,' said a Frenchman. '*Pourquoi, Monsieur? Parcequ'il est le moins Chrétien possible.*'

" Moore is a delightful, gay, voluptuous, refined, natural creature; infinitely more unaffected than Wordsworth; not blunt and uncultivated like Chantrey, or bilious and shivering like Campbell. No affectation, but a true, refined, delicate, frank poet, with sufficient air of the world to prove his fashion, sufficient honesty of manner to show fashion has not corrupted his native taste; making allowance for prejudices instead of condemning them, by which he seemed to have none himself: never talking of his own works, from intense consciousness that every body else did; while Wordsworth is always talking of his own productions, from apprehension that they are not enough matter of conversation. Men must not be judged too hardly; success or failure will either destroy or better the finest natural parts. Unless one had heard Moore tell the above story of Talleyrand, it would have been impossible to conceive the air of half-suppressed impudence, the delicate, light-horse canter of phrase with which the words floated out of his sparkling Anacreontic mouth."*

One of Moore's happiest efforts of an anecdotal kind was his relation of a scene of a very extraordinary description, which took place in Dublin in 1836, and was witnessed by the Editor: of this scene some account will be found in the Appendix.

LETTERS FROM THOMAS MOORE TO LADY BLESSINGTON.

" Sloperton Cottage, Devizes,
" November 18th, 1829.

" My dear Lady Blessington,

" It is now six months since (after a conversation with Lord John Russell about you) I exclaimed, ' Well, I shall positively

* Autobiography of B. R. Haydon.

write to Lady Blessington to-morrow!' Whether I have kept my word, you and the postman know but too well. The fact is, I live, as usual, in such a perpetual struggle between what I like to do and what I ought to do (though communing with you would come under both these heads)—between junketing abroad and scribbling at home, that for any thing but the desk and the dinner-table, I am not left a single instant of time.

"In addition to our neighbours at Bowood, we have got, lately, their relatives, the Fieldings, who have settled themselves near us; and having some very pretty girls for daughters (things I have not yet lost my taste for),—they contrive, with music, visits, &c., to disturb me not a little.

"I have had but one short glimpse of Mrs. Purves for the last year, as she has taken flight to some distant and outlandish place (called Fulham, I believe), to which a thorough *town* man (such as I always am for the few weeks I stay there) could never, even with the help of the 'march of intellect,' think of arriving. I wish she would return into the civilized world, for I miss her very, very much, I assure you. To talk of *you* and old times—of those two dazzling faces I saw popped out of the hotel windows in Sackville Street—of the dance to the piper at Richmond, &c. &c. All this is delightful to remember, and to talk about, and if ever 'we three meet again,' we shall have a regular *cause* of it.

"Lord John Russell told me (and this I own was one of the reasons of my above-mentioned fruitless ejaculations) that you saw a good deal of Lord Byron during his last days in Italy, and that you mentioned some anecdotes of him, (his bursting into tears as he lay on the sofa, &c.), which he (Lord John) thought might be very interestingly introduced into my life of him. He also told me that you had some verses addressed to yourself by Lord Byron, which were very pretty and graceful, in short, in every way worthy of this subject.

"Now, my dear Lady Blessington, if you have anything like the same cordial remembrances of old times that I have—if ever the poet (or the piper) found favour in your ears, sit down instantly and record for me, as only a woman *can* record, every particular of your acquaintance with Byron, from first to last.

M 2

You may depend upon what you write never meeting any eye but my own, and you will oblige me more than I have time at this moment to tell you.

"Above all, too, do not forget the verses, which will be doubly precious, as written *by him* and *on* you.

"Lord Lansdowne told me, some time ago, that he had had a letter from Lord Blessington, which gave, I was sorry to hear, but little hopes of seeing either him or you in England. My most sincere and cordial regards to him, and believe me ever,

"My dear Lady Blessington,
"Faithfully yours,
"THOMAS MOORE.

"I hope to hear that you liked my last *pious* story; it has been very successful."

"Sloperton Cottage, Devizes,
"July 4th, 1828.

"MY DEAR LADY BLESSINGTON,

"Having been some days away from home, I did not receive your kind letter till yesterday; and I am just now so surrounded with shoals of letters, all gaping for answers, that I have not a minute to spare for more than just to say, How charmed I was to hear from you; how comforted I feel in the thought that you are *even so* much nearer to me, and how delighted I should be (if such a dream was but within the sphere of possibility just now) to run over to you for a week or two. However, who knows? as the old woman said, who expected a prize in the lottery, though she had no ticket: 'sure nothing's *un*possible to God.' I will, therefore, hope; and, in the mean time, pray send me the promised packet, directing, under cover, to the Honourable Frederick Byng (our dearly beloved Poodle), Foreign Office, Downing Street.

"I am so glad you like my verses! I repeat them over and over to myself continually.

"Lord Blessington's packet arrived safe, and the sooner he sends me another, tell him (with my most cordial regards) the better.

"THOMAS MOORE."

"Sloperton Cottage, Devizes,
"October 18th, 1828.

"My dear Lady Blessington,

"I have been kept, as I told you in my last, in a state of great anxiety about our little girl, who has been for months confined with an obstinate lameness, which is only just now yielding to the remedies we have employed. Since I wrote, too, I have had an alarm about our eldest boy, who was brought home from school in consequence of a fever having made its appearance there, and who, for some time after his return, shewed symptoms of having caught it. He is now, however, quite well, and is with his mamma and my daughter at Southampton.

"I see, by the newspapers, that there is some chance of your coming to England, and trust that there is more truth in the intelligence than newspapers in general contain. Best regards to Lord Blessington, and

"Believe me ever,
"Most truly yours,
"Thomas Moore."

"Sloperton Cottage, Devizes,
"April 15th, 1830.

"My dear Lady Blessington,

"I received a most kind letter from you the other day, through our pretty *spirituelle* young friend in Palace Yard; so kind, that, hurried as I am with all sorts of distinctions, I cannot resist the impulse of dispatching a hasty line to thank you for it.

"I am also glad of the opportunity to tell you that *it was* all *owing* to a mistake (or rather a difficulty in the way of business) that you did not receive from the author himself one of the first copies of 'The Life of Byron.'

"It is too long a story for a man in a hurry to relate, but you will understand enough, when I tell you that the dispensation of the presentation copies was a joint concern between hurry and me, and that having by mistake extended my number, I was unwilling to embarrass my account by going further.

"But, mind, whatever copy you may have *read* me in, the one that you must go to *sleep upon* (when inclined for a doze) must be a portable octavo presented by myself.

"You deserve ten times more than this, not only for our old friendship, but for the use you have been to the said volume, by the very interesting and (in the present state of the patrimonial question) apropos contributions you have furnished.

"I was sorry, some time ago, to see that the pretty verses to you had found their way into some French periodicals, and from them into ours; but I trust most sincerely that the same accident will not occur to the lines about Lady Byron.

"They gave me some hope at the Speaker's, that we might soon see you in England. Is there any chance?

"Ever yours most truly,

"THOMAS MOORE."

"Sloperton Cottage, April 15, 1832.

"DEAR LADY BLESSINGTON,

"You were one of the very first persons, during my late short and busy visit to London, whom it was my intention, as soon as I discovered you were in town, to call upon; but just as I was about to have that pleasure, your letter, forwarded from home, reached me; and the tone of it, I confess, so much surprised and pained me, that I had not courage to run the risk of such a reception as it seemed to threaten. I can only say, that, had I the least idea that the very harmless allusions in Byron's letter to the very harmless pursuits of Lord Blessington's youth, could have given him (had he been alive) or yourself the slightest uneasiness, I most certainly would not have suffered those passages to remain; nor can I now understand, with all allowance for the sensitiveness which affliction generates, either the annoyance or displeasure which (you will, at least, believe more from wrong judgment than any intention) I have been so unfortunate as to excite in you.

"I have lost no time in searching both for the letters and MS. book which you wished for; but as yet, have been unable to find only the latter, and rather think that the letters of Lord Blessington, to which you allude, shared the fate of many others on the same subject, which I tore up when done with them. Again expressing my sincere regret for the pain I have given,

"I am, dear Lady Blessington,

"Very truly yours,

"THOMAS MOORE."

Those who only knew Moore in fashionable circles, or through his Diaries, are very unlikely to be acquainted with the best part of his character, and what was most estimable and deserving of honour in his principles. The following letter, expressive of his views respecting Cuban slavery, and the conduct of the Irish in America, in relation to slavery, is so creditable to his sentiments, that I presume it may be subjoined, without impropriety, to the preceeding letters.

LETTER FROM THOMAS MOORE TO THE EDITOR.

"Sloperton, March 8th, 1840.

"DEAR DR. MADDEN,

"I have but time to acknowledge and thank you for the very interesting paper on slavery, which you were so kind as to send me through the hands of my sister. I am not surprised that you should have returned bursting with indignation — more especially against those fellow-countrymen of ours (and fellow-Catholics), who by their advocacy of slavery bring so much disgrace both upon their country and creed.

"Wishing you every success in your benevolent efforts,

"I am very truly yours,

"THOMAS MOORE."

THOMAS CAMPBELL.

In the spring of 1832, I introduced Campbell to Lady Blessington. The acquaintance commenced inauspiciously. There was a coolness in it from the beginning, which soon made it very evident to both parties there was no cordiality between them to be expected. The lady, who was disappointed with Byron at her first interview with him, was not very likely to be delighted with Campbell—a most *shivery* person in the presence of strangers—or to have her *beau ideal* of the poetic character, and outward appearance of a bard, realized by an elderly gentleman in a curly wig, with a blue coat and brass buttons, very like an ancient mariner out of uniform, and his native element—being on shore.

Campbell, on the other hand, had a sort of instinctive antipathy to any person who was supposed to be an admirer of Byron, and he could not divest his mind of the idea that Lady Blessington did not duly appreciate his own merits. After dining at Seamore Place twice, I believe, and freezing her Ladyship with the chilliness of his humour, the acquaintance dropped, and left no pleasing recollections on the minds of either of the parties. Lady Blessington occasionally indulged in strictures on the vanity and the selfishness of Byron; Campbell frequently broke out into violent invective, and very unmeasured abuse of his brother bard, after his death. But Lady Blessington could not bear any one to speak disparagingly of Byron in any respect but herself. And there was always a large quantity of eulogy mingled with her small amount of censure. But that was not the case with Campbell. He could see nothing to admire, to pity, or to spare, in Byron.

"If poets only were allowed to pronounce sentence on poets, we are afraid the public would often endeavour to apply to a higher court for a new trial, on the ground of the misdirection of the judge, or of the verdict being brought against the evidence; and this will be found to be the case, even when very high powers and capabilities are found on the judgment-seat." Those very truthful words were spoken by a generous-minded and a manly-thinking writer—Eliot Warburton—in relation of some disparaging remarks of Goldsmith on the odes of Gray.*

* Memoirs of H. Walpole, &c. vol. ii. p. 150.

LETTER FROM THOMAS CAMPBELL TO LADY BLESSINGTON.

"May 19, 1832.
" Sussex Chambers, Duke Street,
" St. James's Square.

"DEAR MADAM,

"I have no engagements for a month to come, excepting for Monday and Thursday next. On Monday, I have a very long-standing and particular engagement, otherwise I should break it with no scruple, to accept your Ladyship's invitation. How unfortunate it is for me to have been engaged. I must not be too pathetic over my misfortune, for that might seem to be saying, 'I pray you ask me some other day,' and that would be very saucy, though it would be very sincere.

"But it cannot be forwardness to thank you most gratefully for speaking so kindly of my works.

" With great respect,
" I remain,
"Your Ladyship's obliged and faithful servant,
"THOMAS CAMPBELL."

B. W. PROCTER, ESQ. (BARRY CORNWALL).

A variety of detached poems, of various merit, and many of them of the highest, constitute the claims of this most amiable and accomplished man to literary reputation. Some years ago, he was appointed to the office of Commissioner of Lunatic Asylums.

A lady, well acquainted with him, whose observations on some others of the celebrities of Gore House, I have already quoted, thus speaks of Barry Cornwall:—" One of the kindest, gentlest, and most amiable of natures; a warm, true, and indefatigable friend; an excellent family man, and in all his relations guileless and simple as a child. His writings, principally in verse, and some charming prose sketches of his, likewise partake, for the most part, of the gentle spirit of the man, with much of playfulness and phantasy; but at times they rise into a tragic force and graphic energy. Some of his descriptions, of scenes in the dark dens of London crime and vice, are very forcible and dramatic."

The English epitaph on the tomb of Lady Blessington was written by Barry Cornwall.

EXTRACTS FROM LETTERS OF B. W. PROCTER, ESQ. (BARRY CORNWALL) TO LADY BLESSINGTON.

"28 January, 1833.

"Your little letters always find me grateful to them. They (little paper angels, as they are) put devils of all kinds, from blue down to black, to speedy flight.

"4th February, 1836.

"Your little notes come into my Cimmerian cell here, like starlits shot from a brighter region—pretty and pleasant disturbers of the darkness about me. I imprison them (my Ariels) in a drawer, with conveyances and wills, &c., and such sublunary things, which seem very proud of their society. Yet, if your notes to me be skiey visitors, what must this *my* note be to *you?* It must, I fear, be an evil genius."

"17th April, 1836.

"I am vexed—more than I can express—at the hurry of your publishers. I do not like that a book of yours should go to press without some contribution from me: yet I am so circumstanced as literally to be unable, for some days, to do anything that is worth your acceptance. I have tried once or twice to hammer out some verse for you, but I am generally so jaded by my day's work, as to be unfit for anything except stupid sleep. I am not visited even by a dream."

[No date.]

"So poor Miss Landon is dead!—what a fate!—she went to certain death. No one ever lived on that dreadful coast, except men of iron, who have been dipped and tempered in every atmosphere, till nothing could touch them."

[No date.]

"I am glad to hear that you enjoy in prospect your garden. You may safely do so. Nature is a friend that never deceives us. You may depend upon it, that her roses will be genuine, and that the whisper of your trees will contain neither flattery nor slander."

"18th December, 1839.

"How is it that you continue to go on with so untiring a pen? I hope you will not continue to give up your nights to literary undertakings. Believe me (who have suffered bitterly for this imprudence), that nothing in the world of letters is worth the sacrifice of health, and strength, and animal spirits, which will certainly follow this excess of labour."

CHAPTER VII.

JOSEPH JEKYLL, ESQ., F.R.S. L.F.S.A.

It is passing strange, how little is to be known, a few years after their decease, of persons greatly celebrated for their wit and humour, while flourishing in society, and courted and petted by the literary circles and coteries of their time. The reputation of a mere man of wit, without any concomitant claims to distinction, whether as an author, an artist, an orator in the senate, or an advocate at the bar, is of small value. There is no element of immortality in it. It is more than strange, it is truly surprising, how men of wit, genuine, exuberant, and irrepressible, spirituelle men, who in society eclipse all other men of letters and remarkable intelligence, by the brilliancy of their conversation, the smartness of their repartees, and the extraordinary quickness of their apprehension; once they cease to throw intellectual somersaults for society to divert it, and make fun for its lords and ladies, and other celebrities, their services are forgotten, all interest in their personal concerns are lost; there is no obligation to their memories, the privileged people of fashion and literature *à-la-mode*, who thronged round them with admiration in their days of triumph, are missing, when they are borne to the tomb, or cease to be funny or prosperous, or in vogue. No man of wit of his time was more talked of and admired than Jekyll. The court that was paid to him, the homage that was yielded to him, were sufficient to lead one to believe that his memory would live long after him; yet a few years had not elapsed after his decease, before he was forgotten. It would seem to be the same with great wits, as with eminent vocalists and musicians: while their peculiar talent is being displayed, while the performance in which they play may last, their talent is fully appreciated; but no sooner is the exhibition over, and the performance at an end, than it becomes a matter of the utmost indifference to the public, whether the person to whom they owe so much enjoyment has fallen into sickness and infirmity, or is of the living or the dead. No book of Jekyll's has found its way into publicity; no writings of any value have turned up among his papers.

During the latter years of his life, he was confined to his house by gout; and during that period Lady Blessington was in the habit of visiting him regularly. She enjoyed exceedingly his society and conversation, the brilliancy of which remained unimpaired by his great age and grievous bodily infirmities.

"Mr. Jekyll was the son of a Captain in the Navy, and was descended from Sir Joseph Jekyll, Master of the Rolls, in the reign of George the First. He was educated in Westminster school, and at Christ Church, Oxford, where he took the degree of M.A., in 1777. He was called to the bar in 1778. He practised in the Western circuit, and in the court of King's Bench."*

He entered parliament in 1787, on the popular interest, in opposition to the Lansdown family. He attached himself to the Whig party, and voted with Mr. Grey, in favour of Reform. So early as 1782, he made himself known to the reading public, as the author of a Memoir, and the editor of the letters of "Ignatius Sancho," (in 2 vols. 8vo.), the African of intellectual celebrity, who corresponded with Johnson,

* Gentleman's Magazine, August, 1837, p. 208.

Sterne, and Garrick. Mr. Jekyll became a fellow of the Royal Society, and of the Society of Antiquaries, in 1790. But it was not his legal, literary, scientific, or antiquarian attainments which gained a reputation for Mr. Jekyll. His ready wit and talent for repartee, his cleverness for hitting off grotesque resemblances of things naturally dissimilar, of seizing on droll peculiarities, salient outlines, and odd circumstances, and making them the subject of sparkling bon-mots and sprightly epigrams, gained him, not only in society, but at the bar, the character of a man of brilliant wit. He was not only witty himself, and the legitimate parent of an innumerable offspring of witticisms—but the putative father of everything really funny and spirituelle, which could not be traced to its true origin.

In 1805, Mr. Jekyll's merits as a humourist became known to the Prince of Wales. He was appointed Attorney-General to the Prince, was made King's Counsel, and also a Commissioner of Lunatics.

Mr. Jekyll held the office for many years of Treasurer of the Society of the Temple, and it was under his directions the venerable hall and celebrated church underwent very important and extensive repairs. In 1811, he published a work in 4to., entitled, " Facts and Observations relating to the Temple Church, and the Monuments contained in it."

Jekyll, like Dr. Johnson, gloried in London life. He said, " If he were compelled to live in the country, he would have the approach to his house paved like the streets of London, and would have a hackney-coach to drive up and down all day long." Doctor Johnson's great dogma, " Sir, the man who is tired of London, is tired of his existence," was ever held by him; and in the exuberance of his metropolitanism, he had a sort of reverential feeling even for the stones of London, which would have made the name of M'Adam odious to him, had he lived a few years later. He agreed with his friend

James Smith in most things, but in one thing he entirely concurred with him in opinion, namely, that—" London is the best place in summer, and the only place in winter."

In short, he never went out of town, that, like Sir Edward Bulwer Lytton, he did not " miss the roar of London."

Mr. Jekyll married, about 1803, the daughter of Colonel Hans Sloane, M.P. for Lostwithiel, and with that lady obtained a very considerable fortune.

He died the 8th of March, 1837, aged eighty-five years, at his residence in New Street, Spring Gardens.

Jekyll's wit in conversation must have been more effective than that of Sydney Smith, and Curran's more marvellously successful than that of either. Byron, no bad judge of merit of this kind, awarded the palm of excellence to the wit of Curran in conversation, over that of all the men of humour and repartee he had ever met. But in composition Sydney Smith surpassed the whole of them in genuine humour and felicitous irony. He had often a higher purpose, moreover, to serve in his writings, than any of his cotemporary facetious friends in their conversation, with one exception, that of Charles Lamb. The excellencies of Sydney Smith have been well observed in the following observations :—

" What Channing is to the democracy of America, with his sober, sustained, and clear dialectic, Sydney Smith is to the tribes of Noodledom, with his irony, his jeering, and his felicitous illustrations. It is his, pre-eminently, to abash those who are case-hardened against grave argument, and to wring the withers of the very numerous and *respectable* class, who

> " ' Safe from the bar, the pulpit, and the throne,
> Are touched and shamed by ridicule alone.'

There are thousands upon thousands whose intelligence is not to be awakened to the perception of wrong by the force of an elenchus, unless like a wasp it carries a sting in its tail—who perceive nothing false that is not at the same time obviously absurd. To all such, Sydney Smith is an Apostle: be they as bigoted and as obtuse as they may, he breaks through the barriers of their inapprehensiveness, presents them with a vivid and well-defined idea, and leaves them without a 'word to throw to a dog.' Could the people of these realms (that singularly disintegrated aggregate of discordant sects, factions, castes, corporations, and interests, by courtesy called a nation) be redeemed from their prejudices, their hypocrisies, and their sophisms, from their plausibilities and their downright nonsense, and brought back into the sphere of a manly common sense —Sydney Smith is just the man to have helped them to the change. His wit, like the spear of Ithuriel, has startled many a concealed misleader of the people; and the false and the fraudulent, who in their panoply of speeches and pamphlets thought themselves syllogism-proof, have been pierced through and through by the lightest of his well-pointed jokes."*

The excellencies of Charles Lamb have been elegantly and generally eulogized by W. S. Landor, in a letter to Lady Blessington, from which the following extract is taken :—

"I do not think that you ever knew Charles Lamb, who is lately dead. Robinson took me to see him.

"'Once, and once only, have I seen thy face,
Elia! once only has thy tripping tongue
Run o'er my heart, yet never has been left
Impression on it stronger or more sweet.
Cordial old man! what youth was in thy years,
What wisdom in thy levity, what soul
In every utterance of thy purest breast!
Of all that ever wore man's form, 'tis thee
I first would spring to at the gate of Heaven."

* Literary Gazette.

I say *tripping* tongue, for Charles Lamb stammered and spoke hurriedly. He did not think it worth while to put on a fine new coat to come down and see me in, as poor Coleridge did, but met me as if I had been a friend of twenty years' standing; indeed, he told me I had been so, and shewed me some things I had written much longer ago, and had utterly forgotten. The world will never see again two such delightful volumes as 'The Essays of Elia;' no man living is capable of writing the worst twenty pages of them. The Continent has Zadig and Gil Blas, we have Elia and Sir Roger de Coverly."

LETTERS FROM JOSEPH JEKYLL, ESQ., TO LADY BLESSINGTON.

"Spring Gardens, July 12, 1822.

"Rogers tells me of 'Magic Lanthorns and Sketches.' You are as false as fair, and send me no copy, though perhaps you think I died last spring, and had plenty of 'noble authors' in the other world.

"Your Ladyship's, while alive, most truly,

"JOSEPH JEKYLL."

"Spring Gardens, July 22, 1822.

"A thousand thanks for the delightful little books; I return one, and cherish the other.

"Fortune is a lavish jade. She might have contented herself in bestowing beauty; but she grew extravagant, and threw talents and taste into the bargain.

"JOSEPH JEKYLL."

"Spring Gardens, January 16.

"Never did any Amphytrion of ancient or modern times furnish so delicious a plate.

"Never was sent a more beautiful memento of that scarce commodity, a bosom friend—she shall soon be thanked in person.

"J. JEKYLL."

"Spring Gardens, December 17.

"Don't think me a barbarian, because I have not fallen at

your feet; but on my return to town the gout amused me for a fortnight, and though I am quite well again, yet hardly heroic enough for a morning visit; but the good time will come.

"JOSEPH JEKYLL."

"Spring Gardens.

"You would have seen me long before now, but the horrible east wind, a fortnight ago, encored an interlude of the gout. It was not severe, but the weather is still so cold, that I cling to my household gods, though entirely recovered.

"*Vive la Vaccine.* Beauty should

"'Make assurance doubly sure,
And take a bond of Fate.'

"JOSEPH JEKYLL."

"Monday.

"Sincere thanks to my kind and good friend, for her enquiries; the gout has confined me to my chamber for a week, attacked the right arm, and, as you see, 'my right hand hath lost its cunning;' but convalescence I flatter myself has commenced, and though its progress be commonly tedious, yet I hope it will not be long before I am visible, and then, that you will come and look at, yours ever,

"JOSEPH JEKYLL."

"Spring Gardens, November 2.

"My dear friend, and a better one than yours in the 'Keepsake,' How do you do?

"Like other idiots, I went once or twice into the country, as it is called.

"And then I had an *amourette* with the gout, and was lame at morning visits.

"But I begin to hobble gracefully, and must soon come to you for what the Indians call 'a talk,' and to learn when your Beauty is to be public.

"JOSEPH JEKYLL."

"Spring Gardens, June 13.

"The horrible extinguisher, dear Lady, annihilated yesterday, and seeing no chance of survivorship, I fled, exclaiming, with the Emperor Titus—

"'I have lost a day!'

Lord Dover's Dissertation is uninteresting, and he leaves the mystery much as he found it.

"JOSEPH JEKYLL."

"Spring Gardens, Saturday.

"I forgot to send yesterday a little unpublished sketch, which you will read and return. I send it, because it alludes to the Countess Guiccioli, and your Ladyship's account of her.

"It is written by a friend of my son, Mr. Hayward, a clever young barrister and linguist, who has lately translated with success the 'Faust' of Goëthe—*en attendant*, 'The Friends,' with impatience.

"JOSEPH JEKYLL."

"Spring Gardens, Friday.

"A thousand grateful hymns to la belle and bonne Samaritaine for her repeated kindness.

"My enemy has fled, but a Parthian arrow, in his flight, left me, of course, disabled on the field, and I have now only to subdue that inveterate *indolence*, which loves to luxuriate in the repose of my chamber, 'and laugh at ease in Rabelais' easy chair.'

"But I shall soon achieve this victory, and when I have gained it, one glimpse of Lady B. will accomplish my restoration.

"D'Orsay, too, called yesterday. Pray thank him for me.

"JOSEPH JEKYLL."

"Spring Gardens, June 20.

"Don't upbraid me, my charming friend, for I am so lame, and so sensible, that I have not inflicted two morning visits any where, since I did homage in Seamore Place.

"On Friday I will pay my vows to a brace of fair Countesses, who have been immortalized by the adoration of wits and poets.

"Ever yours affectionately, JOSEPH JEKYLL."

"Spring Gardens, January 1, 1832.

"The apparent guilt, dear Lady, shall be expiated on Saturday next.

"JOSEPH JEKYLL."

"Spring Gardens, November 25.

"Thanks for indeed a Book of Beauty. Our painters, enamoured of the editress, naturally became bosom friends, and like scientific zoologists, follow Cuvier in classing belles as mammalia of the highest interest, as they have eclipsed Sir Peter Lely's busts for Charles II.

"Yours ever, J. JEKYLL."

"Spring Gardens, January 2, 1832.

"In consequence of a discovery that I could hobble, I have been inundated these three days by invitations to dinner, though I had determined and promised that my first sortie should be to Seamore Place.

"But if you will give me soup any day after Thursday next, I shall be delighted to come to you.

"JOSEPH JEKYLL."

"Romsey, September 19, 1833.

"How kind and considerate to launch a letter from the prettiest *main possible* in the world, and relieve the monotony of a chateau by 'quips and cranks' as interesting as the 'wreathed smiles' I enjoy in Seamore Place.

"Yet I have as many *agrémens* here as content me: a good library—total uncontrol, and daily gratitude to William Rufus for the drives he left me in the New Forest.

"Thanks for the royal talk—we had at the bar a learned person, whose legs and arms were so long as to afford him the title of *Frog Morgan.* In the course of an argument, he spoke of our natural enemies, the French; and Erskine, in reply, complimented him on an expression so personally appropriate.

"We breathe here an Imperial atmosphere—one Queen sailed

away, and the embryo of another reigns in the Isle of Wight, who endures royal salutes from a yacht club every half hour.

"The French Admiral, Mackau, squalled horribly at Cherbourg, when he founp himself invaded by a squadron of *Cowes.* They have swamped the pretty town of Southampton with a new *pier*, though they had Lord Ashton, an old Irish *peer*, residing there, whom they might have repaired for the purpose.

"Sydney Smith was asked what penalty the Court of Aldermen could inflict on Don—Key, for bringing them into contempt by his late escapade?

"He said, 'Melted butter with his turbot for a twelvemonth, instead of lobster sauce.'

"I was asked gravely if Quinine was invented by Doctor Quin?

"In poor Galt's Autobiography, I find a scene at your soirée between Grey and Canning—and I find in Byron's attack on Southey, great fulmination against your correspondent Landor.

"No matter who deserts London—for with such imaginative powers you are never alone—and I am sure, often by no means so solitary as you wish—though I suppose even the Bores have ceased to infest ——— House.

"I left you among thieves, as the Levite did of old the stranger, and had no hope that Bow Street would play the Samaritan.

"I am a fatal visitor to Dowager Peeresses, for while I was lunching with Lady Ellenborough, a rogue descended her area for silver forks. A toady of old Lady Cork, and [ ], whom she half maintains, complained to me of her treatment: 'I have,' she said, 'a very long chin, and the barbarous Countess often shakes me by it.'

"It seemed without remedy, as neither the paroxysm nor chin could be shortened.

"The zephyrs and landscape agree with me better than I expected. But the mind begins, to stagnate as you will suspect by these *Matinées du Chateau.* But gratitude and affection are in full bloom, and totally yours.

"JOSEPH JEKYLL."

"Spring Gardens, Wednesday, June 22.

"Don't upbraid me, for I am so lame, &c., and so sensible,

that I have not inflicted two morning visits any where, since I did homage to Seamore Place.

"On Friday I will pay my vows to a brace of fair Countesses, who have been immortalized by the adoration of wits and poets.

"JOSEPH JEKYLL."

"Spring Gardens, Thursday.

"No love lost between us. This cursed gout has vanished, but left me so lame, that though I have limped into my carriage these last two days with difficulty, I cannot yet lay the flattering unction to 'my *sole*' of a visit to my delightful friend.

"Guess my horror at discovering that, in spite of the new Anatomy Bill, they had burked your 'Beauties.' Do you know who is your dissector? Tell him I will give any sum for so charming a skeleton, or the least portion of your heart, if the whole be not already disposed of.

"JOSEPH JEKYLL."

"Spring Gardens, Nov. 7.

"I should have been at your Ladyship's feet before now, if the rascally gout had not disabled mine soon after my return to town, ten days ago. But I am convalescent already.

"Why is there no more Byron in the 'New Monthly?'

"James Smith sends me a smart epigram on the two famous gunsmiths.

"JOSEPH JEKYLL."

"Spring Gardens, Tuesday.

"I have not yet dined out, though convalescent; but there is no resisting your invitation for Sunday, pressed as it was so powerfully and kindly by D'Orsay. My son will be happy to accompany me.

"My blushes on the last 'New Monthly' have not yet vanished. The style rivals De Staël, and poor Byron seems to say from his grave—

"'After my death, I wish no other herald,
No other speaker of my living actions,

To keep mine honours from corruption,
But such an honest chronicler as Griffith.'

"The W. Gell most interesting—many thanks.

"JOSEPH JEKYLL."

"Spring Gardens, September 24.

"My delightful friend, I thought, was as inveterate a metropolitan as myself, and it petrified me to read that she was betting at Doncaster, but, as usual, '*winning golden opinions*' from all sorts of men.

"It had before puzzled me to see that the bedchamber window was closed, when I threw my eyes up from the Park,

"'My custom ever in the afternoon.'

The 'damask cheek' had deserted the pillow, and the interesting night-cap had been sacrificed to the interested handicap.

"Yesterday was unlucky, as I drive about till five. But I am very well, and very lame, and as fond of you as ever.

"JOSEPH JEKYLL."

"Spring Gardens, Monday.

"Colds, catarrhs, &c., the usual compliments of the season, in addition to my customary *lame* excuses, have prevented a morning visit, which I am too sensible to bestow on anybody but yourself.

"Your good taste, like Falstaff's wit, I find is also 'the cause of good taste in others.' You have made Jack Fuller a Mecænas of science. He has founded a Professorship of Chemistry at the Royal Institution, and struck a gold medal of himself; one of which, I have no doubt, now reposes on your beautiful bosom.

"JOSEPH JEKYLL."

"Spring Gardens, December 27, 1833.

"It is time I should give my charming friend a bulletin.

"The gout has inflicted no greater severity than imprisonment, which to a lame, lazy, literary lounger, is no very important grievance. However, as the enemy has now retreated, I must soon abandon the invaluable quietism of my chamber, and proclaim myself visible to that pack of Cossacks 'yclept morning visitors. Thrice in vain has the hippopotamus Jack Fuller bellowed at my gate.

"It refreshes me to see the 'Conversations' in a handsome octavo, which will challege a place in every library.

"If there be anything of your pen in the new 'Keepsake,' lend it me. The courtesy of Mansel Reynolds used to send it, but I prohibited the continuance of his costly present, as I was not a contributor. The enclosed pompous diploma, with its brilliant list, was sent me lately from Paris, and remains unanswered. It seems an effort to resemble our Royal Society.

"Can you or D'Orsay tell me how it has originated, or give me an outline of M. Cesar Moreau, who appears to be the principal actor?

"JOSEPH JEKYLL."

JACK FULLER.

This old London celebrity of some thirty years ago, was an eccentric humourist, of large means and dimensions, John Fuller, Esq., with the world outside his circle, but "Jack," sometimes "Old Jack," and occasionally "honest Jack Fuller," with his friends and familiars.

Good living, pleasant society, and music to match, were the enjoyments of the latter days of the original, who obtained from his kind friend Jekyll the pet name of "the Hippopotamus," for by this endearing designation he speaks of old Jack Fuller.

In the possession of a large fortune, he lived wholly for his enjoyments, for some years before his death. He was in the habit of having concerts at his house, in Devonshire Place, on Sunday evenings, generally by young amateur performers, or young persons studying vocal and instrumental music of the Academy of Music; and his musical soirées were occasionally attended by ladies, frequently by Lady Blessington.

LETTERS FROM "JACK FULLER" TO LADY BLESSINGTON.

"Devonshire Place, Jan. 6, 1832.

"Mr. Fuller presents his compliments to Lady Blessington, he dines at half after five, and never dines out, otherwise he would have had great pleasure in meeting his old friend Mr. Jekyll, who in a long life has been the source of so much pleasure and amusement to the present age."

"February 13, 1832.

"Inclosed is Mr. Hatchet's kind letter to me, who is one of the Vice-Presidents of the Parochial Schools, at Chelsea. Perhaps it would be for the best, to let him choose that school which is the easiest to be had, and for which he will lay himself under the least obligation.

"I remain sincerely yours,

"J. FULLER."

"I called this morning to thank you for the present of your portrait, and to say that if you are not going into the country, and can look in for a moment only on Sunday evening, it will be doing great service to my juvenile band, Miss Stephens' nephews and nieces, in giving them the sanction of your support and, possibly, recommendation. If the author of the poems published in the 'Gems,' is a protégé of yours, and requires separate publication for them, I will subscribe to them with much pleasure, but in any other case, I have determined to purchase no other work till it is actually finished, I have so many scraps of work laying about me.

"J. FULLER."

(No date.)

"I send you a brace of pheasants, in order to have an opportunity of enquiring after yours and your sister's health, and at the same time to assure you how much the public feel indebted to you for your continued literary labours in London during one of the finest summers ever known, for the purpose of their edification and instruction, and I have the honour to remain, with my kindest compliments to your sister, &c.

"J. FULLER."

"Devonshire Place, May 26, 1833.

"I shall have a little music here this evening, and if you and Count D'Orsay will look in between nine o'clock and ten, I shall be very happy to see you.

"The Smiths, who will be here, distinguished themselves much at a concert the other evening, at which Pasta and Farrelli sang, and I know you to be an encourager of rising genius and merit: they are nieces to Miss Stephens.

"J. FULLER."

"Rosehill, Sussex, July 25, 1833.

"I send you by the Hastings coach, the fore-quarter of the finest buck I have killed this year. No viands can possibly contribute to your own personal and mental charms, but this may be of service in increasing the conviviality of your friends, which will always give great pleasure to

"JOHN FULLER."

THE HON. W. R. SPENCER.

William Robert Spencer was born in January, 1770, in Kensington Palace. He was the youngest son of Lord Charles Spencer, and nephew of the Duke of Marlborough.

He was educated chiefly at Harrow, for some time was under the care of Dr. Parr, and completed his education at Oxford. From earliest youth he manifested an intense love of literature; some good evidences of this passion are to be found in his translations from Euripides, when he was at Harrow, only fourteen years of age.

Of his wonderfully retentive memory, he gave a proof at Oxford, by undertaking for a wager, which he won, to learn off by heart an entire newspaper. There is hardly a more remarkable or lamentable instance to be found of the prematureness of talents than that of the Hon. W. R. Spencer. He was not only in boyhood a good classical scholar, but he had a perfect knowledge of German, French, and Italian.

One of his earliest productions was a spirited translation of Burgher's "Leonora," published in 1796, a production which Walter Scott thought of very highly. He wrote a comedy in two acts, called "Urania, or the Illuminée," which was performed with success at Drury Lane Theatre, in 1802. This piece was a burlesque on German spectral literature. In 1811 he published a volume of poems, including "Leonora." For the production of those occasional epigrammatic lines which are called "Vers de Societè," he had a great facility. And to those lively pieces, the *agrémens* of his conversational talents, and his fine classical taste and literary attainments, he was indebted for his popularity in all circles, and to his winning manners and amiable accommodating disposition, for something more than mere admiration of cleverness and person, for affectionate regard and esteem. Lady Blessington hardly did him justice in a notice of him in his latter days.

The wit, the poet, the pet of English fashionable society, for nearly a quarter of a century, in 1828 is described by her as a wreck of humanity, fallen into the sere and yellow leaf, depressed in spirits, dull in conversation, addicted to unpoetical indulgences. The courtly muse, she observes, had abandoned her spoiled child. The author of the graceful poems sparkling with wit and imagery, those favourite "*Vers de Societé*," which once found a place in every boudoir, now presented a mournful spectacle of decayed powers, mental and physical, his once bright eyes glazed and lustreless, his cheeks sunken and pale, yet straining and wearying his declining powers with efforts to be facetious that were unsuccessful, forced, and ineffectual.

Mr. Spencer died in Paris, the 23rd of October, 1834. His remains were removed from Paris to Harrow, and interred in the church of that place, which he so much loved. The inscription there truly states:—

"Once a distinguished poet, a profound scholar,
A brilliant wit, and a most accomplished gentleman,
Now, alas! removed from the sight of men,
Is interred where he passed the happiest days of his life,
His early days of youth and hope,
Deeply lamented by those friends
Who knew the warmth and kindness of his heart,
And the real excellence of his nature."

LETTER FROM W. R. SPENCER, ESQ. TO LADY BLESSINGTON.

"Hotel Windsor,
"Rue Rivoli, November 5.

"My dear Lady Blessington,

"I have been ages wishing to see you; pray let me see you this evening, and allow me to present to you two very interesting persons, first cousins of poor B. North's, Mr. and Miss Poulter. He is a very agreeable person, and she a prodigy of learning and talent, and withal perfectly amiable. *You* well know that all these advantages are not incompatible with each other. Miss Poulter would say to you on that subject—'Nosce te ipsam.' I hope D'Orsay will be at home.

"Ever yours,
"Most faithfully,
"W. R. Spencer."

HENRY LUTTRELL, ESQ.

Henry Luttrell, one of the *habituès* and most favoured of the circle of the literati, wits, and bookish people of Holland House, the intimate friend of the late Lord, was the cotemporary of the celebrities of that well-known place of literary resort in the palmiest days of its intellectual society, some thirty years ago, of Rogers, Campbell, Moore, and a vast number of eminent persons, of whom very few indeed are now in existence.

To brilliant wit, ever prompt and effective in its display, a cultivated mind, a fine taste, graceful style of writing, and peculiarly pleasing and impressive conversational talents, Luttrell added much kindness of heart and urbanity of manners, amiability of disposition, and sound good sense. He delighted in society, and was the delight of it. He was ever a welcome and honoured guest at the houses he frequented.

"I know no more agreeable member of society than Mr. Luttrell," says Lady Blessington. "His conversation, like a limpid stream, flows smoothly and brightly along, revealing the depths beneath its current, now sparkling over the objects it discloses, or reflecting those by which it glides. He never talks for talking sake.... The conversation of Mr. Luttrell makes me think, while that of many others only amuses me."*

Luttrell, who was not only celebrated for his wit, but remarkable for that species of wisdom derived from a perfect knowledge of the world, acquired by extensive travel and observation, and a very intimate acquaintance with society, literature, and literary people, makes the following observation in the preface to his "Letters to Julia," (3rd ed. Lon. 1822).

"Circumstances, in this lower world of ours, though not everything, are assuredly a great deal; and have a more powerful influence on the popular estimate of character and conduct, than those who are the most lavish of praise and blame appear to suspect, or it might somewhat restrain their prodigality in both. People are too often admired and found fault with, by incompetent judges, like pictures, not on account of their real excellence, or the want of it, but from the light, good or bad, in which they happen to be placed."

Luttrell is frequently spoken of in Moore's Diary; in August, 1820, his new work, "Advice to Julia," is mentioned, as "full of well-bred facetiousness, and sparkle of the very first water." Elsewhere, Moore says he has seen a journal, kept by Luttrell while he was in Italy, which seemed to him very clever.

* The Idler in France, vol. ii. p. 116.

In the "Advice to Julia," we find some lines thus quoted and commented on :—

" When roguery cannot be kept under,
Our pious statesmen share the plunder,
And thus extracting good from evil,
Compound with God, and cheat the Devil !"

Luttrell, taking up this Hudibrastic text, thus prays in rhyme :—

" O ! that there might in England be,
A duty on Hypocrisy !
A tax on humbug, an excise
On solemn plausibilities,
A stamp on every man that canted !
No—millions more, if these were granted,
Henceforward would be raised or wanted."

The following notice of his decease appeared in the "Athenæum :"—

"Mr. Henry Luttrell—a wit among lords, and a lord among wits—died at his house at Brompton Crescent, on the 19th of December, 1851, in the 81st year of his age. He was the friend of Sydney Smith and of Mr. Rogers, and the wit who set the table in a roar at Holland House, when Whig supremacy in the patronage of letters was rather laughed at in political circles. Like many other men of reputation for happy sayings, his printed performances do little justice to the talents which he himself possessed. Yet there are wit and remarkable ease in a tripping style of versification in his 'Letters to Julia.' "*

* Athenæum, No. 1261, p. 1376.

LETTER FROM HENRY LUTTRELL, ESQ. TO LADY BLESSINGTON.

"Holland House, Thursday, June 20.

"MY DEAR LADY BLESSINGTON,

"Many thanks for your kind present, which, being absent from home, I have but just received. To be so agreeably remembered by you, is most flattering to me. I assure you, that I shall reap both pleasure and profit from the perusal of your little work: I feel so satisfied, that I shall delay my harvest for as short a time as possible.

"Your very faithful and obliged,

"HENRY LUTTRELL."

GEORGE COLMAN, ESQ.

Old George Colman *the younger* (to the end of his 74th year), terminated his facetious career in October, 1836, at his residence in Brompton Square. He was born in 1762. His father was a dramatist and a scholar, a joint proprietor and manager of the Haymarket Theatre. George the younger, who had been educated in Westminster school, in his boyhood was brought by his father into the company of Johnson, Gibbon, Goldsmith, and their most renowned associates. He was placed for some time in Christ Church, Oxford, and subsequently in King's College, Aberdeen, but his father's tastes and pursuits had more charms for him than hard studies in colleges. He began to write plays in 1781. In 1784, he made a Gretna Green marriage. His father, desirous of giving him a profession, entered him a student at Lincoln's Inn, and took chambers for him. A supply of law books that had belonged to Lord Bute was provided for him—Blackstone was particularly recommended to his attention—but George the younger had devoted all his attention to the composition of a musical comedy, called "A Turk or no Turk," which was acted in 1785. From 1786 to 1824, his career was one of incessant dramatic literary labour, of embarrassments and arduous struggles—law-suits—theatrical squabbles—and at the close of 1807, of close acquaintance with bailiffs and the King's Bench. In 1824, he was relieved from his difficulties by an appointment conferred on him by the Crown, of Licenser and Examiner of Plays, the emoluments of which were upwards of £300 a year.

The number of his comedies, farces, and musical dramas, exceed thirty. Those of his father amounted to thirty-five. He published also various facetiæ, in prose and verse—"My Nightgown and Slippers," in 1797; "Broad Grins," &c. in 1802; "Poetical Vagaries," in 1812, &c. &c.

LETTER FROM GEORGE COLMAN, ESQ. TO LADY BLESSINGTON.

"14th August, 1819.

"Dear Lady Blessington,

"I dined yesterday at General Grosvenor's, where his brother told me your Ladyship had commissioned him to say that no excuse would be admitted, if I did not attend you and Lord Blessington on Sunday, and I informed him that I should be most happy in that honour.

"Now the impression on my mind was, (I know not why), that Sunday se'nnight was the day intended.

"To have mistaken one Sunday for another, particularly while communicating with a parson, may be unpardonable in the opinion of the Church; but if to-morrow be the day intended, I must entreat your Ladyship to afford me remission for my fine of non-attendance, for to-morrow I cannot avoid dining out of town, in consequence of a promise which I am now absolutely obliged to fulfil.

"With kindest regards to Lord Blessington, I have the honour to be, dear Madam,

"Your Ladyship's faithful and obedient servant,

"G. Colman."

THEODORE HOOK.

Funny men, "diseurs des bons mots," smart sayers of good things, "fellows of wit and humour," always expected to be jocular in conversation, and rich and racy "et toujours prets," in anecdotal lore are indispensable, even in the best circles of fashionable intellectual celebrities.

"Your professed wags are treasures to this species of company," says Sir Walter Scott.

Extremes meet by no means unfrequently in such circles.

These droll people who have to "set the drawing-room in a roar," wherever they are invited, are not often remarkable for the very highest order of moral or intellectual excellence. The thing that is truly surprising in fashionable circles, is, how much of vulgar mechanism there is in the facetious performances which are produced for their intellectual entertainments; how theatrical-like is the éclat of the getting-up, and the coming-off of those amusements.

The lionizing propensity of people in fashionable and literary society, had no commendation from Sir Walter Scott.

The Russian Princess Galizani, being in the heroic vein, on the arrival of Sir Walter in Paris, sent to assure him—"Elle vouloit traverser les mers pour aller voir, Sir W. S.," &c.

"This is precious Tom-Foolery," quoth the good Sir Walter.

James Smith's account of the palmy days of "the Poet of Fashion," might serve for an illustration of those fleeting epochs of success in fashionable society, of all the tribe of humourists in high life.

"His book is successful, he's steep'd in renown,
His lyric effusions have tickled the town;
Dukes, dowagers, dandies, are eager to trace
The fountain of verse in the verse-maker's face;

While, proud as Apollo, with Peers *tête-à-tête*,
From Monday till Saturday dining off plate,
His heart full of hope, and his head full of gain,
The Poet of Fashion dines out in Park Lane.

Enroll'd in the tribe who subsist by their wits,
Remember'd by starts, and forgotten by fits,
Now artists and actors the bardling engage,
To squib in the journals, and write for the stage."

The author of "Sayings and Doings," "The Parson's Daughter," "The Widow and the Marquis," "Gilbert Gurney," "Gurney Married," "Maxwell," "Jack Brag," "All in the Wrong," "Fathers and Sons," "Precepts and Practice," "Peregrine Bunce," "Horace Vernon," &c., whose rich humour, ready wit, singular talent for repartee, and facility of improvising verse, are so well known, occasionally frequented Gore House. Like many fellows of "most excellent fancy," "wont to set the table in a roar," Hook—the humourist, all mirth and jocularity abroad—at home was subject to violent revulsion of feelings, to gusts of sadness, and fits of dejection of spirits, which temporary excitement, produced by stimulants, did not much tend to remedy or remove. The results of his disordered and embarrassed circumstances became too manifest to his private friends, in impaired energies of mind and body, in his broken health, and depressed spirits, and furnished a melancholy contrast with the public exhibition of convivial qualities that rendered him a welcome guest at all tables.

Theodore Hook was the son of a celebrated organist and musical composer. He was born in 1788. In 1809, he made his appearance at Roll's theatre. He attended public dinners, improvising and reciting for a short time, and made his way eventually into the highest circles, where his wit and humour were greatly admired. He commenced writing for his bread before he was of age. His first work was "The Man of Sorrow." In 1812, the lucrative situation of the Treasurership of the Mauritius was given to him, an office of nearly £2000 a year, for which he was wholly unsuited. His unfitness was soon discovered by a large deficit in his accounts; this led to the loss of his situation, and to heavy claims of government, and large liabilities which continued hanging over him during his life. Hook, on his return to England, found a good market for his satirical talents; he sold them to his Royal Highness the Prince Regent, and gave the first value for the Prince's patronage, in a publication entitled "Tentamen," against the Queen, espousing the cause of his patron Prince against his Royal Highness's "greatest enemy," the Queen.

Various publications of Hook's, advocating high Tory politics, appeared, but seem to have failed for his support. Again he took to the stage. In 1820, "The John Bull" was established. He became connected with it, and for many years he derived a clear income of £2000 a year from it. This paper was set up specially to abuse the Queen's friends, against "*The Brandenburg House Party*."

In 1824, "Sayings and Doings" were published: the several series produced altogether about £2000. "The Ramsbottom Letters" attracted universal attention.

"Maxwell" appeared in 1830. "Gurney," and the sequel to it, had a very large sale. "Jack Brag" did not succeed. "Births, Marriages, and Deaths," in 1839, was likewise unsuccessful. "Peregrine Bunce" was not more popular. He owned one-half of "The John Bull," but sold his moiety for £4000, about 1830.

His embarrassments from this period went on from bad to worse—sometimes he was in actual want. The 13th August, 1841, he died at Fulham. He ended his miserable career, warred to death by creditors, attorneys, and bailiffs.

After his death, all his effects were seized by the government for his Mauritius debt, and sold by auction. They realized the large sum of £2500.

He left five children. A sum of £3000 was subscribed for his family—few of his noble friends contributed; they refused on the grounds of his extravagance, &c.; their protest against it was coincident with their interests.

FROM THEODORE HOOK.

"Dear Madam,

"Athenæum, Monday.

"I was on the point of writing to Mrs. Fairlie, when I received your Ladyship's note, and therefore, in order to save time, will say *here* what I was about to say to her.

"It is neither unwillingness nor occupation (for all other business should be laid aside for that) which has hindered me from doing the lines, but absolute want of power to do them. I have tried over and over again, and can make nothing fit to be published.

"This is the plain, real truth, and I never regretted my own stupidity more earnestly; perhaps your Ladyship will have the goodness to say this, and assure Mrs. Fairlie how happy I shall be to be of use in any other way to her publication, to which I wish all manner of success.

"Believe me to remain,
"Dear Madam,
"Your Ladyship's faithful Servant,
"Theodore Hook."

"P.S. I have not the engraving in town, but it shall be sent to Gore House on Wednesday."

JAMES SMITH.

In the calendar of Saints, it has been said, there is no lawyer to be found. In the Martyrology there are, no doubt, a vast number of their clients; and probably if we turn to Lactantius, we shall find in the long list of persecutors of the church, in its richest days, many legal gentlemen, and very eminent literati.

With respect to the category of poets, very many lawyers and jurists, and what is more singular, London solicitors, nay, even conveyancers' clerks, are to be found among the inditers of odes, lyrics, satires, and sentimental pieces, and miscellaneous writings.

James Smith was a London solicitor.

Procter, alias Barry Cornwall, was a London solicitor.

Henry Neele, the author of various "Poems, dramatic and miscellaneous;" the editor of "Friendship's Offering," the author of "The Romance of History," was a solicitor.

Sharon Turner, the Anglo-Saxon historian, who not only wrote, but published poems, was, in his early days, a London solicitor.

Among barristers, Blackstone, Sir John Davis, and Sir William Jones, all flirted with the muse. Sir Walter Scott was a clerk of the Court of Session, when he wooed and became wedded to the divinity.

James and Horace Smith were the sons of Robert Smith, an eminent solicitor, who held for many years the office of solicitor to the Ordnance. This gentleman was a member of the Royal and Antiquarian Societies, "had an occasional dalliance with the muse," and was one of those legal literati ever and anon—

"Who pen a stanza, when they should engross;
Compose by stealth, and blush to find themselves in print."

His eldest son, James, thus named after his maternal grandfather, James Boyle French, a wealthy London merchant, was born in that city, in 1775. He was in early life placed at a school of some celebrity at Chigwell, in Essex, and there displayed considerable smartness, aptness to learn, and a very pranksome disposition.

On his removal from school, he was articled to his father—subsequently taken into partnership, and eventually he succeeded his father in business, and his appointment of solicitor to the Ordnance.

In 1801, he took a leading part in private theatricals, got up on a grand scale, by a society called the Pic-Nic Club, established chiefly by Colonel Henry Greville, at the Old Concert Rooms, in Tottenham Street. The Pic-Nic Society was abused by the press. Col. Greville established a weekly Pic-Nic paper for its defence, and his coadjutors were the two Smiths, Mr. Cumberland, Sir James Bland Burgess, Mr. Croker, Mr. J. C. Herries, and some others. The editor, Mr. Combe, a very eccentric person, of bookish habits, was the only salaried person connected with it. He resided in the rules of the King's Bench, and for his convenience the weekly meetings, at Hatchard's, were always held after dusk. "The Pic-Nic" paper merged into the "Cabinet;" and, like all merging of unsuccessful periodicals into others differently named, the change in the case of the "Pic-Nic" was only a verging to dissolution, which event took place in July, 1803.

James Smith manifested, in his earliest writings, a decided tendency to parody and burlesque. He and his brother wrote many of the prefaces to a new edition of "Bell's British Theatre," published under the sanction of Cumberland's name.

From 1807 to 1810, the Smiths contributed to "The Monthly Mirror," in which periodical originally appeared, a little later, the poetical imitations, entitled, "Horace in London." "The Rejected Addresses," by the brothers, appeared in 1812—one of the luckiest hits in literature. "Judicial Anticipation, or Candidates for the new Judgeship," in 8vo. 1812; "Horace in London," in a separate form of publication in 8vo. 1813. James Smith was the author of "First Impressions," a comedy; "The Runaway, a novel," in 4 vols. 12mo. "Trevanion, or Matrimonial Errors," 4 vols. 12mo.

The authors of "the Rejected Addresses" have been gathered to their fathers some years. James died first. His brother Horace, whom I had the pleasure of knowing, resided in Brighton for many years before his death. The Smiths possessed the same description of talents; they both were humourists, ready witted, quick of perception, observant of character, prone *à envisager* every subject on the ridiculous side, tolerably acquainted with the classics, and intimately so with genteel society; they wrote verses with facility, they composed *jeux-d'esprit* for literary and fashionable conversazione, they read up ancient *ana* and *facetiæ,* of various times and climes, for dinner parties; they were the soul of London society twenty years ago. Horace was not only a man of wit, but a man of wealth. He dabbled in the stocks in the morning, and dallied with the muses in the evening. Tom Campbell used to say of him—" Horace's odes were inspired by a divinity, who dwelt in Bull Alley. His addresses to her never were rejected. She winked at his flirtations with the nine young women of Helicon." James Smith was a man of versatile talents, with a remarkable vivacity of mind and manner, quick in seizing ludicrous aspects of persons and things, excellent at repartee, but a little too fond in society of engrossing conversation, and, in all companies, of bringing in his old jokes and comic songs, in season and out of season.

Lady Blessington observed of James Smith, that "had he not been a man of wit, he would have achieved a much higher reputation." He contented himself with the fame of "a fellow of excellent humour," which procured for him "a welcome reception wherever he went, and a distinguished position in society."

He contributed largely to Charles Mathews' Entertainments; his "clever nonsense" surpassed all other nonsense in cleverness. The merry conceits were more merry, and less conceited, than the quips and cranks of other professed jokers.

He was a man of singularly fascinating manners, excellent temper, and a cheerful, amiable disposition, with a comely aspect, and a dignified and manly carriage and deportment.

In the notice of James Smith, written by his brother Horace, prefixed to his "Memoirs, Letters, and Comic Miscellanies, in Prose and Verse," published in 1840, to which I am indebted for some of the information I have given, it is observed:—

"In the wide circle of his London acquaintances, one of the houses at which he most delighted to visit was that of Lady Blessington, whose conversational powers he highly admired, and to whose 'Book of Beauty' he became a contributor. To this lady he was in the habit of sending occasional epigrams, and complimentary or punning notes." . . . . "He liked to mingle with persons of celebrity, and at these houses his wish was seldom ungratified. Among his personal friends, he had the highest regard for Count D'Orsay, not only adducing him as a specimen of a perfect gentleman, but often declaring that, in the delightful union of gaiety and good sense, he was absolutely unrivalled."*

For some years before his death, he suffered a great deal from gout; he became a cripple; but while hobbling on his crutches, or wheeled about in his Bath chair, he retained an almost youthful buoyancy of mind, referring with glee to the merry meetings of former times, indulging in his pleasant modes of jest and anecdote, or singing with his nieces from morning to night."

He died on the 24th of December, 1839, in his house in Craven Street, as he had lived, a merry bachelor, "with all the calmness of a philosopher," we are told; but of what school we are left in ignorance. Peace, however, to the ashes of James Smith, which are deposited in the vaults of St. Martin's Church.

* Memoirs of J. Smith, vol. i. p. 50.

Mr. Horace Smith died at Tunbridge, of disease of the heart, the 12th of June, 1849, aged seventy. His principal works of fiction were, " Brambletye House," " The Tor Hill," " Zillah," " Jane Lomax," and " Adam Brown."

Any person who has a remembrance of the scenes in Seamore Place, when James Smith, Count D'Orsay, and Dr. Quin were the chief actors, and poor Monsieur Julien, Le Jeune de Paris, the Secretary, in the early days of the Revolution, of Robespierre, was an unconscious performer in those exceedingly comic exhibitions, which took place for the entertainment of Lady Blessington and her guests, may appreciate some observations of a very distinguished literary man, in a letter to Lady Blessington, in relation to D'Orsay's tact in drawing out *les petites ridicules* of peculiar people in society.

At a large assemblage of celebrities, including Dickens and Forster, at Gore House, on one occasion, there was a remarkable display of D'Orsay's peculiar ingenuity and successful tact in drawing out the oddities or absurdities of eccentric or ridiculous personages—mystifying them with a grave aspect, and imposing on their vanity by apparently accidental references of a gratulatory description to some favourite hobby or exploit, exaggerated merit or importance of the individual to be made sport of for the Philistines of the fashionable circle; which exhibition is thus noticed by one of the parties present, in a letter to Lady Blessington, dated April 13, 1848.

" Count D'Orsay may well speak of an evening being a happy one, to whose happiness he contributed so largely. It would be absurd, if one did not know it to be true, to hear D—— talk as he has done ever since of Count D'Orsay's power of drawing out always the best elements around him, and of miraculously putting out the worst. Certainly I never saw it so marvellously exhibited as on the night in question. I shall think of him hereafter unceasingly, with the two guests that sat on either side of him that night."

On an occasion similar to the one referred to, the scene of which, however, was Seamore Place, among a large evening circle at Lady Blessington's, there were present James Smith, Monsieur Julien, and Dr. Quin.

Julien scarcely ever presented himself at Lady Blessington's, that he was not called on to recite a dolorous poem, to which I have referred elsewhere, entitled, " Mes Chagrins Politiques;" and poor Julien invariably considered himself, while thus compelled to recite his public sorrows, necessitated to weep and groan in a very dismal manner. There was one part of the poem, towards the conclusion, descriptive of his unsuccessful pursuit of happiness throughout his early revolutionary career,—intended to be very pathetic, but which appeared to his audience to be ludicrously absurd,—wherein he was supposed to be chasing the capricious fugitive, happiness, in all directions; and these words were frequently and very vehemently repeated:

" Le bonheur! le voila!
Ici! Ici! La! La!
En haut, en bas en bas!"

At this particularly moving part of the *Chagrins*, Dr. Quin, a person of remarkably juvenile appearance for his years, had entered the salon; the venerable figure of James Smith, with his fine bald forehead, and his crutch stick in his hand, was to be observed on one side of Julien, and the noble one of D'Orsay on the other. Julien had no sooner concluded, with the usual *applaudissimens*, than D'Orsay whispered something in the ear of Julien, pointing alternately to Quin and Smith. Julien, greatly moved, repeated the words aloud, " Ah que c'est touchant! Ah mon Dieu! Cet tendre amour filial comme c'est beau! comme c'est touchant!" Here D'Orsay, approaching Quin, and pointing to James Smith, exclaimed, " Allez mon ami embrasez votre père! embrasez le, mon pauvre enfant!" Smith held out his arms—Quin looked very much amazed. D'Orsay approached him nearer, and in a *sotto voce* uttered some words, which were a kind of jocular formula he frequently used in addressing the Doctor,—" Ah ce sacre Quin ! Imbecille ! Ah quil est bete !" and then, sufficiently loud to be heard by Julien, " C'est toujours comma ça, toujours comme ça ce, pauvre garçon—avant le monde il a honte d'embrasser son père." Quin needed no further intimation of D'Orsay's design ; he sprang from his chair, made a desperate rush at Smith, and nearly capsized the poor old gouty man, in the violence of his filial transports, and then, while they were locked in each other's arms, tender exclamations were heard, frequently repeated—" Oh fortunate meeting ! oh happy reconciliation ! oh fond father ! oh affectionate son! And all this time D'Orsay was standing before them, overcome with apparent emotion, smiling blandly ; while Julien, with his handkerchief to his eyes, kept gulping and sobbing, and crying out — "Ah mon dieu, que c'est touchant ! pauvre jeune homme ! pauvre père !"

This was one of the latest appearances and performances of James Smith in Seamore Place, and a very memorable one it was.

LETTERS FROM JAMES SMITH TO LADY BLESSINGTON.

" 27, Craven Street, Thursday, 14th February.

" Dear Lady Blessington,

" I write to return you my thanks for your obliging personal enquiries after my health, and I much regret that I was absent when you favoured me by a visit. I had gone to the Union Club, on a ballot ; all the candidates, by a stretch of good humour very rare in these degenerate days, were admitted. It was observed, that the College of Physicians made but a sorry sight (externally), compared with its neighbour, our newly-painted club. 'Oh !' quoth a wag, 'the reason is obvious—they have painted theirs in distemper.'

" General Phipps called on me last Tuesday, and told me the following. Horace Smith, walking with a friend at Brighton, the latter pointed out to the former the following inscription over a public-house, 'Good *Bear* sold here,' commenting, at the same time, on the bad spelling. 'Phoo!' replied Horace, 'he ought to know best—it's his own *Bruin*.' And now for my last.

"You ask me why *Ponte-fract* borough could sully
Her fame by returning to Parliament Gully?
The ethnological cause I suppose is,
The breaking the *bridges* of so many noses.

"I have had an inflammation in my leg, which, however, Bransby Cooper has allayed. I mean that this limb, aided by its sound fellow, shall soon convey me to Seamore Place.

"Your Ladyship's faithful and devoted,

"JAMES SMITH."

"Craven Street, 5th April.

"DEAR LADY BLESSINGTON,

"Please to send me the portrait. My hand is daily improving, and I should like to have time to study the subject. I have not yet seen the 'New Monthly.' Has any scribbler, as Martial in London, animadverted upon your 'Conversations with Lord Byron?' The newspapers tell us that your 'new carriage is very highly varnished.' This, I presume, means your wheeled carriage. The merit of your *personal* carriage has always been, to my mind, its absence from all varnish. The question requires that a jury should be im-*panelled*.

"JAMES SMITH."

A COLLOQUY OF THE SUN AND MOON, BY JAMES SMITH, ESQ.

"Dear Brother, quit with me the Sky,
(Thus spoke the Queen of Night),
And radiant walk the Earth, while I
Dispense my milder light.

On Malta's rock I'll take my stand,
To calm the seamen's fears;
And you shall brilliantly command,
O'er barbarous Algiers.

Each godhead straight on Earth alights,
With such a potent blaze,
That Malta long was ruled by *Nights*,
And Algiers long by *Days*."

"27, Craven Street,
"Wednesday, 15th February.

"Many thanks for your message. I regret to learn that you have been unwell. I too am a sufferer from gout in my ancle and knee, which has confined me at home since yesterday.

"I have just seen a plan of the projected Richmond railroad, and find that it passes through your garden and the Count's. Tom Moore says, 'they may rail at this life;' and Shylock talks of railing a seal off a bond: but to rail away half a garden is to imitate the Dragon of Wantley:

"'Houses and churches
Were to him geese and turkeys.'

"I am told Lord L——— has returned from Paris with a model of a wig. Have you seen him?

"B——— told Poole that he meant to call his new magazine 'The Wit's Miscellany;' but that, thinking the title too ambitious, he altered it to 'B———'s Miscellany.' 'Was not that going from one extreme to another?' enquired Poole. Jerdan has withdrawn from the Garrick Club, because the Committee found fault with his noticing in his paper a dinner given to Charles Kemble. Considering the object, and the place of meeting (the Albion Tavern), I do not think it was much of a secret. General Phipps came up from Brighton to canvass for his nephew, Augustus, last Monday, at the Athenæum, who got in, notwithstanding. There is a waiter at Graham's, whose sole business it is to pare the thumb nails of the members. This is paring off without going to St. Stephen's. I have no more news.

"James Smith."

NOTICE TO CORRESPONDENTS.

"30 April, 1836.

"You who erst, in festive legions,
Sought in *May Fair*, *Seamore* Place,
Henceforth in more westward regions
Seek its ornament and grace.

Would you *see more* taste and splendour,
Mark the notice I rehearse—
Now at Kensington attend her—
'Farther on, you *may fare* worse.'

"J. S."

"27, Craven Street,
"Friday, 19th June, 1835.

"When you next see your friend, Mr. Willis, have the goodness to accost him as follows:

"In England Rivers all are Males,—
(For instance, Father Thames),
Whoever in Columbia sails,
Finds there *Mamselles* or Dames.

Yes, there the softer sex presides,
Aquatic, I assure ye:
And Mrs. Sippy rolls her tides,
Responsive to Miss Souri.

"Your Ladyship's
"Faithful and devoted servant,
"JAMES SMITH."

"27, Craven Street,
"Wednesday, 7th February, 1838.

"Many thanks for your kind enquiries. I have been confined to the house by gout and rheumatism for a month. My first visit abroad shall be to Gore House. How are you in health? The latest news with me is a letter from the widow of George Colman (late Mrs. Gibbs); they are about to put up a tablet in Kensington Church, and have asked me for an epitaph. I have sent her the following:

"Colman, the Drama's lord, the Muses' pride,
Whose works now waken woe, now joy impart,
Humour with pathos, wit with sense allied,
A playful fancy, and a feeling heart;
His task accomplish'd, and his circuit run,
Here finds at last his monumental bed.
Take then, departed shade, this lay from one
Who loved thee living, and laments thee dead.

"Sincerely yours,

"James Smith."

LINES OF JAMES SMITH,

ON MRS. GRAHAM IN THE COURT OF ALDERMEN.

INCLOSED IN A LETTER TO LADY BLESSINGTON.

"She fell on a slope land,
Said Alderman Copeland.
That Duke is a man sly,*
Said Alderman Ansley.
He looks with a queer eye,
Said Alderman Pirie.
He tumbled out drolly,
Said Alderman Scholey.
Leaving her in the lurch,
Said Alderman Birch.
To get out as she could,
Said Alderman Wood.
Without leave or with,
Said Alderman Smith.
'Twas funny fakins,
Said Alderman Atkins.
The heat made it warp,
Said Alderman Thorp.
She could not away get,
Said Alderman Heygate.
I felt for her then,
Said Alderman Ven-
Ables. Soon she came down,
Said Alderman Brown.

* The Duke of Brunswick, the companion of the æronaut.

What baldness that Duke has,
  Said Alderman Lucas.
From air kept and son,
  Said Alderman Thompson.
Terra firma for me,
  Said Alderman Key.
I'll not mount in Aur-*ie*,*
  Said Alderman Laurie.
I agree with you there, brother,
  Said Alderman Farebrother.
I would not five inches stir,
  Said Alderman Winchester.
Nor I, sir, I tell ye,
  Said Alderman Kelly.
She tumbled a sow on,
  Said Alderman Cowan.
I saw it the hills on,
  Said Alderman Wilson.
You're talking too harsh all,
  Said Alderman Marshall.
Your tone will alarm her,
  Said Alderman Harmer.
Then hush, don't affront her,
  Said Alderman Hunter.

"8th Sept. 1836. J. S."

"18, Austin Friars, Thursday morning.

"It will give me great pleasure to join your party at the Adelphi Theatre this evening, provided I can shake off a stiff neck, which I obtained by riding yesterday in a Paddington omnibus. The 'air' proceeded from a quarter uncongenial to singers, namely, from the back of the head, in lieu of the inside of the throat. I, as a melodist, ought to have known that Horace long ago warned the Sons of Song from venturing in such vehicles—'*Omnibus* hoc vitium est *Cantoribus*.'

"James Smith.

* Aldermanic Latin, for the English word air.

ALPHABETICAL ANSWER,

FROM J. S. TO LADY B.

"8th January, 1836.

"Dear Lady B.,
'Twixt you and me,
The difference all may tell.
Both canvass gain,
From artists twain,
Whose names begin with L.

But Locks, I vow,
Adorn your brow,
By Beauty's judges prized ;
While bare to view,
And void of Q.,
How bald appears my Y. Z.!

The River D.
Runs to the C.,
Expansive to the view:
Thus led by grace
To Seamore Place,
I always follows *U.*

Your style's so terse,
In prose and verse,
No critic sting can trouble you:
'Twould take a score
Of pens and more,
In grace of style to W.

As final Grants,
Four Consonants,
Fast dropping from my pen see.
To nature's part,
(Conjoined with art),
U. O. your X. L. N. C.!

"J. S."

"27, Craven Street,
"Monday, September 13th, 1836.

"Mrs. Torre Holme (whom we last night likened to Minerva) has a daughter, Emily, now at Ramsgate, but soon to return to Shere. This premised, read the following:

"EMILY, A MYTHOLOGICAL SONNET.

Round Thanet's cliff disputing Naiads twine;
Huge Triton on the billow sails his shell,
And yellow Ceres, on that face of thine
Gazing in fondness, sighs a sad farewell,
Oblivious of her long-lost Proserpine.
  Nymphs elastic, heel and eye of fire,
Hygeia, Esculapius' daughter, now
Invokes for thee her death-averting sire,
And pours the cup of gladness on thy brow.
But hark, maternal love from inland shire,
Jove's favourite daughter chides thy longer stay:
A goddess calls thee, hearken and obey.
Severe Minerva bids thee halt not here,
And woos thee homeward to the shades of Shere.

"I have sent a copy of this to the goddess, apprizing her of her installation.

"Your faithful and devoted,
"JAMES SMITH."

"Saturday (P. M. 1836).

"I send you a report.

"REX *v.* WARD.

"'This was an indictment for projecting a pier into the River Medina, at Cowes.'—*Morning Herald.*

"Debrett the wondrous fact allows,
You'll find it printed in his book:
The *Pier* that stemm'd the tide at Cows,
Could only be *Lord Bull in brook.*
"J. S."

"27, Craven Street,
"Monday, 26th September, 1836.

"I have accidentally alighted upon the foundation of Madame de Staël's 'Corinne,' Dodsley's Annual Register, 1776, Chronicle, p. 176, 31st August.—'They have a custom at Rome, of solemnly crowning extraordinary poetical genius in the Capitol: nor is the honour confined to men. Porfetti and Petrarch were the last Italian poets who obtained it. This day it was conferred on a young lady of the name of Morelli Fernandez, called *Corilla* Olimpia, by the Academy of the Arcades, who had long gained the admiration of Italy by her extempore verse on any subject proposed. She was conducted to the Capitol by the Contessas Cardelli, Dandini, and Ginessi. The Chevalier Jean Paul de Cinque placed the laurel upon her head,' &c.

"I wish Madame de Staël had retained the original name. Corinne is debased (at least to English ears) by Swift's Corinna, Pride of Dunbar, not to mention Curll's Corinna.

"JAMES SMITH."

EPIGRAM TO COMTE D'ORSAY.

"September 27, 1837.

"From Mount Street, Phipps to distant Venice hies,
And breathes his last sigh on the Bridge of Sighs.

"J. S."

FROM HORACE SMITH TO LADY BLESSINGTON.

"Tunbridge Wells, 27 June, 1843.

"DEAR MADAM,

"Your Ladyship's letter has been forwarded to me at this place, and I deeply regret to learn that you have been such a sufferer lately, both from ill health and the more trying privation of relations so dear to you; most sincerely do I hope that your early convalescence, and the healing influence of time, will completely restore your usual spirits.

"Never having had the honour of seeing Lady Arthur Lennox, I fear that I could hardly do her justice in attempting to illustrate her portrait; and it would be a bad compliment to trust to my imagination for lines that cannot be other than encomiastic.

"Not having my papers with me here, I have nothing to offer as a substitute, so I have scribbled a few lines of the prescribed shortness, which, if you think them worthy insertion in your annual, are very much at your Ladyship's service.

"I have the honour to remain,
"Yours very faithfully,
"HORATIO SMITH."

"Youth, beauty, love, delight,
All blessings bright and dear;
Like shooting-stars by night,
Flash, fall, and disappear.

While cynics doubt their worth,
Because they're born to die;
The wiser sons of earth
Will snatch them ere they fly.

Though mingled with alloy,
We throw not gold away;
Then why reject the joy
That's blended with decay?
"H. S."

MONIMIA,

BY ONE OF THE AUTHORS OF "REJECTED ADDRESSES."

TO LADY BLESSINGTON.

[No date.]

"A sorrow has shadow'd thy heart,
A thorn in that bosom is set;
Monimia that sorrow impart,
To speak is, in time, to forget.
When sympathy soothes and it cheers,
The wounds of affliction she cures;
How freely a man of my years,
May talk with a woman of yours!

I see that I truly have scann'd,
  The cause of thy sad discontent;
That cheek that reclines on thy hand,
  That dark eye on vacancy bent:
Those lips in mute silence compress'd,
  Those tresses dishevell'd that rove,
All speak of a feeling distress'd,
  And tell me that feeling is Love.

Alas! that Adversity's storms
  Thy happy horizon should cloud!
Envelope that noblest of forms,
  That finest of faces enshroud.
To hear thee thy sorrow relate,
  My long dormant feelings hath wrung;
I heed not the rich and the great,
  But I feel for the lovely and young.

All tokens of memory shun,
  Those jewels, so tastefully set,
Seem but to remind you of one,
  Whom now 'tis your task to forget.
In frightful effulgence they gleam,
  No longer imparting a grace;
Like the vest of Alcides, they seem
  To poison the form they embrace.

You smile at expressions like these,
  At wisdom so threadbare and poor:
And ask, since she sees the disease,
  If wisdom can point out a cure.
Ah no! such a cure is unknown;
  A theme too well known I pursue:
I once had a heart like your own—
  I once was a Lover, like you.

With an eye, while I write, filled with tears,
  At the long-faded passion of youth;
I look thro' a vista of years,
  And scarcely believe it a truth.

Yet, tho' Love's enchantment I miss,
  Mild Reason her solace has lent:
I shrink from the Palace of Bliss,
  To thrive in the Vale ot Content."

CHAPTER VIII.

CAPTAIN MARRYATT, R.N., C.B., AND CHEVALIER OF THE LEGION OF HONOUR, F.R.S. AND F.L.S.

CAPTAIN MARRYATT, born in London, in 1792, was descended from one of the French refugees, who settled in England after the revocation of the edict of Nantes. He was the second son of Joseph Marryatt, Esq., an eminent West India merchant; Chairman of Lloyd's, and M.P. for Sandwich. "A little Latin and less Greek," a good deal of mathematics, and some "polite literature," more than sufficed for him when he entered the navy, in 1806, as a first-class boy, on board the Imperieuse. For more than a quarter of a century, Marryatt followed his profession, braved all its perils, discharged all its duties, risked his own life repeatedly to save the lives of others; attained honours and preferments, and, in 1830, set his foot on shore for good and all—in every respect—a first-class man.

Captain Marryatt turned his leisure to a very profitable literary account. He may be said to have created a new kind of novel literature, illustrative of naval life. And in that line, though followed and imitated by many, he has been equalled by none. The excellence of his productions, and the great success they met with, considering the large number of them, are remarkable.*

* "Frank Mildmay," "Letters in Canada," "Masterman Ready," "Children of the New Forest," "Newton Forster," "King's Own,"

The "Metropolitan Magazine" was ably edited by Captain Marryatt for some years. He was a contributor to several other periodicals, and a writer, in reviews of a graver character, of articles of great merit, on subjects relating to his profession. In politics he was strongly Conservative; but however strongly he wrote against Whigs and Whiggery, in his friendships he knew no difference between Whigs and Tories, no more than he did of distinction in his dealings with men of different religions. It was not in his nature to be deliberately otherwise than just and generous towards all men with whom he came in contact, whom he believed to be honest. But when he had to do with political opponents on paper, whom he did not know personally, and allowed himself to be persuaded by others of his party, who were not sincere and upright, he opened on them all his guns, and raked the enemy fore and aft, very desperately exasperated during the engagement, and often surprised, when it was over, at the extraordinary vehemence of his anger.

Captain Marryatt was one of Lady Blessington's most intimate friends and especial favourites. "Full of talent, originality, and humour," says Lady B., "he is an accurate observer of life—nothing escapes him. Yet there is no bitterness in his satire, and no exaggeration in his comic vein. I have known Captain Marryatt many years, and liked him from the first."* Miss M—— might not have agreed with Lady Blessington's opinion with respect to the character of the satire.

"Peter Simple," "Jacob Faithful," "Pasha of many Tales," "Japhet in search of a Father," "Mr. Midshipman Easy," "Snarley-Yow, or the Dog Fiend;" "The Phantom Ship," "Poor Jack," "Joseph Rushbrook," "Percival Keene," "Privateersman," "Olla Podrida," "Little Savage," "Valerie," "The Mission," "Diary in America," "Narrative of Travels of Monsieur Violet," "Borneo," &c. &c. &c.

* Idler in France, vol. ii. p. 86.

One of Lady Blessington's correspondents, the first and most distinguished of living literati, indulged in some quaint and jocular observations on one of Marryatt's sea-life novels, and the effects on a landsman of a long voyage of perusal over three volumes of salt-water subjects, in which the author was continually splashing in grand style.

"I have been reading 'Peter Simple.' It is very good. But one is never on land for a moment. I feel *grogged* and *junked* after it."

Nevertheless the writer eulogized the talents and the worth of the author.

The surest and best test of moral worth and social excellence, is to be found in the appreciation of a man's character by his own people in the immediate precincts of his own hearth and household, in the small circle of friends and relatives—those nearest and dearest to him.

By that test, if Marryatt be judged, the fine, manly, and kindly qualities of the man will be found, in no respect, inferior to those intellectual ones of the author, which are now generally admitted.

Captain Marryatt died at his residence, Langham, in Norfolk, August 2, 1848, in his fifty-sixth year.

FROM CAPTAIN MARRYATT.

"Spa, June 17, 1836.

"MY DEAR LADY BLESSINGTON,

"I have received all your packets of letters, and am very much obliged to you, not only for the letters, but also for thinking about me when I am so far out of the way, which you know is not very usual in this world, and therefore particularly flattering to me. As you will perceive, I am now at Spa, after a month's sojourn at Brussels. Spa is a very beautiful and a very cheap place, but it is deserted, and it is said that there will be no season this year. There are only two or three English families here, and they are all *cocktails*, as sporting men would say.

"We are, therefore, quite alone, which pleases me. I was tired of bustle and noise, and excitement, and here there is room for meditation e'en to madness, as Calista says, although I do not intend to carry my thoughts quite so far. I write very little; just enough to amuse me, and make memorandums, and think. In the morning I learn German, which I have resolved to conquer, although at forty, one's memory is not quite so amenable as it ought to be. At all events, I have no master, so if the time is thrown away, the money will be saved.

"I believe you sometimes look at 'the Metropolitan;' if so, you will observe, that I have commenced my *Diary of a Blasé*, in the last month; they say at home that it is very good light Magazine stuff, and is liked. I mean, however, that it shall not all be *quite nonsense*. I hope the 'Book of Beauty' goes on well. I know that you, and Mrs. Norton, and I, are the three looked up to, to provide for the public taste.

"Stanfield, I understand, is getting on very well indeed with the drawings for my History. I think, with respect to yours, I would next year make some alteration. Instead of having the letter-press in detached pieces, I would weave them together, much in the same way as the 'Tales of Boccacio;' some very slight link would do, and it should be conversational. It is astonishing how much a little connection of that kind gives an interest and a reality to a work. In the 'Tales of the Pasha,' a great part of the interest is in the conversations between the Pasha and those about him, and the stories become by it framed like pictures. In any work whatever, there should never be a full stop. It appears to me there will be a new era in Annuals, and that, in future, they will become more library works, and not so ephemeral as their present title indicates; but it will first be necessary that the publishers of them discover their own interest to be in making them what they ought to be, and going to the necessary expense.

"Of course I do see the English papers, and I am very much disgusted. Nothing but duels and blackguardism. Surely we are extremely altered by this reform. Our House of Lords was the beau ideal of all that was aristocratical and elegant. Now we have language that would disgrace the hustings. In the House of Commons it is the same, or even worse. The gentleman's repartee, the quiet sarcasm, the playful hit, where are they? all gone; and, in exchange for them, we have—*you lie*, and *you lie*. This is very bad, and it appears to me, strongly smacking of revolution; for if the language of the lower classes is to take the precedence, will not they also soon do the same? I am becoming more Conservative every day; I cannot help it: I feel it a duty as a lover of my country. I only hope that others feel the same, and that Peel will soon be again where he ought to be. I don't know what your politics are, but all women are Tories in their hearts, or perhaps Conservatives is a better word, as it expresses not only their opinions, but their feelings.

"I never thought that I should feel a pleasure in idleness; but I do now. I had done too much, and I required repose, *or rather repose to some portions of my brain.* I am idle here to my heart's content, and each day is but the precursor of its second. I am like a horse, which has been worked too hard, turned out to grass, and I hope I shall come out again as fresh as a two-year old. I walk about and pick early flowers with the children, sit on a bench in the beautiful *allées vertes* which we have here, smoke my cigar, and meditate till long after the moon is in the zenith. Then I lie on the sofa and read French novels, or I gossip with any one I can pick up in the streets. Besides which, I wear out my old clothes; and there is a great pleasure in having a coat on which gives you no anxiety. I expect that by October I shall be all right again.

"I am afraid this will be a very uninteresting letter; but what can you expect from one who is living the life of a hermit, and who never even takes the trouble to wind up his watch; who takes no heed of time, and feels an interest in the price of strawberries and green peas, because the children are very fond of them? I believe that this is the first epoch of real quiet that I have had in my stormy life, and every day I feel more and more inclined to dream away my existence.

"Farewell! my dear Lady Blessington; present my best wishes to the Count D'Orsay *beau et brave*. I have found out a fly-fisher here, and I intend to be initiated into the sublime art. There is a quiet and repose about fly-fishing that I am sure will agree with me. While your line is on the water, you may be up in the clouds, and every thing goes on just as well. Once more, with many thanks, adieu.

"F. MARRYATT."

"Wimbledon, January 3, 1840.

"Many thanks for your kind wishes, and your invitation, which I am sorry to say that I cannot accept, being confined almost totally to my room. I regret this the more, as you are aware how very much I admire Mrs. Fairlie, and how happy I should have been to meet her and her husband, as well as Count D'Orsay and you.

"And now permit me to enter into my defence with respect to the lady you refer to. I was fully aware that I lay myself open to the charge which you have brought forward, and moreover that it will be brought forward, as one in which the public feelings are likely to be enlisted; if so, my reply will be such in tenor as I now give to you.

"The lady has thought proper to vault into the arena especially allotted to the conflicts of the other sex. She has done so, avowing herself the *champion* of the worst species of democracy and of infidelity. In so doing, she has *unsexed* herself, and has no claim to sympathy on that score. I consider that a person who advocates such doctrines as she has done, at this present time, when every energy should be employed to stem the torrent which is fast bearing down this country to destruction, ought to be hooted, pelted, and pursued to death, like the rabid dog who has already communicated its fatal virus; and allow me to put the question, whether you ever yet heard when the hue and cry was raised, and weapons for its destruction seized, that the populace were known to shew the unheard-of politeness of inquiring, before they commenced the pursuit, whether the animal so necessary to be sacrificed was of the masculine or feminine gender? I wage war on the doctrine, not the enunciator, of whom I know nothing, except that the person being clever, is therefore the more dangerous.

"As for your observation, that the lady never wrote a line in 'The Edinburgh,' I can only say, that, although it is of no moment, I did most truly and sincerely believe she did, and my authority was from her having been reported to have said to a friend, that 'she had paid me off well in "The Edinburgh."' That she did say so I could, I think, satisfactorily prove, were not my authority (like all other mischievous ones) under the pledge of secresy; but the fact is, I cared very little whether she did or did not write the articles, though I confess that I fully believe that she did.

"As for the attacks of petty reviewers, I care nothing for them. 'I take it from wherever it comes, as the sailor said when the jackass kicked him;' but I will not permit any influential work like 'The Edinburgh' to ride *me roughshod* any more than when a boy, I would not take a blow from any man, however powerful, without returning it to the utmost of my power. But a review is a legion composed of many; to attack a review is of little use—like a bundle of sticks strong from union, you cannot break them; but if I can get one stick out, I can put that one across my knee, and if strong enough, succeed in smashing it; and in so doing, I really do injure the review, as any contributor fancies that he may be the stick selected.

"The only method, therefore, by which you can retaliate upon a review like 'The Edinburgh,' is to select one of its known contributors, and make the reply *personal* to him. For instance, I have advised 'The Edinburgh' to put a better hand on next time. Suppose that it attacks me again, I shall assume that their best hand, Lord B———, is the writer of the article, and my reply will be most personal to *him;* and you must acknowledge that I shall be able to raise a laugh, which is all I care for. You may think that this is not fair; I reply that it is; I cannot put my strength against a host: all I can do is to select one of the opponents in opinion and politics, and try my strength with him. This I am gratified in doing, until the parties who write a review put their names to the article; as long as they preserve the anonymous, I select what I please, and if I happen to take the wrong one, the fault is theirs and not mine. So recollect, that if I am attacked in 'The Edinburgh' (should I reply to the article when I publish my 'Diary of a Blasé' in June next), my reply will be to Lord B———, and will be as bitter as gall, although I have the highest respect for his lordship's talents, and have a very good feeling towards him. Many thanks for the 'Governess,' which I have just read. My mother finished it last night, and pronounced it excellent. I prefer giving her opinion to my own, as none will ever accuse her of flattery, although you have me. I read it with some anxiety, owing to my having intended to have made the sister of 'Poor Jack,' a governess for a short time, and I was afraid that you would have forestalled me altogether. As far as the serious goes, you have so; but you have left me a portion of the ludicrous. I think I shall pourtray a stout well-formed girl of nineteen, kept up in the nursery by a vain mother, with dolls, pinbefores, and all other *et ceteras*—that is, if I do venture to come after you, which will be hardly fair to *myself*. Are you not tired of writing? I am most completely, and could I give it up, I would to-morrow; but as long as my poor mother lives, I must write, and, therefore, although I detest it, I wish to write a long while yet.

"I have just returned from Norfolk, where I was wet through every day, and to escape cold, filled myself with tobacco smoke and gin—these antagonistical properties have had the effect of deranging me all over, and I am miserably out of tune, and feel terribly ill-natured. I feel as if I could wring off the neck of a cock-robin, who is staring in at my window.

"This is a long letter, but it is your own fault; you have sowed wind, and have reaped the whirlwind. If I have written myself down in your good opinion, I must, at all events, try to write myself up again.

"F. MARRYATT."

"Monday, Jan. 3rd, 1842.

"I write you this shabby-looking note, to thank you for your kind present. I intended to call upon you, but have been prevented, and must now defer it till my return from the country, at the end of the week. I leave now directly.

"You will be surprised to hear that Mr. Howard is dead. He went out to dine with a friend on Christmas day, and after dinner was, I believe, well, and broke a blood-vessel. He could not be removed from the house, but lingered until Thursday evening, when he expired.

"That is all I have heard—poor man! perhaps it is all for the best, as his prospects were any thing but encouraging.

"Kind regards to Miss Power and *the* Count, par excellence.

"F. MARRYATT."

"Manchester Square, June 8, 1841.

"If you cannot command the services of your friends when you are unfortunate, they are of little value.

"I do not therefore think you are wrong in asking me again, and I assure you that if I can find anything to help your book, I will do it with pleasure.

"The misfortune with me is, that I cannot force ideas—they must be spontaneous; and the very knowledge that I am to do so and so by a certain time, actually drives all ideas out of my head, and leaves me as empty as a drum.

"If you do not have it, I can only say it will not be my fault.

"F. MARRYATT."

"3, Spanish Place, Manchester Square, Sept. 6th.

"In reply to your kind inquiries, allow me first to observe, that I have two most *splendid grumbles* on my last, so splendid that I hardly know how to part with them. *Now for grumble the first.* When Sir James Graham was at the Admiralty, he was pleased to consider that my professional services entitled me to some mark of His Majesty's approbation, and accordingly he asked His Majesty to give me the star of the Guelph, and knighthood. To this request His Majesty King William was pleased to reply, in his usual frank, off-hand way, 'Oh yes—Marryatt, I know—bring him here on Thursday,' (the day of application having been Monday). But, it appears that while my 'greatness was ripening,' some kind friend informed His Majesty that I had once written a pamphlet on impressment. And when Sir James saw His Majesty on the Wednesday, the King said to him—'By the bye, Marryatt wrote a work on impressment, I hear,' (whether for or against, His Majesty did not deign to inquire). 'I won't give him anything;' adding, in his wonted free and easy style, 'I'll see him d——d first!' Now the request of a Cabinet Minister is supposed to confirm the claim, and it is not usual for the Sovereign to refuse; indeed His

Majesty seemed to be aware of that, for he said, 'The *Guelph* is *my own* order, and I will not give it unless I choose.' Sir James Graham, of course, did not press the matter after His Majesty's opinion so frankly expressed. And there the matter dropped—so that instead of the honour intended, I had the honour of being d——d by a sovereign, and have worn my travelling name ever since. You'll allow that that is a *capital grumble.* Now for grumble *No. two*:

"Twenty-six years ago, soon after the peace, I was requested by Lloyds and the ship-owners, to write a code of signals for the merchant service. I did so, and in the various annual reports of these societies, they have stated that the saving of lives and property by the means of these signals has been enormous. They were, at the request of Lloyds, supplied to the British men-of-war, to enable merchant vessels to communicate their wants, &c.; and eventually they have been used in all the English colonies and dependencies by the government, to communicate with vessels, &c. along the coast. The French, perceiving their advantage, had them translated, and supplied to their men-of-war and merchantmen.

"Now, independent of the value they may be to the country, in saving lives and property, and the claim which I have on that account, I have one also in a pecuniary way, for during *the twenty-six* years that they have been established they have always been supplied *gratis* to the British navy—and if it is considered how many vessels we have had in commission, had this been paid for, it would have amounted to a very large sum. For this service I have never received any remuneration whatever from our own government. When I was at Paris, some years ago, Admiral de Rigny, the French First Lord, sent for me, and without any application on my part, informed me that, in consequence of the important advantages derived by the use of my signals, the King of the French had been pleased to give me the *Gold Cross* of the Legion of Honour, (equivalent to the C.B. in England); so that I have been rewarded by a nation for whom the signals were not written, and from my own government have received nothing.—I beg pardon, I did receive something; a letter from Lord Palmerston, *forbidding* me to wear the distinction granted to me by the King of the French. Now I call that also a *capital* grumble. I have asked Sir Robert Peel to give me employment, and I did so because I consider that I have done some service to the Conservative cause—at all events, I have worked hard, and suffered much in purse. The contest of the Tower Hamlets cost me between *six and seven thousand pounds,* which is a serious affair to a man with seven children, all with very large ideas, and very small fortunes; and I have felt the loss ever since. I have invariably laboured very hard in the cause, never neglecting to infuse conservative ideas in all my writings. I have written much in the newspapers, and never yet sent any article to the 'Times,' which was not immediately inserted. One Conservative paper, which was dying a natural death, the 'Era,' weekly paper, I re-established, and it now circulates upwards of five thousand; I did this out of good will to the proprietor and zeal for the cause, for I never received a sixpence for many months' labour. The 'Era' is the Licensed Victuallers' paper, and I argued that wherever that paper was taken in, the 'Weekly Dispatch' would not be; and that where the man who draws the beer is a Conservative, those who drink it will become the same. It is well known that it was chiefly through the exertions of the Licensed Victuallers that Captain Rous was returned for Westminster.

"As to my professional services, it is to the Admiralty that I must look for remuneration, and as for my literary reputation, it is an affair between me and the public; but I think you must acknowledge that I have claims for *omission* and claims for *commission,* and when I see the Whigs giving away baronetcies to Easthope, &c., for literary services, and Clay, my opponent at the Tower Hamlets, for contesting elections; I do feel that the party which I have supported, now that I have decided claims upon the country, should not throw me away like a sucked orange; if they do, why—virtue must be its own reward. It will be all the same, a hundred years hence.

"I have now let it all out, and I feel a great deal better.

"F. MARRYATT."

"February 1, 1833.

"Split a cod's head, and put it with two haddocks, my dear Countess, into a kettle containing two quarts of cold water, and an onion chopped fine. When it has boiled a quarter of an hour, take out all the fish, cut off the heads, trim and fillet the haddocks, pick out the best part of the cod's head—such as underjaw, tongue, &c., lay them aside. Put back into the kettle the remains of the cod's head and trimmings of the haddocks, and let them boil until the liquor is reduced to a pint and a half, and then strain off.

"Thicken the soup with the yolks of two eggs well beat up, add some chopped parsley and a little salt. Then put in the fillets of haddock (each cut into four pieces), with the portions of the cod's head—boil till sufficiently done, and you will have a capital soup *à tres bonne marché*. F. MARRYATT."

"I quite forgot to ask the Count and B. A. to give a letter or two for my brother Horace. Do you renew the proposal for me, as I shall have no peace. I like Lord O. very much; he is so frank and manly. Kind regards to Mdlles. Marguerite and Ellen."

"February 4, 1841.

"You are very right in what you say. I think not only that the title may be as you wish, but moreover that we may, throughout the whole, soften down the word to *unmentionables*; if you think it necessary, I will do so, if you please, after it is in type, or you may alter it in any way which you think fit, as you have a nicer sense of what a lady will object to, than a rough animal like me. F. MARRYATT."

"Langham, June 5, 1843.

"I wrote to Sir William Seymour for particulars, but only received a piece of note paper, which contained more about his own than the story I mentioned to you. However, I have out of his meagre account contrived to dramatise to four or five pages, putting speeches into their mouths which they never made, and, in fact, saying what they *ought* to have said, if they did not say it. It is short, but by considering how little there was to work from, &c., I think it will be interesting.

" All things are better short, except a woman, who, as Byron says, ought not to be dumpy. Kind regards to the Count and to the two *gals*. F. MARRYATT."

" 120, Pall Mall.

" I send you my new publication, consisting chiefly of old matter. Never mind; if they abuse it, why I wrote it years ago, and therefore it proves that I improve; if they praise it, why then all the better. I don't care which, so long as they try it.

" What has become of Sir E. Bulwer? I have not seen him for an age. I hope he is not ill. I am awful busy, chiefly with a code of signals for the marine, which printers are so stupid, that they cannot comprehend them. I hope D'Orsay (I beg Miss Power's pardon), I hope Miss Power and D'Orsay, as well as you, are all *bien portant*. No war, and therefore no ship for me, which is a bore, as I wished to go afloat, and wash out all my sins of authorship in salt water. F. MARRYATT."

FROM LADY BLESSINGTON TO CAPTAIN MARRYATT.

" Gore House, November 18, 1840.

" MY DEAR CAPTAIN MARRYATT,

" Many thanks for the 'Olla Podrida,' which I doubt not will afford me the same pleasure that all your books do. I have not seen Sir E. Bulwer for three weeks. He was then about a week returned from Germany, and I thought him looking ill. He has been staying at Knebworth with his mother.

" I send you a 'Keepsake,' not that I think you will take the trouble to read it, but that I believe you will like to offer it to your mother. Did you get your copy of the 'Book of Beauty?' Will you name to-morrow (Thursday), Friday, or Saturday to dine with me *en famille?* Alfred D'Orsay leaves town on Sunday, so I specify these days, that he may have the pleasure of meeting you.

"My brother has returned from New Brunswick, and is now staying with me. He sends you kind greetings.

"Believe me, always your cordial friend,

"M. Blessington."

"Gore House, July 19, 1843.

"I have seldom been more annoyed than in receiving the inclosed half an hour ago. I had thought that, with the omission of the objectionable word, the story, which is full of racy humour, would have been a real treasure for the book, but the ridiculous prudery of a pack of fools compels me to abandon it; for well do I know, that were I to insist on the insertion of the Buckskins, Heath and his trustees (should the sale of the book be less than formerly) would attribute it to you and me.

"After all the trouble I have given you, I dare not ask you for any thing else, though there is no name which I would be more proud to see in my list of contributors than yours; but I must ask you to pardon me for all the trouble I have inflicted on you. M. Blessington."

A LETTER SIGNED R. P. ADDRESSED TO LADY BLESSINGTON, IN REFERENCE TO CAPTAIN MARRYATT.

"Whitehall, Sept. 24th.

"I beg leave to return you the accompanying letter from Captain Marryatt.

"The applications which I have received for employment in the public service, from parties qualified for it in point of character and acquirements, and with claims on a Conservative government (which each party deems unquestionable in its own case), so far exceed any probable means on my part of meeting even a small portion of them, that I do not feel justified, by vague assurances of a disposition to oblige, in encouraging expectations which I have little hope of being able to realize.

"For the consideration of professional services, I must refer Captain Marryatt to the department to which he is attached.

"I cannot say that I think foreign distinctions ought to be recognized in this country, except under very special circumstances. I have the honour to be, dear Lady Blessington,

"Your faithful servant,

"R. P."

A. FONBLANQUE, ESQ.

John de Grenier Fonblanque, Esq., an eminent equity lawyer, senior King's Counsel, and senior Bencher of the Hon. Society of the Middle Temple, died in January, 1837, in his seventy-seventh year. He was descended from an ancient noble French family of Languedoc, and inherited the title of Marquis, though he never assumed it in England.

He was called to the English bar in 1783.

He published several works on professional subjects, and entered Parliament in 1802, and represented the borough of Camelford, until the year 1806. His eldest son, John Samuel Martin Fonblanque, who was called to the bar in 1816, is a Commissioner of Bankrupts.

Albany Fonblanque studied for the bar, but relinquished his profession for that of a public journalist, and in the conduct and management of "The Examiner," made a character, than which no higher was ever gained by the effective discharge of editorial duties, and the devotion to them of brilliant talents and sound judgment.

In 1837 he published a remarkable work, "England under Seven Administrations."

Mr. Fonblanque was one of the most highly-esteemed friends of Lady Blessington; of his intellectual powers there are ample evidences in her papers, that she entertained a very high opinion.

Her knowledge of eminent or prominent persons figuring in literary, political, and artistic life was not more extensive than her power of appreciating worth and talent, and of estimating most things at their proper value.

She certainly possessed great power of discrimination and observation, singular tact in discovering remarkable mental qualities, and excellent judgment in forming opinions of the merits of those who presented themselves to her notice.

Her estimate of the intellectual powers of Fonblanque was perhaps higher than that of most of the celebrities with whom she came in contact. His profound penetration, sound judgment, sobriety of mind, his power in composition as a public journalist, his ability in influencing public opinion, his caustic style, perspicacity, and force of expression, his effective sarcasm, and withal apparent simplicity of character, were well calculated to be appreciated by her. An American writer very ill-advisedly thought fit to lower the estimate of the former editor of "The Examiner," in his own land. The attempt was rebuked by some friend of Fonblanque in a way not likely to be forgotten by the writer of the obnoxious strictures.

FROM A. FONBLANQUE TO LADY BLESSINGTON.

"Rue d'Algra, Oct. 31st, 1831.

"My dear Lady Blessington,

"Though I am almost blind, I must write to say how much I admire Count D'Orsay's letter on the Brougham affair. It seems to me that nothing could be happier in tone and modest dignity. Here it was the subject of universal praise.

"The falsehood that Count D'Orsay had anything to do with the hoax was sufficiently refuted by all who knew him, by the two circumstances that it was stupid and cruel; and the unique characteristic of D'Orsay is, that the most brilliant wit is uniformly exercised in the most good-natured way. He can be wittier with kindness than the rest of the world with malice.

"Lady Canterbury gave me a most friendly recognition, and we dined with them, and found the family very agreeable. If I had been a Tory, Lord Canterbury could not have been more attentive; my recommendation being the stronger one, of which I am not a little proud, of being numbered among your friends. You will be glad to hear that Bulwer is doing extremely well here, and making himself, as he must be every where by his amiable qualities, very popular. My dear Lady Blessington,

"Ever faithfully yours,

"A. Fonblanque."

JOHN GALT.

Mr. Galt was born at Irvine, in Ayrshire, in 1779. During his school-boy days he wrote several poetical pieces, some of which were published in a provincial paper. He was educated for mercantile pursuits, and embarked in trade in London with a Mr. MacLaghlan. This speculation proving unfortunate, he entered at Lincoln's Inn, and commenced the study of the law. This pursuit, however, he soon abandoned, and set out for the Continent. In 1809, he met Lord Byron at Gibraltar, travelled with his Lordship in the packet to Malta, parted with him there, and met him the following spring at Athens.

In his diary, 1st December, 1813, Byron says, "Galt called . . . . We are old fellow-travellers, and with all his eccentricity, he has much strong sense, experience of the world, and is, as far as I have seen, a good-natured, philosophic fellow." *

In 1812, he published his "Voyages and Travels in the years 1809, 1810, and 1811, containing Statistical, Commercial, and Miscellaneous Observations on Gibraltar, Sardinia, Sicily, Malta, and Turkey." Soon after his return to England, he became connected with the "Star" newspaper, and married the daughter of the editor of that paper, Dr. Alexander Tilloch. For some time he was editor of the "Courier." After several engagements in the affairs of public institutions and mercantile companies, Mr. Galt was appointed agent to a Canadian company for the management of emigrant colonization in Canada. In this occupation he quarrelled with the government, and after some time returned to England.

The author of "The Ayrshire Legatees," "The Annals of the Parish," and "The Entail," is not likely to be soon for-

* Moore's Byron, p. 211, ed. 8vo. 1838.

gotten by the novel-reading public. The quaintness of style and phraseology, humour and liveliness, and the rich vein of common sense that runs through all his productions, were sufficient to obtain for his works the hearty commendation of Sir Walter Scott. (See Gentleman's Magazine, 1839, p. 93.)

The old malady that ends the career of so many literary men, paralysis, having prostrated the powers of poor Galt by repeated shocks, the fourteenth attack of that disease proved fatal to him the 11th of April, 1839. He died at Greenock, aged sixty, leaving a widow and family in adverse circumstances.*

FROM JOHN GALT, ESQ., TO LADY BLESSINGTON.

"Liverpool, 27th July, 1822.

"My dear Madam,

"On Monday evening I was so distinctly impressed with the repugnance which your Ladyship feels at the idea of going

* The same year he published his voyages and travels (in 1812), he produced "The Life and Administration of Cardinal Wolsey," 4to., and "Reflections on Political and Commercial Subjects," 8vo., and no less than four Tragedies the same year, "Maddalen," "Agamemnon," "Lady Macbeth," "Antonio and Clytemnestra."

"Letters from the Levant" appeared in 1813; "The Life and Studies of Benjamin West," in 1816. "The Magola," a tale, appeared in 1816, in 2 vols. 8vo. All the above-mentioned works were published previously to his departure for Canada; and subsequently to his return to England, the following works of his appeared: "Pictures from English, Scotch, and Irish History;" "Lawrie Todd," a tale; "Southennan," a tale; "Annals of the Parish;" "The Entail, or Lairds of Guppy;" "Sir Andrew Wylie;" "The Provost;" "The Earthquake;" "The Ayrshire Legatees;" "The Steamboat;" "The Last of the Lairds;" "Mansie Waugh;" "Ringan Galbaize, or the Covenanter;" "Rothelan, a Romance of the English Historians;" "The Spaewife;" "The Bachelor's Wife;" "The Radical;" "The Life of Lord Byron" (1830); "Bogle Corbet, or the Emigrant;" "Stanley Buxton;" "The Stolen Child;" "Apotheosis of Sir Walter Scott;" "Autobiography of John Galt" (1833).

to Ireland, that I entered entirely into your feelings; but upon reflection, I cannot recall all the reasonableness of the argument, a circumstance so unusual with respect to your Ladyship's reasons in general, that I am led to think some other cause at the moment must have tended to molest you, and to lend the energy of its effect to the expressions of your reluctance. For I have often remarked that the gnat's bite, or a momentary accident, will sometimes change the whole complexion of the mind for a time. But even though nothing of the sort had happened, the scores and hundreds, and the thousands of the poor Irish in quest of employment whom I have met on the road and seen landing here, and the jealousy with which they are viewed by the common people, and the parochial burdens which they may occasion in the contemplation of the best of the community, many of whom are loud in their reflections on the Irish absentees, all combine to form such a strong case for my Lord's journey, that nothing but the apprehension of your Ladyship's indisposition can be filed against it. The journey, however, to be really useful, should be one of observation only, and I am sure you will easily persuade him to make it so, and to be resolved not to listen to any complaint with a view to decision in Ireland, nor to embark in any new undertaking. If he once allow himself to be appealed to on the spot, he must of necessity become affected by local circumstances and individual impartialities, by which, instead of doing general good (all a personage of his rank can do), he will become the mere administrator of petty relief, which in their effect may prove detrimental to higher objects; and were he to engage in new undertakings, to say nothing of pecuniary considerations, his thoughts would become occupied with projects, which, of every kind of favouritism, is the most fatal to the utility of a public character, such as my Lord seems now fairly set in to become. In speaking thus, I address you more as an *intellect* than a *lady*, and the interest I take in all that concerns my friends must be accepted as the only excuse I can offer for the freedom.

"Since my arrival, the object of my journey has occupied much of my time. I find many of the merchants disposed to renew the appointment, from the experience they have had of its advantages; and also to allow the agent to be free with respect to other business, which is not the case at present. In this way, it would be a most desirable appendage to my other concerns, but as an exclusive office, it would not be of sufficient consequence. My reception has been exceedingly flattering, and not the least influential of my friends is that excellent bodie, Sir Andrew Wylie; but the election is a more serious affair than I had imagined.

"The merchants consist of five different chambers, constituted by their respective branches of trade. Each chamber, by a majority, chooses a delegate, and the delegates choose the agent; and as he is required to be agreeable to the member, the election will not take place till the successor to Mr. Canning is returned. At present, the public opinion looks towards Mr. Huskisson, and his favour towards me could be decisive, in the event of returning him. Should Mr. H. not stand, Mr. Robinson is spoken of; but Mr. Gladstone, the merchant, is understood to have some intention of offering himself, in which case, from what I know of his sentiments, the office would not suit me.

"I really know not what apology to make to your Ladyship for all this impertinence; but somehow, since I have had the honour and pleasure of knowing you and my Lord so freely, I feel as if we were old friends; indeed, how can it be otherwise, for no other human beings, unconnected by the common ties, have ever taken half so much interest, or at once adding to my enjoyments and consideration. I am sensible not only of having acquired a vast accession of what the world calls advantages, but also friends who seem to understand me, and that too at a period when I regarded myself as in some degree quite alone, for all my early intimates were dead. Your Ladyship must therefore submit to endure a great deal more than perhaps I ought to say, on so short an acquaintance; but as minds never grow old, and frankness makes up at once the intimacy of years, I find myself warranted to say that I am almost an ancient, as I am ever,

"Your Ladyship's faithful and sincere friend,

"JOHN GALT."

"Edinburgh, 13th August, 1822.

"I need not say that, although I regret that the journey to Ireland is not to take place, I am much more concerned on account of the cause which has occasioned the change, than the loss of the pleasure I should have had in visiting Mountjoy. Perhaps I may still go that way; in the mean time, I wish you every benefit and enjoyment that the excursion to France is expected to produce. But for my agency project, I should have rejoiced to have had the honour of accepting my Lord's invitation, had it been only as far as Paris. I shall, however, write to himself to-morrow, when I hope to be able to send him a review of his pamphlet,* which Blackwood has obtained from Dr. Maginn, of Cork;—a man, he says, of singular talent and great learning; indeed, some of the happiest things in the magazine have been from his pen.

"Here, all are on tip-toe for the King; but my worthy countrymen proceed so very considerately in their loyalty, that nothing amusing has yet occurred. The best thing I have heard of is, the ladies who intend to be presented, practising the management of their trains, with table-cloths pinned to their tails. Some tolerable poetry has been spoiled on the occasion. I enclose two specimens; the one is by Sir Walter Scott, and the other (is in his old style, but I think of a more elevated character than his poetry in general), I think it is by Lockhart, but *Ebony* is very mysterious on the occasion. The worshipful magistrates of Glasgow, and other royal boroughs, are wonderfully grand.

"But nothing in all the preparations is so remarkable as the sacrifice of lives; what thousands have been swept away by the besom of destruction and the mop of cleanliness!

"The most Machiavellian trick of all, however, is a picturesque flight of the poetical baronet. In order to get his 'own romantic town' rid of the myriads so disturbed, he has contrived a stupendous bonfire on the top of Arthur's Seat, and induced the magistrates to issue a proclamation, inviting the

* I have not been able to ascertain on what subject was this pamphlet of Lord Blessington.—R. R. M.

loyal lieges to send their old furniture to augment the blaze. This is certainly one way of turning the royal visit to the benefit of the country.

"I see by the newspapers that Lord Mountjoy has come to Edinburgh; I will call to see him. I believe the Montgomeries, Lord Blessington's relatives, are to be with my friend Mr. Gordon, where I shall meet with them.

"JOHN GALT."

The poem entitled "Stanzas for the King's Landing," which Galt supposes to have been written by Lockhart, consists of ten stanzas. The first is as follows:—

"The eagle screams upon Benmore,
The wild deer bounds on Cheviot fell;
Step boldly, King, on Albyn's shore,
Son of her Lords, she greets thee well.
The voice that hath been silent long,
Awakes to harbinger thy path;
Once more she weaves th' ancestral song,
Once more 'tis Righ Gu Brath."

The following is the first verse of the poem attributed to Sir Walter Scott, entitled "Carle, now the King's come!" or, "New words to an old Tune."

"A Hawick gill of mountain-dew,
Heised up auld Reekie's heart, I trow,
It minded her of Waterloo—
Carle, now the King's come!

CHORUS.

Carle, now the King's come! Carle, now the King's come!
Thou shalt dance and I will sing, Carle, now the King's come!"

"London, January 6th, 1823.

"Just as I had sent off my letter last week to Lord Blessington, I got a note from the publisher, telling me that he had written his Lordship relative to the state of the publications. 'The Sketches' are all printed but the last sheet, and 'The Magic Lantern' also, all but a few pages: the latter would have been published before this time, but he was in expectation of additional papers. He has, however, given orders to publish them together, to save the expense of double advertising. By the way, I observed in the Sunday's paper, notice of a new periodical, under the title of 'The Magic Lantern.' I shall see it, and in my next tell your Ladyship what sort of a luminary it is.

"I mentioned to my Lord what passed with the Speaker. The manner in which he has acted in the business, and in which he explained to me what he had done, had a degree of delicacy and kindness in it, that has given, if I may use the expression, something of the sentiment of friendship to the sense of a great obligation. This I owe to your Ladyship, and how many other gratifications? But I should only deserve a rebuke were I to say more, and yet I know not why it is thought indecorous to express as one feels the pleasure of being under agreeable obligations. In summing up at the close of the year, my estimate of its anxieties and enjoyment, I found such a vast amount of favours owing to your Ladyship, that I confess at once my bankruptcy.

"Since my return from Scotland, indeed for some time before, I have been quite an invalid, with feverishness and rheumatism, by which I have been almost constantly confined to the house, and unable to bear the motion of a carriage, but my illness has not been idleness. Since this day week, when I sent off the letter to Lord B., I have been all-heart engaged in my new novel, 'The Scottish Martyrs.' The style I have chosen is that grave, cool, and in some degree obsolete, but emphatic manner which was employed by the covenanting authors; a little like (but of a bolder character) the manner of that most pious and excellent minister, your Ladyship's old friend Balquodder. I have got nearly the first volume finished, and Mrs. G. says she likes it better than anything I have yet attempted. I mean to publish on the 2nd of May, the anniversary of John Knox's return to Scotland, and my own birth-day.

"I take it for granted that you have seen 'Cupid's Loves of the Angels.' What beautiful air-grown bubbles! was ever such a string of pearly words so delightfully and so absurdly congregated before. The first seraph's *faux pas* is the old story of a moth burning itself in a candle; who ever heard of a lady becoming enamoured of a star, except of the Garter, or some other order? Tommy should have put his star on the angel's left breast, and given him 'a cherubim wig,' and called the damsel Lady Elizabeth. The second story is better, but then Jupiter and Semele's is much better as a tale. As for the third, it is a darling for Misses and Masters in their teens. But still the poem is admirable as mere poetry, and is another proof, if such were requisite, to show, that in art, the execution, not the conception, is the primary quality. Byron's 'Heaven and Earth' I can scarcely say I have yet seen, but what I have read is superior in energy and passion to Moore's, owing solely, I think, to the ladies being the chief actors. It is not to be endured that such a genius as his should have stooped to prey on carrion in the manner he has done. To blend himself with the scurrilous politics of the passing day, 'to give up to a party,' and such a party, 'what was meant for mankind.' It is indeed the eagle sharing the spoil of a carcass with grubs and reptiles. I have no patience with him. I have enclosed a copy of my account of the king's visit, or rather of certain of his visitors, in a separate paper, which I shall send with this to Mrs. Purves, and if the postage, for it is not worth the tax, can be got rid of it will go forward.

"Dr. Richardson told us on Sunday, that you were not expected home till about the end of March. I am both sorry and pleased at this; sorry on my own account, sheer selfish sorrow, and pleased because if there is any consideration of health in the resolution, it will do both you and my Lord good, and also because in these times when all the landed lords are crying out as if they had each severally a fit of the gout, the consequences of their war banquets, I am glad that my Lord will be kept out of joining their unpatriotic clamour, a thing which he could by no resolution on the spot avoid. For now that he has embarked his mind in national objects, it is of great consequence that he should be removed from the temptation of mixing in such unworthy politics as those that seem to be so current at present. But I forgot that it is to him, rather than to your Ladyship I should so speak, and therefore I shall conclude, begging your acceptance of Mrs. Galt's best respects and wishes, and my own particularly to the sage and *pawkie* Miss P——.

"JOHN GALT."

"Greenock, 24th March, 1835.

"I have sent by this post the second part of my strictures on the 'Two Friends,' to which I have given a most conscientious perusal *con amore*, and have not said one word more than I do think. It was my intention to have given more extracts, but the paper could not afford space, and therefore being obliged to omit them, I enlarged my remarks. Your Ladyship is, I believe, aware that in whatever regards character or feeling, I am on principle never anonymous. I know not if the rule be a good one, but it was very early formed, and will account to your Ladyship for the authentication by my signature. In this case I do not, however, regret my resolution; for in the first place it binds me to speak sincerely, and I am told my name in this district will be influential. Having no way here of seeing any of the London Reviews, I trust that they coincide in opinion with me regarding the general character of the book. A friend in London, to whose taste I am disposed to pay much deference, has read the work, and has given me a very favourable idea of the ability displayed in it.

"I am glad to see by the papers the elevation to the peerage of your friend, and I do think he will do much good in Canada. I consider him as destined to remain as Civil Commissioner. A very clever person, whom I knew in Canada as one of the editors of the papers, is here at present, and pretends that the mission will be unsuccessful; but I have a personal knowledge of Papineau, and other chieftains of that party, and I think them much less to blame than Englishmen allow. If Lord Canterbury considers them worth a little more attention than they have had, and without shewing any want of attention to the British, and no man can do it better, he may be able to effect much good.

"I shall soon have occasion to send your Ladyship my little work, which is now making up, for my unfortunate restlessness of mind must have something to do, and I can do nothing that is not sedentary, for to add to the trouble of entire lameness, my memory is often very ineffectual, and things of the nature of amusements more than business must, I fear, even with convalescence, be my occupation for the remainder of my life, if able to attend to them. JOHN GALT."

NICHOLAS PARKER WILLIS, ESQ.

Mr. Willis is a native of Boston. While a student at Yale College, he made his first appearance on the stage of literature in a religious character. Some pieces, illustrative of passages in Scripture, published in periodicals, formed his first volume, and amongst these verses of his will be found some which could not be written by a man who deserved the character that has been given of him in some of the leading critical reviews of those countries.

The author of "Pencillings by the Way," "Melanie," "The Slingsby Papers," "Inklings of Adventure," "People I have Met," "Famous People and Places," "Laughs I have put a Pen to," &c. was at one period a frequent visitor at Gore House, a favourite guest there, and regular correspondent of Lady Blessington.

I had the pleasure of meeting Mr. Willis on many occasions at Gore House, to which reference is made in the rather too celebrated "Pencillings by the Way," and also at the soirées of the late Lady Charleville, in Cavendish Square.

Mr. Willis was an extremely agreeable young man in society, somewhat over-dressed, and a little too *demonstratif*, but abounding in good spirits, pleasing reminiscences of Eastern and Continental travel, and of his residence there for some time as attaché to a foreign legation. He was observant and communicative, lively and clever in conversation, having the peculiar art of making himself agreeable to ladies, old as well as young; degagée in his manner, and on exceedingly good terms with himself and with the élite of the best society wherever he went.

during nearly two years that Mr. Willis spent in London, the impressions which London fashionable society made on him having been duly noted down, took a definite shape on the other side of the Atlantic, and came out under the title of "Pencillings by the Way," I think in 1835. The work was published soon after in London, and a second edition in 1839. The matter of this work had been originally communicated in the form of letters to a Monthly Review in the United States, with which Mr. Willis had been previously connected as editor.

In observing, in the preface to the second edition, on the severity with which this production had been handled by the Quarterly Review, Mr. Willis says, "There are some passages (I only wonder they are so few) which I would not re-write, and some remarks on individuals which I would recall at some cost, and would not willingly see repeated in these volumes."

Again, at page 357, he observes, "There is one remark I may as well make here, with regard to the personal descriptions and anecdotes with which my letters from England will of course be filled. It is quite a different thing from publishing such letters in London. America is much farther off from England than England from America."

This publication, to my own knowledge, was attended with results which I cannot think Mr. Willis contemplated when he transmitted his hasty notes to America, to estrangements of persons who, previously to the printed reports of their private conversations, had been on terms of intimate acquaintance. This was the case with respect to O'Connell and Moore. Moore's reported remarks on O'Connell gave offence to the latter, and caused bad feelings between them which had never previously existed, and which, I believe, never ceased to exist. In another instance of indulgence in strictures upon individual character, and in the case, too, of offence given to one of the most able and estimable persons connected with journalism in London, a remonstrance was addressed to Mr. Willis, a copy of which exists among the papers of Lady Blessington, and which appears to have been forwarded to her without the name of the writer, who, in all probability, was some intimate friend of hers.

"April 28th, 1835.

"Sir,

"I delayed replying to your letter until I had read the paper in question, which, agreeably to your request, Lady Blessington permitted me to see. With respect to myself individually, I required no apology; I have been too long inured to publicity to feel annoyed at personal reflections, which, if discourteous, are at least unimportant; and as a public man, I should consider myself a very fair subject for public exhibition, however unfavourably minute, except, indeed, from such persons as I have received as a guest. But in exonerating you freely, so far as any wound to my feelings is concerned, I think it but fair to add, since you have pointedly invited my frankness, that I look with great reprehension upon the principle of feeding a frivolous and unworthy passion of the public from sources which the privilege of hospitality opens to us in private life. Such invasions of the inviolable decorums of society impair the confidence which is not more its charm than its foundation, and cannot but render the English (already too exclusive) yet more rigidly on their guard against acquaintances who repay the courtesies of one country by caricatures in another. Your countrymen (and I believe yourself amongst the number) are not unreasonably sensitive as to any strictness on the private society of Americans. But I have certainly never read any work, any newspaper paragraph of which America is the subject, containing personalities so gratuitously detailed as those in which you have indulged. I allude, in particular, to the unwarrantable remarks upon Mr. Fonblanque, a gentleman who, with so rare a modesty, has ever shrunk even from the public notice of the respectful admiration which in this country is the coldest sentiment he commands; and, I rejoice to add, for the honour of England, that, despite the envy of his fame and the courage of his politics, no Englishman has yet been found to caricature the man whom it is impossible to answer. Your description is not, indeed, recognizable by those who know Mr. Fonblanque, but it is not to be considered so much on account of its inaccuracy, as by the insensibility it appears to evince to the respect due to eminent men and to social regulation. You have courted my opinion, and I have given it explicitly and plainly. I think you have done great disservice to your countrymen in this visit to England, and that in future we shall shrink from many claimants on our hospitality, lest they should become the infringers of its rights.

"To N. P. Willis, Esq."

It will be seen by a letter of Mr. Willis, without date, which, though probably not the latest of his letters, I have placed at the end of his correspondence, with a view to greater facility of reference, that in alluding to the preceding letter, which he had forwarded a copy of to Lady Blessington, he makes observations which do great credit to his character, and show him to be a man very capable, on reflection, of perceiving errors he may have fallen into without consideration, and not so divested of right feeling and good qualities, as he has been represented in some very angry and wholesale denunciations of him.

FROM N. P. WILLIS, ESQ., TO LADY BLESSINGTON.

"Gordon Castle, September 23rd, 1834.

"My dear Lady Blessington,

"I am in a place which wants nothing but the sunshine of heaven and your presence (the latter by much the greater want), and I should while away the morning in gazing out upon its lovely park, were I not doomed to find a provoking pleasure (more than in anything else) in writing to you.

"I am laid up with the gout (parole) and a prisoner to my own thoughts—thanks to Lady Blessington, sweet and dear ones.

"I left Dalhousie a week ago, and returned to Edinburgh. I breakfasted *tête-à-tête* with Wilson, who gave me execrable food but brilliant conversation, and dined with Jeffrey, who had all the distinction of auld Reekie at his table, besides Count Flahault and Lady Keith. His dinner was *merveilleux* for Scotland, but I heard nothing worth remembering, and spent my time talking to an old solicitor, C., and in watching the contortions of a lady who out-B.'s B. in *crispations nerveuses.*

"I went afterwards to a ball, and then sat down, as I do after coming from your house, to make a mem. of the good things I had heard; but the page under that date is still innocent of a syllable. Oh! you have no idea, dear Lady Blessington, in what a brilliant atmosphere you live, compared with the dull world abroad. I long to get back to you.

"From Edinboro' I meant to have come north by Lochleven, but my ankle swelled suddenly, and was excessively painful, and the surgeon forbad me to set it to the ground, so I took the steamer for Aberdeen, and lay on a sofa in that detestable place for four days, when the Duke of Gordon wrote to me to come and nurse it at the castle; and here I am, just able to crawl down slipshod to dinner.

"The house is full of people. Lord Aberdeen, who talks to me all the time, and who is kind enough to give me a frank to you, is here with his son and daughter, (she is a tall and very fine girl, and very conversable), and Lord and Lady Morton, and Lord Stormont, and Colonel Gordon, Lord Aberdeen's brother, and the Duchess of Richmond, and three or four other ladies, and half-a-dozen other gentlemen, whom I do not know: altogether, a party of twenty-two. There is a Lady something, very pale, tall, and haughty, twenty-three, and sarcastic, whom I sat next at dinner yesterday—a woman I come as near an antipathy for, as is possible, with a very handsome face for an apology. She entertained me with a tirade against human nature generally, and one or two individuals particularly, in a tone which was quite unnatural in a woman.

"I have had a letter from Chorley, who says Rothwell has done wonders with your portrait, and has succeeded in what I believed he never would do—getting the character all into his picture.

"I wish the art of transferring would extend to taking images from the heart; I should believe then that an adequate likeness of you were possible. I envy Rothwell the happiness of merely working on it. If he takes half the pleasure in it that I do in transferring to my memory the features of your mind, he would get a princely price for his portrait.

"I am delighted with the Duke and Duchess. He is a delightful, hearty old fellow, full of fun and conversation; and she is an uncommonly fine woman, and, without beauty, has something agreeable in her countenance. She plays well and sings tolerably, and, on the whole, I like her. *Pour moi meme*, I get on every where better than in your presence. I only fear I talk too much; but all the world is particularly civil to me, and among a score of people, no one of whom I had ever seen yesterday, I find myself quite at home to-day—*Grace à Dieu!*

"I have no idea when I shall leave here, my elephant leg being at present the arbiter of my fate. I hope, however, to be at Dalhousie by the 1st of October. Shall I find there the presence I most value—a letter from your Ladyship?

"Pray give my warmest regards to D'Orsay and Barry; and believe me, dear Lady Blessington, ever faithfully yours,

"N. P. Willis."

"Saturday morning.

"A letter turned up among my papers this morning, of which I once spoke to you; and, at the hazard of its offending you by its American impertinence, I enclose it to you, as an exponent of the tone of reputation you have abroad. The remarks I refer to are on the back of the letter. The man is an extraordinary genius, self-educated, but full of talent, and his enthusiasm was suggested by my speaking of Rothwell's picture of you, and wishing he was here, to try his hand at a better.

"I am just through with my monthly labours, and with the corrections to my volume, and at leisure (the first hour these two months). The first use I make of it is to go quietly through your book, and I shall make to-morrow the *digest* for the 'Herald,' which I have so long wished to do.

"I shall send you, to-morrow or Monday, the sheets of 'Melanie,' which I hope you will like. The close is better than the beginning.

"N. P. WILLIS."

"Friday.

"My mind has run a great deal on your book, since the delightful morning I passed with you; and several titles have occurred to me, only two of which I think at all eligible; one is 'Risks in High Life,' and the other 'Under-Currents in High Life,' both of which seem to me taking titles, and descriptive of the plot. You will have seen that your plot is so varied and complicated, that it is exceedingly difficult to find a brief title that at all defines it. Reflection confirms me in the opinion, that it is an admirable and racy design; and I will promise you success without having seen a line of it. Pray elaborate well the poetical passages which so struck me! Depend upon it, the reading world feels them, whatever the critics may do.

"Moore has called twice on me at the club, but I have not seen him. I look forward with the greatest delight to meeting him on Monday.

"I have not seen Procter; but I have met him in thought, I doubt not, at the shrine where we both worship.

"N. P. WILLIS."

"Old Charlton, Blackheath, Friday morning.

"Though I knew what to expect of your warm-hearted nature, I was not the less gratified and grateful in receiving your kind reply to my request. With Count D'Orsay's generous influence added to your own, I am sure Lieut. S— can scarcely fail to get the appointment.

"I don't know whether you and D'Orsay have discovered the *rechauffées* of your own stories in my last book. Do you remember the Count's telling us one evening the story of the Bandit of Austria, the Horse-stealer of Vienna? Your tale of the Roman girl is almost literally repeated in '*Violani Cesarini*,' wanting, it is true, the unrivalled charm of your manner as a *raconteuse*. You would recognize too, I think, the description of your house in Lady Roodgold's Romance. Indeed, dear

Lady Blessington, you must look on everything I have done since I first knew you, as being partly your own creation, for never was a mind so completely impressed upou another as yours upon mine. But all this you know.

"N. P. Willis."

"Charlton, Thursday morning, April 2nd, 1840.

"I must express to you the pleasure I had in making [ ] acquainted with you. She, like all who approach you, having formed an immediate and strong attachment, she begs me to renew her adieus to you, and tell you how happy she shall be to meet you again on her return.

"I cannot leave England without hoping, dear Lady Blessington, that I am counted among your friends the warmest and most attached. The best part of the many kind services you have rendered me, is the presumption it gives me that you consider me a friend. Believe me, there are few I ever loved more, and none whose remembrance I more covet when I am absent. Once more, adieu.

"N. P. Willis.

"Kindest remembrance and farewell to Count D'Orsay. Should you see D'Israeli soon, will you tell him I still trust to his promise of visiting us on his way to Niagara?"

"137, Regent Street,
"Friday evening, January 24th, 1846.

"After some argument, with a reluctant heart, I have persuaded myself that it is better to say adieu to you on paper, partly from a fear that I might not find you alone, should I call to-morrow (my last day in England); and partly because my visit to you the other day forms a sweet memory, which I would not willingly risk overlaying with one less sympathetic.

"As a man is economical with his last sixpence, I am a miser of what is probably my last remembrance of you, believing as I do, that I shall never again cross the Atlantic.

"I unwillingly forego, however, my expression of thanks and happiness for your delightful reception of my daughter's visit; and you were too tenderly human not to value what I could tell you of your impression on my mulatto servant. She saw you to love you, as any human being would, who saw you as she did, without knowing the value of rank. Little Imogen talked a great deal of her visit when she returned, and your kind gift to her will be treasured.

"I hope, dear Lady Blessington, that the new though sad leaf of life that death has turned over for you, will not be *left wholly uncopied for the world.* You would make so sweet a book, if you did but embody the new spirit in which you now think and feel. Pardon my mention of it; but I thought, while you were talking to me the other day, as if you could scarce be conscious how with the susceptibilities and fresh view of genius you were looking upon the mournful web weaving around you.

"I leave here on Sunday morning for Portsmouth to embark, with the most grateful feeling for the kindness with which you have renewed your friendship towards me.

"N. P. WILLIS."

"New York, May 8th.

"In your gay and busy life you will scarce think me gone when this letter reports my arrival on the other side of the world; seven thousand miles of travel having been accomplished between my letter and myself.

"The bearer of this is a person in whom Mrs. W—— is a good deal interested, an American actress. I hope to interest you in her, and I am sure you will at a glance understand a character which has been misunderstood and misinterpreted very often by the world. You may have heard her name, for she was in England some few years since, and played some melodramatic parts at one of the theatres; but she was then very young, and very ill-directed as well as badly introduced. She has since made great advances in her art, and is now, I think, a very clever actress, or can easily be made one, by encouragement and judicious management. She is very well off in point of fortune, I believe, and can afford to wait her opportunity to appear to advantage in England. There are other circumstances which should be told you, however, which may come to you in the shape of malicious rumour, but the truth of which should, and will, commend her to your pity and kindness. She is the daughter of a person of low character, and has been brought up by vulgar and stupid people. She is excessively handsome too, and with these elements of ruin she has been considered easy prey by most of the roués who have seen her on the stage only; my unwavering belief, however, and that of the American public, is, that a more innocent girl to this hour does not exist. She has travelled all over this immense country, playing every where, and has kept her name free from all reproach, even among the young men who have known her most intimately. I think she will always do so, and is a safe object of interest and regard. Would it be asking too much to request you to allow her to call on you, and get your counsel as to her theatrical career in London? She wants fame more than money; and with your wide-spreading influence, you can as easily make her the fashion as give her advice. One glance at her will show you that she is clever; and a more complete 'bon enfant,' midshipman-hearted creature does not exist. I am sure you will like her; and if she plays but tolerably, her very remarkable beauty will, I think, soften the critics' judgment, and propitiate her audience. I introduce her to you in the confident belief that you will think her, considering the circumstances by which she has been surrounded, a curiosity, as well as an object of kindly interest and protection. I shall write to Count D'Orsay to beg him to aid in giving her a vogue, and on his kindness of heart in any matter I know well I can rely.

N. P. Willis."

"Dublin, January 25, 1848.

"Your very kind note was forwarded to me here by Saunders and Otley, and I need scarce say it gave me great pleasure. One of the strongest feelings of my life was the friendship you suffered me to cherish for you when I first came to England; and while I have no more treasured leaf in my memory than the brilliant and happy hours I passed in Seamore Place, I have, I assure you, no deeper regret than that my indiscretion (in Pencillings) should have checked the freedom of my approach to you. Still my attachment and admiration (so unhappily recorded) are always on the alert for some trace that I am still remembered by you, and so you will easily fancy that the kind friendliness of your note gave me unusual happiness. My first pleasure when I return to town will be to avail myself of your kind invitation, and call at Gere House.

"By the same post which brought me your note, I received another from America, signed 'Lady Blessington,' and I must perform a promise to the writer of it, at the risk of your thinking both her and myself very silly, if not intrusive. She is one of the most beautiful girls I ever saw, and the daughter of one of our few acknowledged gentry, a gentleman who lives upon his fortune on the ———. She chances to be singularly like your picture by L. Parris, much more like than most originals are like their pictures. She has been told of this so often, and complimented so much in consequence, that her head is quite turned (literally indeed, for she always sits in the attitude of the picture), and for two years I have refused to do what she has prevailed on me to do at last, to ask you to write to her!! She thinks of nothing but the hope of procuring this honour, and I positively think it has become a monomania. So now I have put myself into the 'category of bores,' but I have discharged my errand, and after you have laughed at it, you will, I presume, think no more about it; still, if you took it into your head to gratify her, I should feel it as a very condescending and important favour to myself. She is a high-spirited, romantic, fearless girl, *tete montèe* as you may suppose, but magnificently beautiful, and as she has a large fortune, and will probably travel the first year of her marriage, she would doubtless call on you soon in London, and present her thanks very eloquently. Her name is Miss W——, of G—— H——; and if you should write, if you will be kind enough to enclose the note to me, I will forward it.

"I am in Ireland, picking up materials for one of Virtue's pictorial books, and next week I go to the Giants' Causeway, &c. I shall be in the country perhaps a fortnight, and in London probably in the course of a month.* N. P. WILLIS."

* I had some conversation with Tom Campbell, on the subject of the above-mentioned undertaking of Willis "to do Ireland" for Mr. Virtue. Campbell worked himself into one of his fits of red-hot wrath, at the idea of an American making a run over to Dublin, and taking on him to enlighten an English public on so extensive a subject as the history,

"Manor House, Lee, Kent, Monday, 18th.

"I enclose you a copy of a letter I have sent to Captain Marryatt, who is abroad. I don't know whether you have seen his attack, but I have been advised to print and send to my friends the letter you now receive, while I am waiting for his answer. It will eventually be published, but meantime his abuse rests on my reputation. I scarce regret his attack, since it gives me an opportunity, once for all, of meeting these matters in a tangible shape; and once for all, I shall carry the point well through.

"I have written quietly, and given Marryatt an opportunity to explain, which I hope he will do; but an explanation I must have. Pray write me your opinion of my document, for I am not much skilled in this kind of correspondence.

"N. P. Willis."

"I send you a rough draft of my idea for Lady Buckingham's picture. If you think it will do, I will elaborate it before you want it; it is at present a little indistinct.

"Fonblanque has written me a note, which, without giving me ground for a quarrel, is very unjustifiable I think. Another friend of yours has written me too, and a more temperate, just (though severe), and gentlemanly letter I never read. He gives me no quarter; but I like him the better for having written it, and he makes me tenfold more ashamed of those silly and ill-starred letters.

"I shall soon have the pleasure to see you, I trust, and remain, dear Lady Blessington, ever faithfully yours,

"N. P. Willis."

antiquities, monuments, manners and customs of the people of Ireland. "What could he know of Ireland? How could any American know any thing about it?" On occasions of this sort, I was accustomed to add a little fuel to the fire of the poet's amusing outbursts of anger, excited very often without any apparently sufficient provocation. I defended the undertaking of Mr. Willis, and the selection of an American for it, on the ground that he was naturally free from English prejudices, and a stranger to Irish feelings in general, and had actually been studying Ireland, politically, socially, and topographically, upwards of fourteen days on the spot. "Fourteen days!" exclaimed Campbell, "all the knowledge he possesses of Ireland might have been acquired in fourteen hours."—R. R. M.

FREDERICK MANSELL REYNOLDS, ESQ.

This gentleman, the son of a well-known dramatist, owes his principal literary celebrity to a remarkable work, which attracted a good deal of attention a few years ago, entitled "Miserrimus."

Mr. Reynolds was rather an amateur in literature than a professor. In his hands "The Keepsake" made its first appearance—the first and last of the tribe of Annuals—some thirty years ago. He continued to edit it till the year 1836, when Mrs. Norton became editress. In 1837, Lady E. S. Wortley became editress. For many years of his latter life, Mr. Reynolds resided on the Continent, and, for some time, in Jersey. He died at Fontainebleau, in 1850. A lady who was well-acquainted with the friends of Lady Blessington, thus speaks of Mr. Reynolds:—

"He was a man of very kind heart and generous disposition, hospitable, obliging, and very true in his friendship; but extremely eccentric, and especially so during the latter years of his life. His extreme sensibility and nervous susceptibility, had so augmented with years and ailments, that he lived latterly with his family, wholly retired from the world. His last illness was long, and of painful suffering. He was very highly educated, and well informed, and had a good knowledge and excellent taste in painting and music, though not a performer in either art. He versified gracefully, but his prose writings partook much, in general, of a forced style, and a fantastic humour. He has left a young wife, who was one of the most perfect models I ever saw of conjugal affection, obedience, attention, patience, and devotion, whom he had known from her childhood, and whose education he had superintended."

FROM F. MANSELL REYNOLDS, ESQ. TO LADY BLESSINGTON.

"Hillan House, St. Helen's, Jersey, March, 1847.

"My dear Lady Blessington,

"After having so recently seen you, and being so powerfully and so painfully under the influence of a desire never again to place the sea between me and yourself and circle, I feel almost provoked to find how much this place suits me in every physical respect. But truth is truth, and certainly I feel that this place is made for me! for illness has effected greater inroads on my strength, than 'all the doctors in the land' can ever repair.

"You and Count D'Orsay speak kindly and cheerfully to me; but I am *une malade imaginaire*, for I do not fear death; on the contrary, I rather look to it as my only hope of secure and lasting tranquillity.

"In the lull which has hitherto accompanied my return to this delicious climate, I have had time and opportunity for ample retrospection, and I find that we have both laid in a stock of regard for Count D'Orsay which is immeasurable: any body so good natured and so kind hearted I never before saw; it seems to me that it should be considered an inestimable privilege to live in his society. When you write to me, pray be good enough to acquaint me whether you have been told verbatim what a lady said on the subject; for praise so natural, hearty, and agreeable was never before uttered in a soliloquy, which her speech really was, though I was present at the time.

"At the risk of repeating, I really must tell it to you. After Count D'Orsay's departure from our house, there was a pause, when it was broken, by exclaiming, 'What a very nice man!' I assented in my own mind, but I was pursuing also a chain of thought of my own, and I made no audible reply. Our ruminations then proceeded, when mine were once more interrupted by her saying, 'In fact, he is the *nicest man I ever saw.*'

"This is a pleasant avowal to me, I thought, but still I could not refrain from admitting that she was right. Then again, for a third time, the mental machinery of both went to work in silence, until that of the lady reached a *ne plus ultra* stage of admiration, and she ejaculated in an ecstacy, 'Indeed he is the nicest man that can possibly be!'

"The progress of this unconsciously expressed panegyric from the modest positive to the rhapsodical superlative, struck me as being extremely amusing, and I only now derive pleasure from repeating it to you, because it is literally true, and utterly unembellished by me.

"I have written to Heath on the subject of the 'Royal' Book of Beauty, to endeavour to dissuade him from the use of an epithet so vulgarized, and to induce him to substitute the word 'Regal.' Ever entirely putting aside your association with a title in such bad taste.

"With our kindest and most affectionate regards to yourself and Count D'Orsay, and also to the Miss Powers,

"Believe me, my dear Lady Blessington,

"Always most faithfully yours,

"MANSELL REYNOLDS."

"St. Helen's, Jersey, March 30, 1849.

"What has been determined with regard to the Annuals? will they be continued? If they be, and you still think that I am capable of rendering you any assistance, it is scarcely necessary for me to state, that I am now, as always, considerably at your service.

"Only the other day I was re-reading one of your last biographies, and I repeat to you, what I previously stated, that the improvement you have made in the art and tone of composition, since I first had the pleasure and honour of becoming acquainted with you, is really wonderful.

"MANSELL REYNOLDS."

CHAPTER IX.

DR. WILLIAM BEATTIE, M.D.

One of the most valued friends of Lady Blessington, in whose worth, moral and intellectual, she placed the highest confidence—was the author of "The Heliotrope," Dr. William Beattie. I had the good fortune to be the means of making Lady Blessington acquainted with Dr. Beattie.

In 1833, on the occasion of a morning call at Gore House, while waiting for her Ladyship, I found a volume laying on the drawing-room table, of newly published Poems, without the author's name, entitled "The Heliotrope, or the Pilgrim in search of Health, in Italy." The volume was a presentation copy to Lady Blessington, with these words on the fly-leaf—"I too have been in Arcadia." I had time, before the appearance of Lady Blessington, to read several of the poems at the commencement of the volume, and was greatly struck with the harmony of the versification, the elegance of style, the evident kindliness of nature, and amiability of disposition manifested in them. I inquired of Lady Blessington if she knew any thing of the author, and was informed she had no knowledge of him whatever. Some days subsequently, I proceeded to the publishers in the Strand, and expressed a desire to know the author of "The Heliotrope." I was told the author had no intention of making his name known; he had intimated in the preface to the volume recently published, his purpose, if the work was favourably received, to complete the poem in another volume; but as the work was not pushed on public attention, and did not sell, the author had given up all idea of continuing it. I had obtained a loan of the volume from Lady Blessington, and perused the entire poem with attention. After that perusal, my impression was so strong as to the merits of the poem (over-modestly introduced to the public), that I addressed a letter to the author, to the care of his publisher, encouraging him to proceed with his performance to its completion, and counselling him, so far from being disheartened by the bad reception given to his first volume, to rest assured of ultimate success. In return I had a gratifying letter from the author, and subsequently a visit, and was indebted to my communication for a friend, whose friendship from that time to the present has been to me a source of uninterrupted satisfaction.

"The Heliotrope" was cast upon the waters by author and publisher, without any apparent anxiety about its fate—to sink or swim on the stream of current literature, as it might please the stars of criticism: no effort was made for its success or safety. Two of the leading periodicals of the time, however, discerned the merits of this poem, and did justice to them.*

Dr. Beattie is a native of Scotland; while he was at school

* The "Metropolitan Magazine" said of it:—"Every line in this book is written in the language of poetry: every expression is idiomatic of the Muses. Cadences cannot be sweeter, nor verse more polished. The author has dipped his right hand in the waves of the Heliconian fount, and has drawn it forth, strengthened with the waters glittering fresh upon it. He has caught the sweetest echo of the spirit of poetry, when she sings her most dulcet song in her secluded shades."

The "Athenæum" said of it:—"The faults of this poem are few, and the beauties numerous; among the beauties are a manly vigour of sentiment, and an elevation and flow of language. The picture of the fallen condition of Genoa is masterly. The destruction of Pompeia is well described. The eye of the poet and the hand of the painter unite in these fine stanzas."

he had the misfortune to lose his father. That loss, the result of an accident, was the beginning of severe family trials; "and from that hour," to use Dr. Beattie's words in reference to his own career, "the battle of life commenced, and has ever since continued."

But one observation of his, in regard to that career, every one who knows him must dissent from—"All I am entitled to say of myself may be comprised in four words—'Laboriosè vixi nihil agendo.'" Dr. Beattie has led a life of labour and anxiety, never wearying of doing good to others; and in that respect he might indeed say,

> "I count myself in nothing else so happy."

His life has been an exemplification of the theory of the duty of benevolence, inculcated in the words of Shakespeare:

> "We are born to do benefits."*

"There are many members of our profession who, although not eminently distinguished in strictly professional circles, nor even in medical science or practice, have nevertheless exhibited talent of no ordinary kind in collateral pursuits, and the gentleman whose name heads this notice is one of such. Dr. Beattie was educated at Clarencefield Academy, between the years 1807-13, and from the latter period to 1820 studied at the University of Edinburgh, where he took his degree. He pursued his studies in London in 1822, and subsequently in the years 1823, 24, 25, and 26, made the tour of Europe, visiting France, Italy, Germany, &c., and acquainting himself with the various modes of practice and theories taught in the most celebrated continental schools. We may judge, therefore, that he was eminently qualified for a part he afterwards filled for eight years—that of Physician to the Duke and

* Timon of Athens, act i. sc. 2.

Duchess of Clarence, whom he attended during their three visits at foreign courts."

The writer of the preceding passage in an eminent medical periodical, has omitted to state the royal remuneration received by Dr. Beattie for his eight years' assiduous attendance on his late Majesty, when Duke of Clarence, and on the Duchess — the late Queen Adelaide. The amount does not require many figures to specify it—a cipher, in the form of a circle, will express it. He was a wise physician, and had much dealings, no doubt, with royal English Dukes and German Princesses, who said of his royal *Clientèle,* "Dum dolent solvunt."

Dr. Beattie commenced practice in London in 1830. He is a graduate of the University of Edinburgh, and a member of the Royal College of Physicians of London. His practice has been very extensive, and highly advantageous and profitable to the poor and the unfortunate who have seen better days; to indigent clergymen, artists, actors, authors, and literati of all grades. Dr. Beattie belongs to a class of men who, having become renowned for their benevolence, in spite of their modesty, are looked on by all their friends in all their troubles, as having a special mission given them to spend their time, and to be spent in alleviating human sufferings.

"The Heliotrope, or Pilgrim in Pursuit of Health," in two cantos, comprising Liguria, Campania, and Calabria, written in Italy in 1823-4, was published in 1833, in 1 vol. 12mo. A second edition in four cantos, (the two last comprising "Sicily" and "The Lipari Island,") under the title "The Pilgrim in Italy, with other Poems," appeared some years later. "John Huss," a poem, was published in 1829. "Polynesia," a poem, appeared in 1839. "The Courts of Germany," visited in 1822, 25, and 26, in two vols. 8vo. appeared in 1827.

A series of splendidly-illustrated works,—the letter-press by Dr. Beattie, the engravings chiefly from drawings on the spot by the late W. H. Bartlett—historical, topographical, and descriptive of scenery and inhabitants,—was commenced in 1836, with the publication of "Switzerland," in 2 vols. 4to. This was followed by "Scotland," in 2 vols. 4to. 1838: and next, "The Waldenses," 1 vol. 4to. 1838: then "The Castles and Abbeys," in 2 vols. 4to. 1839: "The Ports and Harbours," in 2 vols. 4to. 1839: "The Danube," in 1 vol. 4to. 1844. Another illustrated work, entitled "Historical Memoirs of Eminent Conservatives," was subsequently produced by the same publishers, but Dr. Beattie only contributed a portion of the Memoirs.

In 1838, one of those publications made its appearance, to which Campbell was induced to give his name as editor, and not his labours:—"Campbell's Scenic Annual, for 1838, containing thirty-six exquisitely-finished engravings of the most Remarkable Scenes in Europe, &c., with a rich fund of Literary Matter, corresponding with each Subject; and comprising Original Poetry by the Editor, Thomas Campbell, Esq., author of 'The Pleasures of Hope.'"

Among the eulogistic notices of this Annual, which appeared at the time of its publication, is to be found the following, in a leading critical journal. "The name of Campbell is a sufficient pledge for the poetic, literary, and generally tasteful character of this Annual."

It was hailed in the "Gentleman's Magazine:"—"We were most agreeably surprised by the sight of this Annual. In selection of scenery, in skill and elegance of composition, and in pleasing and picturesque effect in the engravings, it yields to none of its rivals; while in the splendour of the editor's reputation it far surpasses them all."

Nevertheless, all the original poetical pieces, for which Campbell got the credit, and the publisher by his name the profit, with the exception of three, were written by Dr. William Beattie.

Dr. Beattie was a frequent contributor to the periodicals

edited by Lady Blessington; and, without any disparagement to the abilities of the other contributors of acknowledged merit to those Annuals, it may be asked, if the lines addressed "To the Fountains in the Place de la Concorde," where the guillotine was erected "en permanence," hastily written at the request of Lady Blessington, in an emergency referred to in one of the letters, which will be found among those addressed by her to Dr. Beattie, have been equalled by any similar contribution in the whole series of those periodicals?

This brief notice may be concluded, I trust not inappropriately, with some lines addressed by Dr. Beattie to the Editor, on his return from Africa in 1840—lines well calculated to shew the talents of a writer who was a favourite contributor to Lady Blessington's periodicals, and a most intimate friend and correspondent of hers.

LINES ADDRESSED TO R. R. MADDEN, BY DR. W. BEATTIE, ON HIS RETURN FROM AFRICA, IN 1841.

"A pilgrim I stood, in a desolate realm,
Where faith had no anchor, and freedom no helm;
Religion no altar, no spirit, no voice,
To cheer the benighted, and bid them rejoice.
For that region with darkness and idols was rife,
Its traffic the blood and the sinews of life—
Where the curse of oppression had blighted the plain,
And the cry of the captive was uttered in vain.

'Is there no one,' they cried, 'to our anguish responds,
No hand from on high to unrivet our bonds?
Like beasts of the forest—like sheep of the fold—
How long shall our children be slaughtered or sold?
How long shall the spoiler pursue his career,
And our traders supply him with sabre and spear?
How long shall the veil of hypocrisy rest,
On the craft or the guile of that trafficker's breast?'

How sad was that voice! But its thrilling appeal,
Has struck on the ear of a Stranger whose zeal,

Long tried and unflinching, was still at his post,
When the victims of slavery needed him most.
He heard, and, like Howard, he turned not away,
For high thoughts in his spirit were kindling that day;
He rushed to the spot, in the struggle to share—
For the victim was bound—and his doom was despair.

The Stranger was moved, and to sever the chain
Of the captive, he laboured and toiled not in vain;
While the man-stealer's sordid accomplice stood by,
And scowled on the stranger with truculent eye—
And by features distorted by impotent rage,
Foamed, fretted, and chafed, like a wolf in his cage:
Exclaiming, 'Right dearly the price thou shalt pay,
For the wrong thou hast done to my interests to-day.'

'Thy threats I regard not,' the Stranger replied,
'My duty is done, by my act I abide:
I have laboured, indeed, to unfetter the slave—
If wrong, let the record be writ on my grave.
But on that of the wretch, who for lucre retains
The man, his Redeemer once ransomed, in chains,
No record be read, save the record of guilt—
Of the hearts he has broken, the blood he has spilt.'

And yet, while I gazed on that terrible scene,
And the slave-stealer frowned with a murderous mien,
While he trampled on freedom, and scoffed at the rood—
For its sign was rebuke to his traffic in blood—
These words were pronounced, and the Stranger was cheered:
'To the genius of Freedom thy cause is endeared,
Through sunshine and tempest pursue thy career,
The billows may roar, but the haven is near!"

LETTERS FROM LADY BLESSINGTON TO THE AUTHOR OF "THE HELIOTROPE."

"April 14th, 1833.

"Lady Blessington has again to acknowledge the polite attention of the author of 'The Heliotrope,' and to thank him for the very acceptable present he has made her. Lady B. feels much gratified that the beautiful poem is given to the public, for in the present degenerate days, when a taste for fine poetry is almost as rare as the genius for writing it, a few specimens like 'The Heliotrope' must do much towards leading back the mind to the true point of inspiration—nature—pure and refined, as portrayed in the admirable poem now published."

"Seamore Place, June 12, 1833.

"The high opinion Lady Blessington entertains of the genius of the author of 'The Heliotrope,' must plead her excuse for the request she is about to make him. Lady B. has undertaken to edit the 'Book of Beauty' for this year, and many of her literary friends have kindly consented to assist her by their contributions. The work is to consist of twenty-five engravings from pictures by the best artists, the engravings to be illustrated by tales in prose, or by poetry. The pictures are all female portraits of great beauty, and Lady Blessington is most anxious that a poem, however short, from the elegant pen of the author of 'The Heliotrope,' should grace the pages of her book.

"Lady B. has many apologies to make for this liberty; but the author of 'The Heliotrope' must bear in mind that few who have had the gratification of perusing that admirable poem, could resist the desire of endeavouring to procure a few lines from the same pen, for a work in which Lady B. is much interested."

"Sunday, June 16th, 1833.

"Lady Blessington feels deeply sensible, not only of the consent the author of 'The Heliotrope' has given to comply with her request, but the amiable manner in which that consent has been conveyed. Lady B. cannot abandon the hope of becoming personally acquainted with an author whose admirable poem has so much delighted her, and requests that if the author of 'The Heliotrope' is resolved to retain his incognito, she may at least have the pleasure of seeing his friend, Dr. Wm. Beattie, whose name brings associations most agreeable, not only of the 'Progress of Genius,' but its happiest results, as exemplified in 'The Heliotrope.' Lady Blessington sends a picture, which she is most anxious should be illustrated in *verse*. The subject is beautiful, and therefore not unworthy the pen she wishes to consign it to."

"Seamore Place, Tuesday, Aug. 20th.

"DEAR SIR,

"I enclose a proof-sheet of the beautiful poem you were so kind as to give me, that you may see if it is correctly printed. Will you be so good as to return it at your earliest convenience? I greatly fear that the *lateness* of my hours has more than once deprived me of the pleasure of seeing you; and to prevent the recurrence of such a loss occurring to me again, may I entreat you to bear in mind, that I receive *every evening from ten o'clock until half-past twelve*, and that it will be most highly gratifying to me to see you at Seamore Place, as frequently as you can favour me with your company.

"Your sincere and obliged,

"M. BLESSINGTON."

"Saturday Morning.

"It appears that I am never to address you, except to acknowledge some favour conferred. I have now to thank you for the lines sent to-day, and to express my gratitude for the admirable poem, with which I shall be proud to grace the pages of my 'Book of Beauty.'

"I should be wanting in candour were I not to acknowledge the high gratification your commendation of 'The Repealers' has given me. It is *such praise*, and from *such a source*, that it repays an author for being misunderstood by the common herd, among whom my book is not calculated to make much impression. M. BLESSINGTON."

"Wednesday, July 3, 1833.

"With such a gem in my book as the sketch you have sent me, I defy criticism, for *one* such contribution would redeem my work. How can I thank you sufficiently?

"I dare not believe the flattering things you say of my 'Repealers;' but pray remember it was written in *five weeks*—the only excuse I can give for its errors.

"I am generally at home, except on opera nights, and your

presence can never fail to be most acceptable at Seamore Place, whenever you have a spare evening at your disposal.

"M. BLESSINGTON."

"Seamore Place, 29th November, 1833.

"I feel that the partiality of the friend (for so you must permit me to consider you) has silenced the criticism of the Erudite Reader, and, therefore, I fear to accept the commendations you offer me—commendations so valuable from an Author, whose brilliant genius is only equalled by the chaste elegance of the language in which it is displayed.

"The truth is, it is difficult for a mind like yours to peruse any work without decking it with some portion of that grace and beauty which evidently peculiarly belongs to your imagination, like the vase which having long contained precious odours, lends a portion of their fragrance even to water when it passes through it.

"I regret that you are compelled to live in darkness, but with 'the light within,' who can so well dispense with that without? Milton described what *he imagined,* and gained immortality; had sight been spared him, he might have only described what he saw, and gained only temporary fame.

"Though I pray that you may never resemble him in the cause, I trust you will emulate him in the *effect*, which was produced on his genius by loss of vision; for I am persuaded the more frequently you draw on 'the light within,' the more will all lovers of true poetry be illumined.

"I hope you will indulge me with your society whenever you are able to face the *lamp,* that most destructive of all economical inventions, which sears the eyes and dulls the head.

"M. BLESSINGTON."

"January 1st, 1834.

"The elegant lines I received this day, can come from no pen save yours, so let me thank you for them. They arrived at a moment when the day had awakened *a melancholy train of reflections, in which the recollections of the past year, and the fears for the future* had shed a gloom, which the fanciful and gay visions of your muse dispelled. 1833 has peculiar claims to my gratitude, for having bestowed on me the advantage and pleasure of your (will you permit me to say?) friendship; and for this I have bade adieu to it with regret.

"I am writing in a room with a circle of friends, who are talking so loudly that I fear my note will be almost as unintelligible to you as my ideas are to myself; but three feelings are distinct in my mind, which are *gratitude* for your kindness, admiration for your genius, and genuine esteem for your mayn fine qualities, which no one, my dear sir, can estimate more highly than M. BLESSINGTON."

"January 16th, 1835.

"The bearer is Mr. Miller,* the poet (and basket-maker), for whom I am anxious to procure *your* countenance. Who so well as you can appreciate a true poet, or who reward with kind words of encouragement, one to whom *Fortune* has been so much less kind than nature?

"M. BLESSINGTON."

"January 1, 1836.

"One can forgive the coming new year, which reminds us of much that we wish to forget, when it brings verses like yours. Verses in which a refined taste and a true genius are equally conspicuous. I put genius last; for though it is considered 'the gift, all other gifts above,' yet I rank it beneath that inestimable gift, a *heart*, that endears you to every friend who has ever had the happiness of knowing you; and I do assure you, honestly and truly, that I have never been able to decide which I most valued, the brilliant genius you possess, or the noble, warm heart, that shines through all your actions and thoughts.

"M. BLESSINGTON."

"Gore House, March 28, 1836.

"I last year gave you a subject, which only a muse like yours would adorn; I now send you one that might inspire a much less gifted one. It is the portrait of the Marchioness of

* Miller, the basket-making bard, author of "Fair Rosamond," &c.—R. R. M.

Abercorn and her daughter, by E. Landseer, and to my taste is charming. The Marchioness is daughter to the Duke of Bedford, and a descendant of Rachael Lady Russell, whose virtues she inherits. If I counted less on your friendship, of which I have had so many proofs, I should hesitate in demanding this new one; but I know that your muse is ever propitious to the call of friendship.

" I hope you will soon come and see my new abode, and your cordial friend,

" M. Blessington."

" Gore House, Friday, April 15, 1836.

" Will you forgive me for being so importunate? But your verses are to open my book, followed by Mr. Bulwer, and Sir William Gell's Essay.

" Printers have sometimes devils *in*, as well as about them, and are prone to perplex those who dip their fingers in ink.

" M. Blessington."

" Gore House, February 15, 1837.

"I am a petitioner to you on the part of Mrs. Fairlie, my niece, for three or four stanzas. The children (for the illustration) are the three sons of the Duke of Buccleugh, whose Duchess is a daughter of the Marquis of Bath. An allusion to the family adds interest to the subject, and *no one* can make such allusions with the grace that you do. The work for which the plate is meant, is to be named ' Buds and Blossoms,' and is to give the portraits of all the children of the English aristocracy. It will be a beautiful work, and as it is the first which my niece has undertaken to edit, I am most anxious for its success. A few lines from your gifted pen will secure this.

" M. Blessington."

" Gore House, July 10, 1837.

" I shall fancy that my ' Book of Beauty' can have no luck, and be sure it can have no *grace*, unless it contains some lines from your pen. The number of plates is now curtailed to twelve instead of nineteen as formerly, and I have not one to be illustrated, having distributed my twelve before I knew that an alteration was to be made. My drawers are full of prose and verse, from the generosity of contributors, but I prefer one page of yours *on any subject*, to piles from others. Let me, therefore, have a page, a sonnet, any thing of yours, and then I shall feel confident of success.

"M. BLESSINGTON."

"Gore House, July 17, 1838.

"I send an engraving of a fair lady as a petitioner to you for a few lines. If I knew any poet who could write half so well, you should not be so often troubled; but the truth is, you throw so much grace, truth, and beauty into your verses, that I cannot resist trespassing on your kindness for an illustration which is so precious for my book. The portrait is Lady Valetort, whose husband is the son of Lord Mount Edgecomb. She is the daughter of Lady Elizabeth Fielding, and a very lovely as well as amiable young woman. The child is her first-born.

"M. BLESSINGTON."

"St. Leonard's-on-Sea, Victoria Hotel,
"September 15, 1839.

"It was only yesterday that your 'Polynesia' was forwarded to me from home, and having perused it last evening, and again this morning, I cannot allow a day to pass without thanking you, as I most heartily do, for the exquisite gratification it has afforded me. You have, indeed, found an irresistible mode for exciting the liveliest interest in favour of the *missionaries* and their converts, for I defy the coldest-hearted Utilitarians to read your beautiful poem without feeling themselves melted into sympathy for the toils and triumphs you have so eloquently described. Poesy is, indeed, a blessed as well as a glorious gift, when, as in this case, it is made subservient to the highest interests of humanity, and I am delighted that your muse (always skilful in awakening the tender feelings) has led you to adopt a subject so fraught with all that could inspire them. Her flight has this time been a very high one, but like the angels who can soar to Heaven, and bask in its glories without becoming insensible to the ills of unhappy mortals, she, though flying through the highest regions of imagination, overlooks not the sufferings of those who are denied its gifts, and while dazzling us by her splendour, forgets not to touch the heart, while charming the mind; so that even when we are most delighted with the muse, we reverence the Christian. M. BLESSINGTON."

"Gore House, November 30, 1839.

"Your verses on the portrait of Lady Clanricarde, have met with universal admiration. No one ever wrote more appropriate or more delicate compliments. Her Ladyship is beautiful and clever, so that your address to her portrait is happily applicable. M. BLESSINGTON."

"Sunday, July 19.

"Nothing can be more happy or more graceful than 'The Planet.' Does not this prove, that 'Poets excel most in fiction?'

"The loveliest portrait could not have inspired more charming lines. How beautiful are the two numbers you have sent me of your 'Switzerland' and 'Scotland,' two works more deservedly popular than any that have appeared for ages, and calculated to produce the most happy effect (that of refining the taste) on all who read them.

"How sweet is 'The Vesper Hymn;' it is a perfect gem, set in a frame of the finest granite (for your prose will last as long as that imperishable substance); and your poetry is not only the most graceful and highly finished, but the most perfectly musical I know; yet neither its high polish nor music are attained by the sacrifice of that greatest of all essentials in poetry, good sense, which joined to a brilliant imagination and exquisite taste, pervade every line you write.

"M. BLESSINGTON."

"Friday evening.

"Read Dr. Hogg's and Sir William Gell's letters. I think the works named by both, might be proposed to Messrs. Saunders and Ottley, who are my present publishers. They appear to be very excellent people, and have just brought out a beautiful work of Sir William Gell, on the 'Topography of Rome,' in a most creditable style.

"M. Blessington."

"Gore House, July 24, 1841.

"I come a *beggar* to you at the eleventh hour, for a few lines to illustrate a portrait of the Honourable Miss Forester, a very charming young lady. Will you therefore write me a page of verse for the portrait in question? The young lady is seated, with a little dog on her lap, which she looks at rather pensively; she is fair, with light hair, and is in mourning. She is sister to Lord Forester, and her sisters, Lady Chesterfield and the Hon. Mrs. George Anson, are remarkable for their beauty. Pray excuse this unreasonable request, and let your brilliant imagination picture the young beauty, whose portrait is to be illustrated.

"M. Blessington."

"Gore House, May 24, 1842.

"I send you a portrait of the Queen, the Prince of Wales, and the Princess Royal, which is to form the frontispiece of the 'Book of Beauty.' Will you extend to me and my book the same kindness so often extended hitherto, and write a page or two for this picture? If I knew any poet who would do half so well, I would not trouble you, for I am really ashamed of trespassing so often on your kindness.

"M. Blessington."

"Gore House, Monday.

"Your kind letter of Saturday found me in the hour of need, for never did I more require your services. The proprietor of the annual, and his printer, and his engraver, have all three been ill, which has delayed the progress of these works; until now, at the eleventh hour, I find myself pressed by a quantity of work hardly to be got through, even with industry. Will you then kindly come to my aid, and illustrate the plate I send, and which only came to my hand this morning? It represents the Place de Louis XV., so celebrated from being the scene of so many remarkable events. It was, during the first revolution, converted into the Place de la Revolution, a permanent guillotine being erected, which served for the execution of Louis XVI. and his unfortunate Queen, and also for a great many of their nobility. In 1800, it became the Place de la Concorde. In 1815 it resumed its original name, Place Louis XV. Under the reign of Louis Philippe, the place has undergone great improvement. It has been admirably paved, lighted by forty magnificent candelabras for gas, and the obelisk of Luxor, seventy-two feet in height, graces the centre, with two noble fountains on either side. A page of verse to illustrate this plate, or two pages, if requisite, would greatly oblige me—treated as you wish. Might not the fountains be supposed to send their showers to efface the innocent blood shed on the spot? I ought to apologize for any hint or suggestion, to one whose mind is stored with poetical images, as well as with historical events.

"M. Blessington."

LETTERS OF DR. W. BEATTIE ADDRESSED TO LADY BLESSINGTON.

"My dear Lady Blessington,

"I have endeavoured to carry your wishes into effect, and have done so; if not successfully, at least speedily.

"Yours truly obliged,
"W. Beattie."

LINES TO THE FOUNTAINS

IN THE PLACE DE LA CONCORDE, WHERE THE GUILLOTINE WAS ERECTED "EN PERMANENCE."

"Flow on, ye bright waters! in harmony flow;
Now mounting like crystal—now falling like snow:
Cheer the night with the music and dance of your spray,
And cool, with your freshness, the long summer day!
Fan the sick with your breath—bid the weary repose,
And wean the sad heart from a sense of its woes!
Wash out, if ye may, the dark record of blood
That reddens the spot where the *guillotine* stood!

"But no!—although Genius and Fancy may toil—
Though trophies and sculptures embellish the soil;
Though kings, or republics, surround you with light,
And deck you with treasures that dazzle the sight—
Their labour is vain.—Through the splendid disguise,
That enchants the beholder, what spectres arise!
Stern HISTORY opens her volume, and lo!
That FOUNTAIN is changed to a scaffold of woe!—
An army of martyrs—starred, mitred, and crowned—
Dragged on by assassins, encumber the ground!
Their dungeon exchanged for the steel and the block,
And the dismal arena, that thrills to the shock—
For the axe is descending—and Mercy takes wing—
Foul hands are imbrued in the blood of their KING!

"Again! for the vision grows darker in hue—
And the regicide weapons are whetted anew!
There—fairer and brighter than fancy may paint—
With the face of an angel, the faith of a saint—
The soul of a martyr—anointed of Heaven—
Their beautiful QUEEN to the scaffold is driven—
On the block, like her consort, to bow and to bleed....
Oh, Mercy—Humanity—blush for the deed!
Weep—weep for the crime whose indelible trace
No tears can extinguish—no time can efface!
The Fountain may flow—and the Sculptor may toil—
But the red stamp of Infamy clings to the soil!

"W. B."

"6 Park Square, Jany. 1839.

"I beg to return you my grateful thanks for a very handsome, and a very useful present. Having failed in two other attempts to do so in person, allow me on paper to wish you many happy returns of the season, and believe that your health, and fame, and happiness, are objects of the most sincere interest at this fireside. Your 'Governess' has produced a most favourable impression—we cannot, however, imagine how you can possibly write so much and so well—unless you have a familiar spirit; and that a *spirit* does abide in much that you write, is apparent.

"I saw Madden for a few minutes since his return from the Havannah, but he is now, I believe, in Dublin. I suppose he showed you the volume of MS. poems, inscribed to him by the bards of Cuba, (and some earlier lines addressed to him by a bard of Caledonia). I thought him greatly improved in health.

"W. Beattie."

LINES ADDRESSED TO R. R. MADDEN, ON HIS DEPARTURE FOR THE WEST INDIES IN 1833, BY DR. W. BEATTIE.

"Strong as some sainted amulet,
The link in memory's chain,
That tells where kindred spirits met,
No time can rend in twain.
And mindful of her pledge, the muse
One passing wreath would twine,
And trace in every flower she strews,
A health to thee and thine.

The union of congenial minds
No distance can divide,
Unshaken in the shock of winds,
Unstemmed by ocean's tide.
It lives beyond the Atlantic main,
Where basking 'neath the line,
A sun-bright shore, a palmy plain,
Shall welcome thee and thine.

Embowered within the glowing west,
And circled by the sea,
Which laves 'the Islands of the Blessed,'
A health to them and thee.
And gentle stars, and generous hearts,
Their genial lights combine,
And all that halcyon peace imparts,
Descend on thee and thine.

Adieu, the breath of friendship fills
The sail that wafts thee hence,
To lands whose radiant sky distils
Arabic's redolence!

Go—but a few brief summers flown,
Once more across the brine—
Thy country shall reclaim the loan
She lent on thee and thine!"

London, Sept. 30th. W. B.

"Park Square, Jan. 6, 1841.

"DEAR LADY BLESSINGTON,

"In looking over some papers of a lamented friend, yesterday, I found some pages of MS. inscribed 'Extracts from Lady Blessington's Works.' He was one of your greatest admirers, and has died in the prime of life of consumption. Brought up in the army, he was a brave soldier, and, as I can speak from long experience, 'a centurion,' and unaffectedly 'devout.' He has left nearly all he possessed to the numerous public charities of London. W. BEATTIE."

Enclosed in the preceding letter.

LINES

ON THE DEATH OF CAPT. J. S. C. 53RD REGIMENT.

BY DR. W. BEATTIE.

"OH, weep not for the fleetness
That closed his brief career!
For memory sheds a sweetness
And fragrance round his bier.

Tho' mouldering in their lowly bed
His lifeless relics lie—
Tho' cold in dust, *he* is not dead—
For virtue cannot die!

Oh, never cloud with sadness
The heart that should rejoice,
For Hope, and Faith, and gladness,
Spoke in his parting voice!

His soul has found that brighter sphere
Where Faith her Sabbath keeps;
While angels whisper round his bier—
'He is not dead, but sleeps!'

If we but lead 'the life *he* led,'
We'll meet him on that shore—
That land—where death itself is dead,
And sin can tempt no more!

He passed our world in pilgrim haste,
Like one whose measur'd way
Was fleeting thro' this dreary waste,
To reach eternal day!

Then, weep not for the fleetness
That closed his brief career,
For memory sheds a sweetness
And fragrance round his bier!"

W. B.

"Park Square, 30th February, 1841.

"To-morrow (D.V.) I will take Prince Albert's likeness at a sitting. From a Conservative, and the editor of 'Conservative Statesmen,' it will be a curiosity! But I will take care that the sketch shall be executed in good taste (!) and shall be as pithy and concise as the enunciation of his R. H.'s accomplishments will allow. W. BEATTIE."

"November 20th.

"There are two 'Sonnets' of yours in the 'Book of Beauty' for the present year, which are gems of feeling and expression; and to my mind afford more real pleasure than all that the artists have done, wonderful as their art undoubtedly is. Mr. Chorley's 'Stanzas to Marguerite' are pointed, graceful, and appropriate; and he is much happier than a hundred others, who have drawn their inspiration from a similar source. I was struck with the 'Lines to Mrs. Fairlie,' so playful and elegant in the structure and sentiment, as well as with the greater portion of the other contributions; but the 'Sonnets' I can repeat, and never repeat anything that does not make a strong impression upon my mind. W. BEATTIE."

I subjoin to those letters a copy of some remarkable lines of Dr. Beattie, which Lady Blessington requested me to procure for her from the author, at the time of their appearance.

TO THE POETS OF AMERICA,

BY DR. WILLIAM BEATTIE.

[Inscribed to R. R. Madden.]

"Bards of Freedom's boasted land!
Brothers! foremost of the free!
Ye who, with impassion'd hand,
Sweep the chords of Liberty.
Ye, to whom the boon is given,
To win the ear and melt the heart!
Awake! and waking earth and heaven!
Perform the minstrel's noblest part.

Why stand ye mute? when on the ear
A thunder-peal from sea to sea—
A peal earth's darkest haunts shall hear,
Proclaims—the slave shall now be free!
Long has he drain'd the bitter cup!
Long borne the scourge and dragg'd the chain!
But now the strength of Europe's up—
A strength that ne'er shall sleep again!

Your Garrison has fann'd the flame!
Child, Chapman, Pierrepont, catch the fire;
And, rous'd at Freedom's hallow'd name,
Hark! Bryant, Whittier, strike the lyre!
While *here*, hearts, voices, trumpet-toned,
Montgomery, Cowper, Campbell, Moore,
To Freedom's glorious cause respond!
In sounds that thrill to every core.

Their voice has conjured up a power
No foes can daunt, no force arrest!
That gathers strength with every hour,
And strikes a chord in every breast;
A power that soon on Afric's sand,
On Cuba's shore, on Ocean's flood,
Shall crush the oppressor's iron hand,
And blast the traffickers in blood.

Oh! where should Freedom's hope abide,
Save in the bosoms of the free!
Where should the wretched Negro hide,
Save in the shade of Freedom's tree?
And where should minstrel wake the strain,
That cheers Columbia's forests wild?
Oh, not where captives clank their chain,
For Poetry is Freedom's child!

The minstrel cannot, must not sing,
Where fetter'd slaves in bondage pine!
Man has no voice, the muse no wing,
Save in the lights of Freedom's shrine!
Oh! by those songs your children sing,
The lays that soothe your winter fires!
The hopes, the hearths to which you cling,
The sacred ashes of your sires!

By all the joys that crown the free,
Love, Honour, Fame, the hopes of Heaven!
Wake in your might, that earth may see
God's gifts have not been vainly given!
Bards of Freedom's foremost strand!
Strike at last your loftiest key!
Peal the watchword through the land!
Shout till every slave is free!

Long has he drained the bitter cup!
Long borne the lash and clank'd the chain!
But now the strength of Europe's up—
A strength that ne'er shall sleep again!

"Park Square, June 24th, 1840. W. B."

LETTERS FROM LADY BLESSINGTON TO R. R. MADDEN.

"Seamore Place, Friday.

"I was both grieved and disappointed this day on discovering that you and Mr. Campbell had called, before I had left my bed-room.

" I expressed to you last evening the extreme desire I have long entertained to make the acquaintance of a Poet, whose admirable productions no one can more highly value and admire than I do. Two months ago, Mr. Jekyll, one of my oldest friends, at my request wrote to Mr. Campbell, stating my impatience to be favoured with his acquaintance; indeed, so well versed am I in Mr. Campbell's works, that I regard him with feelings of such respect and admiration, as merit at least the advantage of being personally known to him.

" I must, therefore, request that you will present him my best compliments, and solicit the favour of his naming any day or time that I may hope to have the honour of seeing you. If it be possible, pray endeavour to bring him this evening to tea.

" Believe me, your sincere friend,

" M. Blessington."

" Monday, March 4th, 1833.

" When I tell you that I have six hundred pages to write and compose, between this and the last day of the month, for a work which, unless completed by that period, I forfeit an engagement, you will understand why I cannot read over the story that you have so kindly sent me; and which I feel persuaded is, like all that I have seen from your pen, graphic and full of talent. The moment I have got rid of my plaguing book, I will sit down to it, with true gusto, and en attendant, have to express my grateful sense of the active kindness with which you have rendered me this essential serviee.

" I am so pressed for time, that I must conclude, though I have a thousand things to say about your interesting Greek heroine; the whole story of her redemption from slavery, her English marriage, her visit to you in London, &c. is a charming little romance.* M. Blessington."

* The person referred to was a Greek girl, named Yanulla, sold into Turkish slavery, and rescued from it in Alexandria, who was subsequently married to a British merchant of Alexandria, Mr. Agnew, a partner in the house of Messrs. Briggs and Co., and after a sojourn in England for two or three years, in Mr. Agnew's family, had been sent to England with a view to her education. I had seen her and her

"Seamore Place, March 12, 1834.

"I saw Dr. Beattie a few days ago; he continues to feel a lively interest in your welfare, and I am persuaded you have few more sincere friends.

"He is a man whose heart is as warm as his head is sensible and clever, and one such as the present times rarely offers in the number of our friends. He has just brought out the first Number of a work, entitled 'Switzerland,' illustrated by beautiful engravings, and the style of the book is admirable, and highly creditable to him. Mr. Campbell I never see, and seldom hear of, either in the literary or social world. I hope he will soon give us his 'Memoirs of Mrs. Siddons,' for it is time they should come forth.

"I trust your pen is not idle; I look forward to a lively novel descriptive of 'Life in the West Indies,' with no trifling impatience. It will give me pleasure to hear from you whenever you have a leisure half hour to give me.

"M. Blessington."

"Gore House, Dec. 17, 1840.

"Many thanks for the very interesting work you have sent me, and which I have perused with pleasure. It will do a great deal of good to the ill-used race you have already exerted yourself so much for, by proving that they are worthy of sympathy.

"I was sorry not to have found you at home when I called. I hope you have no engagement for Saturday next, and that you will give me the pleasure of your company at dinner on that day, at half-past seven o'clock.

"M. Blessington."

"F. O., June 8, 1837.

"I have consulted with Mr. Byng on the subject of your note to me, and it appears to both of us, that your friend *is in*

mother in slavery in Candia, subsequently in Egypt. I was present at the liberation of both in Alexandria, and was visited in England by the former and her husband, Mr. Agnew, a few days after their marriage in London. They were then about to proceed to Candia, where, shortly after, Mrs. Agnew died.—R. R. M.

no danger from any representation against him, as you perhaps apprehend.

"He has lately been *approved* of for his conduct, and things will, I hope, go on better when the new Chief Commissioner shall have arrived.*

"Very sincerely yours,
"W. Fox Strangways."

"Gore House, Dec. 19, 1840.

"I regret exceedingly not to have seen you before your departure for Africa. I had been unwell for some days, and am still an invalid, but snatched the first moment I was able to see any thing, to ask you to come, little thinking you were so soon to leave London.

"It gives me great pleasure to hear that you have arranged matters so satisfactorily at Downing Street, and it proves how highly your services are appreciated there. Long may you continue to enjoy them in the full enjoyment of health, is my sincere and hearty wish.

"It would give me a melancholy satisfaction to learn every particular you can find out relative to poor L. E. L., for I entertained a deep sentiment of affection for her. I should like exceedingly to have a plain, simple marble slab placed over her grave, with her name inscribed on it, and I would willingly defray the expenses, as I cannot bear to think there should be no record of the spot. When you arrive at Cape Coast Castle, you can ascertain if this were possible, I mean as regards her husband.

"It will give me great pleasure to hear from you, whenever you are disposed to write; and if I can, at any time, be of use to you or yours, do not hesitate to employ me, for be assured

"I am your sincere friend,
"M. Blessington."

* The above letter was forwarded to me by Lady Blessington, when residing in Cuba, holding the offices of "Superintendent of Liberated Africans," and acting "Commissioner of Arbitration in the Mixed Court of Justice at the Havannah," while battling with slave-trade interests against very powerful and unscrupulous opponents.—R. R. M.

"Gore House, Dec. 28, 1842.

"Indisposition has prevented me from sooner answering your letter. My advice is, that you render your letter to Lord John as concise as possible. You need not enter into the merits of your case with him, or refute the calumnies of your assailants,* as he is master of the subject; but merely state your motive in publishing a defence, which their attacks have rendered necessary. Inform Lord John as briefly as you can, the persecution, in all forms, you have undergone, previously to defending yourself in the papers. Lord John is so good a man, that I wish you to stand well with him.

"M. BLESSINGTON."

"Gore House, Tuesday.

"I have read with great interest, the books, &c., which you confided to me, and which I now return. I send you a pedigree, on the authenticity of which you may rely.

"Mr. Edmund Sheehy referred to as having been executed for rebellion, was my unfortunate grandfather. He lived at the Lodge, Bawnfoune, county Waterford, about seven or eight miles from Clonmel. I cannot make out in what degree of relationship he stood to Father Nicholas Sheehy, as my mother never referred to the subject without horror. She lost her father when she was only two years old.

"Musgrave refers to Edmund Sheehy in his book. I have heard that my grandfather was a chivalrous-minded man, to whom pardon was offered if he would betray others. I also know that he was nearly related to Father Nicholas Sheehy; but as no mention of this is made in the pedigree, I know not the degree of relationship. I should much like that justice could be rendered to the memories of my unfortunate relatives, without any violation of truth. I shall look for your new book with impatience, and do what I can to forward its circulation.

"I am so agitated by the increasing illness of my dear niece, that I have had hardly time to write you these few lines.

* Opponents of all bona fide efforts for the abolition of the slave-trade on the coast of Africa.—R. R. M.

"Father Sheehy was buried in a church-yard in the neighbourhood of Clogheen. I regret that I can give you no other clue. I trust when you next visit England I shall see more of you, but Mrs. Fairlie's illness has kept me from seeing any of my friends of late.*

"M. BLESSINGTON."

"Gore House, March 7, 1843.

"I thank you for the book on Rome, which I have not yet had time to look at. I wish I could give you any information, or clue to acquire it, relative to the family of Father Sheehy, but unfortunately I cannot, as for thirty years I have entirely lost sight of every one connected with them.

"M. BLESSINGTON."

* The work referred to in this letter was written by the author: to the second series of it there was an historical memoir prefixed, containing an extensive notice of the trial and execution of the Rev. Nicholas Sheehy and Edmond Sheehy, Esq., from the original records of the legal proceedings, in both cases, still extant in the office of the Clerk of the Peace in Clonmel. At the time this notice was written and published, the author was not aware that Lady Blessington was the grand-daughter of Edmond Sheehy, and a relative also of the Rev. N. Sheehy. These facts he learned for the first time from Lady Blessington after her perusal of the notice. While speaking at considerable length of those lamentable events and disastrous times, thus accidentally recalled, she was crying bitterly during the whole time that our conversation lasted.

It was on that occasion, that Lady Blessington promised the author the pedigree of the Sheehy family, which he subsequently received, and published in the work above referred to, omitting, however, though not by her desire, the last passage in the document, which connected her name with the account of the family of the ill-fated Sheehys. There is matter for reflection in the vicissitudes of fortune, which marked the career of the persecutors and the descendants of them in this case of frightful injustice; and also in those singular circumstances attending the elevation to the British Peerage of two grand-daughters of the unfortunate Edmond Sheehy, who had been falsely accused, iniquitously convicted of a white-boy offence, and ignominiously put to death for the same.

"Gore House, October 19, 1843.

"Those who imagine that you will descend one step in life, by accepting the occupation you are about to fill in Portugal, entertain a very different opinion from me. Some of the most distinguished men have written for the press, and your doing so, will, according to my notion, give you a new claim on the political party you have hitherto served.

"I am not sorry that you will be removed from Ireland, at present, when affairs wear an aspect that must grieve and irritate every Irishman with noble and generous feelings. But women have, in my opinion, no business with politics, and I, above all women, have a horror of mixing myself up with them. I must content myself in wishing well to my poor country, which no one more heartily does. Wherever you go, or in whatever position, you will take with you my cordial good wishes for your prosperity and welfare, and for that of your family.

"I am now oppressed by writing to fulfil an engagement I entered into, without being aware of the excessive fatigue it would entail on me; and am even at this moment so occupied, that I have not time to say more than, that I hope to see you before your departure, and that

"I am always your sincere friend,

"M. Blessington."

"Gore House, June 8th, 1847.

"I have been wondering why I have been so long without seeing you, and had I known your address, which unfortunately had been lost, I should certainly have written to you to say so. I do not lightly form friendships, and when formed, I do not allow any differences in political opinions to interfere with them. I have known you too long and too well, not to feel a lively interest in your welfare, however we may disagree on some subjects.* When I last saw you I was suffering such annoyance

* The difference alluded to, was on account of some observations made by Lady Blessington, with respect to the peasantry of Ireland, and their recent sufferings during the famine. The only altercation I

from being above a year without receiving a shilling of my rents from Ireland, that I felt unusual irritation on the subject on which we conversed. It was, however, but momentary, and never could produce any change in my sentiments towards an old and esteemed friend.

"I am not surprised, though greatly pleased, at the appointment offered you by Lord Grey,* for he is a man capable of appreciating merit, and you left so high a character whenever previously employed, as to deserve future confidence. I only regret that you are going so far away. I have heard such favourable accounts of the climate, that I hope your absence from home will not be interminable, and that I may still see you return in health and comfort. It will give me great pleasure to see you before you depart, and to assure you of my unimpaired regard. Count D'Orsay charges me with his kindest wishes for your health and happiness, and my nieces send theirs. God bless you, my dear Dr. Madden. Let me hear sometimes from you, and count always on the good wishes of your sincere friend,

"M. Blessington."

LETTERS FROM R. R. MADDEN TO LADY BLESSINGTON.

"East Ascent, St. Leonards, May 6th.

"I took Campbell to Seamore Place at a very unseasonable hour of the morning, having to leave town at noon, but I thought that having once brought him to your door, like every other person who has once crossed its threshold, he would be very likely to find it again of his own accord.

"I cannot tell you, Lady Blessington, what pleasure it gave me to pass once more a few hours in your society. Much as I have used my locomotive organs since we met in Naples in

ever had with Lady Blessington was on that occasion. She was a little out of temper, and I was not a little vehement, I believe, in expressing an opinion, that those who belonged to the people, and came out of their ranks, should deal leniently with their faults, and sympathize with their sufferings.—R. R. M.

* That of Colonial Secretary to Western Australia.—R. R. M.

1823 and 1824, I do not avail myself of the privilege which courtesy accords to travellers, when I assure you I feel indebted for some of the most agreeable recollections of my life, to the many pleasant hours I have passed in the Villa Belvedere; but like all other pleasures, these are now dashed by the painful recollection that death has broken up that once happy circle, and left all who were acquainted with it so many reasons for regret. I have met few men who possessed more genuine kindness of heart than poor Lord Blessington, or who was less indebted to his rank for the regard of those around him.

"I am indebted, dear Lady Blessington, to your kind note for this opportunity of assuring you I am not forgetful of the obligations I am under to you. I feel I might have remained to this day a very obscure son of Machaon in Naples, had I not known your condescending notice at that period in early life, and at the outset of my career, when it was of most value to me.

"Yours, dear Lady Blessington, ever sincerely and gratefully,

"R. R. MADDEN."

"48, Sloane Square, Chelsea. (1843).

"I thought you might like to see a work, and one that treats of the Eternal City, written by the *grand-nephew* of Father Nicholas Sheehy. The author is, I understand, a layman, now living in Rome, a secretary to the noble ecclesiastic of Scotch origin, to whom his book is dedicated. I am very anxious to ascertain his address, and perhaps your Ladyship's acquaintance with persons either resident there, or going thither from this country, might enable you to obtain some information for me on this point. The author of this book is represented to me as a man of refined taste, a scholar, and strongly attached to the faith of his fathers. But my informant knows nothing of his present abode.

"What relation can he be to Edmund Sheehy?*

* The work above referred to is entitled, "Reminiscences of Rome, by a Member of the Arcadian Academy," post 8vo. London, 1838. It is dedicated to His Grace Charles Edward Drummond, Duke of Melfort and Earl of Perth in Scotland, and domestic prelate of His Holiness Gregory XVI., Apostolical Prothonotary. The work is the production of a man of refined taste, well stocked with recondite Italian lore. He

"In the pedigree there is an unfortunate hiatus, where the latter's father is referred to. It does not mention whom he married, or how many children he had. Edmund alone is mentioned as his son.

"In the early part of next week I am going over to Ireland, and I am likely to be at Clonmel within eight or ten days. Can your Ladyship give me the address of any person in that part of the country, likely to assist me in my further inquiries there? I think the people of Ireland ought not to have left the graves of these martyred men without a monumental stone.

"Your Ladyship will perceive by the note in the fly-leaves of the volume, that there is nothing of the kind. The note is written by a very distinguished scholar; and as there are some curious remarks detailed in it, regarding the deaths of the Tipperary persecutors, I took the liberty of sending it for your Ladyship's perusal. R. R. MADDEN."

EXTRACT FROM A LETTER TO LADY BLESSINGTON, ON LEAVING IRELAND IN 1843. (Vide answer to letter, dated 19th October, 1843.)

"London, October, 1843.

"If Ireland was governed on just, fair, impartial principles, all my experience of other countries would lead me to believe that greater happiness might be expected for its people, than for the inhabitants of any other country in Northern or Western Europe. The people are naturally a joyous, sprightly, social, easily amused, and easily contented people. The middle classes and mercantile communities of the cities and large towns some five-and-thirty or forty years ago, were generally tolerably well educated, and many of both had a dash of gentle blood in their veins. They enjoyed life, and having acquired a competency, they had no idea of slaving themselves to death for the purpose of leaving enormous wealth to their children, or to distant relatives. They were not disposed to carry on business

was a layman when he published those "Reminiscences of Rome." He is now a member of the order of the Brothers of Charity, founded by the Count Rosmini, and is attached to the R. C. College of Ratcliffe, in Leicestershire.

longer than was absolutely necessary to realize a comfortable subsistence for their families. I have never seen, in any foreign country, a state of society in middle life so good as that which existed in Dublin and Cork at that period, in the mercantile and manufacturing communities of those cities. . . The Irish people only want to be fairly ruled, and to be dealt with by their rulers irrespective of their creeds. They are a tolerant, equitable, largely trusting, simply acted-on people; prone perhaps to indulge a little too much in their social tendencies. The system of government that had been long adopted, had been one devised, not for improving them morally or intellectually, but for weakening them, by separating them, by educating them so as to make them detest one another's religions, by incensing them against each other, by making religious discord an element of strength for governmental purposes, by giving one faction which it favoured power, the faction that was small numerically, but important in point of wealth and position. This favoured faction, or, in other words, the Orange faction, was not only fierce and fanatical, and insatiably covetous, but continued, after it ceased to be an element of government, to be still greedy of power, ambitious, and unscrupulous as to the means of attaining its ends, whether by blood, intimidation, hypocrisy, and cajolery, or by indirect back-door official influence, by corruption, subserviency, and imposition.

"The people of England are utterly in the dark about the magnitude of the evil of Orangeism, or, as they please to call it, Protestant ascendancy—as the Roman Catholic people of Ireland, and especially the intellectual educated middle and upper classes are affected by it. The magnitude of the evil is owing to the momentum and power that had been long given to this intolerant system by the British government.

"With such governmental power and influence given to Orangeism under its various denominations, as have been given to it, with exceptions, few and far between, like those of the rule of Wellesley, Anglesey, and Normanby—it was positively a calamity for an intellectual, high-minded Roman Catholic, firmly believing in his religion, and sensible of the wanton and outrageous insults offered to it, to live in his own land, without having his feelings exasperated. There is nothing in this world so galling as the endurance of an asserted superiority, moral, intellectual, and religious, on the part of an overbearing and besotted spirit of intolerance, pretending to be enlightened and religious.

"The fact of England lending its countenance to Irish Orangeism, was always inexplicable to me, on any ground of policy having for its ultimate object and its aim the promotion of British imperial interests. I am most firmly convinced that course, if persisted in, will ultimately prove one of the main agencies that must contribute towards the decline and fall of British influence in the affairs of Europe.

"But supposing it were unfortunately attempted to govern anew this land through the agencies of Orangeism, as in the days of the Duke of Richmond, I have no doubt the attempt would fail.

"In the long run, all kinds of oppression are broken down; the laws of justice are not violated for ever with impunity; whether the day of retribution come slow or fast, it will come surely. All history, ancient and modern, has this teaching for injustice and intolerance. The cry that is 'væ victis,' becomes, in due time, 'væ victoribus.' . . .

"But, in the meantime, of what avail is it to our people to hear our brawling patriots, our newspaper Tells and Hofers praising the fertility of our soil, the multiplicity of our havens, the loveliness of our rivers, valleys, and mountain scenery; the magnificence of our bays and estuaries, the beauty of the shores of Ireland! Would to heaven she were less beautiful, less fertile, less admirable for her havens and her shores, and more distant from all who will not be at peace with her religion and its professors! Would that she were more independent, better educated, more familiar with the history of other nations, and the evils in them of all connection between Church and State, and of all interference of the ministers of religion in temporal and political affairs! Would that she had more food for her people, and more force and union to employ against her foes! Ireland has its analogies with Italy, and the sighs of her children have their similitude with the aspirations of the poets and the people of Italy.

"You have written against Roman Cathalic demagogues and

agitators, but you never wrote a line against Orangeism and Protestant ascendancy; you never wrote a line against the persecutors of your religion, and of your own race.

"Do now, dear Lady Blessington—you to whom nature has given noble gifts, use them for a new account in literary labour, for a better one than fashion, for the advantage of the country that gave you birth, and against those pernicious interests that have been so long inimical to its peace.

"By the influence of your opinions, the distinguished people you draw around you, may be made serviceable to Ireland; and pardon me, Lady Blessington, if I remind you that Ireland has a claim on your pen, and *a controversy with it*. Your country is now entitled to other services at your hands than the production of political novels, pleasing to her enemies and painful to her friends to read. Employ some portion of your leisure in the reprobation of a system of government which administered its powers against the great bulk of the people of a country on account of their religion, and with a special view to the promotion of selfish purposes, hypocritically pursued under the name and guise of Protestant zeal for the interests of true religion.

"R. R. MADDEN."

CHAPTER X.

B. SIMMONDS, ESQ.

This gentleman possessed talents of a higher order than are frequently found belonging to those who are known only in literature as contributors to Annuals. He was a man of considerable talent, refined taste, and cultivated mind; one of Lady Blessington's contributors, for some years, to the periodicals edited by her, and the author of several tales and sketches, and short poetical pieces, of a great deal of merit. Some of his stories, illustrative of Irish character, are extremely clever, and his descriptions graphic. Mr. Simmonds never pursued literature as a career. He held a lucrative appointment in the Inland Revenue department in London. In society, his quiet and reserved manners gave the impression of a man fond of retirement—*peu demonstratif.* But when he felt at ease in company, and found himself in the midst of those he knew and esteemed, and was drawn out by his friends, he was highly agreeable and effective in conversation, and exhibited talent and intelligence of a high order. Mr. Simmonds was certainly a man of more than ordinary ability, and deserving of being better known in the literary world than it was his fortune to have been hitherto.

A writer in the "Notes and Queries" (for April, 1854, page 397), thus refers to the subject of this notice:—" Will you allow me to ask for a little information respecting

B. Simmonds? I believe he was born in the county of Cork, for he has sung in most bewitching strains his return to his native home, on the banks of the Funcheon. He was the writer of that great poem on the 'Disinterment of Napoleon,' which appeared in 'Blackwood' some years ago." The writer adds, "I believe he died in London, in July, 1852." But he is mistaken in the date. The public will be indebted to the inquiry, for a search after information on the subject of it that has not been fruitless.

The following details are the result of extensive inquiries made of the early associates and towns-people of Bartholomew Simmonds:—He was a native of the small town of Kilworth, in the county of Cork. His ancestry had connection with the aristocracy, but no relations, save those of servant and master. His grandfather, Bartholomew Simmonds, had been the butler of the Earl of Mountcashel, whose seat of Moore Park lies near the town of Kilworth (which place gave the title to the eldest son of Lord Mountcashel). After Bartholomew Simmonds had retired from the service of the Earl, he became proprietor of an inn in the town, which was the theatre of a frightful tragedy some thirty years ago—the death of Captain Fitzgerald by the hand of the late Earl of Kingston. His Lordship's sister had been the victim of an unhappy passion, and the person who was supposed to have wronged her was Colonel Fitzgerald, a cousin of the lady. He had gone down to Kilworth with the expectation of seeing her, and the Earl of Kingston, then staying at Moore Park, hearing of his arrival, proceeded immediately to Simmonds' hotel, where the Colonel lodged. He rushed to the bed-room of Colonel Fitzgerald with a loaded pistol in his hand, burst into the room, and took deliberate aim at the Colonel, who was in bed reading. Fitzgerald had only time to exclaim, "Fair play, at all events," and was in the act of springing on his feet, when Lord Kingston fired, and the unfortunate man fell dead on the floor.

The inn of Simmonds was patronized by the Kingston and Mountcashel families, and prospered accordingly. Old Bartholomew Simmonds left two sons; one succeeded his father in the business, the other was made a guager. The latter married a Miss Cuddy, sister of a Doctor Stephen Cuddy, of the Royal Artillery. From that union there were three children—two sons and a daughter; the elder son, Bartholomew Bootle Simmonds, the subject of this notice. His father died while he was young, but his widow and children were not lost sight of by the Earl of Mountcashel. They were located in a small but comfortable house, near the entrance to the Moore Park demesne. The boys, Bartholomew and Stephen, were sent to a school kept in Kilworth by a Mr. Birmingham, an excellent English teacher. The Simmonds' were delicate boys. Bartholomew was a quiet, studious lad, devoting to books and pictures all the leisure time which his class-fellows gave to play. He wrote a beautiful hand, and was very proud of that accomplishment. He was not fond of the society of his schoolmates; few of them were, however, of a respectable station in life. Young Simmonds' taste for poetry was then forming, and manifesting indications of the passion which it proved a few years later. From Birmingham's school he was sent to a classical one, kept by a gentleman of the name of Quigley, where he acquired a knowledge of Greek and Latin, a general proficiency in learning, and a love of literature, that made him ambitious of a wider sphere for the exercise of his talents than Kilworth afforded.

Simmonds' family, in the parlance of Kilworth people of the old faith, "ought to be Catholic;" but Irish innkeepers have more confidence in the patronage of lords on earth than in that of saints in heaven. The Lords Mountcashel carried the day with them against the whole calendar, including the martyr whose name was given to the young Simmonds. So Bartholomew was brought up in the way a child should go in

Kilworth, who might possibly one day or other become a guager, like his uncle. Some of the Kilworthians of ancient days are sceptical on this point, but there is evidence of the fact in his poems. In one of them, entitled "Columbus," a stanza thus begins, apostrophizing the great discoverer;

"Thou Luther of the darkened deep!
Nor less intrepid too than he
Whose courage broke earth's bigot sleep,
While thine unbarr'd the sea."

Through the interest of the old patrons of his family, the Mountcashel family, he obtained an appointment in London, in the correspondence office of the Excise department.

He had become a contributor to "Blackwood" before he quitted his native place; and it does great credit to the editors of that ably-conducted magazine, that they encouraged the very earliest productions of this unknown young contributor of theirs, writing from a small provincial town in Ireland, appreciated his talent, and never paused to inquire whether he was an aristocrat or a plebeian, a Tory or a Whig, an Orangeman or a Roman Catholic—leaving those considerations for the miserable provincial politics that creep into the control of the periodical literature of his own land. It was sufficient for the large-hearted Christopher North that his young Irish contributor was a man of talent and of worth, and we find him introducing one of the early poems of Simmonds to his readers with these words: "Here are verses by one who writes after our own heart."

Mr. Windele, of Cork, a celebrated antiquary and literati, informs me that "Simmonds and himself, many years ago, were contributors to 'Bolster's Magazine,' which was published in Cork; and that Simmonds, at that period, resided at Kilworth. Simmonds' first effusions were published in that magazine (one of considerable literary merit), which made its appearance in February, 1826." In the introductory observations to this periodical, which, for an Irish magazine, had rather a long existence of six years, and reached its fourth and final volume in the year 1832, the following passages occur, the sentiments of which are very analagous to thoughts expressed in several of his poems, and which would apply to the early separation of Simmonds from his native land, and from those literary pursuits in it which find so little encouragement:—

"While political economists contend that the system of absenteeism produces no ill effects on the prosperity of a country, it will not, we think, be denied by the most desperate theorist that the expatriation of native talent causes a positive decrease in the great fund of national intellect." . . . "The ills attendant on the emigration of a *lackland* man of genius are balanced by no such comfortable compensations (as those attendant on the absenteeism of a lord of the land); his wealth lies in a small compass, but it is indivisible, and must accompany the possessor. He leaves no representative behind to cherish the blossoms of literature, or cultivate the plants of science, which would have sprung up at his bidding. . . . In truth, it is a melancholy fact, that the talent for which this country is confessedly remarkable, seems to droop till it is transplanted, and has become, as it were, an exotic in the land that produced it."

He was a constant contributor to "Blackwood's Magazine," in which his name appears (always at the head of his articles) for the years 1834, 1836, 1839, 1840, 1841, 1842, 1843, 1844, 1845, and 1848.

In "Blackwood," June, 1834, there is one of the longest of Simmonds' poetical compositions, extending to 370 lines —"The Vision of Caligula, a Fragment." There are some beautiful lines in this poem, but the whole piece is dull, unimpassioned, and wearisome.

In "Blackwood," December, 1836, there are lines of Simmonds, on a visit of Lady E. S. Wortley to Mad. Letitia, the mother of Napoleon, with the following comments by Christopher North:—"We are delighted once more to number Mr. Simmonds among our poetical contributors. These lines are not unworthy of the author of the noble 'Ode on Napoleon,' which none who read it once in our pages can ever forget."

In "Blackwood's Magazine," February, 1840, there is a poem of Simmonds, entitled, "Song of a Returned Exile," descriptive of the feelings of a native of Kilworth returning after a long absence to his native place, on catching the first glimpse of the mountain of Corrin, and the hills which enclose the beautiful valley of the Blackwater and the Funcheon. Most assuredly the man who wrote these lines was no ordinary verse-maker.

In the same magazine for the following month, there is an "Ode on the Marriage of the Queen of England," by Simmonds, very laboured, heathenishly pious, and mythological.

In "Blackwood," for February, 1841, appeared his remarkable lines on "The Disinterment of Napoleon's Remains at St. Helena;" and in the same number, also, lines of his, entitled "The Flight to Cyprus;" and lines written in 1828, addressed "To an Emigrant Lady." In a later number of the Magazine for the same year, he published a short poem—"The Suit of the Minstrel."

In the January number for 1843 appeared "The Curse of Glencoe."

In the same year, he published (printed by Blackwood) a small 12mo. vol. entitled "Legends, Lyrics, and other Poems." In these we find frequent mention of the scenes of his early years: the Galty Mountains, Cairn Thiarka, the Blackwater, Funcheon, Cloglea Castle, &c.

The "Athenæum," of May 26th, 1843, in noticing this

volume, said :—" Of these poems, the larger number of them have previously appeared in 'Blackwood's Magazine.' The author has many poetic qualities, fancy and freedom of hand —that *daren doe* which puts no restraint upon its own imaginings, and a command of melody for their utterance. It might be worth while, had we space or a more profitable occasion, to inquire why with these and some other elements of poetic success, of a high order, the result is so unsatisfactory. But we will merely remark, that the legends are the best portion of this volume; because the author affects a picturesque style—an almost pageantry of language—which lends itself well to the romantic legend or heroic ballad, but overcharges the simplicity, and disturbs the tenderness of the lyric."

In " Blackwood," for June, 1844, there are two poetical pieces, one entitled " Columbus," very verbose, grandiloquent, and dull; another, " To Swallows on the Eve of Departure," in which the peculiar merits of his poetry, and his penchant for early scenes and associations, are abundantly displayed—tenderness of feeling and a love of nature—a constant turning of thoughts to absent friends—a yearning after home.

The following are the concluding lines of the last stanza but one of the poem, " To the Swallows," &c.

" A few short years when gone,
Back, back like you to early scenes—
Lo, at the threshold stone,
Where ever in the gloaming,
Home angels watched his coming,
A stranger stands and stares at him, who sighing passes on."

In the January number for 1845, a contribution of his appeared, " Vanities in Verse, or Letters of the Dead;" and in the June number, " Stanzas to the Memory of Thomas Hood," perhaps the most beautiful lines he ever wrote.

In the September number for same year, there were lines of his, entitled " Mahmoud, the Ghaznavide."

In 1846 and 47, his contributions to any periodical were very few; but in "Blackwood" for September, 1848, some excellent lines of his appeared, "To a caged Sky-lark, in Regent Circus, Piccadilly."

Simmonds made his way in London into the best literary society. He was a favourite guest at Gore House. But he never forgot his native village, and his mother and sister. He was mindful of them; affectionate, kind, and generous to them; and his liberality was long continued and carefully regulated. The following notice of the estimation in which he was held in the home of his childhood, is from the pen of an estimable lady, who knew him intimately and from his earliest years:—"When it was known in the village, that Bartholomew Simmonds was about to revisit his native place, his arrival was watched with solicitude; and when he came back, he was welcomed by all who had known him in youth, and was regarded with pride as well as affectionate interest, for he was not only talented and enlightened, but he was an amiable man, sincere in his friendships, modest and unobtrusive,—and above all, he was a good and a loving son, and a fond brother."

He never married. A few years before his death, he met with an accident, by the blowing up of a small steamer on the Thames. The external injury, fortunately, was not much, but the shock seriously affected a constitution naturally delicate—he had in him a consumptive tendency—and it is supposed this accident was the remote cause of his death.

So early as 1841, he had been obliged to return to his native place, and to remain there for some time, on account of impaired health. In 1842, we find by his letters he was still residing there. He was frequently obliged to obtain leave of absence, on account of indisposition, and always betook himself at such periods to his much-loved native place.

He died in London, rather in embarrassed circumstances,

but still retaining his appointment, the 21st of July, 1850, in his 46th year.

FROM B. SIMMONDS, ESQ. TO LADY BLESSINGTON.

"4, Ashley Crescent, Saturday Morning.

"DEAR LADY BLESSINGTON,

"Business of an urgent and tormenting nature (which very seldom troubles me) has prevented me from thanking you before now for your new book with a copy of which I was favoured some days ago. It is the only thing I have had time to look into for several evenings, and it has refreshed and delighted me at every perusal. I prefer it, for several reasons, to its predecessor, principally for a strain of graceful feminine fearlessness that pervades several portions of it. It is perhaps impertinent in me to make this remark, but you cannot know how inseparably you, who have so triumphantly asserted by those most potent of earthly spells (when united) beauty and genius, our poor country's supremacy, are associated with the natural pride of your countrymen. Indeed I could give you some amusing instances of this feeling, which I have noticed amongst my compatriots since I came to London—if it were not presumptuous in me thus to take up your Ladyship's time.

"The picture is here, enclosed and addressed as you have directed. I wish I knew whether you preferred prose or verse; but as I suppose you are pretty well deluged with the former, I shall commit a very few lines of rhyme, and send them shortly—taking the view as it is—one upon the Hudson.

"With every sentiment of respect,
"Your Ladyship's
"Faithful and very humble servant,
"B. SIMMONDS."

"4, Ashley Crescent, City Road, June 26.

"With the proof which I return, I received through the medium of your fair secretary, the second print you wished me to illustrate for the Annual, and it is with grief and contrition, I have to confess that, as yet, I have been unable to do any thing for it. I not only agreed to supply the people beyond

Tweed with a Hymn of Triumph on the Queen's escape (a most impracticable subject), but also an article for six consecutive numbers of their Magazine, and which has absorbed nearly all my spare time: and now I dare say your people are waiting for *copy*, and all is at the eleventh hour. If this is not the case, I should be glad to show you, I am not insensible to your wishes. But should you be at a loss for the services of some of your 'Genii of the Lamp,' I think Mr. Plunkett would be happy to give his talents and attention to illustrate the print in question, which I retain until I hear further from you.

"B. SIMMONDS."

"4, Ashley Crescent, City Road, April 27.

"I beg to return 'Gersant,' with a thousand thanks; with half the De Stael's works at my fingers' end, I could not have believed the French language capable of the power of passionate eloquence of the book—it is full too of melancholy truth, which, though perhaps not very new, I never remember meeting brightened up with such enchanting fancy before.

"B. SIMMONDS."

"Saturday Night, June 26.

"To offer the enclosed verses for one of your books, is perhaps like placing a gauntlet among the *bijouterie* of the graces. If, however, you don't think there's too much clangor in them, it is not unlikely they will please at the other side of the Atlantic, where I believe you are as popular as in Europe.

"I have lauded the States, and one who is above all praise—Washington Irving—and have quoted an old and valued friend of mine (and countryman) Isaac Wild, perhaps you know him? the traveller, who published the beautiful quarto on Killarney long ago.

B. SIMMONDS."

"4, Ashley Crescent, City Road, April 2, 1840.

"My health has been very unfavourable this time back to composition; but if you will be kind enough to let me know *the very farthest time* at which I must produce the illustration, I shall be glad to be industrious in your cause. I may, perhaps, ask you for a corner in both the Annuals (for I understand the

'Keepsake' is now under the same auspices as the 'Book of Beauty'), sufficient to give me a claim for a contributor's copy of those books, which are a source of gratification far away, deep in the mountains, among a host of country cousins. I thank you for associating me with your Ladyship and Ireland. I passed last autumn there, and assure you that you interfere with the popularity of Messrs. Moore and O'Connell (and that is saying much), those magnates of the villages. The priest and the doctor drink your health, and never by any chance say 'Lady,' but the 'Countess of Blessington,' a kind of oriental grandiloquence that the Irish are the more profuse of, the poorer they grow. B. Simmonds."

"4, Ashley Crescent, City Road, April 27, 1840.

"I send you an alarming manuscript as an illustration for the drawing, and I hope the verses may meet your approbation. The stanza is a rude imitation of that in Sir L. Bulwer's beautiful poem of 'Milton' (which you will doubtless remember), and has been carried to the highest point of art in *Lycidas*.

"I shall offer two very short things for the 'Book of Beauty,' should you be graciously disposed to receive them.

"You should know how deeply I remember you as the friend of the two greatest poets of the age—Lord Byron and Moore; and with what pride I contemplate your magical influence over our literature and times, to learn the pleasure I derive at finding that any of my unworthy compositions can afford your Ladyship a moment's gratification.

"B. Simmonds."

"4, Ashley Crescent, City Road, 12th Nov. 1840.

"Do you remember that greedy creature, in Roman story, who, on her betraying the city to the Gauls, for the sake of the gold chains upon their bucklers, sank under the shields which they flung upon her as they entered, and so perished miserably?

"I assure you, I feel at this moment something like the traitress in question; you have overwhelmed and punished me for my shabby request of last summer, by the reproachful costliness of the books I have just received. But as, in the words of your familiar adage, 'little said is soon mended,' I shall merely say, that your present is worthy of that magnificent spirit which characterizes everything connected with you; and that if anything were wanting to enhance its value, you have supplied it in the gratification afforded me by the perusal of one of the articles in those volumes—your admirable, faithful, and useful story of *The Old Irish Gentleman.*

"B. SIMMONDS."

"January 2nd, 1841.

"I have just seen my friend, Mr. Arthur Plunkett, who tells me there is some alarming superstition connected with the bestowal of presents with points; which, however, he says, may be averted by the exchange of a small piece of silver. If the mischief, then, be neutralized in proportion to the smallness of the coin, let me hope that the *monies* I beg to enclose will completely propitiate the fairy people, whose influence, I presume, is dreaded upon such occasions.

"B. SIMMONDS."

"Sunday, July 5th.

"Under the supposition that the Rhapsody I sent you on yesterday has found favour in your sight (you are generally indulgent to my vagaries), and being on the eve of departure for Ireland, for some weeks, I am going to make what in our country is called a modest request—it is, that you will order me, when the book is printed, *a large paper copy* of the Annual that contains the verses inscribed to Lady Jane Moore—as I would not think of offering her a small paper one.

"B. SIMMONDS."

"Kilworth, January 1st, 1842.

"I have just been honoured with the flattering and valuable proofs of your kind remembrance. I wish I had deserved them better. In thanking you deeply, as I now do, for giving my humble name a place in your recollection, and for your recent note of inquiry through Miss Power, I beg of you to believe that, though silent and at a distance, I never forget your friendship; and that when louder and livelier visitors have passed away, you will be remembered, as ever, with pride, admiration, and gratitude. B. SIMMONDS."

JOHN KENYON.

In 1838, John Kenyon published a volume of poems, many of which were of a much higher order than the ordinary "Vers de Societé," written by the mere literary hangers-on of coteries of fashion, where there is a kind of under-current, which carries off the floating productions of those ephemeræ of literature. Several of Mr. Kenyon's pieces, illustrative of Italian scenes and scenery (well known to the author), are executed with great spirit, elegance, and taste; and some of them might pass for portions of Rogers' Italy. Those pieces of least merit, and least worthy of their amiable, refined, and kindly-disposed author, are satires, some of which have an air of malignant virulence about them.

Among the miscellaneous poems, there is one entitled "Music," singularly beautiful, from which I venture to extract two stanzas, the first and last, to show what talent this man possessed, who was one of Lady Blessington's especial favourites.

"Awake! thou harp with music stored,
  Awake! and let me feel thy power;
Fling forth, or turn from ev'ry chord,
  The thronging notes, in ceaseless shower!
Following thy measures as they rise,
  Upfloating forms of ev'ry hue
Shall flit before my half-closed eyes,
  And I will dream the vision's true.

. . . . . .

'Tis soft as evening's dewy sigh,
  Sweeter than summer's balmiest breath,
Half-conscious—half-entranc'd I lie,
  And seem to touch the verge of death.
And thus beguil'd, how blessed it were
  To cross that dark and dreaded sea!
Then just escaped this world of care,
  To wake, and—Nea! dwell with thee."

The detached poems of this gentleman lead one to form an opinion of his talents of a very favourable kind. No separate work of his, I believe, exists. He was a man of refined literary tastes and acquirements, and was held in high estimation by eminent literary people, for his high character and his amiable disposition.

FROM JOHN KENYON, ESQ., TO LADY BLESSINGTON.

"38, Rue de Neuve, St. Augustin, Paris, 15th June, 1840.

"Dear Madam,

"You will wonder at this note from one who ought in all modesty to conclude that you have, by this time, forgotten him. But if you happen to have thought of me at all, I trust you will have inferred that my absence from Gore House has been caused by absence from London. It will be one of my duties, on my return home, to shew, as far as an early call may do so, that I have not forgotten all your obliging attentions. My present object is to offer a few stanzas to you, a pepper-corn offering, which perhaps I am, after all, not justified in doing; for, probably, the Muses, like other ladies, should wait till they are asked, and to inquire whether you can make any use of them, such as they are, for your forthcoming annual. I have endeavoured to condense into them the associations which grow out of Italy. Who can judge better than you can, whether I have succeeded well or ill? But do not, I beg of you, think yourself bound to accept my offering. I shall not turn vindictive, like Cain, though your discretion may refuse it. I shall still continue to think the verses excellent verses, and only conceit that they do not happen to suit your particular views for this year's book, and you will have too much courtesy and kindness to clear away my delusion.

"Should you, however, care to make use of them, may I be allowed to request that they may be printed as I send them. Is this modesty or vanity? Whatever *casuists* or *motive-mongers* may choose to decide, I hold for the former. The robust wings of the eagle will bear handling: the butterfly's are ruined, touch 'em ever so lightly.

"Very truly, yours, John Kenyon."

CHAPTER XI.

MISCELLANEOUS LETTERS.

From Lady Blessington to Charles Bianconi, Esq.

"Gore House, Kensington, Dec. 2nd, 1846.

"Dear Sir,

"Accept my best thanks for the statistical statement you have sent me. I have perused it with warm interest, and feel, as all must who have read it, that my native land has found in you her best benefactor. I thank you for discovering those noble qualities in my poor countrymen, which neglect and injustice may have concealed, but have not been able to destroy. While bettering their condition, you have elevated the moral character of those you employ. You have advanced civilization, while inculcating a practical code of morality that must ever prove the surest path to lead to an amelioration of Ireland. Wisdom and humanity, which ought ever to be inseparable, shine most luminously in the plan you have pursued, and its results must win for you the esteem, gratitude, and respect of all who love Ireland. The Irish are not an ungrateful people, as they have too often been represented. My own feelings satisfy me on this point. Six of the happiest years of my life have been passed in your country, where I learned to appreciate the high qualities of its natives, and consequently I am not surprised, though delighted, to find an Italian conferring so many benefits on mine.

"When you next come to England, it will give me great pleasure to see you, and to assure you in person how truly I am, dear Sir, Your obliged,

"Marguerite Blessington."

To Lady Blessington, from a Correspondent whose signature is F. W. T.

"November 24.

"Your sister took me by surprise!! but what I blundered out was still the truth: I felt the necessity of withdrawing myself from the fascination of your society, and from motives which I could not explain, but left you and her to guess. To your sister they were such as should rather flatter than offend.

"I have now nothing more to add *but this*, that no suspicion of your want of friendship *has ever* crossed my mind. I feel conscious that I have never deserved to forfeit your good opinion, and so far from believing you capable of saying or doing towards me ought that would lessen you in my opinion, I should not hesitate at this very moment to place my life, or (what I value more) my honour in your hands. But still I must persist in the course I have marked out for myself, and avoid you.

"As a friend, I have never betrayed, as a foe should disdain to deceive any one, and I am confident these expressions do not refer to me.

"I shall only add, that in reflecting on our relative positions, my judgment and my feelings, my * head and my warm heart equally press on me the conviction, that he who has known you as I have done, and felt the influence of your attractions as I have done, cannot degenerate into an acquaintance. My philosophy knows but one way to escape the fascination of the Syren, and that is to avoid her.

"I am just setting out for B———, to pay my Christmas visit to your old friend. Adieu, may every blessing be yours.

"F. W. T."

From Lady Blessington to a Contributor to the "Book of Beauty."

"Gore House, Saturday.

"MY DEAREST FRIEND,

"I have this moment received the proof, which I send you. Are you not sorry for poor Prince Louis's madness? for I look on his attempt as nothing short of it. How are you?

"M. BLESSINGTON."

* Word illegible.

From Lady Blessington to Lady ——.

"November 29th, 1841.

"My dear Madam,

"Severe indisposition has prevented me from sooner thanking your Ladyship for the two charming books you were so kind as to send me. I would not employ any pen but my own to tell you the delight that their perusal has afforded me—delight that has often soothed the hours of pain and languor peculiar to long illness. I found in both books thoughts as original as they are beautiful, and sentiments fraught with grandeur and truth. Our sex may indeed be proud of one who paints woman in all her excellence, and yet excites an interest for her that 'the sinless monster which the world never saw' never creates.

"Your heroines are the very beau ideals of women, but there are so many natural and exquisite touches in the painting, that, like some of the finest pictures in the world, they bear evidence of being true portraits. I beg to subscribe myself, dear madam,

"Your Ladyship's obliged,

"Marguerite Blessington."

To Lady Blessington, on the subject of the publication of her Memoirs, from a distinguished literati.

"Brighton, December 1st, 1844.

"I am very much flattered that you should wish to have my suggestions with respect to your next work. I suggest 'Anecdotes and Recollections of a Literary Life.' You may add the latter part of the sentence, or not. I think two most interesting volumes might be written by you on such a subject, commanding a great sale, and yet not laborious. You have only to remember all the distinguished persons you have known, (now dead, I would not, except in rare cases, take living persons), and give sketches and recollections of such. Consider the artists, actors (such as Kemble), authors, statesmen, royal persons, foreigners, &c.

"If you disliked this, I think a very pretty taking work might be written, called 'Modern Life,' consisting of short tales, illustrative of manners and morals of our time—for which the 'Contes Moraux' of Marmontel furnish an admirable example. They exactly describe the philosophy and manners of his day. Something of the same kind, equally faithful to ours, might be prettily got up, and even illustrated, if desirable.

"I can also imagine a charming lady's book written, called 'The Book of the Drawing-room.' In this, we suppose the authoress in her drawing-room; her recollections of it—snatches of dialogue with the people who have been there—recollections, reflections—*the life in-doors of an intellectual feuille woman.* If these do not strike you, turn over the French correspondence and memoirs of the last century, ponder a little over that delightful chit-chat and philosophy of the *salons,* and I think something similar will occur to yourself, which your peculiar mind would yet make original; much which a woman only can do, may be done in this line, new with us, but always captivating.

From the same to Lady Blessington, on same subject.

"Kingston, February, 1848.

"I think that you might find good terms, and a ready publisher, for a work after the plan I once suggested to you, viz. reminiscences of eminent persons, and specimens of their conversations. You could do this, I think, without infringing the least on your own dignity, or the rules of social intercourse. You need only take public characters, and those chiefly dead.

"If your memory and your journal supplied materials for this, you might, in disposing of it, make a condition to take the other biography too, which could follow it; consider. At all events, I think you will find it desirable to hit on some other work, which a publisher will agree to *beforehand,* and make the condition of taking the one the condition of taking the other you have done or commenced. What say you to Mr. Newby? —I see he publishes and adventures with spirit. I know nothing of him."

From D. Stuart, of Erskine, Esq., on the part of Editors of the "Glasgow University Souvenir," to the Countess of Blessington.

"University of Glasgow.

"MADAM,

"The high honour which your Ladyship formerly conferred

on the students of this University, by contributing to a small volume of original compositions edited by them, and entitled 'The University Souvenir,' induces them, while they desire to express their most sincere acknowledgments for past favours, again to request, for a similar publication, a renewal of your Ladyship's distinguished patronage, and a contribution, however small, from your very able pen.

"We remain, Madam,

"Your Ladyship's most obliged and obedient servants,

(Signed in the name of Editors), D. STUART, of Erskine."

From the Duc de Guiche (present Duc de Grammont) to Lady Blessington.

"Versailles, 16th February, 1835.

"MY DEAR LADY BLESSINGTON,

"I cannot send you this letter for Alfred, without telling you how highly pleased we are at the hope he has given us of possessing shortly your last work, which I understand has had so much vogue in England. I feel quite sure it would likewise be gratefully accepted by the public here, was it translated into French; for our literary men, or amateurs, are generally indifferent English scholars. It is quite a good fortune to us, with our retired and monotonous habits, to pass a few hours reading a book, with the double interest the work and the success of its author will excite in us. We have not heard anything more about your friend. She is, I am told, grown very handsome at first sight, and seemingly inclined to leave people under the influence of that first impression.

"My sister * is gone to London as Embassadrice ——. Is it not strange? but what will appear to you still more so is, that this extraordinary change, at their time of life, is the operation of love, by which influence no couple of sixteen had ever been more subdued. I, who feel daily old age creeping on, I hope that some like occurrence will in twenty years' time set me up again. I however trust that, through our numerous acquaintances and connections with English society, she will be *bien recu,*

* The Comtesse Sebastiani.—R. R. M.

and that people will recollect the Comtesse de Sebastiani is *nè de Grammont.*

"Believe me, my dear Lady Blessington,
"Your ever faithfully attached friend,
"GUICHE."

From the Duke de Grammont, (written in the spring of 1849, a few weeks before the death of Lady B.).

"MY DEAR LADY BLESSINGTON,

"My aunt, the Duchesse de Polignac, desires me to tell you, that, unwilling to have recourse to the formality of a letter between you and her, to request you to dine with her on Sunday next, she called this day upon you, to make herself the invitation; not having had the pleasure to find you at home, she hopes that yourself, your amiable nieces, and Alfred, will not forget that you had agreed upon accepting that reunion de famille.

"I received a letter from Lady Tankerville, quite enchanted with the prosperous sale of your furniture at Gore House, but lamenting upon the cause of it. I cannot agree with her in that respect, for a little egotism is allowable in such circumstances, and we gain too much by it.

"Your ever most attached and devoted,
"Wednesday, A.M. GRAMMONT."

From W. C. Macready, Esq.

"5, Clarence Terrace, Regent's Park,
"April 18th, 1843.

"DEAR LADY BLESSINGTON,

"The news of your sad bereavement gave me the deepest concern. I was not at first aware of the full extent of your loss, but even in the partial account that reached me, I feel how much you had to grieve for.

"All who are acquainted with a disposition like yours, so quick to befriend and so sensible of kindness, would wish that such a nature should be exempt from suffering, whilst they feel with what extreme severity affliction such as you have been called upon to bear, must press upon you.

"I do indeed sympathize with your griefs, and wish with condolence there were consolation to offer; that is only to be drawn from the resource of your own mind and heart, so rich in all that is most amiable. But there must be something akin to comfort, in the reflection of how very many mourn for your sorrows.

"Among those, you may truly number, dear Lady Blessington,

"Yours most sincerely,

"W. C. MACREADY."

From the same.

"Bristol, March 11th, 1840.

"MY DEAR LADY BLESSINGTON,

"It is a real regret to me that I am engaged on Sunday next, and obliged to relinquish the pleasure you hold out to me in your invitation. What a pity it is, that we have not a choice of languages, like the Italians,—conversational and poetical,—instead of being obliged to resort to the same expressions for declining what we would wish or would avoid.

"Let me tell you, that if you say such kind things to and of my boys, you will counteract my grand philosophical experiment in their education, which is the extirpation of vanity, for you corrupt the teacher, and make him proud, while you ruin his pupils.

"Always, my dear Lady Blessington, most sincerely yours,

"W. C. MACREADY."

From Washington Irving, transmitting a contribution for Lady Blessington's "Annual."

"Newhall, May 2nd, 1835.

"MY DEAR SIR,

"I enclose a nautical anecdote, written down pretty much as I heard it related a few years since, by one of my sea-faring countrymen. I hope it may be acceptable to Lady Blessington, for her 'Annual,' and only regret that I had nothing at hand more likely to be to her taste. However, in miscellaneous publications of the kind, every humour has to be consulted, and a tarpaulin story may present an acceptable contrast to others more sentimental and refined.

"I beg you to present my kindest remembrances to Lady Blessington, and believe me, my dear Sir, with high interest and regard, very faithfully yours, WASHINGTON IRVING."

From William Godwin.

"13, New Palace Yard, May 7th, 1835.

"DEAR MADAM,

"I ingenuously confess that I trespassed upon your Ladyship's good-nature too far, when, as Polonius says, 'by laboursome petitions I wrung from you your slow' consent to write to me your observations on London. It would have given me great pleasure to have received them in that form. But I feel that I took an unbecoming liberty in so pressing you. I therefore by these presents give you a full discharge from the effect of your promise, in the same manner as if it had never been made. I am, dear Madam, with sincere respect and admiration,

"Your Ladyship's most devoted servant,

"WILLIAM GODWIN."

From Ronald Cutlar Ferguson, Esq.

"London, January 25th, 1830.

"DEAR LADY BLESSINGTON,

"There begins to be a little stir in the political world. It is said that the Duke's strength in the House of Lords is unassailable, and as he has got, it is also said, almost all the borough holders, his majority is expected also to be great in the House of Commons.

"There will be possibly a split among the Whigs. Several of the Whig Lords are believed, and I think truly, to be with him. Among others, the Duke of Bedford and Lord Fitzwilliam, and also Lord C———. It is said that Lord Darlington will move the address, and that Mr. Ward, the City Member, will second it. Lord Palmerston is to lead the opposition in the Commons, and Lord Melbourne in the Lords.

"It is said that the King has been very averse to the nomination of the Prince of Saxe Coburgh to the throne, or whatever else it may be called of Greece, but that he has at last yielded. The Duke of Cumberland is much with the King.

It is thought there will be a division on the first day of the session of the House of Commons, but these are all reports, and they are given you by a person who is not in the secret of any party. I have seen Lord Rosslyn and Sir J. Scarlett, and delivered your 'Souvenir' to them. My kind remembrance to the Count and Countess, and to your sister.

"Very truly yours,

"RONALD C. FERGUSON."

From Colonel Mackinnon.

"Sunday morning.

"Colonel Mackinnon's compliments to Lady Blessington, and encloses the lock of Lord Nelson's hair given to him by Captain King, who was First Lieutenant of the Victory at the battle of Trafalgar."

From Colonel D'Aguilar.

"Dublin, January 12, 1837.

"DEAR LADY BLESSINGTON,

"I was with your sister yesterday. She repeated to me her intention of going to you after her visit to Mrs. Dogherty, whither she proceeds on Monday next. Her stay there will be six weeks or two months, after which she means to join you by way of Bristol.

"The success of Bulwer's play has gratified me extremely, although the first accounts were any thing but satisfactory. I have since read the critique, and extracts in the 'Examiner;' of the former I say nothing till the play is before me. Of the latter I can have no hesitation in deciding, that they unite the profoundest tact and delicacy with the profoundest wisdom.

"I can perfectly understand at the same time, how entirely the coarseness of an actor might destroy the one and neutralize the other.

"Enclosed is a lock of poor Mrs. Hemans' hair, which you desired to have. I give it to you, as to one who knows how to appreciate her virtues.

"By the bye, is the fair S———, the lady my friend is said to have been once partial to? She is no beauty, but beauty,

I believe, is, after all, the least attraction. There are a thousand things short of beauty, that decide a man's fate ten times in his life, if nine were not sufficient for the purpose.

"Remember me always most kindly to Count D'Orsay,

"And believe me ever, dear Lady Blessington,

"Faithfully yours,

"GEO. D'AGUILAR."

"I have sent you 'Fiesco,' for no earthly reason than because you were good-natured enough to ask to see it.

"It is a very boyish production, being translated so far back as 1805, when I was an ensign in India; and it is as crude and unfashioned as the worst-natured critic could desire; but I did not venture to alter a line."

Letter signed R. C. M. to Lady Blessington.

"Camp, Isthmus of Corinth, September 18, 1827.

"DEAR LADY BLESSINGTON,

"I was exceedingly gratified to find that, notwithstanding my bad conduct in never writing after I went to England from Naples—I not having had the pleasure of seeing you when I passed through Pisa—that you still remembered me, and that with friendship. You may be assured that I have always preserved the same, the very same sentiments for you, Lord Blessington, and that little circle of friends with whom I have passed so many happy days; and every now and then I am faithless in my thoughts about our neighbours, the Turks, to think of friends as unlike Turks as people can possibly be.

"My cousin, if you see him, will tell you how we are going on; had we money, our heads would be worth more than the Turks; without money, we are not always sure of keeping out of a scrape. How little people know of this country, who think that the Turks could ever conquer it, if trifling resources, in comparison to the wants of other armies, were sent to it. Our situation here is picturesque and interesting. The Isthmus of Corinth, and a large gun-boat marching across it from one gulf to another; the army in very rustic bivouacs of all colours and shapes. Turks near us, but indolent; our people anxious to march, but the want of bread repels every attempt at activity. The field of Athens was surely a *blood-stained* field; but honour made us fight, and not necessity, as appeared afterwards, although at the moment we thought the garrison of Athens could not hold out a day, for want of provisions. Two victories have been obtained by my troops *within a march*, and above one thousand Turks and Arabs have been killed. My position (what stuff to write to a lady) is that which keeps the Turkish main army at bay. In a day or two, however, I hope to be moving if (and it really depends upon it) I can raise sufficient money to give the men enough to buy a pair of shoes each.

" Make my cousin tell you every thing. I was exceedingly delighted with Lord Blessington's letter. I hope often to hear from him, and sometimes from your Ladyship. Our head-quarters is not brilliant. We have no tents, consequently a wet day is a great bore; still worse, a wet night. Our horses are good, and when we are marching we are gay enough. I care not one fig about the Turks or Arabs.

" A thousand remembrances to Lady Gardner and to Miss Power—I hope they are both in good health—and to D'Orsay, if you have not all forgot me.

" Adieu, dear Lady Blessington,

" Ever very sincerely yours,

" R. C. M."

Letter, signed C. Nizzensitter, to Lady Blessington.

" 12th March, 1827.

" Of news, the first and best I can give you is the health and spirits of all at Wilton Green. I am sure you would not think Mrs. Purves in looks an hour older since you saw her last; whilst in every other respect that can engage admiration and respect, there is a constant increase and improvement, or rather addition, for as to improvement; there is not room for it. Well, that's my judgment, and I hardly think there lives in the world the person who could or would attempt to gainsay it, if they knew her as well as I do. Louisa and Mary, what the world calls very nice girls, though such a description does not one quarter do them justice—admirably disposed, well-educated, well-mannered, and good-tempered, Louisa bearing the palm, as you will readily conceive, as to beauty; the lesser ones of the troop, Margarette and Elly, dear little girls—and John wonderfully improved by Eton, and a fine healthy, ingenuous boy. God prosper them all! I say, from the bottom of my heart. Now, for a few words more interesting to others, though not so to me. Who is to be Prime Minister? every body asks; but it is all question, for none of us can get an answer; and yet the mystery cannot last much longer. The government has been walking without a head for more than three weeks, and even legendary lore does not give a precedent for so lengthened a walk (*sans tété*).

"Lord Normanby dined with me on Saturday; but he is come over alone, leaving Lady Normanby at Florence, where they seem almost to be domiciled; so, I suppose, the private theatricals thrive there as well as they did at Rome.

"I cannot help wondering that you did not prefer Florence to Pisa. Well, be this as it may, and be you where you may, from the bottom of my heart you have always, and in all places, my most hearty good wishes, of whatever value they are. You will be glad to hear my trio of children are quite well. The two boys at Eton. C. Nizzensitter."

Extract from a Letter respecting a proposed Notice of Lady Blessington's Novels in "Edinburgh Review."

"Edinburgh, April 10th, 1838.

"It was not from any sort of neglect, you may be assured, that your letter of the 7th was not immediately answered. Your proposal was only for the summer number, and I, therefore, concluded that it would be time enough to write you when this number shonld be off my hands. Such is the plain fact.

"Had the proposal for an article on Lady Blessington's novels come from any one but yourself, I should have given it a negative, because, though her Ladyship's claims are undeniable, they are not so permanent as to justify an article upon a class of works in which there are female competitors, who, I think, rank above her. But I defer to your judgment; and, believing you would not propose an article without having something to say that you yourself think the public would like to hear, I gladly accede to your obliging proposal. Permit me, however, to stipulate, *first*, that the article shall be of moderate length; and *next*, that it will for certain be with me in time for the next number. I have already commenced printing, having one or two articles on hand. . . . .

From General Phipps to Lady Blessington.

"Brighton, January 11th, 1836.

"Dear Lady Blessington,

"I was delighted with the good sense, the good feelings, and the good writing in which your book—'The Conversations of Byron'—abounds. I usually, in books worthy of such notice, make pencil marks on the margin, to note passages that strike me as peculiarly good, and never marked so many in any other book, or omitted to mark so many I thought worthy of notice, that I might not mark every paragraph.

"I knew Lord Byron a little; you have made me know him thoroughly. In your book you have made his 'evil manners live in brass,' but you do not 'write his virtues in water.' Could he have known how justly you would represent him, he would have said, 'After my death, I wish no other herald, no other speaker, of my living actions to keep mine honour from corruption, but such an honest chronicler as Blessington.' Whom 'men' most hated living, thou hast made 'them,' with thy religious truth and modesty, now in his ashes honour.

"There would be no need of short-hand writers if there were such good reporters from memory as you shew yourself to be. What gave the greatest value of the book to me, was the writing on the leaf before the title-page.

"I was much concerned to read in the newspaper the alarm you had on the next house being on fire; but as you had not suffered, and were 'quitte pour la peur,' I did not trouble you with a letter. I am glad to see, by the newspaper, that in removing from Seamore Place you do not go out of the reach of a morning call or an evening visit.

"Ever, dear Lady Blessington,

"Yours affectionately,

"Edmund Phipps."

"Saturday, August 13.

"I called yesterday on your sister, the bride and bridegroom, to congratulate them on the approaching nuptials. I wish to give them a dinner *de noces* in the course of next week, if you and your party will do me the honour and the favour to meet them; that will make us, myself seven, there will be room for three more, as I can accommodate ten (enough for a small room, in this warm weather), who shall the other three be? It is in vain to invite the Speaker. Who else do you suggest? What think you of Lord Wilton? Lord Tullamore? and either Jekyll or James Smith? As I can neither carve joints, nor cut jokes, I must ask some one to do so for me. Jekyll can do the latter, but not the former. James Smith can do both, and therefore the preferable person of the two upon this occasion. Our friend George Colman is in France; I would have invited him to cut jokes and joints, had he been at home.

"E. Phipps."

From D. Wilkie, Esq.

"7, Terrace, Kensington, Nov. 28, 1836.

"Dear Madam,

"I fear I shall appear very troublesome in what I am about to ask; but wishing to introduce into a picture I am now painting, an Italian greyhound, might I request that your Ladyship would give permission for the very beautiful one which you possess to be brought to me by one of your people, to give me one or two sittings for that purpose?

"Requesting your particular and obliging excuse,

"I have the honour to be,

"Your Ladyship's very obliged servant,

"David Wilkie."

From B. R. Haydon, Esq.

"March 28, 1836.

"Dear Lady Blessington,

"I have not had the honour of calling on leaving town, but I hope you are well—indeed I heard yesterday you never looked better.

"I wish now to ask you if you have seen a miserable caricature of one of my best little pictures, 'Lord Grey musing?' I have sold the picture to Lord Audley; it was well engraved, and I sold the copyright. Would you believe, after I had sold it, the head was totally altered to a peevish expression?....... I wrote to Lord Grey, as I found I had no remedy by law, who answered me most kindly, told me I had been incautious, as he had no doubt it was bought to be caricatured, but he begged me to be easy about it, as it would be only one caricature added to the one thousand and one with which he had been honoured.

"I offered to repay the purchase money, and remit the purchaser above the expense incurred, but he refused ..... You will be pleased to hear I am flourishing, having orders enough for two years at least.

"I am faithfully yours,

"B. R. Haydon."

"I shall be ready to begin your Ladyship any day next week you will honour me by fixing.

"I have settled the attitude such as I saw you one day in the drawing-room; your Ladyship shall now see if I understand you with your cap on well.

"Yours faithfully,

"B. R. Haydon."

From J. Uwins, Esq.

"10, Paddington Green, April 3, 1839.

"Madam,

"May I be allowed, without the charge of impertinence, to tell your Ladyship, how much delight I am getting from the 'Idler in Italy?'

"To hear tell of scenes and characters so well known to me, and to follow your Ladyship's discriminating pen through delineations as faithful as they are interesting, is a pleasure that none can enjoy more than your humble servant.

"Year after year, since my return from those delightful regions, I have been looking for such a book from Lady Blessington; the delay, perhaps, judicious, at any rate the book loses none of its freshness, and, in many cases, may even be read with additional zest derived from the lapse of time. Like every thing done by your Ladyship, it seems to appear exactly at the proper moment.

"May I hope your Ladyship will find time to come and see what I have been doing this year in the same ground? I have got eight small pictures ready for exhibition, all Neapolitan; one of the bay, executed for Lord Landsown, the beginning of which you saw last year.

"They will be visible till the 9th instant.

"Your Ladyship's humble servant,

"J. Uwins."

From George Dallas, Esq.

"My dear Madam,

"I find Mr. Mills has mentioned to your Ladyship a poem of my son's, awfully beautiful in my estimation of it, but which, for personal reasons, I did not intend shewing to you while he is here. Since, however, Mr. Mills has mentioned it to you, and applied to me for the loan of it to bring under your eye, I think it better to do this myself. It appeared twice in the paper which gave it to the world, with the following notice, viz., 'We reprint the admirable poem we gave to the public a few days since, from the great demand for it in our office.'

"Its origin was as follows:—Mrs. L—— W—— was an old and intimate friend of ours, for whom we had a very great regard, and who leaned much on us during her misery. My son R. had been known to her from his childhood; and in the interest he took in her cause, he attended the trial while it was on in Chancery, and at its close, before tardy judgment was given, under the virtuous indignation of a young and generous mind, horrified by its details, he took up his lyre at its close, to avenge in the manner you will read, the wrongs and the memory of his martyred friend. On this explanation, I submit it to your Ladyship. Have the goodness to return it to me when done with.

"I have the honour to be,

"My dear Madam,

"Your Ladyship's most faithful and humble servant,

"George Dallas."

From Henry Cook, Esq.

"18, Corso, Rome, May 27th, 1843.

"My dear Lady Blessington,

"But yesterday I heard there was a possible chance of your visiting the Eternal City, and as I have taken apartments for a year, I look forward with hope and pleasure to the delightful prospect, of perhaps in your society gazing on the relics of the marvels of the past.

"I will forward you a copy of a poem which I wrote in Florence; it is short, and I think will please you, at least as much as 'The Bride,' or any of my juvenile efforts. Beyond all conception am I delighted with the mode of life in Rome; no words can describe the pleasure resulting from its entire freedom from almost all the vices and drawbacks of London society. We have had again some most delicious '*Idlers*,' with a pleasure immeasurably heightened by being or having been one. Often have I been struck with the perfect truth and justness of your opinions on that most intricate subject 'fine art;' could you have laid bare my heart ere I left London, and could compare it with that now beating within me, what a change would you behold; you could scarcely conceive the extent to which this visit has humbled me. I then knew perfectly well I had much to surmount, but I now know that I have everything to surmount; that I have been like a child playing with a prism, unconscious of the glorious rainbow which was arching above my head. I have, I believe, mastered the Italian, and most delighted am I with it, as it pleases me far more than the French. Will you, dear Lady Blessington, should you find time to write to me, be so very good as to tell me your impression as to the progress of art, as deducible from the exhibitions, and also from the cartoons? I had made many studies for a cartoon, and most bitter was my disappointment in being compelled, by the impossibility of finding a studio, to give it up. The subject I have chosen is one of boundless scope.

"Ever, dear Lady Blessington, yours, &c.

"Henry Cook."

From C. R. M. Talbot, Esq.

"Morgan Park, Taiback, Glamorganshire,
December 4th, 1848.

"My dear Lady Blessington,

"I beg you to accept my best thanks for the present of your two beautiful books, which I received very safely. Nothing can exceed the manner in which they are got up; and as works of art, it is no exaggeration to say the engravings are not to be surpassed. I am particularly struck with the one representing Lady Constance Gower, and also with that of Lady Elizabeth Lascelles, as being the very perfection of female loveliness. Certainly the 'Keepsake' ought to be a popular work with *ces dames*. But if anything can prove the superiority of imagination over reality, it would be the pictures of the Queens of England. Only regard those magnificent eyes of our earlier Queens (I marvel that you can speak of Queen Mary as unlovely).

"Believe me ever most truly yours,
"C. R. M. Talbot."

From C. White, Esq.

"Place de Hamur, Brussels, 3rd October, 1845.

"My dear Countess,

"A young and very pretty acquaintance of mine is desirous to appear in your next year's 'Book of Beauty;' and, in truth, will do full honour to the title. Her name, so long as she may remain single, is, and will be, Miss Anne M———, a daughter of the defunct General of that ilk, and a niece of the Watson Taylor. The celebrated Gallait has done a full-length of her, now in the Brussels expositer, and some one else has done a miniature very charmingly. The latter will be forwarded to you, on your consenting to the damsel's longings. I will add some four or five couplets about rose-buds and beauty.

"Ronge is making head. I am not disinclined to think that he is the tool of a party. It is curious to see Ronge in Germany and Pusey in England, acting as sets-off to each other; and certainly Ronge has numbers on his side, and perhaps reason — I mean, as relates to religious matters. These subjects are, however, quite secondary for the moment, in comparison with the lamentations over failing potatoes. One hears no other subject mentioned. So that instead of saying, 'How is your wife and children?' men greet each other with, 'Good day! how are your karloffiler?'

"Pray remember me to Count D'Orsay, and believe me always truly and gratefully yours,

"C. WHITE."

Letters signed L. R. to Lady Blessington.

"17th April.

"DEAR MADAM,

"Although the stormy tides of the world have swept me away so far and so long from the eminence where your Ladyship stands, I take the chance of your still retaining some recollection of me.

"To ask you to give me any trifle of yours either in prose or verse, for the work I am now editing, and accept in return one of mine, I am afraid you will think is reversing the story of the Arabian Nights, and offering old lamps for new ones—but as the vendor in that case counted upon the covetousness of his desired customers, I rely upon the generosity of mine.

"At the same time, I beg you will not suppose there is any necessity for granting *both* clauses of my request, unless you should be so inclined: it is hard enough to lose a real gem without being compelled to exhibit a false one in lieu of it.

"Believe me to be, dear Madam, with grateful recollections of your kindness and politeness, your Ladyship's faithfully,

"L. R."

"Monday.

"My friends have long been anxious that I should abandon literature, and take to some more reputable profession; and truly, after the experience of half-a-dozen years, I begin to think that they are not far in the wrong. At any rate, a letter I received a day or two ago, has brought me to the point, by requiring me to say 'yea or nay,' whether in the event of their procuring me a small collectorship of the customs, or other similar situation, I would accept of it.

"Now in my situation it would be extremely unwise to run counter to the advice and wishes of my friends, but at the same time I desire, if possible, to modify their plan a little. I would not like to go into a small country town for the rest of my life, to consort with oxen like a second Nebuchadnezzar. Literature is with me a passion, which may be prudently directed, but cannot altogether be repressed; and besides, I am not beyond the age when a man dreams of attaining to distinction, as well as to worldly competency.

"If I could obtain a situation in a public office in London, having been educated for business, I could discharge its duties as many other men do, without withdrawing entirely from the world of letters. In the event of this not being readily come-at-able, one of the smaller consulships abroad would afford room for promotion, if I shewed that I deserved it; or a seat in one of the commissions occurring so frequently at home, two of which are I think at this moment to fill up, would at least, though not permanent in itself, place me in the way of public employment.

"It has occurred to me as possible, that your Ladyship might feel sufficient interest in the fortunes of a literary man to obtain for me the necessary influence. .... Having hitherto struggled through the world, not only without the aid of interest, but in defiance of more than common obstacles, I feel some diffidence in making this request, or in troubling you at all with my small affairs. Were you merely a lady of high rank, I should never dream of such a thing—but it seems to me, whether I am right or wrong, that there is a sort of freemasonry in literature, which removes from between the initiated much of the coldness and seeming heathenism of society.

"L. R."

From George Hill, Esq., to Lady Blessington.

"Omagh, September 7th, 1835.

"Complaints are often made to me of the very tardy manner in which the Chancery suit is going on, and of the very heavy expense attending it. It is now nearly seven years, and nothing appears to have been done.

"The Colonel has lately made an application to sanction his borrowing money to pay off some of the charges on this estate, which looks anything but like things coming to a close. I advised our friend strongly against this. Could not the principal persons most deeply interested, make a grand effort together, and insist on knowing what has already been done, and try everything in their power to get out of Chancery? I often fancy if they do take some decisive step, they might urge on a decree, which certainly would be for the benefit of all parties. I wish, Lady Blessington, you would tell me your opinion on this subject, as I know you are quite capable of forming a correct one, and would easily find out whether Mr. P—— thought anything could be done. Miss Gardiner and her aunt have arrived in Dublin, and Miss G. is expected here in a few days, to stay for a month. In her last letter to Mrs. Hill, she mentioned that Lady H. was to follow her to Dublin in a few days. I believe they all intend to spend the winter in Dublin, though in a former letter she talked of going to Leamington.

"Mrs. Hill had a long and very agreeable letter from Mrs. Power last month, in which she stated that they were all quite well and happy, and that their new house at last was beginning to progress rapidly. Your Ladyship's much obliged and faithful servant,

"George Hill."

From the Abbot of Mount Melleray to Lady Blessington.

"Cappoquin, December 14, ——.

"The Abbot of Mount Melleray presents his most respectful compliments to the Right Honourable the Countess of Blessington, and presumes most earnestly to entreat her Ladyship to honour the abbey with a visit before she quits Ireland. The Abbot ventures to hope that the Countess will not regret such an act of condescension, if it be possible for her Ladyship to accede to his humble request."

Letter from Signore Guiseppo Pazzi, the celebrated Astronomer Royal, of Naples, the discoverer of the Planet "Ceres."

"Napoli, 21 Febrajo, 1826.

"Ubbidisco, Miladi, ai graziosi comandi, di cui vi siete degnata a onorarmi, e quali che siano, eccovi li miei carateri. Possano dessi perfetamente attestarvi, la mia riconoscenza e il mio rispittosa attacamento. Se mi grave che siete per muovere de questa classica terra, mi conforta la speranza che sarete per fare ben presto di ritorno. In questa dulce lusinga col maggiore assequeo ho l' honore di essere. Devotissimo, servo,

"GUESEPPE PAZZI."

Letter from Mademoiselle Rachel to Lady Blessington.

"Londres, 4 Juillet, 1844.

"MADAM,

"Lorsque j'appris que Monsieur de Chozel avait le bonheur de vous voir et de vous entendre quelquefois, je lui témoignais (desirant vivement que cela vous fut repetè), mon chagrin et mes regrets de s'avoir pas osé vous approcher l'année dernière lorsque vous aviez la bonté d'employer quelque-tems à des vers charmants adressés à la jeune artiste. Les jours les mois s'etaient succedés rapidement je n'osais plus reclamer le *pardon* d'une faute *impardonnable* si vous refusez de m'entendre me justifier c'est bien audacieuse à moi, Madame, mais je sens si fortement tout ce que j'ai perdu que rien ne saurait m'arrêter aujourd'hui pour reconquérir votre bienviellance. Avec l'espoir qui me reste permittez-moi, Madame, d'oser vous offrir (quoique trop tard pour vous éspérer le soir) une loge pour la représentation de Bajazet. Si ma bonne étoile me donnait la joie de vous entretenir, j'osérais vous en aller démander le lendemain chez vous l'impression que vous aurait laissé mes fureurs de la veille. Agréez, Madame, avec toute vôtre indulgence, une hardiesse naturelle, puisqu'elle est, avec le désir vif de vous voir, et l'expression de mes sentimens les plus distingués.

"RACHEL."

Lines on various Subjects, by Lord Erskine, given by his Lordship to Lady Blessington.

EXTEMPORE, ON A YARD OF FLANNEL.

"Who, when rheumatic I complain,
Gives sweet oblivion to my pain,
And makes me feel quite young again?
A yard of flannel.

Who, when my tooth begins to ache,
And keeps my anxious eye awake,
Bids me refreshing sleep to take?
A yard of flannel.

Who, when my ear is chill'd with cold,
And her accustom'd sound withhold,
So kindly lends her fleecy fold?
A yard of flannel.

Who, when my throat is stiff and sore,
Does perspiration's reign restore,
And save from quinsy's threat'ning power?
A yard of flannel.

Do you desire to find a friend,
Where warmth and softness gently blend?
Then I would beg to recommend
A yard of flannel."

ON WALTER SCOTT'S POEM ENTITLED "THE FIELD OF WATERLOO."

"How prostrate lie the heaps of slain,
On Waterloo's immortal plain;
But none by sabre or by shot
Fell half so flat as Walter Scott."

ON PRESENTING BUONAPARTE'S SPURS TO THE PRINCE REGENT.

"These spurs Napoleon left behind,
Flying swifter than the wind;
Useless to him, if buckled on,
Needing no spur but Wellington."

AN INSCRIPTION FOR A COLLAR OF THE LAP-DOG OF THE COUNTESS OF BLESSINGTON.

"Whoever finds, and don't forsake me,
Shall have nought in way of gains;
But let him to my mistress take me,
And he shall SEE HER for his pains."

Conclusion of a Speech *attributed* by Lord Erskine to Lord Viscount Stafford.

"The evidence against me, my lords, is so vague, so contradictory, and so confused, that if an angel from heaven were to appear at your lordships' bar, and to attest its truth, you would say he was a fallen angel, and that he would return no more to the sphere from whence he had descended."

Translation of a Portuguese Song, sent under cover to Lady Blessington.

"Know'st thou the land where citrons scent the gale,
Where glows the orange in the golden vale,
Where softer breezes fan the azure skies,
Where myrtles spring, and prouder laurels rise;
Know'st thou the land? 'Tis where our footsteps bend,
And there, my love, and there, my love, and there
Our course shall end.

Know'st thou the pile the colonnade sustains,
Its splendid chambers, and its rich domains,
Where breathing statues stand in bright array,
And seem, 'What ails thee, hapless maid?' to say;
Know'st thou the land? 'Tis there our footsteps bend,
And there, my love, and there, my love, and there
Our course shall end.

Know'st thou the mount where clouds obscure the day,
Where scarce the mule can trace his misty way,
Where lurks the dragon and his scaly brood,
And broken rocks oppose the headlong flood;
Know'st thou the land? 'Tis there our course shall end;
There lies our way, there lies our way, and thither
Let our footsteps bend."

Letter from B. Cochrane, Esq.

"May, 1849.

"My dear Lady Blessington,

"It is so idle to tell you what you so well know, that you have left a vacancy here which can *never* be filled up. It makes me quite sad to know that your absence is for a lengthened period, as I can assure you that it calls forth one common expression of sorrow from all your friends, that is, from all who had the honour and delight of your acquaintance. I quite concur in all you say respecting M.; he is a most admirable and honourable man; but, alas! it is, in these days, in political as in naval matters, the ship that can tack and veer is ever the most valued. Yours ever truly,

"B. Cochrane."

Letters from H. R., Esq., to Lady Blessington.

"Rue de la Paix, Paris, 13th October, 1840.

"I have been here an anxious spectator of the perils which menace this fleet vessel of France, with its gibbering crew, and queer pilots. The wind has caught the chaff once more, and it whirls it upwards. Another breath may fan the spark to flames. Sparks, did I say!—they are no sparks, they are the unextinguished embers of that great funeral pile of the monarchy and aristocracy of France, which has been burning and smouldering for fifty years.

"Ah, no! if I write to you, let me rather talk to you of the sunshine, the leisure, the scenery, the peasantry, the fruit, the billows of the South. From Bordeaux to Marseilles we travelled along the valley of the Garonne, the plains of Languedoc, the shores of the Mediterranean. I revelled in the beauty of the country, the exuberant fertility of the land, the enchanting clearness of the sky. In Provence, I visited the coast of Hyeres, with its woods of orange trees and palms, and I made a solitary pilgrimage to Vancluse.

"Ever most faithfully yours, H. R."

"13th June, 1842.

"Your directions, many weeks ago, to ask me for a few lines to some fair lady's eyebrow, in the 'Book of Beauty,' I have left unfulfilled, and, what is worse, the note unanswered, for I did not quite like to confess to myself, much less to another, that I was grown so dull and old (a Benedict!) that rhymes for me have ceased to flow.

"Prose, my dear Lady Blessington, prose is the true language of happiness; poetry the language of the want of it. Prose pays the rent and the butcher; poetry starves the poet, and, still more, his wife and children. In short, I have only to assure you, that I tried hard to write something, found I could not, and then perceived that the beadle must have whipped away all poetical ideas, which I only regret, inasmuch as it makes me very useless and uncivil. H. R."

"2nd February, 1843.

"In my position, I have at least more aptitude to share in the griefs of my friends than those who are not stricken from the herd. And I most deeply feel for you in the loss you and your nieces have sustained. That child had in her such gifts of affection, and such a clear, active spirit, that even her natural infirmities seemed to be those of a superior being. But she was of those whose maturity must needs be elsewhere, where alone are the best hearts and truest souls. H. R."

"April 28, 1849.

"I chanced to be absent from London, for some little time, previous to your departure, and, indeed, a few days earlier, we might have gone to Paris; but I hope you will allow me the privilege of an old and grateful friend, in expressing to you my sincere and lasting regret for the loss we all sustain by your removal. London is, I believe, the place in the world in which we are least given to express what we feel; and a thousand circumstances and impediments are for ever occurring to make us appear much more dull and miserable than we really are.

"Yet, I believe, no acts of kindness, or recollections of pleasant hours, are lost in that deep and turbid water; and, for my own part, as I wander onwards on my solitary way, I have a thousand emotions connected with the past, which *revolve* though they seldom *exhale*. Amongst how many of those remembrances, dear Lady Blessington, do your kindness and hospitalities keep their place! Our lives are like those hollow Chinese balls, which they carve one within another, each including all that preceded it, and of these the clearest and most ornamental is marked 'Gore House.'

"In after-times, that house will have its place in literary and social history, and I am afraid, in our time, we shall not see its fellow, until you come back to us. H. R."

Letter from R. Monckton Milnes, Esq. to Lady Blessington.

"Dear Lady Blessington, Sept. 12.

"I don't know Mons. Louis Blanc, nor sympathize with his opinions; but having seen him in the Assembly all the 15th of May, and having carefully read the *enquete*, I am convinced in my own mind, that the act of the Assembly was a surprize to him, and that his manner when in the Assembly was deprecatory, and not discouraging. I thought, certainly, he seemed to desire to get them away. I remain yours, very truly,

"Richard M. Milnes."

CHAPTER XII.

EPISTOLARY CURIOSITIES, ETC.

Letter to Lady Blessington, endorsed by her Ladyship,—"A curious communication from a Mr. J——, relative to a mysterious occurrence."

"Brussels, 26th October, 1835.

"My Lady,

"An utter stranger to you, I find it very difficult to apologize for the liberty I am taking, but your Ladyship has seen much of life, and you possess great talent; the latter consideration influences me to address you on a very extraordinary subject, sure you will help me to find out the object of my search.

"Thirteen years ago, I was asked by a very old friend (an apothecary) if I would undertake an accouchement, under very extraordinary conditions. I consented; in a few days I was requested to be at the corner of Downing Street, at ten o'clock in the evening, and a pledge of honour was exacted, that I should never disclose the affair I had undertaken, or make any effort to find out the parties interested; and that if accident ever revealed them to my knowledge, I should never disclose the facts or names to any one; to all this I consented, and made no terms of any kind for myself, leaving the remuneration to the parties. On the night named I was at my post, and my old friend, Mr. Lee, saw me into a carriage, the blinds of which were up, and not a ray of light entered the space in which I was. How far we travelled I am totally unconscious, as I fell asleep. I was awoke by the door of the carriage being opened at a gate, which to all appearance led into a shrubbery; from this my conductor, who was the man that drove the coach, and who had very much the appearance of Mr. Lee, conducted me across a kitchen garden, and thence into a small house; here I was detained about twenty minutes; from thence I was taken a few steps to a large house, and ushered by the coachman or driver into a very large room A female soon appeared, who told me, as my services would not be required probably for a day or two, I had better take some refreshment and repose—a bed was prepared, and I availed myself of it. How long I slept I know not, but I got up when tired of bed, and in a short time breakfast was announced. The windows of the rooms I occupied were never opened; books were provided me. From the luxurious appearance of everything about me, I had no doubt that I was in one of the first-rate houses in the country; three days must have passed in this way. On the 21st March, I was called from my bed, and followed the same female who attended me into a very splendid apartment, where I found my patient and two other persons, females; there was but one lamp in the room, and that at a considerable distance from the bed. The mother was in perfect health, and I should think about from twenty to twenty-eight years of age. She never spoke, or uttered a sound of any kind; in a few hours a female child was born. I gave the proper directions as to her treatment, and quitted the room. I remained four days more, seeing my patient twice every day; I never spoke to any one but the female who attended me, who certainly was not accustomed to that kind of service.

"I was on the fifth night taken to Downing Street, where I arrived at about five o'clock in the morning. I went home, where I found Mr. Lee waiting my arrival; he said I had conducted myself entirely to the satisfaction of the parties, and was charged to present me with £100, for which he gave me his cheque. Of course I asked no questions; he had no occasion to ask me any, I am sure. A few weeks after, he asked me if I would take charge of the child I had introduced to the world; he would undertake to make the charge advantageous. I consented, provided I was to be secured against loss, and to have the entire control as a father. The infant was delivered into my hands, and the sum of £100 per annum settled to be paid six-monthly, until it was ten years of age; then she was to be allowed £200 per annum. Things went on very regularly for four years, when I was requested to take the child to Richmond to be christened; this I could not comply with, so it was agreed that she should be taken to St. George's, Hanover Square, where she was baptized Frances D'E., daughter of Colonel and Lady D'E. The persons who undertook this office I had never seen before, and we parted at the doors of the church, and I have never seen them since. What their motives for baptizing the child were, I know not; but as I had engaged not to ask any questions, I let the whole pass in silence. Two years after that, Mr Lee died suddenly. I tried in vain to find among his papers any trace of the affair; I waited in expectation of hearing from some other quarter; from the day of his death up to this hour I have not heard one word. I brought the child to Paris; placed her under the care of my wife, who is one of the daughters of Mrs. K., widow of Admiral [ ]; she has been with me up to this moment as my daughter. I have given her my name, and I love her as my own child—having lost my own.

"She has received a first-rate education, is highly talented and beautiful. Misfortune has overtaken me; I am now suffering extreme privation; Fanny is at a school, where I pay £100 per annum for her education.

"What I would ask of your Ladyship is, to consider if about the period I name, 21st March, 1822, any lady of rank or fortune was absent, under extraordinary circumstances; if there is any family who might take the name of D'E.; if there is any Colonel or Lady D'E. I think the Register at St. George's Church was about September or October, 1826. Frances has been with me at Paris about eight years; I have never been in England since, as I am attending to chemistry and scientific objects, but I would cheerfully lay aside every thing to secure the child a provision.

"I have never made till this hour any kind of communication or research into this matter; bound by my word, I have kept it. Frances knows and loves me, yet she has some vague idea that my wife is not her mother. I think I am, under these circumstances, absolved from secresy, as it is the fault of the parties to leave the dear child to chance. If I were able to support her, as I have done since the death of Mr. Lee, I would never trouble any one on this head. Mr. Lee died poor, and he never was rich; he was one of the most honourable men I ever knew. I am almost wild about this dear child; her future fate preys upon my heart and spirits. She must be the child of some person of consequence; she shows blood in every thought and action.

"I have thought Lady D'E., or some of that family, may know something of the matter, but I have never made any inquiry into the case; now I am forced to do so, by circumstances. I never saw the features of her mother, or any of the parties, or do I know what part of the country I was taken to; it could not be far from London, from the time, and I should think, from the stars which I saw as I got out of the carriage, the house I was taken to must bear S.W. of London, but I may be deceived in this point; being under a promise of secresy, I determined not to notice anything, so that I might be better able to keep my promise. I am sure no deceit has been practised on me by Mr. Lee, as he was ever beforehand with the payments he undertook, and often has borrowed money of me soon after he has made the payments; he never asked me for a receipt for any monies. It was an affair upon honour, and he also was bound to secresy, as we never spoke on the subject. I have dined with him, and have been introduced to several persons, who have often asked to see my daughter; but whether they had any particular motive for so doing, I know not; she must have some one to whom she is dear. Will your Ladyship find out, if possible, if Lord G. knows anything of this child? I have no grounds for the supposition beyond the name, which is very uncommon in England. The great caution used in this affair, and the profound mystery connected with it, with the obvious riches of the proprietor of the house where the lady was confined, convince me that they cannot be common persons.

"Begging your pardon for this trouble, I am, my Lady,

"Your most obedient, humble servant,

"H. C. J."

From Lola Montes à Monsieur [ ]

"106, Bond Street.

'Monsieur,

"Pourquoi ne finessez vous pas le portrait ici? Quoique un peu indisposée hier. Je compte sur vous de venir demain—soir, ou le matin pour achever votre joli ouvrage, qui est fort admirè par tout le monde. En attendant je vous la renvoie.

"Marie, Comtesse de Landsfeld."

To Lady Blessington,—transmitting two letters, endorsed "Curious Correspondence indicative of the Triumphs of Popery."

Mrs. Martyr's letter the morning after Miss Younge's marriage to Mr. Pope.

"Dear Madam,

"Permit me to be one of the first in offering congratulations. I have no doubt of your happiness, for I will confess that if his holiness had *attacked* me, I should not have had the resolution, as good a Protestant as I am, to die.

"A. Martyr."

Answer.

"Dear Madam,

"Accept my best thanks for your congratulations; this is not an hour for criticism. But I will whisper softly to my friend, that Pope's 'Essays' are in perfect harmony with Young's 'Night Thoughts.'

"Yours, &c.

"E. Pope."

The Pilgrim, alias Octogenarius, of Mount Radford, Exeter.

Among the anonymous correspondents of Lady Blessington, there was one who usually styled himself "The Pilgrim," evidently a person far advanced in years, of eccentric habits and modes of thinking, with a dash of gallantry, and a strong tincture of southern travel and literary tastes in his quaint and laconic compositions. Who the Pilgrim was, I have not been able to learn, nor does it appear that he was personally known to Lady Blessington. Occasional verses, having reference to the current event of the times, or the subjects of leading articles in the Annuals, edited by Lady Blessington, furnished the customary themes of his singular communications.

"The Pilgrim's" Impromptu on the movement of certain Oxford divines towards Catholicism.

"Oxford, renowned in days of yore,
The seat of arts and classic lore!
From Oxford—who could now expect
This Rome—ward march of intellect?"

"Mont Radford, Exeter, Nov. 22, 1843.

"The 'old Pilgrim' rejoices to see the name of 'Lady Blessington' announced as the editor of the new annual 'Book of Beauty.' He remembers with feelings of gratitude the Divine condescension shewn towards him by 'the Priestess of Minerva,' in her acceptance of his minute volume of Poems; and by admitting it within the *precincts* of her temple; having rendered it a visible object in the literary hemisphere."

To the Countess of Blessington from "The Pilgrim," alias Octogenarius, of Mount Radford, Exeter.

"A round delicate aperture is the avenue to a small cavern; wherein, upon a bed of coral, is deposited a 'pearl' of exquisite whiteness; and all 'young mothers' can duly appreciate the value of this beautiful *gem.*

"It would be needless to *tell* Lady Blessington, that the first *tooth* of an *infant* is here described. And, if any one of her fair votaries in the Temple of Minerva, would avail himself of such a sweet subject for a poetical offering in the next 'Book of Beauty,' it is much at her service from

"OCTOGENARIUS."

From G—— J——, Esq. to Lady Blessington.

"Saturday evening, May 11, 1844.

"Mr. G. J. presents his compliments to the Countess of Blessington; and with a full appreciation of the value of time, solicits knowledge regarding that given by her Ladyship as to the receiving of visitors: for with all his desire to breathe the classic air of Athens, he should regret if it were received at the hazard of intrusion in the land of Attica.

"Will not the mind of Lady Blessington appreciate the declaration of Mr. J., when he writes — That the evening of Friday last, is placed within his memory as one of the most intellectual in his enthusiastic life? He will rest in the belief, at least, that his grateful sentiment will be received.

"When Mr. J. saw a certain miniature by Sir William Ross, he conceived it to be the *ideal* of the artist's thought; but having been now convinced that the supposed poetry of Sir William was caught from the *original*, Mr. J. begs to present his compliments to Miss Power—a subject to create a poetic *pen* as well as *pencil*."

From Mr. A—— S——, Professor of Languages, to Lady Blessington.

"MADAM, "March 10, 1840.

"The storm, whose disastrous gloom the smiles of your Ladyship's countenance so sweetly dissipated, has passed away, and a prosperous sunshine seems to have begun.

Non sempre è mal qual che me afflige e duole
Anzi talvolta son nunzie le pene
Di non sognato bene
Doppo la poggia al fin resplende il sole.

"I have been for the last five months professor of languages in ———, with an income of £200 per annum, and pupils increasing. Such is the strange vicissitude of man's uncertain pilgrimage! Tyrants of Syracuse to-day—to-morrow school-master at Corinth; school-master in Canada to-day, to-morrow King of the French! Indeed at every point of his existence man is but a chrysalis, equally claimed by the past and the future, based on nothing, an ill translated book, taken out of one language without being put into another—a rootless tree leaning on a tottering ruin! Five months ago I was a miserable derelict, homeless outcast, now I am richer in wealth than desires, courted by the rich, respected by all, and enjoying myself as your Ladyship does, the secret, the sublimest pleasure of 'clothing the naked and feeding the hungry.'

"My object in addressing your Ladyship again, is two-fold, to give your Ladyship the joy of this intelligence, with which I know you will sympathise, and to evidence my gratitude by the only means in my power. Deprived of my birth-right, and of the accessories of rank, Parnassus has given me a palace, and from that everlasting court I crave your Ladyship's patronage, as of Polymnia, the muse of song.

"I am about to publish a song, entitled 'Oh, life is not a dream!' Shall I be deemed presumptuous in hoping for the honour of dedicating it to your Ladyship? Helicon has honours for none more than for your Ladyship, and all her sons should weave conjointly for a Blessington a wreath of her immortal bays.

"In conclusion, honoured Madam, your Ladyship has touched the heart of one who feels intensely, good or ill, and I have read your kind letter over and over again with intense delight: misfortune batters in vain when woman's entrancing voice of pity is heard in the respite intervals of the storm.

> Tengo dunque ver me l'usato stile
> Amor Madonna, il mondo e mia fortuna
> Che non pensa esser maï si non felice.

"I have the honour to be very respectfully, your Ladyship's most obedient, humble servant,

"A—— S—— ."

From Mr. J. C. W. R————, to the Count D'Orsay.

"July 12th, 1835.

"My Lord,

"I am very sorry to incumber you with a request, but '*ne-*

cessitas non habet leges,' is an old but true proverb. There was a time when I could smile, but now I am like a good many more fools, whom experience has made wise. Upon my honour! there is nothing so provoking as to be reduced to absolute poverty, for it excludes a man of feeling from all intercourse with mankind. Sports of all descriptions were my leading passions, but how the devil can a man act when he has all and every thing before him that is, as he imagines, innocently good? I am a bit of a literati also, so that one quality is always conjoined with another. But, to tell you the honest truth, we are all a set of fools in this world, for as long as we have it to spare, the devil an enemy can you find; and he could not even play the '*vouloir etre*' with all the imaginary powers possible. The short and the long of the story is, I am in want of a trifle of money; if you can spare me a few shillings, I will gladly and thankfully receive it. Can you perhaps spare an old coat off hand, or an old pair of trowsers, or any thing that you have designated a pensioner? Whatever answer you may have for me, please to leave it, *under cover*, with one of the servants of your noble mother-in-law, the Countess of Blessington, from whence I will fetch it. I don't want the servants to know my unhappy situation.

"I remain sincerely yours, my Lord, truly grateful,

(Signed) "J. C. W. R——N."

"P.S. By-the-bye, are you not a Freemason? Excuse this rude question, for I am one."

Letters from L. N. to Lady Blessington. [The writer was evidently an exceedingly eccentric correspondent, labouring under some very singular delusions.]

"Lincoln's Inn Fields, February 22nd, 1839.

"HONOURED AND ESTEEMED MADAM,

"However reluctant I am to intrude on your Ladyship, I trust you will do me the kindness not to consider the present letter an unwelcome epistle; while, in referring to my last of the 29th ult., I beg leave to acquaint you that as I have not been favoured with a reply, it will be requisite for me to prepare for my journey to Paris, where I must endeavour to obtain a livelihood by being instructed in the art of miniature painting. I had the happiness (after much pushing and squeezing, to obtain a seat in the pit) of seeing our beloved Queen at Drury Lane Theatre, and being placed at a convenient distance from the maids of honour, who were in the circle adjoining the royal box. Her Majesty and these ladies had an opportunity of catching a glance of me, which I believe they did; for I perceived more than once their opera-glasses were directed towards me, while there was some conversation held with the Earl of Albemarle, whose attention was also diverted towards the pit; and myself being so well known to the public, hundreds of eyes were riveted there, so that no doubt could be entertained on the subject. In fact, when the Queen entered the house, she almost immediately recognized her lover, while she was unanimously applauded by one of the most numerous and brilliant audiences I ever beheld in that theatre. If I were to confess the emotions of my heart, at beholding the elegant and graceful manners of my sovereign, coupled with the captivating smile by which her features were adorned, expressive of the happiness she felt in meeting with so loyal a reception from her subjects, I should, without hesitation, allege the Queen has made a conquest of it. The delightful scene was highly coloured, and rendered doubly interesting by the applause of the whole theatre, after the performance of the anthem.

"Her stature is short, and inclined to embonpoint; my own is not tall, and therefore might not suppose there would be a great deal of disproportion in our height, if we were married, so as not to appear conspicuous, if my age was not so much beyond her Majesty's. This, however, you are aware, is more apparent in some persons than others. My health is, thank God, much the same, and therefore might not imagine it would be thought an overwhelming obstacle to our union, should it be so arranged, pursuant to the royal marriage act of parliament in that case to be made and provided. I should be anxious, however, before I take my departure from England, to have an opportunity of kneeling at the Queen's feet, and offering the homage of my love and respect.

"This distinguished honour could not be obtained, I believe, without an application to the Secretary of State, and perhaps then there would be some difficulty in the way, without an introduction at Court; and although *I am ready to espouse Her Majesty in a week (if wished)*, I have no opportunity of obtaining a private interview, which might hasten the completion of my hopes, viz. marriage with the Queen, Victoria the First.

" To describe to your Ladyship the effect the recent work, published by Messrs. Longman, Orme, and Co., entitled 'Love's Exchanges,' has had on the public mind, is not within my capability. Every lady that I meet, seems full of anxiety on the subject, observing, ' Not yet in the petticoats ?' The gentlemen say ' What! still in the same dress ?' Thus I will leave your Ladyship to judge what I go through, from day to-day, while my likeness is pourtrayed as an elegant woman, in all the picture shops in London. Why, therefore, I may say, should not the first ladies in the land have the society and friendship of one of the fairest flowers ? should I, by being in petticoats, be transgressing the rules of morality or propriety ? Probably not; *could I, by acting as I wished, obtain forgiveness after M.....* A guarantee to that effect, would tend to relieve my anxiety of mind, and remove my scruples, if I am now thought over-fastidious. Being without incumbrance, could I not say, why should I hesitate ? my dress would be respectable without being gaudy.

" My time is short, and my funds are exhausted, while I am fearful I shall have a painful struggle to provide for my necessities ! Should I be generously aided with pecuniary means to forward my prospects in France (in the event of not being united to her Majesty), that help, when forwarded to me by your Ladyship and your friends, will be refreshment to the weary, as Petrarch beautifully expresses it in his commentaries—' Crede mihi non est parvæ fiducie volliceri opem decertantibus consilium dubius umen cœcis spem dejectio refigerium fescis magna quidem hæc sunt si fiant parva si promittantur.'*

" In the fervent hope this will find your Ladyship in good

* *Sic* in original letter.—R. R. M.

health, please to accept my prayers for a continuance of your happiness in this world and the world to come.

"I have the honour to be, with sincere regard,

"Your faithful and affectionate friend,

"L. N.

From the same.

"Lincoln's Inn Fields, June 7, 1840.

"HONOURED MADAM,

"The duty and profound respect I must always feel bound to entertain for my Sovereign Lady the Queen (for the public say that illustrious lady now patronizes me), as well as sincere regard towards yourself, would induce me without hesitation to consent to the apparent wish of clothing me in petticoats, if I could be favoured with a specific authority for such a very important change in my habits, as well as exterior appearance (for I am sure I should look like an old washerwoman in female attire); and notwithstanding which, I could not but feel highly honoured by her Majesty's condescension in thus selecting me to occupy a situation (governess, I presume, in the royal family, and to reside in the palace), if such duties could with strict propriety be considered to fall within the scope of my knowledge, which, matured by experience, might be useful in such a capacity; and if it even were so, my endeavours to meet the Queen's approbation would be at all times exercised with sound judgment and energy; but I may, while thus expressing my ideas confidentially on so interesting a subject, be still greatly mistaken, while my awkwardness in petticoats would expose me to the ridicule of all the distinguished guests at the palace.

"The ladies of the capital say, I shall look like a fine woman. The gentlemen say I could not wear stays without springs, and they don't think I should look handsome in a bònnet, and therefore I had better remain in breeches.

"If they are all in error on the subject, then, I trust, you will do me the kindness to afford me a solution of the mystery. If the public are wrong (errant quidem gravissimè), who is to put them right?

"In the event of funds being forwarded to me (in a parcel sealed up and directed as above), I will occupy furnished lodgings at Kensington, for I am in impoverished circumstances, and if £50 is sent to me it will be very acceptable and useful, these hard times.

"Hoping this will find your Ladyship in good health,

"I remain very truly,

"Your faithful and affectionate friend,

"L. N."

From the same.

"London, May 28, 1841.

"HONOURED AND MUCH ESTEEMED MADAM,

"Although still (after a lapse of three years' written communication), without a single reply either in the affirmative or the negative, and having been personally present at your abode nine times, without being favoured with an appointment or an interview, I take leave to offer an explanation to your Ladyship on the subject of a bond of indemnity (which I mentioned in the postscript of my last letter), a legal instrument cased with armour, to be a defender against the poisoned darts from the venomous tongue of the rocky-hearted slanderer. A shield against the malicious and mischievous deeds of the secret enemy.

"The obligor is the party bound, whereby he or she obliges themselves, their heirs, executors, and administrators to indemnify and save harmless the obligee, which surety without the condition is called simplex obligatio; but with the covenant, a specialty, the damages therein being particularly specified in writing, and the contracting parties' seal, while regularly acknowledging the same, and duly confirming the contract, being affixed thereto, thus rendering it a security of a higher nature than those entered into without the solemnity of a seal.

"But if it be to do a thing that is malum in se, the obligation itself is void, for the whole is an unlawful agreement, and the obligor could take no advantage from such a transaction; and if the condition be possible at the time of making it, and afterwards becomes impossible, by the act of God, the act of law, or the act of the obligee; there the penalty of the obligation is saved, for no prudence or foresight of the obligee could guard against such a contingency.

"My playing, therefore, a second character in this drama (by acting a woman's part), would depend *in toto* on my own conduct for honour and integrity. Could I therefore, with safety, enter upon such an engagement, without the liability of being a particeps criminis in any unlawful action which might subsequently follow? My opinion from the first was, that it would be an impracticable scheme, and I think my friends will admit I have taken a correct view of this extraordinary design of the projectors; for baffled and frustrated in all my efforts to become the husband of the lady agreeable to the wishes of the public, the disguise of a gentleman, in the apparel of a lady, with an intention of having a conversation with his sweetheart at a ball (such a plan being suggested in my letter of July 8, 1839), would, as that lady is married to another, be now entirely out of season; what motive, therefore, there can be now for exhibiting my portrait (in flagrante delicto) in female clothes, is to me incomprehensible, and I remain, in hope your Ladyship will do me the kindness to afford me a solution of the enigma.

"Whatever is the object, it has inflicted on me manifold injury and mischief, by the construction put upon it. Even at this time more calumny is issuing from the press, and the work entitled 'De Clifford, or the Constant Man,' has very much astonished the public.

"My proposal to raise £1000 by way of loan being unattended to, I am of opinion the most judicious plan of arrangement and relief would be for me to quit my native country; and if I had £50 a quarter allowed me for my maintenance, in the city of Brussels, I would go and reside there, from which capital I would correspond with my amiable friend.

"Your Ladyship's most obedient, humble servant,

"L. N."

"P.S. If your Ladyship could honour me with your company for a few weeks in the summer season at Ostend, not only for the benefit of sea-bathing, but also to assist you and your friends in the completion of works for the press, I should esteem it a favour, and learn much from you."

CHAPTER XIII.

CORRESPONDENCE WITH THE MATHEWS.

From Lord Blessington to Charles Mathews, Sen.

"Mountjoy Forest, August 2, 1823.

"My dear Mathews,

"I am determined to build a house here next spring, and I should like to give your son an opportunity of making his *débût* as an architect.

"If you like the idea, send him off forthwith to Liverpool or Holyhead, from which places steamers go, and by the Derry mail he will be here (with resting a day in Dublin) in five days; but he must lose no time in setting off. I will bring him back in my carriage.

"Remember me most kindly to Mrs. Mathews,

"And believe me,

"Ever yours truly,

"Blessington.

"I suppose it would be utterly useless my asking you to come with Charles; but if you wish to spend a week in one of the most beautiful spots in Ireland, eat the best venison, Highland mutton and rabbits, and drink the best claret in Ireland, this is the place; and you would be received with undivided applause, and I would give some comical dresses for your kit.

"Yours, B."

Letters from Charles James Mathews, Esq., to Lady Blessington.

"Torre del Annunciata, Napoli,

"Wednesday Evening (1824).

"Dear Lady Blessington,

"On Wednesday last, at half-past twelve o'clock precisely,

we started for Pompeii, and arrived in excellent health, covered with dust, hoping your Ladyship is the same. After a scientific walk through a few of the houses, we returned to our quarters, and sat down to dinner, which we performed with ease in less than five-and-thirty minutes. We then went to bed, thinking that the best way of passing the evening, and though we had no 'curtained sleep,' we managed uncommonly well, and it perfectly answered our purpose. Angell says that I snored, but persons are very fond of throwing their own sins upon the backs, or rather the noses, of others.

"On the following morning, at break of day, we were again at Pompeii, and spent the whole of the day in combining, analyzing, and arranging our plan of study. The result was this, that we found nothing in the whole city worthy of being measured and drawn 'architecturally' (by which I mean outlined with the scrupulous accuracy of measurement usually adopted by architects), except the two theatres and the amphitheatre, picturesque sketches and notes of the other subjects of interest being quite sufficient for our object.

"On Friday morning we commenced, and by our united efforts have completed the measurement of the small theatre, which, by-the-bye, was unquestionably an odeum. We are now engaged upon the other, which I hope to see concluded in three days. From all which, it appears probable that I shall have the happiness of seeing you all again about Wednesday next—which was to be demonstrated.

"Our weather has been 'charming and very,' and seems likely to continue so. We are at a delightful inn (Locanda I call it, when I speak Italian), and live in the public room, which is quite private. The bed-rooms are fitted up with peculiar taste; mine contains an iron bedstead with one leg shorter than the other (which on the first night of my arrival deposited me safely on the floor—N.B. stone), a wash-hand basin one inch and a quarter deep and six inches in diameter, a small piece of broken looking-glass, and half a table. It is an airy room, with four doors, which we should in England call glass-doors, only these have no glass in the openings. However, they are easily closed, for they have shutters which won't shut above half way;

still, a couple of towels and a bit of board keep them together very snugly. The walls are stuccoed and painted in the same manner as the houses at Pompeii—only that they are quite white, and entirely without ornament of any kind.

"We take two meals a day, besides a luncheon. In the morning a little boy, with dark (I won't say dirty) looking hands and face, brings us some coffee in a little tin pot. The coffee is poured over into the saucer, which saves the boy the trouble of washing it out. We can always tell how much we have had, for the coffee leaves a black mark on the cup wherever it has touched it. Upon the whole, it would be a very nice breakfast, if the eggs were new, the butter fresh, and the bread not quite so sour. But the dinner makes up for all. We begin always with maccaroni—I have learnt to eat it in the Neapolitan fashion—it is the prettiest sight imaginable, and I am making great progress. We then have lots of little fish (from which they tell me they make *seppia*) fried; they taste pleasantly, and black all your teeth and lips. They dress their fish with their scales on, too, which makes them look very pretty. We next generally choose a 'pollastro deliziozo,' because it is the tenderest thing we can get. We each take a leg and tug till it comes asunder, which it usually does in a few minutes. They are very fine birds, and when you happen to hit upon a piece which you can eat, it makes a particularly agreeable variety. When the chicken has disappeared, we call for fruit, and they sometimes bring it. The hot baked chesnuts would be delicious if they were ever warm—they never are so; but then the grapes are so hot, that it comes to the same thing. When we tell the man to bring some water to wash off the dirt that is always about them, he wipes them in his own apron, which is certainly better and surer.

"We finish our repast with a ditto of the coffee that we have had in the morning, only thicker and of a darker colour. This is not the dinner we always have. There are varieties in the bill of fare which your Ladyship little dreams of. I will mention two or three, with their prices, as specimens.

	Grains.
Frogiolino al brodo—small embroidered frogs .	5
Fetti de cazzio carvallo—feet of a cart-horse . .	7

	Grains.
Bolito de vacina—a boiled cow, only	5
Fetti de Genevese—Genoese feet	2½
Calamaro arrostito—a roasted inkstand	6
Frita de negro—a fried negro	5

Other delicacies are to be had by paying higher prices for them; but as we are only artists, and not gran' signori, we are contented with little.

"I am delighted with my new acquaintance and his well-informed friend. Angell is a very intelligent, amiable man; I like him so much, that I even let him smoke in the dining-room—a thing unheard-of, as you may suppose, in these refined regions. Poor fellow! I am sorry to say that the cause of his breathing so hard is but too well accounted for—he has a decided asthma, which at times troubles him sadly. We get on famously together, and work very hard.

"I hope you are all quite well, and enjoying the 'gloomy month of November.' I long to be back and comfortably seated at my firm *whole* table, surrounded by kind friends. Pray thank Lord Blessington for his knapsack, which is invaluable here.

"With best remembrance to Count D'Orsay and Miss Power, believe me, dear Lady Blessington, your most affectionate and respectful servant,

"Charles James Mathews."

From Charles J. Mathews (recovering from illness) to Lady Blessington.

"Palazzo Belvedere.

"Dear Lady Blessington,

"I'm so much better, that I should like to come and have a snack,
Only Dr. Reilly says that I mustn't eat, or do any thing but lie on my back;
So I'll stop here in the dark as quiet and patiently as ever I am able,
Though I shall certainly think most affectionately of you all, about the time that the roast potatoes are put upon the table."

Lady Blessington in reply.

"MY DEAR CHARLES,

"I will run all risks, and send you something to eat, as I cannot bear to think that we are all eating while you are starving. God bless you, and enable you soon to join us."

From Charles Mathews, Jun., to Lady Blessington.

"Kentish Town, Nov. 26, 1824.

"The only clog to the happiness I have experienced on my return, has been the impossibility, up to the present moment, of imparting any portion to your Ladyship, from whom I trace the greater part of it. But I am sure you will have made allowance for the bustle and confusion of the first week's visiting and calling. At Paris, I fully intended writing, but as I found that Mrs. Purves had left before my arrival, I thought it would be better to wait till I had seen her, as the interest of my letter almost entirely rested upon the power of assuring you all of her health.

"Last Wednesday I arrived in London, after a most fatiguing journey full of hardship, and consequently of amusement. Various incidents might be worked up into good stories, if I thought my paper would last me: such as passing the Garigliani, in the character of a German officer, without paying; quelling a dispute at Beauvoisin, as prefect of the village, and very narrowly escaping a broken head upon the discovery of the cheat. I shall, however, only touch upon one, which is interesting, inasmuch as it is linked with the never-to-be-forgotten Borghetto. At Florence, not having time to get my passport visèd, the courier persuaded me take a one-horse carriage, and drive out of the town, as if to some villa, and wait for him without the walls. Of course, it was all the same to me how I effected my journey, so that I did but 'keep moving,' and I therefore accepted his offer, to the great astonishment of Mr. Bailey, with whom I was to have dined, and who, after staring at me for a quarter of an hour, very gravely assured me, that I should most probably be secured, and thrown into prison, or, at least, be arrested at Genoa, as the Austrians (he supposed—I was well aware) thought nothing of sending a man back three hundred miles if his passport were not in order. Notwithstanding his prudent assurances, I pro and suc-ceeded in my rash measure, nor should I perhaps have much minded, except on account of the delay, a day or two's imprisonment; being, as you know, very fond of witnessing foreign customs and manners. All, however, went well, and I secured my place as far as Turin, but the next morning, on arriving at Pietro Santo, a village consisting of a post-house and two ruined cottages, in the midst of a pouring rain, the courier, with that natural politeness for which foreigners are so justly celebrated, informed me that there was no place for me any further. I began to feel 'rather contemptible than otherwise.' 'But,' said I, 'I have just paid for my place as far as Turin, and we are not yet half way to Genoa.' '*Mi dispiace, Signore,*' said he, 'but there is no room for you.'

"The idea of being left in this wretched hole, in such weather, without any means of conveyance, was a great deal too absurd, and I was beginning to grow excessively disagreeable to the courier; but finding that bullying did not advance me one jot with my little fat friend, who was comfortably buttoned up in his independence and his over-alls, and seeing that my situation was much too critical and dangerous to be serious about, I began to banter and joke the little choleric officer, till I absolutely laughed myself into his good graces and his mail. When I say his mail, I mean it literally, for as there was no room in the regular part of the gig, we emptied the letters from behind, and I travelled ninety miles over the most dreadful Borghetto road, now worse than ever—in the courier's letter-box!

"Arrived at Genoa, I found the mail-carts all engaged, so went on by vetturino to Turin, and with many little adventures, reached Paris in nineteen days, having only slept one night on the road—at Turin; I was tired enough, but not half so much so as some of my fellow-travellers, who had only been up two nights, and a *bain de voyageur* at Paris perfectly restored me to what Sir William Gell would call my 'natural loveliness.' After waiting a couple of days at Calais, eight hours carried me over from thence to Dover, nor was I at all anxious to lengthen the passage.

"I will, however, put an end to my journey, or you will be more fatigued from the recital than I was myself from the reality. I will only add, that from my excellent management and forethought I found myself at Genoa without a farthing—my letter being on Turin, ditto Lyons, &c. &c., and so I only reached London by borrowing money from the coach-office upon my luggage.

"As soon as I arrived in town, I called on Mrs. Purves, and am sorry to say found her excessively low; though, on dining with her on Tuesday, I was happy to see her much gayer, and her spirits altogether improved. I shall refrain from saying a word upon the cause. She has already explained it to you, and it is unnecessary for me to say what pain I feel on account of it, dear Lady Blessington.

"I shall do myself the great pleasure of bestowing some more of my tediousness upon you very soon, and will try and write better, and more composedly.

"Charles J. Mathews."

"Ivy Cottage, December 25th, 1824.

"Week after week has passed away, since I last wrote to you. My thoughts, however, have the more continually been with you, if indeed those thoughts can be so at one time more than another, which are unceasingly reverting to the happy time passed in your beloved family.

"We are going to spend a delightful day with Mrs. Purves, and could impossibilities be effected merely by the sincerity of the wishes suggested by our affection, you would all be there, to make our happiness complete. But buoyant fancy cannot overcome dull reality, and therefore I must take advantage of the mode which nearest resembles being with you—that of writing to you, and converse as if with a deaf and dumb person, upon paper, with this only difference, that I shall have all the talk to myself.

"First and foremost then—Business. Books. I have been buffeted about in the most unfeeling manner from Mr. Longman to Mr. Lee, and back again from Mr. Lee to Mr. Longman, till I am tired of their very names. Mr. Lee tells me a vessel starts on a certain day, and Mr. Longman says he will be ready, and is not. Ditto Mrs. Purves, milliner. Upon this, vessel No. 1 is to set sail. Vessel No. 2 will be off in a few days, I am told, and both the dress-maker and the bookseller have promised me to be ready the day after to-morrow; but the first declares she is dependant upon her 'young women,' who are all engaged with their sweethearts at Christmas time, and the second assures me that his delay is all owing to his dilatory binder.

"But I have given the dress-maker a good *dressing*, and *trimmed* her in such a manner that she is quite *hemmed* in, and I think cannot *try the thing on* any longer; and as to the binder, he is plainly *bound*, for he has been so *pressed* and *lettered* by me, that should he fail, it would stamp disgrace upon his name, and I should certainly pull his *dog's ears* well, and cover his *calf-skin* back with stripes. Thus being, I think, pretty secure of my people, I have been to the vessel, and the package, I am happy to say, is at last booked.

"Now that business is done, let me proceed to pleasure, and tell you what you already know, the state of happiness and comfort I am in at dear home. On my journey, my feelings were divided;—sweet glowing tears at the approaching meeting frequently mixed themselves with the bitter brine of parting; but now I have time to dwell upon all I have left at Naples, I cannot, while I rejoice at being where I am, resist the wish that I were still with you. But the advantage of being in two places at once, is known to 'birds alone.' The pleasure with which I reflect upon all the scenes that passed at the dear old Palazzo and the dear new villa, is not unmixed with melancholy —that of knowing that I never shall visit them again with the same dear party. Everything that I have seen in Naples has a double interest for me, from the associations connected with it. The scholar remembers with enthusiasm all he has beheld, because it is the confirmation of all he has previously read. But I have still more to dwell on; I have the gratifying remembrance of having visited these magic scenes in the society of the dearest and kindest friends in the world, under circumstances which of themselves alone would form subjects for pleasing retrospection for my whole life.

"I am very much to blame in not having yet written to Lord Blessington, after his flattering command, which I had before this intended to obey; I well know, that in writing to you, dear Lady Blessington, I do, in fact, the same thing.

"Pray give my best regards also to Count D'Orsay, and say that his kind permission gave me at once the greatest pleasure and the greatest pain;—pleasure that he should conceive a letter from me worth receiving, and pain at knowing that I never shall be able to express in French half the admiration and regard I feel for him. Pardon my making your Ladyship my message-bearer; but I do it because I know you are always ready to be the conveyer of kindness to every one. To Mary-Anne, if you please, my best love; and to Sir William Gell and Mr. Strangways, if still at Naples, my affectionate remembrance.

"To Lord Blessington and yourself, I can only say that I am, and shall always be, affectionately yours,

"CHARLES JAMES MATHEWS."

"Great Russell Street, Friday Evening (1835).

"We left my father in most satisfactory health, and able to gratify his wish of proceeding to Devonshire, and returned to town quite in spirits about him; but this morning we have received a letter from Plymouth, where he now is, which announces that he is not so well. Any change for the worse in his state is alarming, and my mother and I are therefore on the point of setting out, at an hour's notice, to join him there.

"It is a sad journey for her to undertake; but, unfortunately, we have not been able to persuade him to come to London, where he ought to have been from the first. his distance from us making his situation more cruel. I trust, however, we may find him better again, as his health, of course, varies very much from day to day. C. J. MATHEWS."

Letters from Lady Blessington to Charles J. Mathews, Esq.

"Villa Gallo, January 1st, 1825.

"MY DEAR CHARLES,

"Your account of your journey was most amusing, and excited a portion of that risibility that you have so often excited in *propria persona* in other days, and which has been rather a stranger to us since your departure.

"We can laugh at your perils by flood and field, *now* that we know you are safely nestled beneath the dear maternal wing at Ivy Cottage; but had we anticipated the probability of all the embarrassments you encountered, we should have been, indeed, most uncomfortable.

"You will have seen in the papers the melancholy and shocking account of the murder of Mr. and Mrs. Hunt, close to your old haunt at Pæstum. They were a very young and interesting pair; the gentleman not more than twenty-four, and the lady nineteen years old, and only a year married. They had spent the summer at Naples, and had been to Pæstum, from whence they were returning, when they were assailed by six armed brigands, who demanded their money. Mr. Hunt gave them some money, and remonstrated with them for ill-treating his servant, when they threatened to shoot him if he did not keep silent; seeing them still continue to beat his servant, he stood up in the carriage, which was an open one, when two of the miscreants (one at each side) fired, and at the same instant mortally wounded the husband and wife. Mr. Hunt fell from the carriage on the road, and his wife sunk on the seat, in which state they were found by three midshipmen of the 'Revenge,' who were also returning from Pæstum, and who arrived in half an hour after the fatal catastrophe. The brigands fled almost immediately after the murder, fearing that the midshipmen would arrive; for it appears that they had a perfect knowledge of the number of the persons, and the property they possessed, which it is thought they got intelligence of at Eboli, where they had slept the night before. The midshipmen assisted Mr. Hunt, who was perfectly sensible, and who detailed the affair, and placed him in the carriage with his wife, of whose wound the whole party were ignorant. Thinking she had fainted from fright, they opened her cloak to give her air, and found her weltering in blood, the ball having taken off some of her fingers in passing through her breast, and passed out through her shoulder-blade, carrying away the lobe of her lungs. A gold chain and locket which she wore, as also the part of her dress next the place, were forced into the wound, and the poor unhappy woman suffered the most violent torture. The midshipmen, finding the danger they were in, thought it best to return to

Pæstum, which was the nearest place; and Mr. Hunt becoming delirious, they placed him in your old wretched lodging at Pæstum, while his wife was conveyed to the farm-house next it. The husband only lived four hours and a half after the wound, and the poor wife thirty-three. I must not omit telling you that the midshipmen, who were total strangers, behaved like brothers to the poor couple, but particularly Mr. Hornby, who you may remember in the 'Revenge,' who never left Mrs. Hunt until she breathed her last. Some of the brigands have been taken up on suspicion, and the event has made a deep impression here.

"Pray tell me all that is going on in the literary way in London, and be assured that your letters will always be welcomed by, my dear Charles, your sincere and affectionate friend,

"M. BLESSINGTON."

"Friday Evening, June or July, 1833.

"A thousand thanks, my dear Charles, for the verses, which are beautiful, but alas! a *leetle* too warm for the false prudery of the public taste. Were I to insert them, I should have a host of hypercritical hypocrites attacking the warmth of the sentiments of the lines, and the lady-editor; and therefore I must ask you to give me a tale, or verses more prudish, —prettier ones you can hardly give me. I have been so long a mark for the arrows of slander and attack, that I must be more particular than any one else; and your pretty verses, which in any of the Annuals could not fail to be admired, would in a book edited *by me* draw down attacks. I find I have another clear week to give you for the composition of an illustration for Alice, and entreat you to write. I keep the verses, for they are too beautiful not to find a place in my album.

"What a misery it is, my dear Charles, to live in an age when one must make such sacrifices to cant and false delicacy, and against one's own judgment and taste.

"M. BLESSINGTON."

"Pray urge your father and mother to give us frequent tidings of you, as you may be well assured that after *them* there are *none* who can feel a deeper, truer interest in you than we do."

Letters from Lady Blessington to Mrs. Mathews.

"Villa Gallo, Naples, October 18, 1823.

"Dearest Mrs. Mathews,

"I can, at the present moment, enter much better into the feelings that dictated your letter addressed to me a year ago, than when it reached me. You were then parting with Charles, and wrote under all the feelings of anxious affection; judging by what I now feel, when, after a year's residence with us, he is on the point of leaving us, I am sensible of what a sacrifice you made in resigning him, and what your joy must be in having him restored to you. I believe that your letter desiring his return, was the first that you ever dictated that gave pain; it threw a gloom over our whole circle, Charles excepted, whose heart is too devoted to you, not to throb with rapture at the idea of again seeing you after so long an absence, and I see the embarrassing situation he is placed in, between his wish of not appearing ungrateful by participating in our regret at parting, and the delight he naturally feels at rejoining you. Long may his honest and noble heart be filled with the same ingenuous sentiments, that dictate all his actions at present, for it would be indeed a pity, if it ever became sullied by a contact with the world. Without one-half of the estimable qualities which Charles possesses, his talents, various, brilliant, and amusing as they are, always render him a guest too agreeable to every society, to be resigned without real regret, as he is found to enliven and be the charm of every circle in which he moves; but when one knows, as I do, that those talents, delightful as they are, constitute his least merit—that to those he unites the kindest heart, the most ingenuous nature, the best principles, and unvarying good temper, and perhaps what endears him still more to me, a delicacy of sentiment almost feminine, it is impossible not to feel sad and sorrowful at giving him up, even to a mother whose happiness he forms. It is my consolation, that I restore him to you, my dearest friend, as pure, as amiable, and as unsophisticated, as when he left you; and it is with as much pleasure, as truth, that I declare that, in a year's residence beneath my roof, and almost constantly beneath my eye,

I have not discovered a single fault, action, or inclination, that would give a moment's pain to your heart, which gives me the gratifying conviction, that through life he will prove a source of pride and comfort to you, and all his friends, and among that number (and after yourself the most affectionate and interested), I beg you will consider me. I send you two little souvenirs of Naples; they have no other recommendation than that of being the production of this country, and a very trifling memorial of an affection, which, though less inflammable than the lava that forms them, retains its warmth much longer; as for you it never can end. Say every thing that is kind for me to Mr. Mathews; and when Charles and you are enjoying one of those dear, quiet, happy *tête-à-têtes* in your dear, snug little room, pray give a thought to a friend, who would gladly steal away from the bustle and noise of a heartless world to make a trio with you. Write to me often; Charles has promised to do the same, and ever believe me,

"My dearest Mrs. Mathews,

"Your sincere and affectionate friend,

"MARGUERITE BLESSINGTON."

"Apres avoir passé une année dans l'intimité avec Charles, il ne m'est pas possible de vous considerer come etrangere, c'est pour cette raison Madame, que je prends la liberté de vous dire combien nous regrettons votre fils, qui emporte avec lui notre sincere amitié ainsi que notre parfaite estime, s'il nous quitte à present, c'est pour le retrouver plus tard j'espere, et lui prouver s'il est possible, la verité de l'amitié que je lui ai vouée. J'espere aussi etre bien recu de vous, presenté par votre sincere amie Lady Blessington, et par votre cher fils les deux personnes que je connais qui vous sont le plus attachés—et c'est en même temps que je me feliciterai connaitre Mr. Mathews de qui la voix publique, et l'amitié privée donne tant le desir d'etre connu de lui.

"L'Ami de votre fils,

"COMTE D'ORSAY."

"Palazzo Belvedere, Naples, Nov. 21, 1823.

"Your amiable and excellent Charles has been at Pompeii for ten days past, so do not be uneasy at not hearing from him. With the affection and esteem I feel for you, my dearest Mrs. Mathews, as well as the regard I entertain for Mr. Mathews, you may be assured that I shall take a warm interest in your son, and do all in my power to contribute to his present and future comfort; but putting those sentiments aside, Charles has so many excellent qualities, and is so agreeable a member of society, that he must always be esteemed and valued for himself; and, I assure you, so much do we prize his society, that nothing but the sense of the advantage he would derive from a ten days' residence at Pompeii, could have induced us to relinquish it; and we find his absence leaves a chasm in our little circle, that although he has only been some days gone, renders us already impatient for his return. Sir William Gell has taken such a fancy to Charles (as indeed has every individual to whom we have presented him), that he takes quite an interest in his plans. It was Sir William who introduced him to a very clever intelligent young architect (Mr. Angell), with whom he has gone to Pompeii, which is much more agreeable than would be a solitary sojourn there; and I expect to see Charles return with a portfolio of sketches that will hereafter charm your eyes, and convey to you a lively idea of this land of wonders. Never does Charles see an interesting object or beautiful view without wishing for you; and I hope I need not add, that in those wishes I most heartily join.

"Pray write to me whenever you have resolution enough to seize the pen, and in return I will from time to time give you an account of Charles. Lord B. promises to take us to Sicily in February, and we anticipate with delight seeing that interesting country, where there are some of the most admirable remains of antiquity to be viewed.

"Marguerite Blessington."

"December 6th.

"Lord B. unites with me in congratulating Mr. Mathews on having so far carried his point, as to look upon it as now settled, that the monument to our immortal bard will be erected, and Mr. Mathews will be entitled to the thanks of all the admirers of Shakspeare, in which list are comprised all the people of taste and genius the country can boast, for being the means of carrying so desirable an object into effect. I do not know Sir C. Long, but I understand he is not only a man of very fine taste, but a most amiable person, and I think Mr. Mathews will have great satisfaction with him in this project. I return you the dear little Count's letter, which is like himself, very short, very sweet, and full of heart.

"M. Blessington."

"Villa Gallo, January 1st, 1825.

"Your letter of the 8th of December reached me on Christmas day, and was truly gratifying, though you far overrate the services that you conceive we have rendered Charles. You had laid the foundation so solidly of every good and essential quality, that you have left nothing to be added, except, it may be, a few of the ornamental decorations, that are given to finish a work; and those he has an intuitive tact and quickness in acquiring, that renders the assistance of friends unnecessary. I speak to you, my dearest Mrs. Mathews, with all the candour and frankness that I should do in addressing myself to a sister, and without one shade that the flattery of friends in general think necessary, when speaking to a mother of her son; and, in the true spirit of candour, I declare to you, that after a year's daily intercourse with Charles, I regard him as one of the most faultless characters I ever met, and possessing more amiable, as well as more amusing qualities, than have fallen to the lot of any of my friends and acquaintances. Enjoying the charms of his society as you now do, you may conceive what a chasm his absence has left in our circle; there is not a day in which we do not miss the sunshine of his well-timed gaiety, or an evening in which we do not name him with affectionate regret. I assure you, that it gives me real pleasure to hear from you, that Charles feels for me a portion of the regard and interest that I entertain for him; and pray tell him that I will yield to no other, except his mother and his wife, the place I wish to hold in his affection; as through life he may count upon me, after the two I have named, as the woman in the world the most sincerely his friend. I am glad to hear that you have been staying with my dear sister, at a moment when she needed the consolation the presence of valued friends can alone afford. Separated from her by such a distance, it is a balm to my heart, to think that she has in you a friend who can supply my place, and I trust you will see her as often as you can. MARGUERITE BLESSINGTON."

"Paris, July 6th, 1829.

"I thank you for your kind letter, and feel deeply sensible of the sympathy of you and your excellent family, under the cruel and heavy blow that has fallen on me, in the loss of the best of husbands and of men; these are not mere words of course, as all who know him will bear witness, for never did so kind or gentle a heart inhabit a human form; and I feel this dreadful blow with even more bitterness, because it appears to me, that while I possessed the inestimable blessing I have lost, I was not, to the full extent, sensible of its value; while now, all his many virtues and good qualities rise up every moment in memory, and I would give worlds to pass over again the years that can never return. Had I been prepared for this dreadful event by any previous illness, I might perhaps have borne up against it; but falling on me like some dreadful storm, it has for ever struck at the root of my peace of mind, and rendered all the future a blank. It is not while those to whom we are attached are around us in the enjoyment of health and the prospect of a long life, that we can judge of the extent of our feelings towards them, or how necessary they are to our existence. We are, God help us! too apt to underrate the good we have, and to see the little defects to which even the most faultless are subject; while their good qualities are not remembered as they ought to be, until some cruel blow, like that which has blighted me, draws the veil from our eyes, and every virtue, every proof of affection, are remembered with anguish, while every defect is forgotten. Oh! could we in our days of health, but ask ourselves the question of how we could support the loss of a friend to whom we are attached and endeared by habit, the examination of our hearts would render us more anxious to show that tenderness, and give those proofs of an affection that often lies dormant there, and the extent of which we are not aware, until the object is for ever torn from us. What renders my feelings still more bitter is, that during the last few years my health has been so bad, and violent attacks in my head so frequent, that I allowed my mind to be too much engrossed by my own selfish feelings, and an idea of my poor, dear, and ever-to-be-lamented husband being snatched away before me, never could have been contemplated. Alas! he who was in perfect health, and whose life was so precious and so valuable to so many, is in one fatal day torn from me for ever, while I, who believed my days numbered, am left to drag on a life I now find a burthen. Excuse my writing to you in this strain; I would not appear unkind or ungrateful in not answering your letters, and my feelings are too bitter to permit my writing in any other. Believe me, dearest Mrs. M., deeply interested in your affairs, and in that of your excellent husband and son. Your truly affectionate friend,

"M. Blessington."

"Paris, October 7th, 1829.

"Your letter is so like yourself, kind, gentle, amiable, and soothing, that its perusal has had nearly the same effect on my feelings, that an interview never failed to produce, during the too brief period of your stay at Paris. I quite agree with Mrs. M—— S——, that you are admirably adapted to afford consolation to the afflicted. I too have experienced it, and never will neglect any opportunity of benefiting from its salutary influence. If you knew how often and fondly you have been remembered by us all, you would at least give us credit for warm hearts; but above all, Comte D'Orsay rarely passes a day without speaking of you, with all the esteem and admiration you are so well calculated to inspire, and even Charles admits that he can appreciate you as well as if he were English, which is a great deal for a foreigner. Pray do not, dearest Mrs. Mathews, feel any apprehension as to the effects of any communications you may make to me; alas! I have no longer any illusion as to the real feelings of one who for so many years I considered as my second self, and explanations are as useless, and would be almost as undignified as reproaches, neither of which shall I ever condescend to make to her. I view her conduct with much more of pity than of anger, and nothing she can do shall ever urge me to a reprisal; on the contrary, had she occasion for my services to-morrow, she should experience that, though I cannot forget, I can forgive. If, however, it is painful to you to tell me anything she writes, let it pass; unhappily all that I can learn must fall infinitely short of what I already know; and as I have no longer any illusion, I never can again be deceived or wounded in that quarter. She cannot dislike my going to England as much as I do, for death has deprived me of the *friend* who could have rendered my visit there as happy and prosperous as all my days were when he lived. The contrast between the past and present would and will be most poignant, but should our affairs require it, I shall certainly go; but I wish that she would be persuaded that *business* alone could take me, and that I never can accept the civilities or hospitality of those who were wanting in both to the *truest* and *dearest friend I* ever had, and her *greatest benefactor*, whose name I am proud to bear, and shall ever respect. Poor Charles has been, and still is unwell, but his illness is not serious, and with care he will, I trust, soon get well. I hope you know he is in good hands, Comte D'Orsay and his doctor, and we all take as much care of him as we can. I have been much annoyed at its appearing in the papers that I had been to the theatre; this is to believe that I am equally wanting in feeling and decency. I wish it could be contradicted. M. Blessington."

"Paris, Monday, October 20th, 1829.

"I have great pleasure in telling you that your dear and excellent Charles is nearly quite well, and that you may make your mind perfectly easy about him, as a few days cannot fail to restore him to his wonted health and strength. You may be assured that I would not suffer him to depart while I saw a trace of illness hanging over him; he is too dear to us all, to admit of our letting him commit any imprudence. He proposes setting off on Thursday, but I have requested that he may wait until Monday, to make assurance doubly sure of the impossibility of any relapse. We have too much enjoyment in his society, and desire it too much, not to seize with avidity any opportunity of retaining him, the moment we had your sanction for so doing; but he appears so very anxious to set off, and his health is so much better, that I can oppose nothing but my wishes for retarding his departure. M. Blessington."

"Paris, December 14th, 1829.

"You can so well make allowance for omission in correspondence, for having unhappily too often felt the difficulty of writing even to those most loved, that I will make no other apology for not having sooner replied to your letter of the 19th of November, than that it found me, as I still am, ill in mind and body, and unequal to the exertion of writing even to you. Indeed, my health suffers so much, that I fear I shall be obliged to give up residing at Paris, and be compelled to try the effects of English air; and this will be very painful to me, after having gone to so much expense and trouble in arranging my rooms here, where I am so comfortably lodged, besides which, a residence in England, under my present circumstances, would be so different to all that I have been accustomed to, that I cannot contemplate it without pain. But, after all, without health there is no enjoyment of even the quiet and sober nature which I seek—a cheerful fire-side, with a friend or two to enliven it; or, what is still, perhaps, more easily had, a good book, for I am a little of Mr. Mathews' opinion, that conversation and society, such as I should prefer, cannot be had in Paris. I have never had a day's health since I have been in France; and though I do all that I am advised, I get worse rather than better. I heard from Mr. Powell yesterday, and find he has as yet done nothing either in discovering the author of the scandalous attacks against me, or in preventing a renewal of them. You are wrong in thinking that Col. C——— has been actuated by annoyance of slighted attentions, &c. &c.; he never paid me any more than politeness required during the many years of our acquaintance, so that wounded vanity cannot have caused his conduct.

"Mary Gardiner has been at Paris for three weeks, and left last Saturday: she is all that is most perfect, her dear father's kind, noble, and generous heart, with a manner the most captivating; I adore her, and I believe she loves me as few girls can love a mother. All charge me with a thousand affectionate regards to you. M. BLESSINGTON."

"Paris, January 18th, 1830.

"MY DEAR, DEAR FRIEND,

"A report has reached me that has filled my mind with terror and regret; and, perhaps, of all created beings, I am the one who can the most truly and deeply sympathize in your feelings at this crisis. It is because I know, by bitter experience, the utter hopelessness of all attempts at consolation at such a moment, that my writing to you has only one object—that of assuring you, that my heart bleeds for and with you; and as I know the sincerity of your affection for me, my sympathy, which is, God knows, true and heartfelt, cannot be deemed obtrusive. You, like me, have lost the kindest and truest of friends—a loss that will be felt with anguish all your days I, who knew your affection and devotion to him, can well feel all the bitterness of your grief; and I, who knew also how well he merited it, and who felt for him the most sincere friendship and respect, can fully estimate your cruel bereavement. But you, my dearest friend, have a consolation that was denied to me; you have a son, who will share, and, if possible, lighten your sorrow, while I am alone, with estranged and ungrateful friends. Think of Charles, who has only you left him for consolation, and let this thought give you force to bear up against your grief. Change of scene would, I am certain, be of use to you; my house and heart are open to receive you, and here you will meet with the truest sympathy. M. BLESSINGTON."

"Paris, May 7th, 1830.

"I lose not a moment in replying to your letter of the 3rd, and regret that I cannot at all enlighten you on the subject you name. All that has occurred on the subject of the attacks in the 'Age,' I shall now lay before you. Mr. P——— is the only person to whom I ever named you as having given me any information relative to the subject; and this I only did, because I conceived, from a passage in one of your letters, that he had had a conversation with you on the affairs. I wrote to Mr. P———, urging him to commence a prosecution against the editor, and stated to him that Lord S—— de R—— had advised me to do so, as the only means of putting a stop to these attacks. Mr. P—— was of a different opinion, and advised our treating the attack with contempt; and so the affair ended. I never heard of Lord S—— writing to England on the subject, and am sure he is too indolent to take the trouble when he was in no way interested.

"When Col. C———— returned to Paris, in February, and came to see me, I told him my information as to his being the author of the attacks; but this I did without ever even hinting at my informant. He declared his innocence in the most positive terms, gave his word of honour that he had never written a line in his life of scandal for any paper, and never could lend himself to so base and vile a proceeding. His manner of denial was most convincing, and so it ended. Two months ago, Capt. G————, of the Guards, who had been very severely attacked in the 'Age,' went to London, and took a friend with him to the editor of the 'Age,' who even gave him a small piece of the letter sent from Paris, which Captain G———— sent Comte D'Orsay, and which is a totally different writing from Colonel C————'s; and so here ended the business, as it was useless to do anything more, except commence a prosecution, which I still think ought to have been done. Mr. P—— has never given either Comte D'Orsay or myself the least information, since last January, on this subject; and now you know all that I do on this point. I have never seen a single number of the 'Age,' do not know a single person who takes it in, and never hear it named, so that I am in total ignorance as to the attacks it contains.

"I can name as yet no definite period for my going to England; pecuniary affairs prevent me at present, though I am anxious to go, in the hope that change of air may do me good, my health and spirits being very, very poorly. *This month*, as your heart may tell you, is a great trial to me; it has renewed my grief, with a vividness that you can understand; for it is dreadful to see all nature blooming around, and to think that the last time I welcomed the approach of spring, I was as happy as heart could wish, blessed with the best and most delicate of friends, while now all around me wears the same aspect, and all within my heart is blighted for ever! M. Blessington."

"Paris, Monday, August 9th, 1830.

"Thanks, my dearest Mrs. Mathews, for the kind solicitude expressed in your letter of the 2nd, which reached me this day, and which I hasten to remove as speedily as possible, by assuring you that we never were, during the whole tumult, exposed to the least personal danger, and that now everything is so perfectly tranquil here, that we have nothing to dread. The scenes we have witnessed form an epoch in our lives; we may truly say, the revolution was a triumph of liberty over despotism, and unstained by a single act of cruelty or pillage. Private property has been respected in every instance, and while the mass of the people have been, as it were, animated but by one feeling, a just indignation against their oppressors, no example of robbery or cruelty can be cited against them. It is impossible to have witnessed their conduct, without feelings of warm admiration and respect, and without remarking the striking effects of the march of intellect. M. Blessington."

"Sunday, 14th August, 1831.

"I fully enter into all the feelings and troubles that have oppressed you, up to the last. Perhaps I can the more deeply enter into them at this period, as your letter found me sinking under all the nervous excitation natural for a sensitive person to feel, under such painful and embarrassing circumstances as I find myself placed in. M. Blessington."

"Seamore Place, December 7th, 1831.

"What shall I say, in return for the many sweet but too flattering things your partiality has prompted you to address to me? All I shall say is, that if it had been my lot in life to have met with many hearts like yours, I might have become all that your affection leads you to believe me; or if in my near relations, I had met with only kind usage or delicacy, I should now not only be happier, but a better woman, for happiness and goodness are more frequently allied than we think. But I confess to you, my beloved friend, a great part of the milk and honey of nature with which my heart originally overflowed is turned into gall; and though I have still enough goodness left, to prevent its bitterness from falling even on those who have caused it, yet have I not power to prevent its corroding my own heart, and rusting many of the qualities with which nature had blessed me. To have a proud spirit, with a tender heart, is an unfortunate union, and I have not been able to curb the first or *steel* the second; and when I have felt myself the dupe of those for whom I sacrificed so much, and in return only asked for affection, it has soured me against a world where I feel alone—misunderstood—with my very best qualities turned against me. If an envious or a jealous crowd misjudge or condemn, a proud spirit can bear up against injustice, conscious of its own rectitude; but if in the most inveterate assailants one finds those whom we believe to be our trusted friends, the blow is incurable, and leaves behind a wound, that will, in spite of every effort, bleed afresh, as memory recalls the cruel conduct that inflicted it. Cæsar defended himself against his foes, but when he saw his friend Brutus strike at him, he gave up the struggle. If any thing can preserve me from the *mildew of the soul* that is growing on me, it will be your affection, which almost reconciles me to human nature. M. Blessington."

"Monday, 14th November, 1831.

"Count D'Orsay has just arrived, and has described to me (not without tears) the distressing scene he witnessed at Ivy Cottage.

"I am miserable at your continuing there this night, and would give any thing on earth that you were with me. Do let me entreat of you, come to me to-morrow, and remain here until all is over; believe me, it is best for every reason. As long as your presence could be of use to the faithful and excellent creature who is departed, I would not have proposed your leaving him for a day; but now all is over, your staying in such a scene will only destroy your already shattered nerves and injured health, which must be preserved, to console poor dear Charles. M. Blessington."

"Thursday Evening, April 26th, 1832.

"It is strange, my dearest friend, but it is no less strange than true, that there exists some hidden chord of sympathy, some 'lightning of the mind,' that draws kindred souls towards each other when the bodies are separated. I have been for the last four days thinking so much of you, that had this day been tolerable, I should have gone to you, as I had a thousand misgivings that something was wrong, when lo! your little note arrives, and I find that you too have been thinking of your absent friend. I shall be so glad to hear that Mr. Mathews is returned, and in better health and spirits. I feel all that you have had to undergo; that wear and tear of the mind, that exhausts both nerves and spirits, is more pernicious in its effects than greater trials. The latter call forth our energies to bear them, but the former wear us out without leaving even the self-complacency of resisted shocks. I shall be most glad to see you again, and to tell you that in nearness as in distance your affection is the cable that holds my sheet anchor, and reconciles me to a world where I see much to pity, and little to console. La Contessa Guiccioli is arrived in England, and this day came to see me; she is a very interesting person, gentle, amiable, and unhappy; you would, I am sure, like her, and if you think so, you shall meet her here at dinner with me when you like.

"M. Blessington."

"Monday Evening, April 3rd, 1832.

"You have such a good and kind heart, my dearest friend, that I know it will give you pleasure to hear that your friend has seen her error, made the *amende honorable*, *without* any communication from me, and that all is at present *couleur de rose*. I could not sleep without telling you this. Why do we live so far asunder? I am sure it would add years to my life, and oh! how much happiness to those years, to see you often; your presence not only makes me happier, but makes me *better*; there is a soothing influence in your looks, manner, tones, and voice, that comforts and tranquillizes my feelings, like a delicious twilight, that is so dearly valued, because felt to be so fleeting; not that I should appreciate your dear society or twilight less, were both as lasting as they are delightful; but alas!

"'All that's bright must fade.'

"M. Blessington."

"Sunday, June 24th, 1832.

"I have had all the horrors of authorship on my hands the last week, so that I really have not had an hour to call my own, and retire at night so fatigued as to be unable to sleep.

"I have disposed of my 'Journal of Conversations with Lord Byron' very advantageously; they are first to appear in the 'New Monthly,' and after in a separate volume. I tell you all this, knowing the interest your dear, kind heart takes in all that concerns me. You may be assured that it delights me to hear of dear Charles's success in every branch to which he turns his talents; and I foretold from his earliest youth that he must succeed in all that he tried. M. Blessington."

"Seamore Place, Sept. 20, 1832.

"I have had my father with me for the last fortnight, and he only left me to-day. My brother is at Palace Yard, but I see him every day. You must never imagine for a single moment that there exists that person that could rival you in my affection — there is but *one* Mrs. Mathews in the world, though there may be, and is, a thousand amiable and charming people; and though La Contessa Guiccioli is among the thousand, and perhaps unites more good qualities than fall to the share of many of the number, still she is not formed to occupy a place that ever had been filled by you. Alfred charges me with all that is grateful, affectionate, and sincere to you. You have not, after Charles, on earth, a *male* heart more truly devoted to you, nor a *female* one that feels for you a more *true, warm,* and constant affection than your most cordial friend,

"M. Blessington."

"Friday, Sept. 20th, 1832.

"You will, I know, be sorry to hear of the death of dear, good Madame Crawford. She died at Paris, on the 13th, lamented by all who knew her, and deeply so by me, to whom she was most deservedly endeared by a friendship as warm as it was unchanging, of which she gave me many proofs. Though, from her advanced age, being in her eighty-fifth year, a protracted existence was not to be expected, still her heart was so warm, and her affections so fresh and devoted, that one could never consider her as an old woman; and if age was to be considered by feelings instead of years, how much younger was dear, good Madame Crawford than many of those who have not half her years. Your friend, and I may safely use the term in its true acceptation of the word, as he is your true and affectionate friend, Cte. Alfred, is deeply grieved, for he truly loved his grandmother, as she did him. He begs me to offer you his most affectionate remembrances, and to Mr. Mathews his kind regards. Pray make mine also acceptable to him. I had seen notices of dear Charles's whereabouts in the newspapers, and was truly glad to have them confirmed by you. That his expedition will be most serviceable to his health and spirits admits not of a doubt, and that it will be advantageous to his future prospects, is, I think, equally sure; for the intimacy of the influential family with whom he is domesticated cannot fail to be cemented by a warm friendship, as Charles has as many solid qualities to ensure esteem, as he has brilliant talents to win admiration; and those he met as acquaintances, he will leave as friends. M. BLESSINGTON."

"Saturday, 29th Sept. 1832.

"I wrote a line to Charles to Newport, to apprise him of the necessity of his appearance at Lincoln's Inn on the 1st. I must repeat the regret I feel at taking him from you and his father, when the helplessness of the latter renders his son's attention so necessary for you. I so well know the devotedness of your affection for those you love, that a sacrifice of personal comfort costs you, perhaps, less than any one else; but when I reflect on the fearful accident, and its consequences, that has reduced Mr. Mathews to his present distressing state, I feel pained beyond expression at depriving him and you of Charles's assistance at such a crisis, though but even for a few days. The newspapers, that in general magnify misfortunes, in the case of poor Mr. Mathews reduced them, by stating that a few hours after his accident all traces of it had disappeared;—would to God it had been so, as I really feel more than all, *save you,* could imagine, at finding how much more serious the misfortune has been. Yes, you are right, my beloved friend, in supposing that your silence can never by me be mistaken for want of affection or interest. I *know your heart*, and I *rely on it*, because I judge it by my own, which neither time, distance, nor circumstances can change towards you. I detest writing, but I do not love my friends less, because I do not tell them so more frequently; the sentiment is engraved in indelible characters on my heart, and each profession is but as a new seal with the same legend. I like to hear often, very often, from those I love; but when they do not write, I conclude that, like me, they are silent, but not forgetful. My friend, Mr. John Fox Strangways, is third cousin to Lord Holland, being brother to the present Earl of Ilchester, who, with Lord Holland, descends in line direct from Sir Stephen Fox (of the reign of Charles the Second), whose eldest son was created Earl of Ilchester, and the second was created Baron Holland.

"Your constant and attached friend, Alfred, paid a visit to the cottage five days ago; the cage was there, but, alas! the bird was flown; and he came back to tell me that, lovely as the day was, the cottage looked gloomy and melancholy without its owners.

"I like the Isle of Wight—it is endeared to me by the recollection of having passed a delightful fortnight there, with my ever-to-be-lamented husband; the only *tête-à-tête* we ever enjoyed during our marriage, and which we both felt as children do their first vacation from school. How many souvenirs does each thought of it excite. M. BLESSINGTON."

"To-morrow, Saturday, I have the nuisance of having some people to dinner, invited days ago; but I shall leave my sister and Count Alfred to entertain them, as I am too suffering to attempt it; indeed, my spirits are as low as my health, and my thoughts are much more with you and your house of mourning, than with anything passing around me. Conquer the feelings that the last sad event will excite, by recollecting what I had to bear when all I most valued was torn from me, and I left with strangers in a foreign land.

"M. BLESSINGTON."

"Thursday, August 19th, 1835.

"Well can I understand, my dearest friend, the total break-up in your habits and hours. All that you are now undergoing, I have undergone, with the additional misery of having *him* whose loss I must ever deplore, snatched away from me in the midst of apparent health, without the preparation for such a fatal event by one day of illness, or the melancholy consolation of having cheered his bed of sickness, or soothed his last hours by a knowledge of how he was valued. Time is the only consoler. Every day brings us nearer to those we have lost, and who have only preceded us by at most a few fleeting years. I shall call on you at four o'clock on Saturday next, unless I hear that you are engaged, and cannot receive me.

"M. Blessington."

"Tuesday night, Dec. 2nd, 1835.

"I can well enter into your feelings, every one of which finds an echo in my heart. Little do we think, when we are enlivening birthdays and anniversaries, that we are laying up cause for future sorrow, and that a day may come when those who shared them with us, being snatched away, the return of past seasons of enjoyment bring only bitterness and sorrow. All that you feel I felt and do feel, though years are gone by since the blow that destroyed my happiness took place. Without the constant occupation I have given myself, I should have sunk under it, when the memory of it comes back to me with all the bitterness of the past, though I try to chase it away. Lady Canterbury charges me to offer you her congratulations on Charles's success, and her affectionate regards. God be thanked, that his efforts have been crowned with unequalled success: every one talks of his acting, in raptures.

"M. Blessington."

"Monday night.

"It was only on Saturday that I first read of your intended voyage to America; and my knowledge of the delicacy of your health during the last year, led me to think the statement totally destitute of truth, so that until your letter of yesterday reached me I disbelieved it. But what cannot affection and a sense of duty effect in a mind like yours? I am not surprised at your determination, because I know you; but I believe there is not another woman in England, in your delicate health, that would have courage to undertake such a voyage, and such an absence from Charles. May God bless and reward you for it, and may you reap all the advantages from it that you deserve. I had wished much to see you, for I was anxious to tell you honestly, and in all sincerity, the real delight I experienced at seeing the performance of Mr. Mathews the last night. Never—no, not even the first year of his performance, was it more brilliant, more vigorous, or more successful, and I was enchanted to find that this was the sense of the whole house. I have thought all day of your departure, and mourned over it as though we were often together, instead of being, as we have lately been, almost as much separated as if different countries held us; but even though friends do not meet, it is always a comfort to know that they are within reach, and a pang shoots through the heart when a year of absence is contemplated.

"M. Blessington."

"Monday Night.

"I had thought it very long, my dearest friend, since I heard from you; and dear Charles having told me that you had been ill and suffering, did not console me. I have been so constantly and fatiguingly occupied in copying and correcting since I saw you, that I have not had a moment to myself, and the only recreation I have enjoyed, is the having gone to see 'The Wolf and the Lamb,' which, I do assure you, delighted all our party, some of whom did not know the author. I should have sent you the 'Monthly,' but that I could not bear that you should read anything of mine in the same book that unfavourably noticed Charles's production. I cannot account for the editor's ill-judged and ill-placed severity; but I believe that so high a report of Charles's talents has gone forth, that miracles are expected of him, and that anything short of a comedy of five acts would be considered as *infra dig.* for him. M. B."

"Tuesday Night.

"Your agitated letter of this day has just reached me, and

never did I feel the annoyance of indisposition so heavily as during the last two days, that it has kept me from going to you, perhaps (and God in heaven grant it may be!) the last occasion on which I could be of use in consoling you, or rather let me say, in sharing your sorrow, for, in cases like this, there is no consoler but time. But still, when one's feelings are understood —and who can understand yours like me, who have drank the cup of bitterness to the very dregs?—though sorrow is not *removed*, it is *lightened* by being shared. Alas! I have too keenly, too deeply felt the want of friends, to consider the rank or position of any one who had served or loved me or mine, and, therefore, well can I understand *all* that you feel at the loss of the amiable, the noble-minded creature who has gone before us to that kingdom where rank loses all its futile, its heartless distinctions, and we are judged of by our deeds and our hearts, and not by our names. Though I have not been with you in person, my mind, my soul, has been with you, and my tears have flowed in sympathy with yours. M. BLESSINGTON."

"Gore House, July 1st, 1840.

"You do me but justice in thinking that you are not forgotten, though my not going to you would seem to imply it; but when I tell you that I have no less than three works passing through the press, and have to furnish the MS. to keep the printers at work for one of them, you may judge of my unceasing and overwhelming occupation, which leaves me time neither for pleasure, or for taking air or exercise enough for health. I am literally worn out, and look for release from my literary toils more than ever slave did from bondage. I never get out any day before five o'clock—have offended every friend or acquaintance I have, by never even calling at their doors—and am suffering in health from too much writing. M. BLESSINGTON."

From Lady Blessington to a young friend of Mrs. Mathews.

"Paris, November 30, 1829.

"You are one of the few, dearest, who do not quite forget me. I have experienced such ingratitude and unkindness, that, added to the heavy blow that has fallen on me, I really dread becoming a misanthrope, and that my heart will shut itself up against all the world. If you knew the bitter feelings the treatment I have met with has excited in my breast, you would not wonder that it has frozen the genial current of life, and that I look, as I am, more of another world than this. Had God spared me my ever-dear and lamented husband, I could have borne up against the unkindness and ingratitude of friends estranged; but, as it is, the blow has been too heavy for me, and I look in vain on every side for consolation. I am wrong, my dearest, in writing to you in this gloomy mood, but if I waited until I become more cheerful, God alone knows when your letter would be answered. You are young, and life is all before you; take example by me, and conquer, while yet you may, tenderness of heart and susceptibility of feeling, which only tend to make the person who possesses them wretched; for, be assured, you will meet but few capable of understanding or appreciating such feelings, and you will become the dupe of the cold and heartless, who contemn what they cannot understand, and repay with ingratitude the affection lavished on them. I would not thus advise you, if I did not know that you have genius; and who ever had that fatal gift without its attendant malady, susceptibility and deep feeling? which, in spite of all mental endowments, render the person dependent on others for their happiness; for it may appear a paradox, but it is nevertheless true, those who are most endowed can the least suffice for their own happiness.

"The Princess Esterhazy has been a fortnight at Paris, and was scarcely a day away from Madame Crawford, who she considers just as a mother. The poor old lady has been ill, and still keeps her room, but is getting better. She inquires every post-day for you, as does the General.

"M. BLESSINGTON."

With this letter I bring the correspondence of Lady Blessington to a close. I have stated at the commencement of this work, that, however brilliant was the position of this highly-gifted and generous-hearted woman, at the onset even of her triumphs of the *salon*, and of her career of fashion in London intellectual society, her life was not happy: and I have to terminate my labours with a repetition of that opinion.

I have had, on many occasions, to refer to acts of benevolence, liberality, and generosity of hers that furnished ample evidence, at every stage in her career, of a noble nature, largely endowed with genial feelings, kindly sympathies with suffering poverty and depressed worth, and neglected merit in every pursuit and occupation—evidence that cannot be contravened, of active impulses to do good, and untiring energies in her efforts to be serviceable to others. One proof more of this generous disposition may be fitly referred to in this place.

Various applications had been made to Lord Blessington and his agents, by the members of a religious order in Dublin, for an eligible site on his Lordship's property in the metropolis, for the erection of a place of worship. A promise had been early obtained from his Lordship, but his agents had found difficulties in the way of carrying his intention into effect; and the site, in fact, could not be obtained.

At length, on the arrival of Lord Blessington in Dublin, after his second marriage, accompanied by his lady, he was waited on by a deputation from the members of that order; their suit was strongly urged on his Lordship, and the unperformed promise given to them was referred to.

On that deputation was the learned and venerable Dr. Esmond, a brother of the present Sir Thomas Esmond. Even his eloquence was employed in vain on that occasion. The Lord spoke generally of his former willingness to give the site, but stated that he could not interfere with those who had charge of his affairs, and a thorough knowledge of them.

At that moment, a door of the drawing-room, which had been ajar during the interview, was opened, and a lady of surpassing beauty, grace, and elegance of form and manner, made her appearance. "My Lord," said the lady, "did you make a promise of this ground for the purpose stated?" His Lordship replied in the affirmative, and was beginning to notice the difficulties that had been discovered.

The lady interrupted him, and said, in a very decided tone, "What my Lord has promised will undoubtedly be performed. The word of a Mountjoy was never broken. I would be ashamed to bear the name if it were otherwise."

The deputation departed. The grant of the promised site was duly made in a few days, and one of the finest churches in Dublin, that of Gardiner Street, stands on the site which was procured for it by Lady Blessington.

APPENDIX.

No. I.

LETTERS TO AND FROM LORD BLESSINGTON.

Letters from the late Duke of Richmond.

"Dublin Castle, March 24th, 1810.

"MY DEAR MOUNTJOY,

"I perfectly remember your speaking to me on the subject of an earldom, which I understood from you, the Duke of Portland had given you hopes of when any promotion to that dignity should take place, and am glad to find it is recognized by Mr. Perceval.

"With respect to the next vacancy in the order of St. Patrick, I can assure you that it is not promised, and that I shall be glad to take your wishes into consideration with other claims; at the same time I must say that there are several staunch supporters of the present administration who have not, so lately at least as yourself, received a mark of their good wishes. I am sure I need not say that I shall on many accounts be glad to attend to your wishes when I conceive I can, with fairness to the general good of the country and of other well-wishers to government. Yours, dear Mountjoy, very sincerely,

"RICHMOND."

"Phœnix Park, January 12th, 1811.

"I will take a note of your wishes respecting your chaplain, Mr. Ellison, and also Humphries.

"The difficulties are, however, great. Formerly the supporters of government claimed sinecures for themselves. Those are nearly done away, so that they now ask for livings for their relatives and friends. By this means the claims for church preferment have increased enormously.

"As for Humphries, I do not exactly see what can be done for him. Few things are compatible with the situation he holds.

"If any thing should occur that would answer for him, and which, consistent with necessary arrangements I could appoint him to, I shall have much pleasure in so doing.*

"RICHMOND."

"Phœnix Park, June 30th, 1811.

"I am sorry it so happens that you will not be in Ireland at the time I shall be in your part of it. The reasons, however, are good; I hope we shall yet meet before your return to England.

"I am very much obliged to you for the bust of Charles the Second.

"Charles Gardiner and one of the 7th have hired a cottage at Clontarf; it is generally called 'Rattletrap.'

"RICHMOND."

"Phœnix Park, August 3rd, 1811.

"At present it is impossible for me to settle about the winter shooting; but if I remain in Ireland, and can manage it, I shall be happy to accept your invitation, and that of Mr. Browne.

"As for a room, I care not one farthing about it, and can sleep quite as well on a floor as in a bed. I am obliged to him for his offer of the Tyrone mountain. RICHMOND."

From Mrs. Siddons to Lord Mountjoy.

"Westbourne House, Paddington, July 1st, 1812.

"MY DEAR LORD,

"It is impossible for me to express the vexation which I have

* In a letter of a previous date, October 28th, 1809, the following passage relating to the Major above-mentioned occurs: "I have appointed Brigadier-Major Humphries to your district—he is an active, jolly man, and will, I am convinced, give you satisfaction. Pray let me recommend him to your notice."—RICHMOND.

felt from being deprived of the honour of your presence at the theatre, on the 29th. And it is more, much more grievous to me, that you, to whom I feel indebted for so many polite and gratifying attentions, should be the only person who has had cause to complain of the arrangements of that night. Allow me, my Lord, to trouble you with the enclosed vindication of my conduct and intentions, and with my most grateful acknowledgments for your temper and forbearance on so vexatious a predicament. Indeed, indeed, my Lord, your gentle and considerate goodness upon that occasion has left an impression of your character upon my mind of higher value than all those gifts, whether of birth, or taste, or talents, with which you are endowed, and ever possibly have made.

"I have the honour to be, my Lord,

"Your Lordship's most obliged and obedient servant,

"Sarah Siddons."

Letters from Lord Blessington to Charles James Mathews, Esq.

"Villa Gallo, Tuesday, October, 1824.

"My dear C. Mathews,

"In returning to you your sketch of the house we proposed to build, I wish to say a few words respecting the deferring of a project which I had last year so much at heart. You may recollect that it was determined, in case the site and ground-plan were approved, the foundation should be commenced this summer, so that in five years, at furthest, the building should be completed; at the same time I said, whatever faults there were in the plan, should be attributed to me, leaving you any praise which it might receive.

"It appeared to me the project was not warmly received, and I said no more about it, but wrote to your father, telling him to say nothing to you, as after the trouble taken it might be disheartening.

"There was a point which I did not mention to your father, but one of some consequence, namely, that I found the plan suggested by Mr. Branson to raise funds to meet the annual expenditure would not succeed. I told your father that I would patch on, looking forward to better times for a building suitable to the grounds. I still look to that 'golden age.'* I also told him, that if you would give me your opinion and advice in my patch-work I would be much obliged; but I should be cautious not to injure your reputation as an architect, by letting people believe you could be to blame for the faults commited by me.

"This will make your family and friends perfectly understand that no change took place in my opinion of you, or my confidence in your zeal and abilities.

"The project has caused one solid good; it led to a year's study in Italy, and has enlarged your mind without endangering your morals. You will therefore return to your home improved in taste and uncorrupted in heart.

"May you live to be a blessing to the mother who adores you, and a true friend and a comfort to so fond and kind a father as yours. And believe me to be your sincere friend,

"BLESSINGTON."

"N.B. With respect to the elevation, I wish, at your leisure, you would put in the wing, as intended, of the Gothic work, and I think the appearance would be better if the tower for the staircase and chimney was altered. B."

"Villa Gallo, February 1, 1825.

"To prove to you, my dear C. J. M., how I value your letter, I will merely say, that I have just received it; and while Michael is preparing my coffee, which Johnny Purves used to call Daddy Olay, I sit up to reply. Your pretty mother has bestowed on you her *eloquence de billet,* but she has also given you some portion of her reserve, for you say nothing of the garden or of herself—now you know I have a tenderness for both, *mais nous ne parlerons plus.*

"It is true they do dig up fresh treasures, and we hear of, and intend to see them; but with all our love for the sublime and beautiful, a fresh assortment of potatoes would be most

* That "Golden age" of Irish landlordism, which had loomed so long in the distance, and has merged at last in the era of the Encumbered Estates Court!—R. R. M.

agreeable to our humble appetites. Artichokes we have, but alas! no gravel pits, and few coal mines; consequently the walks are bad, and the fires expensive. Our volcanic mountain does not smoke, but my chimney, does. The Count does wear calicoes and nankeens. I continue as I did in summer, with my flannel and patent hosiery. We have our Gaetanos—Giovannis—Amelioras, but wish fervently for English servants, for a John and a Betsy, and Sal. Naples is a delightful place—not to eat in—although I name it with awe. I dined on Sunday with Sir W. Drummond, and went to the Opera, where I heard the *Sekart*—is that right? and saw the *Telamon*, Colonel S———'s passion. The last played in the new ballet, founded on the Exile of Siberia; but the Empress is made a man, in the performance. You, however, allude to Naples as the point recollective, and if you did feel that you incurred my displeasure, you must acknowledge that my intention was to supply the place of those who value you more than I can describe; and though you might for the moment consider me severe, your cooler moments must have admitted that I would have no object but your advantage. Your father told me that you had the best heart in the world, and your conduct has proved it. I feel that you left us as innocent of vice as when you left your mother's fostering care; and, if improved in temper and manners, as well as knowledge, your parents must acknowledge that your time was not misspent.

" I have just read your letter to Lady Blessington, and she is as much pleased with it as myself, and desires me to say ' mille choses.'

" Fortunately for your comparatives, the day is lovely, the sky blue propre, the barometer nearly two sections above 29½, but we have had snow, thunder and lightning, wind, hail and rain. The Revenge ran to Malta in thirty-six hours, nine knots an hour under bare poles, and thirteen with a foresail. The *post-captain* has been thinking of going for more than a quarter of an hour, but is by no means gone, although he has the prayers of every one in the house for a speedy voyage. His grievances are much too numerous to relate, and ' imaginary ones' in abundance. Scene—The Horns at Kennington, or the Elephant and Castle, where he wishes to insinuate mysterious events have happened. There has been *one scene*, I hope not to hear of a second, not that I think he is much improved by the rehearsal; and he may perhaps live to consider himself fortunate, if his 'Much Ado about Nothing' concludes with 'All's Well that Ends Well.'

"I am happy to hear that you are in favour with the Speaker, for he is a man high in the estimation of the world, and whom I am sure you will always treat with marked respect, and, in return, be assured of receiving kindness.

"As your mother has resigned my bantling to C. B., I am satisfied she did not think it worthy of being read; as Kemble said to Curran of Miss O———, 'Time was, Mr. Curran, when they strangled such reptiles in their birth.' If the poor baby dies a natural death, you may write its epitaph.

"Great events have happened here. Ferdinand is gone, and Francis reigns in his stead. The spies are sent to the right about, and Abbé C——— in the grumps. He has had a pitched battle with his dear Mary, and we are encouraging her to call him out.

"I have made an architectural plan of the Belvidere for certain purposes, and wished much that you had been here, as I might have put you *en train*. We are great friends with Sir Richard Church, and he has the charge of the plan—more of that hereafter. We have finished the billiard table, and established a handsome library.

"We have found out the means of living better for less money, and as we are to remain, determined to be comfortable. The Count is sitting for his picture to M. le Comte, who has succeeded *a merveille*. Lady B. is to sit to him, and I also. All we want is books. We have got permission from Medici for them to land. Before Mr. Hamilton went away, I asked him to dinner, and thanked him for his kindness to you. Sir William Gell has the gout. We have seen Saint Angelo's collection. He is a nice little man, and has beautiful things. I dine to-day with M. Antrobus, the Chargé d'Affaires. You will say, what a resolution. I have written a second tale in three volumes, and am employed in a political and historical work. We leave this, I believe, for Rome in the beginning of April; from that I go to England. Write me word what you are doing, and tell me about your father, mother, &c. Give my kindest remembrance to both. Lady B. generally speaks for herself better than I can speak for her. Gibbon's 'Decline and Fall' is the thing at present. Remember two things; this letter is for you, and not for St. James's Square, and that I am

"Most truly yours,

"BLESSINGTON."

"Florence, June 21, 1827.

"After a tedious expectation of your arrival at Pisa, we received a long letter, which deserves an answer, addressed Milan. It would give us great pleasure to see you before your pilgrimage, and we hope that it may happen. Whether you can catch us at Parma, or cross so as to meet us at Turin, depends upon your own plans. If you have not seen Turin, you ought to see it, as an architect.

"I hope your father will have his usual success, and that your mother and her garden are as pretty as ever. Sir W. Gell talks of going to Egypt, thence to Syria. In Greece you will find Sir R. Church in high feather, and if you go to the Ionian Islands, our friend Sir Charles commands one of the most agreeable.

"Count D'Orsay is sitting for his bust to Bartolini, and I hear it is admirable. You must see it as you pass through. Mr. Hayter is also at full work at a new picture. A Mr. Salter has made an admirable copy of the Titian Madonna and Child. The plays have wound up with 'The Honey-moon,' and 'The Maid of the Inn.' Our Charles played the young smuggler with good effect. You would have been a wonderful addition.

"BLESSINGTON."

To W. S. Landor, Esq.

"Paris, Hôtel de la Terrasse, July 14th, 1828.

"Oh! it is an age, my dear Landor, since I thought of having determined to write. My first idea was to defend 'Vavasour,'* but the book was lent to one friend or another, and always out of the way when the pen was in hand. My second inclination was, to inquire after you and yours; but I knew that you were not fond of corresponding, so that sensation passed away. And now my third is to tell you that Lady B. has taken an apartment in the late residence of Marshal Ney, and wishes much that some whim, caprice, or other impelling power, should transport you across the Alps, and give her the pleasure of again seeing you. Here we have been nearly five weeks, and, unlike to Italy and its suns, we have no remembrance of the former, but in the rolling of the thunder; and when we see the latter, we espy at the same time the threatening clouds in the horizon. To balance or assist such pleasure, we have an apartment *bien decoré* with *Jardin de Tuileries en face*, and our apartment being at the corner, we have the double advantage of all the *row*, from morn till night. Diligences and fiacres—coachmen cracking their whips, stallions neighing—carts with empty wine-barrels—all sorts of discordant music, and all kinds of cries, songs, and the jingling of bells. But we hope this is our last day of purgatory; for though the skies are loaded with more water than one could expect, after so much pouring, yet, midst thunder, lightning, and rain, we are to strike our tents and march.

"So much for us and Paris. What think you of public affairs? The Miguelites and Pedroites seem to talk bigly of war, but 'by my honour' they seem very chary of their flesh. *Pauvres Diables* of Portugal, they seem upon the eve of falling into a worse state than their Spanish neighbours, who have more room to run away from their oppressors.

"Turning from the Peninsula to the island of Erin, we see the Roman Catholics, under the orders of their priesthood, defeating one of the most honest and honourable members of the Irish representation.

"It is not permitted to our Church to interfere at an election.

* A novel by Lord Blessington, entitled "Vavasour," in 3 vols. 8vo., Colburn, 1828; not very successful.—R. R. M.

Why should the members of another, which from its situation ought to be moderate, I should say humble, be allowed to preach the damnation of souls for the exercise of intellect? and what intellect could be so muddy, as to see public or private service better performed by a lawyer, who, if he can take his seat, will not be listened to; or by a civilian, who has served the public, and Ireland in particular, for so many years, honestly and zealously?—but a truce to Irish politics.

"Of French affairs it is needless to speak—the Chamber of Deputies seem to agree upon the necessity of economy; and there appears a probability of an advance in the system of liberality.

"In Greece, affairs seem asleep. Ibrahim is looking hunger in the face;—what the rest are doing, no one seems to know. On the frontiers of Turkey, the trowser gentlemen seem to fight well behind their walls; but if the army follow the fashion of their Sultan, and ride with long stirrups and English saddles, adieu to the effect of the cavalry. The Turk will no longer be a part of his horse, and his coup de sabre will be parried as easily as the thrust of a small sword; but now my paper says halt—and so do you—and so do I—so all three are agreed.

"Adieu, and believe me, ever truly yours, B."

"P. S. We are now fixed in 74, Rue de Bourbon. I leave Paris for England to-morrow."

To W. S. Landor, Esq.

"My dear Mr. Landor, Saturday.

"As I am one of those unfortunates who never miss an opportunity of catching a cold *en passant*, I have been suffering these last two days, and do not think that I shall be early enough in the field to take the Palazzo Pitti before my departure. You will be surprised to hear that Benjamin Constant and two of his party have been at a card-party of his most Christian Majesty, so that I think his most Catholic Majesty will be left in the lurch, and that the Cross will triumph over the Crescent.

"But everything political now gives way to the new administrations of England and France—Lord Lansdowne, they say, will be Foreign Secretary, and Lord Holland, Privy Seal. The Bar is not pleased by the appointment of Plunket to the Rolls, with a peerage; but he will be a fine make-weight against Eldon in the next debate upon one Irish question.

"They talk of Lord Mountcharles coming here. I think he will be Vice-Chamberlain. Sir J. Leach will not go to Ireland: he is wrong, for he would do well there, and get excellent claret, as well as agreeable society, both of which *agrémens, on dit*, his honour has no objection unto.

"On Tuesday, the 15th, L. N. plays the 'Iron Chest.' I do not know yet whether I shall come over for it or not—I love plays so much, that I think I shall.

"Believe me very sincerely yours,

"BLESSINGTON."

Letters from Lord Rosslyn to Lord Blessington.

[No date, but must have been written in 1829, immediately previous to the introduction of the Catholic Emancipation Act.]

"MY DEAR LORD BLESSINGTON,

"Knowing the deep interest you have always taken in the peace and prosperity of Ireland, and the anxious zeal with which you have upon every occasion exerted yourself in favour of the repeal of the civil disabilities upon the Catholics, I take the earliest opportunity of apprizing you of the present situation of that question.

"It has become of the utmost consequence to obtain the best attendance of the friends of civil and religious liberty, in order to give all possible support to the measure proposed by the Duke of Wellington.

"I am persuaded that you will feel with me that the present is a crisis that calls for every possible exertion and sacrifice from those who have as strong feelings and as deep a stake in the peace and prosperity of Ireland as you have; and you cannot fail to be aware, that the object of the Orange and Brunswick Clubs, in both countries, is to defeat the salutary measures proposed by the Duke of Wellington, and consequently to endanger the security of all property in Ireland, and the peace of the empire.

"If you see this subject in the same light that I do, you will not hesitate to come over to take your seat; and I should venture to suggest to your Lordship, if that should be your determination, that you should come before the second reading of the bill, and remain till after the committee; and if you will do me the honour to signify your commands to me, I will take care to give you timely notice of the day on which it may be necessary for you to be in the House of Lords, for the purpose of taking the oaths, and will take the charge of seeing that your writ is ready.

ROSSLYN."

"St. James' Square, 23rd September, 1829.

"I write to thank you for your letter, and to express the satisfaction I feel in your promise of support to this important and interesting question; and I have no doubt that the public expression of your sentiments will do credit to your talents, and be of advantage to the great cause to which you have so long devoted your attention—the peace and prosperity of Ireland.

"I trust you will not leave Paris later than the 12th, for it is desirable that you should be in London by the 17th, to take your seat.

Yours faithfully,

"ROSSLYN."

No. II.

LETTERS OF SIR WILLIAM GELL TO DR. FREDERICK FORSTER QUIN.

"Rome, January 1, 1823.

"CARO MIO CUGINO E DOTTORE,

"I arrived here notwithstanding my malady, and all the prophecies that I should not set out, somewhat better in health than when you saw me, though I was carried in and out of the carriage, and have not till lately been out, without my arms round the necks of two servants. However, I now stumble over my garden with two canes as supporters, for without them, and particularly without high heels, I walk in the shape of the figure 7, in spite of the German doctor and his remedies.

" *Mawbles** is in great glory, and is going to give two *smole bolls* to open the *cawnival.* I believe she is very useful to society in all points of view.

" When you see Lady Mary Deerhurst, tell her I hope she is coming soon, and that there are a great many families here, besides her aunt, Lady Caroline, and that the world is very gay indeed. Lady W. I saw on the stairs yesterday, and she was dressed in a shroud of white satin, with a great deal of blonde lace, having bled herself with leeches till her face was all of the same colour. We have at present a sort of melting snow here, but not so melting but that all my walks are white, all my lemons frozen to death, and all my geraniums retired into the next world. I fear much my lemon trees will follow the fruit, and I have positively got out my skates this morning, that if the ice bears, as it will if it freezes again in the Villa Borghese, I may lend them to somebody who will shew the Romans what skating is. Pray give my love to Miss Douglas, and Sir William and Lady Drummond.

" Most truly yours,

" My dear Doctor,

" W. Gell."

The mention in a succeeding letter of an Esculapian tour in Greece, is in relation to an application made by some friends of Lord Byron to Dr. Quin, to accompany his Lordship to Greece in the capacity of travelling physician. The subject is referred to in a letter of the Duchess of Devonshire to Dr. Quin, from Rome, dated July the 17th, 1823.

" You must feel, I am sure, it is quite impossible that I could give you the advice you ask for. It is one of those cases in which the opinion of men of wordly experience is of much more value, and it appears evidently that Sir W. Drummond and Sir W. Gell are against your accepting what appears an uncertain and hazardous engagement.

* Gell thus designated an English Duchess, on account of her peculiar pronunciation of the word marbles, and the letter R in general, to which she gave the sound of W.—R. R. M.

"The Cardinal* is wonderfully recovered, and the Pope is going on as well as possible. It is quite miraculous; but yesterday there was a cruel event for Rome. San Paolo took fire, and exists no longer; it is impossible to give any idea of the destruction and devastation. I went with the Duc de Laval yesterday, and the Cardinal, whom we met there, conducted us to all the parts where, amidst burning beams and falling pillars, it was still possible to go. The roof in falling broke down the columns, and, on the opposite side, the violence of the fire calcined those beautiful fluted columns which had stood for fifteen centuries—all, all destroyed in five hours."

In another letter, dated July 22, 1823, the Duchess refers to the same subject.

"I shall be anxious to hear what your decision has been about Lord Byron's offer, and what Sir W. Drummond and Sir W. Gell advised you. I came from Rome the day before the Pope died. The change was sudden, for we had great hopes of preserving him, and I believe he might have been so, had the proper medicines been given in time. The excellent Cardinal is in a state of great affliction for the loss of his tried friend; living twenty-two years in the service of his Sovereign, he never left him hardly, and sat up the last three nights at the bed-side, till quite exhausted, he nearly fainted. I am delighted that Lord Byron is going to Greece; his noble and inspiring genius, when it may be wanted, will reanimate the exertions of the Greeks—heroic efforts they have already made, and they will, I hope, be rewarded by freedom and independence.

"The acrimonies here are fierce and awful—the conclave begins, I believe, this day week; it is to be held at the Quirinal. They will, I hope, suffer less from the confinement there than elsewhere. Adieu, my dear Sir,

"Yours very sincerely,

"E. D."

* The Cardinal Gonsalvi.—R. R. M.

On the same subject, Sir William Drummond wrote to Dr. Quin, at Naples, July 18, 1823.

" I am very inadequate to give you any advice on the proposal which has been made to you. The salary which you require, in consequence of giving up your practice here, does not appear to me too much. You must expect to meet with some difficulties, and to endure some privations, if you go to Greece. Still there is something very attractive in such a voyage, and something even more attractive in making it with a man of such extraordinary talents and genius as Lord Byron. But I really do not feel that I ought to offer any opinion on the subject. You have other friends here, who are better able to advise you. Have you consulted the Duchess of Devonshire, and what does her Grace advise?

" Believe me, ever yours,

" W. DRUMMOND."

From Sir W. Gell.

" Rome, March 19, 1823.

" MY DEAR DOCTOR QUINIBUS,

" My cruel stars, and the tyranny of the two Miss Berrys, who will not be at all grateful for my exertions, force me to return to Naples in the beginning of April, sore against my will, as April and May are the only months when it is worth while to assist at Rome. I made them a promise so long ago to accompany them to Naples, that I was in hopes, indeed almost certain, that they would either have forgotten it, or hired a more active cavaliere servante to assist them in their projects; but it seems I am detected, and that I have very little hope left of being able to divert them from their undertaking. Have, therefore, your mind's eye upon the houses of your neighbours.

" My medicine is come to an end, and that brute of a Doctor Necker will not send any more, so that I am at present reduced to his Ledum Palustre; and, I suppose, in consequence have the gout in both my elbows, a knife in my knees, and a nail in my instep, besides a cold back, and a sort of general weakness, if I become at all cold from the external air. Nevertheless I am not prevented yet from going about; and when you hear that I climbed on my own crazy legs to the top of St Peter's, to take some angles with a sextant, and besides that, I have been out in a storm, between rain and snow, with an icy wind, in a gig, for five hours together, you will be inclined to think I deserve what may follow.

"Our weather still continues to be bad, and the peaches are only now just coming into blossom, whereas on the 24th of March, I have seen the oak trees even on the hill of Albano in leaf. Even the grass shews no symptom of growing yet, and the country looks as wintry as ever.

"*Mawbles* is well, though dried to a stick by a cold, so as to have been in great danger of calling upon you to set her up again. Dr. C. seems to be going on with great success, though he has lost a patient or two of consequence, and I observe on his green chaise a bend in the arms, crossing the wrong way, which ought to be a sign of illegitimacy. But I rather think Esculapius himself was in that predicament.

"This place seems filling for the Holy week, when the dullities become an object to the sheep who follow others to the waters of Babylon.

"I hope the Rocca conducts himself, with his ugly face, according to your wishes, and that the old cat sometimes pays you a visit, and jumps on your breakfast table.

"I hope you have all the success you deserve with your patients, and as you are not too old to learn, I send you a receipt of your friend, Dr. Pomposity, to Lord Newburgh—'Eat a little at breakfast, and a little at luncheon, and, in short, do everything you can to spoil your dinner.'

"Under these awful sentiments I take leave, being most truly, my dear doctor, your sincerely affectionate,

"WILLIAM GELL."

From the same.

"28th March, 1823.

"MY DEAR DOCTOR QUINIE,

"I fear neither your prayers nor my sins will keep me from Naples. I shall have to set out the first Sunday in April, and shall lose all the beauty of the spring in April and May at Naples, where there is none, as summer and winter, dust and rain, join on without spring in your country. Nobody regrets it more than I do, not even yourself; but so cruel fate wills, and you go out and I come in with mutual disgust. Should you decamp much before my arrival, which we will call on the 9th, pray recommend to the fatherly protection of the beauteous Rocca the conservation of my goods and chattels! I conclude, having been your chamberlain, he will soon rebel, and not last above a week after my return. The people here do nothing but take *Misereres*, not *Minderaras*, in large doses; they dine at the Cawdinal's, and thence to the church, to be illuminated by about two hundred tin lamps in the shape of a cross; there they walk about and chatter till they are turned out, and then go to parties at night.

"Mawbles is in all her glory, and heads the *Misereres*, the fire-works, and the illuminations; but the best authorities state the very diminished effects of her *chawms* in the Cawdinal's *hawt*. The Princess G. is arrived, and as Miss D. says she has bought up all the tea on a speculation, let us hope she will be able to dispose of a bargain to her. The Duchesse of Chablais has found in her excavations two Bacchuses, two Nymphs, and an anomalous small deity, about three feet long, sitting up like a dog, with little wings. It strikes me as rather outré for a lady's collection, but I dare say 'tis the fashion. The Bacchus is so fine, that the people dispute as to its being a first-rate work or not, but I dare say it will fall in price quickly. I find I have nothing to add, but that I am, most truly yours,

"My dear Doctor Q.,

"WILLIAM GELL."

From the same.

"Naples, Tuesday, July, 1823.

"DEAREST OF DOCTORS,

"Your kind note I received yesterday, and being free from pain, I thought myself already arrived at Castella Mare, and the difficulty I should have in getting a stable. But though the spirit is willing, the body is so confoundedly crazy, that I find nothing is to be done with it, and I am now fretting myself almost ill again, having promised to dine with the Douglass's to-day, without a foot to stand upon, and how I am to do it the Lord only knows. I am very much flattered by the kind remembrance of Prince and Princess Razamousky, which pray tell them, and how hard I take it of fate to have made me ill, prior to the time of their play.

"You know, I suppose, that the ancient and respectable tumble-down Basilica of San Paolo *fuori delle mure* is burnt down at Rome, for which I should grieve but little, if with the timbers of the roof they had not contrived to calcine all, or nearly all, the beautiful columns, which, if decently arranged, would have been quite invaluable. Pray let us know how the Esculapian tour with Lord Byron goes on in Greece, and what the Duchess of Devonshire says about your going. So no more at present, from yours to command, WILLIAM GELL."

From the same.

"Rome, June 6th, 1824.

"GREAT QUINSBURG,

"I still continue uncertain whether I shall have the good fortune to meet you at Lady Harry Deerhurst's at dinner. If not, a good voyage to you, and many pleasant hours. Look in drawer A (a sketch of a table with drawers numbered is given) and try to find a book of pedigrees, which is green leather on the outside, and red velvet within, and has arms and genealogies in it. This please to send me by a safe hand, that I may see what I can do for my relation's imaginary peerage of D. Excuse the infernal trouble I give you. I cannot help it. Believe me ever, your affectionate aunt, W. GELL."

From the same.

"Rome [no date].

"The great Dr. Quin is requested to give the enclosed letter to the illustrious Watson, who will perhaps do me the favour to set down in French or Italian for Dr. Necker, my brother's numerous answers to questions already sent.

"The Quinibus flestrin is moreover requested to deliver these books to Mr. Craven, with permission to take out of my library for his use a small book, in blue paper boards, of heraldry for Craven's use, which will answer all the questions said Craven put to me. Thirdly and lastly, the great Doctoribus will arrange, according to his skill and exquisite taste, certain terra cottas of Pæstum in the library. WILLIAM GELL."

From the same.

"Rome, June 15th, 1820.

"GRANDISSIMO QUINIESTRO,

"Don't you want a remarkably nice, active, clean, young, and attentive servant, who can drive and take care of horses well, and lived as postilion with the Duchess of Chablais? He has served several people here this year, and has from all the very best recommendations possible. He can cook for one or two, on occasion, and would be really a very good servant for you, being just out of place. Besides all these things, he is a very respectable youth in appearance, and is very honest, so that you, being a careless man about your money, might make him your secretary, without fear of his becoming Rocca over you. You had better provide yourself an abode on the 1st of July, when I propose (the thieves willing) to return about eight in the morning to you and my dusty house at Naples, and languish out the summer, as Egypt is, I fear, and you may fear also, gone upside down for the present, if the Pasha is deposed. Believe me, most affectionately yours,

"WILLIAM GELL."

"We took possession on Sunday, and I wish you had seen the Monsignors with purple gowns on horseback fall off."

From the same.

"Rouen, May 10th, 1824.

"MY DEAR DOCTORIBUS,

"I don't know whether your compliments on the flourishing state of my health were the signal for the devil to recommence his torments, for I was, after reading your epistle, seized with a slow, deliberate fit, which began by being nothing at all, and is now arrived in both knees, both feet, and an elbow, not to mention the fatal consequences produced by an ass-ride of seven hours in the sun, so that I can neither walk, stand, sit, nor lie down; and it requires no small share of genius to know how to proceed under so many untoward circumstances. Nothing can exceed the beauty of our climate just now, as they have put off May this year till July; but Craven, who writes from the banks of a little lake called Wallensee, near Munich, says, there is a hard frost every evening, snow yet reaching down to the lake, even the elder not in flower, and the apples yet in bloom; and all this, he says, two days after he had been eating oranges, cherries, roasting himself in Italy. Oh, the delights of a German climate! He says, neither peas nor salad yet exist at Munich, and that, in consequence of the change of atmosphere, he has got every sort of cough, cold, and consumption possible, and longs for a box of your celebrated Leake's patent pills. I scrambled all over this country on jack-asses, while I was well, in a very agreeable manner. We went in a party to somebody's overgrown feudal palace, which the people very kindly lent us, and Lady Mary Deerhurst became the hostess of the castle, while we passed our days in exploring the country.

"I have long ventured an opinion, that wherever there was an ancient town, some traces of its walls or buildings will be found, if any one would take the pains to search; but I only spoke of Greece, whereas now I think the same may be said of Italy; and I should not despair of finding out, in time, all the towns which Romulus and the Tarquins took. We have found in the Via Appia that, by turning three miles to the right, at about eight miles from Rome, and making for the highest of the eminences towards the sea, there is an ancient city, the walls of which are quite perfect, as far as two, three, four, or five courses all round. The stones are great square masses of tufo, and have all the appearance of an ancient Greek city; it is about half a mile round, and in the form of a parallelogram, or nearly so. It is quite singular that the Roman antiquaries always stick to the modern carriage road, as if they had all the gout like me.

"The gout being in my elbow, I cannot write any better, so you must excuse me. Craven saw Lady W. at Venice and Vicenza, but she was so entirely taken up with Mr. Battier's case, and the decease of Lord Byron, before he had time to reform, that she had little time left for Egypt, so means to take England on her way there, having first gone to the military governor for a courier, which she is sure is the only way to avoid being cheated. In short, she is to winter at Catania, on her way to Egypt, if she is not exhausted before that time by the double cases of Mr. Battier and Lord Byron. What fun she must have, and all unknown, as you say, to the inhabitants of Cheshire, in being able to agitate her nerves so much out of a newspaper. Speaking of which, I send you a Greek inscription, which some think sepulchral, and some a dedication. It is newly discovered, and you scholars may comment on it, and you and Sir William Drummond may make it out together. You will perceive that it is of a period when the Romans thought it right to affect Greek literature. The Greeks have begun to write to Dodwell and myself to assist them, as their *maladetta revoluzione* has left them nothing to live on abroad, and the total want of any government at home, hinders them from staying there. They are Athenians who write, and are fled to Genoa.

"WILLIAM GELL."

Letter of introduction of Dr. Quin from Sir W. Gell to Lady Manvers.

"Naples, July 22, 1824.

"MY DEAR LADY MANVERS,

"I send you in this letter Dr. Quin, the medical gentleman who came out with the poor Duchess of Devonshire, and who was with her at her death. He is going to England for a few months, and will give you all the news of Italy, and tell you that the new Torlonia house, at the Porto del Popolo, is finished, and that a pendant to it has started up on the other side, exactly similar. There will be no dancing this year, on account of the Anno Santo, so I don't know what your Ladyship and I shall do to achieve our long engagement. Eating turkeys, however, is not yet forbidden, and, I dare say, we shall have all sorts of queer figures, and strange people of all countries, as pilgrims, to console us for the loss of our hops. I am very much improved in general health, and am delighted to hear that you are also much better. Your house at the Sentinella, at Ischia, is tenanted by the Duchess of Sagan, the great lady of Courland, who is cured of all her misfortunes, when she has any, by Dr. Quin's prescriptions.

"I think my expedition to Egypt is expiring, and shall hope to put in practice our plot for meeting at the Holy City. You will find Dr. Quin a very clever and agreeable person, and not one who sits still and says nothing, as a certain person did who I once introduced to you.

"Truly and affectionately,
"My dear Lady Manvers,
"Your slave and dog,
"WILLIAM GELL."

From the same to Dr. Quin.

"Rome, 4th January, 1825.

"DOCTISSIME QUINIE,

"The book about which you order me to write is in three volumes, and if Dr. Nott, Nell, or Noll be a friend of yours, you may lend it to him; only make him return it when he has finished his studies. I wish you would make Sir William Drummond send you back the volume of Cellarius, for fear he should forget it, which would ruin the whole work, and I have suffered so much from the lending of odd volumes, that I have a right to look sharp. I am quite delighted, as well as surprised, at the progress of the illustrious Rocca* in arts and humanities, which pray tell him from me. We have lost, somehow or other, a certain number of pages of bad writing-paper, on which was written a part of a novel, about a family of the name of Tregannock. The author being at Rome, it was laid out in my house at Naples, to be brought to him, but somehow mislaid, and never arrived, and being now wanting, we are distressed for it; there may be about twenty sheets of letter-paper sewed together very ill, and perhaps doubled lengthways down the middle. It begins with the words—'Well said, Mr. Nathaniel Randall Tregannock'—and that is all we can recollect of it; and if you can find this most precious MS. about the house, pray send it by Mr Frederick Dundas, or any other traveller.

"So Mawbles is at the very pinnacle of glory, dealing out protection, dispensation, and plenary indulgence, in the bosom of her admiring family. I hope my geraniums are not all dead of the frost at Naples, as they are here all defunct, without confessing their sins, at the pressing instance of a hoar frost.

"You have now balls and routs enough, as I hear, to keep

* A servant Sir William Gell had recommended to Dr. Quin.

the world alive, and to swell the lists of Galen and Co. One does not desire that either an earthquake or an eruption should take place, but if it must, one wishes to be witness of it; and so, if the people will persevere in being ill, I wish they would at least have the good sense to fall into your hands. Senna and syrup of buckthorn are your fellows, for they have all over-eaten themselves, and are over-gorged.

"Don't imagine I neglect my Doctor Necker, whose poisoned sugar I take every five days with great success, and the most innocent results. I am uncommonly well withal, and go out every day to dinner, without finding myself worse. Moreover my pains seem diminishing gradually, and I waddle about with tolerable success. Last night I went to the opera of the Princess Volkonsky, 'the Camilla' of Paer, in which she performed admirably, and though ill supported by the rest of the company, succeeded on the whole very well, being the first opera I have ever seen at a private theatre. Don't tell any one that I am not coming back to Naples soon, but you need not begin to fear for yourself till April. Believe me most truly yours, great descendant of Queen Quintiquiniestra,

"W. Gell."

From the same.

"Rome, Friday night.

"My dear Quinibus,

"I have written to the Drummonds some days ago, and sent them a silver medal of Lord Byron, therefore I have no right to dumpify. I have deluded my tyrant the gout for some time. If the Abbate Giustio calls, listen to all he has got to say about the library, which is to be sold, and let me know the result. Lord D. says he would rather trust the negotiation to you than any body he knows, which is sensible of his Lordship, is it not? Write soon, and then I will tell Mawbles that you are a good boy. God bless you, magnanimous Quin his Curtius! your sincere friend, William Gell."

Epistle in verse from the same.

BIBLIOTHECA QUINIENSIS.

"Though of all things, dear Dr., I know you know much,
I should never have dreamt you had studied low Dutch;
Or supposed that the subjects your studies would choose,
Was a large folio Jewish account of the Jews!
I know, my dear Quin, and we all of us know,
That Jewish accounts are on long folio:
And too well do I know for my dear money bags,
That in Jewish accounts the interest ne'er flags.
But those great thick fat tomes about Aaron and Moses,
What connection on earth can they have with small doses?
Four close printed volumes of folio pages,
Composed by the sagest of Israel's sages;
The story of those who sell second-hand togs,
Done into language of Dutchmen and frogs.
Oh, tell me, dear Doctor! oh, tell me, are such
The books you most fancy in English or Dutch?
—There must be some reason—I'm certain there is,
Why books such as these are, show their ugly phiz.
And after reflection, I think I have hit on
The reason you bought them to carry to Britain.
It is this—as you say, that all maladies must
Yield to infinitesimal doses of dust,
It may be that those volumes the patient espies,
Are only put there, to throw dust in his eyes.

W. G."

From the same.

"Rome, April 8th.

"My dear Dr. Quin, I have now to ask,
If you won't think I'm going to put you to task,
To take in my servant, and give him his room,—
His name is Luigi, my coachman and groom;
Who is going to Naples, for carriage and horses,
And to spend a large sum of my money, which worse is.
So if you'll be so good to order your man,
To get his room ready as fast as he can;
Above or below, 'tis to me all the same,
And then send him back just as fast as he came,

You'll oblige me, and serve me, and much I shall thank you,
And among my particular friends I shall rank you.
As to balls and to dinners, and fêtes and such bawbles,
This city's most truly indebted to Mawbles,
Who being a person of great notoriety,
Contrives to be useful to all the society,
Inviting the people to parties and routs,
Promiscuously treating the ins and the outs.
In short, I may say we are going on well,
And that I'm most truly your friend,

"William Gell."

TO THE GREAT DOCTORIBUS.

"Apollo had two famous sons,
Phaeton and Æsculapius;
The first dared drive his horses once,
The other drove the vapours.

Now Æsculapius is grown gay,
He too must manage horses,
Sport chariot and cabriolet,
And be a friend of D'Orsay's.

Apollo's learned son, beware,
Why dash at such a rate on?
Be wise for once, and have a care,
Lest you should fall like Phaeton.

"Hygeia."

"Apothecaries' Hall, St. Valentine's day."

No. III.

LINES TO LADY BLESSINGTON, BY W. S. LANDOR.

In Vol. I. page 295.

"What language, let me think, is meet
For you, well called the Marguerite.
The Tuscan has too weak a tone,
Too rough and rigid is our own;
The Latin—no—it will not do,
The Attic is alone for you.

"W. S. L."

A Latin version by Mr. Landor, of the above lines, followed the latter, which escaped notice in time for insertion in the proper place, and is therefore placed in this Appendix

" Quoniam carmine te alloquar decenter
Vero nomine dicta Margarita!
Sermo est durior Anglicanus: atque
Tuscus displicet: est enim vigoris
Expers: aptior est quidem latinus
Atque non satis est mihi sibique
Te sermo Atticus unicè decent.
" W. S. L."

The charms, mental and personal, of Lady Blessington, were fully appreciated by another literary celebrity, as we learn from the following lines, terminating some others, descriptive of the frivolous amusements of belles wholly devoted to the varying *mode*, and each recurring change in the empire of fashion.

" But thy bright mind eclipsing e'en thy face,
The muse with justice claims thee from the grace.
Thought gives the gems which love in beauty set,
And every fairy at thy cradle met.
From the dull world around escaped awhile,
I breathe the air which brightens in thy smile:
Ah! half already of that gift possess'd,
Which conquering space, is destined to the blessed,
How little thought—this gaoler flesh can bar
Our souls how rarely, where our bodies are."

No. IV.

REV. THOMAS STEWART.

The Rev. Thomas Stewart, who was assassinated in Italy, some five-and-twenty years ago, was a nephew of Sir William

Drummond, and a brother of Sir William Drummond Stewart, of Grandtully, Perthshire. On conforming to the Roman Catholic religion, he was admitted into the Benedictine order in Sicily, and later at Rome, was received into the order of St. John of Jerusalem.

His assassination took place on the shores of the Adriatic, between Senigalia and Ancona. Some lines of this gentleman, addressed to Lady Blessington, written while he was a layman, will be found in Vol. i. page 306, of more than ordinary merit.

No. V.

Statuary, Vases, and Bronzes, the property of General Count D'Orsay, the father of Count Alfred, confiscated in 1793, and appropriated by the state; claimed by the Count in July, 1844.

CONSULTATION POUR M. LE COMTE D'ORSAY CONTRE LA LISTE CIVILE.

" M. Pierre Gaspard Marie Grimod, Comte d'Orsay, d'Autrey et Nogent-le-Rotrou, Baron de Rupt, Seigneur de la principauté souveraine de Delaine et autres lieux en Franche Comté, Seigneur d'Orsay Courtabœuf, la Plesse, les Villefeux, etc. etc., et qui comptait au nombre de ses aïeux maternels le Duc de Sully, ministre et ami de Henri IV., ne put échapper aux mesures révolutionnaires qui en 1793 menaçaient la noblesse Française. Atteint par les lois rendues contre les émigrés, ses biens furent confisqués par l'état et mis sous le séquestre.

" Lors de son émigration, M. le Comte d'Orsay était propriétaire, entre autres biens, de l'hôtel d'Orsay situé à Paris Rue de Varennes, Faubourg St. Germain, et de la terre seigneuriale d'Orsay près de Palaiseau, arrondissement de Versailles, et dont dépendait un château considérable, et aussi célébre par le luxe de sa construction que par les souvenirs historiques qui s'attachaient.

" L'hôtel et le château d'Orsay, les jardins et le parc qui en faisaient partie, contenaient une grande quantité de statues, de groupes, de bustes et de vases, en marbre et en bronze, d'une immense valeur, que la famille du Comte d'Orsay y avait réunis à grands frais, et que ce dernier avait augmentés encore par les nombreuses acquisitions qu'il avait faites en Italie en 1780, avec le goût qui a toujours été l'apanage de cette illustre maison.

" Maître de cette collection précieuse et unique, le Gouvernement Français se garda bien de la vendre. Il la conserva avec le plus grand soin, et bientôt après en enrichit ses musées, ses palais, et leurs jardins. Plusieurs des statues, groupes, bustes, vases qui se trouvent aujourd'hui dans les palais et les jardins des Tuileries du Luxembourg et de St. Cloud, qui en font l'ornement, et qui sont l'admiration des artistes et des étrangers, ont appartenu à la riche collection de M. le Comte d'Orsay.......

" Nous pensons donc, qu'en fait comme en droit, M. le Comte Alfred d'Orsay, par répresentation de M. le Lieutenant-Général Comte Albert d'Orsay, son père, est fondé dans sa réclamation contre la liste civile ou le domaine de l'Etat, qui est en ce moment en possession des objets d'art confisqués pendant la révolution sur M. Pierre Marie Gaspard Comte d'Orsay, son aïeul.

" Délibéré à Paris le 7 Juillet 1844.

" CHARLES LEDRU,

" Avocat à la Cour Royale de Paris."

" Catalogue des Statues, Groupes, Bustes, Vases, Futs de Colonnes, Gaines en Bronze et en Marbre, Appartenants à Monsieur le Comte D'Orsay.

" D'après le Catalogue imprimé qu'en avait faire M. le Comte D'Orsay père, avant la Révolution en 1791 ; et l'indication des lieux, &c., où ces différents objets se trouvent placés.

" Ces divers objets d'art furent saisis dans l'Hôtel du Comte D'Orsay pendant la Revolution Française, et plaçés dans les Palais Nationaux.

BRONZES.

Apollon du Belvedère, fondue à Rome par Villadier; à la Malmaison.—Antinoüs, fondue à Rome par le même; Jardin des Tuileries.—Une Amazone; à la Malmaison.—Mars en Repos, fondue à Rome par Villadier; aux Invalides.—Deux Bustes, l'un de femme; à la Bibliothèque Mazarine: l'autre en recherche.—Louis XV., donné à la section par un homme d'affaires de mon père.—Deux Vases, restés dans l'Hôtel.—Deux Girandoles; restées dans l'Hotel.—Deux Girandoles, idem.—Neptune au Milieu d'un Rocher; resté dans le Jardin de l'Hôtel.—Un Casque; en recherche.—Un Mascaron D'Eole, qui soutenait le Mercure, en bronze, qui a été volé dans le jardin de mon père; au Muséum.

FIGURES ET GROUPES, EN MARBRES BLANCS ET DE COULEUR.

Lucius Verus, statue colossale antique; au Muséum, salle des fleuves.—Auguste Empereur, grande statue moderne; Vestibule du Luxembourg.—Minerve, petite statue de 4 pieds en albatre Oriental antique; en recherche.—L'Amour et Psyché, groupe moderne, fait à Rome par Belaitre, et son piédestal; Galerie des tableaux du Luxembourg.—Athalante et Hyppomène, groupe en marbre; Jardin de St. Cloud.—Apollon et Marcias, groupe moderne en piédestal; Magasins du Luxembourg.—Castor et Pollux, groupe moderne; Jardin des Tuileries.—Bacchus et un Faune, groupe moderne; Jardin des Tuileries.—Arethuse et un autre groupe moderne.—Phèdre et Hyppolite, groupe.—Néron, grande statue antique; au Muséum.—Un Centaure sur son piédestal; Jardin de St. Cloud.—Deux Petites Figures Antiques, l'une au musée, l'autre dans les Magasins du Musée.—L'Amitié, statue (sous le No. 107); Galerie des Tableaux du Luxembourg.—Antinoüs petite statue antique; au Muséum.—Apollon (petite statue) tenant sa lyre, antique; Magasin du Musée.—Vénus Anadiomède antique; Jardin du Luxembourg.—Bacchus, statue antique; en recherche.—Cérès, statue moderne; Jardin du Luxembourg.—Achille, statue antique ; au Musée.—Cérès une statue antique ; Jardin du Luxembourg.—Coriolan, statue moderne ; idem.—Antinoüs, statue moderne. — Cérès, statue moyenne antique ; au Musée.—Venus Victrix, statue moyenne antique ; idem.—Apollon, petite statue antique ; idem.—Vénus de Médicis, copie.—Appoline.—Vénus Callipige.—Le Gladiateur Blessé ; Jardin de St. Cloud.—Hercule Farnèse, petite statue.—Deux Prêtresses.—Deux Figures Modernes, une Bacchante et un Faune ; Appartemens des Tuileries.—Deux Autres Figures Modernes, Bacchus et Flore ; en recherche.—Medaillon D'Antinoüs ; resté dans l'Hôtel.—Deux Lions, modernes ; à l'entrée des Tuileries dans le Jardin.—Deux Sphinx, vendus.

84 Bustes de Marbre Blanc sur leurs Gaines, Groupes et Figures au Magasin de Louvre Magasin de Musèe—aux Tuileries restèes dans l'Hôtel.

VASES, COLONNES, ET PIEDESTAUX EN MARBRE.

37 Vases Magasin de Luxembourg—au Musèe aux Tuileries —restées dans l'Hôtel.

" Un Grand Vase, forme de Medicis, avec un bas-relief, représentant le sacrifice du Minotaure, sur un fut de colonne Torse, le tout antique en marbre de Paros ou Pantélique ; au Musée, vestibule au bas de l'escalier.

" Il se trouve aussi dans le Musée trent-six fûts de colonnes cannelées en marbre blanc veiné qui peuvent valoir 200f. pièce.

" Quarante-deux gaînes plaquées en marbre de différentes couleurs qui peuvent valoir 150f. pièce.

" Il se trouve à Versailles une statue en marbre blanc dans l'atelier du marbrier venant du château, et destinée à être placée au tombeau de Madame la Comtesse D'Orsay, la mère.

" Portraits de famille à Versailles, entr'autres celui de Madame la Comtesse D'Orsay, sa mère.

" Plusieurs tableaux provenants du château D'Orsay, à Versailles.

No. VI.

COUNT D'ORSAY'S GORE HOUSE PICTURE.

A garden view of Gore House, the residence of the late Countess of Blessington, with Portraits of the Duke of Wellington, Lady Blessington, the Earl of Chesterfield, Sir Edwin Landseer, Count D'Orsay, the Marquis of Douro (now Duke of Wellington,) Lord Brougham, the Miss Powers, &c. &c.

In the foreground to the right are the Duke of Wellington and the Countess of Blessington in the centre, Sir Edwin Landseer seated, who is in the act of sketching a fine cow, which is standing in front with a calf by its side, while Count D'Orsay, with two favourite dogs, is seen on the right of the group, and the Earl of Chesterfield on the left; nearer the house, the two Miss Powers (nieces of Lady Blessington) are reading a letter, a gentleman walking behind. Further to the left appear Lord Brougham, the Marquis of Douro, &c. seated under a tree in conversation. On canvas, 3 feet 8 inches by 3 feet 2 inches, in a noble gilt frame.

This interesting picture, one of the favourite productions of Count D'Orsay, was sold at the Gore House sale in 1849, and is now in the possession of Mr. Thomas Walesby, No. 5, Waterloo Place, London.

No. VII.

LORD BYRON'S YACHT "The Bolivar," (subsequently Lord Blessington's property). From Mr. Armstrong, Author of "The Young Commander," "The Two Midshipmen."

Mr. Armstrong, the author of several nautical novels, gives the following account, in a letter, dated August 1,

1854, of his first meeting with Lord Byron, in Italy, and some particulars of his yacht.

"It was in the year 1822 or 1823 I was residing at Nice scarcely then twenty years of age, when I received a letter from Lord Byron. He said he heard I had a schooner yacht to dispose of, and wished to know the tonnage and price. I had not made up my mind to sell the yacht, but I thought this too good an opportunity to be thrown away, as his Lordship was said to be going to aid the Greeks, and my yacht would get a name, as she was remarkably fast.

"I answered his Lordship at once, stating tonnage and price. Shortly after, I received his Lordship's reply. This letter I gave, some years ago, to the late Mr. Murray, the publisher.

"In it, I think, his Lordship stated, that a friend of his, a captain in the Sardinian service, said he could build a new one in the arsenal of Genoa for a less sum—£800, or something to that purpose. I answered this, and shortly after received another letter, requesting to know if I would take less for the schooner; and amongst other things, his Lordship asked me what society there was in Nice, as he had an idea of taking up his residence there.

"I wrote in reply, that I offered my yacht for £300 less than she cost me. I built her at Savona, a rather pretty place, some thirty miles from Genoa. As to the society of Nice, it could not be better any where; highly aristocratic, as many of the English nobility were there, and also the Ex-King of Sardinia, and last, though not least, Lady Blessington had a house there.

"Her Ladyship was much liked, and behaved very liberally to one or two artists, who were there at the time; one a first-rate portrait painter, but very poor; so much so, that he could not make his appearance anywhere. She relieved him from his difficulties, and enabled him to proceed to

Rome with a well-filled purse; this was not the only charitable act her Ladyship performed. But I am wandering away from my subject.

"The last letter I received from his Lordship stated, he had begun to build his schooner in the arsenal of Genoa, under the superintendence of Captain Wright, who then commanded a Sardinian vessel, and regretted giving me so much trouble, and also that he had abandoned his intention of residing in Nice. Some months after this, I went to Genoa, and hearing that Lord Byron's yacht was nearly ready for sea, and was lying in the arsenal, I went with a friend to have a look at her. She was lying near the platform, and she surprised me, she was so much smaller than my own schooner. There were three planks along-side, and on these stood a gentleman, very intently occupied with the putting on of a narrow gold moulding round the yacht.

"'Well,' said I, rather loud to my friend, 'if that yacht sails with that heavy foremast slipped so far forehead—it's curious; she is not half the size of mine, after all; but I should like to see her inside.'

"The gentleman on the plank turned round, looked me in the face, and said, 'Would you like to come aboard, sir?' Very much indeed,' I replied, 'thank you;' and without thought, or more words, I jumped down on the plank, by which thoughtless proceeding, I very nearly sent the gentleman and myself into the arsenal, only saving myself by taking a good grip of him, and he of the shrouds, and then we both scrambled on deck, leaving the frightened painter holding on by the bulwarks.

"We then went into the cabin, which was most luxuriously fitted up, couches soft and tempting, marble baths, &c.; in fact, not an inch of space was lost. In the course of conversation, the gentleman said, opening a desk, and taking a letter—'I think I have the pleasure of speaking to Mr.

Armstrong.' Before this, I guessed the gentleman I was so near ducking was Lord Byron, and I said, 'Then I have the honour of speaking to Lord Byron;' he bowed, and said, 'Why did you not mention in this letter, the length, beam, depth, &c., of your schooner, which you say is twice as large as this?'

"'Well, I might have done so certainly, my Lord, but you merely said tonnage, and then saying you could build one for £800 put me out; this has cost you more.' 'Double,' said his Lordship, 'and not yet finished.' This schooner turned out afterwards a very dull sailer.

"ARMSTRONG."

No. VIII.

Notices of Lords Holland, Grey, Lansdowne, Erskine, and Mr. Perry, in the hand-writing of Count D'Orsay:—probably the production of Lady Blessington.

LORD HOLLAND.

C'est impossible de connaitre Lord Holland sans éprouver pour lui nu vif sentiment de Bienveillance il a tant de bonhomie que l'on oublie souvent les qualités superieures qui le distinguent, et c'est difficile de se rappeller que l'homme si simple, si naturel, et si bon, est un des senateurs les plus estimés de nos jours.

LORD GREY.

Si M. B. Constant eut mieux connu Lord Grey, il ne vondroit pas laisser ses droits à l'estime et à l'admiration de la posterité rester sur la limite bornée d'un orateur eloquent. Ci Titre qui est le plus beau pour beaucoup d'autres, est le moindre pour Lord Grey, qui est reconnu en outre pour ses principes nobles et inalterables, dignes et éclaircis, et par une grandeur de caractère qui force le respects même de ses ennemis et inspire l'admiration de ceux qui sont honorés de son amitié.

Quand je parle de ses ennemis je devrais dire ceux de la liberté et de la justice pour laquelle il est le vrai champion, sans peur et sans reproche.

MR. PERRY.

Mr. Perry a bien merité des éloges, je l'ai beaucoup connu sa vie privée était aussi aimable, que son caractère publie était digne et respectable. Il est mort dans l'année 1821. Après une longue maladie, regretté par tous ses amis nombreux, et estimé par tous ceux au quels son nom était connu.

MARQUESS OF LANSDOWNE.

Le Marquis de Lansdowne a bien realisé les ésperances données par Lord Henry Petty. Honnête, sage, franc, liberal, moderé, et surtout toujours consistant, il offre un vrai modele d'un homme d'etat. Il est bien rare de trouver un homme qui unit autant, de connoissances profondes et variés et de talents distingués avec un caractère aussi doux, si égal, et si digne.

LORD ERSKINE.

Lord Erskine n'était pas moins remarquable pour son grand esprit et son savoir qui ont si bien éclaircis les lois, et si courageusement defendu la liberté de son pays, que pour sa bonté de cœur, et generosité de caractère. Doué de tous les talents les plus brillants, qui le rendoit le charme dans chaque societé, par sa conversation qui laissoit toujours dans l'esprit de ceux avec lesquels il parlait des images frappantes, lumineuses, et agréables. Il est mort en 1824 suivi dans le tombeau par les regrets de tous ceux qui venerent le genie, qui respectent les talents, et qui admirent leur union avec les meilleures qualités du cœur.

No. IX.

MADAME DU DEFFAND AND MADAME GEOFFRIN.

MADAME DU DEFFAND.

Lord John Russell, in his "Life of Lord William Russell," (Pref. ix.) tells us, "What most contributes to render biography amusing, is a certain singularity and some degree of forwardness and presumption in the hero."

Campbell said to me, when he was preparing for the press his biography of Mrs. Siddons, "The uniform propriety of my heroine admits of no incidents which her biographer can avail himself of to create an interest and an excitement, for the public."

Madame du Deffand cannot be complained of in those respects by any of the numerous tribe of writers of *Memoires Pour Servir.* There is a certain singularity, some degree of forwardness and presumption in the heroine, and certainly no lack of indecorum in her at any period of her career. It always seemed as if this singular woman's power and dominion in the exalted circle over which she presided, was owing, in a very great degree, to the fear she inspired, and the belligerent qualities that were mixed up with her personal attractions.

"Many things," it is said, "are regarded with awe and deference, mainly, perhaps, on account of the occasional arrogance of dogmatism bred in solitary ruminations, and promulgated with an oracular tone and air." Many women, too, and ladies of brilliant salons in particular, may inspire sentiments of admiration—wonder—may effect subjection to their powers, by an exercise of their talents, that would be intolerably pretentious and presuming, overbearing and unbearable, only for the beauty, gracefulness, or *esprit* that accompanies it. We need not travel to France, or go back to the days of Louis XV. or XVI. for instances of this sort of dominion in society, and admiration, mingled with apprehension, excited by it.

The great enemy of Madame de Geoffrin, because her successful competitor in the Parisian salons of literature and philosophy *à-la-mode*, about a century ago, Madame la Marquise du Deffand, in fashionable society a queen, having dominion over men of the first order of intellect of her time, had been, for a short period *only*, a mistress of the regent; and throughout a long career, a woman of wit, of remarkable powers of conversation, wonderful vivacity, and extraordinary agrémens, considering, that for a very considerable period of that prolonged career, she had been stone blind. In her old age and blindness she went to operas, plays, balls, and public entertainments. When she was obliged to give these up, she had parties and conversaziones at her own house, gave suppers twice a week, had all new works read to her, and approached eternity making epigrams, songs, and jeux-d'esprit, corresponding with Voltaire, and laughing at the " superstitious mummeries " of religious rites and ceremonies.

Madame du Deffand was born in 1697; she died in 1780, retaining to the last her vivacity, conversational power, love of literary society, and repugnance to religion and its ministers.

Madame du Deffand has been immortalized in memoir notoriety by the Baron Grimm and Horace Walpole. The hotel in Paris of the Marquise du Deffand, about the middle of the last century, was the head-quarters of the fashionable infidel philosophy, the political gallantry and sprightly literature of the day. Her salons were the resort of wits, wags, savants, and literati. In 1754, this patroness of literature *a-là-mode*, renowned no less for her hospitality, her influence over men in power, her gallantry, and the grace and elegance of her manners and appearance, was totally deprived of sight.

She continued, however, the *role* of a *bel esprit*, received intellectual celebrities of all nations at her salons as heretofore, and corresponded with distinguished people, with some, in very impassioned language — Horace Walpole, especially, among the number, for a great many years, subsequent to her blindness, from 1766 to 1780. In 1769, Walpole thus describes Madame du Deffand :—

"She makes songs, sings them, remembers all that ever were made; and having lived from the most agreeable to the most reasoning age, has all that was amiable in the last, all that is sensible in this, without the vanity of the former, or the pedant impertinence of the latter. I have heard her dispute with all sorts of people on all sorts of subjects, and never knew her in the wrong. She humbles the learned, sets right their disciples, and finds conversation for every body. Affectionate as Madame de Sevigné, she has none of her prejudices, but a more universal taste; and with the most delicate frame, her spirits hurry her through a life of fatigue that would kill me, if I was to continue here." *

"In a dispute, into which she easily falls, she is very warm, and yet scarce ever in the wrong; but judgment on every subject is as just as possible, in every point of conduct as wrong as possible; for she is all love and hatred; passionate for her friends to enthusiasm, still anxious to be loved,—I don't mean by lovers,—and a vehement enemy, but open. As she can have no amusement but conversation, the least solitude and *ennui* are insupportable to her, and put her into the power of several worthless people, who eat her suppers when they can eat nobody's of higher rank, wink to one another, and laugh at her; hate her because she has forty times more parts, and venture to hate her because she is not rich." †

MADAME GEOFFRIN.

An able writer in the "Quarterly Review" for May, 1811,

* Memoirs of Horace Walpole, by Warburton, vol. ii. p. 316.

† Ibid. p. 278.

describes the intellectual qualities of Madame Geoffrin in the following terms:—"This lady seems to have united the lightness of the French character with the solidity of the English. She was easy and volatile, yet judicious and acute; sometimes profound, and sometimes superficial. She had a wit, playful, abundant, well toned; an admirable conception of the ridiculous, and great skill in exposing it; a turn for satire, which she indulged not always in the best-natured manner, yet with irresistible effect; powers of expression varied, appropriate, flowing from the source, and curious without research; a refined taste for letters, and a judgment both for men and books in a high degree enlightened and accurate. As her parts had been happily thrown together by nature, they were no less happy in the circumstances which attended their progress and development. They were refined, not by a course of solitary study, but by desultory reading, and chiefly by living intercourse with the brightest geniuses of her age. Thus trained, they acquired a pliability of movement which gave to all their exertions a bewitching air of freedom and negligence, and made even their faults seem only the exuberances or flowerings-off of a mind capable of higher excellencies, but unambitious to attain them. There was nothing to alarm or overpower. On whatever topic she touched, whether trivial or severe, it was alike *en badinant;* but in the midst of this sportiveness, her genius poured itself forth in a thousand delightful fancies, and scattered new graces and ornaments on every object within its sphere. In its wanderings from the trifles of the day to grave questions of morals or philosophy, it carelessly struck out, and as carelessly abandoned, the most profound truths; and while it aimed only to amuse, suddenly astonished and electrified by rapid traits of illumination, which opened the depths of physical subjects, and roused the researches of more systematic reasoners. To these qualifications were added an independence in forming opinions, and a boldness in avowing them, which wore at least the resemblance of honesty; a perfect knowledge of the world, and that facility of manners which, in the commerce of society, supplies the place of benevolence."

Horace Walpole thus speaks of Madame Geoffrin:—"Madame Geoffrin, of whom you have heard much, is an extraordinary woman, with more common sense than I almost ever met with."

No. X.

EDWARD RUSHTON, OF LIVERPOOL.

The memory of this illustrious man of humble rank and fortune, is indebted to a correspondent of Lady Blessington for a well-written notice of his merits, and some eulogistic lines not devoid of truth and poetry.

This communication is signed "Thomas Noble," and dated the 2nd of December, 1844.

RUSHTON'S MEMORY.

"The man to whose memory these lines are a sincere tribute, united in a perfection of which there are few examples, those distinguishing characteristics of a reasoning, sensitive being, fortitude and affection. His mind and his heart were equally capacious; the former, endowed with activity and energy of thought, was comprehensive of every moral and political truth; the latter, excited by the purest benevolence, was ardent in domestic love; open, liberal, and independent in social intercourse; boundless in devotion to the freedom and welfare of mankind, his soul had an elasticity of temperament which not bodily infirmity, nor misfortune, nor even affliction, could subdue.

"It was this, his elasticity of soul, that has imparted to his poetic composition an unabating vigour of expression. With indignation against the oppressions of mankind, the perverters of intellect, the subjugators of reason, the violators of humble affection, and plunderers of industry, he who, 'midst clouds of utter night' well knew what mournful moments wait the blind, poured forth from his luminous and contemplative mind eloquent streams of reproof, of commiseration, of hope to the wretched, and of freedom to the enslaved.

"I knew him for little more than three years, but it required only to know him once to esteem him for ever. The generous liberality of his opinions proved in an instant the extent as well as the strength of the principles on which they were founded.

"For my own part, I felt immediately convinced that he had taken his stand with truth, and that he had the tenacity of mind ever to abide by her. I was not deceived: what he was one day, that he was continually; and had he lived, my esteem for him could not have increased.

"In his death, what an example of sincerity, energy, and independence have not I, and all who knew him, to deplore?

"THOMAS NOBLE."

Is there a spot to thee, oh Freedom, known—
That owns no terrors and that dreads no throne.
Where servile men to tyrant man ne'er bend,
Nor mock the God they cannot comprehend?

Is there a spot uncurst by martial fame,
Where conquest never cast its meteor flame—
Where mighty heroes would be paltry things,
And thrown, unnamed, aside with slaves and kings.

Is there a spot hypocrisy hath ne'er
Profaned, nor made a mart of—one place where
Religion seeks for ministers the true,
The pure, the faithful, and the humble too?

Is there a spot where man's unclouded mind,
Conscious of social bonds that blind his kind;
Frames, firm in all his rights, the law that sways,
Is independent still, and still obeys?

O! in that spot let freedom's vot'ries place,
A column on an adamantine base;
'Gainst its firm shaft let independence stand
Our Rushton's lyre, eternal, in his hand.

Oft from its chord a dirge and daring sound,
Shall burst upon the wretched nations round;
Till startled slaves th' arousing thunder hear,
And all oppressors scared shall learn to fear.

Perhaps it may not be irrelevant to this subject to place before the readers of the preceding notice, an account of a single act of the remarkable man who is the subject of it, well worthy of attention and admiration.

A very remarkable letter of Edward Rushton, of Liverpool, was addressed to Washington, in 1797. The writer was then labouring under blindness. He was embarrassed, and nearly indigent in his circumstances—a liberal in politics, an admirer of Washington, and an enthusiastic advocate of the American Revolution.

Washington was then at the height of his glory: President of the United States, and Commander-in-Chief of the American army.

Rushton, being a plain, honest, simple-minded sort of man, could not understand the anomaly of a liberator on a grand scale being a holder, a buyer, and a seller of slaves—a man interested in the robbery of the rights of other people. So Edward Rushton wrote to George Washington a letter in his plain, straightforward way of setting forth his views; and a nobler letter is not to be found in the English language. It is painful to learn that the illustrious American Republican had the littleness of mind to send back the bold but respectful letter of the poor blind republican of England, without deigning to write one word in reply to it. Yet Washington must have been aware of the character of his unsought-for correspondent —that he was a man who had suffered in some degree for his devotion to republican principles—that he had lost his sight in consequence of his humanity in attending to sick slaves, during the prevalence of a pestilential malady on board a crowded slave-ship—that he was a consistent philanthropist, and a good hater of injustice of all kinds.

The following extracts from his letter are well deserving of reproduction, at the expiration of half a century; and perhaps those who read them will be disposed to think less enthusiastically of the magnanimity of George Washington.

"It is not to the Commander-in-chief of the American forces, nor to the President of the United States, that I have aught to address: my business is with George Washington, of Mount Vernon, in Virginia; a man who, notwithstanding his hatred of oppression, and his ardent love of liberty, holds at this moment hundreds of his fellow-beings in a state of slavery. Yes, you who conquered under the banners of Freedom, you who are now the first magistrate of a free people, are, strange to relate, a slave-holder. That a Liverpool merchant should endeavour to enrich himself by such a business, is not a matter of surprise; but that you, an enlightened man, strongly enamoured of Freedom—you who, if the British forces had succeeded in the Eastern States, would have retired with a few congenial spirits to the rude fastnesses of the Western wildernesses, there to have enjoyed that blessing without which a paradise would be worthless, and with which the most savage region is not without its charms;—that you, I say, should continue to be a slave-holder, a proprietor of human flesh and blood, creates in many of your British friends both astonishment and regret. It has been said by some of your apologists, that your feelings are inimical to slavery, and that you are induced to acquiesce in it at present merely from motives of policy. THE ONLY TRUE POLICY IS JUSTICE; AND HE WHO REGARDS THE CONSEQUENCES OF AN ACT RATHER THAN THE JUSTICE OF IT, GIVES NO VERY EXALTED PROOF OF THE GREATNESS OF HIS CHARACTER. . . . . . . Of all the slave-holders under heaven, those of the United States appear to me most reprehensible; for man is never so truly odious, as when he inflicts on others that which he himself abominates. The hypocritical courtesan who preaches chastity, yet lives by the violation of it, is not more truly disgusting than one of your slave-holding gentry bellowing in favour of democracy."

Rushton died in 1814. He was a man of great virtue, a patriot on a large scale, a philanthropist in the true sense of the term, a practical Christian; his life was spent in advocating justice at home and abroad, and doing works of mercy and kindness to his fellow-men. I have dwelt so much on the consistency of the philanthropy of Rushton, because it is so rarely encountered of a perfectly unsectarian character. The lives of Clarkson, Buxton, Sturge, Rushton, and Romilly, afford striking exceptions to this rule. There is, however, in the variable atmosphere of the mind, influences which seem to excite the pity of men for one class only of unfortunates, or at one period for a particular train of calamities, or peculiar description of suffering; and at another time, and in the case of persons in misfortune, of some particular community, which seem to stifle every emotion of sensibility. If we love justice and liberty abroad, we cannot be otherwise than faithful to their interests at home. If we hate the injustice that is offered to black men in Africa or the West Indies, it is also incumbent on us to reprobate all the oppressions that are done under the sun to white men in European countries. If the cruelty of slave-trading is the cause of enormous suffering which we deplore, and use all our efforts to put an end to, the wickedness of legislation, which admits of dreadful wrong and suffering being inflicted in the shape of evictions, dispossessions and destitution of thousands of our fellow-creatures at our own doors, —which leaves a million and a half of the people of a Christian land in a state of beggary for six months in the year, and in permanent pauperism one million of its inhabitants,—is an evil that is the occasion of tremendous calamities, which we are surely called on to devote a large portion of our philanthropy to remove and alleviate. But if, instead of doing this, we share in the guilt of sustaining and supporting a system which suffers such evils to exist, what is to be said of our philanthropy? Why, either that we are mistaken enthusiasts—like Granville Sharp and William Wilberforce, who united the advocacy of the abolition of slavery in Africa with that of the maintenance in Ireland of the sanguinary atrocities of the penal code—or sanctimonious hypocrites, who speculate in theoretical benevolence, and exercise practical inhumanity in all our political conduct, with respect to millions of our fellow-subjects, guilty only of a creed not fashioned like their own. Oh! it is time to put away these unfounded pretensions to philanthropy. The basis for all true philanthropy must be large and deep, capable of sustaining tolerance in affairs of religion, in matters that affect political opinions, in all things that concern national distinctions and differences of class and clime, capable of enabling charity to deal with all, in a Christian spirit.

No. XI.

A correspondent of Lady Blessington, one of England's foremost men, and of the master-spirits of his time, in a letter to her ladyship, thus estimates the labours of Monsieur Eugene Sue, the author of "The Wandering Jew:"

"Sue's 'Wandering Jew' seems to me a failure, and I don't

like the attack on the Jesuits, whom I have always honoured for their immense services to science, letters, and humanity. Here, I dare say, you do not agree with me.

"But though I shall never, I suppose, turn Catholic, I feel if I had been a Catholic, I should never have been anything else. I love the grand enthusiasm of its earnest believers, and the child-like faith of its simple flocks. I love its ascent into faith above reason."

No. XII.

SEPARATE NOTICES OF SOME OF THE EMINENT OR REMARKABLE PERSONS WHO WERE CORRESPONDENTS, FRIENDS, OR ACQUAINTANCES OF LADY BLESSINGTON.

In the following notices, I have endeavoured to set before my readers some of the leading features in the character or career of persons intimately acquainted with Lady Blessington, of whom mention has not been made, in connection with the correspondence. The object held in view, in giving these slight sketches, was to represent the persons referred to as they were known to Lady Blessington and her immediate friends; and to recall such traits of character, or traces of events in their career, as might bring them to the reader's recollection, and renew the acquaintance that many of those readers, who were visitors at Seamore Place or Gore House, may have had with them.

The society had some undoubted claims to pre-eminent excellence, that could boast of such *habituès* as the elder D'Israeli and his son, Landor, Dickens, the Bulwers, the Smiths, Luttrell, Spencer, Moore, Galt, Ritchie, Reynolds, General Phipps, Landseer, Lawrence, Maclise, Ainsworth, Thackeray, James, and so many others of the celebrities of various countries; and such occasional guests as Grey, Canning, Russell, Wellington, Wellesley, Durham, Burdett, Abinger, Lyndhurst, Auckland, Brougham, and their fellow-magnates of the aristocracy, intellectually gifted, or patrons of intellectual pursuits connected with art or literature.

Of many of these celebrities some outlines have been prefixd to their correspondence.

LORD LYNDHURST.

It has been my object, in those notices I have given of eminent persons intimately acquainted with Lady Blessington, and peculiarly regarded by her with favour and confidence, and an implicit reliance on their friendship, to give expression to her opinions of their merits, as I find them scattered over her correspondence, or noted down in detached memoranda among her papers, or treasured up in the remembrance of her gifted niece, Miss M. Power.

Lady Blessington felt a pride, as well as a pleasure, in the friendship of persons of exalted intellect; and probably she felt more pride in the position in which she apparently stood in the estimation of Lord Lyndhurst, with two or three exceptions, than on account of the intimacy of her relations with any other intellectual celebrity, for she entertained an opinion of his Lordship's mental powers so exalted, that it would be difficult to exaggerate its elevation. On the other hand, it is obvious that his Lordship's friendship was based on an appreciation of Lady Blessington's talents, generous nature, and noble disposition, that did justice to them. Indeed, when we find men of such exalted intellectual powers among the celebrities most highly favoured who were to be found in the *salons* of Seamore Place and Gore House,—we have evidence that the attractions of the fair lady who presided over those reunions were of a high order.*

* The attractions which such persons found in Lady Blessington were assuredly of a higher order than those of the reigning beauties of any of the salons which Grammont has so graphically described, and Sir Peter Lely depicted. Those of Sir Peter's beauties of "the sleepy

The son of John Singleton Copley, Esq., the painter and Royal Academician, might have made an indifferent artist, had he been brought up to his father's profession. Happily for him, he was brought up for the bar, and became one of the first lawyers, perhaps the first lawyer, of his time. Of unquestionable talents, and great powers of mind, an excellent scholar, of sober judgment, clear and sound, active, serious, and earnest in business, in society no one is more agreeable, animated in conversation, and evidently conversant with the literature of the day, as well as with the lore of ancient times. He has the art of inspiring confidence and winning regard by his simplicity of manner, playful humour, and warm interest in the concerns of those with whom he associates. This eminent man was born on the other side of the Atlantic, in Boston, in 1772, and is now in his 83rd year, in the full possession of all his great faculties. He was called to the bar in 1804, and after attaining signal success in his profession, and passing through its several gradations and preferments, he was appointed Master of the Rolls in 1826, and the following year the successor of Lord Eldon, when he was raised to the peerage: having resigned the seals in 1830, he

eye, that spoke the melting soul,"—of Grammont's enchantresses:—"The languishing Boynton," "the lovely Jennings," "the serious Lyttleton," "the fair Stewart," "pretty Miss Blague," "the beautiful Hamilton," "the agreeable Miss Price," though "short and thick,"—"the susceptible Miss Hobart," and no less so "the unlucky Miss Warmestre," the irresistible damsel

With her young wild boar's eyes;

the fascinating Lady Chesterfield, Lady Shrewsbury, Lady Carnegie, Mrs. Roberts, and Mrs. Middleton, so sprightly and spirituelle, so very *piquant* in conversation—these needed all the graces of the style of Anthony Hamilton, to make us understand the power of their *agrémens* even over such modish men as the Earl of Ranelagh, "that mad fellow, Crofts," "the beau Sidney," "Little Jermyn," "the incomparable Villiers," and other adepts in gallantry, who had grown grey in the service of the sovereign beauties of the salons.

filled the office of Chief Baron of the Exchequer till 1834, when he resumed the seals for another year, again resigned, and in 1841, for a third time, was appointed Lord High Chancellor of England, which office he retained till 1846. He married, first, a daughter of C. Brunsden, Esq., widow of Lieutenant-Colonel Thomas, who died in 1834: secondly, a daughter of Lewis Goldsmith, Esq., in 1837, and has issue by his first marriage four children, and by the second, one daughter.

LORD ERSKINE.

The name of Lord Erskine often occurs in the journals and letters of Lady Blessington. At the early period of her London career, Lord Erskine was an intimate friend of her ladyship, and one of the peculiarly favoured and most highly honoured of the visitors at her mansion in St. James's Square.

The Hon. Thomas Erskine, born in 1750, third son of the Earl of Buchan, having served both in the army and navy, turned to the legal profession, and was called to the bar in 1778. He rose to the summit of his profession as an advocate, in which capacity he continued till 1806, when he was elevated to the office of Lord High Chancellor, and to the peerage in the same year. He married first in 1770, a daughter of Daniel Moon, Esq., M.P.; and secondly, Miss Sarah Buck, and died at Almondell, near Edinburgh, the 17th of November, 1823, in his seventy-fourth year.

Lord Byron spoke to Lady Blessington of Erskine as "the most brilliant person imaginable, quick, vivacious, and sparkling; he spoke so well, that one never felt tired of listening to him, even when he abandoned himself to that subject, of which all his other friends and acquaintances expressed themselves so fatigued,—self . . . Erskine had been a great man, and he knew it; and talking so continually of self, imagined that he was but the echo of fame." He was deceived in this (continued Byron), as are all who have a favourable opinion of their fellow men; in society all and each are occupied with self, and can hardly pardon any one who presumes to draw their attention to other subjects for any length of time.

Lord Erskine is thus spoken of by Lord Brougham:—

"The disposition and manners of the man were hardly less attractive than his genius and his professional skill were admirable. He was, like almost all great men, simple, natural, and amiable; full of humane feelings and kindly affections. Of wit he had little or none in conversation, and he was too gay to take any delight in discussion; but his humour was playful to buoyancy, and wild even to extravagance; and he indulged his roaming and devious and abrupt imagination as much in society, as in public he kept it under rigorous control . . . .

"The striking and imposing appearance of this great man's person has been mentioned. His herculean strength of constitution may also be noted. During the eight-and-twenty years that he practised at the bar, he never was prevented for one hour from attending to his professional duties. At the famous State Trials, in 1794, he lost his voice on the evening before he was to address the jury. It returned to him just in time, and this, like other felicities of his career, he always ascribed to a special Providence, with the habitually religious disposition of mind which was hereditary in the godly families that he sprung from."*

"The ministry of Mr. Pitt did not derive more solid service from the bar in the person of Mr. Dundas, than the opposition party did ornament and popularity in that of Mr. Erskine. His Parliamentary talents, although they certainly have been underrated, were as clearly not the prominent portion of his character . . . .

"He never appears to have given his whole mind to the

* Historical Sketches of Statesmen in the Time of George III., p. 130.

practice of debating; he had a very scanty provision of political information; his time was always occupied with the laborious pursuits of his profession; he came into the House of Commons, where he stood among several equals, and behind some superiors, from a stage where he shone alone, and without a rival; above all, he was accustomed to address a select and friendly audience, bound to lend him their patient attention, and to address them by the compulsion of their retainer, and as a volunteer coming forward in his own person, a position from which the transition is violent and extreme, to that of having to gain and to keep a promiscuous, and, in great part, hostile audience, not under any obligation to listen one instant beyond the time during which the speaker can flatter, or interest, or amuse them."*

"It remains that we commemorate the deeds that he (Mr. Erskine) did, and which cast the fame of his oratory into the shade. He was an undaunted man; he was an undaunted advocate. To no Court did he ever truckle, neither to the Court of the King, neither to the Court of the King's judges. Their smiles and their frowns he disregarded alike in the fearless discharge of his duty. He upheld the liberty of the press against the one; he defended the rights of the people against both combined to destroy them. If there be yet amongst us the power of freely discussing the acts of our rulers; if there be yet the privilege of meeting for the promotion of needful reforms; if he who desires wholesome changes in our constitution be still recognised as a patriot, and not doomed to die the death of a traitor; let us acknowledge with gratitude, that to this great man, under heaven, we owe this felicity of the times. In 1794, his dauntless energy, his indomitable courage, kindling his eloquence, inspiring his conduct, giving direction and lending firmness to his matchless skill, resisted the combination of statesmen, and princes, and lawyers, the league of cruelty and craft, formed to destroy our liberties, and triumphantly scattered to the winds the half-accomplished scheme of an unsparing proscription."†

* Ibid. p. 131.

† Ibid. p. 135.

HENRY ERSKINE.

The brother of Lord Erskine, the Hon. Henry Erskine, for many years the leader of the Scotch bar, died in 1817, the same year which deprived Ireland of the great leaders of its bar, Curran and Ponsonby. Henry Erskine was a man of distinguished talents and brilliant wit. He was appointed Lord Advocate of Scotland, the same time his brother was made Lord Chancellor of England. He was an ardent and able advocate of civil and religious liberty. The conversational powers of Henry Erskine were of the highest order; his epigrams and witticisms, his clever impromptus, in verse as well as prose, were hardly inferior, it is said, to those of any of his brilliant cotemporaries of the bar or the senate.

THE EARL OF DUDLEY.

This nobleman (born in 1782) acquired distinction in the House of Commons as Mr. Ward. He gave great promise of ability in early life, possessed powerful talents, varied accomplishments, generous sentiments, and active sympathies with the wronged and the unfortunate. He visited Naples, and resided there for several weeks, in 1823; he was no less loved by those who knew him, than marvelled at by all who came in contact with him, for his singularity of character, absence of mind, and abstraction in society.

In the spring of 1827, in Mr. Canning's newly-formed administration, Viscount Dudley filled the office of Minister for Foreign Affairs. On Mr. Canning's death, in August, 1827, in Lord Goderich's administration, he held the same office as he did in the Canning Ministry. In January, 1828, at the onset in the formation of the Wellington administration, Lord

Dudley was continued in his post; but on the resignation of Mr. Huskisson, he retired from the ministry, along with Lord Palmerston and Mr. C. Grant.

Sir W. Gell wrote to Lady Blessington, in July, 1834, that he had received a letter of introduction from some friend in England, which was duly presented to him by the recommended party. The letter of introduction ran thus:—

"DEAR GELL,—I send you my friend, Mr. [———]: you will find him the greatest bore, and the most disputatious brute you ever knew. Pray ask him to dinner, and get any one you know of the same character to meet him."

This production is so exceedingly like some of the epistles and sundry of the audibly-thinking escapades of the late Lord Dudley and Ward in conversation, that I am induced to cite the following anecdote from Moore's Memoirs.

"*Dec.* 9. Lord Dudley, it is well known, has a trick of rehearsing over to himself, in an under-tone, the good things he is about to *debiter* to the company, so that the person who sits next to him has generally the advantage of his wit before any of the rest of the party. The other day, having a number of the foreign ministers and their wives to dine with him, he was debating with himself whether he ought not to follow the continental fashion of leaving the room with the ladies after dinner. Having settled the matter, he muttered forth, in his usual soliloquising tone, 'I think we must *go out* all together.' 'Good God! you don't say so!' exclaimed Lady ———, who was sitting next him, and who is well known to be the most anxious and sensitive of the Lady Whigs, with respect to the continuance of the present Ministry in power. 'Going out all together' might well alarm her. A man not very remarkable for agreeableness once proposed to walk from the House of Commons to the Travellers' Club with Lord Dudley, who, discussing the proposal mentally (as he thought) with himself, said audibly, 'I don't think it will bore me *very* much, to let him walk with me that distance.' On another occasion, when he gave somebody a seat in his carriage from some country-house, he was overheard by his companion, after a fit of thought and silence, saying to himself, 'Now, shall I ask this man to dine with me when we arrive in town?' It is said that the fellow-traveller, not pretending to hear him, muttered out in the same sort of tone, 'Now, if Lord Dudley should ask me to dinner, shall I accept his invitation?'"

Lord Dudley's eccentricities were of the most singular kind, and were productive of strange and ridiculous occurrences. While holding the office of Minister for Foreign Affairs, an amusing instance occurred of his absence of mind, even in his official capacity. Some misunderstanding had taken place between the Russian and the French governments—the object of the English ministry being to mediate between these powers—Lord Dudley had to forward private dispatches to both governments of great importance, which rendered it necessary to keep each government ignorant of the communication made to the other power. Lord Dudley, in one of his customary fits of absence of mind, enclosed the letter for the Russian Minister in the envelope addressed to the French, and vice versâ. When the mistake was discovered, Lord Dudley was greatly agitated. But his anxiety was speedily terminated, by a communication from the English Ambassador at Paris, stating that his Excellency the French Minister had returned the letter for the Russian Minister, which had been sent to him, saying—"Je suis trop fin, pour etre pris par tel artifice de Milord Dudley."

His Lordship's eccentricities increased very much from the period of his retirement from the ministry in 1827; nevertheless, one of his ablest speeches was made in 1831, against Lord Grey's government, in resistance of what he deemed the republican tendency of the Reform Bill.

His mental infirmities, after that period, rapidly augmented; his friends had the pain of seeing this able and accomplished man snatched from his exalted position and from society in the prime of life, bereft of reason, and eventually reduced to imbecility, by a succession of paralytic attacks. Death happily terminated this most awful of all human sufferings and humiliations in March, 1833, when he died in his 52nd year.

LORD AUCKLAND.

This amiable nobleman, who filled the high post of Governor-General of India, under the Melbourne administration, for many years was a warm and faithful friend of Lady Blessington, and her sister, Lady Canterbury. After his return from India, he resided at Eden Lodge, Kensington Gore, the grounds of which were only separated from those of Lady Blessington by a hedge, across which his Lordship and Lady B. often conversed. Lady Blessington has left a record of one of those conversations, in her Diary of December 24, 1845.

"Lord A., speaking of the efforts to form a new Ministry, said he was not sorry they had not succeeded; they should have been too weak for any useful purpose. They might have endeavoured to carry one great measure, and should probably have failed in their attempt to carry even that. Peel might have intended to support them, but his followers would not have been followers of him when out of power, though they might be so when he was Prime Minister. Peel has a better chance, therefore, of carrying a measure on the Corn Laws than they had, and he only hoped that Peel's measure would not fall very far short of what they should have proposed.

"Of the manner in which Lord John's attempt to form a government failed, he would say nothing. It was not good for public opinion and public discussion, and it was not agreeable to personal feeling, and he wished that the impressions which it had left might pass away."

The favourite pursuit of Lord Auckland was the culture of flowers, and the great perfection to which he brought them was a source of no small pride and satisfaction to his Lordship.

Lord Auckland was born in 1784, and died in 1849, at the seat of Lord Cowper. In 1830, he filled the office of President of the Board of Trade; in 1835, he was appointed Lieutenant-Governor of India, was recalled in 1841, and made First Lord of the Admiralty in 1846.

One who knew him well, has left this attestation of his worth—" A more kind, a more true, and a more just man never lived than Lord Auckland."

LORD HOLLAND.

The present Lord, when Mr. Henry Fox, was intimately acquainted with Lady Blessington in Italy in 1824: frequent mention is made of him in her diaries. In August of that year she speaks of him as having been an inmate of their abode—a most agreeable, entertaining, and lively companion, humorous and piquant in conversation—turning peculiarities of persons at all bordering on the class of *ridicules*, to an amusing account, and rivalling D'Orsay even in his own particular province of drawing-out people who can be made ridiculous, and laughed at, without being conscious of the use made of their society.*

In one of Lady Blessington's works, Henry Fox is spoken of as " such a forced plant as might be expected from the hot-bed culture of Holland House, where wit and talent are

* How far hosts and hostesses can reconcile the bantering privilege they accord to friends, who are reputed droll and witty, the sanction given by them to the practice of making any particular guest ridiculous, and drawing out any peculiarities of his, that may render him absurd in the face of a company, while pretending to pay attention to him, and to bring the merits of his conversation or opinions into notice, can reconcile, I say, this practice with the obligations and the duties of hospitality, is a question that may be answered in a few words. The conferring of such a privilege—the giving of such a sanction—is a vulgar and a gross violation of the rights of hospitality, and an unpardonable breach of faith with people who having been invited to partake of it, are entitled to its protection.

deemed of such importance, that more solid qualities are sometimes, if not sacrificed to their growth, at least overlooked in the search for them. Accustomed from infancy to see all around him contributing to the amusement of the circle they compose, by a brilliant persiflage, a witty version of the on-dits of the day, epigrammatical sallies, which, though pungent, never violate *les bienséances de societé*, and remarks on the literature of the day, full of point and tact, it cannot be wondered at, that he has become what he is—a most agreeable companion. As, however, he possesses no inconsiderable portion of the sweet temper and gaiety of spirits of his father, he may yet attain the more worthy distinction of becoming an estimable man."*

It is very probable that the preceding remarks were made at a later period than some others of Lady Blessington, in reference to the same distinguished person. The intimate acquaintance and friendship that had subsisted between the Blessingtons and Mr. Fox in Naples, had been interrupted. An estrangement had taken place, which existed for some years, and was followed by some explanations that were creditable to the feelings of both parties.

About the same period that Lady Blessington refers to in her notice of Mr. Fox, Moore also having met him in Italy, makes the following mention of him in his Journal:—

"I have also seen Henry Fox, Lord Holland's son, whom I had not looked upon since I left him, a pretty, mild boy, without a neck-cloth, in a jacket, and in delicate health, seven long years agone……"I think he has the softest and most amiable expression of countenance I ever saw, and manners correspondent."†

Lord Holland was born in 1802; he married, in 1830, Lady Mary Augusta Coventry, only daughter of the Earl of

* The Idler in Italy, Par. Ed. p. 354.

† Moore's Life of Byron, p. 576.

Coventry. He entered the diplomatic service in 1831, was some time attaché at St. Petersburg, was minister plenipotentiary at Florence from May 1838 to June 1846, and succeeded to the title as fourth Baron, October 28th, 1840, on the death of his father in his 67th year.*

Lord Holland lived much abroad for some years previously to his father's death, principally at Florence. His lordship's abilities and agreeableness of manners and conversation seem destined to conciliate the opinions and regards of his father's former friends and associates. But to render Holland House as heretofore, a place of intellectual and social *agrémens* of the most varied kind—to keep up its ancient celebrity as a rendezvous of the most distinguished personages of the day, the resort of " the high-thoughted spirits of the time, of all

* Lord Holland was born in 1773; his father was the elder brother of Charles James Fox. In March 1793, he set out on a continental tour, visited Spain, passed into Italy, and resided for some time in Florence with Lord Wycombe. While in Italy, he formed an intimacy with the wife of Sir Godfrey Webster, of Battle Abbey, co. Sussex, in consequence of which the latter brought an action against him, and obtained damages to the amount of £6000.

She was the daughter and heir of Sir Richard Vassall, Esq., of Jamaica; and was first married, June 27, 1786, to Sir Godfrey Webster, co. Sussex, Bart. By that marriage she had issue, two sons, the late Sir Godfrey V. Webster, Bart., formerly M.P. for Sussex, who died in 1836, and Colonel Henry Webster; and one daughter, Harriet, married in 1816 to Capt. the Hon. Sir Fleetwood Pellew, R.N. and C.B.

Lady Webster's marriage was dissolved by act of parliament in June 1797, and her Ladyship was re-married the following month to the late Henry Richard, third Lord Holland, who died October 22, 1840, and had four children by that marriage, of whom two died at an early age. Her ladyship had issue before her second marriage, Charles Richard Fox, Colonel in the army and Aide-de-camp to the Queen, who married, in 1824, Lady Mary Fitzclarence, daughter of King William IV. and Mrs. Jordan.† The dowager Lady Holland died on November 16, 1846, in her 76th year.

† Gen. Mag. for 1846, p. 91.

renommées in letters or in arts, of exalted positions in political life, is a consummation hardly to be expected.

The accomplishments and qualities of heart and mind which were united in the late Lord Holland, are not so transmissable as titles and estates; and without them Holland House never could have been what it was, or be again what it had been. They are characterized well and truly, in a few words, by an able writer in "The Examiner," which appeared at the time of the death of the late Lord. The charm of his conversation had a power of fascination in it; his mind was full of anecdotes, which were always happily introduced, and exquisitely narrated. "Lord Holland was a benignant and accomplished man; the last and best of the Whigs of the old school. He was something more and better than a Whig of any school. He was ever true to the cause of civil and religious liberty—a friend of merit, wherever it could be found—a lover of literature, of an understanding thoroughly masculine, yet his taste was of a delicacy approaching to a fault. His opinions were maintained earnestly and energetically but with a rare and beautiful candour—a wit without a particle of ill-nature, he was of a joyous and a genial nature. He possessed the sunshine of the breast, and no one could approach him without feeling it."

LORD ROSSLYN.

Sir James St. Clair Erskine, Bart., created Earl of Rosslyn in 1801, succeeded to the title and estates of his uncle, Lord Loughborough, in 1802, as second Earl. His Lordship was a General Officer, Colonel of the 9th Regiment of Dragoons. He married, in 1790, the eldest daughter of the Hon. Edward Bouverie. He was a Councillor of State to the King in Scotland, and Lord Lieutenant of Fifeshire; he died in January, 1837, in his seventy-sixth year. Lord Rosslyn, on entering into politics, linked himself with the Tory party, and for some time, on all great questions and important occasions, he acted as whipper-in to his party. In 1829, we see by his letters what an active part he took in that capacity on the Catholic Question. His amiable qualities in private life, endeared him to all who knew him, and caused him to be one of the most esteemed friends of Lady Blessington.

MARQUIS OF NORMANBY.

Constantine Henry Phipps, son of Henry, 1st Earl of Mulgrave, was born in 1797. He was educated at Harrow, and Trinity College, Cambridge. He married a daughter of Lord Ravensworth in 1818, and entered Parliament for the borough of Scarborough. His first speech in the Commons was on the Catholic Question, in which he strongly and ably advocated that object. His next great display in the House was when he seconded Lord John Russell's earliest resolutions in favour of Reform, and went farther than the terms of those resolutions, in promulgating his views on the general subject of Reform. The embarrassing circumstance of opposition to the political opinions of his father, caused him to retire from Parliament for some time. He proceeded to the Continent, and resided two years in Italy, during which period an acquaintance with the Blessingtons took place. At the end of 1822, he again entered Parliament, and again distinguished himself as an able and undaunted advocate of Reform.

In April, 1831, he succeeded his father in the Earldom of Mulgrave.

In 1832, at a very critical period, he was appointed Governor-General of Jamaica.

Lord Mulgrave having returned to England from Jamaica, and remained for some time not on very cordial terms with the ministry—was invited to take office under Lord Melbourne, and was appointed Lord Privy Seal, which office he held till the first break-up of the Melbourne ministry in 1834.

In May, 1835, on Lord Melbourne's return to office, he was appointed to the office of Lord Lieutenant of Ireland.

I have an intimate knowledge of the intentions and views of Lord Mulgrave, when he entered on the duties of the office of the new Viceroy in the government of Ireland. These intentions were—*To deal with Ireland as if it was an English county: in a straight-forward, manly, impartial manner; to know of no anomalies in its condition, which could render it necessary to have one rule of right and justice, and one line of policy for the regulation of affairs of government when dealing with the people in Ireland, and another, when the power of government was to be exercised in England over Englishmen: but to administer the laws in a spirit of equal and impartial justice towards all the King of England's subjects in Ireland: to make the magistracy respected, and to keep it respectable: to remove unfit men from the bench of magistrates—whether on account of their being bankrupts in fame or fortune, or fanatics, and furious political partizans: and by making no distinction between candidates for office, on account or on pretence of religion, and by giving a civil character, as much as possible, to various subordinate services in the Castle, which had formerly been of a military kind: and by discountenancing the practice of packing juries, to make English government reverenced as well as feared in Ireland.*

These intentions were calumniated by the selfish leaders of one party, and depreciated by the disappointed *pretendants* to exclusive Castle influence of another. The interests of Orangeism and Ribbonism, the pretensions of political factions, were not promoted by his rule. But England's imperial interest was greatly served by the government of Lord Mulgrave in Ireland.

In April, 1839, he resigned the Vice-Regal office, and was shortly after appointed Secretary to the Colonies, which office he held only from September till December of that year; when he was made Secretary of State for the Home Department, and continued in that office till September, 1841.

In 1846, he was appointed Ambassador to the court of France, and held that appointment till after the *coup-d'-état*, when he was succeeded by Lord Cowley.

Lord Normanby's first novel was, "Matilda, a Tale of the Day;" the next, "Contrast;" the last, "Yes and No."

The literary antecedents and dramatic tastes of his Lordship might not have led to very large expectations of sudden and signal success in a political career, for the young Lord. But seven years did not elapse between the theatricals in Florence and those in Jamaica, in which the part of Governor was played with great ability at a very critical period, and in front of a very unruly and adverse audience. As an eye-witness of the performance, I feel qualified to express an opinion on its merits.

The short, but important government of Lord Normanby in Jamaïca in 1833 and 1834, that had to prepare the way for the Emancipation of the Negroes, and to carry that measure into effect in the midst of difficulties that can hardly be overstated, was conducted with remarkable ability and courage; courage that had to encounter face to face, armed opponents of that measure, and astuteness that knew how by blandishments and affability to conciliate adversaries in Council and Assembly, and to make wives and daughters of refractory members ancillary to governmental objects.

To form any opinion of those difficulties that were encountered and overcome by Lord Normanby, it is necessary to have some idea of the constitution of the West India Houses of Assembly, and to bear in mind the enormous change that was about to take place in West India affairs and interests.

In 1832, Lord Normanby's services were transferred to

another stage, hardly less trying to the talents of a state actor than that of Jamaica. It is the fashion to underrate those talents that are very prominently and ostentatiously exhibited, and to argue that demonstrative men, who shew them off to the most advantage they can on all occasions, are only intellectual coxcombs, whose inordinate vanity is incompatible with great qualities of mind. The fact is, that great qualities of mind are often found accompanied by an inordinate amount of self-esteem, sometimes prejudiced indeed by it, but not destroyed. From the political arena of party strife in Ireland, the Lord—now Marquis of Normanby—after a repose of some years, in 1846, passed to another scene of turmoil—in the diplomatic line, and performed the arduous duties of an Ambassador in Paris, during the revolutionary horrors of 1848.

The eldest son of the Marquis of Normanby, George, Earl of Mulgrave, M.P., was born in 1819, and married in 1841.

THE EARL OF WESTMORELAND.

Lord Burghersh, born in 1784, succeeded his father as eleventh Earl of Westmoreland in 1841. In 1811, he married a daughter of William Wellesley Pole, late Earl of Mornington, and for several years subsequently to his marriage resided on the Continent. He entered the army in 1803, served in the expedition to Hanover in 1806 and 1807, as assistant Adjutant-General in Sicily; on board Admiral Duckworth's fleet, in the action and passage of the Dardanelles; in Egypt, with the force under General Wauchope; served in Portugal in 1808, as Adjutant-General, under Sir Arthur Wellesley; and in 1809, as extra Aid-de-camp to Lord Wellington, at the battle of Talavera; was appointed to a Lieutenant-Colonelcy in 1811; in 1813 was accredited as Military Commissioner to the head-quarters of the allied armies in Germany, under Prince Schwartzenberg; served in France in the campaign of 1814; was appointed Envoy Extraordinary and Minister Plenipotentiary at Florence in August, 1814; served with the Austrian army in the campaign against Naples in 1815; was made a Privy Councillor in 1822; he was British Minister at the court of Florence in 1825; became a Major-General in 1825; was made a K.C.B. in 1838, and Lieutenant-General the same year; was appointed Envoy Extraordinary and Minister Plenipotentiary at Berlin in 1841; succeeded to the peerage in 1841; made G.C.B. in 1846; and transferred from Berlin to Vienna in 1848.

This nobleman, though not remarkable for exalted intellectual powers, or high attainments of a literary kind, is much esteemed by those who know him, for his upright principles and honourable character, his kindness of heart and amiable disposition. He is a great musical amateur, has composed several pieces, and has done much to promote musical art in England.

Lady Blessington, in her diary at Genoa, thus makes mention of the arrival in that city of Lord and Lady Burghersh, and of their popularity there being the same it was in every other part of Italy:—

"They have done much to efface the impression entertained by Italians, that the English aristocracy are not much devoted to the fine arts, or prone to encourage them; for Lady Burghersh is said to be not only a *connoisseure* in painting, but to have arrived at no mean excellence in it herself; while the kind-hearted and excellent Lord Burghersh is a proficient in music, and has composed some very charming things."

LORD HOWDEN.

John Hobart Caradoc, Lord Howden, K.C.B., entered the army in 1815, served as aid-de-camp to the Duke of Wellington in 1817 and 1818; was attached to the Embassy in Paris in

1825; charged with a special mission to Egypt and Greece in 1827; was present at the battle of Navarino same year; at the siege of Antwerp; was sent on a special mission to Spain in 1836; appointed Envoy Extraordinary and Minister Plenipotentiary to Rio Janeiro in 1847; and was transferred to Madrid in May, 1850. In Italy he was well acquainted with Lady Blessington.

THE EARL OF CHESTERFIELD.

The celebrated Philip Dormer Stanhope, fourth Earl of Stanhope, a renowned wit, a statesman, and man of letters, born in 1695, died without issue in 1773.

The present Earl, George Augustus Frederick, was born in 1805, succeeded to his father, Philip, fifth Earl of Chesterfield, in 1815. He married, in 1830, a daughter of the first Lord Forrester.

His Lordship travelled in Italy previously to his marriage, and was intimately acquainted with Lady Blessington.

Chesterfield House was one of the places of fashionable resort of Count D'Orsay, during his sojourn in London, which was most frequented by him. The old *renommée* of this house as a place of assemblage of distinguished persons, the foremost fashionables and wits of the day, was maintained for some years by the present Earl. The friends of Lord Chesterfield speak warmly of his amiable, generous, and kindly disposition. Of his friendship for Lady B., and his generosity in the mode of evincing his regard and admiration, I have seen some very remarkable tokens. Among others, at the sale of the effects in Gore House, there was sold a portfolio of massive chased silver covers, with gold bands and clasp, which was stated by the auctioneer to have cost upwards of £300.

LORD GLENELG.

This nobleman, when Mr. Charles Grant, Chief Secretary

for Ireland, as well as after his elevation to the peerage in 1835, and while he filled the office of Colonial Secretary, was intimately acquainted with Lady Blessington, and greatly esteemed and respected by her.

He is the son of the late Charles Grant, Esq., M.P. for Invernesshire, a member of a junior branch of the family of the Grants, who were Sheriffs of Inverness in the thirteenth century.

Lord Glenelg is a living instance of the facility with which a cry can be got up in England against a particular member of an administration beginning to be unpopular, by powerful or unscrupulous parties, whose views or interests may be impeded or prejudiced by the integrity and straightforwardness of his views in the discharge of his duties: and of the meanness of his colleagues, who may be led by selfish considerations to allow their colleague to be made a scape-goat and a sacrifice of atonement for their short-comings, and the sin of their unpopularity.

During the whole period of Lord Glenelg's tenure of office in the Colonial Office, I had ample opportunities of knowing officially and practically, in the West Indies, the efficiency of his conduct in his office, and the deep interest he took in the abolition of slavery, and the traffic in slaves; and having often need of all the countenance and protection I could get from my superiors at home, for the discharge of very arduous and invidious duties, I had always reason to know any appeal of mine to Lord Glenelg could never be made in vain. It is a gratification to me to have an opportunity of making this avowal of my sentiments with respect to a very honest, ill-used, and misrepresented public servant.

THE EARL OF CARLISLE.

The Honourable George William Frederick Howard, son of George, sixth Earl of Carlisle, made the acquaintance of

Lady Blessington in 1824, at Naples, and, as her journals inform us, was one of her most intimate acquaintances, and constant companions to the remarkable places and monuments of antiquity in the vicinity of Naples.

In May, 1824, Mr. Howard accompanied her Ladyship to Pæstum, and on that occasion presented Lady Blessington with a poem written by himself, entitled "Pæstum," which will be found at page 108 of vol. i. of this work. The original document is endorsed by Lady Blessington—"A Prize Poem, given by Lord Morpeth to me at Naples, in 1824."

The present Peer graduated at Christchurch, Oxford. From his earliest years he was addicted to literary pursuits, and cultivated a taste for poetry with some success. He contributed to the Annuals edited by Lady Blessington articles in prose and verse, till political cares and senatorial duties seemed to him incompatible with flirtations with the Muses; and as such, he declined Lady Blessington's last pressing application for a contribution to her album. As Lord Morpeth, he was well and advantageously known in Ireland, in the office of Chief Secretary, from 1835 to 1841—the period of the career of his Lordship most honourable to his character, and creditable to his talents and integrity. Subsequently he filled the office of Chief Commissioner of Woods and Forests. He was born in 1802, and succeeded his father in 1848.

THE MARQUESS OF CLANRICARDE.

The Marquess was one of the friends of Lady Blessington, in whose stedfast kindness and regard she placed the highest confidence. This nobleman is known better and more advantageously to private friends than to the public. To the latter he is merely known as a respectable, upright, painstaking, and efficient servant of the State, in every high office he has filled, whether of a Minister at a Foreign Court, a Postmaster-

General, or a member of the present government. To private friends he is known as a man of amiable disposition, prompt to serve his friends, and unchangeable in his friendship.

The Marquess was born in 1802, succeeded his father in the Earldom in 1808, was created Marquess in 1825, and married, the same year, the only daughter of the Right Honourable George Canning, and has issue seven children, the eldest of whom, Lord Dunkellin, born 1827, is a Captain in the Coldstream Guards (recently a prisoner in the hands of the Russians). The Marquess was formerly Ambassador Extraordinary at the Court of St. Petersburgh, and in 1850 filled the office of Postmaster-General.

From the house of Clanricarde (the family of De Burgh), was derived, the Viscounts Bourkes, of Mayo, long since extinct in Ireland, but not so in Spain. The title, honours, and arms of the Viscount Bourkes, of Mayo, are still claimed by a descendant of the representative of the ancient family, who was expatriated after the battle of the Boyne, and having acquired distinction in the Spanish service, was ennobled by the Spanish Sovereign.

In 1845, I was introduced in Madrid to the Spanish grandee who claims the title of Viscount Mayo.

LORD JOHN RUSSELL.

Lord John, third son of the late Duke of Bedford, by the second daughter of George, Viscount Torrington, was born in August, 1792. He was placed at school, first at Sunbury, from whence he was removed to Westminster, and thence to Cambridge, where his education was completed. Long before Lord John made his débût on the stage of Parliament, took a leading part in politics, or addressed polemical epistles to Episcopal performers in state-church panics; he figured in theatricals of another sort (on one occasion in the character of

" Friz"), and composed epilogues, which were recited by him at private plays " with due emphasis and discretion." It is curious to see in this notice of Lord John's first appearance on any stage, an account of another young gentleman, on the same occasion, reciting an epilogue also, and favouring the company with some songs of his own composition—who was destined to become a great poet, and, some forty-five years later, to have Lord John Russell, a great statesman, for his biographer.

When Moore and Russell made their appearance on the same stage in Dublin, January 22, 1807; Moore was then twenty-eight, and Lord John, under fifteen years of age.

During the Vice-Royalty of the Duke of Bedford, the Royal Hospital at Kilmainham, near Dublin, was the scene of fashionable festivity, accompanied with private dramatic entertainments, which are recorded in the pages of the " Dublin Evening Post " of that period.

In the " Post" of January 22, 1807, an account is given of a fancy ball, and a " dramatic exhibition," attended by the Duke and Duchess of Bedford.

" On Monday evening there was a select party of about one hundred, at which the Duke and Duchess of Bedford also were present, as part of the audience, to see a dramatic exhibition, cast in the following manner for the farce ' Of Age To-Morrow :'—

Men.

Frederick . . .	Marquis of Tavistock.
Baron Pistleberg . .	Hon. Mr. H. Stanhope.
Malkus	Hon. Mr. F. Stanhope.
Friz . . .	Lord Wm. Russell.
Waiter	Hon. Mr. A. Stanhope.

Women.

Lady Bromback . .	Lady C. Stanhope.
Sophia	Lady C. A. Stanhope.
Maria	Lady A. M. Stanhope.

"The quarrel of Brutus and Cassius was admirably recited by the Marquis of Tavistock and the Hon. Mr. Henry Stanhope—the former particularly excellent.

"The farce 'Of Age To-Morrow' was pleasingly executed by the dramatis personæ, and gave universal satisfaction to the company.

"Lord John Russell delivered with due emphasis and discretion, a very neat epilogue of his own composition, which did equal honour to his poetic taste and recitation; and Anacreon Moore also repeated some lines by way of epilogue, which, we understand, were from the pen of Mr. Atkinson, and we hope some future day to be favoured with a copy of both those pieces.

"Between the acts, Mr. Moore favoured the company with some of his lyric compositions, which, as usual, charmed every ear.

"The ballet, conducted by Mr. J. Crampton,* in which the charming family of the Stanhopes joined, was elegantly executed and highly applauded; and, in fine, the tout ensemble of the evening's amusement was every way entertaining."

Doubtless the *tout ensemble* of that evening's amusements were far more entertaining than the performances in which Lord John has played so distinguished a part since the year 1813, to the present period.

Lord John's Parliamentary career commenced in 1813. He set out in political life an adherent of the party who supported Mr. Fox's principles, and adopted his watch-words—Civil and Religious Liberty, and Parliamentary Reform. He represented Tavistock from July, 1813, till March, 1817, and also from 1818 till March, 1819; Huntingdonshire from 1820 till 1826, and sat for Bandon Bridge from 1826 till 1830; was made a Privy Councillor in 1830; filled the office of Paymaster of the Forces, from December, 1830, till the end of December, 1834; was returned for Devon in 1831; sat for South Devon from 1832 till 1835; filled the office of Secretary of State for the Home Department, from 1835 to August, 1839. He represented Stroud from 1835 to 1841; filled the office of Secretary of State

* The brother of one of Ireland's most celebrated medical men, Sir Philip Crampton.

for the Colonies from 1839 to September, 1841; and has represented the City of London, since July, 1841. He was First Lord of the Treasury from July, 1846, to February, 1852; was Secretary of State for Foreign Affairs, *ad interim*, from December, 1852, till February 20, 1853; and is now President of the Council.

The principal great events of Lord John's career are comprised in the following data:—

In 1815, he opposed the war against Napoleon, when the latter escaped from Elba, on the principle of non-interference in the affairs of self-government of foreign nations.

In the same year, he published his first literary work, "The Life of Lord William Russell."

In 1817, he denounced Lord Castlereagh's Suspension of the Habeas Corpus Act.

In 1819, he made his first motion in favour of Parliamentary Reform.

In 1820-1, he took an active part in behalf of Queen Caroline.

In 1822, he made another motion for Parliamentary Reform with great effect, and had 164 supporters.

In the same year, he proposed a measure of Reform; one of the propositions of which was, the abolition of the rotten boroughs, and a pecuniary compensation to the owners of them, deeming it would be "a wise economy to expend a million of money in the purchase," &c.

In 1826, he renewed his efforts for Parliamentary Reform, and procured the second reading and committal of a Bill for transferring the principle of returning members for small corrupt boroughs to others more popular and wealthy.

In 1828, he proposed a measure for the repeal of the Test Acts, which was carried in the Commons, but only passed the Lords after such mutilations as to render it in the opinion of many of its supporters, a nullity.

In 1829, he zealously advocated the cause of Catholic Emancipation, of which measure he has been an old, able and consistent advocate.

In 1830, he moved for leave to bring in a Bill to enable Manchester, Birmingham, and Leeds, to return Members to Parliament; but the motion was lost by a majority of 48.

In the same year, he spoke in favour of a motion for the removal of Jewish Disabilities.

In the same year, he opposed O'Connell's proposed plan of Parliamentary Reform, including the ballot, universal suffrage, and triennial parliaments.

On the 1st of March (1831), being appointed Paymaster of the Forces in Lord Grey's administration, he submitted to the House his scheme of Parliamentary Reform—the first governmental proposition of that kind; when the second reading was carried by a majority of one, in a House of 603 members.

On the 24th of April following, Parliament having been dissolved, he again submitted his measure, and had a majority of 136. After going through Committee, it was read a third time, the 20th of September, and passed by a majority of 109. In October the Bill was lost in the Lords.

In October, same year, Ministers again brought in their Bill, "revised and improved;" and Lord John carried it through the Commons without a division, the 23d of March, 1832.

On the 27th of March, Ministers being defeated in the House of Lords, resigned; but, by the advice of the Duke of Wellington, they were recalled—brought forward their measure *de novo* in the Lords, and carried it.

In 1833, Lord John gave his strenuous aid to the governmental measure for the abolition of Negro Slavery.

In 1834, he brought forward a measure to enable Dissenters to marry in their own places of worship.

The 30th of March, 1835, he moved for "a Committee of the whole House to consider the Temporalities of the Church of Ireland." He argued, on that occasion, that the surplus revenues ought to be appropriated to purposes of general education. His motion was carried by a majority of 33, in a House of 611 members; a result which eventually caused the resignation of Sir Robert Peel's government.

In June, 1835, being Secretary of State for the Home Department, he brought forward his great measure of Municipal Reform in England, which was carried through both Houses, and was followed eventually by a Municipal Reform Bill for Ireland.

In 1841, he attempted unsuccessfully the reduction of the Sugar Duties, and subsequently, the same year, proposed a fixed duty of 8*s.* on corn, instead of the protection sliding scale.

In 1845, Peel being in office, Lord John wrote a letter from Edinburgh, declaring his conversion to total repeal of the corn laws.

In 1850, Lord John addressed a lettter to the Bishop of Durham, which answered a temporary purpose in Parliament, and furnished Mr. D'Israeli with a model epistolary combustible for similar use on a like emergency in "the Recess."

In 1851, Lord John, being First Lord of the Treasury, proposed a plan for a Local Militia Force, which was successfully opposed by Lord Palmerston, and being defeated, he resigned.

The recent career of his Lordship is too well known to need any reference to.

LADY CHARLEVILLE.

The late Dowager Lady Charleville was the daughter of Thomas Tomlins Dawson, Esq., a member of the family ennobled in the person of the first Lord Cremore. She was educated chiefly in France, and, though a Protestant, received the best part of her education in a French convent, previously to the French revolution. Soon after her return to Ireland, she was married to James Tisdale, Esq., of the county Louth. He died in 1797, and one daughter by this marriage, Maria Tisdale, who married Dean Marlay, survived both her parents, and her husband also. In 1798, she married Charles William, Lord Tullamore, who, in 1800, was created Viscount Tullamore, and, in 1806, Earl of Charleville. Prior to her marriage, in the early part of 1798, her name was disagreeably connected with a translation of Voltaire's "Pucelle D'Orleans," made and printed for private circulation some time previously to her second marriage, by Lord Tullamore.

Her co-operation in the translation was intimated in a

satirical poem, published in 1804, entitled, "A Familiar Epistle to Frederick Jones, Esq.," Manager of the Theatre Royal, Dublin, ascribed to an Irish barrister, briefless, but not brainless, now a Privy Councillor, an Admiralty official, a renowned and a redoubtable Quarterly Reviewer. In a recent number of "The Gentleman's Magazine," it is stated, —that in a note to the satire above referred to, Lord Tullamore's English version of the "Pucelle" was said to be indebted to "lawn sleeves and gauze petticoats." The lawn sleeves being understood to belong to the late Bishop Marlay, and the petticoats to Lady Charleville.*

The note in question, which I copy from the fourth edition of the satire, published in 1805, makes no allusion to "lawn sleeves and gauze petticoats," but to the "bipennifer arca," of the reputed translation of the "Pucelle."†

Lady Charleville invariably denied having had any thing whatever to do with the work referred to; and there can be very little doubt, but that the imputation was utterly unfounded. Lady Charleville, though partly educated in a Roman Catholic convent, was what is termed "a staunch Protestant" in her religious opinions, but she was no bigot; and while residing among her husband's tenantry, at Charleville, in the King's county, she promoted the interests of the poor of all denominations, without respect to creed or franchise politics. She died in London, in 1852.

* Vide Gentleman's Magazine, 1851, Part i. p. 429.

† "'Multa morum elegantia,' and perhaps I may even add 'ingenio in lustris,' will Lord Charleville permit me to say, that I do not approve the expenditure of his taste and talents on a certain translation attributed to him. I know, that, like Ovid's personage, it has been said to be Bipennifer arca; but this I can hardly believe. I am happy, however, to be able to offer to my Lord Charleville the unmingled praise of being a generous and knowing patron of learning, and a most amiable and honourable gentleman."—*Familiar Epistles to F. Jones*, 4th Ed. Dub. p. 61.

She had lost the use of her lower extremities for a great many years before her death; and though she went into society, and frequently rode out, she had to be carried to her chair or carriage, or moved about her apartment in a sort of Bath chair at her soirées and conversationes; which at the period I had the honour of her acquaintance, from 1833 to 1835, were hardly exceeded by any in London for their agreeableness and the brilliancy of intellectual enjoyments that were found in them.

The Earl of Charleville died in October, 1835, reduced to a state of helplessness by disease of a paralytic nature, that was painful to witness for many years before his death. He was a generous and a kind-hearted man, addicted to literature, and partial to the society of literary men.

THE PRINCE MICHAEL SOUTZO.

The Prince Michael Soutzo was formerly Hospodar of Moldavia; a man of very superior abilities and most polished manners, whose varied life and vicissitudes of fortune were full of interest, and many of the episodes in whose career were as romantic as remarkable. In 1826 and 1827, the Prince and his family were residing in Pisa, where a little colony of Greeks was established, among whom were some of the highest families of the Fanaar. The Prince Carragia, the Hospodar of Wallachia, the Greek Archbishop of Mitylene, and the Prince Carragia, resided in the Palazzo Lanfranchi, in which Byron had lived.

In May, 1827, Lady Blessington gave a dinner in the Forest of Pisa to the Prince and Princess Soutzo, the Duchess de Guiche, the Prince and Princess Constantine Carragia, and several Greek notabilities of the Fanaar and of Wallachia—some of whom probably were indebted for the advantage of having heads on their shoulders, to the circumstance of having had the happiness to realize the blessings of exile in a foreign land.

Lady Blessington speaks of the Greek acquaintances she made at Pisa as friends. " They were clever, intelligent, and amiable." " The talents of the Prince Soutzo were too remarkable not to place him in a distinguished position, whenever his country was sufficiently tranquil to permit a government to be established : in which doubtless he would be called to fill an important situation. She had never known a more interesting family than his, nor one in which talent and worth were so united."

GEORGE BYNG, ESQ. M.P.

Poodle Byng is better known to London celebrities than George Byng, Esq. of Wrotham Park, Middlesex. Mr. Byng, brother to Lord Strafford, was born in London, in 1764, the eldest son of the Right Honourable Robert Byng, by Anne, daughter of the Right Honourable William Conolly, of Castletown, in Ireland, grand-daughter of Thomas, Earl of Strafford, and sister to the Countess of Buckinghamshire. In 1788, he became a candidate for the representation of Maidstone, but was defeated. In 1790, he was returned for Middlesex, on the Liberal interest, on the retirement of John Wilkes. From that time till he expired, he never ceased to represent the great metropolitan county. Mr. Byng could boast what few members of parliament were ever able to boast : for a period of fifty-six years he enjoyed the confidence of his constituents, and was returned by their suffrages to sixteen parliaments. Middlesex contains three-parts of the city of London. Its two representatives, therefore, are regarded as the most influential members in the House, as representing especially the commercial interests of England. All Mr. Byng's sympathies were with the Whigs, yet he was respected and esteemed for his integrity and consistency by his political opponents. "He was a thorough-bred true-hearted gentleman, a staunch partizan, and on the whole, diligent in the discharge of his public duties, yet neither learned, eloquent, nor profound."*

On the last day of the year, 1846, Mr. Byng, finding old age and infirmities *beginning* to interfere with his parliamentary duties, then in his eighty-third year, addressed the electors of Middlesex, and in his address observed: "I am, I believe, the oldest member of either house of the legislature, and I entertain the deepest feeling of gratitude and thankfulness to Divine Providence, that my life has been spared to witness the accomplishment of all the great measures of public policy which I was early taught by my most dear and valued friend, Mr. Fox, to be essential to the security and perfect development of the English constitution." This was a fitting close of a long career of a consistent Whig politician. Mr. Byng, ten days after he published this farewell address to his constituents, had departed this life. He died on the 10th of January, 1847. Mr. Byng married in early life, Harriet, eighth daughter of Sir William Montgomery, Bart., of Maybec Hill, county Peebles, whose sister had married the first Viscount Mountjoy, father of the late Earl of Blessington.

THE RIGHT HON. R. CUTLAR FERGUSON.

This gentleman, descended from an old and honourable Scotch family, in the early part of his career was an ardent admirer of Mirabeau, one of "the friends of the people," a sympathizer with the Scotch Reformers, and with those of Ireland who were rather in advance of Reform. So early as 1792, he published a pamphlet, entitled, "The Proposed Reform in the Representation of the Counties of Scotland considered." In 1798, being intimately acquainted with Arthur

* Gent. Mag. 1847, p. 309.

O'Connor and his associates, then proceeding on a treasonable mission to France, he attended the trial of O'Connor at Maidstone; and at the termination of it, an attempt being made to effect the escape of O'Connor, the Earl of Thanet and Mr. Ferguson were charged with joining in the attempted rescue, for which they were tried, convicted, and sentenced to twelve months' imprisonment. Lord Thanet was imprisoned in the Tower, Mr. Ferguson in the King's Bench prison. In 1799, Mr. Ferguson published an account of the proceedings against him and Lord Thanet. In 1797, he had been called to the bar, but his reforming principles excluded him from all patronage, and any chance of practice at his profession at home. He went to India, and followed his profession there with honour and emolument, and returned after twenty years absence, with an improvement in his position, but no change in his liberal principles. He was returned for his native county to parliament in 1826. In parliament and out of it, he was an able, eloquent, and energetic champion of the cause of Poland and its unfortunate people. In 1834, he was appointed Judge-Advocate-General, and also a Privy Councillor. He died at Paris, in his seventieth year, in November, 1839.

SIR THOMAS NOON TALFOURD.

The father of Sir Thomas was a brewer, at Reading, in Berkshire. Thomas was born in January, 1795. He gained a scholarship at the grammar school at Reading, under Dr. Valpy. While a boy, he shewed a taste for versifying, and a turn for literature and politics. At eighteen, he came to London, to study law under Chitty, the pleader. He published in periodicals of that period, some papers in favour of religious toleration. In 1815, he wrote critiques on poetry and literature, which led to his first acquaintance with literary men in London. In 1821, he was called to the bar, and the following year married a Miss Rutt, eldest daughter of J. I. Rutt, Esq. of Clapton. He found time, while pursuing his professional avocations, to produce the successful tragedy of "Ion" in 1836, and subsequently, two plays, "The Athenian Captive," and "Glencoe," which were of inferior merit to the former drama. His "Vacation Rambles" did not contribute much to his literary fame. He acquired eminence in every position in which he was placed as a leading member of the bar—a member of parliament—a serjeant-at-law, and finally, in 1849, as one of the Judges of the Court of Common Pleas. The career of this eminent and good man, from his onset in life to the recent close of it on the bench, was in keeping—uniformly entitled to the admiration of all thinking and good men. Talfourd seeking eminence in his profession, distinction in literature, renown in his judicial capacity, was always true to the interests of humanity and of literature. He had strong sympathies with his fellow men—with poverty and suffering. He had a sound taste in matters appertaining to art and letters, and kindly feelings towards those who cultivated those pursuits. It has been truly said, that "the noble sentiments uttered by Justice Talfourd in his last moments, gave a charm to his sudden death, and shed a hallowed beauty about the painfully closing scene of this great man. They forcibly illustrated the loving soul, the kind heart, and the amiable character of this deeply-lamented judge." After speaking of the peculiar aspect of crime in that part of the country where he delivered his last charge, he went on to say:

"I cannot help myself thinking, it may be in no small degree attributable to that separation between class and class, which is the great curse of British society, and for which we are all, more or less, in our respective spheres, in some degree responsible, and which is more complete in these districts than in agricultural districts, where the resident gentry are enabled to shed around them the blessings resulting from the exercise of benevolence, and the influence and example of active kindness. I am afraid we all of us keep too much aloof from those beneath us, and whom we thus encourage to look upon us with suspicion and dislike. Even to our servants we think, perhaps, we fulfil our duty when we perform our contract with them; when we pay them their wages, and treat them with the civility consistent with our habits and feelings; when we curb our temper, and use no violent expressions towards them. But how painful is the thought, that there are men and women growing up around us, ministering to our comforts and necessities, continually inmates of our dwellings, with whose affections and nature we are as much unacquainted as if they were the inhabitants of some other sphere. This feeling, arising from that kind of reserve peculiar to the English character, does, I think, greatly tend to prevent that mingling of class with class, that reciprocation of kind words and gentle affections, gracious admonitions, and kind inquiries, which often more than any book-education, tend to the culture of the affections of the heart, refinement and elevation of the character of those to whom they are addressed. And if I were to be asked what is the great want of English society,—to mingle class with class, I would say in one word, the want of sympathy."*

From Sergeant Talfourd to Lady Blessington.

"Reading, 16th October, 1836.

"My Dear Lady Blessington,

"On my return from Scotland, on Saturday, I found your charming work, some foretaste of the delicate beauties of which I had enjoyed in the extracts of the Examiner, and for the full enjoyment of which I have now heartily to thank you.

"The airy graces of its style, and the loveliness of its illustrations, came upon me very opportunely between the perils and distresses of a most tumultuous passage, and the stormy duties which compelled me to leave home to-day for this place, where I have to undergo many dinners, &c. for the next ten days. From those whom it was delightful to visit, when they

* Notes and Queries, April 29, 1854.

were no more than friends, and whom now I shrink from as if they were creditors, I turn to your book for recreation.

"I remain, dear Lady Blessington,

"Ever faithfully yours,

"T. N. TALFOURD."

GENERAL THE HON. EDMUND PHIPPS.

Edmund, the fourth son of Constantine, first Lord Mulgrave, was born in 1760. He entered the army in 1780. He served in Jamaica, Gibraltar, in the Low Countries, and in England and Ireland; obtained various honours and preferments, and attained the full rank of General in 1819. He entered parliament in 1794, for the borough of Scarborough. He was re-elected at each subsequent election till that of 1832, when he retired.

General Phipps was the uncle of the present Marquess of Normanby. He possessed refined literary tastes, and an excellent judgment in literary matters, and extensive information; mingled for upwards of half a century with the most eminent and talented men of his time, and was greatly loved by all who knew him. He died in Venice, the 14th September, 1837, after a few days' illness, without issue.

WILLIAM GODWIN, ESQ.

The author of "Caleb Williams" was born at Wisbeach, in 1756. He was the son of a Calvinist minister, and was educated for the ministry at the Dissenters' College at Hoxton, under Rees and Kippis.

In 1778, he was appointed to a congregation at Stowmarket, in Suffolk. About 1782, he abandoned the church, and devoted himself to literature. His first published work, entitled "Sketches of History," appeared in 1784. Soon after the outbreak of the French Revolution, he was engaged as a writer in "The New Annual Register." A work of his attracted very extensive notice, entitled "Political Justice," in 1793. This performance, on account of the novelty and boldness of its doctrines, brought down a tempest of wrath and reprehension on his head; this work was followed by "Caleb Williams," which fully established his reputation. In 1797, his work "The Inquirer" appeared; a little later, "St. Leon;" in 1801 a tragedy, produced at Drury Lane, called "Antonio:" and in 1804, "The Life of Chaucer," and "Fleetwood." Till 1817, he was almost lost sight of by the public, when he published his novel, "Mandeville." In the interim, he was engaged in London on a small scale in the bookselling trade, but was unsuccessful in it. For many years subsequently, he gave himself up wholly to literature; at various intervals appeared, "An Essay on Sepulchral Monuments," "A Reply to Malthus on Population," "The History of the Commonwealth," "Cloudesley," "The Lives of the Necromancers," &c. Mr. Godwin was thrice married. His first wife, whom he married in 1797, was the celebrated Mary Wolstonecraft, by whom he had one daughter, the late Mrs. Shelley. In 1801, he married a widow lady, who survived him.

While struggling for his support in London, in a small bookselling business, he published several little books for the instruction and amusement of children, under the name of Edward Baldwin. He was continually engaged in literature, likewise as a contributor to various publications, and a compiler of several biographies.

His private worth, lofty sentiment, and originality of mind, his courteous manners and pleasing address, gained him the friendship of some of the great men of his age—Fox, Sheridan, Mackintosh, Grattan, and Curran.

For his very ably-written and successful novel, "Caleb Williams," he received only £84, while for the most hastily-written, and perhaps the most trashy of all his works, "An

Inquiry into Political Justice," he was paid £700; and for a novel of far inferior merit to that of "Caleb Williams," "St. Leon," he got 400 guineas.

His last years were made comfortable by an appointment of Yeoman Usher in the Court of Exchequer, during Earl Grey's tenure of office: which office he retained till his death, which took place in Palace Yard, April 7th, 1836, in his 81st year.

Godwin was one of the earliest of the literary friends of Lady Blessington in London.

JAMES PERRY, ESQ.

Mr. Perry, born in 1756, was a native of Aberdeen, at which University he was educated, and then removed to London, where he applied himself to the law, and was called to the bar; but devoting himself to politics, and becoming proprietor of the "Morning Chronicle," he relinquished the legal profession. He settled in London in 1777. He wrote for the "General Advertiser," and "London Evening Post," for some years; subsequently established the "European Magazine," and soon afterwards became Editor of "The Gazette." Having purchased the "Morning Chronicle," he raised that paper to the first eminence amongst the public journals.

In 1810, an ex-officio prosecution, for an alleged libel on the House of Lords, was instituted against him in the King's Bench; and the result of this prosecution was, the imprisonment for three months of Mr. Perry in Newgate.

Shortly before Lord Blessington's second marriage, Mr. Perry, then a stranger to his Lordship, did an act worthy of an honourable man: he refused to allow his paper to be made the vehicle of a foul calumny, intended to give annoyance to the feelings of his Lordship, and injury to the character of another person, respecting the death of a gentleman who had recently met his death in the Fleet Prison, by falling through a window in a state of inebriety—Captain Farmer.

Mr. Perry died the 4th December, 1821, in his 66th year.

The original publisher and proprietor of the "Morning Chronicle" was Mr. William Woodfall.

In the latter years of Mr. Perry's life, he drew a very large income from the paper, (larger than the future prosperity of the paper justified, upwards of £10,000 a-year).

On the death of Mr. Perry, in 1821, the "Morning Chronicle" was purchased by William Clement, Esq., editor and proprietor of the "Observer," for £40,000, payable by instalments of £10,000 each. In 1834, struggling with great difficulties, Mr. Clement sold the "Chronicle" to Mr. John Easthope, for about a quarter of the sum he had paid for it.

Mr. Clement died in 1852.

JOHN ALLEN, ESQ.,

One of the visitors at Seamore Place, was the intimate friend of Lord Holland, the inmate for many years of his house, "one of the most acute and learned of our constitutional antiquaries,"* died the 3rd of April, 1843, in his 73rd year, in South Street.

Mr. Allen was born in 1770, at Redford, a few miles west of Edinbro'. He graduated at the University of Edinburgh, as M.D., in 1791, and in 1792 was associated with the Scotch reformers, Muir and Palmer, in their political efforts for reform. Since the beginning of the present century, he was almost a constant inmate of Holland House, and after the death of Lord Holland, continued to reside there for some years. Mr. Allen contributed largely to the "Edinburgh Review." He was profoundly versed in history, and singularly clever in unravelling difficulties, and applying his knowledge of past times to present circumstances, and passing subjects of public or literary interest.

* Sir James Mackintosh.

For upwards of forty years, Mr. Allen mingled with the scientific and literary society of Holland House; in the library of Holland House, and in its salons, with the best books, "in which every talent and accomplishment, every art and science had its place,"* and the most distinguished people. Mr. Allen passed as long a period in literary and social ease and enjoyment, as Moses passed in the wilderness, wandering in dismal and dreary places. Mr. Allen was one of the members of the commission of public records, and a master of Dulwich College.

SIR DAVID WILKIE, R.A.

Lady Blessington made the acquaintance of Wilkie in Italy. In her journal at Pisa, in March, 1827, she mentions the celebrated painter spending a few days with her. Elsewhere she frequently alludes to his remarkable simplicity, and amiability of disposition.

When deeply engaged in his professional pursuits, his whole mind was absorbed in them. He was so abstracted when thus engaged, that passing occurrences, or the entrance of visitors, and presence of persons in his studio, often seemed unperceived by him. His friends recounted many amusing traits of his absence of mind, and characteristic simplicity, and no doubt embellished many of them.

He is represented as lamenting in his studio, an act of savagery committed in his absence—" his model had been eaten in it." The model thus made away with, turned out to be a biscuit which he had been " painting from nature."

Wilkie had extreme difficulty in comprehending the point of a good joke—and a strange propensity to make puns, which, however well begun, always ended abortively.

* Macaulay, of Holland House.—Ed. Rev.

Lady Blessington used to tell of his being found once at a friend's house in a deep reverie—contemplating some repairs that were being made on the roof of the house, and while striving hard to effect a pun on the word roof, repeating aloud, "Rufus! Rufus! yes, there was a monarch of that name: dilapidated houses might well cry out . . ." then looking up at the roof, exclaiming, "yes, truly, something might be made of it;" and then abandoning the attempt, failing to do anything successful with his embryo pun.

Wilkie commenced his career in London in 1805, with his Village Politicians. He was one of those fortunate children of genius, who commence their career with complete success—who go to bed on a particular night unknown and unappreciated, awaken the next day, rise with the sun shining on their fortunes, and find themselves famous all at once.*

From 1825 to 1828, ill health of mind and body compelled Wilkie to cease his more arduous labours, and to make a continental tour in Spain and Italy. In the latter country his head-quarters were chiefly at Rome.

In 1841, he was again obliged to abandon his occupation, and to travel for his health. He proceeded to the East, and returned to his own land no more.

* The following was the succession of Wilkie's principal works from 1805 to 1825:—"The Village Politicians," in 1805; "The Blind Fiddler," 1807; "The Card Player," 1808; "The Cut Finger," 1809; "The Rent Day," 1809; "Boys Digging for Rats," 1811; "A Game-keeper," same year; "Blind Man's Buff," 1812; "The Village Festival," 1813; "The Letter of Introduction," 1814; "Distraining for Rent," 1815; "The Rabbit on the Wall," 1816; "The Breakfast," 1817; "The Errand Boy," 1818; "The Abbotsford Family," 1819; "The Penny Wedding," 1820; "The Reading of the Will," 1821; "The News-mongers," 1822; "The Chelsea Pensioners," 1823; "The Parish Beadle," 1824; "The Smugglers," 1825; &c. &c. &c.

The works of Wilkie, like those of Hogarth, possess one great claim to admiration, which caprice or fashion, and the revolutions in art, and style, and taste, can never seriously affect. They are true to nature, and they are indicative of generous feelings and general sympathies with humanity at large.

Wilkie was born at Culls, near Cupar, in Fifeshire, in 1785. He died in the roads of Gibraltar, the 1st of June, 1841, on board the Oriental, on his return from Egypt, in his fifty-fifth year.

DANIEL MACLISE, R.A.

The city of Cork has given some very eminent men to art and literature. Daniel Maclise was born in Cork, in 1811. From his earliest years, he manifested a great taste for art and considerable talents for drawing. The desk of a banking-house was relinquished by him for the easel, before he was sixteen. He commenced his career as a professional artist, by painting portraits, and drawing landscapes and sketches of the peasantry in his rambles in search of the picturesque along the banks of the Blackwater, and, at a later period, of the Avon and Avoca, and the grotesque in all congregations of the people, at fares, wakes, weddings, and patterns.

Young Maclise studied, not only in his profession, in galleries and studios, but for it in anatomical schools, and even in dissecting rooms; and likewise in libraries, he made himself thoroughly acquainted with the history of art and artists.

The first drawing of his that was exhibited in the Royal Academy, Somerset House, was in 1828. He was successful from the start in London in that year. He obtained two prizes before he was twelve months in London; one for a drawing after the antique; another for a copy of a Guido.*

After having studied in the Paris galleries for some time, he commenced his career in London in oil painting, on a large scale, and obtained the gold medal of the Academy in 1831, for his " Choice of Hercules." From that period his status in English art was determined—his succeeding works were so many successive triumphs. His principal productions appeared in the following order:—

1832, " Allhallows' Eve;" 1833, " Love Adventure of Francis;" 1834, " The Installation of Captain Rock," and " Illustrations of Bulwer's Pilgrims of the Rhine;" 1835, " The Ladies and the Peacock:" between that period and 1840, when he was elected a Royal Academician, he painted some of his best works, among which were the " Interview between Charles I. and Cromwell;" " Macbeth and the Witches;" since 1840, his numerous works have established his early fame. Few modern artists have produced so many works, so few of which have been unsuccessful.

The artist who painted " Malvolio smiling on Olivia;" " The Banquet Scene in Macbeth;" " Scene from Undine;" and " Macready as Werner," has condescended to lend his talents to the illustration of Magazines and Annuals, and even, in his early days, to contribute his poetical talents to some of them.

Lady Blessington was frequently indebted to him for sketches for her " Keepsake" and " Book of Beauty," which illustrations contributed not a little to their success.

* Cork can boast of having given birth to many very distinguished artists. Rogers, " the father of landscape painting in Ireland;" his pupil Butts, who commenced his career as a scene painter, at Crow Street Theatre; Nathaniel Grogan, a self-taught artist, a man of considerable talents; John Corbet, an eminent portrait painter; Barry, the celebrated painter; Hogan, one of the first of living British sculptors; and lastly, Maclise, the subject of this brief notice.

Maclise was a constant visitor and a favoured guest at Gore House. D'Orsay had a great regard for him, and was an enthusiastic admirer of his works.

SIR EDWIN LANDSEER, K.B., R.A.

The father of the renowned and unrivalled painter of animals,was an engraver of celebrity. Edwin Landseer was born in 1803. His great merits not merely as a painter of deer, and dogs, and horses,but as a great artist, most skilful in his delineation of human figure,and of original genius in the representation of vast subjects, in small isolated series of individualized parts of them, conceived and wrought with such powers of comprehension and concentration, that in a single episode of " Peace," and " War," all the blessings of the former, and all the horrors of the latter, are conveyed to the mind of the person who looks on small pictures of Maclise, on those master-pieces of his, " Peace," and " War." Landseer, true to the dignified character of high art, has not lent its aid to the glorifications of war, in the great picture of his which bears that name. He represents war in one of its results—a desolated rural scene, distant gleams of conflagration, a lurid sky, a wasted garden, a ruined peasant hut ; and all that we have of the immediate horrors of battle—is a dead horse, and the rider slain, with the foot stretched across the saddle.

This eminent artist was elected a Royal Academician in 1831, and was created a K.B. in 1850.

It has been my good fortune on several occasions to have met this distinguished artist at Lady Blessington's.

Few of the frequenters of Gore House were more sincerely esteemed and more kindly received, on all occasions, than Sir E. Landseer. Independently of his great eminence in his profession, the wonderful fidelity of his representations, so true to nature, so full of originality, poetry, and quaintness of conception, so perfect in touch and execution ; his social qualities, his facility for diffusing pleasure, and being pleased by those around him ; his anecdotal talent, his refined tastes and manners, secured him a hearty welcome in every circle, and the most distinguished society. There is in Landseer's compositions an exquisite delicacy of organization, an acute sense of perception of all that is harmonious in nature or art, a nervous susceptibility of all impressions, pleasing or poetical, such as it would be difficult to find in other artists. His chefs-d'œuvre are "The Highland Drovers," "Laying down the Law," "Bolton Abbey," "Lady and Spaniels," "The Sanctuary," "The Challenge," "High Life and Low Life," "Jack in Office," "Shepherd's Grave, and Chief Mourner."

BENJAMIN ROBERT HAYDON, ESQ.

The recently published life of this great artist, from his Autobiography and Journal (edited by Tom Taylor and Son, 1853), exhibits the struggles of a man of high purposes and bold independent mind, who braved all sorts of enmities and opposition, for one glorious object—the elevation of the art of his country. He waged this war, that began in manhood, and ended with his life, without wealth, title, powerful patronage, or protection.

The style of painting, with all its grandeur and with least of its defects, is best exhibited in his "Solomon," "Jerusalem," "Dentatus," "Macbeth," "Napoleon," "Lazarus," "The Mock Election," "Eucles," "Aristides," and "Curtius." Haydon's style of writing—perspicuous, vigorous, and pithy, is shewn to best advantage in his diaries, and to least in his letters.

SIR GEORGE HAYTER.

The earlier works of this eminent painter gave great promise of excellence; but it is the calamity of artists who have been early patronized by royal personages, to abandon nature in her simple forms and humble aspects, for subjects appertaining to state ceremorials, court pageants, or royal progresses suggested by courtiers, or commanded by sovereigns, or their consorts. Sir George Hayter has been much patronized by the Queen and Prince Albert.

RICHARD J. WYATT, ESQ.

Mr. Wyatt went to Rome in 1822, and worked for some time in the studio of Mr. Gibson. A recent account of his career, in the "Gentleman's Magazine," makes mention of him as "the eminent British sculptor, whose works are so well known at home, and whose fame is spread in every part of the world where the fine arts are valued." He is said to have executed commissions to the extent of £20,000 sterling.

Frequent mention will be found of him in Lady Blessington's "Idler in Italy."

He died in Rome, the 27th May, 1850, in his 57th year.

THOMAS UWINS, ESQ. R.A.

Among the many artists either already eminent or rising to eminence, who made the acquaintance of Lady Blessington in Italy, was Mr. Uwins the painter, who in 1824 was introduced to her Ladyship at Naples, by Sir William Gell. Mr. Uwins had already acquired celebrity by several works, in which the glowing scenery and picturesque inhabitants of Rome and Naples, were delineated in a style of the highest excellence.

FRANCIS GRANT, ESQ.

This eminent artist, remarkable for his excellence in painting horses, and the style of his portraits in general—the striking resemblances given in them, and the grand simplicity of character with which they are invested—is of ancient Scotch family. He commenced life with a large fortune, and having lost it, he determined to turn his talents to account, and became a professional artist. One of the first portraits he painted professionally, was the well-known equestrian one of Count D'Orsay, who was an intimate friend of his. The Count had previously, I think, executed a fine bust and statuette of the artist. Mr. Grant has the advantages of a fine person and gentlemanly manners. He is highly esteemed by those who know him for his integrity and worth. He has been twice married. His present wife is a niece of the Duke of Rutland.

EMILE DE GIRARDIN.

This eminent French Journalist was born in Paris, about 1802. Early in life he established a literary journal, and had proceedings taken against him by his own father, for assuming the name of his litigious parent. He became connected at different periods with a great number of literary journals; at the time of the Revolution of February, he held the office of "Inspecteur des Beaux Arts." In the several periodicals conducted by him, he has invariably displayed a great fund of cleverness, of common sense, of practical business-like habits; but all his journals broke down in the long run, and some of his distinct works—his "Emilie" among others.

He married a celebrated literary lady, Mademoiselle Delphine Gay,* and entered into another kind of joint-stock partnership

* Byron, in a letter to Moore, speaks of a romantic Parisian corre-

with a gentleman, a clever, speculative man, who, in conjunction with his friend, established the "Presse" newspaper in 1836, one of the most influential of all the journals of France. In a previous joint-stock speculation he had been unsuccessful, and was prosecuted for defrauding the shareholders, by paying dividends out of capital, and was acquitted of the charge.

The foolish notion that a newspaper was to be established and sustained, in order to advance particular political opinions, and not solely with a view to the promotion of pecuniary interests, or individual advantages in political speculations, was never professed, much less entertained, by Monsieur Girardin. Few ministries, and prominent leaders of parties, have not been occasionally dallied with or denounced, turned for some time to an account, advocated in it, or, being found to be impracticable and untractable, warred on with great energy and ability. This eminent journalist claims the merit of being "no party man." *He gives to mankind* all he has to give—his "Presse," and gets as much as he can for it. Parisian newspaper advertising, under his editorship, vied to some extent with that of the "Times." This very clear sighted journalist, several years ago, perceived that the different factions of the Chambers were bringing parliamentary intrigues, alias French constitutional politics, into disrepute. The public—"hors des factions"—were becoming sick of reading of their sayings and doings. He invented the *feuilleton* system; he cut off half a foot or more of politics on each paper, and devoted the space to spicy novels, of the convulsive, compendious style of modern French romance, and discarded dull political writers for the sentimental celebrities and thrilling-interest authors of the greatest vogue at the time—Balzac, Dumas, Dudevant, Sue, Soulie, &c.

spondent of his, Sophia Gay. This lady was the mother of the celebrated poetess and beauty, Mademoiselle Delphine Gay, we are told by Moore.

About five years ago, the "Presse" was making, clear of all expenses, nearly 200,000 francs a year. Louis Napoleon in December, 1852, took some measures for the improvement of public morality, against the promulgation of political opinions which might not be in harmony with his own views of the interests of order, and his own Idées Napolèens. He wrote a few lines—published them in the "Moniteur"—the independent journals were suppressed. Poor Monsieur Girardin and his partners lost 200,000 francs a year; but then they have the great consolation of knowing that Les Idées Napolèens have prevailed, and the Empire is established, even though it be on the ruins of the press.

M. Girardin lent his aid in the Chamber of Deputies, and in his journal, to pull down the ministry of Guizot, and to discredit the power and authority of his master. At the period of the downfall of Louis Philippe, he was busy in the closing affairs of the unfortunate Citizen-King; without any ostensible mission from any party, or authority for taking on himself the office of counsellor of the ruined sovereign, he assumed that office, and received the act of abdication from the hands of Louis Philippe. He gained nothing by this service to the Republican cause. It inspired no confidence, and obtained no recompense.

During the short régime of Cavaignac, M. Girardin was for some time under arrest, and the surveillance of the police.

M. Girardin has once more taken to newspaper writing, as it now is permitted to exist in France—handcuffed journalism—every effort of which reminds the writer of the shackles on the hand that holds the pen, and makes the reader feel as if the attempt at freedom of discussion was akin to the mockery of that amusement which is witnessed in Carolina—the dancing of slaves in the presence of their drivers, in sight of the lash, and perhaps of some of their fellow-slaves in the stocks.

In 1834, M. Girardin turned his attention to his advancement in the senatorial line; he became a member of the Chamber of Deputies. Two years later, he commenced a fierce war of aggression on the character of the editor of a rival newspaper—Armand Carrel, of the "National,"—a man of great ability, and, for a French journalist professing patriotism, a man of singular integrity and sincerity of principle, and of singleness of mind. Carrel challenged the aggressor, and the young republican editor of the "National" was killed by the editor of the "Presse."

SAMUEL CARTER HALL, ESQ.—MRS. A. M. HALL.

Mr. Hall was born at Topsham, Devonshire, in 1800. In conjunction with Mrs. Hall, some of the most popular illustrated works on Ireland have been published by him. Mr. Hall edited the "New Monthly" for several years. He established the Art Union. He edited the "Book of Gems," the "Book of British Poets," "Book of British Ballads," "Baronial Halls," and several other illustrated works.

The principal works of Mrs. Hall are, "Sketches of Irish Character," in 2 vols.; "The Buccaneer," in 3 vols.; "The Outlaw," in 3 vols.; "Uncle Horace," in 3 vols.; "Lights and Shadows of Irish Life," in 3 vols.; "Marian, or a Young Maid's Fortunes," in 3 vols.; "The Whiteboy," in 2 vols.; "Stories of a Governess," &c. in 1 vol.

Mr. and Mrs. Hall were for many years on terms of very intimate acquaintance with Lady Blessington. Lady Blessington's regard for Mrs. Hall, and appreciation of her talents, were often warmly expressed, when that lady was not present; and Mrs. Hall's kindly sentiments towards the memory of Lady Blessington, have been recently expressed to me in a way which does great credit to that lady, and affords matter for reflection, by comparison, by no means favourable to many who professed to be the friends of Lady Blessington while she lived in splendour, but when the crash came, and the brilliant salons of Gore House were no longer open to them—and a little later, when the grave had closed over the remains of the poor mistress of that noble mansion—were unwilling to be reminded of their former protestations of regard, and perhaps considerately thus acted, conscious as they were of the hollowness of those professions.

A person in humble life, but of high principles and right notions, on all subjects within the scope of her knowledge and observations, having a perfect knowledge of Lady Blessington and all that concerned her, for the last eighteen years of her life, thus expresses herself to me, on the subject that has been glanced at in the preceding remark:—" My opinion is, that no woman ever was overwhelmed with such professions of friendship and attachment from so great a number of insincere acquaintances."

There are many exceptions, I must observe, to the rule—if such it may be considered, in this assertion.

LADY E. S. WORTLEY.

Lady Emmeline Charlotte Elizabeth Stuart Wortley, a daughter of the Duke of Rutland, born in 1806, married the Hon. Charles Stuart Wortley, a brother of the present Earl of Wharncliffe, who died in 1844. Lady Emmeline has travelled much, and contributed a great deal to our periodical literature. Her performances are chiefly poetical; some of them of considerable merit. If there be not evidence in them of the highest order of talent, there are ample proofs in them of an amiable disposition, of kindly and benevolent feelings, and of a generous and noble nature.

Of the many fair contributors to the "Book of Beauty," there are few whose compositions rank higher than those of Lady Emmeline Stuart Wortley.

There are some lines on death, of this gifted and amiable

lady, in the volume for 1843, of much beauty, beginning thus:—

> "Say, what shall still this bounding heart,
> Bounding as boundless—strong and wild?
> Or what shall heal each wounded part,
> With gentlest healings, soft and mild,
> And still this restless storm of breath;—
> Death!"

Lady Emmeline Stuart Wortley edited "The Keepsake" in 1836 and 1837.

Among her prose articles in that annual, 1837, there is an article of much interest, entitled, "A Visit to Madame Letitia, Mother of Napoleon, May 26, 1834."

She has published "Travels in the United States, during 1849–50," in three volumes; and a continuation of her "Travels in America, and other Sketches," in one volume.

G. P. R. JAMES.

Few novelists, with the exception of Dumas, have equalled Mr. James in fertility, and apparent facility in production. It is impossible that so many compositions should not be of very unequal merit. Few of them, however slightly constructed, or hastily executed, are devoid of interest. The titles alone of his novels will serve to exhibit the extraordinary rapidity of production above noticed.

As the demand in this case, as well as in that of other commodities, must regulate the supply, it follows that the novel-reading public are satisfied with these brain stuffs of their hard-worked author.

With several of his works they have a good right to be content—and with some, it is probable, the writer himself is not. These are the novels of Mr. James, "and their name is Legion :"—Richelieu ; Darnley ; Delorme ; Henry Masterton ; The Gypsey ; Philip Augustus ; Mary of Burgundy ; John Marston Hall ; One in a Thousand ; The Desultory Man ; The Robber ; Attila ; The Huguenot ; Charles Tyrrell ; Rose D'Albert ; The Step-mother ; The Smuggler ; Delaware ; Agincourt ; Arrah Neil ; Heidelburg ; The King's Highway ; The Man-at-Arms ; Corse de Leon ; Henry of Guise ; The Ancient Régime ; The Jacquerie ; Morley Ernstein ; Forest Days ; Eva St. Clair ; The False Heir ; Arabella Stuart ; The Castle of Ehrenstein ; Russell ; The Convict ; The Whim and its Consequences ; Margaret Graham ; Sir Theodore Broughton ; Gowrie, or the King's Prize ; Beauchamp ; The Forgery ; The String of Pearls ; The Woodman ; The Old Oak Chest ; Henry Smeaton ; Fate ; Revenge ; Pequenello. In all, 138 volumes !

Sidney Smith's account of the anti-diluvian diffusive style of writing, (*à propos* of Dr. Parr's Character of Fox,) should be commended to the attention of all voluminous, as well as of lengthy and extensive writers.

" There is an event recorded in the Bible, which by men who write books, should be kept constantly in their remembrance. It is there set forth, that many centuries ago, the earth was covered with a great flood, by which the whole of the human race, with the exception of one family, were destroyed. It appears also, that from thence, a great alteration was made in the longevity of mankind, who, from a range of seven or eight hundred years, which they enjoyed before the flood, were confined to their present period of seventy or eighty years. This epoch in the history of man gave birth to the twofold division of the ante-diluvian and the post-diluvian style of writing, the latter of which naturally contracted itself into those inferior limits, which were better accommodated to the abridged duration of human life and literary labour. Now to forget this event,—to write without the fear of the deluge before his eyes, and to a handle a subject as if mankind could lounge over a pamphlet for ten years, as before their submersion,—is to be guilty of the most grievous error into which a writer could possibly fall. The author of this book should call in the aid of some brilliant pencil, and cause the distressing scenes of the deluge to be pourtrayed in the most lively colours for his use. He should gaze at Noah, and be brief. The ark should constantly remind him of the little time there is left for reading: and he should learn, as they did in the ark, to crowd a great deal of matter into a very little compass:"—a valuable suggestion to more authors than Dr. Parr.

Sismondi tells us, his great History of the Italian Republics occupied him for eight hours a day during a period of twenty years; and when he finished that work, he sat down to a new literary labour, "The History of France," which occupied him for the same length of time daily for a period of twenty-four years.

Now, if we deduct the Sundays from the period devoted to each work, and allow the hard worker of the brain one day in the week to rest his wearied mind, we shall find that this great historian devoted to his work on the Italian Republics, 50,080 hours of his life; and to that on French History, 61,086 hours; the sum-total of which labour, on two works, amounts to 111,166 hours!!!

Yet, we are told by Southey, "the best book does but little good to the world, and much harm to the author."

W. M. THACKERAY, ESQ.

An artist and an author, with talent sufficient for success in either pursuit, Mr. Thackeray commenced his career in London some years ago, and for some time had to struggle through many difficulties. He began by the publication of some illustrated tales and sketches of slight merit. His peculiar talents soon found numerous persons to appreciate them. His "Vanity Fair" made his reputation, and surpassed his other works. Perhaps, in merit, his "Pendennis" approaches nearest to it, and next to that production, his "Harry Esmond." He began his career as a painter, but soon abandoned that pursuit for literature. He illustrated some of his early works. He has travelled much, and is a good linguist. Few persons who entertain the ordinary opinions that are held concerning humourists, would imagine the sterling qualities of solid worth and faithfulness in friendship which belong to Mr. Thackeray. With strangers, reserved and *uncommunicative;* to those who know him, he is openhearted, kindly-disposed, and generous. To great sensibility, and an innate love of all that is good and noble, he unites sentiments of profound hatred and contempt for falsehood, meanness, worldliness, and hypocrisy; and a rare power of satirizing and exposing it. In analyzing character and describing its various shades of difference, he possesses great strength and originality of style and expression.

His latest occupation has been the delivery of Lectures in the United States, on the wits and miscellaneous humourist writers of the last century, which had been commenced by him in England.

His principal productions are, "Our Street," in one vol.; "Vanity Fair," one vol.; "Book of Snobs," one vol.; "Pendennis," two vols.; "Great Hoggarty Diamond," one vol.; "Doctor Birch," one vol.; "Rebecca and Rowena," one vol.; "Comic Tales," two vols.

WASHINGTON IRVING.

A glance at one of the eminent of our transalantic celebrities in the "Homes of the New World," will give a tolerable idea of the external man, his manners, and mode of life.

IRVING AT HOME.

"His house, or villa, which stands on the banks of the Hudson, resembles a peaceful idyll; thick masses of ivy clothe one portion of the white walls and garland the eaves. Fat cows fed in a meadow just before the window. Within, the rooms seemed to be full of summer warmth, and had a peaceful and cheerful aspect. One felt that a cordial spirit, full of the best sentiment of the soul, lived and worked there. Washington Irving, although possessing the politeness of a man of the world, and with great natural good temper, has, nevertheless, somewhat of that nervous shyness which so easily attaches itself to the author, and in particular to one gifted with delicacy of feeling and refinement. The poetical mind, by its intercourse with the divine spheres, is often brought somewhat into disharmony with clumsy earthly realities. To these belong especially the visits of strangers, and the forms of social life, as we make them in good society upon earth, and which are shells that must be cracked if one would get at the juice of either kernel or fruit. But that is a difficulty for which one often has not time. A portrait which hangs in Washington Irving's drawing-room, and which was painted many years since, represents him as a remarkably handsome man, with dark hair and eyes, a head which might have belonged to a Spaniard. When young, he must have been unusually handsome. He was engaged to a young lady of rare beauty and excellence; it would have been difficult to find a more handsome pair. But she died — and Washington Irving never sought for another bride. He has been wise enough to content himself with the memory of a perfect love, and to live for literature, friendship, and nature."*

WILLIAM HARRISON AINSWORTH, ESQ.

The author of "Rookwood," "Crichton,"† "Jack Sheppard," "The Tower of London," "Guy Fawkes," "Old

* "Homes of the New World," by Frederika Bremer.

† Mr. Ainsworth, it is said, in this character intended the portraiture of Count D'Orsay.

Saint Pauls," "The Miser's Daughter," "Windsor Castle," "Saint James and Saint Giles," &c., was well known to Lady Blessington, and appreciated by her.

Mr. Ainsworth, it need hardly be observed, is a man of talent and research, of great facility in composing, successful in dealing with historical incidents, depicting character, presenting striking scenes with historical incidents, giving to works of imagination a life-like air, and sustaining an interest in his stories.

J. H. JESSE, ESQ.

The subject of this notice is a young man of remarkable abilities and strong contrasts of character. A few years ago, to the most singular passion for boyish freaks and fantastic frolics, practical jokes, and ludicrous recreations, he added the very opposite predilection for hard study and close research. Historical literature has occupied him chiefly. He has published "The Court of England, from the Revolution in 1688 to the death of George the Second," in three volumes; "Memoirs of the Pretenders," in two volumes; "Memoirs of the Court of England during the reign of the Stuarts," in four volumes, an extensive and interesting picture of the period, full of research, yet amusing and gracefully written; "Memoirs of George Selwyn and his Cotemporaries," in four volumes; his other works present the same general features of interest and instruction.

In 1848, Mr. J. H. Jesse published "Literary and Historical Memorials of London;" and in 1850, a second series of that work, under the title of "London and its Celebrities," two vols. 8vo., Bentley.

HENRY F. CHORLEY, ESQ.

As a litterateur and musical critic, Mr. Chorley holds a high place, and still higher, in every society he frequents, as an amiable gentleman, of honourable principles, strongly attached to his friends, and entirely confided in by them. Though reserved and silent in the presence of strangers, in the company of those he is intimately acquainted with, he is communicative and agreeable. He has travelled on the Continent, and made good use of his powers of observation and keen perception of the ridiculous. He possesses a fine musical organization, a delicate ear, and refined taste, though not a musical performer of much excellence on any instrument. His style of writing is quaint, original, and always in good taste. His principal works are, "Pomfret, or Public Opinions and Private Judgments," a novel, in three volumes; "Sketches of a Sea-Port Town," in three volumes; also some plays, and numerous poetical pieces in various periodicals. Mr. Chorley was very intimately acquainted with Lady Blessington, and was held in high regard by her.

WILLIAM JERDAN, ESQ.

This gentleman, for many years editor and principal writer in the "Literary Gazette," in his recently published "Reminiscences," has given the world an account of his career as a journalist. My acquaintance with him extends over a period of twenty years. In conversation, as well as in writing, he exhibited considerable talents and information. He was well versed in the literature of the day, and the state of art and science of his time, and for many years the paper he edited was one of the most able journals dedicated to these subjects. In society his conversation was sprightly and agreeable, with a dash of dry humour in it, that savoured more of Scotch than of Irish wit; but there was often a piquancy in his remarks, which gave a peculiar zest to his conversation, and rendered his society amusing to people in general.

Mr. Jerdan, prior to 1815, had conducted the "Satirist." Afterwards he became a partner in the "Sun" evening paper, of which he was the joint editor with Mr. Taylor. He published, nearly forty years ago "The Paris Spectator," in three vols. 12mo., also a translation of Mon. Jouy's well-known work of "Il Hermite de la Chaussèe D'Antin." Mr. Jerdan, from 1817 to the close of 1850, was editor of the "Literary Gazette." In April, 1853, a pension of £100 a year was conferred on him in consideration of his literary labours. For some years before his retirement from the "Literary Gazette," he was harassed by pecuniary difficulties, and heavily afflicted by domestic calamities. On the occasion of his retirement, he received testimonials of regard from the foremost of his contemporaries, literary, scientific, and artistic. Mr. Jerdan lately edited "Tallis's Weekly Newspaper."

WILLIAM CHARLES MACREADY.

This eminent tragedian was born in London in 1793, and educated chiefly at the celebrated school at Rugby. His father, who was a lessee and manager of several provincial theatres, had intended to bring up his son to the legal profession, and was about sending him to Oxford, when his affairs became embarrassed, and caused these plans to be relinquished. The boy was taken from school to assist his father, and transferred to the stage in 1810, and made his first appearance in a provincial theatre in the character of Romeo, when he was scarcely seventeen years of age. His *débût* was successful, and his career continued to be so in many of the theatres of the chief towns in England for four or five years. In 1815 he visited England and Scotland with great success; and in 1816 made his first appearance on the London boards at Covent Garden, in the character of Orestes, in "The Distressed Mother." His first appearance in London was a decided hit; but the establishment of his fame and position on the London stage, with such competitors as Kemble, Kean, and Young, was a long and arduous struggle, and for nearly ten years it had to be maintained before he could be said to be a great tragedian, worthy of representing the great Shaksperian tragic characters. The highest place in tragedy was held for nearly a quarter of a century by Mr. Macready. This eminent actor studied for his profession, and considered that to be a great actor it was advisable for him to become a good scholar, an accomplished gentleman, a well-ordered man, with a well-regulated mind, and finely-cultivated taste. In France and in America, as well as in his own country, Mr. Macready not only won golden opinions from all kinds of people, but wore his honours well to the end of his theatrical career. He retired from the stage a few years ago, universally esteemed, admired, and respected.

In March, 1851, a banquet, on an extraordinary scale of magnificence, was given at the Hall of Commerce in London, on the occasion of Mr. Macready's retirement from the stage. Of the merits of Mr. Macready, which received so much applause on that occasion, "The Athenæum" observed—

"We look back to what we remember of other actors,—we look round to what is still to be seen, and it is precisely because we do not think that Mr. Macready has brought his art to the highest measure of excellence, that we refuse to concede to him the attribute of genius in its strictest sense, as distinct from talent. An actor may have a good figure, expressive features, a fine voice, a keen intellect, a cultivated taste, an educated eye for the picturesque, large experience of the external signs of passion, and great power in expressing them; he may have knowledge of life, of history, literature, and art; Mr. Macready *has* all these—yet will not their possession establish a claim to the so often rashly misapplied epithet of genius. Hard to define, its presence is never to be mistaken. Its power in the performer is akin to that of the dramatic poet. You do not see the individual character in the man he is portraying, any more than you see the individual poet. Sentence by sentence, and scene by scene, the character developes before you. Not this burst, nor that look, arrests you by the way; you are borne resistlessly along by a power which at once satisfies the imagination and the heart. Critical you cannot be, while under its spell; but when all is over, and the imagination cools, the image of the man's whole nature is left a living reality in your memory, and you feel that such he was, and that he could be no otherwise. Whence comes this power, but from the quick and deep sensitiveness of a nature that sympathises with, and can lose itself in all forms of humanity—a quality which belongs to the great actor in comedy as well as in tragedy—nay, which, we believe, makes him who is greatest in the one great also in the other? This quickness and breadth of sympathy—this power of losing himself in his part, we have always missed in Mr. Macready. He lent it to him, he did not lend himself to it. We recognised the able illustrator, but we never bowed before the unconscious inspiration of genius. In his greatest scenes there was nothing, as Horace Walpole said of Mrs. Siddons, 'which good sense or good instruction might not give.' Looking steadily to the laurel from the first, sparing no labour, avoiding no self-denial, Mr. Macready's ambition has not only been crowned with success, but with success have come all those collateral advantages which embellish and sweeten life."

R. M. MILNES, ESQ., M.P.

Mr. Milnes devoted much of his time and talents to literary pursuits some ten or twelve years ago. He published several poetical pieces in the periodicals, of merit, in the early part of his career, and even of late years has occasionally relinquished political pursuits for those of literature. In 1839 he published his collected Poems.

For some years he was a regular contributor to the Annuals edited by Lady Blessington, and his pieces, whether in prose or verse, were always marked by a high moral tone, by liveliness of fancy, originality of mind, and correctness of taste and style. In politics, he was a strenuous supporter of the late Lord George Bentinck, and ally of Mr. D'Israeli.

In private circles, he stands high as a man of amiability, as well as talent, of straightforward views and honourable principles, kind hearted, and agreeable in society. In the past year, he married the Hon. Miss Crewe, daughter of Lord Crewe.

Louis Blanc, in August and September, 1848, when an exile in England, was known to Count D'Orsay and Lady Blessington. In reference to an attack that had been made on him, charging him with inciting the populace against the government of which he was a member, Lady Blessington had recourse to the recollections of her friend Mr. Monckton Milnes, who had been in Paris at the time; and a statement was made in September, 1848, of his remembrance of the occurrences, referred to of the 15th of May, which exculpated the exiled republican from the charge brought against him.

RALPH BERNAL OSBORNE, ESQ.

Mr. Bernal Osborne, both in society and in public, is remarkable for those qualities which manifest originality of mind, great quickness of perception, and liveliness of imagination, energy of thought and language, and enthusiasm in any cause or side of a question espoused by him. He was a frequent and talented contributor for several years to the Annuals edited by Lady Blessington.

Captain Robert Bernal, on his marriage with the only daughter and heiress of Sir Thomas Toler Osborne, of Newtown, county Tipperary, the eighth Baronet of the name—

a near relative of the notorious Judge Toler, the Lord Norbury of 1798—formerly Chief Justice of the Common Pleas, —assumed the name of Osborne, and is now Secretary of the Admiralty, and M.P. for Middlesex.

The old family estates of this branch of the Tolers passed away by this marriage.

ALEXANDER BAILLIE COCHRANE, ESQ.

This gentleman, of great promise in his early days, the son of Sir Thomas Cochrane, R.N., travelled in the East and Greece, and sojourned in Southern Europe sufficiently long to acquire a taste for its arts and literature. He has written many pieces of merit in the Annuals and other periodicals, and those "vers de société," which serve, at least, as presages of talents fitted for future occupations of more importance and utility. His first introduction into public life, is said to have been in the ranks of the Protectionists, under Lord George Bentinck.

Mr. Cochrane, in the literary society of Gore House, passed for "a young man of refined tastes and good abilities, of a romantic turn of mind, and enthusiastic temperament; somewhat given to exercise his intellectual faculties in startling paradoxes, and the maintenance of propositions requiring ingenuity and courage to sustain." A work of fiction, entitled "Ernest Vane," by Mr. Cochrane, in two volumes, appeared some years ago.

TERRICK HAMILTON, ESQ.

Mr. Hamilton was for some time in the East India Company's service; was officially employed abroad in 1811; was appointed Oriental Secretary of Embassy at Constantinople in 1815, and Secretary of Embassy in 1815, when he obtained a pension.

HENRY REEVE, ESQ.

The letters of Mr. Reeve correspond to his conversational talents. He is an amateur in literature, writes prose and verse with grace and facility; and though possessing excellent abilities, has figured hitherto as an author only in Annuals and Albums. His knowledge of language, and acquaintance with continental literature, and general information, and agreeableness of manner, are exhibited fully, but not ostentatiously, in conversation. His high character as a man of honour and integrity, gives an additional advantage to his intellectual qualities in society. His popularity in it is of that kind which is most readily accorded to talent, when united with amiability of disposition, kind heartedness, and good nature.

Mr. Reeve, a few years ago, held a post in the Privy Council Office, and there he enjoyed the good opinion and confidence of the Marquis of Lansdowne, Lord John Russell, Lord Minto, and other influential men.

HENRY CHESTER, ESQ.

Mr. Henry Chester was attached to the late Lord William Russell's special mission to Lisbon, in 1833; had been a Clerk in the Council Office from 1826; and is now Assistant Secretary to the Committee of Council on Education.

C. GREVILLE, ESQ.

The position of this gentleman in society, his high character for intelligence and literary acquirements, his knowledge of public affairs and eminent public men, his high standing too, in official life, as Clerk of the Council, give him much consideration and influence in the circles of his acquaintance. Mr. Greville is a well-known member of the turf. He is of a noble family. His mother, Lady Charlotte Greville, I believe, was daughter of the third Duke of Portland, who married Charles Greville, Esq., in 1793.

T. N. LONGMAN, ESQ.

Mr. Thomas Norton Longman, who died in 1842, in his seventy-second year, was well known to Lady Blessington, and highly respected by her. From the period of the death of his father in 1797, he had been at the head of the great publishing firm of Longman, Hurst, Rees, Orme, Brown, Green, and Longman (all of whom had been at various times his partners). Mr. Longman's personal property amounted to nearly £200,000. He left two sons, Thomas and Charles, his successors in the business, who had been his partners. His eldest daughter was married to Andrew Spottiswoode, Esq., the Queen's Printer.

COUNT VON KIELMANSEGG.

The Count was an intimate acquaintance and a correspondent of Lady Blessington. He was a General in the Hanoverian service, and died at Linden, aged 83, in September, 1851. He was born at Ratzebourg, in 1768; entered the army in 1793; served against the French in Holland, and commanded a brigade at Waterloo.

F. MILLS, ESQ.

In Rome, Mr. Mills resided in a beautiful villa, on the Mount Palatine; "it occupies," says Lady Blessington, "the site of the palace of the Cæsars, and is arranged with exquisite taste. The gardens are charming beyond description, presenting an unrivalled view of Rome and the Campagna, and containing some most interesting fragments of antiquity, seen to peculiar advantage, mingled with trees and flowering plants, of luxuriant growth. The owner of this terrestrial palace is worthy of it; possessing a highly cultivated mind, great suavity of manners, and qualities of the head and heart, that have endeared him to all who knew him."

Mr. Frank Mills has been confounded with Charles Mills (born in 1788, and deceased in 1828), the author of "The History of Mahommedanism," "History of the Crusades," "Travels of Theodore Ducas, at the period of the revival of Arts in Italy," and "The History of Chivalry."*

Mr. Charles Mills has had the honour likewise, of being taken for the author of "The History of India," and complimented on its merits—for James Mill, who died in 1836.

THE DUC DI ROCCO ROMANO.

The Duc di Rocco Romano, one of Lady Blessington's intimate friends when residing in Naples, in 1824, was a Neapolitan General of some celebrity, and, in the opinion of Lady Blessington, the very personification of a *preux chevalier*, "brave in arms, and gentle and courteous in society." Though upwards of sixty years of age at the period referred to, the old General was full of life and vivacity—a man of gallantry in every sense of the word, and equally at home in camps or fashionable circles. Those acquainted with the Villa Belvidere, will not easily forget the military air and carriage, and venerable appearance, of the old Duc di Rocco Romano, now many years gathered to his fathers.

* Like several others of our great literari, he was destined for the legal profession, and had been articled to a conveyancer.

HON. WILLIAM THOMAS HORNER FOX STRANGWAYS.

This gentleman, a son of Henry Thomas, second Earl of Ilchester, was attached to the Embassy at St. Petersburgh in 1816; at Constantinople in 1820; at Naples in September, 1822; was appointed paid Attaché at the Hague in January, 1824; Secretary of Legation at Florence in March, 1825; at Naples in February, 1828; and Envoy Extraordinary and Minister Plenipotentionary to the Diet of the Germanic Confederation in August, 1840, which post he held till 1848, when he retired on a pension.* He was an intimate acquaintance of Lady Blessington, as was likewise his brother, John Charles Strangways, born in 1803, married in 1844 to a daughter of E. Majoribanks, Esq.

CAPTAIN THOMAS MEDWIN.

In November, 1821, Captain Thomas Medwin found Byron sojourning in the Lanfranchi palace, at Pisa, which he had taken for a year.

Medwin published in 1823, "Conversations with Lord Byron, noted during a Residence with his Lordship at Pisa, in the years 1821 and 1822." At a later period, he published in the "Athenæum," his "Recollections of P. B. Shelley;" and in 1823, "Translations of the Agamemnon and Prometheus of Æschylus," which display considerable talent, and frequently preserve the beauty of the original.

The author of "Coversations with Lord Byron," resided with me in Naples, for some time, about thirty years ago. He was then a young man of gentleman-like manners and good address, of bookish habits, and in conversation and in society, agreeable, well-informed, and good-natured.

* Foreign Office List, 1854.

His work treating of Byron, was partly composed in the apartments he shared with me; and it seems to me now, that his verbal anecdotes of Byron, and oral description of his mode of life, were more interesting than his published account of them.

Captain Medwin published also a work in fiction, entitled "Lady Singleton, or the World as it is," in three volumes.

ALBERT SMITH, ESQ.

Whether in society or on the summit of Mount Blanc, in a monster balloon, the columns of "Punch," or in the company of the "Marchioness of Brinvillieres," "Christopher Tadpole," or of "A Gent about Town," Mr. Albert Smith is equally amusing. He is the son of a general medical practitioner at Chertsey, and was intended for the medical profession. He studied medicine in London and in Paris, and abandoned his profession about 1818, for that of literature. He was one of the original contributors to "Punch," and for some time one of its principal managers. Easier circumstances and less necessity to struggle with the world in very early life, might perhaps have given his talents a better chance to ripen and turn to a good account, and have afforded them a higher direction. By Lady Blessington and her surviving friends, he was looked on as—"a man of considerable comic talent, a humourist, an excellent mimic, quick of perception and comprehension, apt to see things in a ludicrous light, sprightly and animated in conversation, as a writer possessing much facility in composition; but he was known also to them as a kind-hearted person, an excellent son and brother, possessing sterling qualities, seldom found in those who pass in society for humourists and jest makers."

CAPTAIN WILLIAM LOCK.

The Locks of Norbury Park had been at a very early period of Lady Canterbury's career in London, very intimate friends of hers and her sister's.

One of that family, Captain William Lock, a young man remarkable for great comeliness, was drowned about seventeen years ago, in the Lake of Como, in sight of his newly wedded bride.

The mother of Captain Lock was a Miss Jennings, daughter of a person of some notoriety in his day, the celebrated "Dog Jennings," thus called on account of having brought from Greece a fragment of an ancient sculpture, which was named the dog of Alcibiades. A brother of this gentleman married a Miss Ogilvie, a daughter of the Duchess Dowager of Leinster.

DR. EDWARD HOGG, M.D.

The author of "A Visit to Alexandria, Damascus, and Jerusalem, during the successful campaign of Ibrahim Pasha," 2 vols. 8vo. 1835, died at Chester, aged 65, in March, 1848. Dr. Hogg set out from Naples in April, 1832, on his Eastern visit, and returned to Italy the year following. A man whom Gell regarded with esteem, and looked on as a friend, could neither be destitute of companionable qualities or intellectual gifts. He had practised his profession with success and reputation for some years in England, and retired from it in easy circumstances, but in very impaired health. He was an amiable man, of literary tastes, deeply interested in antiquarian researches, especially those connected with the history of early civilization in the East, and the examination of the proofs of that early advancement of which he speaks in the graceful, modest preface to his "Travels," "still existing in the stupendous monuments of Egypt and Nubia."

C. M. TALBOT, ESQ.

Mr. Talbot was at one period a frequent visitor at Gore House. He is a member of an ancient family, and of ample means—generous, simple in his tastes, and unaffected, but somewhat peculiar in his habits. He has travelled a good deal, and now lives retired in Wales.

WILLIAM THOMAS FITZGERALD, ESQ.

This well-known literati, one of the Vice-Presidents of the Literary Fund, died in London in 1829, aged 70.

Mr. Fitzgerald claimed to be a descendant of the Desmond branch of the illustrious family of the Fitzgeralds, of Ireland, and was the son of a Colonel John Austen Fitzgerald, who served in the Dutch armies.

He was educated partly at Greenwich, and at the Royal College of Navarre, in the University of Paris. Mr. Fitzgerald had figured at the court of the unfortunate Louis the Sixteenth and his Queen, and even in the select circles of the Petite Trianon.

In 1782, having returned to England, he obtained an appointment in the office of the Navy-Pay Office, in which he continued for a great many years. His exuberant loyalty was only exceeded by the exuberance of his poetry. His poetical pieces published in newspapers, prologues, political squibs, odes to Sovereigns, and invocations to Princes to arm against France, lines on battles, and pæans for victories, would make several volumes.

JOHN BUSHE, ESQ.

The son of the late Chief Justice, better known, perhaps, by the more familiar appellation of Johnny Bushe, was at one time a celebrity in the sporting and the fashionable world.

He has travelled much, on the Continent, in the East, India, China, &c.; and wherever he had been, his hereditary turn for humour and drollery, in addition to the singularity of his adventures, his warmth of feeling, frank and generous disposition, eagerness to oblige, truly Irish indifference about the cares of life, and characteristic ease in the enjoyment of all its present advantages, rendered him popular and well-remembered.

THEOPHILUS GODWIN SWIFT, ESQ.

The family of Godwin Swift, we are told in a recent remarkable work, who came to Ireland during Ormonde's power, and acted as Attorney-General for the Palatinate of Ormond, was descended from a Yorkshire family, originally from Belgium (Swft or Suyft), settled at Rotherham.

The Attorney-General of Ormond, Godwin Swift, married first, Miss Deane, of the Muskerry family, by whom he had issue: Godwin, the ancestors of the Swifts, of Lion's Den, and three other children. He married, secondly, a Miss Delgarno, daughter of a rector of Moylisker.*

The celebrated Dean, according to Sheridan, (Life of Dr. J. Swift), was a member of a younger branch of an ancient Yorkshire family. His grandfather, the Rev. Thomas Swift, was distinguished for his general exertions in favour of Charles the First, and his subsequent sufferings and ruin. Five of his sons went to seek their fortunes in Ireland, one of whom, Jonathan, was the father of the famous Dean. He had married a Leicestershire lady, of little fortune, a Miss Abigail Errick, a relative of the wife of Sir William Temple, and had died in distressed circumstances, about two years after marriage, seven months before the birth of his only son, Jonathan. After his death, his widow came to Ireland, and was received into the family of her husband's eldest brother, Godwin Swift,

* Lyon's Grand Jury Lists of Westmeath, p. 303.

(who had married a relative of the old Marchioness of Ormond, and to the great offence of his family, subsequently a sister of Admiral Deane, one of the regicides), a lawyer of great eminence and large income, which he squandered away, however, on idle projects. At his house, in Hoey's Court, Dublin, Jonathan was born in November, 1667. At the death of Godwin Swift, it was found his affairs were in a ruinous condition; the mother of Jonathan returned to England, established herself in Leicester, and there remained. The place of Godwin was supplied for some time to young Swift by a cousin, Willoughby, the eldest son of Godwin Swift, who resided in Lisbon. In the year 1688, young Jonathan left Ireland, and proceeded on foot from Chester, to visit his mother, then residing in Leicester; and soon after, his intimacy with Sir W. Temple commenced.

Those who are curious to know the grounds on which the surmises rest of Sir W. Temple being the father of Jonathan Swift, and the celebrated Stella being the half-sister of the latter, may refer to Exshaw's "Gentleman's and London Magazine," 1757, p. 555, and to Wilde's "Closing Years of Dean Swift," (2nd edit. 1849, p. 108), a work of singular interest and considerable research. The Dean died in October, 1745, in his 78th year.

The representative of this family in Ireland was a person of considerable notoriety about half a century ago, Theophilus Swift, Esq. Barrister-at-law.

In a letter to Sir Walter Scott, respecting the celebrated Dean, he thus spoke of his own father, Mr. Deane Swift:—

"'My father, having an easy fortune, had taken to no profession. He was an excellent scholar, but a very bad writer. He was a very moral man, and, from an innate love of religion, had made divinity his immediate study. He had taken a degree of A.M. at Oxford, and was every way qualified for an excellent divine.' Theophilus goes on to state that Sir Robert

Walpole offered his father preferment in the Church, and that his friend the Dean prevented him from availing himself of the Minister's offer, because he had a grudge against Walpole, on account of the neglect he had experienced at the hands of the latter. And he adds, that his father dared not disoblige the Dean at that time, because he owed the Doctor £2500, for which he had given a mortgage on his estates, and that he left his son to pay the debt after his death."*

Theophilus Swift was a native of Herefordshire, but settled at an early age in Ireland. This singular person, who claimed descent from the celebrated eccentric of the same name, the renowned Dean of St. Patrick, laboured under an inveterate disease, which political nosologists term pamphleteering. He commenced his career of a pamphleteer by a satirical production, entitled "The Gamblers." "A Poetical Letter to the King" followed, in which he slandered Colonel Lennox—the subsequent Duke of Richmond, Viceroy of Ireland, and being challenged by the Colonel, fought a duel in July, 1789, and had the honour of being wounded by his distinguished opponent. He next published a letter to W. A. Brown, Esq., on the duel of the Duke of York with Colonel Lennox, in 1789; next, "A Vindication of Renwick Williams, commonly called the Monster," in 1790.

He signalized his progress in the career of a pamphleteer in 1794, by assailing, in a pamphlet of 192 pages, "The Fellows of Trinity College, Dublin," charging them with perjury, violation of the college statutes, marrying against the same, &c. &c.; and being prosecuted by one of them, Dr. Burrows, he was cast into prison, but had the consolation of prosecuting successfully the Doctor for a libel, and having him imprisoned also while he was undergoing the penalty of his offence.

Theophilus Swift had two sons, Edmund Lenthall, and Deane Swift. The former was educated at Oxford, the latter

* Nichols' Illustrations of Literature of the 18th Century.

was an under-graduate in Trinity College, Dublin, where he quarrelled with Dr. Burrowes, one of the examiners; and his father, on the son's account, waged war on all the heads of the University, and the whole of the Fellows in particular. Theophilus ended his career by tormenting a daughter of a respectable Protestant clergyman of Dublin, the Reverend Mr. Dobbyn, with violènt protestations of love, and bitter complaints of not being accepted by the lady, embodied in a pamphlet addressed to her father, for which he was challenged by a relative of the young lady, (she being then about to marry a Mr. Lefanu); but Theophilus declined to *accept* any thing from the Dobbyns except the young lady's hand, and died, like his pamphlet, in the summer of 1815.

Deane Swift was a young man of considerable ability, an excellent scholar, a good Latin versifier, and an able writer. From the time of the war with the Fellows, and the composition of divers sarcastic epigrams on them, no more was heard of young Deane Swift till the memorable year of 1798, when his name occurs in certain governmental documents, representing him as a person not particularly loyal in his opinions; and then he disappears from the stage of Irish politics and the page of Irish history, and is only known to have quitted Ireland, at the period above referred to, and not to have returned to it. About twelve years ago, the late General Arthur O'Connor informed me, that the author of the stirring treasonable letters against Lord Camden's government, published in "The Press" newspaper, the Dublin organ of "The United Irishmen," under the signature—MARCUS, was Mr. Deane Swift, who had fled from Ireland, and was no more heardof. He and Dr. Drenman were the chief penmen of the Dublin Leaders; but the strongest and most stirring leading articles in that paper were written by Swift.

Peter Finnerty, the printer of the "Press," in the early part of 1798, was prosecuted for the publication of the libellous letters against Lord Camden, signed "MARCUS,"—in which letters the words in capitals, "REMEMBER ORR," (the first person executed, charged only with taking the oath of the United Irishmen), were frequently repeated in the way of appeal to the passions of the people, and thus were rendered so familiar as to become the great cry of the lower orders of the disaffected.

O'Connor supposed the writer of those letters had been long dead. Shortly after my interview with the former, however, on my return to London, a friend of mine brought me an invitation to dine with the Keeper of the Regalia of the Tower, and in making the acquaintance of that excellent gentleman, it was no small surprise to me to find an official charged with the custody of her Majesty's crown, Edmund Lenthall Swift, Esq., the brother of the formidable penman of the "United Irishmen," Mr. Deane Swift, the "MARCUS" of the "Treasonable Press," whose writings had so seriously troubled the repose of Lord Camden, endangered his government, and for which eventually the writer had to fly to save his life, after having to some extent compromised his brother by them. I found General O'Connor's statement to me confirmed by Mr. Edmund Swift, and further learned, that his brother was living, and then residing at Gravesend, in comfortable circumstances, highly respected by all classes.

The last time I saw Mr. E. L. Swift was in 1847; his brother was then living.

Edmund L. Swift, Esq. was Keeper of the Regalia of the Tower so far back as July, 1817. He died in the enjoyment of his office of great trust, about seven years ago. He was an occasional contributor in verse and prose, to the "Gentleman's Magazine."*

In the November number of that Periodical, for 1817, he published some verses on the death of the Princess Charlotte,

* Gents. Mag., July, 1817, Part ii. p. 3.

entitled "The Heart," strangely contrasting with the effusions of his brother in the "Press" newspaper of 1797 and 1798, under the signature of "MARCUS."

A few years before his death, Mr. E. L. Swift had the misfortune to lose his eldest son, Mr. Theophilus Godwin Swift, aged thirty-two, at Hobart Town.

P. B. SHELLEY, ESQ.

Though Lady Blessington was personally unacquainted with Shelley, so many references to him are to be found in her letters and journals, and especially in her "Conversations with Lord Byron," that the following brief notice of him may not be misplaced. Lady Blessington was intimately acquainted with Shelley's career previously to his second marriage, and had much valuable authentic information given her, both oral and written, respecting his early career, by some of his most confidential friends, of which she has left some very curious records in her papers.*

"Sir Timothy Shelley, the second Baronet, died April 24, 1844, at his seat, Field Place, Warnham, Sussex. He was born in 1753, and married in 1791, Elizabeth, daughter of Charles Pitford, Esq., of Effingham, Surrey, by whom he had issue — Percy Bysshe, the celebrated poet; and five other children.

"The one true friend of Byron; the only one to whom Byron appears to have been truly attached, and faithful

* Lady Blessington was a great admirer of the works of Shelley. She had heard so much of him from his dearest friends, that she took a deep interest in every thing that concerned his brief and remarkable career; and from his immediate friends and companions she obtained a good deal of information respecting it, which throw much light on that strange and eventful history. From various memorandums of hers on that subject, the following particulars are collected.

in his friendship. P. B. Shelley was born in August, 1792, at Field Place, the seat of his father, in Sussex.

" After passing some years at the preparatory school of Leon House, in Brentford, he was sent to Eton at thirteen years of age, and, in due time, commenced his College course at Oxford. His passion for poetry first manifested itself about the age of fifteen, in some effusions indicative of a taste for ghost stories, and German relations of marvellous enchantments, and " Hopes of high talk with the departed dead."

His near relative, Captain Medwin, remembers no display of precocity of genius in his earlier years. " His parents were not remarkable for any particular talents." One of his earliest characteristics was a sovereign contempt for the universal idol (Mammon). Another, of rather a later growth, was an abhorrence of tyranny and injustice. In his childhood even, he tells us he formed resolutions—

" To be wise
And just, and free, and mild, if in me lies
Such power, for I grow weary to behold
The selfish and the strong still tyrannize
Without reproach or check."

In his novel of " Lastrozzi," a very wonderful work for a boy of sixteen, he embodied much of the intense passion that had already taken possession of his heart—his hopeless passion for his beautiful cousin Miss G. ; his expulsion from College, on a charge of Atheism; the misery of seeing the girl he adored married to another; the unhappiness of his relations with his father; the apparent inveteracy of that parent's animosity to a youth before he could be said even to have approached the age of reason, to have attained maturity of mind or body; all these things are familiar with the lovers of Shelley's poetry, who are interested in his unhappy fate, and need no further reference in this notice of the salient points in his career.

There is a curious coincidence in the early tastes of children, who, in after-years, become distinguished for exalted genius, or some great qualities which lead to signal intellectual successes in after life; they shun in childhood the scenes of uproarious merriment of their juvenile companions; they shew no liking for rural sports and games, and the ordinary outdoor amusements of boys, especially those of boisterous habits. They seem to need silence and seclusion for their meditations and communings with nature, and with themselves.

Shelley's natural disposition in childhood was a striking instance of this kind of turn for gravity and retirement, and premature concentrativeness of ideas.

Of this kind also was the childhood of Dante and of Savonarola. Byron was an exception to the rule; his youth was venturous, daring, pugnacious, turbulent, and demonstrative of a desire to distinguish himself among his schoolfellows in all athletic sports and exercises.

The prevailing turn of Shelley's mind towards mystic speculations and strange abstractions, at a very early period of his career, appears to have had at times an unhappy influence alike on his bodily health and mental sanity.*

Shelley married, or according to Captain Medwin, he was inveigled into marriage, at eighteen. The union we are told was not made in heaven, nor apparently on earth with any reasonable prospect of felicity. It is easy to visit the sins of such an ill-starred union on the unhappy wife of an inferior rank to that of her husband, on the weaker vessel, on the woman of few friends in her former position, and who when driven from it, on the wide world, having no hope left, died

* Moore's Life of Byron, Ed. 8vo. 1838, p. 7.

by her own hand. But it may be, that the sorrows of that unhappy union are mistaken for the sins, and the victim has been wrongly regarded by us.

Harriet Westbroke, the first wife of Shelley, was the daughter of a retired coffee-house keeper. With this lady it is stated he lived very unhappily; and after bearing him two children, a separation took place, and a little later the wife, thus abandoned, died by her own hand in 1817.

Shelley married while yet a stripling, and his friend Leigh Hunt, says, " the wife he took was not of a nature to appreciate his understanding, or perhaps, to come into contact with it uninjured in what she had of her own."* They separated by mutual consent after the birth of two children. We are told by way of apology for Shelley's conduct in this mutually voluntary separation, and something more, in the letter of licence accompanying it, that Mrs. Shelley was a person of inferior rank, and that Shelley's family disapproved of the match.

Whatever her rank was, the unfortunate discarded wife believed herself to have been ill-used by her husband; and while Mr. Shelley was residing in Bath, paying court to another lady, news came to him that his wife had destroyed herself. " It was a heavy blow to him," we are told, " and he never forgot it."

The first Mrs. Shelley is represented by Mr. Hunt in a very unfavourable light, especially in an intellectual point of view. I have had evidence before me which would go very far to contradict that unfavourable opinion. In the year 1812, and early part of 1813, Mr. Shelley was reduced by pecuniary distress to the necessity of frequently supplicating a friend for the loan of small sums of money to meet his current expenses, he and Mrs. Shelley living at that period in the most straitened circumstances.

* The reasoning of Mr. Leigh Hunt on this untoward event,—this "one painful passage in Shelley's life,"—is hardly less revolting than the conduct which led to it.

In March, 1813, Mr. and Mrs. Shelley were residing in Dublin, at No. 35, Great Cuffe Street, Stephen's Green, a locality sufficient to shew the nature of the pecuniary circumstances in which Shelley was then placed. He and Mrs. Shelley were then, to use his own words, "overwhelmed by their own distresses, but still not indifferent to those of others, suffering or struggling in the cause of liberty and virtue," and therefore he sent instructions from Ireland to apply £20 to the benefit of the Hunts.

Shelley was then slowly recovering from an alarming illness accompanied by great nervous excitement and depression of spirits, brought on by dread of assassination and night watchings, and terrors, occasioned by an imagined attempt made on his life, the 26th of February, 1813, between ten and eleven o'clock at night, while residing in Wales.

Mr. and Mrs. Shelley, and a sister of Mrs. Shelley, had retired to rest about half an hour, when Shelley, imagining he heard a noise in the lower part of the house, rushed out of bed, and armed with two pistols *which he had loaded that night, expecting to have occasion for them,* ran down stairs and entered a room, from whence it seemed to him the noise had proceeded. Mrs. Shelley in narrating the occurrence, stated, that Shelley saw a man in the act of making his escape through a window that opened into a shrubbery. The man, according to that account, fired at Shelley without effect; Shelley then attempted to fire at his assailant, but the pistol did not go off. The man then rushed on Shelley, knocked him down, and while on the ground a struggle took place between Shelley and his assailant. Shelley managed during this struggle to fire his second pistol, which he imagined had wounded the man in the shoulder, for he screamed aloud, rose up and uttered terrible imprecations and threats, in the grossest language, calling God to witness that he would be revenged—that he would murder his (Shelley's) wife, that he would bring disgrace on his sister, and ending with these words:—" By G— I will be revenged!"

The villain had fled as they (Mr. and Mrs. Shelley) hoped for the night. The servants had not gone to bed when this occurence took place, yet Mrs. Shelley makes no mention of them having made their appearance at all on the scene of this rencontre during the struggle, notwithstanding the firing of the shots, nor did she mention being present herself, till about eleven o'clock, when " they all assembled in the parlour where they remained for two hours." Mrs. Shelley stated that her husband then desired them to retire, as there was no farther attack likely to be apprehended. She went to bed and left Shelley and a man servant, who had only became an inmate of the house that day, sitting up. Mrs. Shelley was in bed about three hours when she heard a pistol go off, and immediately ran down stairs, where she found her husband greatly excited. She saw that his dressing-gown and the window-curtains had been perforated by a ball. The servant man who had been left sitting up with Shelley, by her account was not present when the shot was fired. He had been sent out to see what o'clock it was, and after having done so, on hearing some noise at the window, Shelley, as she states, went forward in that direction, *when a man thrust his arm through the glass and fired at him.* The ball passed through the curtain and his dressing-gown—Shelley fortunately standing side-ways at the moment the assassin fired. Shelley immediately attempted to fire his pistol at the man, but it would not go off. He then made a lounge at him *with an old sword which he found in the house;* the assassin tried to wrest the sword out of his hand, and while in the act of so wresting it, the servant man, Daniel, rushed into the room, and the man then took to flight and disappeared.

When Mrs. Shelley saw her husband after this second attempt, it was four o'clock in the morning. The night had been most tempestuous, a most dreadful night, the wind was so loud, it seemed to her like thunder, and the rain came rattling down in torrents.

The next day the occurrence was a subject of general conversation in the locality. A Mr. L— spread a malicious report that the whole story was a fabrication of Shelley, and the object of it was to furnish an excuse for leaving the place without paying his bills—this Mr. L— having an enmity to Shelley, on account of being slighted by the latter, and once having obtained a pamphlet which Shelley had published in Dublin, of a political nature, and having sent the same to the government, denouncing its principles and its author. On the Saturday following the Shelleys took their departure for a neighbouring place, and determined shortly after to proceed to Dublin for change of scene, that might lead to some new train of thought most urgently required at that time, for the restoration of his health and spirits.

Shelley in his account of the attempted assassination said, he had been fired at twice by the assassin, and one of the balls had penetrated his night-gown *and pierced his waistcoat.* He was of opinion it was no common robber they had reason to dread, but a person seeking vengeance, *who had threatened his life and his sister's also.*

Within a week of the date of the occurrence above mentioned, Shelley's state of mind was not only one of depression, but of desperation ; he spoke of his escape from an attempted atrocious assassination, and the probability of being then heard of no more, in a very incoherent manner.

The whole alleged attempt at assassination, there can hardly be a doubt, was an imaginary occurrence—the creation of an over-worked mind, greatly excited, controlled by no religious sentiments—of a state of mental hallucination remotely occasioned by excessive metaphysical abstraction, immediately aggravated by impaired bodily health and extreme physical debility.

Those who contributed perseveringly and industriously to undermine the religious sentiments of this noble-minded being, for such he was with all his faults, one originally good and excellently gifted, naturally endowed too with sentiments of a reverential kind for the Creator, and with feelings of grateful admiration of the glorious and beautiful works of creation; those persons, some of whom are still living, might well lament for the success of their efforts to unchristianize Shelley, if they had the grace to be conscious of their own grievous errors in matters of religion.

Moore says of Shelley, "With a mind by nature fervidly pious, he yet refused to acknowledge a supreme Providence, and substituted some airy abstraction of 'universal love,' in its place."*

We are told by Leigh Hunt, that "Shelley was subject to violent spasmodic pains, which would sometimes force him to lie on the ground till they were over, but he had always a kind word to give to those about him when his pangs allowed him to speak."

One of the earliest and most intimate friends of Shelley, in whose house in London, at the period of his first married life, and subsequent to the separation, Shelley was in the habit of staying when in town, informed me that he was subject to violent paroxysms of pain in the head, so violent and overpowering, that while they lasted, he would lie down on a sofa and writhe in an agony of suffering, that seemed almost to drive him to distraction.

Polidori, the Italian physician of Lord Byron in Genoa and Milan, in his Preface to the "Vampire," gives a curious account of one of Shelley's occasional hallucinations, for the truth of which Byron vouches.

* Moore's "Life of Byron," p. 316, 8vo. Ed. 1838.

"It appears that, one evening, Lord B., Mr. P. B. Shelley, two ladies, and the gentleman before alluded to, after having perused a German work called 'Phantasmagoria,' began relating ghost stories, when his Lordship having recited the beginning of Christabel, then unpublished, the whole took so strong a hold of Mr. Shelley's mind, that he suddenly started up, and ran out of the room. The physician and Lord Byron followed, and found him leaning against a mantel-piece, with cold drops of perspiration trickling down his face. After having given him something to refresh him, upon inquiring into the cause of his alarm, they found that his wild imagination having pictured to him the bosom of one of the ladies with eyes (which was reported of a lady in the neighbourhood where he lived), he was obliged to leave the room, in order to destroy the impression."*

The belief to which he clung with most tenacity, we are told by his friend, Hunt, was in the existence of some great pervading "spirit of intellectual beauty." The sweet cadences of melodious music, the lustre of the stars, the loveliness of flowers, the beauties of nature, the excellencies of art—these, we are told, were the spiritual influences which went to the formation of his religious opinions. The works of Bernard de St. Pierre contributed, perhaps, to make him a natural religionist; and one work of Mr. Godwin, on "Political Justice," made him a philosophic radical and a metaphysical republican. Of his personal appearance it is said :

"Shelley's figure was tall and almost unnaturally attenuated, so as to bend to the earth like a plant that had been deprived of its vital air; his features had an unnatural sharpness, and an unhealthy paleness, like a flower that has been kept from the light of day; his eyes had an almost superhuman brightness, and his voice a preternatural elevation of pitch and a shrillness of tone; all which peculiarities probably arose from some accidental circumstances connected with his early nurture and bringing up. But all these Hazlitt tortured into external types and symbols of that unnatural and unwholesome craving after injurious excitement, that morbid tendency towards interdicted

* Moore's Life of Byron, p. 316, 8vo. edit. 1838.

topics and questions of moral good and evil, and that forbidden search into the secrets of our nature and ultimate destiny, into which he strangely and inconsequentially resolved the whole of Shelley's productions."*

Shelley's lines—" *Written in dejection*, near Naples"—contain some passages exquisitely beautiful and pathetic, some, too, of a mournful interest, and calculated to recall his own sad fate :—

I see the deep's untrampled floor,
  With green and purple sea-weeds strown ;
I see the waves upon the shore,
  Like light dissolved in star-showers thrown.
I sit upon the sands alone :
  The lightning of the noon-tide-ocean
Is flashing round me, and a tone
  Arises from its measured motion,
How sweet !—did my heart share in my emotion.

Alas ! I have nor hope, nor health,
  Nor peace within, nor calm around,
Nor that content surpassing wealth,
  The Sage in meditation found,
And walked around with inward glory crowned ;
  Nor fame, nor power, nor love, nor leisure.
Others I see whom these surround ;
  Smiling they live, and call life pleasure :—
To me that cup has been dealt in another measure.

Yet now despair itself is mild,
  Ev'n as the winds and waters are ;
I could lie like a tired child,
  And weep away the life of care
Which I have borne, and still must bear,
  Till death, like sleep, might steal on me,
And I might feel in the warm air
  My cheek grow cold, and hear the sea
Breathe o'er my dying brain its last monotony.

* " My Friends and Acquaintances," by P. G. Patmore, iii. 134.

The second Mrs. Shelley was the daughter of William Godwin, by his union with Mary Wolstonecraft, the author of the "Rights of Women." This gifted lady became the wife of P. B. Shelley in 1818. Soon after their marriage, they left their residence at Great Marlow, in Buckinghamshire, for Italy, where they resided till the fatal accident by which Shelley perished, in his thirtieth year, in the Gulf of Lerici, with his friend, Edward Elleker Williams, the 8th of July, 1822. Mrs. Shelley's first work, written during her residence in Italy, was "Frankenstein," one of the most remarkable works of fiction of the time. After Shelley's death, she had to devote herself to literature, to enable her to provide for herself and two young children. She produced, at intervals, "Valperga," "The Last Man," "Lodore," one or two other works of fiction, biographies of foreign artists and men of letters, for the "Cabinet Cyclopædia." She edited, moreover, the poems and various fragments of Shelley, and, lastly, published, in 1843, in 2 vols. 8vo., her "Rambles in Germany and Italy, in 1840, 1842, and 1843." Mrs. Shelley's elder son, William, died in childhood; the survivor is the present Sir Percy Florence Shelley, Bart., who succeeded his grandfather, Sir Timothy Shelley, in that title, in 1844. Mrs Shelley died at her residence, 24, Chester Square, London, aged 53, the 1st of February, 1851.

Willis thus refers to the disposal of Shelleys ashes:

"The remains of Shelley are deposited near those of his friend, Keats, in the cemetery at the base of the pyramidal tomb of Caius Cestius, in Rome. In his preface to his lament over Keats, Shelley says, 'he was buried in the romantic and lonely cemetery of the Protestants, under the pyramid which is the tomb of Cestius, and the massy walls and towers, now mouldering and desolate, which formed the circuit of ancient Rome. It is an open space among the ruins, covered in winter with violets and daisies. *It might make one in love with death, to think that one should be buried in so sweet a place.*' The inscription on the monument of Keats, who died in Rome, in 1821, briefly tells the sad story of the short career of the young English poet, the friend of Shelley :—'*This grave contains all that was mortal of a young English poet, who, on his death-bed, in the bitterness of his heart at the malicious power of his enemies, desired these words to be engraved on his tomb:* HERE LIES ONE WHOSE NAME WAS WRITTEN IN WATER.' "

"I have been here to-day, to see the graves of Keats and Shelley. With a cloudless sky and the most delicious air ever breathed, we sat down upon the marble slab laid over the ashes of poor Shelley, and read his own lament over Keats, who sleeps just below, at the foot of the hill. The cemetery is rudely formed into three terraces, with walks between; and Shelley's grave occupies a small nook above, made by the projections of a mouldering wall-tower, and crowned with ivy and shrubs, and a peculiarly fragrant yellow flower, which perfumes the air around for several feet. The avenue by which you ascend from the gate is lined with high bushes of the marsh rose in the most luxuriant bloom, and all over the cemetery the grass is thickly mingled with flowers of every dye."*

No. XIII.

THOMAS MOORE.

MOORE's anecdotal talents have been referred to at page 162 of vol. iii. In 1835, I dined with Moore, in Dublin, at a large party of upwards of twenty persons, many of whom were distinguished intellectual people. At dinner, I sat between Moore and a barrister, not remarkable for talent, but highly respected, an amiable, inoffensive, meek, well-mannered, gentleman-like, good-humoured person, naturally timid and retiring, and rather advanced in years, who was named Cornelius, but was no Centurion, and though familiarly called Con by his intimate friends, was never supposed to be a descendant of him "of the hundred fights." On the opposite side, near the head of the table, sat

* Willis's Pencillings by the Way, p. 84.

an important-looking personage, tall, gaunt, and bony, once evidently of herculean strength and stature, now bent and somewhat shrunken, but still of formidable breadth of shoulders and size of hands, if one might be allowed to use that expression in speaking of such enormous appendages to human wrists. This portentous-looking gentleman, of a grim aspect and a gruff voice, was the redoubtable Tom, commonly spoken of as a younger brother of Jack the Giant-Killer. Tom was the representative of a class now happily defunct in Ireland—the Sir Lucius O'Trigger school, of pleasure-loving, reckless, rollicking, elderly gentlemen of good family, who always went into society on full cock, and generally *went off*, leaving some striking proofs of their valour, and the value they set on their own opinions, behind them—men of a great fame for fighting duels, of indisputable authority in all controversies concerning hair-triggers and matters of etiquette in affairs of honour, in pacing the ground, and placing a friend well on it; capital judges of prime port and claret, flaming patriots after dinner, greatly disposed to be oratorical and tuneful, and with a slight dash of sedition in their songs and speeches. He belonged to that school whose disciples, like the good Master Shallows of former times, as they grow old, remember "the mad days that they have spent," when they were "such swinge bucklers in all the Inns of Court," and "heard the chimes at night," and "drew a good long bow, and shot a good shoot"—veterans who had seen much service in the field with the hounds, after the fox and the hare, and in the hunt elsewhere, after other game, in their early days, when "the watchword was 'Hem, boys!'" lusty fellows once, "who would have done anything, and roundly too," but who, in their latter years, "poor esquires in the county," and justices of the peace, begin to think, "as death is certain, that all must die;" all their "old friends are dead," and then, being dejected, and becoming sanctimonious, kindly take the interests of religion and the state under their immediate protection, and ultimately obtain some celebrity as *Cawtholic* notabilities, "*voteens*, suffering loyalists," and arbiters of all matters in controversy in society affecting their opinions of what is genteel, pious, or well affected to the constitution, and the Hanoverian succession, as established in the House of Brunswick.

Moore had been particularly joyous and brilliant in conversation during dinner. The cloth was removed, the contagion of his wit and humour had spread around him, the dullest person in company had become animated, every one had some anecdote to tell. Poor Con, the barrister, the mildest and most harmless of men, told a story of Father O'Leary and the Protestant Bishop of his diocese, dining together, and joking on a point of discipline, the gist of the story being some facetious observation of the prelate, which had been taken in jest, and had been enjoyed as a joke by Father O'Leary himself. Every body at table laughed at the story but one person, and that unpleased and very unpleasant individual was Tom, who looked unutterable things, the obvious meaning of which was, "Shall we have incision ?" "Shall we imbrue ?" "Have we not hiren here?" "Now let the welkin roar!" Now for "a goodly tumult!"

Slowly, and with alarming solemnity of aspect, the great bony frame of the fire-eater of former times was seen rising up. Supporting his great bulk on the knuckles of both hands planted on the table, far inwards towards the centre, and stretching across decanters and glasses in a most formidable attitude in the direction of the unhappy Cornelius, who looked exceedingly astonished and alarmed. Moore gazed around him on the faces of the guests inquiringly, and, if he dared to speak, would evidently have asked—what the deuce was the meaning of the coming row. The generality of the guests awaited the explosion, as if a thunderbolt was about to fall on the head of the petrified barrister. Tom took a minute or two to fix himself in his terrible position, and to concentrate his fiery glances and scathing frowns on the pale and shrinking victim, the ill-starred Con. Not a word was spoken, but a hollow grumbling noise could be distinguished, a kind of preface to a horrid growl—"mugitus labyrinthi"—such a grumble as a sick giant, in the recesses of some deep cavern, might be expected to utter, in extremity; and now the bellowing of the mountain of a man marvellously distempered by his choler, commenced in good earnest. His volcanic fury thus disembogued in a torrent of incoherent threats, denunciations, and invective.

"How *dar* you speak disrespectfully of the clergy of my church? How *dar* you do it, sir? I say, Con, how *dar* you insult my religion?"

Poor Con, terror-stricken, held up his hands imploringly, and, in most tremulous accents, vainly protested he meant no offence whtever to the faith or feelings of any man, woman, or child in Christendom.

"How *dar* you, Con—tell me what you mean? How *dar* you attempt to interrupt me? You had the baseness, Con, and you know it, sir, to insult the ministers of my religion. How *dar* you deny the cowardly attack, sir?"

Con, pale as death, but with no better success than before, made another imploring appeal to be allowed to deny the alleged insult.

"There was a time, Con, when, with this hand [lifting his right arm as he spoke, clenching his fist, and shaking it vehemently across the table at his victim]—there was a time, Con, and well you know it, when I would have smashed you for this outrage. But I scorn you too much to take any other than this slight notice of your heinous offence against everything sacred and profane!"

Frowning awfully, the indignant champion resumed his seat, and the dismayed barrister, who began to pluck up his courage from the moment Tom declared his excess of scorn prevented him from having recourse to actual violence, began to sit up more perpendicularly in his chair, for, previously to that, he had been sinking gradually, fading away before the face of his infuriated assailant's overwhelming wrath, till it was to be feared he would eventually have sliddered down altogether from his seat and slipped under the table.

Silence reigned; the guests looked at one another, discreetly holding their tongues; Moore seemed to be exceedingly annoyed and sickened. After a little time, he whispered to me to follow him, and, to the great disappointment of the company, he rose before any of the guests had stirred, and took his departure. I followed him, and the first words he uttered when we were in the street, were the following:—"So disgusting an exhibition I never witnessed in my life."

We went to the theatre; it was a command night, and Lord and Lady Mulgrave were there in state. Moore was soon recognized by the audience, and greeted with loud cheers and plaudits. After a short time, one of the aides-de-camp came to the box where we were sitting, and conveyed an invitation to Moore to sup with his Excellency at the vice-regal lodge. Moore then accompanied the aide-de-camp to the box of the vice-regal party, and, on his appearance there, the cheering for him was renewed. He returned to the box I was in before his Excellency made his exit, and brought me an invitation from Lord Mulgrave (whom I had the honour of knowing in Jamaica) to the supper-party that night at the Park. I accompanied Moore to that entertainment, without exception the most delightful I ever enjoyed. The principal guests at supper were Lord and Lady Cloncurry, the Lord who was a prisoner in the Tower in 1798, and his lady, the near relative of the foully-murdered Sir Edward Crosbie; Sir Guy Campbell and his lady, the eldest daughter of Lord Edward Fitzgerald; Thomas Moore, the historian of the rebel lord; and the humble individual who, a little later, was the author of the "Lives and Times of the United Irishmen." There were present also Miss Ellen Tree, Mr. Macready, and Sir Philip Crampton.

If the ghosts of the Duke of Richmond, of the good old times of the Orange régime, in the Castle and the Vice-regal Lodge, and the unhappy shades of William Saurin and Lord Manners, could only have come up and gazed that night on the company by whom the Viceroy was surrounded, and amongst whom there was not one purple marksman, or representative of an Orange lodge, how shocked they would have been. Moore, that night, sang and played several of his own beautiful melodies, in his own most exquisite style—more than one that had reference to persons who had figured in the stormy affairs of 1798—songs which brought tears into the eyes of the daughter of Lord Edward Fitzgerald.

No. XIV.

L. E. L.

SINCE the notice, in the second volume of this work, of Mrs. Maclean's death, at Cape Coast Castle, and the circumstances attending it, was written, a publication has appeared, entitled "Recollections of Literary Characters and Celebrated Places," by Mrs. Thomson, author of "Memoirs of the Court of Henry the Eighth," "Correspondence of Sarah, Duchess of Marlborough," &c. In the second volume of this work,* there is a biographical sketch of L. E. L., the author's reminiscences of her, and (at page 92) an account of her decease, wherein some matters are stated in regard to the immediate causes of Mrs. Maclean's death, for the first time said to be presented to the public, which deserve attention, and the more so, on account of Mrs. Thomson's claim to authentic sources of information for many of the alleged facts detailed by her. The author, previously referring to the marriage of Miss Landon with Mr. Maclean, says: "The common surmise is, that L. E. L. *married* the Governor of Cape Coast, *to be married*, to fly from the slander, to have a home and a sanction. No—these were not her reasons, for she was truly and ardently attached to one whom she declared was the only man she ever loved. She confided in him, she pined in his absence, she sacrificed for him the friends, the country, the society, to which she had been accustomed. But she made one false step."

The false step spoken of diffusely rather than explained, was the fact of the acceptance of a suitor, who having been ardently loved by poor L. E. L., the only one she had ever loved, all of a sudden, after being so accepted, and having carried on a correspondence with her, without any assigned or assignable cause or explanation, had ceased to hold any intercourse with her, and had betaken himself to Scotland, without any intimation of his departure from London, and thus left her in a state bordering on despair.

The mystery of the sudden breaking off of the marriage,

* Recollections of Literary Characters, &c., vol. ii. p. 86.

however, terminated in Mr. Maclean's return from Scotland, the renewal of his engagement, a joyful wedding with a man who had seemed to Mrs. Thomson, at the time of the marriage, "like one who had buried all joy in Africa, or whose feelings had been frozen up during his last inauspicious visit to Scotland."

The marriage, which was attended by Sir E. B. Lytton, the kind and constant friend of Miss Landon, and which had been made a mystery of, according to Mrs. Thomson's account, for about a month after its celebration, was apparently the false step referred to. Had it been called a fatal one, there would have been something in the account not to be impugned. But that Mrs. Thomson's impressions of this marriage being the result of strong feelings of attachment, the ardent affection of first fond love on the part of the lady are entirely erroneous, there cannot be the slightest doubt. That Mrs. Thomson has stated correctly the words of Miss Landon, declaratory of such sentiments, I have no doubt; but I know that pride has its anomalies as well as other passions, and does not bear, in great extremities, to be too literally interpreted; and it is difficult to conceive any greater extremity than the sacrifice which Miss Landon made of her happiness, in abandoning friends, country, and pursuits for the hand and name of Captain Maclean, a dreary home, and, as she anticipated, an early grave on the coast of Africa.

Mrs. Thomson, to a short passage of about a dozen lines in the text of her notice of L. E. L., adds a long note of six pages on the subject of her death. In the former we are told—"All that is known of her death is this: she was found '*half an hour after taking from a black boy a cup of coffee brought by her order*,' leaning against the door of her chamber, sitting as if she had sunk down in an effort to rush to the door for help. A bruise was on her cheek, a slight bruise on the hand which was pressed on the floor—(these details are not in the inquest, but are true)—an empty phial (so said the maid who found her) in her hand."

If Mrs. Thomson's account is correct, Mrs. Maclean was found by the English servant-woman, Mrs. Bayley, in a sitting posture at the door. But, on the inquest, Mrs. Bayley swore she had found the body of her mistress lying on the floor near the entrance; and no evidence was given by any person examined on the inquest of any coffee having been brought to her that morning by a native servant.

Mrs. Thomson further adds, the black boy was about ten years of age who had brought the coffee, and that when Mrs. Bayley returned to the dressing-room, she found the cup standing empty on Mrs. Maclean's table. I never heard one syllable of this at Cape Coast. If such a circumstance took place, it was suppressed at the inquest, and it was withheld from me. But Mrs. Thomson says Mrs. Bayley mentioned this circumstance to the late Mrs. Liddiard of Streatham.

Mrs. Bayley certainly did not say one word that has been reported, in her evidence on the inquest, about a cup of coffee having been brought to her mistress in the interval between her first entering Mrs. Maclean's room that fatal morning and her second appearance there, when she found Mrs. Maclean lifeless, to all appearance, on the floor. If any other servant previously entered the room that morning, and brought any liquid to the poisoned person, that servant ought surely to have been examined on the inquest. If the circumstance took place that is stated by Mrs. Thomson, the suppression of such evidence would be calculated, no doubt, to excite a suspicion that the inquiry was not intended to ascertain the real facts of the case.

When Mrs. Bayley left the room of Mrs. Maclean, her mistress was apparently well; about half an hour, at the utmost, elapsed before she returned to the room; her mistress was then apparently dead.

Did the boy bring the coffee before Mrs. Bayley's first appearance in Mrs. Maclean's room? Who was that boy? Was he a son of a native woman who had to quit the castle on the arrival in the arsenal of Mrs. Maclean? Are the poisons known to the natives on the west coast of Africa of that deadly virulence and swiftness in destroying life, that death was likely to result from the administration of one of them within a period of half an hour after the time of taking it?

Were there good authority for the statement made to Mrs. Liddiard, these are matters which it might be desirable to have inquired into if Mrs. Bayley could answer them, could be relied on, and could not be intimidated or tampered with. Some of the questions my own knowledge of the facts enables me to throw some light on. The boy who brought the coffee was not the son of the woman referred to. There was no child of hers by Captain Maclean living at the time I was on the Gold Coast, nor long previously to that period. The poisons known to the natives of Africa are not generally productive of instantaneous death.

Mrs. Thomson states several circumstances relating to her last letters to her friends, which are unquestionably true, as far as they go, shewing those communications "were not the letters of a newly-married and happy wife."

In one of these letters she complained bitterly, that, in spite of her entreaties, Mr. Maclean had ordered her attendant, Mrs. Bayley, the only woman in the settlement, to return to England; and Mrs. Thomson truly states, "that decision seemed to give her, Mrs. Maclean, inexpressible vexation, as, indeed, it naturally might." The decision was inexplicable to the friends of Mrs. Maclean, and might reasonably be so.

Mrs. Bayley was the wife of the steward of the vessel in which the Macleans went out to the Gold Coast from England. On arrival, Mrs. Bayley went to live at the castle, and appeared to every one there in the capacity of lady's-maid to Mrs. Maclean. Her husband, at the same time, became a kind of factotum to Mr. Maclean, and eventually was put in charge of Captain Maclean's yacht schooner, and became the master of that vessel.

He was master of that vessel long after his wife's departure from the settlement. I think I heard he had returned to England on Mr. Maclean's business, had come back to the colony, and resumed his command of the yacht.

Not very long before the death of Mr. Maclean, a friend of his at Cape Coast, much in his confidence, recently deceased, a gentleman with whom I was well acquainted, stated, that some revelation (in the shape of a letter) had been made to Mr. Maclean of a serious nature, which he, Mr. Maclean, was not prepared for by any previous rumours with which he had been made acquainted in England.

Whether the alleged revelation had anything to do with the

decision come to with regard to the return of Mrs. Bayley to England, no one living, with one exception, now can say. I allude to this statement, because I think it very probable that for Mr. Maclean's decision there may have been some excuse, if not a cause, of which the public are unaware. Mrs. Bayley's discretion may not have been more remarkable at Cape Coast Castle than it proved on her return to this country.

Mrs. Thomson lays great stress on the fact that the medical attendant of L. E. L., while residing in London, Dr. A. T. Thomson, had stated in a letter, which he published in the "Times" shortly after the death of Mrs. Maclean, "that he had attended her (Miss Landon), as a friend, for a period of fifteen years, and that he had never ordered prussic acid for her in any form." Mrs. Thomson states also, that the medicine-chest, which had been fitted up for her by Mr. Squires, of Oxford Street, did not contain that medicine, and that none of the prescriptions for her, for years, which had been compounded by that eminent chemist, by whom all prescriptions for her were usually made up, included prussic acid; and that "Mrs. Sheldon and her daughters, who had watched over Mrs. Maclean during a long illness, and who knew her habitual course of life thoroughly during the two years that she resided under their roof, asserted positively that they had never known her to take it."

The inference that Mrs. Thomson leaves, or rather leads, her readers to draw, is, that Mrs. Maclean, having no prussic acid in her possession ordered by her physician or supplied by her druggist, could not have poisoned herself with that drug, either unintentionally or wilfully.

But Mrs. Bayley deposed, at the inquest, that she had found in the hand of Mrs. Maclean an uncorked bottle, when she discovered the body lying on the floor, and the bottle, when produced, was found labelled "Hydrocianic Acid." She further deposed: "She afterwards corked the bottle, and put it aside." She added also, that she had seen her mistress take a drop or two of the medicine in the bottle, in water, two or three times, when ill with the spasms, to which she was subject. Mr. Maclean deposed, that when he had been called to Mrs. Maclean's dressing-room, on the occasion of her death, he saw a small phial upon the toilet-table, and asked Mrs. Bayley where it came from. "Mrs. Bayley told him that she had found it in Mrs. Maclean's hand; and that phial (she added) had contained Scheele's preparation of prussic acid. His wife had been in the habit of using it for severe fits of spasms, to which she was subject. She had made use of it on the voyage from England, to his knowledge. He was greatly averse to her having such a dangerous medicine, and wished to throw it overboard She requested him not to do so, as she would die without it."

Dr. Cobbold, the medical officer of the Castle, deposed, that, from his examination, he came to the opinion that death was caused by the improper use of the medicine, the bottle of which was found in her hand. He deposed further to a smell of prussic acid about her person.

In the face of this evidence, it is more difficult to admit Mrs. Thomson's inference, than to deny the possibility, nay, the probability, of Mrs. Maclean's having procured a bottle of Scheele's preparation of prussic acid, on some one of those numerous occasions of her spasmodic seizures to which she had been subject in England, especially after those severe mental disquietudes to which I have elsewhere referred. Any very intimate friend who visited her on such occasions, and found her suffering from those spasmodic attacks, might have spoken of their experience of the effects of that medicine in such seizures; and if she acted on their suggestion while so suffering, the probability is, she would not have waited to procure the sanction of her ordinary physician, but would have sent to the nearest apothecary's for the medicine, and not to a druggist in Oxford Street, upwards of two miles from her place of abode.

But, supposing that the idea of self-destruction had ever entered the head of L. E. L. while residing in England, and previously to her marriage, is it not quite clear that it is not from her regular medical attendant she would have sought a prescription for such a drug? and it is not at the druggist's where she had her prescriptions made up for many years she would have sought this dangerous drug. In such a case, it is quite evident the inference of Mrs. Thomson would be deserving of no consideration.

But there are two difficulties connected with this subject which present themselves to my mind, and I am quite at a loss to solve them. The uncorked phial which Mrs. Bayley deposed she had found in the hand of her dead mistress, when produced at the inquest was found labelled—"*Acid Hydrocianicum delulum Pharm: Lond.* 1836: *medium dose* 5 *minims.*" But not one word was mentioned in any of the depositions as to the name and address of the druggist or apothecary, which invariably, I believe, are to be found at the top and bottom of all labels of poisonous drugs of this description.

This bottle was not produced to me by Dr. Cobbold nor by Mr. Maclean when I was at Cape Coast Castle; and Dr. Cobbold had professed to afford me all the information he could give me on the subject of my inquiries touching the death of Mrs. Maclean. And very unfortunately the great importance of that circumstance had totally escaped my attention at Cape Coast Castle; it never occurred to me to inquire for that bottle, and to examine the label, with the view of ascertaining the name of the druggist or apothecary from whom it had been obtained.

The other difficulty above referred to is this: Mr. Brodie Cruickshank, in his recent work, commenting on the evidence at the inquest, of which he was one of the jurors, says, that the manner in which Mrs. Bayley alluded to the important circumstance of finding the bottle in her mistress's hand, only doing so in answer to a question from Mr. Maclean, and the manner Mrs. Bayley behaved also after her return to England, making some flagrantly false statements—"These considerations (he adds) induced him to discredit altogether Mrs. Bayley's testimony, and to believe that the phial had not been found in Mrs. Maclean's hand at all." But Mr. Cruickshank (the friend and advocate, be it observed) of Mr. Maclean, makes no doubt whatever that Mrs. Maclean had been poisoned by prussic acid, and had taken that drug inadvertently in an excessive quantity.

Here ends all the evidence that has been given to the public on this mysterious and melancholy affair. Many of those with whom I have communicated on the subject at Cape Coast Castle are no longer living. Mr. Maclean has been long dead; the magistrate before whom the inquest was held, the 15th of October, 1838, Mr. Swansey, is dead; Dr. Cobbold, the medical officer of the Castle, who was examined at the inquest, is dead, and Mr. Brodie Cruickshank, one of the jurors on the inquest, whose work, "Eighteen Years on the Gold Coast of Africa," &c., was only published about eighteen months ago, has just ended an early career in Lisbon.

Mrs. Bayley, on her arrival in England, immediately after the death of Mrs. Maclean, manifested some striking evidences of an inordinate passion for notoriety. Other persons have shown an undue desire to make a public opinion of their impressions, and to have Mr. Maclean regarded, as he was by them, not only with favour, but with deep interest and affection. Efforts like these may carry everything before them for a time, but, eventually, they not only fail, but the pertinacity with which they are made engenders doubt, stimulates inquiry, and determines its pursuit. The minds of people, in the long run, revolt at attempts to force conclusions on them which are not legitimately arrived at. From the following extracts from official papers, the reader will be enabled to form his own judgment as to the character of the person, in his public capacity, which, as in his private one, has been the subject of a great deal of unjust opprobrium—of unmerited eulogy.

In the archives of the Colonial Offices there are various documents connected with the subject of the administration of the Gold Coast government, while Mr. Maclean held the office of President of the Council, and of complaints brought against it, especially on account of the execution of a native under peculiar circumstances, and the death of another native a few hours after a flogging, administered by Mr. Maclean's orders, and in his presence. A great deal of matter that has reference to other serious complaints against Mr. Maclean, I omit, and confine myself entirely to extracts fairly taken from the original officia documents, without offering any comments on them.

Extracts from a Letter of J. J. H. Burgoyne, Esq., (late of Cape Coast), to James Stephen, Esq.

"London, September 21, 1837.

"Sir,

"Without one exception, every English merchant on that coast (Cape Coast Castle) was possessed of a retinue of 'pawns' or slaves: and from persons under the latter denomination, Mr. Maclean, the president himself, sold into the Dutch Batavian service, contrary to his will and inclination, a man named 'Coffee Sam,' and was possessed moreover of several other natives, as 'pawns,' who served him in a variety of domestic purposes.

"Corporal punishments of an inhuman description have been repeatedly inflicted during my residence on the coast upon natives, on account of their owing debts to merchants, and for other trivial offences, for which chains and imprisonment too were uniformly their portion: and, in one instance, the death of an unhappy victim ensued within twelve hours after a corporal punishment of five hundred lashes, which had been inflicted on the sole responsibility of Mr. Maclean himself (Quabino, a slave of Mr. Hanson).

"Vessels engaged in the Slave Trade, under the flags of Spain and Portugal, have frequently anchored at Cape Coast Castle, during my sojourn thère; the masters received from within the very fort the articles of merchandize that were requisite for the prosecution of the traffic in which they were engaged, and those masters were accommodated in the apartments of the President himself.

"Wretched slaves who, flying from the cruelty of savage owners in different neighbouring states, have thrown themselves upon the protection of chiefs friendly to the British, Mr. Maclean made a uniform practice of causing to be delivered up; with respect to which system (so directly in opposition to the commands conveyed in Lord Bathurst's circular, despatched the 31st of December, 1825), I am in possession of documents in the hand-writing of Mr. Maclean, which prove of themselves how invariably he pursued it: in one of which documents that gentleman says, 'I have recovered the two runaway slaves that you wrote to me about; the man slave has been redeemed, and the money paid for him; the woman slave I now send by the messengers.' And that wretched woman slave was put to death by the savage chief to whom she belonged, on the instant of her arrival at Coomasie!

"Mr. President Maclean, assisted in his judicial office solely by the merchants composing the Council, of which he was the head, I have known to condemn natives to death; which condemnation has been executed without any reference whatever to the authorities, either at Sierra Leone or in England.

"A mulatto man, named Graves, committed a murder at the British settlement of Commendale in 1836, by cruelly beating one of his slaves, and afterwards suffocating him with burned peppers. Graves was brought before Mr. Maclean, the President, and the Council, at Cape Coast Castle; but a reference in his case to the authorities at Sierra Leone would have formed a dangerous precedent, and might perchance have thrown a light upon the death of poor Quabino, Mr. Maclean's own victim; so Graves was liberated after a short confinement, which he was informed he underwent on account of certain debts that he owed to English merchants of Cape Coast, and not for having caused the death of his slave!!!

"I have the honour to be,
"&c. &c. &c.
(Signed) "J. J. H. Burgoyne."

Affidavit of Sergeant Hobbs.

"The Affidavits forwarded to England by Mr. Gedge, as a Justice of the Peace, to the Colonial Office, and to the African Committee, set forth, that Quabino was, on a certain day, tied over a three pounder field-piece, by order of Mr. Maclean, outside of the fort of British Accra, where (Mr. Maclean standing by) he, Quabino, received first 300 lashes; that after this, a fresh cat was obtained from Mr. Bannerman's, and 200 lashes more inflicted. From the said place of punishment, he (Quabino) was conveyed to a cell, where at day-light, on the very next morning, he was found lying on his face, *dead.*"

Affidavit of Henry Pocock.

"One of the *Buglars,* who inflicted the lashes, and who swears to their number (500), also testifies to having seen Quabino dead on the following morning.

"The other *Buglar,* who assisted at the punishment, stated the same facts, and was about to be examined, on oath, respecting them by Mr. Gedge, as a magistrate, when Mr. Maclean having heard of his (Gedge's) intention, confined Paine in the guard-room of the Castle, and there left him for weeks."

Affidavit of Thomas P. Grant, of Annamboe, a British Merchant.

"A merchant at Annamboe declared, on oath, that he had seen the punishment inflicted; that Maclean was present, and directing the punishment: that on the following morning, he saw the same man (Quabino) dead: that a kind of coroner's inquest assembled to view the body; that of this jury he was a member, that neither himself nor any of the others were sworn; that they entered on the face of the proceedings a verdict of—'Dead from suffocation,' and this without re-assembling; other proceedings were drawn up, and signed by the said members, he signing as well as the rest; these last proceedings (which he declared, on oath, he never even read) recording an altered verdict of—'Died by poison;' and that no evidence of the wretched Quabino's having taken poison had ever been adduced to justify this last verdict; he had no other reason why he consented to either verdict, than because he was told by Ridley (the foreman and Coroner) that it was 'all right.'"

Extracts of a Letter from George Maclean to the Committee of Merchants.

"London, Oct. 14, 1837.

"Gentlemen,

"I shall now proceed to notice and refute, *seriatim*, the several accusations contained in Mr. Burgoyne's letters, accusations I may say, which as yet are unsupported by proof: for the few documents of which Mr. Burgoyne has furnished copies, prove little or nothing, even if taken in the perverted sense in which he affects to understand them. * * * *

"I observe that the character assumed by Mr. Burgoyne, in bringing forward his charges, is that of champion of the 'deeply injured and oppressed race' of Africans on the Gold Coast. Now it will be readily admitted, that the previous conduct of a person appearing in such a character ought to be able to bear the strictest scrutiny, and that his motives ought to be above suspicion. At present, I shall only touch on Mr. Burgoyne's character as an officer; and I think that not only your records, but those of the Colonial Office and Horse Guards will bear me out in saying, that his conduct has not been such as to entitle him to the favourable notice of any department of Government. A reference to the records of the Horse Guards, will shew, that when a Lieutenant in the 33d regiment, Mr. Burgoyne was tried by a General Court Martial, and cashiered by the sentence of that Court: that when, by the clemency of the Commander-in-Chief, he was reinstated in his rank, though placed at the bottom of the list of Lieutenants of the 93d regiment, he was obliged to leave the army after serving some time, receiving the value of his commission. I now proceed, as I proposed, to reply to his charges *seriatim.*

"First,—I am accused of having wantonly, or, at least, by an undue severity, caused the death of a native at Accra, named Quabino, inasmuch as I, by my own sole authority, caused 500 lashes to be inflicted upon him, in consequence of which he died in twelve hours thereafter.

"It will scarcely be believed that the occurrence misrepresented by Mr. Burgoyne in every particular, actually took place two years before he arrived in the country, and that consequently he could know nothing of the matter, save what he might have heard from vague report, as might be expected under such circumstances; the charge is false in almost every particular. It is false, that I 'on my own authority ordered that man alluded to to be punished.' It is false, 'that he received 500 lashes.' It is false, utterly false, that he 'was punished with undue severity,' or that 'he died in consequence of such punishment.'

* * * * * *

"I am enabled to produce an official document addressed by Mr. Gedge himself to you, gentlemen, (of a date long subsequent to that of the proceedings in question), wherein he repudiates in the strongest terms the whole of those proceedings, expresses his deep regret that he should have been unwarily led by Mr. Burgoyne to institute them, and states, in fine, that subsequent inquiries had fully and generally satisfied him that no grounds whatever existed for the accusation attempted to be got up against me. But further, I will presently show that Mr. Burgoyne did, in subsequent letters to the president and council, express himself in nearly similar terms, in which he fully acquitted me, not only of the charges in question, but of all or nearly all of the other charges, which he now for the vilest of purposes thinks proper to revive, in a country where he deems his own character unknown, and where he, perhaps, thinks it will be difficult to disprove his reckless allegations. After what has been already stated, I need scarcely add, that the documents called 'affidavits,' were papers drawn up by Mr. Burgoyne himself, and assented to by these men (who being ignorant of their contents, and not being Christians, could not make 'affidavits' of such) through fear; at least, they afterwards came to me, requesting to be made acquainted with the substance of those documents, and expressing their readiness and wishes to swear to any counteracting statements which I might think proper to draw up; to which offer I, of course, paid no attention.

"I trust you will be of opinion that this, Mr. Burgoyne's first charge, is sufficiently answered.

"2nd. Mr. Burgoyne's second charge is, 'that a system of pawning' the natives, and thence of coercive labour, prevails on the Gold Coast.

"The prevalence of this system, even if there were (which there is not) anything morally wrong or illegal in it, cannot be charged against the government of Cape Coast Castle, since it has prevailed in that country from time immemorial, and the local government possesses neither the right nor the power to interfere with it. This system (which, under different names and modifications, prevails more or less in every country in the world) is peculiarly adapted to a state of society so constituted as that on the Gold Coast of Spain; and Mr. Burgoyne might as well exclaim against the system of apprenticeship in England, as it also induces a system of coercive labour.

"The system which Mr. Burgoyne impotently attempted to make a handle, in order to excite a prejudice in this country against the resident merchants on the Gold Coast, is simply this; a man owes a debt, perhaps, which is utterly out of his power to pay, he thereupon applies to a person of property, and offers to serve him as a labourer or domestic servant, as the case may be, at a low rate of wages, provided he (the person of property) will pay the debt, the debtor binding himself to serve his new employer until he shall have saved enough, or otherwise acquired property sufficient to repay the sum advanced on his own account. But his master has no more power over his 'pawn,' than he has over any other servant: if he were to ill-use him, the servant has only to apply to the next magistrate, and the master would at once be punished; or, if the 'pawn' is dissatisfied with his situation, he has only to apply to any one whom he would prefer as his master, and he will, in nine cases out of ten, pay his debt (which the former master is obliged to accept), and take him as his servant. Many persons become 'pawns' when there is no necessity whatever for the step, merely for the purpose of securing regular and steady employment. In short, to relieve a debtor of his obligations and to accept of his services in lieu of the debt, is not uncommon, I presume in England, or any country in the world; and the system of pawning in Africa is nothing more or less—at all events, as I have already said, the local government is not answerable for it.

"Mr. Burgoyne goes on, in his usual reckless manner, to assert, that natives are indiscriminately flogged, for owing sums of money to the merchants. This I do most distinctly and fearlessly deny; and I defy Mr. Burgoyne to produce a single instance of what I would be myself the first to denounce as gross and wanton cruelty. Mr. Burgoyne alleges, as a charge against the head government, what he must or ought to have known to be utterly destitute of foundation. He alleges, namely, that I, assisted by the council, did upon our own authority, try, condemn, and execute a man, for murder. It is utterly false that we ever did so, in any one instance. The case alluded to by Mr. Burgoyne, you will find in our dispatches of the 12th of August, 1834, which most distinctly prove that our interference in that case was strictly confined within the limits prescribed by your dispatch of the 21st January, 1835: to see, namely, that no injustice was committed towards the wretched criminal, and that he did not suffer unnecessary torture, or cruelty, which, but for such interference, would most certainly have been practised. What was done, was done in the face of day, in the presence of assembled hundreds; and it is surprising how Mr. Burgoyne could have ventured to a statement so capable of being at once and most completely refuted.

"I now come to a case of a man named Graves, who, according to Mr. Burgoyne's statement, committed murder, at British Commendale, from the merited consequences of which crime he was screened by me, inasmuch as a strict inquiry into the case might have induced a similar inquiry into the case of the Accra man Quabino. * * * *

"I have frequently known Her Majesty's cruisers to lie at anchor in Cape Coast roadstead, along-side of vessels which both the commander of the former and myself had every reason to think were employed in the slave trade, but with which we had no power to interfere; but when I could interfere, I have always shown myself zealous and anxious to do so. And the report of more than one of the commanders of Her Majesty's ships to the Admiralty, will show that my exertions in that cause have been unremitting, and not in vain.

"I have the honour to be,

"Gentlemen, &c.

(Signed) "GEO. MACLEAN."

Extract of a Letter from the London Committee to the President and Council of Government at Cape Coast Castle.

"21st January, 1835.

"Upon perusal of your proceedings in Council of 12th Aug. 1834, we observe that the president brought under your consideration the case of a man who had committed murder, and then a prisoner in Annamboe Fort; and it was agreed that the murderer should be tried by the native authorities, and that you should only interfere in so far as to prevent injustice and inhumanity.

"We conclude that the criminal was found guilty, but we trust that the execution of the sentence was solely in the hands of the natives, and that you took no responsibility upon yourselves. These occurrences, however, although they may be perfectly proper, expose you and us to a serious responsibility, and it is impossible but that they should be conducted with too much caution.

"We therefore direct, that in every case which seems in the least likely to affect the life of an individual, that three magistrates may be present, and that we may receive a certificate, signed by them, that they had been present during the whole of the trial, that to the best of their opinion the judgment of the Pigmies and Caboosees was correct, and the criminal justly punished. * * *

Extracts from the Proceedings in Council at Cape Coast Castle, the 11th November, 1833.

"After which, he, the president, read a letter which he had received from Mr. Hansen, of Accra, soon after his arrival at that place, requesting his interference in recovering some of his servants who had escaped from prison, and who had made themselves over to the fetish in a village in Aquapino; in which letter Mr. Hanson stated that he had applied to the Danish government to recover them, but without effect.

"The president stated that he had succeeded in bringing them to justice; that one of them, on being punished, had poisoned himself. Upon which occurrence taking place, the president intimated that he had summoned a jury of all the gentlemen then at Accra to hold an inquest on the body, Commandant Ridley being coroner. A copy of the coroner's inquest was then read.

"Present,—Geo. Maclean, *President*;—J. Swanzy, R. Roberts, J. Jackson, *Members*."

Letter from J. Jackson, Esq., of Cape Coast Castle, laid before the London Committee.

"Cape Coast Castle, 23rd November, 1833.

"GENTLEMEN,

"The public mind is so ill satisfied with the cause of the death of the man flogged by the president at Accra, in October last—it is said 500 lashes, and died in a close and loathsome gaol, in less than twelve hours after enduring his punishment —that I think it my duty to acquaint you therewith, and to declare my firm persuasion, a fair, full, and impartial inquiry cannot be obtained while the president remains in authority here; the dread of the consequences of rendering themselves obnoxious to him—no man considering himself safe, his conduct has been so arbitrary—would alone suffice to restrain them from giving evidence. However, it is not of this subject only I find fault; and as I am told other gentlemen will forward to England the particulars, I, therefore, will no longer dwell upon it; but of his tyrannical, arbitrary, and oppressive proceedings generally I complain, in entire disregard of the Council, as stated in my letter addressed to the President and Council in July last, and again touched upon in that of the 23rd of September.

"That, in my own behalf, and in behalf of the natives of Africa, I entreat your consideration of the matter, with the view of affording us protection, restraining the President within the just exercise of his authority, and, I hope, restoring the conduct of affairs here, as they were originally intended by his Majesty's Government, to the wholesome management of a council.

"I have the honour to be, &c.,

(Signed) "J. JACKSON."

"London, 2nd April, 1834.

"At a committee held this day—

The committee had under consideration Mr. Jackson's letter of the 23rd November, also the minute of council of the 11th of the same month, respecting the man flogged at Accra, when Mr. Gibson stated,—

"That he was at Cape Coast in October, and until the early part of January, and also was at Accra both before and after the punishment: that the subject was frequently mentioned in conversation at both places, and the general opinion was, that the man did not die from the flogging, but from taking poison. That the public mind did not appear dissatisfied with the inquiry that had taken place; and that he considered Mr. Maclean a most humane and able man, and in every respect highly qualified for his office.

(Signed) "TIMOTHY GIBSON."

"London, 5th April, 1834.

"The committee resumed the consideration of the above-mentioned subject, when Captain Longridge, of the 'Prince Oscar,' who, they had been informed by Mr. Gibson, was present at the punishment, and was one of the members of the inquest, attended, and stated,—

"That he was present at the commencement of the punishment, and passed again before it was finished: that it was inflicted with a cat that had been very much used, so that it had become quite soft: that the man received, he believes, about 250 lashes: that the punishment did not exceed that which he had seen inflicted upon a schoolboy: that he afterwards saw the man walking through the court-yard of the Fort to the prison, after having received his punishment. He further stated, that the man cried out at the early part of the punishment, but not afterwards, while he attended: that the Cabooses, Pigmies, and chief men of the place attended the inquiry upon which he received his sentence: that the man was confined during the night, with about twenty others, in prison, and in the morning was found dead: that an inquiry was held by Mr. Ridley, Commandant of the Fort—President, Mr. Fry, M.C., Mr. Hanson, Mr. Bannerman, Mr. Grant, Mr. Barnard, and Captain Longridge, who, after hearing the evidence of the other prisoners, gave it as their opinion, that the man died from having taken poison.

"That there was no surgeon at Accra, or at the Danish Fort. That the members of the inquiry were not sworn: that he was not aware that the public mind was at all dissatisfied on this subject. (Signed) J. LONGRIDGE."

Copy of a Letter from Sir George Grey to the Committee of Merchants for Superintending the Affairs of the Gold Coast.

"Downing Street, 4th December, 1837.

"GENTLEMEN,

"I have laid before Lord Glenelg your letter of the 16th ultimo, inclosing various documents, in answer to the charges preferred against the local authorities at Cape Coast Castle by Mr. Burgoyne, in his letters of the 2nd, 16th, 21st, and 25th September, 1837.

"After fully considering the statements made by Mr. Burgoyne and your own, and Mr. Maclean's counter-statements, and the evidence adduced on either side, Lord Glenelg has formed the following conclusions, which his Lordship instructs me to communicate to you.

"First,—With regard to the case of Quabino, Lord Glenelg finds that, in the month of October, 1833, Quabino, a native servant, belonging to Mr. Hanson, a British subject, residing under the protection of James' Fort, Accra, was punished at that place by flogging; that, after the punishment, he was committed to gaol; that within twelve hours of his commitment he died; that an inquiry was held by seven gentlemen, of whom the Commandant of the Fort was the president, into the cause of Quabino's death; that the members of the court of inquiry were not sworn; that they examined the fellow-prisoners of the deceased; that the court formed the opinion that Quabino died from having taken poison; that no medical examination was or could have been made, because there was no surgeon at Accra or at the neighbouring Danish Fort; that this transaction engaged the attention of your predecessors, who received the statement of Messrs. Longridge, Roberts, and Gibson on the subject, and from their concurrent evidence drew the conclusion that the punishment of Quabino was not the occasion of his death. Notwithstanding the necessarily imperfect nature of the investigation, owing to the impossibility of medical examination, Lord Glenelg sees no ground sufficient for doubting the correctness of this conclusion. At the same time, I am to observe, that it does not appear by what authority of law the punishment was inflicted, nor to what extent Mr. Maclean is responsible for that sentence. And that his Lordship is of opinion that the infliction of so many as 250 lashes (the number assigned by Mr. Longridge) was a measure of a very severe nature, in defence of which, some very urgent reason ought to be adducible. Lord Glenelg, therefore, must call on Mr. Maclean to state what was the offence of Quabino, under what law he was tried for it, and by whom the trial was conducted, and what precautions, if any, may have been taken to prevent the punishment being urged beyond the point at which it would become dangerous to the life or health of the sufferer.

"Secondly,—Lord Glenelg cannot regard that which is called in these papers the 'pawning system,' without considerable doubt as to its propriety. It is, in effect, that of engaging to serve an employer until the labourer shall, by the wages of his labour, have redeemed any debt which he may owe to the person whom he undertakes to serve. To such an engagement there can be no valid objection, if regard be had merely to the abstract justice and reasonableness of conduct. It is simply an agreement to pay in labour a debt which there is no other means of liquidating; but in a country in which slavery so long prevailed, contracts of this kind may be readily made a pretext for perpetuating, under a new name, the ancient system; and it appears to Lord Glenelg that no such contract ought to be valid, unless made for some short, definite period, and in the presence, and with the consent, of some magistrate, who should be responsible for the fairness of the transaction.

" Thirdly,—Mr. Maclean would appear to maintain that, upon the Gold Coast, slavery is still lawful. If his reasoning be, that it is lawful within any territory in the Gold Coast, within Her Majesty's dominions, this is a very serious misconception. Nothing can be more complete or unequivocal than the terms in which Parliament has provided for the Abolition of Slavery in every part of Her Majesty's dominions.

" Fourthly,—The restitution of fugitive slaves when reclaimed by the neighbouring chiefs, is a practice which Mr. Maclean admits, and vindicates the existence. Without undertaking to say that the defence is unsatisfactory, it appears to Lord Glenelg that the practice requires a more ample explanation than it has yet received. Especially it is necessary to state, on what grounds is supposed to rest the legality of sending any person from a British possession into a foreign country, there to be dealt with as a slave; what are the specific evils which the surrender of these persons designed to obviate, and what are the grounds on which it is apprehended that any such evils would result from refusing to restore them into slavery.

" Lord Glenelg further directs me to state, that subject to the preceding remarks, he considers the answers to Mr. Burgoyne's charges as entirely satisfactory. And his Lordship regrets, that he should, however unintentionally on his part, have been made the channel of conveying to Mr. Maclean imputations on his character at once so injurious and so unfounded.

" With reference to your suggestion, that Rear-Admiral Elliott should be instructed, on his arrival on the Gold Coast, to enquire into the system of Government pursued by Mr. Maclean during his Presidency, I am to inform you, that Lord Glenelg has intimated his opinion to the Lord Commissioners of the Admiralty, that such an inquiry would be highly satisfactory if it can be effected without inconvenience to the naval service on that station.

" I am, &c.

(Signed) " Geo. Grey."

Letter from G. Maclean, Esq. to the Committee of Merchants, &c.

"Craven Hotel, Craven Street, London,
"December 16, 1837.

"Gentlemen,

"* * * The additional particulars respecting the case of the man Quabino, called for by Lord Glenelg, are as follow:—

"The crime, or rather series of crimes, which subjected him to trial and punishment were singularly aggravated, and, in that country, of rare occurrence. In the month of March, 1833, he with three accomplices (all in the employ of Mr. Hanson), planned and executed, in the dead of night, three distinct burglaries; two in British, and one in Danish Accra.

"In the commission of these crimes they grossly maltreated several unprotected women, and finally, having collected all the plunder upon which they could lay their hands, they escaped into the mountainous district of Aquapim; after much trouble and expense, they were captured in the month of May, and sentenced to work as prisoners until the amount of property whereof they had robbed their victims should be made good, as well as a sum of money, in the shape of compensation for the injuries they had inflicted upon the sufferers.

"The case upon this occasion was heard before the new Commandant (the late Mr. Ridley), and another Magistrate, assisted, as is usual, by several of the Cabooceers or head men; and the latter, though greatly exasperated against the prisoners, agreed to the mode of punishment above stated as affording the only means whereby the unfortunate sufferers could receive reparation of their losses. The four prisoners had not been confined two weeks in pursuance of this sentence, when they contrived to break out of prison during the night-time, and having committed a fresh burglary in British Accra, they again escaped into Aquapim, taking care, however, upon this occasion, to take refuge with the fetish or priests, &c. * * *

"The Aquapims persisted in their refusal to surrender the fugitives, whereupon I dispatched a force fully adequate to the object in view, with strict injunctions to confine itself to the particular service in which it was sent, viz., to secure and bring to Accra the four criminals.

"This service, after considerable trouble and difficulty, was accomplished. But it ought here to be mentioned, that the man Quabino, whose death occurred subsequently, attempted, when he saw his capture was inevitable, to commit suicide by hanging himself, which he had nearly accomplished, when discovered by the sergeant of the party, to whom he thus declared, 'that his master should never get another day's work out of him.'

"Such were the circumstances under which the four prisoners were brought before myself and another, and the Caboceers of Accra, when the extreme atrocity of the crimes committed by the prisoners in the first instance, joined to their prison breaking, and subsequent burglary, led to an unanimous sentence, on the part of their judges, that they should be severely whipped in different parts of the town, as well for the sake of example, as to shew the inhabitants generally, that, under no circumstances, could such atrocious criminals escape from merited punishment. To obviate the possibility of danger to the lives or health of the criminals from the severity of the punishment, previously to the execution of the sentence, I directed Mr. Mark Clelland (a young man who had formerly been attached to the army medical department, and had often attended military punishments when the King's troops were in the country), to attend the punishment of the prisoners, and to stop it whenever he saw the slightest cause, my orders being, that they were not to be so severely punished as to prevent their speedily resuming their work as labourers. When Mr. Clelland made his report to me, after the punishment of the man Quabino, and when I inquired whether he was so much hurt as to require medical treatment, he assured me that he required no extraordinary attention or treatment whatever: and having seen the man myself, I can with truth declare, that he had been very slightly punished; indeed, so slightly, as to justify the words of Captain L., one of the witnesses, 'That he had seen a schoolboy more severely flogged.' * * * * * * *

"I have, &c.

(Signed) "Geo. Maclean."

No. XV.

ASSASSINATION OF THE ABBÉ STEWART.

About two years ago, at Previtalè's Italian Hotel and Restaurant, Panton Square, Haymarket, there was an Italian waiter, who had been a servant to the Abbé Stewart, at the time of his assassination in Italy, as it was said by brigands, (as I was informed by the proprietor of the hotel he had learned from this waiter), and who, on account of the great care he had taken of the Abbé, during the short time the latter survived after the mortal wounds inflicted on him, had been left a pension, I think, of £50 a-year, and after the Abbé's death who had come to England, with the view of securing the bequest.

Mr. Previtalè had asked me, as a favour, to advise the man as to the best means of applying to the family of Mr. Stewart, and in compliance with this wish, I suggested his sending in some memorial to the brother of the Abbé, a Scotch baronet, residing in Perthshire.

The account which this man gave me of the murder of the Abbé, whom I had known in Naples, before he became an ecclesiastic in 1824, was not a very clear one. I could not understand from him what had brought him to the spot where he found his wounded master, or whether he had accompanied him to the place, and had fled when the brigands made their appearance. But as I had found some difficulty in understanding this man's Italian, and as he appeared to me, moreover, a half-witted sort of fellow, I attached no importance then to that confused account. But now, after the perusal of the account of the recent "horrible murder" in Foley Place, by Luigi Baranelli, formerly valet of Thomas Stewart Drummond, Esq., of Perth, by whom he is said to have "been allowed an ample pension," a suspicion arises in my mind, that he may have been the assassin likewise of the Abbé Stewart—the identical Thomas Stewart Drummond above referred to.

9th January, 1855. R. R. M.

INDEX

TO THE THREE VOLUMES.

A.

Abell, Mrs., Napoleon's pet English child at St. Helena, "Betsy Balcomb," ii. 323.

Aberdeen, Lord, Gell's references to family, ii. 32.

Abinger, Lord, notice of, iii. 108; letters of, 113.

Acton, Lady, her theatricals at Naples in 1834, ii. 78.

Acton, Sir Frederick, notice of, ii. 114.

Aguilar, Colonel, enclosing a lock of Mrs. Hemans' hair to Lady B., iii. 311.

Ainsworth, W. H., Esq., notice of, iii. 475.

Allen, John, Esq., notice of, iii. 459.

Alpinula, Julia, remarkable sepulchral inscription, ii. 353, 378.

Anson, Henry, acquaintance with Lady B. at Florence, i. 117.

Arlincourt, Vicomte De, notice of, and letter to Lady B., ii. 180.

Auckland, Lord, notice of, iii. 429

Auldjo. John, his ascent to summit of Mont Blanc, ii. 88; letter to Lady B., 201.

B.

Barings, the, at Florence in 1828, ii. 185.

Bathurst, Miss, account of her death by drowning at Rome, ii. 26; reference to her death, 116; account of finding her dead body, 145; Lord Aylmer's account, 384.

Beattie, Dr. William, notice of, letters and poems, iii. 253.

Biography, observations of Editor on its legitimate inquiries, i. 1; of Sir Egerton Brydges, 5; of a German writer, 7; reference to Goldsmith's Life, 9.

Blakeney, General, present at the marriage of Miss M. Power, i. 437.

Blessington, Lady, Miss Power's account of her family: early life, i. 11; pedigree of the Sheehy family, 12; account of her mother's family, the Sheehys, 15; details of persecution of Father Sheehy, 389; education, home, family circle, 17; removal from Knockbrit to Clonmel, *ib.*; first marriage and results, *see* Power, 1804, 30; residence at Cahir, 35; in Dublin, 58; at Sidmanton, Hants, *ib.*; second marriage with Lord B. in 1818, *ib.*; peculiar character of her beauty, 59; first presentation to his Irish friends, 61; accompanies Lord B. to his Tyrone estates, *ib.*; costly preparations made at

Mountjoy Forest, 62; singular contrasts of splendour and misery, *ib.*; numerous claims on Lady B.'s bounty, i. 41; removal of, from Manchester Square to St. James's Square, 69; launched into fashionable life, 70; the éclat of her beauty, and graces of her conversation, *ib.*; turn for grave irony, *ib.*; reference to her by Moore, visits her with W. Irving in 1822, *ib.*; brilliant society in St. James's Square, 71; surrounded by the first celebrities of the time, *ib.*; first acquaintance with Count D'Orsay in London, *ib.*; illustrious personages visitors at St. James's Square, 72; leaves England on a continental tour in 1822, 73; Miss M. Anne Power accompanies them, *ib.*; Count D'Orsay joins their party in France, 79; extensive preparations in Paris for their tour, 75; renews her acquaintance with Denon, 76; mentions two visits to Paris, previous to 1822, *ib.*; Moore's frequent visits to her at Paris, *ib.*; in Moore's company, descends "La Montagne Russe," 77; observations on art in the galleries of the Louvre, 78; admires a Madonna and child, by Raphael, in spite of her "stern Protestantism," *ib.*; sets out for Switzerland, 79; joined by Count D'Orsay, and sets out for Italy, 80; her works, "The Idler in France," "The Idler in Italy," *ib.*; is introduced to Byron, 1st April, 1823, at Genoa, 81; her description of Byron, 82; Byron's account of this interview, 83; first mention of D'Orsay in her Diaries, 84; arrangements for the Count's accompanying the party to Naples, *ib.*; Byron's liking for D'Orsay, 85; Byron's epigram, "Il diavolo e entrato in Paradiso," *ib.*; lines of Byron to, 86; letter of Byron to, *ib.*; parting with Byron, 88; Byron's farewell letter to, 89; second visit to Genoa, visits his former abode, 90; observations on Byron's death, *ib.*; refers to "*consequences resulting from the violation of ties, never severed without retribution,*" *ib.*; no cordial friendship between her and Byron, 91; departure from Genoa for Naples, 2nd June, 1823, 92; arrival in Rome, 5th July, 1823, 93; disappointed, departs after nine days for Naples, 95; fastidious tastes, occasional aims at stage effects, *ib.*; arrival at Naples, delighted with its scenery, climate, site, &c. *ib.*; her glowing description of the bay, 96; yachting excursions, 103; her account of "The Bolivar," *ib.*; residence in the Palazzo Belvidere, 105; singular beauty of its site and scenery, 106; her description of it, *ib.*; visits to Pompeii, Herculaneum, with Gell, 107; her lines on Pompeii, *ib.*; visits to ancient monuments, with eminent savans and artists, *ib.*; visits Pæstum, with Lord Morpeth, Mr. Millingen, &c. 108; notice of ruins of Pæstum, 110; ascent of Mount Vesuvius, *ib.*; celebrities who frequented the Palazzo Belvidere, 113; removal to the Villa Gallo in March, 1825, 114; departure from Naples in February, 1826, *ib.*; proceeds via Rome to Florence, sojourn there, 115; revisits Genoa, meets Lord John Russell, 116; returns to Pisa, remains there till June, 1827, 117; returns to Florence, acquaintance there, *ib.*; returns to Rome, December, 1827, rents the Palazzo Negrone, 125; enormous expenditure there, *ib.*; the seeds of the Encumbered Estates Court sown in Italy, *ib.*; Editor, on return from Egypt, visits the Blessingtons in Rome, *ib.*; saw there the first time the young Countess D'Orsay, then three months married, i. 125; preparations for departure from Rome, May 7th, 1828, 127; parting entertainment given to her by Mr. Mills, 128; among the guests, Sir William Gell, Mr. and Mrs. Dodwell, *ib.*; Gell and Count Esterhazy see her take her departure, *ib.*; Gell's fears expressed that they should meet no more, *ib.*; refers to her visit that day to Sir W. Drummond's grave, *ib.*; visits the shrine of the Santa Casa at Loretto, 129; philosophizes *a l'Anglaise* on superstitious mummeries, *ib.*; witnesses the execution of three men at Ravenna, 130; renews her acquaintance at Venice with W. S. Landor, 131; visits the Ambrosian library at Milan, *ib.*; her account of a lock of the golden hair of Lucretia Borgia, and several letters of hers to Cardinal Bembo: obtains some of the hair, reference to it in the "New Monthly Magazine," for 1825, *ib.*; visits the shrine of San Carlo Boromeo, in the Duomo of Milan, 132; at the close of 1828 re-visits Genoa, 133; five years previously knew Byron there, 132; on last occasion saw Lady Byron and her daughter there, 134; departure for Paris, and close of her Italian life, *ib.*; returns to Paris in June, 1828, after an absence of six years, 135; first visitors, Duke and Duchess de Guiche, *ib.*; rents the Hotel Ney, *ib.*; great expenditure in adorning Hotel, *ib.*; the magnificence of the decorations, &c. ordered by Lord B., suitable for royalty, *ib.*; her description of the chambre a coucher and dressing-room: the bed, with its gorgeous hangings, supported on the backs of large silvered swans, &c. 136; the luxurious adornments and furniture, compared with those of the Imperial Palace at Fontainbleau, 138; publication of her memoirs suggested by one of her friends, iii. 305, 306; return to London in 1830, i. 153; conversational powers: love of intellectual society, *ib.*; three leading circles of London intellectual celebrities some twenty years ago: the remarkable women who presided over them, *ib.*; conversational powers of Fox, Mackintosh, Sydney Smith, Lord Holland, Madame de Staël, 156; her love of London life, like De Staël's love of Paris, 159; establishment in Seamore Place in 1831: beginning of third phase in her literary career, 167; her picture of "the modern Mecænases of May Fair," patronesses of "tame poets and petits littérateurs, who run about drawing-rooms as docile as lapdogs, *ib.*; reasons for giving up house in St. James's Square, 168; description of the réunions of London: celebrities at her house in Seamore Place, 169; Willis's reference to those réunions, and their celebrities, 174; B. Haydon's references to her soirées, 181; her house robbed in Seamore Place, 182; removes to Gore House, *ib.*; changes in her tastes at different epochs, *ib.*; different periods of Editor's renewed acquaintance with her, 183; character of Gore House society, 184; laudable aim of Lady B. in bringing people together, of opposite pursuits, opinions, and interests, 186; one of her foreign guests, Monsieur Julien le Jeune de Paris, in his youth a secretary of Robespierre, said to be a regicide and a terrorist, a philanthropist, a poet, and a sentimentalist in his old age, *ib.*; his recitations in the first revolution, 187; at Lady B.'s, of his dolorous poem, "Mes Chagrins Politiques," i. 187; his gift of tears, 188; D'Orsay's talent in drawing out Julien: a scene with Dr. Quin, Editor, &c. &c. 191; Julien and L.E.L., 192; Lady B.'s embarrassments consequent on expensive establishment of Gore House: D'Orsay's difficulties, claims of many persons on her bounty, 193; punctuality in her accounts, *ib.*; folly of thinking of sustaining a fashionable position by the aid of literature, *ib.*; Charles Lamb's opinion on literature as a calling for a livelihood, 194; expenditure at Gore House, 195; costly efforts to maintain a literary position: Scott's reference to Lydia White, *ib.*; pressure of misfortunes, and pecuniary losses of Lady B., 196; beginning of literary career in St. James's Square, with the publication of "Sketches of Scenes in the Metropolis," &c.: the first sketch, descriptive of the ruin of a fashionable London establishment, and an auction of its magnificent furniture, might serve for that of the sale at Gore House twenty-seven years later, 210; vicissitudes and changes of fortune of occupiers of Gore House, 461; arrives in Paris middle of April, 1849, 213; takes an *appartement* near Champs Elysèes, and furnishes it with much elegance, *ib.*; preparations made in vain: takes possession of the new abode 3rd of June, 1849, and dies the day following, after a sojourn of five weeks in Paris, *ib.*; on arrival in Paris, found coldness and neglect in some quarters, where she had a right to expect kindness and gratitude, 214; *accueil* of Prince Louis Napoleon, *ib.*; plans for a new literary career formed in Paris, *ib.*; vague and unfounded rumours concerning her death, 215; striking coincidences in circumstances of sudden deaths of Lord and Lady B. in Paris, each event shortly after arrival from London, *ib.*; reminded, in a letter to her a few weeks before her death, by a British Peeress, of the necessity of remembering religious duties, 216; on two Sundays, while in Paris, attended the church of the Madeleine, *ib.*; Heath's failure, Irish famine, and difficulties leading to the break-up at Gore House, 196; advice of friends on ditto, 198; in April, 1849, the long-impending crash, 200; execution put in, 201; for two years previously, constant fears of executions, arrest of D'Orsay, and precautions to prevent them, *ib.*; particulars of first intimation of the execution in Gore House, *ib.*; auction at Gore House,—foreshadows of that *denouement* in some of her works: her remarks on the old curiosity shops of Paris, and breaking up of great establishments, 202; the concluding words, "So will it be when I am gone," 203; catalogue of magnificent effects and furniture of Gore House, *ib.*; 10th May, 1849, and following days, Editor attends sale, meets several of the old guests and intimate friends of the house, sees Lawrence's portraits of Lord and Lady B. sold, several of D'Orsay's portraits, the library, Lady B.'s ornaments of gold and silver, 207; letters of a few kind friends to her on the break-up, 208; departure from Gore House, accompanied by her nieces, for the continent, 14th April, 1849, and end of her London career, *ib.*; state of religious opinions for many previous years, weariness of spirit, vague desires for retirement from the turmoil of a life in salons and literary labours, i. 216; remarkable conversation of Editor with D'Orsay, respecting Lady B.'s religious sentiments and creed, shortly before his death, 353; particulars of her last illness and death given in a letter of Miss Power to Editor, 217; account of monument erected by D'Orsay, 219; English inscription by Barry Cornwall, 220; Latin inscription, altered from one by W. S. Landor, 221; Landor's original inscription and translation, *ib.*; reference to an inscription on the tomb of Dryden's daughter, 222; different accounts of the ages of Lady B. and sister, 223; notices in public journals of her death, *ib.*; view of her literary career, tastes, and talents, 227; some analogy with those of Madame Geoffrin, *ib.*; D'Alembert's account of Madame Geoffrin—"*Sa passion de donner,*"—unceasing beneficence: her *soirées,* and *entourage* of authors, artists, literati, &c. 228; testimonies of Mr. and Mrs. Hall to Lady B.'s active and untiring benevolence, 230; her eagerness to discover merit in others, and *enjouement* of her appreciation of it, 233; an outline of a class of habitual depreciators of talent, who ignore all merit superior to their own, *ib.*; Lady B. naturally of a frank, generous, noble, and kindly nature, 234; testimony of one eighteen years about her, to her generous disposition, her numerous charities and sympathies with the unfortunate, 235; various instances of her benevolence, irrespective of all considerations but the necessities of people, 236; embarrassments of late years constantly augmenting: her life a continual struggle with difficulties, and her position in the brilliant society around her a state of splendid misery, 237; vanity of consolation in such circumstances sought in the worldly wisdom of Rochefoucault, 238; the undue importance she attached to the writings of the modern French philosophers, 240; her fatal gift of pre-eminent attractiveness in society, 242; the double influence exercised by her of intellectuality and beauty, *ib.*; the necessity of keeping up a dominion obtained by such influence by constant administrations of cordial professions of affection and admiration, epistolary or conversational, 242; Dr. Parr's designation—"the most gorgeous Lady Blessington," 243; the misery of being continually en scene, 244; her reflections on various subjects. MS. books of hers, named "Night thought books:" some of them well deserving of attention, on the wrongs and woes of women, 246; several short pieces in verse of the same character, 249; notices of her works, 253; notice of the Annuals edited by her: contributors to them: origin and decline of those periodicals—specimen of Lady B.'s poetical contributions, 267; when income from novel writing and the editing of Annuals fell off, efforts to derive emolument from connection with periodical literature of another kind: engagement with the "Daily News," as a contributor of exclusive intelligence, 275; income derived from her literary labours for several years, 277; waifs and strays of thoughts and observations, 278; lines addressed to her by various persons, 295; notice of her correspondence with celebrities of all climes and pursuits, princes and princesses, peers, divines, statesmen, lawyers, literati, artists, military heroes, exiled patriots, actors, &c. ii. 1; letters to Captain Marryatt, iii. 228; to Sir Henry Bulwer, 66; to Sir R. Peel, 135; to Dr. Beattie, 260; to Mrs. Mathews, 357; to Lady W., respecting L. E. L., ii. 295, iii. 289; to R. R. Madden, iii. 276; to Charles Mathews, 351; to Madame Guiccioli, ii. 231; to Charles Bianconi, iii. 303; to W. S. Landor, ii. 340; to John Forster, 398; to a young lady, referring to unhappiness, iii. 404.

Blessington, Lord, notice of origin, Right Honourable Charles John Gardiner, 2nd Viscount Mountjoy, i. 41; notice of 1st Viscount Mountjoy, career, death, 47; succession of his son, large fortune, 50; adopts his father's political principles, *ib.*; elected a representative Peer in 1809, *ib.*; first speech in House of Peers, 51; part taken by him on Queen's trial, *ib.*; young lord's manners, deportment, and education, *ib.*; taste for the drama, lavish in his patronage, *ib.*; habits of self-indulgence, 52; acquaintance with Mrs. Brown in 1808, 53; establishment at Worthing, *ib.*; in Portman Square, *ib.*; his son, Charles John, born there, *ib.*; in Manchester Square, *ib.*; his daughter, Emilie Rosalie, born there, *ib.*; marriage with Mrs. Brown in 1812, *ib.*; birth of Lady Harriet Frances Anne Gardiner, 54; Lord and Lady Mountjoy proceed to Paris, *ib.*; death of Lady Mountjoy at Paris, in Sept. 1814, *ib.*; ages of children, birth and death of son and heir, *ib.*; dates of marriages of daughters, *ib.*; grief for Lady Mountjoy, 55; funeral pageant of great magnificence, *ib.*; remains of Lady M. conveyed to Dublin, *ib.*; vast expenditure, lying in state, extraordinary pomp and splendour, *ib.*; scene at the house of mourning, 56; burial in St. Thomas's Church, Dublin, *ib.*; second marriage, in February, 1817, with Mrs. Farmer, 57; present at marriage, Sir W. P. Campbell, W. Purves, Robert Power, F. S. Poole, *ib.*; his residence, Henrietta Street, Dublin, 61; his prodigality, 62; dinner there, first introduction of Lady B. to his friends, 61; one guest at that bridal party who had been last there when Lady M.'s remains were lying in state, *ib.*; vast expenditure of preparations for visit to Mountjoy Forest, 60; evidence of unsoundness of judgment in lavish expenditure, 63; created Earl, 48; embarrassments at time of marriage, 63; annual income from Irish estates, *ib.*; visit of Editor to Tyrone estates, *ib.*; liberality as a landlord, *ib.*; builds a theatre on one of his estates at Rash, 64; private theatricals there, enormous expenditure, *ib.*; actors and actresses domiciled at Rash, *ib.*; Moore's reference to those theatricals, 65; dilapidation of the house, disappearance of theatre, 67; assists at banquet to John Kemble, on his retirement, 65; assists in the Kilkenny theatricals, 66; played *The Green Knight,* in Valentine and Orson, *ib.*; the Rash theatricals, from 1802 to 1812, *ib.*; theatrical tastes of Lord B.'s father, 475; visits his Tyrone estates with General D'Orsay and a son of the Duc de Guiche, 69; his last visit to them in 1825, *ib.*; sets out for the Continent in Sept. 1822, 73; hires the cook of an Emperor, provides a vast batterie de cuisine, 78; renews his acquaintance with Byron at Genoa, 81; buys Byron's yacht, the Bolivar, 92; receives the news at Genoa of the death of his son and heir, 119; an account of his surviving children, i. 119; his two daughters left in Ireland, in charge of his sister, Lady Harriet Gardiner, *ib.*; makes a codicil to his will at Genoa, 2nd June, 1823, naming Count D'Orsay sole guardian of his surviving son, and his sister guardian of his daughters, reciting engagement entered into with Count D'Orsay, to marry one of his daughters, 120; bequeaths £3000 a-year to Lady B., 121; 31st Aug. 1823, executes a new will, provides for intended marriage, reduces annuity to Lady B., 122; D'Orsay's marriage took place the 1st of Dec. 1827, 125; great extravagance in Paris in 1828, 137; large outlay in decoration of the Hotel Ney, 138; proceeds to England, in 1829, to vote for Catholic emancipation, 139; Editor visits his Lordship at St. James's Square, *ib.*; his deep interest in the Catholic question, *ib.*; letter to Editor: his views for the amelioration of Ireland, *ib.*; letter of introduction to Lord Strangford, *ib.*; having voted on Catholic question, returns to Paris, 141; 23rd May, 1829, on his return to Paris, dies suddenly, *ib.*; remains conveyed to Dublin: deposited in family vault, in St. Thomas's Church, 142; letters of W. S. Landor on the death of, *ib.*; the embarrassment of his affairs at the time of his death, 145; value and extent of his Irish estates, from the schedules to act of parliament for their sale passed in 1846, *ib.*; lists of mortgages, debts, bequests, &c. 146; remnant of the vast properties of the Mountjoys now unsold, 152; detailed account of incumbrances on his estates from schedules of act for their sale, 455; rental of the estates, from ditto, 461; account of his death, in letter to Landor, ii. 342; letters from Duke of Richmond to, iii. 375; letter from Mrs. Siddons, 376; his letter to C. J. Mathews, *ib.*; to W. S. Landor, 382; to Lord Rosslyn, 383.

B. F., letters signed, to Lady Blessington, iii. 139.

Borghese, Prince, "the noble Roman," remarkable for his obesity, i. 117.

Boulter, Primate, recommendation of Mr. Gardiner, i. 46.

Brougham, Lord, notice of, iii. 124; letters of, 127.

Brown, Mrs., née Campbell, early acquaintance with Lord B., i. 53; her family, children, *ib.*; her marriage with Lord B., *ib.*; death of Major Brown, *ib.*

Bulwer, Sir Edward Lytton, in Italy in 1833, ii. 70; entertained by Archbishop of Tarento, 71; notice of, iii. 27; letters of, to Lady Blessington, 33; epistolary poem to ditto, 53.

Bulwer, Sir Henry, notice of, iii. 63; letters to Lady B., 70; letters of Lady B. to, 66.

Bunsen, Chevalier, Prussian minister at Rome in 1828, ii. 252.

Burdett, Sir Francis, notice of, iii. 139.

Burrell, William, Gell's reference to his new vest and cravat for each day of the year, ii. 40.

Bushe, Chief Justice, Marquess Wellesley's reference to, ii. 4, 11; notice of, iii. 489.

Bute, Lady, Gell's reference to, ii. 40.

Butera, Princess of, death at Naples, ii. 5.

Byng, George, Esq., notice of, iii. 451.

Byron, Lord, early acquaintance with Lord Blessington, i. 52;

refers to Lord B. in all the glory of gems and snuff-boxes, *ib.*; becomes acquainted with Lady B. at Genoa, 81; lines and letters to Lady B., 86; observations of Lady Blessington on his death, on revisiting Genoa in June, 1828, i. 133; Lady B. then saw Lady Byron and her daughter there, 134; Byron's references to D'Orsay, 321; Gell's references to his death, ii. 30, 31; anecdote of him passing the Alfred club, 66; letter of, in reference to Polidori, 207; original poem of, 215; death, and removal of his remains, 228; Lady B.'s remarks on his character, 345; Landor's remarks on, 372; Mr. Armstrong's letter respecting the yacht "Bolivar," iii. 405.

C.

Calabrella, Baroness, marries Captain Jenkins, i. 35; notice of her literary talents, *ib.*

Caldwell, Miss Bess, Gell's references to, ii. 50, 52, 58.

Caledon, Lord, Colonel of Tyrone militia, in Clonmel, i. 36.

Campbell, Lady Mary, Gell's reference to, ii. 42.

Campbell, the Abbé, Gell's reference to quarrel with him, ii. 42; notice of him, 98.

Campbell, Thomas, animosity to Lord Byron, i. 91; notice of, iii. 167; letter of, 169.

Canterbury, Lady Ellen, daughter of Edmund Power, widow of John Home Purves, Esq., i. 14; for early life—*see* Purves, Mrs.

Canterbury, Lord and Lady, brief notice of them; Mr. Purves having obtained the office of British Consul at Pemacola, proceeded to his post, and died there in September, 1827; December 6, 1828, Mrs. P. married, secondly, the Rt. Hon. C. Manners Sutton, Esq., Speaker of the House of Commons, i. 379; children's difficulties consequent on Sir C. Sutton's loss of office of Speaker in 1835; his death in July, 1845; followed by that of Lady Canterbury, Nov. 16, 1845, aged 54, 382; some account of her amiable daughter, Mrs. Fairlie; lines of D'Israeli to a beautiful mute, an interesting child of Mrs. Fairlie, of singular beauty and intelligence, 382; death of that child, Jan. 31, 1843; death of Mrs. Fairlie, in April, the same year; some evidences of the angelic nature, amiable disposition, and spiritualized mind of Mrs. Fairlie, 385; Lady B.'s account of her sister's death, Nov. 1845, ii. 358; notice of Lord and Lady C., i. 374.

Caroline, Queen, her career in Italy, from 1814, ii. 8; her chamberlains and household, 8, 131; Miss Demont's diary, 36; Gell's possession of sixty or seventy of her letters, 84.

Charleville, Lady C., intellectual society at her house, i. 165; notice of, iii. 447.

Chester, H., Esq., notice of, iii. 483.

Chesterfield, Lord, notice of, iii. 439.

Chevalier le C., author of voyage to the Troad, ii. 58.

Chorley, H. F., Esq., notice of, iii. 476.

C., letters signed, iii. 142.

Clanricarde, Lord, notice of, iii. 441.

Cochrane, Baillie, letter to Lady B., iii. 324; notice of, 482.

Colman, Geo. the Younger, notice and letters of, iii. 191.

Cook, Henry, letter to Lady B., iii. 320.

Correspondence of Lady B., notice of, ii. 1.

Correspondents of Lady B., letters of theirs omitted, iii. 144.

Cornwall, Barry (B. W. Procter), notice of, iii. 169 ; letters of, 170.

Cork, Dowager Lady, her celebrity as Miss Monckton in Johnson's times ; her soirées of late years, i. 166.

Corry, James, early friend of Lord Blessington's, taste for theatricals, i. 7 ; assists at Lord B.'s private theatricals, 65 ; on a visit at Mountjoy Forest, 68.

Coventry, Lady Augusta, Gell's references to her beauty, ii. 62, 64 ; idem. to intended marriage with Hon. H. Fox, 68.

Cowper, Hon. Charles Spencer, marries the widow of Count D'Orsay ; notice of, i. 54.

Crampton, John, assists in Lord B.'s theatricals, i. 65 ; letter of Sir P. C. in reference to them, *ib.*

Craven, Hon. Keppel, beginning of acquaintance with Lady B., i. 107 ; chamberlain to Queen Caroline in 1814, ii. 8, 10 ; letter to him of Mr. J. Ramsey, *in re* Gell, 14 ; Gell's references to him, 31 ; mythological emblems, mysteries, and explanations of, for Lady Blessington, 37 ; death of his brother, 42 ; buys a large convent near Salerno, 79 ; receives company in his convent, 88 ; Gell's reference to his son's intended marriage, *ib.* ; diplomatic career of his son, 133 ; reference to the convent at Penta, 92 ; notice of, 124 ; letters of, to Lady Blessington, 134.

D.

Dallas, George, letter to Lady B., iii. 318.

Deerhurst, Lady Mary, references to her, by Gell, iii. 25, 30, 41 ; ditto " going over the mountains of China," 52.

Deffand, Madame du, her epistolary and conversational talents, ii. 5 ; iii. 410.

Delavigne, Cassimir, notice and letters of, iii. 190.

Devonshire, Duchess of, her death, attended by Dr. Quin, iii. 26.

Dickens, Charles, notice of, iii. 95 ; letters of, 98.

Dillon, Lord, author of an epic poem at Florence, i. 117.

D'Israeli, Isaac, notice of, iii. 75 ; letters of, 79.

D'Israeli, Right Hon. Ben., notice of, iii. 80 ; letters of, 88 ; Lines addressed to " a beautiful mute," 383.

Dodwell, Edward, the Antiquarian, cuts up a mummy in Rome, ii. 40 ; Gell's references to, 44, 46, 50 ; his death—marriage of his widow, 75 ; Countess Spour at Rome in 1834, 87 ; notice of, 146.

Dogherty, Mrs., relative of Lady Blessington, living near Cashel, i. 42.

Donaghmore, Lord, the patron of Edmund Power, i. 22.

Dormer, Mrs., Gell's reference to, ii. 56.

D'Orsay, Count Alfred, first acquaintance with Lady B. in England, i. 79 ; acquaintance renewed in Florence, *ib.* ; sets out from Avignon with the Blessingtons for Italy, 80 ; first acquaintance with Byron at Genoa, 84 ; Byron's liking for him, sits for his portrait to D'Orsay, 85 ; Byron's allusion to the French Count, a " cupidon déchainée," 83 ; displays his talent at drawing out people, on Lieut. Smith, R. N., 105 ; engagement entered into with Lord B. to marry one of his daughters, recited in codicil to Lord B.'s will, June 2, 1823, 120 ; engagement set forth in a later will, Dec. 1, 1827 ; marriage with Lady Harriet Gardiner, 125 ; his father, Gen. D'Orsay, and the Count Leon, accompanied by Lord B., visit the Tyrone estates in 1825, 69; marriage settlement, monies charged on Lord B.'s estate, &c., 147, 149; deed of separation, 151; his pecuniary difficulties, arrest in London for a debt of £300 to a Paris bootmaker, 197; tradesmen allow his debts to stand over on account of the advantage of his patronage, i. 197; on his keeping at Gore House two years previously to break-up there, 200; on intimation of the execution put in, told by Lady B. he must quit London immediately, 201; departure for Paris before break of day following morning, end of his London career, in April, 1849, 201; arrival in Paris, expectations reasonably formed of Prince Louis Napoleon's friendship, 215; former services rendered to the Prince, *ib.*; his profound grief at the loss of Lady B. 242; notice of the Count: his origin; early life, some account of career in London, of his pursuits in art—the close of his career—observations on his talents, and the application of them, 318; his death, August 4, 1852, 330; religious sentiments in his last illness — remarkable conversation with Editor on religious subjects, 352; attended by the Archbishop of Paris, 330; singular inconsistencies in his character, 332; his embarrassments—reckless extravagance — an utter ignorance of the value of money — inordinate and ill-regulated generosity—forgetfulness of the obligations contracted for the sake of others, 332; his works of art and talents as an artist—portrait and busts of Wellington, busts of Napoleon, Emperor of Russia, Lamartine, Girardin, Napoleon Bonaparte, son of Jerome — pictures, Sir Robert Peel, Lord Lyndhurst, Lord Byron, Dwarkanauth Tagore, 335; verses of Lamartine to D'Orsay on his artistic talent, 340; Haydon's references to ditto, 341; references to his mother's family, Madame Crawford (La belle Sullivan), the mother of Countess D'Orsay, 347; his grandmother, Madame Crawford, compared by Lady B. to Ninon de l'Enclos—conquests of Ninon at 56, 70, and 80 years of age, 348; notice of his death in the "Presse," by Emile Girardin, 352; his funeral, 356; concluding observations on the Count as a man of wit—the wit combats of Gore House compared with those of the days of Dorset, Sedley, Etherege, Denham, and those of the times of Horace Walpole, Selwyn, Bubb Doddington, Townsend, &c., 361; various kinds of wit, in conversation, in displays of eloquence, in bon mots, epigrams, vers de societé, &c., *ib.*; reference to Curran's conversational wit, 363; in Hyde Park, in recent times, as described by Patmore—contrast with Grammont, as described in the same place in 1659, 366; Dickens' tribute to his memory, 369; Patmore's reference to his position in English society, *ib.*; the Alpha and Omega of all moralizing on the career of a young man thrown on life in a position beset with temptations—there is no protection for it—no hope for its safety or success, where there is no dependence on religion and the restraints imposed by it, 370; his remains deposited in the same sepulchral chamber in which those of Lady B. were deposited at Chambourcy, 372; of the architect of this remarkable monument—now the inmate of it—all that remains—" Pulvis et umbra, nomen, nihil," *ib.*; his letters to W. S. Landor, ii. 406; his letters to John Forster, 410; quarrel with Charles J. Mathews at Naples—statement of Mr. Mathews' correspondence and proceedings in this affair in August, 1824, 435; amicable arrangement, 440; letters to Mathews—letters to Dr. Frederick F. Quin, 448; letters to—from Alfred de Vigny, 454; letters of—to Editor, 455; letters from Editor to Count, 457; his embarrassments and amount of debt in 1845, 456; notice of his principal statuettes, 459; dedicatory letter to him prefixed to Godolphin, by Bulwer, 462; memorandum respecting his expected official appointment in the French Embassy in 1841, 463; his friendship for Richard J. Lane, the eminent artist—Mr. Lane lithographs about one hundred and fifty of the Count's sketches of the celebrities and habitués of the Villa Belvedere, Hotel Ney, Seamore Place, Gore House, of which one hundred and thirty-seven have been published by Mitchell, 465; Editor's communication to Lane's inquiries as to the Count's talents as an artist, and Lane's reply, 468; his letter to Lane from Paris, eulogizing Prince Louis Napoleon, 470; another letter of his to Lane on loss of his only son, *ib.*; his first visit to England, 471; notice of his connections, the Grammonts and Mareschal Sebastiani, 472; claims on government for—statues and pictures seized during the Revolution, iii. 399; notice of his Gore House pictures, 405.

D'Orsay, Lady Harriet, early life, i. 54; left under the care of her aunt, 119; arrangements for her marriage in 1823, 121; marriage with Count D'Orsay, Dec. 1827, 125, 325; Editor meets Lady Harriet at the Blessingtons' shortly after her marriage, 126; personal appearance, apparent infelicity, *ib.*; results of that marriage, *ib.*; returns to England with Lady B. in 1830, 168; takes her departure from Seamore Place early in August, 1831, 127; visits the continent with her aunt, latter end of 1833 or beginning of 1834, *ib.*; in September, 1835, residing with her aunt and sister in Dublin, *ib.*; marriage settlement, 147; arrangement entered into by the Count in 1838, 334; becomes a widow, August 4, 1852, 330; concluding observations on the unhappy marriage with the Count, 371; in Naples in 1832, ii. 72.

Druids' origin, Landor's notion of, ii. 369.

Drummond, Sir William, beginning of acquaintance with Lady B. at Naples, i. 113; his death—grave at Rome visited by Lady Blessington in 1828, 128; Gell's references to, ii. 23, 26; quarrel with little Campbell, 43, 48; reference to his death, 58; reference to his works, 59, 60, 96, 109; notice of, 95; letter of Lady Blessington to him, 210; comments on his scepticism by Rev. A. Hare, 209; letter to Dr. Quin, iii. 387.

Drummond, Lady, at Naples in 1832, ii. 72; Gell's account of her "tremendous dinners," 79.

Durham, Lord, letters of, iii. 119.

Dudley, Lord, references to, by Gell, ii. 25, 27; notice of, 426.

D., letter signed, to Lady Blessington, iii. 134.

Dwyer, Miss Anne, early instructress of Miss M. Power, i. 17.

E.

Epistolary curiosities, various letters, iii. 329.
Errington and Co., Gell's reference to Messrs. Errington and Lyne Stephens, Naples, 1834, ii. 84, 87.
Erskine, Henry, notice of, iii. 426.
Erskine, Lord, verses addressed to Lady B., iii. 324 ; notice of, 423.

F.

Fairlie, Isabella, death of Lady B.'s favourite, "the beautiful mute," the daughter of her niece, 31 January, 1831, ii. 356; approaching death of the child's mother notified to Landor, 357.
Falkner, Sir Frederick, notice of, ii. 114.
Farmer, Captain, an officer of the 47th Regiment at Clonmel, i. 29; acquaintance with Miss M. Power, *ib.*; offer of marriage, 30 ; marriage and its results, 31 ; marriage certificate, 436; separation, 32 ; Lady B.'s account of the cause, 32 ; this account impugned by Captain Farmer's brother, 33 ; defended by his brother, his letter, 437 ; quarrel of Captain F. with a brother officer, 33 : sells out—proceeds to India, 39 ; returns home—killed in the Fleet Prison in 1817, 39; inquest on his body, 40.
Farmer, Mrs., refusal to accompany Captain F. to India, 36 ; account of marriage and separation, by Mr. Sheehy, 34 ; account of her residence at Cahir, 35 ; he denies injurious reports against her, 36 ; her residence for some years at Sidmanton, Hants, 58 ; her residence in London, Manchester Square, 38, 58 ; early acquaintance with Lord B., 58 ; Lord B. a visitor at her house, Manchester Square, 38 ; marriage with Lord B. in 1818, 58.
Ferguson, Cutlar Ronald, letter to Lady B., iii. 310 ; notice of, iii. 451.
Filangieri, the, Gell's references to, iii. 58.
Fitz-Gerald, Lord William, at Cuma in 1832, iii. 64.
Fitz-Gerald, W. T., Esq., notice of, iii. 489.
Fitz-Herbert, Mrs., references to her marriage by a Catholic priest, supposed to be the Abbé Campbell, iii. 100.
Fonblanque, A., Lady B.'s eulogium on his character, ii. 349 ; Landor's opinion, "We have nothing like him in the political world," 379 ; Bulwer's reference to, iii. 37 ; notice of, 229 ; letters of, to Lady B., 230.
Forster, John, Lady B.'s reference to, in letters to Landor, iii. 351, 352 ; Landor's references to, 374, 378 ; notice of, 396 ; letters to him from Lady B., 398.
Fox, Gell's reference to "Black Fox," at Naples, ii. 52.
"Fuller, Jack," notice of, iii. 184 ; letters of, to Lady B., 185.

G.

Galt, John, Gell's reference to, ii. 50 ; notice of, iii. 231 ; letters of, to Lady B., 232.
Gardiner, Charles John, son of Lord B., notice of, i. 53, 54.
Gardiner, Miss Emily Rosalie, daughter of Lord B., notice of, 53, 119; marriage with Mr Charles White, and death in Paris, 127.
Gardiner, Lady Harriet, daughter of Lord B., references to, i. 54, 119.
Gardiner, Lady Harriet, sister of Lord B , guardian of his daughters, i. 119.
Gardiner, Right Honourable Luke, son of Lord B., notice of, i. 53, 54 ; death at the age of ten, 119.
Garrow, Miss Theodosia, letters to Lady B. ii. 319.

Garth, Captain, reference to, ii. 123.

Gell, Sir William, beginning of acquaintance with Lady B. in Naples in 1824, i. 107; accompanies Lady B. to Pompeii, &c. *ib.*; constant visitor at Villa Belvedere, 113; renews his acquaintance with Lady B. at Rome, 127; his parting with her in Rome, in 1828, 128; mournful anticipations at parting, *ib.*; his death in April, 1836, referred to by Lady B., *ib.*; notice of his life, ii. 8; his letter to Lady Blessington, 21; lines written in Rome, 43; his dog family, 65; a model letter of introduction to him, 87; at Gell's convent in June 1835, 90; affecting account, in his last letter to Lady B., of the breaking-down of his health, loss of memory—singular illusions, 90; letter of introduction of Editor to grand Admiral of Egyptian fleet, 93; Craven's account of last illness and death, 136; Lady B.'s account of his death to Landor, 348; Bulwer's account of, iii. 35; letters to Dr. Quin, iii. 384.

Geoffrin, Madame, Lady B. compared with, i. 227; notice of, iii. 412.

Girardin, Emile de, notice of, iii. 466.

Glenelg, Lord, letters to Lady B., iii. 13; notice of, 439.

Godwin, William, letter to Lady B., iii. 310; notice of, 455.

Graham, John, account of the death of Lord Mountjoy, at Newross, i. 47.

Grammont, Duc de, married a sister of Count d'Orsay, when in England as Duc de Guiche, previously to Lady B.'s departure for the continent, acquainted with her, i. 79; accueil of Lady B. on her arrival in Paris in April 1849, 213.

Grammont, Duc de, father and mother of the present Duke, accompanied the French Princes into exile. The mother died at Holyrood house in 1803, i. 349; her remains conveyed to France in 1825, *ib.*: Lady Tankerville, sister of present Duke, a beauty of celebrity, much admired, 350; another sister of present Duc, married Marshal Sebastiani, i. 351; letter of, to Lady Blessington, *ib*, letters of, to Lady B., iii. 307, 308.

Grammont, Duchesse de, has the papers of Count d'Orsay. His journal alluded to, by Byron, burned by herself some years previously to her death, i. 324; notice of, 351.

G., letters signed, to Lady Blessington, iii. 130.

Grant, Francis, Esq., notice of, iii. 466.

Greville, C., Esq., notice of, iii. 483.

Guiccioli, Countess, notice of, ii. 213; Byron's first acquaintance with Guiccioli at Ravenna, 215; personal appearance, 217; colour of her hair, 218; proofs of disinterestedness, 220; second marriage with an "Elderly Gentleman," 229; letters to her from Lady Blessington, 231; letters from her to Lady Blessington, 243; second husband of the Countess, the Marquis de Boissy, 255.

H.

Hacket, Alderman, a school-fellow of Robert Power, i. 20; his account of the Powers, *ib.*

Hall, S. C., Esq. and Mrs., notice of, iii. 469.

Hallam, Lady B.'s acquaintance with at Florence, i. 117.

Hamilton, Terrick, Esq., Gell's reference to, ii. 71; notice of, iii. 482.

Hardinge, Lord, present at the marriage of Miss M. Power, i. 437.
Hare, Julius, Gell's reference to, as "Julius Hirsutus," ii. 52.
Hare, Rev. Augustus F., remarkable letter to, in re Drummond's scepticism, ii. 209; Lady B.'s reference to his noble qualities, 341; reference to, in a letter of Lady B., ii. 340.
Haydon, B. R., letters to Lady B., iii. 316; notice of, 464.
Hayter, Sir George, notice of, iii. 465.
Hemans, Mrs. Felicia, Lady B.'s admiration for her writings, ii. 312; place of burial, and inscription on mural slab, 313.
Herculaneum, notice of, visits of Lady B. and Sir W. Gell, i. 113.
Herschel, Sir John, makes Lady Blessington's acquaintance in Naples, i. 107.
Hesse, Captain, singular notice of him by Lady B., and of his correspondence with a royal personage, ii. 119.
Hill, George, letter to Lady B., iii. 322.
Hill, Mr., subsequently Lord Berwick, minister in Naples in 1831, i. 64.
Hogg, Dr., at Naples in 1832-3-4, i. 60, 72, 79; notice of, iii. 488.
Holman, Lieutenant, R.N., the blind traveller, ascends Mount Vesuvius in June, 1821, accompanied by Editor, i. 111.
Holland House Society, Lady B.'s observations on, i. 161.
Holland, present Lord, notice of, iii. 430.
H., letter to Lady B. signed, iii. 142.
Hook, Theodore, notice of, and letter, iii. 193.
Howden, Lord, notice of, iii. 438.
Hunt, Mr. and Mrs., their murder near Pæstum, ii. 21; detailed account of, iii. 352.

I.

Irving, Washington, a contribution to Lady B.'s album, iii. 309; notice of, 474.

J.

J——, Mr., of Brussels, curious communication—mysterious occurrence, iii. 329.
James, G. P. R., notice of, iii. 471.
Jekyll, Joseph, notice of, iii. 172; letters to Lady B., 177.
Jenkins, Thomas, Captain 11th Dragoons, stationed in Clonmel, i. 34; intimacy with the Powers, *ib.*; supposed attachment to Miss M. Power, *ib.*; his family and fortune, *ib.*; his military career, *ib.*; residence in Dublin in 1809, *ib.*; his establishment in Hampshire, *ib.*; subsequent embarrassments, *ib.*; his marriage and death, *ib.*; Meagher's reference to him, 36; Bernard Wright's reference to him, *ib.*; Lord Blessington's acquaintance with him, 56; present at a dinner given in Dublin by Lord B., 57; departure of Capt. Jenkins, and scene, *ib.*; subsequent visit to Mountjoy Forest, 68.
Jesse, J. H., Esq., notice of, iii. 476.
Jerdan, W., Esq., notice of, iii. 477.
Jesuit Church, Gardiner Street, site of, obtained by Lady B.'s aid, iii. 381.
Julien, Monsieur Le Jeune, secretary of Robespierre—figured in the Reign of Terror in a public recitation of revolutionary odes by Madame Fontenay, iii. 186; figures as a dolorous poet with "le don des larmes" at Seamore Place and Gore House—recites his "Chagrins Politiques," 187; another scene with Dr. Quin and James Smith, 201.

K.

Keats (the Poet), Landor's account of W.'s ungenerous criticism, ii. 380.

Kielmansegg, Count von, notice of, iii. 484.

L.

Lamartine, Lady B.'s acquaintance with at Florence, i. 117; poem addressed to D'Orsay, 340.

Lamb, Charles, Landor's and Coleridge's eulogiums on, ii. 369; reference of Landor to an affecting story of his sister, *ib.*; lines of Landor on, iii. 176.

Landon, Miss Letitia E., notice of, ii. 264; marriage of, 7th June, 1838, with Mr. Maclean, ii. 266; death of, 13th October, 1838, 267; Editor visits Cape Coast Castle in Feb. 1841, *ib.*; his account of Mr. Maclean, 268; observations on inquest, &c., 270; charged by Lady B. to get her husband's consent to set up a monument at Cape Coast Castle, ii. 279; called on by Mr. Maclean to inquire into the death of L. E. L., 280; result of inquiry, 288; seized with fever while occupying the room in which L. E. L. had died, 289; neglect experienced during illness, 291; death of her husband 28th May, 1847, *ib.*; a lament for L. E. L. by W. S. Landor, 293; destitute state of her mother after her death, 294; Lady B.'s account of her death to Lady W., 295; letters of Landon to Lady B., 299; Bulwer's reference to, iii. 40; further observations on her death, 511.

Landor, Walter Savage, first acquaintance with Lady B., i. 117; notice of his career, ii. 236; letters from Lady B. to him, 340; verses to him from Lady B., 360; letters from, to Lady B., 361; comments on the paltry grant of George IV. to Coleridge, 362; visit to a Roman Catholic Chapel, 384; D'Orsay's letters to him, 406; imaginary conversation between Lord Mountjoy and Lord Edward Fitzgerald, communicated to Lady B. in Feb. 1839, 475; lines addressed to Lady B. iii. 398.

Landseer, Sir Edwin, notice of, iii. 463.

Lansdowne, Marquess, letter to Lady B., iii. 129.

Lawrence, Sir T., notice of, iii. 153; letters of, 156; lines on waltzing, *ib.*

Lindsay, Lady Charlotte, Gell's reference to, ii. 56, 66.

Lock, Captain William, notice of, iii. 488.

Loewe, Dr., a celebrated linguist, accompanied Sir M. Montefiore to the East, ii. 328.

Lola Montes, a letter of hers, iii. 333.

Longman, T. N., Esq., notice of, iii. 484.

Lucas, Mr. and Mrs., Gell's reference to "very nice people from Ireland," ii. 41.

Lucca, Duc de, his pilgrimage to Rome, ii. 41.

Luttrell, Henry, early acquaintance of the Blessingtons, i. 72; Gell's reference to, ii. 46; notice of, and letters, iii. 189.

Lyndhurst, Lord, notice of, and letters, iii. 129, 421.

M.

M. R. C., letter from Greece to Lady B., iii. 312.

Mackinnon, Colonel, transmitting a lock of Lord Nelson's hair to Lady B., iii. 311.

Mackintosh, his conversational powers, i. 156.

Maclise, D., notice of, iii. 461 ; on toleration for opinions, i. 186.
Macready, W. C., letters to Lady B., iii. 309 ; notice of, 478.
Madden, R. R., lines of Dr. Beattie addressed to, iii. 260. 272; correspondence with Lady B., iii. 276; correspondence with D'Orsay on the part of C. Mathews, 433; letters from D'Orsay to, 455.
Manners, Lord, the Orange régime in Ireland, iii. 4.
Manning, Mr., the celebrated Chinese scholar, Gell's reference to, ii. 53.
Manvers, Lady, Gell's reference to her, ii. 40.
Margravine of Anspach, Gell's reference to 36, 50, 54 ; notice of, ii. 124.
Marryatt, F., notice of, and letters to Lady B., iii. 220.
Marsault, Madame la Comtesse St., Mary Anne, youngest daughter of Edmund Power, i. 14 ; her marriage and separation, 41 ; lives with her father in Ireland, 42; return to England in 1839, *ib.*; accompanies the Blessingtons on a continental tour, 74; her personal appearance in 1822, *ib.*
Mathews, Charles James, joins the Blessingtons at Naples, i. 74; his early career, sojourn with the Blessingtons in Italy, *ib.* ; amiable character, comic talents, 75 ; an inmate of the Palazzo Belvedere, 108 ; accompanies Lady B. to Pæstum, *ib.* ; notice of, ii. 423 ; quarrel with D'Orsay—proceedings and correspondence in that affair, 433 ; subsequent amicable correspondence with the Count, 441 ; letters of to Lady B., iii. 343.
Mathews, Mrs., letters of Lady B. to, iii. 357.
Matthias, James, (Pursuit of Literature), Gell's reference to him in Naples, November, 1833, at the age of 81, rather younger than ever, ii. 72 ; idem.—in Naples, June 2, 1834, then "*in his 93rd year*," 86 ; Bulwer's reference to, iii. 35
Matuschewitz, Count, notice, ii. 151 ; letters to Lady B., 152.
Meagher, Jeremiah, vice-consul at Lisbon, account of the Powers, i. 21 ; account of Bernard Wright, *ib.*: further account of Miss M. Power, 36.
Medwin, Captain Thomas, notice of, iii. 486.
Melleray, abbot of Mount, letter to Lady B., iii. 323.
Millengen, the antiquarian, makes Lady B.'s acquaintance at Naples, i. 107 ; initiates her into the mysteries of numismatics, *ib.*; notice, ii. 144; letters from to Lady B., 145.
Mills, Frank, Gell's reference to, ii. 26 ; notice of, iii. 484.
Milnes, Richard Monckton, letter to Lady B., iii. 328; notice of, 480.
Mirabeau, his description of a celebrated beauty, i. 60.
Montefiore, Sir Moses, Gell's reference to, ii. 44; instance of devotion and filial affection, 133; world-wide benevolence and charitableness of heart and mind, 328.
Montmorenci, Duc de Laval, notice, ii. 115.
Montague, Lady M. Wortley, her epistolary talents, ii. 5.
Moore, Thomas, early acquaintance with the Blessingtons, i. 72; reference to Lord B.'s theatricals, 65 ; visits Lady B. with Washington Irving, 70 ; renews his acquaintance with her at Paris, 76 ; lines of his to Lady B., 299 ; notice of, iii. 158 ; his first lines, 161 ; letters of, to Lady B., iii. 192 ; Galt's remarks on "the Loves of the Angels," 237; letter to the Editor on slavery, 167; account of a scene of, witnessed by the Editor, iii. 506.

Morpeth, Lord, acquaintance with Lady B. at Naples, i. 108; his prize poem on Pæstum, *ib.*; notice of, iii. 440,

Mountjoy family, burial-place at Cappagh, near Rash, i. 67; desire of Lord B. to be interred there, 69.

Mountjoy, Dowager Lady, residing at Rash, after her husband's death, i, 64; residing in Dublin in 1807, 67; death in 1839, 119.

Mountjoy, Lady, notice of family, marriage, and death, i. 53—59.

Mountjoy, Lord, *vide* Blessington.

Murray, James, Captain of 47th, suitor to Miss M. Power, i. 30.

Murray, Lord Charles, account of his sojourn in Naples in 1822, career and death in Greece, ii. 126.

N.

Naples, Editor's notice of Naples and its vicinity, i. 96; Willis' notice of the bay, 101; Lady B.'s notice of it, *ib.*; evening passed by Editor on board "the Bolivar," 103.

Napoleon, Prince Louis, the present Emperor of the French, attention paid and services rendered to him when in exile by Lady B. and Count D'Orsay, how repaid on a throne, i. 214, 329, 331, 356—360; notice of his origin and career, 463—475; on his elevation to the Presidency of the Republic, *ib.*; Lamennais' observation to Editor respecting the Prince, 360; Landor's lines, the Quest of Honour, applicable to him, *ib.*; visited in Bath in Aug. 1846, by Landor, ii. 393; Landor's great interest in and anxiety for the welfare of the Prince January 1849, 394; Landor writes to the President, 395; remarkable letter of Duke of Wellington in reference to, i. 357.

Nizzensitter, C., letter to Lady B., iii. 313.

N—— L., an eccentric correspondent of Lady B., labouring under singular delusions, iii. 337.

Normanby, Lord, theatricals at Florence, i. 115, ii. 57; Lady B.'s reference to, i. 117; letter to Lady B., iii. 132; notice of, 434.

O.

Odin's stone pillar, Sir W. Scott's account of, ii. 81.

O'Flagherty, Father, the parish priest of Cappagh, patronized by Lady B., i. 68; Lord B.'s liberality to him, 69; his amusing correspondence, *ib.*

Osborne, T. B., Esq., notice of, iii. 481.

Ossian's poems, reference to, by Sir W. Scott in Italy, ii. 81.

Ossuna, Duc d', notice, ii. 168; letters to Lady B., 169.

P.

Pagani, Padre, President of the Roman Catholic Colleges of Rugby and Ratcliffe, his learning extolled by W. S. Landor, ii. 383.

Parr, Dr. Samuel, Gell's reference to his death, ii. 40; the doctor's "holy kiss," 48; notice of, iii. 146; letters of, 147; Miss Calcraft's references to, 149; Rev. Mr. Horseman's lines on, 151; extract from a sermon, 152.

Peel, Sir Robert, disposal of his papers for publication, i. 5; letters to, of Lady B., iii. 135, 227; statements of, on the subject of Lady B.'s letter, 136.

Perry, James, the editor of the Morning Chronicle, refuses to insert a slander in his paper relative to Captain Farmer's death, i. 40; beginning of his acquaintance with Lord B., *ib.*; notice of, iii. 457.

Phipps, General, letters to Lady B. iii. 315 ; notice of, 455.

Pilgrim, the, his lines and letters to Lady B., iii. 333.

Piazzi, the celebrated astronomer, notice of, i. 107, ii. 118 ; letter Lady B., iii. 321.

Polidori, notice of, ii. 204.

Ponsonby, Lord, minister at Naples in 1832, ii. 64.

Popery, triumphs of, singular instance of one, iii. 333.

Powell, John Allan, law agent of the Milan commission, friend of Lord B., i. 51.

Power, Anne, eldest of the children of E. Power, death, i. 28.

Power, Capt., brother of the preceding, his death in India, a fine young man of twenty-two, ii. 402.

Power, Edmund, father of Lady B., early history, i. 12 ; notice of, 14 ; recklessness, improvidence, 20 ; magisterial terrorism, *ib.* ; patronized by Lord Donoghmore, 21 ; Lady B.'s account of terrorism in his family, 22 ; his pursuits, tastes, and appearance, 23 ; exercise of magisterial duties—rebel hunting, 24 ; shooting a peasant boy, *ib.* ; indicted for murder, 25 ; name expunged from magistracy, *ib* ; inquest on boy shot, 440 ; indictment and sworn informations, 441 ; his paper prosecuted for a libel on Colonel Bagwell,—report of first trial, Bagwell *v.* Power, ii. 449 ; report of second trial, Macarthy *v.* Watson, 476 ; Miss Ellen Power examined on last trial, *ib.* ; death of his first wife, i. 41 ; second marriage, *ib.* ; supported in his latter years by his daughters, *ib.* ; amount of pecuniary aid from Lady B., *ib.* ; end of his unfortunate career, 42.

Power, Edmund, Jun., death of, i. 28.

Power, Miss Margaret, niece of Lady B., memoir of her aunt, i. 11 ; her affectionate regard for her aunt's memory, *ib.* ; obligations of the Editor to her, *passim ;* her poetry praised by Landor, ii. 393.

Power, Miss Ellen, younger sister of Miss M. Power, Landor's reference to, ii. 287. *See* Mrs. Purves.

Power, Marguerite, early life, i. 11 ; her personal attractions, 29 ; attentions of Captain Farmer, 30 ; offer of marriage to her, *ib.* ; repugnance to Captain Farmer, *ib.*; marriage with Captain Farmer, 31 ; unhappy results, *ib.* ; separation, 32 ; Lady B.'s account of same, *ib.* ; return to her father's, *ib.* ; distinguished officers present at her marriage : the present Lord Hardinge, General Blakeney, 31. *See* Mrs. Farmer.

Power, Miss Mary Anne, youngest daughter of Edmund, i. 14 ; marriage with Count St. Marsault, 41, separation, *ib.* ; attention to her father, 42 ; sojourns with Mrs. Dogherty near Cashel, *ib* ; mentioned in Lord B.'s will, 123 ; reference to her age, 223 ; Gell's references to her, under various designations, ii. 22, 33, 36, 44, 47, 52, 54, 65, 69

Power, Michael, amiable disposition, early death, i. 25 ; his duel with Captain Kettlewell, 475.

Pratt, Miss, author of "Inheritance," Gell's reference to, ii. 61.

Procter, Barry W., letters to Lady B. and notice, iii. 169.

Purves, Mrs., Miss Ellen Power, mention of her marriage, i. 14 ; her remarkable beauty, 29 ; admiration she excited at the "coteries" of Tipperary, *ib.* ; early acquaintance with Colonel Stewart, *ib.* ; marriage with John Home Purves, Esq., 14 ; at a dinner given by Lord B. in 1815, 56 ; on a visit at Mountjoy Forest, 68 ; death of Mr. Purves

379; second marriage with Lord Canterbury, 380; death in her 54th year, 16th November, 1845, 381; born the latter part of 1791, 223.

Q.

Quin, Dr. Frederick F., reference to by Gell, ii. 26, 27; notice of him, 110; letters of D'Orsay to, 448; scene at Seamore Place with Julien, i. 186; do. at Gore House, iii. 201.

Quinlan, Mr., a distant relation of Lady B., i. 42; assisted E. Power with money to fee counsel when tried for murder, *ib.*

R.

R. H., letter to Lady B., iii. 324.

R. J. C. W., singular epistle to D'Orsay, iii. 336.

R. L., letter to Lady B., iii. 321.

Rachel, Mademoiselle, letter to Lady B., iii. 324.

Ramsay, James, of Naples, sketch of Sir W. Gell, ii. 14; Gell's reference to him, 87.

Reeve, H., Esq., notice of, iii. 483.

Reilly, Charles, Surgeon, R.N., espouses the cause of Abbé Campbell, ii. 42; notice of his career, 108.

Reynolds, F. Mansell, notice of and letters, iii. 253.

Ricciardi, the, Gell's references to them and the Filangieri of Naples, iii. 58, 59.

Richardson, Dr., attended Lady Mountjoy to the Continent, in 1814: subsequently travelling physician to Lord Belmore in the East, i. 52; letter on death of Lord B., 144; letter to, from Mrs. E. M. S., iii. 324.

Roberts, Emma, notice of, iii. 325; letters to Lady B., 326.

Rogers, early acquaintance of the Blessingtons, i. 72.

Romano, Duc di Rocco, notice of, iii. 485.

Romer, Isabella, Mrs., notice of, iii. 329; letters to Lady B., 330.

Rose, Mr., Gell's reference to "the man of Greek inscriptions," iii. 40.

Rosslyn, letters to Lord B., iii. 383; notice of, 433.

Rothwell (the painter) at Naples, in 1834, 78, 79.

Russell, Lord John, early acquaintance with the Blessingtons, i. 72; eulogized by Lady B., 127; letter to Lady B., iii. 124; notice of, 442.

S.

S. A., letter to Lady B., iii. 334.

Saurin, Attorney-General of Ireland, Marquess Wellesley's account of his Orange régime of fifteen years, iii. 4.

Scarfe, Captain, Gell's reference to, *in re* Abbé Campbell, ii. 42.

Scarlett, Sir James. *See* Abinger, iii. 108.

Scott, Sir Walter, at Naples, in 1832, ii. 60, 61; Idem, 67, 68; Gell's reminiscences, 71, 74, 76, 80, 84.

Sevignè, Madame de, her epistolary talent, ii. 5.

Sheehy, Father Nicholas, relative of Lady B.'s mother, i. 15; persecution and death, *ib.*; detailed account of him, 389.

Sheehy, Edmund, Esq., maternal grandfather of Lady B., i. 14; persecution and death, 15; detailed account of, 389.

Shelley, P. B., Esq., notice of, iii. 495.

Sheridan, Miss Louisa, notice and letters of, to Lady B., ii. 320.

Sigourney, Mrs. Lydia, notice of, ii. 312; letters to Lady B., 314; styled "the American Hemans:" similarity of her genius and her fate, 312.

Smith, Albert, notice of, iii. 487.
Smith, James, notice of, iii. 196; letters and poems, 203.
Smith, Lieut., R.N., commander of "The Bolivar," i. 103; D'Orsay's talent in drawing out people tried on him, 100; referred to by Lord Blessington, iii. 376.
Soutzo, Prince Michael, iii. 449.
Spencer, Hon. W. R., notice of, iii. 186; letter of to Lady B., 188.
Stael, Madame de, conversational talents, i. 158.
Starke, Anna Maria, Gell's reference to: gives parties and misèreres in Rome, ii. 40.
Stewart, Thomas, nephew of Sir W. Drummond, lines to Lady B., i. 306; subsequently becomes a Benedictine monk, ii. 212; his assassination, *ib.*; further particulars of, iii. 400; his servant, Luigi Baranelli, recent murder by, 534.
Stewart, William, Esq. of Killymoon, Colonel of Tyrone militia, i. 36; stationed at Clonmel in 1804, *ib.*; intimacy with the Powers, *ib.*; notice of, 37; intimacy with Lord Blessington, 68; entertained at Mountjoy Forest in 1816, *ib.*; ditto in 1823, 69; Gell's reference to, in Italy in 1829, ii. 56; Gell's inquiry after the amiable Colonel of Killymoon, 89.
Strangford, Lord, notice of and letter to Lady B., iii. 183.
Strangways, Hon. William Thomas Horner Fox, notice of, iii. 486.
Strangways, J., an intimate acquaintance of Lady B. in Italy, i. 117.
Sue, Monsieur Eugene, notice of, ii. 174; letters to Lady B., 178; observations of an eminent literati on his writings, iii. 419.
Swartzenberg, the Prince of, notice of his career, ii. 158; letters to Lady Blessington, 160.
Swift, Godwin, reference to him in a letter of Lady B., ii. 341; Landor's reference to him as "a representative of the earliest patriot in Ireland," 363; notice of family, iii. 490.

T.

Tajore, Dwarkanauth, the celebrated Hindoo Baboo, notice of, i. 194; letters from, to Lady Blessington, 195.
Talbot, C. R. M., letter to Lady Blessington, iii. 320; notice of, 489.
Talbot, Sir George, his "great and good dinners," at Rome, ii. 40.
Talfourd, Sir N., notice of, iii. 452; letter to Lady B., 454.
Tarento, Archbishop of, Gell's references, ii. 22; death of his favourite Annette, 58; his letter on cats, 70; notice of, 147; letters of to Lady B., 148.
Thackeray, W. M., Esq., notice of, iii. 473.
Teggart Arthur, early acquaintance of Lord and Lady B., i. 58; notice of, *ib.*
Torlonia, Duc et Banquier, Luigi Chiave's account of his death, ii. 193.

U.

Uwins (the Painter), makes Lady B.'s acquaintance in Italy, i. 107; his pictures referred to by Gell, ii. 62; letters to Lady B., iii. 316; notice of, 465.

V.

Vespucci, America Contessa, notice of, ii. 307; letter to Lady B., 309.
Vigny, Alfred de, notice and letters of, ii. 192.
Vyse, Colonel, at Naples in 1832, ii. 64.

W.

Wade, General, an old Irish officer—commandant of the Castello del Ovo, Naples, i. 99; some account of origin, 113.

Watson, Dr., a celebrated linguist, ii. 23, 73.

Watson, Solomon, a Quaker banker of Clonmel, libel on Colonel Bagwell in Power's paper, i. 476; action against him, by M'Carthy, 475.

Wellesley, Marquis, notice of, iii. 1; his reference to an "old Orangeman, named Saurin," 4; letters to Lady Blessington, 9.

Wellington, late Duke of, notice of, iii 13; letters of, to Lady Blessington, 18.

Wellington, present Duke of, notice of, iii. 25; letter to Lady B., 26.

Westmacott, Richard, the eminent sculptor, i. 107.

Westmoreland, Lady, Gell's references to, ii. 48.

Westmoreland, Lord, letter to Lady B., iii. 132; notice of, 437.

White, Charles, marries Lady Emily Rosalie (Mary) Gardiner, i. 55; letter to Lady B., iii. 320.

White, Miss, at Rome in 1828, ii. 55; visited by Sir W. Scott, near Pæstum, 60; at Portici in 1834, 77.

Wilkie, Sir D., letter to Lady B., iii. 316; notice of, 459.

Wilkinson, Egyptian Traveller, Gell's reference to his discoveries, ii. 56.

Willis, N. P., notice of, iii. 240; letters of, to Lady B., 243; reference to Sir W. Gell, ii. 12.

Wortley, Lady E. S., notice of, iii. 470.

Wright, Bernard, Alderman Hackett's account of, i. 20; tortured by Sir T. Judkin Fitzgerald, 21; detailed report of proceedings *v.* Fitzgerald, 429; in the employment of Power, 21.

Wyatt, Richard J., Esq., notice of, iii. 465.

Wycherley, the comedian, when verging on eighty—his last counsel to his young wife, ii. 228.

ERRATA.

VOL. I.

P.	L.	*For*	*Read*	P.	L.	*For*	*Read*
97	20	Castello del Novo,	Castello del' Ovo.	244	12	au,	ou.
98	1	Apenines,	Appenines.	246	33	cette,	celle.
212	13	Gore,	Gore House.	265	23	laughted,	laughed.
223	16	youngest,	younger.	341	10	La tombeaux,	Le tombe.
ib.	24	of Marsault,	St. Marsault.	349	38	plead,	pleaded.
228	21	thermometee,	thermometre.	470	16	orderes,	ordres.

VOL. II.

P.	L.	*For*	*Read*	P.	L.	*For*	*Read*
45	27	by Lady B.,	to Lady B.	254	35	Torloresse,	Fortoresse.
87	1	93rd year,	83rd year.	255	25	ressairer,	ressaissir.
88	36	Ferronage,	Ferronaye.	*ib.*	28	heurez,	heureux.
161	23	extermienateur,	exterminateur.	*ib.*	34	L'unanimitie,	L'unanimitè.
164	3	Erois,	Irois.	256	2	D'Ici,	Dit.
ib.	9	aves,	avez.	257	1	peur,	pour.
166	8	pais jai,	puis-je.	258	23	devinir,	devener.
169	32	au este,	au reste.	*ib.*	24	grand,	quand.
171	26	pauvais,	pouvais.	277	11	Mrs.,	Mr.
172	32	pent,	peu.	311	36	aurai,	aurez.
173	8	denez,	devez.	407	6	nos,	vos.
183	35	miasventure,	misaventure.	*ib.*	19	nous vous piquiez,	vous vous pique.
185	2	arrange,	arrangez.	439	11	apprendee,	apprendre.
ib.	29	Les,	Tres.	*ib.*	24	prendee,	prendre.
188	5	Fucheuse,	Facheuse.	444	17	Ji,	Je.
189	12	Le vie,	La vie.	*ib.*	13	banqueronte,	banqueroute.
198	6	expriner,	exprimer.	311	40	a me mes,	à mes.
ib.	20	plur,	plus.	449	19	recoutrè,	rencontrè.
ib	2	saccoutumee	accoutumèe.	452	9	To,	Tu.
208	27	Sdignera,	S'degnera.	*ib.*	29	donuant,	donnant.
ib.	89	Quelcuno,	Qualcuno.	*ib.*	29	Don,	Bon.
241	23	his,	her.	454	18	Et,	Eu.
245	9	inspires,	inspirer.	*ib.*	30	merile,	merite.
248	29	Blessington,	Lady Blessington.				

VOL. III.

P.	L.	*For*	*Read*	P.	L.	*For*	*Read*
35	35	Matthias,	Mathias.	165	36	hurry,	Murray.
51	33	mementoes,	mementos.	181	4	founp,	found.
68	1	Landor,	Landon.	185	4	challege,	challenge.
120	16	indignified,	undignified.	324	10	S'avoir,	N'avoir,